Race/Gender/Class/Media 3.0

Considering Diversity Across Content, Audiences, and Production

Third Edition

REBECCA ANN **LIND**

University of Illinois at Chicago

PEARSON

Boston   Columbus   Indianapolis   New York   San Francisco   Upper Saddle River
Amsterdam   Cape Town   Dubai   London   Madrid   Milan   Munich   Paris   Montreal   Toronto
Delhi   Mexico City   São Paulo   Sydney   Hong Kong   Seoul   Singapore   Taipei   Tokyo

Editor-in-Chief, Communication: Karon Bowers
Editor: Ziki Dekel
Editorial Assistant: Megan Hermida
Project Manager: Debbie Ryan
Marketing Manager: Blair Zoe Tuckman
Art Director, Cover: Jayne Conte
Cover Designer: Suzanne Behnke
Cover Photo: Alamy

Credits and acknowledgments borrowed from other sources and reproduced, with permission, in this textbook appear on the appropriate page within text.

Library of Congress Cataloging-in-Publication Data

Race/gender/class/media 3.0 : considering diversity across content, audiences and production / edited by Rebecca Ann Lind. — 3rd ed.
    p. cm.
  ISBN-13: 978-0-205-00610-6
  ISBN-10: 0-205-00610-8
 1. Race relations in mass media.   2. Gender identity in mass media.   3. Social classes in mass media.   4. Mass media—Social aspects.   I. Lind, Rebecca Ann.
  P94.5.M55R33 2013
  305—dc23   2011041549

5 6 7 8 9 10 V092 16 15 14

PEARSON

ISBN-13: 978-0-205-00610-6
ISBN-10:   0-205-00610-8

Why Do You Need This New Edition?

If you're wondering why you should buy this new edition of *Race/Gender/Class/Media 3.0,* here are six good reasons!

1. Close to 80 percent of the readings are new to this edition.

2. Social class has been added as a third socially-constructed and contested area of difference.

3. The Audience section has been reorganized, with a new chapter on Produsage, or the intersection of producing and using/consuming media content in the Web 2.0 environment.

4. More unique voices and perspectives, including considerations of disability, bullying, and intimate partner violence, and first-person pieces from working journalists.

5. Overall, there is an increased emphasis on new media.

6. The list of resources has been significantly updated.

BRIEF CONTENTS

CHAPTER TEN

CONTENTS

CHAPTER SIX

Film and Entertainment Television   186

CHAPTER SEVEN

Music and New Media   244

PREFACE

Welcome to the third edition of a sampler presenting a wide variety of perspectives that, when taken together, shows just how many ways there are to consider race, gender, and class in the media. It's designed to make you think critically about these issues and to encourage you to decide which of the ideas and perspectives makes the most sense to you. It's designed to spark your interest and stimulate discussion.

New To This Edition:

What's new in the third edition? Plenty!

- The new title, *Race/Gender/Class/Media 3.0: Considering Diversity Across Content, Audiences, and Production,* gives a few hints. The inclusion of social class as a third socially contested area of difference makes the book more broadly reflective of the challenges facing our society. Referring to "3.0" stresses the extent to which the material in this text is new.
- The key issues continue to be covered, but in fresh readings. Indeed, about 80% of the readings are new, with another *10%* updated from the second edition—it's more than a third edition; it's version 3.0.
- The Audience section has been reorganized to create a new chapter representing the intersection of producing and using/consuming media content in our increasingly online, interconnected world.
- The number of articles that discuss new media has been greatly expanded.
- The introduction has been updated, as has the epilogue/list of resources.

This collection contains 51 readings by a wide variety of authors across many disciplines. They approach the matter of race, gender, and class in the media from rhetorical, social scientific, and critical/cultural perspectives. You won't agree with everything you read, and that's just fine.

As with everything, this book represents a tradeoff. If content is covered in greater depth, there can be less breadth. If greater breadth, there can be less depth. Because I wanted to present as many viewpoints as possible, this book contains many short readings; I emphasize breadth. The readings provide an introduction to the field, a taste of what people are thinking and writing about. If you find something particularly interesting, you can consider it a starting point and eventually learn much more about it.

This book can be used in both lower and upper division courses. The authors have been encouraged to speak with their own voices to better reinforce the fact that the scholarship in this field is diverse.

Because of the number of readings, instructors might emphasize or de-emphasize certain things. The book has been designed to contain enough readings so that reading and other assignments can be flexible—depending on the goals of the course, some readings may not be assigned at all.[1] Alternatively, instructors might ask students to learn more about the topic of an especially important reading. Students could be assigned to obtain some of the material referenced by the author, to see whether they can find anything else written by that author, or to search for additional relevant information in the campus library or on the Internet. If desired, students could even become teachers for a time and share what they've learned with the class.

Instructors will have different expectations of students in terms of the items presented in the "It's Your Turn" segment of each chapter. These items can be used or adapted in numerous ways. At the very least, some of the "It's Your Turn" items can provide a basis for fruitful class discussion. Some can become major term projects, on an individual or group level. Some can be handled as traditional assignments. Others can be assigned in lieu of quizzes to encourage students to read and think about the material prior to class. Any of the "It's Your Turn" items that become graded exercises, assignments, or projects could take any number of forms. They could be traditional papers (of varying lengths, determined by the instructor), or complete, full-sentence outlines conveying the essence of the students' ideas (with the expected extent of detail specified by the instructor). They could be traditional oral presentations, or something akin to the "poster session" format that's becoming increasingly popular at scholarly meetings—students could create visual presentations on poster board conveying the essence of their work. If the school has the facilities and the students have the expertise, some "It's Your Turn" items could even result in students producing some audio, video, graphic, or interactive (even online) material. And, as noted earlier, any of these can be done on an individual or small-group basis, or even by the class as a whole.[2]

The chapters comprise multiple readings and are divided into three main parts: Production, Content, and Audience, each of which will be discussed in Chapter 1 (Introduction) as well as in the appropriate section introduction. Because I wanted the emphasis of this book to reflect the overall interests of media students, scholars, and teachers, some sections contain more readings than others. The Content section has the most readings, followed by the Audience section, then Production. Within each section, chapters contain clusters (of varying sizes) of readings, representing thematically coherent emphases. For example, the 27 readings in the Content section are organized into three chapters: *Journalism, Advertising, and Public Relations*[3]; *Film*[4] *and Entertainment Television*; and *Music and New Media*. These multifaceted chapters are a helpful way to approach a book containing so many readings that are purposely diverse. However, there are other ways to approach and organize this material, so the appendix also offers alternate tables of contents, based on what I'll call the *site of struggle* (race, gender, class, or any combination thereof), the *arena* (journalism or entertainment), and the medium (audio, television, print, new media, film, etc.). Alternatively, individual instructors might prefer something completely different. The material in this book is nothing if not flexible, so there's no reason not to completely reconsider the order of the material if it helps instructors better meet the goals of their courses.

I hope you come away from this book more aware of precisely what is being presented in the media content that you (and others) engage with/consume/produce and that you think about how you (and others) not only actively interpret and make sense of what you see/read/hear but also about the effects media might have on each of us. I hope you have a sense of the varied and complex forces at work in the social organizations within which media content is produced—the social forces providing opportunities or constraints for certain people working in media organizations, inhibiting or encouraging the production and distribution of certain types of messages or content, and even those social forces affecting us as we use the capabilities of new media to make the step from being consumers to producers of mediated content.

I also hope you come away from this book thinking more positively about your role in the entire media system. You aren't a passive victim of what you see—at least, you don't have to be. You can be an active and engaged participant in the process of media use. At the very least, you can decide what media and what content to utilize, and when, and you can critically evaluate the messages as well as the messenger's motives.

NOTES

1. When I teach courses using collections containing many readings, I rarely assign everything in the book or packet. Instead, I select a few key items I want to address early in the course, and then I ask each student to select one or two readings/chapters (depending on the number available and the number of students, and striving to have most of the chapters selected). The chapters I select can't be chosen by students, and each of the remaining chapters can't be chosen by more than one student. If each student is selecting two chapters, I hope that they are either similar or different enough to make some kind of coherent whole—in practice, this does get a bit "fuzzy," but it's by no means a severe drawback.

These selections perform two functions. First, they create the list of assigned readings for the term, and in so doing give the students a clear voice in guiding their own learning. Second, they form the basis of an assignment in which each student, informed by the selected chapter, leads the class in a discussion of the chapter content. The length of discussion depends on the number of students in the class as well as the class level; lower division students have the shortest amount of time, and graduate students have the most. I evaluate these discussion more on preparation than on execution (especially in a lower level course when students generally have less public speaking experience and aren't as used to nontraditional classroom activities)—if a student has prepared a list of thoughtful questions, which should have filled the required time, the student will earn a good score. I also find it helpful to follow each student-led discussion by posing discussion questions of my own, to ensure that the points I think most important are indeed raised.

Besides the activities presented after each reading, there are some online resources that instructors may wish to consider adapting for use in their courses. With thanks to the reviewer who suggested adding this, I urge you not to judge these resources, some of which were created for younger students, too quickly.

- Forum on Media Diversity. A Project of the Manship School of Mass Communication. http://www.mediadiversityforum.lsu.edu/
- Critical Multicultural Pavilion (Awareness Activities and more) an EdChange Project by Paul C. Gorski. http://www.edchange.org/multicultural/
- DiversityCouncil.org http://www.diversitycouncil.org/hsActivities.shtml
- White Privilege & Racism Resources created by Peggy Beck Haines & Julie Rion. http://www.chlive.org/pbeck/eastlibrary/WHITEPRIVILEGE&RACISMRESOURCES.htm

- Teaching Tolerance: A Project of the Southern Poverty Law Center. http://www.tolerance.org/
- Dimensions of Diversity (Pennsylvania State University). http://diversityeducation.cas.psu.edu/Resources.html
- Project Implicit. (Implicit Association Test) https://implicit.harvard.edu/implicit/

2. Instructors who are new to teaching a course on race and/or gender in the media might find it helpful to look at a chapter I wrote about teaching race and gender in the media; it contains tips from experienced teachers: Lind, R. A. (2003). Race and gender. In M. D. Murray & R. Moore (Eds.), *Mass communication education* (pp. 63–77). Ames: Iowa State Press.

Additionally, instructors should acknowledge at the outset that these topics, and certain readings in particular, are sensitive. Your school might have resources for addressing sensitive topics in the classroom, or you might investigate other resources such as those prepared by UC Berkeley's Office of Educational Development (http://teaching.berkeley.edu/sensitivetopics.html). Another helpful site is a listserv of women's studies teaching, research, and administration (table of contents at http://userpages.umbc.edu/~korenman/wmst/wmsttoc.html). There you will find discussions on a variety of topics, including dealing with sensitive subjects (I and II), teaching about pornography, race/gender/ethnicity, sexuality/sexual orientation, pedagogical issues and strategies, and more.

3. It isn't unusual for these topics to be linked. Many journalism schools offer emphases in advertising, marketing, and public relations.

4. Several readings focus on film—the films themselves, their production, or their reception. Some instructors will find it helpful to show at least part of some of these films during class, although the readings will "work" on a conceptual level even if the students don't know the text.

Still, most students are probably already familiar with *The Twilight Saga*, *The Lion King*, *The Devil Wears Prada*, and *The Nanny Diaries*. The readings present concepts which can be applied to other media texts. For example, the reading featuring *The Twilight Saga* is really intended to present a tool students can use when approaching any media text. Even if they haven't seen the film, the tool is still conceptually useful, and can be applied to another text instead. Instructors will decide whether and how to incorporate the presentation of any of the media texts discussed in this book.

ACKNOWLEDGMENTS

I extend my thanks to the students who have enrolled in my courses in race and gender in the media—from first-year students all the way to PhD candidates—for their energy and enthusiasm for the subject, and for what they have taught me. I'd also like to thank Ziki Dekel, Toni Magyar, Jeanne Zalesky, and Karon Bowers of Pearson and the reviewers of the first and second editions. In particular, I'd like to thank the following reviewers who offered feedback and suggestions for this edition: Heloiza Herscovitz, California State University Long Beach; Trevy McDonald, University of North Carolina at Chapel Hill; Marilyn Olsen, Chicago State University; Joanna Lian Pearson, Colorado State University; Arthur Santana, University of Oregon; and Carrie Sipes, Shippensburg University. I owe a large debt to my stellar research assistant, Paul Couture, who has continued to help in many ways as I juggled the many pieces of this project. I'm lucky to have had him on board for all three editions. Finally, I'm very grateful to all the contributors to this book. I've made some new friends and built some new connections while corresponding with the authors. Thank you all!

. . . To My Parents & My Students.

Laying a Foundation for Studying Race, Gender, Class, and the Media

Rebecca Ann Lind

THE MEDIA MATTER

Ours is a mediated society; much of what we know about, care about, and think is important is based on what we see in the media. The media provide information, entertainment, escape, and relaxation and even help us make small talk. The media can help save lives, and—unfortunately—also encourage people to cause harm to others. For example:

- A doctor performed a surgical procedure with which he was unfamiliar, saving the life of a teenager in the Democratic Republic of Congo, by following the instructions texted to him by his colleague in the United Kingdom.
- Social networking has been charged with causing physical and emotional harm; although the jury is still out on that, what is clear is that people continue to post inappropriate material and engage in inappropriate relationships on Facebook and other sites. One Florida attorney said that about 90% of her divorce cases involve Facebook in some way.
- The AMBER Alert system uses local radio and TV stations in conjunction with electronic highway signs to rapidly disseminate information about child abductions.
- We all deal with spam in our own ways, at best lamenting the huge waste of time it takes to deal with it, occasionally losing important messages along the way, and at worst being bilked out of our life savings by being caught up in a scam. But, to the planet, it's far more than just a waste of our time. The amount of electricity spam uses worldwide is astronomical. According to Kraemer (2011), who references a study by the technology security company McAfee, "Transmitting, processing and filtering spam has been estimated by McAfee at taking an astonishing 33 billion kilowatt hours—that's 33 terawatt hours (TWh) —of the global energy supply, every year! Enough power, according to McAfee, in their *The Carbon Footprint of Spam* study, to 'power 2.4 million homes.'"
- Charitable giving by text has made it even easier for people to donate to a worthy cause, and although the 2010 earthquake in Haiti was not the first appearance of "text-to-give,"

it proved the effectiveness of the campaigns. However, the wide net cast by text donations might lessen the overall amount received; as Patrick Rooney said in an interview (Dickler, 2011), "After giving $5 or $10 dollars, you are probably less likely to go back and write a check for $50 or $100."

■ The Internet can be an effective tool for social change, but it will be a while before we really understand the impact of social media on the Middle Eastern political upheavals that began early in the decade.

■ A New York City subway clerk was torched and killed after some teens copied what they'd seen in the film *Money Train*. Such "copycat crimes" have occurred frequently enough that they've been the subject of an episode of a book by the A&E series *Investigative Reports*.

■ And then, there's the guy whose posts on Twitter on May 2, 2011, in real time as forces surrounded Osama bin Laden's compound, can't help but remind one of why World War II posters proclaimed "Loose Lips Sink Ships." Some examples of Sohaib Athar's tweets are: "Helicopter hovering above Abbottabad at 1AM (is a rare event)"; "Go away, helicopter – before I take out my giant swatter :-/"; and "A huge window shaking bang here in Abbottabad Cantt. I hope it's not the start of something nasty :-S."

If the world is shrinking, and our "village" is becoming global, it's because the media—especially TV—have brought things ever closer to us. The average American household has the television set on more than 8 hours a day. When you consider how averages are calculated, this means that if you—as a busy college student with lots of homework and perhaps some extracurricular activities, not to mention work and/or family obligations—only have the TV on for about 2 hours, then some other household has it on for more than 14 hours. Now think about your involvement with other social institutions. How much time have you spent in the classroom in your entire life? (Because you're in college, it's a lot more than most Americans). How does that compare to your time spent with TV? How will that change as you leave the classroom but continue to watch TV? How many hours per day do you spend with your parents (and reflect on others who might not be as lucky) or with religious leaders? How can the media *not* affect us in some way?

A primary assumption underlying media research is that the media do matter—what we see, read, and hear have some type of affect on us. Different types of scholars, however, approach the matter of media effects differently. Social scientists try to model their research on the natural sciences and strive to maintain objectivity. They often employ experimental or survey methodologies testing for precise and narrowly defined media effects (such as how people's opinions change as a result of media exposure, how people's perceptions of others or about the world in general are affected by what they see/hear/read, or whether people behave more aggressively after being exposed to violent media content).

Critical/cultural researchers, on the other hand, reject not only the desirability of maintaining an objective, value-neutral position but also the very possibility of accomplishing such a goal. As human beings, they argue, we cannot distance ourselves from our social world; indeed, only by immersing ourselves in its practices can we understand them. A subjective interpretation is thus not just desired but required to learn how the media affect the world in which we live. These are fundamentally different assumptions from those held by most social scientists. The types of media effects that critical/cultural researchers investigate are different, too. They're much more broadly defined and often address the cumulative effects of a lifetime of exposure to media content—content that typically represents a limited range of viewpoints, ideas, and images. Ultimately, the media help maintain a status quo in which certain groups in our society routinely have access to power and privilege while others do not. Because the types of questions critical/cultural scholars ask are often different from those posed by social scientists, these scholars tend to prefer qualitative methodologies such as rhetorical or textual analysis, interviews, and ethnographic techniques. In addition, critical/cultural scholars extend their involvement with their research to include the ultimate goal of making the world a better place. If we can identify the ways in which our social structures function to oppress certain groups, then we can try to do something to make things more equitable.

This book contains work by both social scientists and critical/cultural scholars, although the latter group dominates. As you explore the readings, see if you can identify which perspective seems to be guiding the authors and how it affects the questions asked and the way the answers are sought.

RACE, GENDER, AND CLASS MATTER

Like it or not, we do categorize people on the basis of race/ethnicity, gender, and social class. Our perceptions of our own and others' identities color all our interactions; they affect our expectations of others, our expectations of ourselves, and others' expectations of us.

According to sociologist Joseph Healey (2006), we make snap judgments about people (and things). This is necessary because we live in a complex social world, and we simply don't have time to ruminate about all the fine points of everything and everyone we encounter. So we constantly categorize people and groups, often on the basis of nothing more than their most "obvious" characteristics—markers of race and gender. Furthermore, the classifications we make affect our behavior toward others.

Why do the markers of race and gender stand out, rather than other attributes? Why are these the "obvious" characteristics by which we categorize others? Healey said this is because "our attention is drawn to the characteristics that have come to identify the dividing lines between groups" (2006, p. 79.) We could classify people according to length of hair, height, or even the size of their feet, but we don't. Ultimately, we rely on these characteristics because we have been taught to do so: "The dividing line between groups that were created in the past condition our perceptions and impressions in the present. Our 'knowledge' that skin color can be used to judge others and our sensitivity to this characteristic reflects our socialization into a race-conscious society with a long history of racial stratification" (p. 79).

It's the same with gender—we've been socialized into a gender-conscious society that is also stratified (divided in a hierarchical fashion, with some social groups having more of the goods/services valued by society than others) along the lines of gender.

When our generalizations become overly simplistic, when we ignore evidence that they are incorrect, or when they become exaggerated, they have become more than mere "generalizations"; they've become *stereotypes*. Stereotypes reflect our (erroneous) beliefs that the few traits we stress are the most important, and that they apply to all members of the group. They deny the presence and the importance of individual characteristics. Stereotypes are an important component of *prejudice*, which Healey (2006) defined as "the tendency of an individual to think about other groups in negative ways and to attach negative emotions to those groups, and to prejudge individuals on the basis of their group membership" (p. 26). Notice the two dimensions of this definition—prejudice has both a cognitive and an emotional element. Stereotypes are at the heart of the cognitive aspect of prejudice. Prejudice can lead to *discrimination*, although it doesn't need to, because even a very prejudiced person can refrain from acting on her or his negative cognitive or emotional response to certain social groups. Discrimination occurs when people are treated unequally just because they belong to a certain group. People can be treated differently for many different reasons, but any time unequal treatment is based on group membership (even the perception of group membership), the behavior is discriminatory. Stereotypes, prejudice, and discrimination reflect *racism* or *sexism* (although both concepts go much deeper than that and are defined differently by different people), depending on whether the stereotypes are rooted in race/ethnicity or gender.

A final word about race and ethnicity: Although both are socially constructed, some people find it helpful to distinguish between race and ethnicity. To those who do, race is primarily defined in terms of physical characteristics and ethnicity in terms of cultural characteristics. Markers of race include skin color and hair (delineating individuals as being of African, Chinese, Japanese, European descent); markers of ethnicity include religious practices, language use, mode of dress, dietary habits, and cuisine (delineating individuals as being Catholic, Hindu, Irish Americans). Those who employ this distinction tend to believe that the meanings attributed to both physical and cultural markers remain socially constructed; they are not propagating biological theories of race, which for good reason have largely been rejected.

AUDIENCE, CONTENT, PRODUCTION: THREE FOCAL POINTS

Our media system is complex and incorporates a variety of interrelated components, each of which experiences many pressures from both within and without. Three of the major elements of the system are the producers, the audience, and the actual media content.[1] The chapters of this book are organized around those three elements.[2] *Production* involves anything having to do with the creation and distribution of mediated messages: how the messages are assembled, by whom, in what circumstances, and under what constraints. *Content* emphasizes the mediated messages themselves: what they present, and how; what is included, and by implication, what is excluded. *Audience* addresses the people who engage, consume, or interact with mediated messages: how they use the media, what sense they make of media content, and how they are affected by the media.

The production–content–audience distinction is consistent with commonly used models of communication focusing on the source (or sender), message, channel, and receiver. Scholars have presented these models in a variety of ways and with a variety of additional elements, but at their core they focus on who creates or originates the message (sender/source), how the source has presented the ideas she or he wishes to communicate (message), how the actual message is conveyed (channel), and to whom the message is sent (receiver).[3] These SMCR-type models fit well with the social–scientific approach, and all have their roots in the 1940s' work of Harold Lasswell (1948) and Claude Shannon and Warren Weaver (1949). The Shannon and Weaver mathematical model of communication has been most influential in the field.

The production–content–audience distinction is also consistent with how media studies can be approached within the critical/cultural studies perspective. These three realms are usually referred to as *production, text*, and *reception* by critical/cultural scholars and are considered *points of intervention*. Don't let the overt political stance implied by that term escape you—remember the goal of critical/cultural scholars: They want to understand how social structures serve to oppress and repress certain social groups in order to end that oppression.

KEY CONCEPTS AND RECURRING THEMES

As you read this book, you'll begin to notice a pattern of recurring themes. Although these are typically defined when they're presented, it's important that you have a sense of some of the key concepts you'll encounter. In addition, these concepts often inform the readings even if they're not explicitly mentioned. Thinking about these concepts right up front will help frame the readings in a way that should prove beneficial. And speaking of framing . . .

Erving Goffman argued in his classic 1974 book that the framing of an event or activity establishes its meaning. In other words, *framing* is the process by which we make sense of the events around us. Frames are like story lines that allow us to interpret new information in the context of something we already understand. We use frames all the time, without even knowing it. For example, we might say to our friends that a new band is "like Nine Inch Nails with Kanye West." Or that a singer is the "next Lady Gaga." People pitching ideas for films or television shows often frame their ideas in terms of content the networks or studios already know and understand: "It's a Western set in outer space."

Journalists use frames as they prepare news stories, too, whether they know it or not. Despite journalists' quest for the objective presentation of the "facts" to their audiences, Gamson (1989) claimed that "facts have no intrinsic meaning. They take on their meaning by being embedded in a frame or story line that organizes them and gives them coherence, selecting certain ones to emphasize while ignoring others" (p. 157). Because news stories always emphasize some facts over others, we should "think of news as telling stories about the world rather than as presenting 'information,' even though the stories, of course, include factual elements" (p. 157). A story might frame something as an economic or a moral issue, a local issue, or one with far-reaching consequences. A story might emphasize the "horse race" aspects of a political campaign or the important issues and stances held by the candidates. Framing is important because a great deal of research has shown that the frames employed by the media when telling a story can affect our attitudes and judgments about the issues and people involved in the story—especially, as Gitlin (1980) argued, when people don't have firsthand knowledge of and experience with the issue at hand.

In the case of this book, the information provided in this chapter should frame the readings in such a manner that you're on the lookout for certain concepts and that your understanding of the readings is bolstered by your knowledge of these concepts.

Symbolic annihilation is a concept often associated with sociologist Gaye Tuchman (whose 1978 work is widely cited, with good reason) but which was presented by George Gerbner in 1972 and George Gerbner and Larry Gross in 1976. The concept is rooted in two assumptions: that media content offers a form of symbolic representation of society rather than any literal portrayal of society, and that to be represented in the media is in itself a form of power—social groups that are powerless can be relatively easily ignored, allowing the media to focus on the social groups that really matter. It's almost like implying that certain groups don't really exist—even though we can't go out and actually annihilate everyone who isn't a straight, white, middle-to-upper-class male, we can at least try to avoid them in our mediated versions of reality.

Tuchman (1978) focused on the symbolic annihilation of women, but the concept is applicable to any socially constructed group, whether based on gender, race, sexual orientation, ethnicity, appearance, social class, and so on.

Tuchman argued that through absence, condemnation, and trivialization, the media reflect a social world in which women are consistently devalued. As noted above, when the media consistently fail to represent a particular social group, it becomes easy for us to assume that the group either doesn't exist or doesn't really matter. So, if the media consistently present an image of a social world that is (in terms of numbers) dominated by men, Tuchman argued, the media have symbolically annihilated women. But women are not completely absent from media content. Symbolic annihilation also looks for evidence of condemnation or trivialization. Perhaps women are reduced to incompetent childlike beings needing protection from men. Perhaps they're only valuable when they're attractive, young, thin; when they're sexual rather than smart. Perhaps they only function well in the home, getting into all sorts of trouble—some comic, some tragic—when they dare leave the confines of the traditionally acceptable roles of wife and mother. Even when enacting those "appropriate" roles, however, women's contributions may be seen as less valuable than those made by the men of the house. As you read the following essays about a variety of social groups falling outside of the straight white middle-to-upper-class male norm—whether it's women, homosexuals, the poor, the homeless, the uneducated, African Americans, Muslims, Sikhs, Latin Americans, Native Americans, or even "white trash"—consider the extent to which, and how, the group might be experiencing a form of symbolic annihilation in the media.

Intersectionality. The variety of social groups noted earlier raises an important issue: No one is a member of just one social group; we are all a product of a combination of experiences and identities, rooted in a variety of socially constructed classifications. The social reality experienced by gay white males, for example, differs from that experienced by white lesbians or by straight white males—and that of economically disadvantaged gay white males differs from gay white males with greater access to economic and other resources. The social reality experienced by white women differs from that experienced by Black women. The concept of intersectionality helps us understand the futility of trying to know what it means, for example, to be "Native American." None of us can ever be *only* poor, *only* Native American, *only* female, *only* bisexual, *only* deaf or blind. We all experience multiple identities that combine, or intersect, to help us understand who we are, and who others are, and to help others understand who we are. Our unique combination of identities affects all of our interactions with others. As you read this book, you'll see this is a dominant theme. Notice readings that overtly address intersectionality by acknowledging the interaction of race, gender, and class. Also, see how other readings might be informed by intersectionality even though it may not be a key focal point.

Cultural/social identity is another concept you'll come across repeatedly, and not only in readings addressing intersectionality. We all have the sense that we belong to a particular cultural group (or several such groups), even if we haven't consciously thought about it. The more we've thought about it, though, and the more importance and emotional significance attached to our membership in these groups, the more important this cultural identity is to us. Sometimes a cultural or social identity is so pivotal to us that we never approach any social or communication situation without being aware of ourselves as (for example) a gay man. At other times, an aspect of our identity might hardly be considered.

The way issues of identity are handled can serve to reveal or highlight various social tensions rooted in issues of difference. Think about the character "Pat" originated by Julia Sweeney on *Saturday Night Live*. If gender identity didn't matter, Pat wouldn't be funny. If racial identity didn't matter, we wouldn't still, even after his death, care about Michael Jackson's evolving appearance, so we'd never bother making fun of it, and we wouldn't care whether the lightening of his skin was due to vitiligo or personal preference.[4] We wouldn't have people arguing about who is and is not Black, or who has the "right" to employ traditionally Black modes of dress and speech. Members of one social group (in particular the dominant white group) might go so far as to remove someone else's cultural or social identity. We see examples of this every time some-one (usually white) say something like, "I don't see Bill Cosby as a Black comedian; he's just a comedian." As you read this book, note how frequently issues of identity are considered, even if the authors don't explicitly use that term.

Social Construction of Reality. The previous discussion of social identity at least implicitly highlights the fact that identities are negotiated within a social context.[5] Sometimes identities are forced upon or denied to people (as in the "one-drop rule," which claimed that any individual with at least one drop of African blood was Black, or Native American tribal membership based on blood quantum or direct tribal lineage). Sometimes identities are rejected (as when people of one social group attempt to "pass" for another, or when acquaintances of someone who has undergone gender reassignment refuse to refer to the person as "he" rather than "she"). But most often we understand and accept what it means in our culture to be lower class or middle class, male or female, Black, white, Native American, Latino/a, Japanese, Korean, Chinese, and so forth. How do we do this? We learn what it means to be a member of a certain social group through our inter-actions with others. By consistently being treated in a certain way, we begin to expect to be treated in that way. This is exemplified in the process of engenderment, by which a biological female becomes a socially constructed feminine being and a biological male becomes a socially con-structed masculine being. We learn what boys and girls (and later, men and women) act like, do for fun, think is important, are good at, and so on. A similar process is also at work in constructing our ideas about people of various racial and ethnic groups and different social classes.

The importance of race and gender in our society has nothing to do with physical attributes of race and gender and everything to do with society's interpretation of what it means to be a member of a particular gender or racial/ethnic group. What it *really* means to be a Black man, or a Latina, or a Muslim in our society is entirely dependent on what we *think* it means to be a Black man, or a Latina, or a Muslim. As you read this book, think about what the media are telling us about what it means to be a member of a given social group and how that reflects to us what that group is, does, and values.

The perspective that race, gender, and social class are socially constructed phenomena is in contrast with an alternative viewpoint, one which sees race and gender, in particular, as deter-ministic or essentialistic (unalterable; a law of nature, immutable). There is something akin a nature versus nurture debate between these perspectives. Weighing in on the "nature" side are the determinists. Differences among groups are rooted in biology. Sigmund Freud's statement "anatomy is destiny" is often presented as "biology is destiny." One's character is fixed at birth, based on the presence or absence of male reproductive organs. One's family tree roots one into a specific racial category; members of different races have different traits; it is biology which (it is claimed) makes certain races "naturally" more or less musical, athletic, intelligent, and so forth. Such a position is not one with which I am comfortable. The social constructionist perspective, on the other hand, is more analogous to the "nurture" position.

Importantly, seeing these groupings as social constructions allows us the opportunity to lessen or perhaps move toward removing inequity. If we identify the presence of racism, classism, sexism, and heterosexism, we can hope that with awareness, the social reality we construct through our interactions and our social institutions will reflect a more egalitarian approach to engaging issues of difference.

At the core, each of these phenomena—racism, classism, sexism, heterosexism—is about power relationships. Our society is hierarchical; some groups have more power than others do. The hierarchy allows the dominant group to consider itself superior to the subordinated group(s), and to treat members of the subordinated groups differently just because of their membership in that group. The hierarchy allows the dominant group to determine, among other things, into which group an individual belongs and the "proper place" of the subordinated group. Overt racism, for example, presented the proper place for African Americans as at the back of the bus and away from the "Whites Only" drinking fountains. Overt sexism said that a woman's place was in the home (preferably barefoot and pregnant). The "isms" in our culture are less overt nowadays, but without doubt they remain. As I write this, the hotly contested issue of same-sex marriage highlights the heterosexist hierarchy. The dominant group has the power to make a rule defining marriage as a union between a man and a woman. The dominant group can define whether the lived experiences of the subordinated group do, in fact, represent a "problem" that might be worthy of society's time, attention, and resources—and the ever-present ideology of "the American Dream" makes it all-too-easy to dismiss claims of unequal opportunity made by subordinated groups, and to say that if they would only apply themselves, try harder, they would succeed. The dominant groups can rationalize why so few people from an underprivileged background, or women, or people of color, have advanced to truly important positions in society (there are notable exceptions, of course, but not of sufficient number to demonstrate equality). The dominant groups can proclaim that affirmative action is no longer needed, and that we are living in a post-racial, color-blind, gender-blind, and classless society. As the readings in this book will show, we are not.

Discourse is a concept frequently employed by scholars. It may be used/defined differently by different people, but at the heart of the matter, discourse essentially refers to ways of conceptualizing, discussing, or writing about various social phenomena (such as racism or sexism). Discourses can be seen as interpretive frameworks that have a powerful role in defining the phenomenon of interest, in determining exactly what it is and how it can or should be dealt with—or even whether it should be addressed at all. In a way, the concept of discourse is related to framing. It's probably safe to say that discourse is a more "rich" or "dense" concept that tends to be favored by critical/cultural scholars, while framing is more narrow and tends to be favored by social scientists.

Ideology is a concept of fundamental importance to critical/cultural studies, with roots in Marxism. As with discourse, definitions of ideology abound; different scholars approach the concept slightly differently. For our purposes, ideology is best understood as a set of deeply held ideas about the nature of the world and the way the world ought to be. There are many different ideologies, and they all affect the way any given society has been socially constructed. Some ideologies are more repressive or more egalitarian than others. Even within any given society, multiple ideologies can be found, but one ideology is usually accepted by most of the society's members. We call this the *dominant ideology*.

Discovering and articulating a culture's dominant ideology and how it's perpetuated is important to critical/cultural scholars, because if it serves to oppress and repress certain cultural groups, these scholars would like to see it changed. Media perform a pivotal role in perpetuating the dominant ideology, because media texts so often produce and reproduce that ideology. If we (as members of a society) don't see much that represents an alternative way of approaching or understanding our world, it's unlikely we'll embrace an alternative ideology. Because of this, it's vital to examine the way the media represent members of a culture's social groups. In our culture, we should look at media depictions not only of the dominant social group (straight, white, middle-to-upper-class male) but also of the subordinated groups (homosexuals, women, people of color, people of lower economic classes, and the like.)

We should also look at how the media represent groups that explicitly challenge the status quo. The media can ignore such challenges only up to a point—sometimes the groups become so large and well organized that they must be acknowledged. But when they are portrayed in the media, groups challenging the dominant ideology are often represented as deviant, as fringe elements, as disorganized—anything other than offering a viable and beneficial alternative to the way things are. An example of this occurs when the media represent members of the women's movement as hairy-legged lesbian man haters who want to destroy the sanctity of the nuclear family. In labor disputes, maybe union negotiators are described as "demanding" while management is "only doing what is logical during the current economic climate." In the early days of the environmental movement, its members were seen as hippies, and called "tree huggers." Members of the women's movement were called "bra burners." These portrayals provide examples of what it means to belong to these groups and in doing so represent to us all the dominant ideology in action. Why should we take these weirdos and their crazy ideas seriously? Again, if that's all we see, that might be all we know.

CRITICAL THINKING AND MEDIA LITERACY

One of this book's goals is to encourage you to think critically about the media. *Critical thinking* has been defined in a variety of ways, but at the very least, it involves "the ability to examine issues rationally, logically and coherently" (Stark & Lowther, 1988, p. 23). However, a fuller definition helps delineate the processes involved more clearly. A group of experts gathered by the American Philosophical Association defined critical thinking as "purposeful, self-regulatory judgment which results in interpretation, analysis, evaluation, and inference, as well as explanation of the evidential, conceptual, methodological, or contextual considerations upon which that judgment is based" (Facione, 1990, p. 2). Essentially, for the type of course using this book, critical thinking boils down to asking and trying to answer the following types of questions (which will take a variety of forms, in part due to whether they're directed at media content, media production, or media audiences): What do I see? What do I think it means? How did it get that way? To what extent is that appropriate, a good thing, or handled effectively? What does this tell me about some aspect of our media system, or our society? And finally, why do I say that?

Being critical participants in our media system means constantly asking questions and doing our best to answer them in a logical and defensible fashion. We should engage in a systematic but not necessarily linear process of thinking through these issues, defining terms and concepts, looking at and evaluating evidence, considering the pros and cons of various positions, acknowledging underlying assumptions, and justifying our position.

As elements of critical thinking are tailored to fit the media context, the result is a way of thinking that shares a great deal with the idea of *media literacy*. Although the United States falls far behind much of the rest of the developed world in terms of the extent to which media literacy is developed and integrated into the educational system, we are beginning to understand its importance. For example, Wulff (1997) argued that media literacy is a key component in people's ability to participate actively in a democratic society, as well a within a global context.

But what exactly is media literacy? It involves expanding the general concept of "literacy" (the ability to read and write) to what the Aspen Institute called "the powerful post-print media that dominate our informational landscape" (Aufderheide, 1993, p. 1). Media literacy "helps people understand, produce and negotiate meanings in a culture made up of powerful images, words and sounds" (Aufderheide, p. 1). The Institute provided further guidance as to what it actually means to be media literate: "A media literate person: Can decode, evaluate, analyze and produce both print and electronic media. The fundamental objective of media literacy is critical autonomy in relationship to all media" (Aufderheide, p. 1).

According to the Center for Media Literacy's Web site,

> A media literate person doesn't know all the answers, but knows how to ask the right questions: Who created this message? Why? How and why did they choose what to include and what to leave out of this message? How is it intended to influence me?

The National Communication Association (1998) developed five standards of media literacy, each of which can be reflected in specific competencies or abilities and as a result are particularly valuable for educational purposes. Here are the standards, with some of their associated competencies:

- *Media literate communicators demonstrate knowledge and understanding of the ways people use media in their personal and public lives.* (Specifically, they "recognize the roles of culture and language in media practices"; "identify personal and public media content, forms, and products"; and "analyze the historical and current ways in which media affect people's personal and public lives"; among other competencies.)
- *Media literate communicators demonstrate knowledge and understanding of the complex relationships among audiences and media content.* (Specifically, they "identify media forms, content, and products"; "recognize that media are open to multiple interpretations"; "explain how media socialize people"; and "evaluate ideas and images in media with possible individual, social and cultural consequences"; among other competencies.)
- *Media literate communicators demonstrate knowledge and understanding that media content is produced within social and cultural contexts.* (Specifically, they "identify the production contexts of media content and products," "identify the social and cultural constraints on the production of media," "identify the social and cultural agencies that regulate media content and products," and "evaluate the ideas and aesthetics in media content and products.")
- *Media literate communicators demonstrate knowledge and understanding of the commercial nature of media.* (Specifically, they "explain how media organizations operate" and "compare media organizations to other social and cultural organizations," among other competencies.)
- *Media literate communicators demonstrate ability to use media to communicate to specific audiences.* (Specifically, they "identify suitable media to communicate for specific purposes and outcomes"; "identify the roles and responsibilities of media production teams"; "analyze their media work for technical and aesthetic strengths and weaknesses"; and "recognize that their media work has individual, social, and ethical consequences"; among other competencies.) (pp. 19–23)

As you read this book, consider these media literacy standards and competencies. Notice how the authors reflect these competencies in their writing. Think about how your responses to the items presented in the "It's Your Turn" section of each reading reflect these competencies. Try to exhibit these competencies as you read/see/hear media content and as you create media content for class or other purposes. You'll probably find that the more you do it, the easier it is to respond in a media literate fashion to the "It's Your Turn" items as well as to the media content you encounter in your day-to-day life. Perhaps it'll even become second nature, which would be good, because a more media-literate media user is a more empowered and less vulnerable media user.

NOTES

1. There are other elements affecting media, such as the legal/regulatory system, but even though regulators could be considered a specialized segment of the audience, this book won't address that part of the process.

2. Classification systems such as the one used here are useful devices to help us organize and make sense of ideas and processes, but they're not perfect—some readings don't fit neatly into a single category. In particular, as will be discussed in the *Audience* section, the concept of *produsage* represents a hybrid of production and usage—in which tendrils from two areas which used to be clearly separate have now begun to merge. As you read this book, think about the questions posed in item #3 in "It's Your Turn," that follows.

3. Although this book doesn't have a special section devoted to the channel of communication, some readings do focus on how the channel of communication might change the relationship of the participants within the communication process and perhaps even the communication process itself. Note also that one of the alternate tables of contents organizes the readings by medium.

4. Consider the difference between Michael Jackson lightening his skin and the voluntary skin darkening undertaken by whites everywhere at the beach, in tanning salons, and so on. Why do we not tease whites for becoming darker, and what does this reveal about the power hierarchy in our society?

5. The social construction of reality concept was first presented by sociologists Peter Berger and Thomas Luckmann (1966). Although it's a little book, it has had a large impact on many disciplines.

IT'S YOUR TURN: WHAT DO YOU THINK? WHAT WILL YOU FIND?

1. At this point, does the social–scientific or the critical/cultural studies approach seem to make more sense to you? Why? What do you think are the strengths and weaknesses of each approach?

2. Consider the term "points of intervention" used within the critical/cultural studies tradition. Why do you think they use that term? Would social scientists ever employ such a term? Why or why not?

3. As you read this book, think about how some readings have been categorized as being about production, content, or audience—do you agree with all of the classifications? If not, why do you think it appears in that category? Where would you have put the reading, and why? As you're considering this, think about what this tells us about the integration of the various components of our media system. Also consider what this tells us about the nature of any classification system; reflect on how such systems can be helpful even though they're flawed.

4. *Intersectionality* is presented as a major recurring theme in the chapters that follow. To what extent do you think it's important to acknowledge the variety of influences on our cultural identity? To what extent do you think it's possible to isolate just one element (say, gender or race) for study—what is lost, and what is gained, by doing so?

REFERENCES

Aufderheide, P. (1993). *Media literacy: A report of the national leadership conference on media literacy.* Queenstown, MD: The Aspen Institute.

Berger, P. L., & Luckmann, T. (1966). *The social construction of reality: A treatise in the sociology of knowledge.* New York: Doubleday.

Center for Media Literacy. (n.d.). Frequently asked questions. Retrieved May 2, 2011, from www.medialit.org/faq

Dickler, J. (2011, March 15). Earthquake aid totals $25 million – far less than Haiti. *CNNMoney.com.* Retrieved September 20, 2011, from http://money.cnn.com/2011/03/14/pf/japan_earthquake_donations/index.htm

Facione, P. A. (1990). *Critical thinking: A statement of expert consensus for purposes of educational assessment and instruction.* ERIC Document Reproduction Service No. ED 315423.

Gamson, W. A. (1989). News as framing: Comments on Graber. *American Behavioral Scientist, 33*(2), 157–161.

Gerbner, G. (1972). Violence in television drama: Trends and symbolic functions. In G. A. Comstock & E. A. Rubenstein (Eds.), *Media content and control*, Television and social behavior (Vol. 1, pp. 28–127). Washington, DC: U.S. Government Printing Office.

Gerbner, G., & Gross, L. (1976). Living with television. *Journal of Communication, 26*(2), 172–199.

Gitlin, T. (1980). *The whole world is watching: Mass media in the making and unmaking of the New Left.* Berkeley, CA: University of California Press.

Goffman, E. (1974). *Frame analysis.* Philadelphia: University of Pennsylvania Press.

Healey, J. (2006). *Race, ethnicity, gender, and class: The sociology of group conflict and change.* (4th ed.). Thousand Oaks, CA: Pine Forge Press.

Kraemer, S. (2011, March 19). The world just got back 13 terawatt hours of spam-wasted electricity! *Conservation.* Retrieved September 20, 2011, from http://cleantechnica.com/2011/03/19/the-world-just-got-back-13-terawatt-hours-of-spam-wasted-electricity/

Lasswell, H. D. (1948). The structure and function of communication in society. In B. Lyman (Ed.), *The communication of ideas* (pp. 37–51). New York: Harper & Row.

National Communication Association. (1998). *The speaking, listening, and media literacy standards and competency statements for K–12 education.* Retrieved July 18, 2002, from www.natcom.org/Instruction/K-12/standards.pdf

Shannon, C., & Weaver, W. (1949). *The mathematical theory of communication.* Urbana, IL: University of Illinois Press.

Stark, J. S., & Lowther, M. A. (1988). *Strengthening the ties that bind: Integrating undergraduate liberal and professional study.* Ann Arbor: University of Michigan.

Tuchman, G. (1978). The symbolic annihilation of women by the mass media. In G. Tuchman, A. K. Daniels, & J. W. Benet (Eds.), *Hearth and home: Images of women in the mass media* (pp. 5–38). New York: Oxford University Press.

Wulff, S. (1997). Media literacy. In W. G. Christ (Ed.), *Media education assessment handbook* (pp. 123–142). Mahwah, NJ: Lawrence Erlbaum Associates.

AUDIENCES

Some people might argue that the audience is the most important element in our complex media system. We are, after all, the commodity that is bought and sold—bought for the price of the content provided by the media outlets and sold by the media outlets to advertisers. Because the U.S. media system operates under the marketplace model, economic factors are paramount; and because a larger audience means greater advertising revenues, most media outlets strive to generate the largest possible audiences. If any given media text fails to bring in a large enough audience, it probably won't continue to be offered. It's not so much an "if we build it, they will come" perspective as an "if they don't come, we'll take it away." Because of the importance of knowing how many people are listening/watching/reading/and so on, each medium has its own mechanism for measuring audience size. Television programs, for example, live and die by the Nielsen ratings; the Audit Bureau of Circulations measures both magazine and newspaper circulation, and Arbitron is the key provider of radio ratings.

Yet the consideration of audience size is just one of several important attributes of media audiences. Size does matter, but there's more to it than that; more even than size coupled with demographics. These aspects of the audience might seem the most important to media outlets, but perhaps that's just because they're the easiest things to measure and to quantify. Here, we'll ignore these traditional favorites of media organizations in favor of more scholarly considerations of audiences.

Before presenting the chapters that make up the Audience section of the book, we should think about the nature of media audiences. We traditionally think of audience members as the receivers of the messages sent by the media (although of course the Internet and other new media allow the process of creating media to come full circle, when an audience member becomes a producer—a phenomenon that inspired the idea of *Produsage* [Chapter 4]). Media audiences tend to be very large, heterogeneous, and dispersed. We're also relatively anonymous; although when we're using new communications technologies such as the Internet, we can sometimes be identified, usually the message sender doesn't really know who we are. Providing feedback to a content producer or media outlet is difficult, or at least involves greater effort than in other communication situations. Finally, there is a debate over whether the media audience is active or passive. Some people argue we're nothing more than "couch potatoes," although if some of us are so involved that we actually begin to create content then we can be very active indeed.

At the very least, we are active enough so that we are the ones who initiate the communication process. We are invited to the communication event by virtue of the fact that media have produced content designed to appeal to us, but it is we who decide whether, when, and how we will partake. This book operates from the perspective that members of the media audience are active participants in the communication process. Excluding unintentional media exposure (such as when we're shopping in a store that has the radio on), we are the ones who approach the media. We decide which medium to use (TV? book? Internet?) and what specific content (crime story? textbook?). We are not media victims, swayed to whatever perspectives we encounter. We use, interpret, and make sense of the media texts we use (or produse) as we go about our daily lives.

However, even though we're not passive dupes of the media, we have to remember that the media do matter. The media, taken as a whole, represents one of several social institutions that help us understand what it means to be a member of our society. These social institutions present to us and help instill in us the values, attitudes, and beliefs shared within our culture. In other words, much of the content produced by the media reflects society's dominant ideologies. And when we're exposed to so much material reproducing certain values and ignoring or denigrating others, we can't help but be affected in some way.

The chapters in this part of the book investigate the people who read, watch, listen, or otherwise engage with mediated messages. How do people interpret what they see and hear? Why and how do people use certain media or certain types of content? How are people affected by what they see and hear? How do new media blur the lines between media consumption and creation?

The 17 readings in the Audience section start with two traditional emphases of audience research, and then look into the developing area called produsage. Chapter 2, *Media Effects*, offers five readings reflecting traditional social–scientific studies of media effects, even if addressing larger cultural issues. As mentioned in the preface and introduction, the readings represent a diverse array of viewpoints and voices (you'll agree with some authors more than others and prefer some authors' writing styles over others). Please also note that the alternate tables of contents include a list of which readings address class issues.

In Reading 2.1, Bradley Gorham reviews the social–scientific evidence demonstrating the effects that stereotypical images have on audiences—even on people who reject stereotypes. The next four readings present experimental research. Travis Dixon, in Reading 2.2, investigates whether seeing stereotypical crime portrayals shapes perceptions of African Americans and crime. His findings suggest that participants tend to think of criminals as Black unless provided with overwhelming information that a suspect is white. Lori Bindig (Reading 2.3) created and tested the effectiveness of a media-literacy-based curriculum for people undergoing treatment for eating disorders. In Reading 2.4 Cory Armstrong and Mindy McAdams examined how author's gender influences the perceived credibility of blogs. Their findings suggest that gender stereotypes persist for credibility, especially for novice blog readers; experienced blog readers seemed to evaluate credibility by using indicators other than gender cues. Ryan Rogers, in Reading 2.5, demonstrates that the acceptance of hate speech while playing online games can be influenced by the game's design.

Chapter 3 focuses on what is broadly called *Audience Studies*. It presents a qualitative look at audience reception, use, and interpretation of media content from a critical cultural perspective. These readings reflect on audience identity (considering identity a social and cultural construction), and investigate how audiences understand and make sense of specific examples of media content (showing that people's discussions and interpretations of media content can provide an understanding of contemporary race/gender/class issues). Unlike the experimental studies presented in Chapter 2, the research in Chapter 3 relies on in-depth interviews, ethnographic methods, and critical analysis of audience-produced texts.

Michelle Wolf, Melinda Krakow, and Rebecca Taff lead off the chapter (Reading 3.1) with a discussion of how women with physical disabilities think and feel about media representations of women's bodies, and their own bodies. Reading 3.2, by Helen Ho, considers how Asian American men interpret, and are in part defined by, mediated representations of Asian Americans. Neil Alperstein (Reading 3.3) studies how men evaluate and compare themselves to examples of what he calls "less than ideal" men in ad campaigns (e.g., the GEICO caveman). Reading 3.4, by Dina Ibrahim and Aymen Abdel Halim, looks at Arab Americans' and Muslims' interpretations of how news programming affects their sense of identity and makes them feel about themselves.

In Reading 3.5, Sheena Malhotra reflects on how Bollywood films can evoke "home" for members of the South Asian diaspora (displaced or dispersed people). Pamela Tracy (Reading 3.6) studied how young girls use popular music to understand and negotiate their social and cultural identities. Importantly, Tracy's themes are rooted in how the audience engages with this aspect of popular culture, rather than in the specific pop culture artifacts themselves. In his analysis of audience postings about the use of Native American mascots, Richard King (Reading 3.7) claims that the audience is actually arguing about race. Again, the crucial aspect of the reading is showing how people use mediated messages to negotiate some part of their social reality.

Chapter 4 is about *Produsage*, or the melding of "production" and "usage." Produsage as a concept was introduced by Axel Bruns (2005; 2008; Bruns & Jacobs, 2006), and reflects a key aspect of our evolving media environment. When considering "the creative, collaborative, and ad hoc engagement with content [on] user-led spaces," Bruns (2008, p. 1) argues, "the term 'production' is no longer accurate." In the produsage era, "people are much more actively involved in shaping their own media and network usage" (Bruns, 2008, p. 15). Earlier editions of this book had considered this concept, in various ways, but only now do we have an appropriate label. You may argue that some of the other readings in this book would fit well under the produsage label. I encourage you to make as many connections across all the material as possible.

In reading 4.1, andre carrington explores the world of fan fiction, focusing on a form of creative writing in which fans generate their own scripts for an established media series (in this case, *Buffy the Vampire Slayer* and *Harry Potter*), and what these new stories reveal. Travis Gosa (Reading 4.2) looks at Obama-inspired content on the Internet during the 2008 presidential election, arguing that user-generated content is an important part of political discourse. In Reading 4.3, Sitthivorada Boupha, Ashley Grisso, John Morris, Lynne Webb, and Monica Zakeri analyze how users enact ethnic identity on Facebook. Reading 4.4, by Robert Mejia, considers how mobile communications technologies may actually not result in bringing people closer together, but in keeping disparate people farther apart. Diego Costa, in Reading 4.5, argues that our social world is set up to facilitate male–female relationships, and asks how queers might make sense of their social world—and points out the hierarchies potentially reinforced by the digital divide.

Taken as a whole, the readings in this section of the book illustrate the wide range of audience-oriented scholarship that can be conducted. They also highlight the need to go far beyond merely counting how many people are consuming media texts. Remember, the average American household has the TV on for more than 8 hours a day—and although TV is our dominant medium, it's not the only one we use. We should understand how people are affected by the media, how and why people use (or produse) media in their daily lives, and how people make sense of or interpret what they see/read/hear.

REFERENCES

Bruns, A. (2008). *Blogs, Wikipedia, Second Life, and beyond: From production to produsage.* New York: Peter Lang.

Bruns, A. (2005). *Gatewatching: Collaborative online news production.* New York: Peter Lang.

Bruns, A., & Jacobs, J. (Eds.). (2006). *Uses of blogs.* New York: Peter Lang.

Media Effects

2.1 THE SOCIAL PSYCHOLOGY OF STEREOTYPES: IMPLICATIONS FOR MEDIA AUDIENCES

Bradley W. Gorham

> *The author reviews the social scientific evidence demonstrating how stereotypical images affect media audiences. Don't be too quick to say, "The media don't affect me!"*

On September 25, 1996, as part of a series on race relations in America, ABC's *Nightline* featured a short video clip that I often use in my classes on media effects. The video shows a large, stern-faced Black man in a white T-shirt in a classic mug-shot pose: The man is seen in profile, and then the camera slowly turns to face the man head-on. As the camera turns toward the classic head-on mug shot, the following words are slowly revealed: "Armed robbery . . . Battery . . . Drug Possession . . . Concealed weapon . . . Apprehended . . . March 1994 by . . . Police Officer . . . Robert Williams . . . shown here." Ted Koppel then comes on and asks viewers if they "fell for the premise of that video" and confides that he and much of the *Nightline* staff did. So did I the first time I saw it. So do most of my students.

The trick, of course, is that we are led to believe that the person shown in the video is the perpetrator of these crimes, a belief that's proven wrong by the last set of words. The Black man in the "mug shot" is the police officer, but a few seconds before, most people naturally assumed that he was the criminal. Do we think this because the man is Black? At this point, a small ruckus usually ensues, as my students bristle at the notion that the race of the man might have affected their interpretation of the video. They inevitably point out that if you did the same thing with a white guy, they'd think the same thing. After all, they argue, it's the format of the video—the mug shot, the crimes listed next to it, and so on— that tricks the viewer, not the man's race. They'd think *exactly* the same thing no matter what the race of the man pictured.

Well, not quite.

Although the format of the video clearly plays an important role in steering people toward the belief that the man pictured is the criminal, research in social psychology and media effects suggests a man's race also plays a role. In fact, experiments altering the race of suspects shown

17

in TV news stories have found that people do *not* make exactly the same interpretations; this is true even for people who don't endorse any type of prejudice or bigotry.

In other words, race really does seem to affect how we interpret media, especially in subtle ways. My purpose here is to help explain why this is so and what it means for media audiences.

THE SOCIAL PSYCHOLOGY OF STEREOTYPES

It's important to realize at the outset that stereotypes aren't simply something that only bigots have experience with. We all know about stereotypes, and we're all pretty familiar with the stereotypes of various social groups circulating in our culture. In fact, research has shown that when asked to list the traits defining the cultural stereotype of Blacks, both high- and low-prejudiced people come up with essentially the same list (Devine & Elliot, 1995), including traits such as poor, hostile, uneducated, athletic, and rhythmic. It's only when asked to list their personal beliefs about Blacks that we see a difference: High-prejudiced people tend to list the same traits they listed for the cultural stereotype, while low-prejudiced respondents tend to list other, more positive traits. However, the cultural stereotype seems to play an important role in how we process information about people from various groups regardless of whether we endorse it. To understand this, we need to examine what a stereotype is more generally.

Psychologists Hamilton & Trolier (1986) defined a stereotype as "a cognitive structure that contains the perceiver's knowledge, beliefs, and expectancies about some human group" (p. 133). This definition highlights an important characteristic of stereotypes: They are structures in our minds, and as such, they function in much the same way as other structures in our minds do. Psychologists call these cognitive structures *schema* and believe that schema help simplify a complex social environment by quickly and efficiently processing incoming stimuli based on the presence of a few relevant characteristics. We have schema about objects (chairs, bicycles), events (what happens when we go to a restaurant), and people. Schemas help us categorize the world by telling us the basic characteristics of the things we encounter. This allows us to make judgments about our environment without having to expend much mental effort. Our dog schema, for example, says that dogs bark and have fur, four legs, and a tail. So when we see a creature with these basic characteristics, we don't have to examine it much further to know it's a dog and how we will act or respond. *A stereotype, then, is a schema for people we perceive as belonging to a social group.*

Schemas help structure not only our knowledge of things but also our expectations. Because they tell us what characteristics the category usually contains, schemas lead us to expect certain things once other traits of a category have been encountered. Thus, when we encounter someone of a particular social group, whether based on gender, race, ethnicity, sexual orientation, occupation, or something else, the schema we have for that group tells us what features or traits we should expect to encounter. Using the information stored in our schema for Latinos, for example, we can quickly make judgments about a Latina and our potential interaction with her without having to expend much mental energy to evaluate the person in great detail.

This expectation that we should see additional features associated with a schema once any features of the schema are encountered is called *priming*. Once we see or hear something in the environment that activates a schema, related concepts tend to be primed, or triggered, and we're more likely to expect them and respond to them than to unrelated concepts. This should especially be true when the schema is something we encounter often through repeated and consistent exposure. A primed concept is thought to be more accessible to our consciousness (and our cognitive processing). Furthermore, because we expect them, primed concepts can influence how we perceive subsequent information. That is, because we're looking for the primed concepts, we're more likely to perceive incoming stimuli as containing the traits and features our schema have taught us to expect. *In this way, priming tends to alter our interpretations of things toward what fits (is congruent with) our schema.*

Stereotypes, then, are schema that help organize our knowledge and beliefs about social groups. They also structure our expectations and influence how we perceive incoming messages. A landmark study in social psychology can help make all these concepts more concrete. Devine (1989) thought that because stereotypes are so pervasive in the media and in our everyday interactions with others, they become very well learned. Stereotypes become so well learned, she argued, that when we encounter someone of a particular social group, the stereotype for that group is primed and automatically activated and influences subsequent cognitive processing (the interpretation of the situation).

To test her hypothesis, Devine (1989) first primed research participants (all of whom were white) by showing them a set of words flashed on a screen so quickly that they couldn't consciously identify or recall them. Some people saw words that were consistent with stereotypes of Blacks, while others saw words that were not consistent with those stereotypes. People then read a paragraph about a person of unspecified race doing things that could be interpreted as either an aggressive shove or a playful push and evaluated that person.

What Devine found was that when subconsciously primed with words reflecting racial stereotypes, almost everybody (both prejudiced and non-prejudiced people) evaluated the racially unspecified target person in a fashion congruent with the stereotype. That is, people were more likely to think the person in the story was aggressive and hostile if they'd been primed with the Black stereotype. This was true regardless of whether the person endorsed the Black stereotype. Furthermore, although the prime words avoided references to hostility (part of the stereotype of Black men), people still activated that portion of the stereotype. As a result, Devine concluded that stereotypes are so well learned that they become automatically triggered in individuals whenever a person from that particular group is encountered.

Devine (1989) also found that there were important differences between knowledge of the stereotype and endorsement of it, and between high- and low-prejudiced individuals. She gave a different group of people 1 minute to list as many terms as they could think of, both socially acceptable and not, for the group "Black Americans." Shortly afterward, participants wrote down all of their thoughts and reactions to the term "Black Americans" and the labels they had just generated. While both low- and high-prejudiced people came up with similar numbers of pejorative and non-pejorative terms in the first task (reflecting the automatic and pervasive nature of the stereotype), there were significant differences in the second. Highly prejudiced people were much more likely to include stereotypical thoughts than less-prejudiced people were—despite the fact that the stereotype had been primed in all of them and that their label-listing task showed no significant differences. Devine concluded that low-prejudiced people used some type of controlled cognitive processing to suppress the automatically activated stereotype. They also seemed reluctant to try to describe the group as a whole. Thus, both high- and low-prejudiced people have the schema for the stereotype of Blacks, but it appears that only highly prejudiced individuals endorse it. Low-prejudiced individuals actively try to suppress it.

Since Devine's study was published, research has blossomed about how stereotypes can be triggered without us even being aware of it. The results are pretty clear: Stereotypes of various social groups can be activated automatically, and they can influence how we interpret incoming information (Blair & Banaji, 1996). What is even more disconcerting is that stereotypes can activate and influence processing even when people don't endorse them. Fortunately, research suggests that people can inhibit these tendencies if they know about them (Monteith, 1993) and if they have the cognitive capacity to work against them (Blair & Banaji, 1996). At the very least, people can try to work around stereotypes once they've been activated (Devine, 1989).

It's important to keep in mind that stereotypes often offer explanations about the groups they categorize. This is an especially nasty characteristic of many stereotypes: Not only can they tell us what people of a social group are like, but they also tell us *why* the people are like that. For example, Devine and Elliot (1995) showed that many people chose "poor" and "lazy" as traits describing the social stereotype of Blacks. It doesn't take much effort to link these and say that the stereotype is "Blacks are poor because they are lazy." In a broader sense, one can say that a stereotype asserts that people of a group simply *are* a certain way, and these "natural tendencies" lead to particular behaviors more often for that group than for others.

There's a lot of research about how people explain the behaviors of people belonging to various social groups. The theory of the *ultimate attribution error* (Pettigrew, 1979), for example, explains the behaviors of "ingroups" and "outgroups" as functions of either "internal" or "external" causes. Ingroups are the groups of people we identify with or feel we belong to (males, or Blacks, or Irish, or Chevy truck owners), while outgroups are people who are "not like us." Pettigrew argued that when we see a person doing something, we make an inference about why the person behaved that way. Maybe we think the person is simply responding to the situation, in a sense being pushed by external forces to act that way. On the other hand, we might infer the behavior is the result of the individual's personality or some other internal characteristic of the person and has nothing to do with the situation.

Pettigrew (1979) argued that the inferences we make about people's behaviors are biased in favor of our ingroups—we make the ingroups we identify with look good and the outgroups we don't identify with look bad. In Pettigrew's theory, ingroup members seeing someone doing something bad will be more likely to attribute that behavior to internal causes if the person is from an outgroup. But if it's an ingroup member doing it, they'll attribute the same bad behavior to external factors. At the same time, if we see a man do something good, we're more likely to infer that he had to do it under the circumstances (an external cause) if he's from an outgroup. But we'll think it represents "just how that guy is" if he is from a group we identify with. The relevance of this for racial stereotypes should be clear: white people could be more likely to think a Black person committing a crime did so because "that's what those people are like" (an internal characteristic of Black people), whereas a white person could be driven to the crime by bad parenting, alcohol addiction, or some other external factor. Likewise, positive behaviors will likely be attributed to external causes when performed by outgroup members and internal causes when performed by members of the ingroup. Thus, the ingroup is always held in higher esteem, because good behaviors are seen as internal to the group, whereas bad behaviors are the result of negative external influences.

It's important to keep in mind that, even though these cognitive mechanisms operate outside of our conscious awareness, they appear to support positive views of ourselves. This implies that, even if people don't endorse stereotypes, members of dominant social groups interpret information in ways that support their superiority and, by extension, reinforce the subordinate position of minority groups. Stereotypes are rarely neutral, and so they not only attempt to describe and explain the behavior of groups, but they also evaluate those groups based on the norms of the majority. For example, Peffley, Hurwitz, and Sniderman (1997) found that racial stereotypes played an important role in people's opinions about welfare mothers and criminals, but only when those welfare mothers and criminals were Black. Furthermore, people's opinions about welfare mothers were closely related to beliefs about Blacks' commitment to the work ethic, suggesting that the explanation that "Black welfare mothers do not want to work because they are inherently lazy" was more salient than a similar belief about white welfare mothers. This is hardly a neutral belief in a society brought up to believe in the value of hard work and merit-based rewards, and thus the stereotype of Blacks as lazy and uneducated may make it harder for many whites to accept that the Black community should receive "extra" help or economic aid.

Stereotypes clearly don't give us the "whole picture" of a group, as if such a thing is even possible, and they aren't neutral in their evaluations. Instead, stereotypes give us highly edited and distorted images of groups that tend to support the way groups are treated in society. Cultural stereotypes of minority groups, especially, tend to reflect the biases and the histories of the majority, such that the people being stereotyped are reduced to a few characteristics that are socially relevant for understanding that group's place in society. The important thing to realize about this is that stereotypes often perform this function without our conscious awareness or control. We may not endorse these stereotypes at all, nor have any intention of seeing the world through prejudicial lenses. But unfortunately, *a stereotype, as just another schema that helps us process the world around us, helps maintain a view of that world that works in favor of the majority.*

STEREOTYPES AND THEIR EFFECTS ON MEDIA AUDIENCES

All of this research by social psychologists has not gone unnoticed by media researchers. Although relatively small compared to the body of work studying the stereotypes present in media content, a growing area of media studies uses psychological research to examine the effects of such images on audiences. For example, Peffley, Shields, and Williams (1996) investigated how manipulating the race of a suspect in a television news story affected viewers' interpretation of that story. In a sense, they tested the assertion my students make after viewing the *Nightline* segment described earlier—the race of the suspect doesn't matter because the story's format makes the suspect seem guilty. The researchers asked a sample of white students to fill out a survey about a variety of social issues (including questions measuring prejudice toward African Americans). A week later, the students watched a brief television news story about the murder of a prostitute. The story contained a 7-second video clip of the suspect, which the researchers had "manipulated." Half the students saw the news story with a Black suspect, and the other half saw a white suspect. Otherwise, the stories were identical. Students were asked about their reactions to the news story and the suspect in particular.

Peffley et al. (1996) found that the race of the suspect did indeed make a difference, but so did the level of prejudice of the viewer. People with negative stereotypes of Blacks judged the Black suspect more likely to be guilty and deserving more jail time than the white suspect, thus employing a "racially discriminatory double standard" (p. 316). People with positive stereotypes of Blacks, on the other hand, judged the white suspect as more guilty and deserving more jail time than the Black suspect. The only people who judged the suspects more or less equally were those who held neutral stereotypes toward Blacks. *Even a 7-second visual of a Black man in handcuffs was enough to trigger the Black stereotype, and the stereotype then affected the way the news story was interpreted.*

Power, Murphy, and Coover (1996) also believed that priming played a role in the effects of race-related images. Of particular interest was how the causal attributions (primed by stereotypes) varied based on the race of the people involved. The researchers suspected that when negative racial stereotypes are primed, people's subsequent evaluations of a Black person in a news story would suggest that the bad behaviors discussed in the story were caused by the internal characteristics of Black people. On the other hand, people might be less willing to make such internal attributions of behavior if they were first exposed to a Black person who countered the stereotype. To test this, Power et al. (1996) asked students to evaluate a new campus newsletter featuring an autobiography of an African American student named Chris Miller (his race was indicated by the use of a photograph). The autobiographical information was manipulated such that in one version of the newsletter (the stereotypical condition), Miller was described using information relevant to four traits prominent in the stereotype of Blacks: lazy, unintelligent, aggressive, and engaging in socially destructive behavior. In a different version of the newsletter (the counter-stereotypical condition), Miller was described using the opposite of these four traits: hardworking, intelligent, gentle, and engaged in socially constructive behaviors.

In what they thought was an unrelated study, participants then evaluated two media events—the beating of Rodney King and Magic Johnson's disclosure of his HIV status—and rated the degree to which the two were victims of circumstance or had brought their fate upon themselves. The results showed that people who read the stereotyped version of the campus newsletter were more likely to blame King and Johnson for their circumstances and thus attribute the problems to the men's own failings. People who had seen the counter-stereotypical newsletter were less likely to make these internal attributions, instead believing that King and Johnson were victims of circumstance. Thus, the Power et al. (1996) study suggested that *stereotypes in media can lead to message processing that supports the ultimate attribution error.*

Domke, McCoy, and Torres (1999) wondered whether stories about race-related issues such as immigration could prime racial perceptions of relevant groups even if race was not specifically mentioned. Given that beliefs about race are relatively accessible schema, Domke et al. suggested that discussions of issues such as immigration, which are usually framed with a particular racial group in mind, might activate relevant racial stereotypes just because the issue is so frequently linked with race. The researchers asked subjects their positions on issues and their impressions of how common certain qualities are among members of racial and ethnic groups; they found that when people read news stories linking immigration with economics, their position on immigration was significantly related to their perceptions of Hispanics as violent, nurturing, and lazy. Furthermore, perceptions of Hispanics as violent or intelligent—both of which could make Hispanics seem a threat to U.S. communities or jobs—were related to anti-immigration attitudes and the view that immigration hurts the U.S. economy in general. Other research participants read news stories about immigration that stressed the principles governing admitting the "huddled masses yearning to breathe free" into the nation. For this group, positions on immigration weren't correlated with even one stereotypical characteristic of Hispanics.

Thus, the way immigration was framed in the news stories activated people's racial cognitions differently, and these cognitions subsequently affected people's broader interpretations of the issue. Domke et al. (1999) concluded that news frames can significantly affect the linkages people make between their perceptions of racial groups and race-relevant political issues. This is a concern because it suggests that *how the media talk about an issue can influence whether people use stereotypes to understand that issue, even when people don't endorse the stereotypes.*

If people use stereotypes to understand a political issue, then the decisions they make in their civic life may have negative consequences for the groups being stereotyped—whether we intend it or not. In this way, portrayals in the media might help perpetuate discrimination and negativity toward some groups.

IMPLICATIONS FOR MEDIA AUDIENCES

Perhaps the most important implication to arise from this discussion of research about stereotypes is that stereotypes can influence our processing and understanding of media messages even when we're not aware of it. As the *Nightline* clip demonstrated, we may be led down one path by our processing of stereotypical information only to discover that we went down a path of stereotypes and prejudice that we wouldn't normally endorse and that violates our own ideals and morals. *The way our brains process information may lead us to think things we don't even agree with.* That is, we may automatically make stereotype-congruent interpretations of news stories or film snippets even though we reject the stereotype in question. This is especially troublesome given that stereotypes tend to be negative for all minority groups in society and that the application of stereotypes to political issues tends to hurt minority groups and keep members of majority groups looking good. If crime in Black neighborhoods is seen simply as the result of inherently aggressive Black people who don't want to work, then there's no incentive for people to tackle the economic causes of crime or implement solutions that might prevent crime in those neighborhoods. When performed by white kids in the suburbs, however, crime may instead be seen as preventable if the external forces acting on these kids can be alleviated. Thus, lawmakers may provide resources for these kids but not kids in troubled Black neighborhoods.

Given the number of mass media messages we consume on a daily basis, the potential for negative cumulative effects seems great. Each representation of a member of a social group could potentially trigger the stereotype of that group, giving viewers an example that helps reinforce the majority's dominance. There is much evidence that the media perpetuate stereotypical images, so if audiences interpret those images in ways that subtly support the stereotypes, then a lot of prejudice-congruent messages are being digested. Local television news, for example, often contains images of Blacks that reinforce the dominant cultural stereotype of Blacks as dangerous (Entman, 1990; see also Dixon's piece in this book). If news is seen as an objective and accurate description of "the way it is," then those stereotypical images will help reinforce the truthfulness of the stereotype and the "explanation" that violence in Black neighborhoods is the result of the natural tendencies of Blacks themselves. Such an explanation excuses the majority from intervening, thus helping keep the majority in control.

Our own cognitive processing system may inadvertently reinforce the dominant positions some social groups enjoy, despite our conscious intentions to the contrary. As I've argued elsewhere (Gorham, 1999), this may help explain why prejudice and racism is such an entrenched problem. If the unconscious processing of information tends to push even low-prejudiced people toward making stereotype-congruent interpretations, no wonder we have such a hard time trying to put an end to prejudice. Furthermore, if the images and portrayals of groups in mass media enhance or reinforce our tendency to interpret information in stereotypical ways, then the media are inadvertently helping make the problem of prejudice and discrimination worse. The calls for change in media images are justified, but real progress will only be made when we also understand our role in the perpetuation of prejudice.

IT'S YOUR TURN: WHAT DO YOU THINK? WHAT WILL YOU FIND?

1. Discuss a news story you've recently encountered in terms of how it might prime stereotypes. What sorts of interpretations would you expect people to make based on those stereotypes?

2. What can news organizations do to try to limit the extent to which news stories automatically activate stereotypes?

3. Examine a magazine ad. How and to what extent might it prime our stereotypes to its advantage? How would you change the ad content so that it gets the desired message across without triggering people's stereotypes?

4. What can audience members do to try to counteract the effects of the automatic activation of stereotypes?

REFERENCES

Blair, I.V., & Banaji, M. R. (1996). Automatic and controlled processes in stereotype priming. *Journal of Personality and Social Psychology, 70*(6), 1142–1163.

Devine, P.G. (1989). Stereotypes and prejudice: Their automatic and controlled components. *Journal of Personality and Social Psychology, 56*, 5–18.

Devine, P. G., & Elliot, A. J. (1995). Are racial stereotypes really fading? The Princeton trilogy revisited. *Personality and Social Psychology Bulletin, 21*(11), 1139–1150.

Domke, D., McCoy, K., & Torres, M. (1999). News media, racial perceptions and political cognition. *Communication Research, 26*(5), 570–607.

Entman, R. M. (1990). Modern racism and the images of Blacks in local television news. *Critical Studies in Mass Communication, 7*, 332–345.

Gorham, B. W. (1999). Stereotypes in the media: So what? *Howard Journal of Communications, 10*, 229–247.

Hamilton, D. L., & Trolier, T. K. (1986). Stereotypes and stereotyping: An overview of the cognitive approach. In J. F. Dovidio & S. L. Gaertner (Eds.), *Prejudice, discrimination, and racism* (pp. 127–163). New York: Academic Press.

Monteith, M. (1993). Self-regulation of prejudiced responses: Implications for progress in prejudice-reduction efforts. *Journal of Personality and Social Psychology, 65*, 469–485.

Peffley, M., Hurwitz, J., & Sniderman, P. M. (1997). Racial stereotypes and Whites' political views of Blacks in the context of welfare and crime. *American Journal of Political Science, 41*(1), 30–60.

Peffley, M., Shields, T., & Williams, B. (1996). The intersection of race and crime in television news stories: An experimental study. *Political Communication, 13*, 309–327.

Pettigrew, T. F. (1979). The ultimate attribution error: Extending Allport's cognitive analysis of prejudice. *Personality and Social Psychology Bulletin, 5*(4), 461–476.

Power, J. G., Murphy, S. T., & Coover, G. (1996). Priming prejudice: How stereotypes and counter-stereotypes influence attribution or responsibility and credibility among ingroups and outgroups. *Human Communication Research, 23*, 36–58.

2.2 "HE WAS A BLACK GUY": HOW THE NEWS CONTINUES TO CREATE FEAR OF BLACKS

Travis L. Dixon

> *The author provides social scientific evidence demonstrating that stereotypical crime portrayals shape perceptions of African Americans and crime. This association between crime and race reinforced by the news might influence viewers' conceptions of both Blacks and crime—sometimes without viewers being fully aware.*

In my contribution to earlier editions of this book, I recounted a story of how many of my friends and family became tense when they watched the news and some horrible crime had occurred. Their tense reaction was because they suspected that if the news revealed the perpetrator was Black, it would reinforce the stereotype that most Blacks are criminals. Others, particularly those outside of the Black community, would then use that stereotype to unfairly judge other African Americans they encountered, the vast majority of whom are not criminals.

Knowing for sure whether the news over-associates Blacks with crime is the first step in establishing that news viewing influences whether people stereotype Blacks as criminals. The chapter that I wrote in the first edition, and some of my other work, has documented how the news appears to indeed depict a world in which African Americans are overrepresented as criminals. There is a growing amount of research that establishes support for this first step.

The next step requires that we provide evidence that the news actually influences people's perceptions. This means that we must go beyond content assessments. We need to learn whether seeing these portrayals affects viewer's beliefs and attitudes. The current chapter discusses a few studies that do just that. I report on a series of experiments where I exposed viewers to a news program that contained either a majority of white criminals, a majority of Black criminals, a number of unidentified criminals, or non-crime stories. Afterward, I asked them about the race of the perpetrators in the stories, their views about the police, danger, culpability judgments, support for the death penalty, and racial animus. Before I provide more description of what I did, I will give you some background so you can understand why I approached the topic this way.

BACKGROUND: STUDIES OF CONTENT AND EFFECTS

A number of research studies have concluded that local news programs often misrepresent African Americans as the primary perpetrators responsible for crime (Dixon & Linz, 2000a; Entman, 1992; 1994). For example, in some of my prior work, I found that Blacks were twice as likely as whites to be portrayed as perpetrators of crime on local television news (Dixon & Linz, 2000a). In addition, African Americans were six times more likely to be depicted as perpetrators than as officers on news programs. Furthermore, Blacks were overrepresented as criminals on the news, representing 37% of the perpetrators shown while comprising only 21% of those arrested according to crime reports.

These findings are in stark contrast to the ways in which whites typically appear on local news programs (Dixon & Linz, 2000a, 2000b). Whites appear as officers twice as often as they appear as criminals, and they are overrepresented as officers (69%) on news programs compared to employment records (59%). In addition, whites are more than twice as likely to appear as victims compared to Blacks, and they are overrepresented as victims in news stories (43%) compared to crime reports (13%). These studies, as well as a number of others, indicate that African Americans are much more often associated with criminality on television news in comparison to whites.

Many scholars interested in the effects of distorted racial portrayals have used two theories to guide their investigations: cognitive accessibility theory and spreading activation theory. *Cognitive accessibility* suggests that people use mental shortcuts to make relevant social judgments. So if one encounters something or someone related to the stereotype (e.g., a Black person) you might make a judgment about them based on repeated exposure to the stereotype (e.g., seeing tons of Black criminals on TV). *Spreading activation* says that stereotypes form an associative network of related ideas or schemas linked in memory, and activating one idea spreads to other linked notions. In other words, we understand, remember, and evaluate the world based on the associations that are linked in our brain. So the link between two things (e.g., Black people and crime) can also influence the association between other things (e.g., fear of Blacks and support for the police). In short, people may make judgments about race-related issues based upon their racial perceptions.

Because Blacks are repeatedly shown as criminals in the news, news exposure to either African American criminals or even race-unspecified criminals may activate the cognitive linkage between African Americans and criminality. This linkage may then be used in race and crime judgments.

Under certain circumstances, television news imagery of a majority of African American rather than white criminals might *prime* or activate a "Black criminal stereotype" utilized in making social reality judgments regarding race and crime. The construct linking African Americans with criminality (i.e., the Black criminal stereotype) might be chronically or easily accessible given that it may have been frequently activated in the past due to media exposure. Chronic accessibility means that after exposure to a majority of Black rather than white criminals in the news, the Black criminal stereotype becomes triggered or activated in one's mind without the perceiver even being aware. After this activation, the stereotype gets used to make relevant judgments related to race and crime (Bargh, Chen, & Burrows, 1996; Devine, 1989; Shrum, 2002).

Given that African Americans have been linked with criminality so often in news programming, exposure to crime news devoid of racial identifiers may nonetheless elicit unfavorable thoughts about Blacks. When presented with illegal activity committed by unidentified suspects on a television news program, audience members might unconsciously invoke the stereotype that links African Americans with criminality and hence infer that the perpetrators are African American. This process is also the result of chronic accessibility. Repeated exposure to African American criminals in the news leads to the activation of the stereotype that links African Americans with criminality. As a result, exposure to criminality devoid of racial identifiers may be enough to still trigger the Black criminal stereotype, usually without the perceiver even being consciously aware (Devine, 1989; Shrum, 2002).

Exposure to a majority of Black rather than white perpetrators or race unidentified suspects may conjure notions of crime as a largely Black phenomenon that requires police intervention due to a Black predisposition toward criminal activity (Hewstone, 1990; Pettigrew, 1979). Prior research has found that exposure to Black criminality in the news encourages the endorsement of punitive crime policy and politicians (Gilliam & Iyengar, 2000; Valentino, 1999). This effect may be related to the notion of spreading activation discussed earlier.

As discussed earlier, exposure to a majority of African American rather than white suspects or race-unidentified crime may lead to the activation of a stereotype linking Blacks and criminality. Spreading activation suggests that the activation of this stereotype may lead to the activation of other related ideas in one's mind (Valentino, 1999). As a result of activation of the Black criminal stereotype, viewers may also come to have other notions activated such as "fear of crime" and "protection from criminal activity." These notions may then link to support for the police (crime reducing agents).

In addition, exposure to a majority of Black rather than white suspects or unidentified suspects in the news may cause viewers to misremember a non-Black suspect as Black (Gilliam & Iyengar, 2000; Oliver & Fonash, 2002). The Black criminal stereotype may influence encoding and memory such that stimuli may be recalled in a manner congruent with the schema (Fiske & Taylor, 1991). Once the Black-crime stereotype is activated, it also activates a generalized schema of African Americans (Ford, 1997). The mismemory effect described above results directly from "ambiguous" targets being processed and remembered in congruence with the activated schema (Devine, 1989; Fiske & Taylor, 1991). This occurs partly because under high stress conditions or when decisions have to be made quickly, perceivers utilize what is most available to them in order to make decisions. Once the African American schema is activated, it is available for use, and requires fewer cognitive resources than other decision-making processes.

Thus far I have described a two-part process. First, exposure to either a majority of Black rather than white suspects or a majority of unidentified suspects may prime the Black criminal stereotype. Second, after this stereotype is primed, schematic processing and spreading activation lead to various perceptual effects. Below, I provide an overview of the method and the hypotheses or predictions of the current study.

HYPOTHESES AND METHOD

My studies were designed to assess whether exposure to a majority of Black rather than white suspects or unidentified suspects increased support for the police, perceptions of danger, racial animus, and culpability judgments. They were also designed to determine the extent to which participants tended to cognitively associate unidentified suspects with Black suspects. Based on the priming paradigm and theories of stereotyping described earlier, I propose the following hypotheses:

H1: Exposure to a majority of Black rather than white suspects in the news will lead to mismemory of a non-Black suspect as Black, more support for the police, increased perceptions of danger, racial animus, and greater culpability judgments of criminals.

H2: Exposure to race-unidentified suspects will activate the Black criminal stereotype and lead to mismemory of a non-Black suspect as Black, more support for the police and increased perceptions of danger, racial animus and greater culpability judgments of criminals.

H3: Heavy news viewers exposed to either race-unidentified suspects or a majority of Black suspects will have mismemory of a non-Black suspect as Black, more support for the police, increased perceptions of danger, racial animus and greater culpability judgments of criminals.

I wanted to be sure that people would tell me their real views and not what they thought I wanted to hear. Therefore, I used several experiments. Experiments are powerful because if done properly, they can provide good evidence for whether one thing (e.g., watching the news) causes something else (e.g., racialized perception of Blacks). Participants came into a laboratory and watched a news program, then completed some questionnaires. I did not tell them that I was actually interested in their views about race and crime policy.

The 20-minute program they viewed contained seven crime stories about murder and eight "fluff" or distracter stories (i.e., human interest stories that contained no violence, crime, or disasters). Photographs of suspects in the murder stories were manipulated so that the experiments had four conditions: (a) a majority of Black suspects, (b) a majority of white suspects, (c) race of the suspects was not identified, and (d) non-crime stories. I pre-tested the photographs to ensure that any potential outcomes were not due to differences in how the suspects were depicted. There were no differences between the Black and white photos on how menacing or dangerous they looked. In addition, during the general questionnaire part of the study I asked people how often they watched the news.

After viewing the news program, participants responded to a number of bogus memory items. At the end of this questionnaire, the first murder story that participants had viewed during the manipulation was re-described to them. They were then asked to recount the race of the suspected murderer presented in that one news story. The crime story was the same in every condition, and except in the condition where all perpetrators were race unidentified, the murder suspect was always an identical white man. I was interested in the extent to which participants correctly remembered the race of the suspect as being non-Black.

At this point, a "second experimenter" entered the room. Participants were told that because they had signed up for an hour experiment, they would complete the hour by assisting the second experimenter with another task. The second experimenter explained to them that they were "pre-testing" a questionnaire to determine how long it takes to complete. However, the real purpose was to have participants complete the police support measure, danger measure, and racial animus measures along with a number of distracter/pretend questions. Participants also had a scenario described to them in which a race-unidentified suspect committed some crime. They were asked how convinced they were that the suspect actually did it. After completed the "second study," participants were debriefed. We repeated or "replicated" this study three times. More than 400 people, mostly college students at Big Ten universities, participated.

RESULTS

All statistical tests were conducted at the $p < .05$ significance level. We used Analyses of Variance (ANOVAs) and Regression Analyses to test our hypotheses. ANOVA and Regression are statistics that allow us to compare on average whether any differences exist for those who saw either a majority of Black suspects, a majority of white suspects, race unidentified suspects, or non-crime stories.

Hypotheses 1 and 2 stated that exposure to a majority of Black rather than white suspects or race unidentified suspects in the news will lead to increased support for the police. The ANOVA for police support appears to provide support for these hypotheses. It revealed a significant main effect for the exposure condition, $F(2, 145) = 5.62, p < .01, \eta^2_p = .07$. Those who were either exposed to a majority of Black suspects (M [mean] $= 4.61$, SD [standard deviation] $= .12$) or race unidentified suspects ($M = 4.94$, $SD = .17$) were significantly more likely than those exposed to a majority of white suspects ($M = 4.25$, $SD = .12$) to support the police. There were no statistically significant differences between those exposed to a majority of Black suspects and those exposed to race unidentified suspects in terms of their support for the police.

The ANOVA for mismemory revealed results practically identical to the police support measure. It revealed a significant main effect for exposure condition, $F(2, 145) = 7.71, p < .001$, $\eta^2_p = .09$. Those who were either exposed to a majority of Black suspects ($M = 4.11$, $SD = .22$) or race unidentified suspects ($M = 4.04$, $SD = .32$) were more likely than those exposed to a majority of white suspects ($M = 3.04$, $SD = .21$) to misremember a non-Black suspect as being Black. Most notably, there were no significant differences between those exposed to a majority of Black suspects and those exposed to race unidentified suspects in terms of their mismemory.

Hypothesis 3 suggests that those who watch a lot of television news and who are exposed to either a majority of Black suspects or a number of unidentified suspects will show increased racial animus, support for the death penalty, perceptions of danger, and culpability. Using regression analyses, I found that those exposed to a majority of Black suspects who watched a lot of television news tended to perceive the world as dangerous and view the race unidentified suspect in my scenario as culpable or guilty. In addition, heavy news viewers exposed to unidentified suspects tended to support the death penalty, and they also reported an increase in racial animus against Blacks.

DISCUSSION

In this study, three significant findings appear to have emerged that provide some support for Hypotheses 1, 2, and 3. First, participants exposed to a majority of African American suspects or to a number of race-unidentified suspects showed increased support for the police. This provides evidence that racialized crime news invokes the Black criminality stereotype that in turn activates a cognitive linkage between Black suspects and perceived threat level. The increased sense of threat manifests in support for the authorities responsible for protection. Moreover, the Black criminal stereotype appears to be invoked whether participants are exposed to a majority of Black suspects or whether they simply encounter race-unidentified suspects.

Second, this study provides some evidence that compliments prior research suggesting that viewers tend to think of unidentified suspects as Black suspects (Gilliam & Iyengar, 2000; Oliver & Fonash, 2002). When exposed to a number of unidentified suspects, participants were more likely to "guess" that a non-Black suspect was African American rather than white. This suggests that participants tend to think of criminals as Black unless provided with overwhelming information that a suspect is white. This finding offers support for the notion that a cognitive link has been formed between criminality and African Americans that is reinforced by news programming.

Third, this study provides evidence that many of the above effects are made even stronger the more you watch television news. In addition, watching television news and seeing either Black or unidentified suspects makes you think the world is a dangerous place, encourages support for the death penalty, and makes you feel more distrust toward Blacks. Clearly these findings are related to what social scientists term cognitive accessibility effects (Dixon, 2006a; Gilliam & Iyengar, 2000). In other words, if you see something (e.g., Black criminal) over and over again, when you need to make judgments, this notion of Black criminals is most accessible and is used to make the judgments.

Fighting the Stereotype

So what are our options if we want to resist the effects of negative media coverage? The first step, of course, is to make a conscious decision to resist prejudice and stereotyping. The more we can resist thinking of people in stereotypical ways, the less potent the media message. Many scholars have uncovered evidence that reflective thinking before making a judgment deflates the use of the stereotype (Devine, 1989; Livingston & Brewer, 2002).

The second step is to actually be very careful of what you watch. You should definitely expose yourself to the news, but you should consider what kind of news you consume. Be very careful of crime news and approach it with a critical eye.

Third, as citizens, you should consider becoming involved in actually writing media outlets and advocating for more balanced coverage of topics. In theory, broadcast television operates with a license from the government, and it has a duty to be responsive to people from the community to retain that license. However, no matter what you decide, you should know that the media do have an effect and that we all play a part in dealing with it.

IT'S YOUR TURN: WHAT DO YOU THINK? WHAT WILL YOU FIND?

1. If you wanted to counter the negative effects of the news as a journalist or editor, how would you change the coverage?

2. Have you ever thought about an issue in the news, and a racial group just came to your mind even if they were not shown? If so, what groups? Why do

you think this is, and do you think there is any way to stop it? Would it be helpful to stop it?

3. Watch politicians in the news. Do you see any subtle racial cues when they talk about certain issues? If so, what are the issues? What are the subtle cues?

REFERENCES

Bargh, J. A., Chen, M., & Burrows, L. (1996). Automaticity of social behavior: Direct effects of trait construct and stereotype activation on action. *Journal of Personality & Social Psychology, 71*, 230–244.

Devine, P. G. (1989). Stereotypes and prejudice: Their automatic and controlled components. *Journal of Personality & Social Psychology, 56*, 5–18.

Dixon, T. L. (2006a). Psychological reactions to crime news portrayals of Black criminals: Understanding the moderating roles of prior news viewing and stereotype endorsement. *Communication Monographs, 73*, 162–187.

Dixon, T. L. (2006b). Schemas as average conceptions: Skin tone, television news exposure, and culpability judgments. *Journalism and Mass Communication Quarterly, 83*, 131–149.

Dixon, T. L., & Linz, D. G. (2000a). Overrepresentation and underrepresentation of African Americans and Latinos as lawbreakers on television news. *Journal of Communication, 50*(2), 131–154.

Dixon, T. L., & Linz, D. G. (2000b). Race and the misrepresentation of victimization on local television news. *Communication Research, 27*, 547–573.

Entman, R. (1992). Blacks in the news: Television, modern racism, and cultural change. *Journalism Quarterly, 69*, 341–361.

Entman, R. (1994). Representation and reality in the portrayal of Blacks on network television news. *Journalism Quarterly, 71*, 509–520.

Fiske, S. T., & Taylor, S. E. (1991). *Social cognition* (2nd ed.). New York: McGraw-Hill.

Ford, T. E. (1997). Effects of stereotypical television portrayals of African-Americans on person perception. *Social Psychology Quarterly, 60*, 266–275.

Gilliam, F. D., & Iyengar, S. (2000). Prime suspects: The influence of local television news on the viewing public. *American Journal of Political Science, 44*, 560–573.

Hewstone, M. (1990). The "ultimate attribution error"? A review of the literature on intergroup causal attribution. *European Journal of Social Psychology, 20*, 311–335.

Livingston, R. W., & Brewer, M. B. (2002). What are we really priming? Cue-based versus category-based processing of facial stimuli. *Journal of Personality & Social Psychology, 82*(1), 5–18.

Oliver, M. B., & Fonash, D. (2002). Race and crime in the news: Whites' identification and misidentification of violent and nonviolent criminal suspects. *Media Psychology, 4*, 137–156.

Pettigrew, T. F. (1979). The ultimate attribution error: Extending Allport's cognitive analysis of prejudice. *Personality & Social Psychology Bulletin, 5*, 461–476.

Shrum, L. J. (2002). Media consumption and perceptions of social reality: Effects and underlying processes. In J. Bryant & D. Zillmann (Eds.), *Media effects: Advances in theory and research* (2nd ed., pp. 69–96). Mahway, NJ: Lawrence Erlbaum Associates.

Sunnafrank, M., & Fontes, N. E. (1983). General and crime related racial stereotypes and influence on juridic decisions. *Cornell Journal of Social Relations, 17*(1), 1–15.

Valentino, N. (1999). Crime news and the priming of racial attitudes during evaluations of the president. *Public Opinion Quarterly, 63*, 293–320.

2.3 MEDIA LITERACY IN EATING DISORDER TREATMENT

Lori Bindig

> *The author argues that media literacy should be a key component of eating disorder treatment; this reading describes and tests a curriculum for accomplishing such a goal.*

As a young woman growing up in mass-mediated American culture, I noticed that many of my friends struggled with body image and as I became more involved in dance and theater, I found, that for at least some of my friends, their struggles transformed into clinically diagnosable eating disorders. This is not all that surprising given that according to the Alliance for Eating Disorder Awareness (AEDA, 2005), there are 70 million individuals suffering from eating disorders worldwide. The AEDA (2011) also notes that of the 25 million Americans suffering from eating disorders, approximately 75% are women. Eating disorders are often thought to affect affluent Western white women, but all people regardless of gender, race, class, ethnicity, and sexual orientation are afflicted.

To make matters worse, eating disorders have the highest mortality rate of any mental illness and are the leading cause of death for young women in the United States (Wykes & Gunter, 2005). The AEDA (2005) estimates that of those afflicted, approximately 50,000 will die as a direct result of their illness typically from a heart attack, organ failure, electrolyte imbalance, or infection. Even if not deadly, eating disorders incapacitate young women mentally, physically, and spiritually during the time that they are afflicted. In fact, only one third of patients ever successfully recover after their initial episode with the illness. Another third of patients are caught in a cycle of recovery and relapse, while the final third are destined to suffer from chronic deterioration. One possible reason for the poor recovery rates is that the socio-cultural dimensions of eating disorders are grossly overlooked in current treatment models.

When studying communication in graduate school, I realized that if eating disorder treatment protocols were to incorporate more of a cultural perspective, a central focus would have to be dedicated to one of our most significant social institutions— the mass media. I believe that understanding media is integral to eating disorder treatment because media act as a microcosm of toxic social forces and institutions. In order to fully understand the images and stories media present to us and how they may affect our understanding of ourselves and the world around us, we need to embrace *media literacy*.

Media literacy is grounded in five tenets, which suggest (1) although media help shape our reality, they are not natural or inherent but are actually constructed texts that (2) have commercial interests and (3) ideological implications, as well as (4) unique forms and content that (5) viewers negotiate to make meaning (Aufderheide, 2001). Media literacy encourages viewers to engage in critical thinking about television shows, movies, the Internet, magazines, and advertisements. Being media literate does not mean hating all media or never enjoying media again. Rather, media literacy allows us to make more informed choices about our own media consumption and to have a deeper understanding of the connections between media and society.

Using media literacy to thwart eating disorders is nothing new. In the past, media literacy has had some success in eating disorder prevention. However, there has yet been no published research regarding media literacy in eating disorder *treatment*. Therefore, I developed and implemented my own three-prong media literacy intervention, the ERA (education-recognition-activism) curriculum. It was designed for people formally diagnosed with eating disorders and enrolled in an eating disorders treatment program.

THE ERA CURRICULUM

The ERA curriculum is based on critical cultural studies conceptions of media literacy. This perspective suggests that media literacy can be viewed as a consciousness-raising tool that empowers people and helps them recognize the impact of social structures in their everyday lives. If people being treated for eating disorders become more empowered and are able to lessen the negative impact of media ideologies, their disordered eating attitudes may be diminished. Therefore, my three-prong, four-session ERA curriculum focuses on education (the development of media literacy skills), recognition (reflection on how media ideologies may affect an individual and his or her eating disorder), and activism (the practice of linking the personal and political through engaged citizenship).

Specifically, the first prong of the ERA curriculum, *Education*, addresses the importance of media culture and four of the five core concepts of media literacy (unique codes and conventions of particular media are less relevant to the goals of the ERA, and thus this tenet was not included). Participants apply the tenets of media literacy to familiar media texts (television programs, films, and advertisements). This is done both as part of a group discussion and also individually outside of the treatment setting. The education stage invokes an intersectional approach, stressing the need to understand issues within their socio political, economic, and historical contexts. The program views gender, race, class, sexuality, and consumerism not as mutually exclusive factors, but as overlapping and intertwined. Lastly, the education stage introduces key concepts, such as ideology, hegemony, political economy, and the white supremacist capitalist patriarchy, which are integral to understanding how power operates throughout society and its institutions. This process starts with more familiar aspects of media analysis (critiques of gender or racial representations) and links them to new or less understood concepts (hegemony and/or political economy). Overall, the education stage reflects the tenets of media literacy because it provides participants the tools for becoming critical media viewers.

The second stage, *Recognition*, calls for personal reflection on how ideologies of gender, race, class, sexuality, and consumerism are at play in each individual's life and how these ideologies may affect his or her eating disorder. This stage consists of two parts, each using a full group session to complete. In the first part, participants consider what elements in media "trigger" emotions contributing to their eating disorder (both attitudes and behaviors). They develop strategies to respond to the triggers. In the second part, participants perform a "personal inventory" where they determine their goals for a happy and healthy life. This part of the recognition stage encourages participants to consider how dominant themes in media, as well as other social forces, may work against their goals. This stage concludes when participants identify what they would like to change in order to reach their goals, and design a strategy to help this change occur.

The last stage, *Activism*, is based on the two recognition activities. Participants review personal goals that conflict with the dominant themes presented in media. Participants identify a "perpetrator" of one of these themes and try to combat that theme through an activist project such as writing a letter to a magazine or television program or advertiser that contributes to a toxic media environment. Participants are also encouraged to write to an individual or corporation that promotes socially responsible media messages. The action project is determined and implemented by the individual with suggestions and guidance from the curriculum facilitator. Participants are encouraged to read (or summarize) their letters to the group, and to submit their letters to the facilitator for mailing.

Although the ERA curriculum was primarily designed to increase media literacy and empowerment and diminish the drive for thinness, it may also address other obstacles in eating disorder treatment, such as dealing with issues of loss of control, low self-esteem, emptiness, and isolation. For instance, a sense of control can be gained by becoming an active and engaged citizen; as Bergsma (2004) notes, "... research confirms that actual and perceived control enhance quality of life ..." (p. 152). Furthermore, media literacy itself may combat feelings of low self-esteem; participants may feel "smart" when able to deconstruct a media message, or "creative" when engaging in activism. Similarly, the activism projects may help overcome feelings of emptiness, and encourage a sense of fulfillment through helping others. Lastly, the ERA curriculum contends with feelings of isolation by providing a forum where participants who are facing similar issues can interact with each other. Peer interactions before, during, and after sessions (along with specific activities such as group discussions and the activism project) may help develop friendships or at the very least build alliances around important social issues.

TESTING THE EFFECTIVENESS OF THE ERA CURRICULUM

After creating the ERA curriculum, I wanted to see if it could help people in treatment for eating disorders. Could the curriculum actually increase media literacy and empowerment, and diminish a drive for thinness? To test this, I implemented the curriculum at an eating disorder treatment facility in the Northeast. A partial hospitalization treatment program (PHP) invited me to implement the ERA curriculum. I conducted an experiment with one treatment condition (the ERA) and one control condition (no ERA). In the experimental condition, which lasted 9 months (November 2007 to August 2008), the ERA curriculum was implemented in conjunction with the standard of care (traditional eating disorder treatments such as nutritional counseling, and individual, group, and family psychotherapy). Of the 73 patients enrolled at the PHP while the ERA curriculum was implemented, 33 consented to complete pre- and posttest questionnaires asking about attitudes toward eating, feelings of empowerment, and thoughts about media.

The pretest survey contained 33 closed-ended questions drawn from multiple sources, and used varied question formats, as outlined below in Table 1. Semantic differential items presented subjects with two opposite descriptive terms representing the positive and negative ends of a continuum, and respondents choose which position along the continuum best represents their opinion. Likert-type items presented a 5-point "strongly agree" to "strongly disagree" scale, or a 5-point "always" to "never" scale, depending on which set of options was appropriate. The posttest questionnaire, completed after each of the individual ERA sessions, also asked specific questions about the ERA curriculum. Participants were at different stages of the treatment process; for instance, one person's last day may be another's third. For a number of reasons, including the high cost of treatment, not all participants completed all four ERA sessions; others with the resources and interest repeated some sessions—in itself a telling observation regarding health care available to the "haves" and "have nots" in a society that still calls itself egalitarian and classless.

TABLE 1   **Description of Survey Items**

CONCEPT MEASURED	# OF ITEMS	SOURCE	ITEM TYPE	EXAMPLE
Media Literacy Tenets	9	Bindig (2009)[1]	Semantic differential	Media reflect reality accurately . . . Media distort reality.
Media Economics	5	Duran, et al (2008)	Likert type	I am concerned that most media content is produced by a few big companies.
Empowerment	12	Rogers, et al (1997)	Likert type	I see myself as a capable person.
Drive for Thinness	7	Garner, et al (1983)	Likert type	I am terrified of gaining weight.

The pretest was administered prior to the individual's first ERA session. Because of rolling admissions at the PHP, the four weekly 50-minutes sessions that made up the ERA curriculum were implemented four consecutive times (sessions 1–4 in order). The PHP then returned to its traditional care plan; patients entering the facility during the next 5 months comprised the control groups. Of the 36 patients enrolled at the PHP during this period, 30 consented to complete the pretest question-naire. Therefore, there were 33 subjects in the experimental condition and 30 in the control.[2]

For analysis, the closed-ended questions were statistically transformed into indices: the media economics index (4 items), the media literacy index (8 items), the empowerment index (12 items) and the drive for thinness index (7 items, reverse-coded such that a higher score on this index reveals a *lower, more healthy* perspective on the desire to be thin). Because of the complex nature of this study, I present here only two sets of statistical comparisons—both con-ducted specifically for this reading. The original detailed statistical analysis can be found in my doctoral dissertation (Bindig, 2009). For this reading, I wanted to present a simple pre- and post-test analysis of the ERA curriculum, so the posttests (which in the original dataset ranged from one to seven completed posttests per participant) for each index were examined cumulatively. Thus, this reading focuses on *global results* computed across each of the four indices rather than fluctuations between each posttest within each index.

In addition to the closed-ended items, the questionnaires included open-ended items, which allow participants to answer more freely, help clarify certain issues, and can show the nuances of an issue. Besides asking for opinions about media systems, participants were asked about the value and enjoyment of the ERA curriculum. These responses were not only used as data but as a means of feedback for curricular improvement.

FINDINGS: DID THE ERA PROGRAM MAKE A DIFFERENCE?

As illustrated by Table 2, when paired t-tests were utilized to compare the global pretests and posttests within the experimental group, there were no statistically significant difference between the pretests and posttests for any of the indices. Although the posttest means for media economics and media literacy did increase when compared with the pretest, the posttest means decreased for

TABLE 2   Testing Treatment Effects within Experimental Group

INDEX (N)	EXPERIMENTAL GROUP PRETEST		EXPERIMENTAL GROUP POSTTEST		PAIRED-SAMPLES T-TESTS		
	MEAN	SD	MEAN	SD	T VALUE	DF	SIG.
Drive for Thinness (29)	12.28	5.85	12.14	5.40	0.72	28	0.48
Empowerment (30)	36.43	9.40	35.77	9.45	1.90	29	0.07
Media Economics (32)	15.59	1.85	15.75	2.33	0.55	31	0.59
Media Literacy (31)	34.58	3.19	35.19	3.36	1.32	30	0.20

empowerment and drive for thinness (recall that a lower drive for thinness score reveals a less healthy attitude toward being thin). Although the lower results for empowerment and drive for thinness could be interpreted as an adverse effect of the ERA curriculum, it is much more likely due to the intervention group's long-term struggles with low self-worth and extreme body ideals as well as their brief time spent with the ERA curriculum (again, only four 50-minute sessions in 4 weeks), or perhaps respondent fatigue as the subjects completed the same posttest survey after each session. Thus, even though not statistically significant, two of the global indices changed in the desired direction.

Table 3 reveals that the independent t-tests used to compare the posttests of the experimental group with the pretests of the control group yielded more optimistic results. Although there were no statistically significant differences between the two groups' global scores for the drive for thinness and empowerment indices, the t-tests revealed statistically significant increases in the understanding of media economics and media literacy for the experimental group, which, when coupled with the results from the paired samples t-tests conducted within the experimental group, suggests that the ERA curriculum is successful in increasing participants' understanding of media literacy and media economics.

Furthermore, on the larger sample generated by calculating the global scores for the independent samples posttest, we see higher means on three of the posttest indices reported in Table 3 (drive for thinness, media economics, and media literacy) than were found on the posttest means of the paired-samples test reported in Table 2. Although the difference between the control and

TABLE 3   Testing Treatment Effects across Experimental and Control Groups

INDEX	CONTROL GROUP PRETEST			EXPERIMENTAL GROUP POSTTEST			INDEPENDENT SAMPLES T-TESTS		
	N	MEAN	SD	N	MEAN	SD	T VALUE	DF	SIG.
Drive for Thinness	30	12.53	4.19	72	12.94	5.71	0.36	100	0.73
Empowerment	29	36.66	7.97	82	35.32	8.57	−0.74	109	0.46
Media Economics	30	14.13	2.58	83	16.27	2.20	4.33	111	0.00
Media Literacy	30	31.43	3.20	81	35.52	3.54	5.54	109	0.00

experimental groups for the drive for thinness index was still not statistically significant, the trend is in the desired direction. Thus, perhaps the smaller sample size in the pretest may have hindered the statistical significance of some of the results.

Qualitative results of the open-ended survey questions also suggest a cautiously optimistic reading of the ERA curriculum outcomes. For instance, the qualitative analysis not only reinforces the statistical findings that participants in the ERA curriculum did grasp the tenets of media literacy, but they also suggest that participants valued and enjoyed the curriculum and the conversations it generated as well as the sense of community fostered by the curriculum. The latter reflects an additional benefit of media literacy in eating disorder treatment.

Although the ERA curriculum did not achieve all of its goals, this short-term preliminary implementation of the curriculum does provide a new context for media literacy research. In this case, the intervention can be considered successful since the impetus behind the ERA curriculum was not only to improve the status of those who take part in it, but also to move eating disorder treatment in a new direction. Again, the only way to see a new era for eating disorder treatment is to actively seek out new ways of thinking about eating disorder recovery and implement new interventions. This foray of media literacy in eating disorder treatment was based on a range of literature from the eating disorders, media studies, cultural studies, feminist studies, and critical pedagogy fields. Although further work must be done in order to create a cultural intervention that successfully addresses empowerment and drive for thinness as well as media literacy, this implementation of the ERA curriculum represents a small move toward a new era of eating disorder treatment.

NOTES

1. Although grounded in Aufderheide's (2001) five tenets of media literacy, I created these measures because no general media literacy measures had been published at the time of the study.

2. Each lesson in the ERA curriculum was self-contained. The posttest survey was administered after each individual ERA session. Subjects participating in multiple sessions completed multiple posttest surveys. Many statistical analyses reported in my dissertation used the number of sessions completed as a control variable (Bindig, 2009). When interpreting Table 1, note that one survey item for media literacy was excluded from analysis. Although the survey contained nine items, the index itself contained only eight items.

IT'S YOUR TURN: WHAT DO YOU THINK? WHAT WILL YOU FIND?

1. The author addresses cultural issues (eating disorders) through an experimental framework. Reflecting back on the discussions of these paradigms in Chapter 1, how successful do you think she has been in her attempts to borrow from both worlds?

2. Review media coverage of and references to eating disorders. Look online to discover the actual statistics of people with eating disorders. How does media treatment of the disorder relate to reality? Consider race, class, and gender. Consider success rates of treatments. Why do you think the media's treatment of eating disorders is as it is?

3. Based on what you've learned about the ERA curriculum, how do you think issues of gender, race, or class affect participation in the curriculum? Might different social groups be more or less willing to participate? Might people of different social classes be more or less able to capitalize on the sort of ideas and activities it contains?

4. Explore contemporary media content and discover some examples to use in the education stage of the curriculum. How would you use them? What would you say about them?

REFERENCES

The Alliance for Eating Disorders Awareness. (2005). *Eating disorder statistics*. Retrieved September 21, 2011, from http://www.s126869113.onlinehome.us/18.html

The Alliance for Eating Disorders Awareness. (2011). *What are eating disorders*. Retrieved April 23, 2011, from http://allianceforeatingdisorders.com/what-are-eating-disorders

Aufderheide, P. (2001). Media literacy: From a report on the National Leadership Conference on Media Literacy. In R. W. Kubey (Ed.), *Media literacy in the information age: Current perspectives* (pp. 79–88). New Brunswick, NJ: Transaction Publishers.

Bergsma, L. J. (2004). Empowerment education: The link between media literacy and health promotion. *The American Behavioral Scientist*, *48*, 152–164.

Bindig, L. (2009). A new "ERA": Media literacy in eating disorder treatment. (Doctoral Dissertation). Amherst, MA: University of Massachusetts Amherst.

Duran, R. L., Yousman, B., Walsh, K. M., & Longshore, M. A. (2008). Holistic media education: An assessment of the effectiveness of a college course in media literacy. *Communication Quarterly*, *56*(1), 49–68.

Garner, D. M., Olmstead, M. A., & Polivy J. (1983). Development and validation of a multidimensional eating disorder inventory for anorexia nervosa and bulimia. *International Journal of Eating Disorders*, *2*(2), 15–34.

Rogers, E.S., Chamberlin, J., Ellison, M.L., & Crean, T. (1997). A consumer-constructed scale to measure empowerment among users of mental health services. *Psychiatric Services*, *48*(8), 1042–1047.

Wykes, M., & Gunter, B. (2005). *The media and body image*. Thousand Oaks, CA: Sage Publications.

2.4   BELIEVING BLOGS: DOES A BLOGGER'S GENDER INFLUENCE CREDIBILITY?

Cory L. Armstrong and Mindy McAdams

This study examines how gender and occupational cues influence Weblog credibility. Participants rated the overall credibility of a blog entry for which male and female descriptors of the author were manipulated. Findings suggest that while gender stereotypes persist for credibility, perhaps traditional cues used to discern media credibility may be less effective for blogs.

One of the newer terms in the public vernacular is "blog." It serves as a noun, verb, and adjective: "Did you read my blog?," "I blogged about my trip to Alaska last week.," or "She's a blogger." The number of Internet users who maintain a blog is rising dramatically; experts predict that the "blogosphere" will double every 6 months. Blogs, or Weblogs, are widely varied presentations of an enormous range of content—from personal diaries to supplemental article information posted by news reporters.

Given this variety, researchers are still learning about blogs, blogger demographics, and how they compare with other mass media. This type of information source is particularly compelling given that the vast majority of bloggers is under 30, and more than half are women.

This gender diversity leads to the question of the role of gender in gauging blog credibility. Generally, the overall credibility of Web sites is mixed, depending on the author of the site; government and media Web sites have often been deemed more trustworthy than those created by private individuals (Center for the Digital Future: Digital Future Project, 2005). It is unclear whether those credibility ratings are determined in part by the gender of the blog author. Are gender stereotypes employed by blog readers in determining the credibility of a blog?

So far, few studies have focused on blog users and how much they trust this content. Because Weblogs are becoming a significant source of information among U.S. Internet users, examining their credibility for the general public is important for communication research. Weblogs are a virtually untested medium, so learning more about how they are perceived will provide valuable insight. This study attempted to isolate the credibility of male and female Weblog authors. In particular, we used an experimental design to examine how gender cues might influence Weblog credibility.

CREDIBILITY IN NEWS CONTENT

In news stories, the source of the news story is responsible for conveying information about a story, so who is quoted may determine how the story is interpreted by readers. Most studies of source credibility within mass communication research were conducted in the late 1960s and early 1970s and targeted four dimensions of credibility: knowledge, trustworthiness, attractiveness, and dynamism. More recent studies have focused on key source credibility determinants, such as believability, topical interest, and source selection evaluations. This line of research has also examined credibility from other venues, such as news medium credibility and message credibility.

More recent trends in journalism scholarship have been to examine relationships and predictors of credibility. For example, a 2003 study found that students attending universities in the U.S. Northwest rated political columnists as more credible than did students in the U.S. Southeast (Andsager & Mastin, 2003). A multimedia presentation of Internet news has been found to positively influence source credibility (Kiousis, 2006). Reliance on Weblogs was found to be a strong predictor of Weblog credibility, but reliance on traditional media and political involvement/knowledge and trust in government are weak predictors (Johnson & Kaye, 2004a). In other work examining overall Web site credibility, the authors found that amount of online activity and years spent online were not good predictors of Web credibility (Johnson & Kaye, 2004b). The results are inconclusive at best.

The linkage between credibility and gender has been mixed, depending upon medium. White and Andsager (1991) found that gender was not related to the credibility of newspaper columnists. However, their results indicated that readers preferred columns written by authors of the same sex. A 1988 study found that college-age men viewed men as having more expertise, while women of the same age group found no difference between genders (Carocci, 1988). Later work found that female newspaper columnists—in particular African American women—were ascribed with higher credibility than were men (Andsager & Mastin, 2003). Armstrong and Nelson (2005) found a relationship between credibility and source descriptors (official/nonofficial), suggesting that as credibility for a source decreased, readers processed information within a news story more thoughtfully. However, the results of that study only held true for the respondents who thought the source was male. Flanagin and Metzger (2003) found that men and women had different views of Web site credibility and that each tended to rate opposite-sex Web pages as more credible than same-sex Web sites.

Extending these ideas to Weblogs, the term "source" takes on different meanings. In traditional news coverage, the source is the person to whom information is attributed and, in some instances, the journalist who is conveying the story. However, as noted above, Weblogs are a bit different. Weblogs are generally written by an individual who shares his or her opinions and usually provides additional Internet links for more information. Those links are often to mainstream media or informational Web sites, which may lend credibility to the overall Weblog post, but the links themselves aren't generally examined for source credibility. The human sources quoted in a news story speak to the reader. Rather than speaking *to* the blog user, the links in a blog post speak *for* the blog author.

Generally, the blog author establishes a relationship based on trust with his or her audience. This relationship is intentionally personal, in contrast to the professional objective detachment of a journalist, who must rely on quoted sources to speak to the reader. Bloggers, however, speak directly to their readers. As a result, the blog author is the "source" within a Weblog. It is the author who is being judged for accuracy, newsworthiness, and believability, not others who might be quoted (or linked) in a post.

Gender Stereotypes

Credibility of Weblogs may also be influenced by the use of heuristics such as gender stereotypes. Readers may gauge credibility and trust of information based on the individual descriptors (including gendered words such as *he* and *she*) of sources within the text. Armstrong and Nelson (2005) found that when readers encountered official sources providing information, they were less likely to process the story thoughtfully; but when an unofficial source was quoted, individuals read the story more thoroughly. Furthermore, when "official" or "expert" sources were used, most respondents tapped into their stereotyping heuristics, assuming that the source was male. Because gender is one of the most commonly accessed stereotypes, whether the author of a Weblog is male or female may influence the blog's perceived credibility. Herring and Paolillo (2006) found that diary-focused blogs tend to present female-oriented characteristics, while "filter" blogs—often political blogs that provide commentary and link to other content—seem to contain more male-oriented language and cues.

With the proliferation of blogs, questions arise as to how the credibility of these posts appears to readers. That is, how are these new media being perceived, and what types of cues are readers using to determine the authenticity of content? Given prior credibility scholarship, it seems likely that gender cues can influence the credibility of Weblogs. Individuals may perceive some topics as "belonging" to female or male bloggers or as requiring a particular expertise. Those cues may trigger stereotypes in readers, who may base credibility more on the source descriptors than on the information presented.

Blog Usage

Although mass media studies have found that credibility of a medium is often positively associated with how much an individual uses the medium (Wanta & Hu, 1994), that has not always been true with Internet use. In fact, studies have found conflicting information about whether more frequent Internet use predicted credibility (Flanagin & Metzger, 2000; Johnson & Kaye, 2004b; Kiousis, 2001). Johnson and Kaye (2002) found that traditional media use was a strong predictor of online credibility, but that reliance on the Web was not. In a study of 3,747 blog users, Kaye (2005) found that for some motivations, blog usage (measured in hours used per week) was a predictor but Internet experience (measured in years of use) was not. This suggests that effects of blog usage may not be parallel to that of other media.

A Pew study in 2003 found that "about 11% of Internet users at that time had read blogs," (cited in Rainie, 2005, p. 2). Subsequent Pew studies showed that the percentage had increased to 27% by November 2004 but had not changed by September 2005 (Rainie, 2005). Rainie (2005, p. 2) concluded that "[b]log readers are somewhat more of a mainstream group than bloggers themselves" and noted recent growth in blog readership among women and minorities. Blog readers, therefore, are not rare, but the amount of experience with blogs can be expected to vary widely across the population of U.S. Internet users.

Clearly, differences may exist between those who have had little or no exposure to blogs and those who use blogs on a regular basis. In a study of Internet users, 12% of blog users surveyed said they trusted information received in Weblogs, while 23% reported that they trust most blog content they receive (Consumer Reports WebWatch, 2005). These differences may influence the credibility of blogs. Experienced blog users may have more skill in judging the expertise of a blogger, even on the first encounter with a given blog. Lacking the branding of a well-known journalistic organization, an individual's blog exhibits other cues that encourage or inhibit a reader's willingness to trust the blogger. These include links to archives (How long has the blog existed?), comments (Does the blog have a participating audience?), syndication (Is the blogger sophisticated enough to provide an RSS feed link?), and a "blogroll" (What other blogs are linked to the blog?). Less-experienced blog users may not recognize these features and thus may be more likely than experienced uses to trust a blog that lacks those conventions.

If those features are missing from a blog by an unknown author, then experienced users might be skeptical about the information provided, regardless of traditional cues such as gender or occupation of the blog author. This study suggests that perhaps gender cues—which are typically used to process information quickly—may be tempered by an individual's familiarity with blogs.

OUR EXPERIMENT: MANIPULATING GENDER OF BLOG AUTHORS

In this research, we addressed two specific questions: (1) *Are individual credibility ratings different when the blog is perceived to have been written by a man or a woman?* (2) *What is the role of blog usage in determining credibility?*

To examine these questions, we wanted the views of students, among the largest audiences for blogs. We embedded an experiment within a Web-based survey conducted in November 2005 and had 586 students at a southeastern university participate in the study (58% were women). Respondents read identical versions of a Weblog entry about rebuilding homes in New Orleans in the aftermath of Hurricane Katrina, written by either James Fitzgerald, Ann Fitzgerald, or the gender-neutral pseudonym "Urbanite." The text was seven paragraphs (about 570 words) long and included six external links to other actual Web sites with additional information about topics discussed in the Weblog. We chose a blog post that we expected would be "fresh" to most of our study participants without being obscure. We also chose a topic that had no overt references to gender or politics.

Among other questions, we asked participants to rate the blog post on a 1 ("not at all") to 7 ("extremely") Likert scale for each of the following six dimensions: interesting, accurate, credible, trustworthy, believable, and held the respondent's attention.

OUR FINDINGS: BOTH GENDER & BLOG USAGE AFFECT CREDIBILITY RATINGS

First, we examined how author gender affected respondents' credibility ratings of the post. In all six dimensions, participants reading the male author condition found the blog post more credible than those reading the female author condition and the gender-neutral author condition. Table 1 demonstrates those findings. Certain dimensions demonstrated little difference, whereas there appeared to be great differences in other elements of credibility, including level of trustworthiness and attention. The largest mean difference ($-.51$) occurred between male and female writers on the dimension of ability to hold the student's attention, and, in terms of statistical significance, the dimension of trustworthiness was also found to have a large disparity among conditions. To explore this result, we ran separate analysis of variance (ANOVA) tests on each dimension. ANOVAs allow us to compare whether differences exist across the gender manipulations. Our results indicate that there was a great difference between how students viewed the trustworthiness and the level of engagement (ability to hold attention) of the blog post, depending on whether a man or a woman was perceived as writing it.

This result was interesting because the text was identical across all conditions, except for the manipulation of the authors' gender. These findings suggest that respondents are using source descriptors—in this case, gender—to develop their credibility levels. These various dimensions of credibility that we examined may tell a bit more about the difference. Essentially, no gender difference existed in four of the dimensions—accuracy, believability, interest, and credibility. But, along the dimensions of trustworthiness and attention-keeping, the post by a female author ranked much lower than posts by both the male and gender-neutral authors.

We also looked at whether blog users would rate the credibility of a blog higher than nonusers would. In particular, we were attempting to flesh out whether experienced blog users would use gender as a criterion for determining blog use in the same manner as non-blog users. To explore this idea, we combined all of the credibility dimensions by adding the scores together to come up with an overall rating. Then, we classified a person's rating of the blog as "credible" if the credibility score was above the mean and compared the scores across the three gender manipulations through a Chi-square test. The Chi-square statistic allows us to compare for signifi-

TABLE 1   Means* of Credibility Dimensions by Gender of Blog Writer

CREDIBILITY DIMENSIONS	MALE WRITER	FEMALE WRITER	GENDER-NEUTRAL
Interesting	4.49	4.16	4.26
Accurate	4.30	4.17	4.24
Credible	4.34	4.09	4.13
Trustworthy	3.99[a]	3.64[a]	3.77
Held attention	3.95[b]	3.44[b]	3.78
Believable	4.72	4.50	4.49

*Based on responses to a 1–7 Likert Scale.

Means with like superscripts indicate the condition means for high and low credibility were significantly different from each other at $p < .05$. (Univariate ANOVA; a Scheffe post-hoc test of each condition by dimension.)

TABLE 2   Credibility Ratings by Blog Users and Nonusers

CONDITIONS	NONUSERS	USERS
Female writer	26.1% (42*)	25.7% (35)
Male writer	29.8% (48)	32.4% (44)
Gender-neutral	44.1% (71)	41.9% (57)
Total	161	136

*Number of subjects per condition given in parentheses

Blog Users: X2 (2, N = 253) = 2.19, p = .33

Non-Blog Users: X2 (2, N = 289) = 7.87, p = .02

cant differences across conditions or among groups, so here we ran two separate Chi-square tests, one each for blog users and nonusers. As noted in Table 2, we found that among users, there were no statistically significant differences in credibility. However, among nonusers, more students found the non-gender condition more credible than either of the gendered conditions. Both tests indicated the respondents found the non-gendered condition credible, but among nonusers the non-gender condition was significantly more credible than either male or female writers. This finding suggested to us that perhaps in the blogosphere, non-gendered pseudonyms (such as our "Urbanite") may connote more credibility than actual names.

WHAT DOES IT MEAN?

In terms of gender equality, the findings aren't good. We found that one criterion used to determine the credibility of blogs is gender. That is, when students read a blog post perceived to be written by a male author, they give it more credibility than a post perceived to be written by a woman. The findings demonstrate what many people—primarily women—have alleged for years: There is a perceived gender difference. Men are generally given more credibility than are women. More specifically, our findings suggest that men are seen as more trustworthy, interesting, and engaging, at least when they write a blog post.

What is it about those specific dimensions that bring out these gender differences? It may not be surprising that trust is associated with men more than women, as traditionally men have been placed in more positions of authority, such as law enforcement personnel, national political figures and even network newscasters. Perhaps more surprising is the idea that the post commands a greater level of attention when perceived as being written by a male author. Does that air of authority automatically awarded to men permit them to espouse information and commentary in a way that women cannot, in this society?

The study also illustrates the proliferation of gender stereotypes within our lives. Stereotypes are automatic shortcuts that our mind seeks to help speed up the interpretation of information and make quicker decisions. When confronted with information, people often rely on these heuristics to make choices or evaluations fast. In this case, it appears that part of the decision-making on credibility was related to the gender of the writer, which makes sense, as research has found that gender is a common shortcut used to evaluate information (Armstrong & Nelson, 2005). In this case, despite identical material, the post was rated as more credible when it was supposedly written by a man. Perhaps most surprising, the question "held my attention" illustrated the greatest disparity, with a 17.5% difference between those posts written by men and women.

However, our results do offer some positive news, as it appears that students find higher credibility in blog posts when pseudonyms are employed—in this case, one that is nongendered. Among nonusers, we found that students engaged in gender stereotyping, but more students favored the nongendered condition. However, among blog users, there was no meaningful difference among the three conditions. As blog users become more savvy at reading and interacting with blogs, they may be developing a different way of evaluating blogs—looking at indicators other than gender cues. Although research has found that gender stereotyping is often used as a heuristic when evaluating information, it happened here only among non-blog users. In effect, blog use may lead to more gender-blind evaluations among individuals, while non-blog users may be using the same shortcuts we have seen in older media, such as newspapers.

The connection between gender and blog usage should provide some optimism for those interested in gender-related media issues. Overall, individual use and reliance on the Internet is growing; therefore, the possibility that it may help to mitigate some of the existing gender stereotypes is a positive outcome of this research. Perhaps the growing trend of gender-neutral screen names may help lessen gender stereotyping within the online world.

Those who pursue this line of research may want to try to isolate the indicators by which blog users are determining credibility. These could be based on links to external information, comments, links to other blogs (including the blogroll), or design components. Another cue may be related to the content of the blog. Much of the extant research about blogs relates to political blogs; however, the number of blog topics is large and hardly limited to politics. In this study, we looked at only one blog topic and one post—certainly more study is needed for other types of blogs before we can make a definitive conclusion. But whatever these factors are—and how they vary across topics—they appear to be more important in determining credibility than the gender of the author.

In a classroom setting that focuses on gender in media, the results of this study are provocative, if not puzzling. While the study is exploratory in nature, it seems encouraging to think that gender is becoming less important as a criterion for credibility. On the other hand, why is this still an issue at all? Many journalism schools in the United States now have more female than male graduates, so it isn't as if media work is a predominantly male field. Why does stereotyping happen? Perhaps our findings suggest that blogging may help to lessen the use of gender cues as a factor in credibility. Only time, and more research, will tell.

IT'S YOUR TURN: WHAT DO YOU THINK? WHAT WILL YOU FIND?

1. Use Technorati.com to find five blogs about the same topic. Which ones do you find credible? What are your criteria for credibility? What factors do you examine to determine whether you believe the information you're reading? Make a list. What does your list say about you as a media consumer?

2. Share your list of the criteria and factors with your classmates. To what extent were these evaluative criteria gender-based? Can you identify any patterns of difference among your classmates? Why or why not?

3. What makes someone an expert? Would you trust a male doctor to treat a woman during her pregnancy? Would you trust a female doctor to treat a man for prostate cancer? In what areas does gender *really* play a role in one's expertise? What about blogging? Is there a topic that only women, or only men, should blog about?

REFERENCES

Andsager, J. L., & Mastin, T. (2003). Racial and regional differences in readers' evaluations of the credibility of political columnists by race and sex. *Journalism & Mass Communication Quarterly, 80*(1), 57–72.

Armstrong, C. L., & Nelson, M. R. (2005). How newspaper sources trigger gender stereotypes. *Journalism & Mass Communication Quarterly, 82*(4), 820–837.

Carocci, N. M. (1988). Trust and gender ten years later: The more things change. *Women's Studies in Communication, 11*, 63–89.

Center for the Digital Future. (2005). Press release for the Digital Future Project, Year 5. Retrieved September 21, 2011, from http://www.digitalcenter.org/pdf/Center-for-the-Digital-Future-2005-Highlights.pdf

Consumer Reports WebWatch. (2005). Leap of faith: Using the Internet despite the dangers, October 26, 2005. Retrieved September 21, 2011, from http://www.consumerWebwatch.org/pdfs/princeton.pdf

Flanagin, A.J., & Metzger, M. J. (2000). Perceptions of Internet information credibility. *Journalism & Mass Communication Quarterly, 77*, 515–540.

Flanagin, A. J., & Metzger, M. J. (2003). The perceived credibility of personal Web page information as influenced by the sex of the source. *Computers in Human Behaviors, 19*, 683–701.

Herring, S.C., & Paolillo, J.C. (2006). Gender and genre variation in weblogs. *Journal of Sociolinguistics, 10*(4): 439–459.

Johnson, T. J., & Kaye, B. K. (2002). Webelievability: A path model examining how convenience and reliance predict online credibility. *Journalism & Mass Communication Quarterly, 79*(3), 619–642.

Johnson, T. J., & Kaye, B. K. (2004a). Wag the blog: How reliance on traditional media and the Internet influence credibility perceptions of weblogs among blog users. *Journalism & Mass Communication Quarterly, 81*(3), 622–642.

Johnson, T. J., & Kaye, B. K. (2004b). For whom the web tolls: How Internet experience predicts web reliance and credibility. *Atlantic Journal of Communication, 12*(1), 19–45.

Kaye, B. K. (2005). It's a blog, blog, blog, blog world. *Atlantic Journal of Communication,13*(2), 73–95.

Kiousis, S. (2001). Public trust or mistrust? Perceptions of media credibility in the information age. *Mass Communication and Society, 4*(4), 381–403.

Kiousis, S. (2006). Exploring the impact of modality on perceptions of credibility for online news stories. *Journalism Studies, 7*(2), 348–359.

Pew Center. (2005, June 25). Public more critical of press, but goodwill persists. Pew Research Center for the People and the Press. Retrieved September 21, 2011, from http://people-press.org/reports/display.php3?ReportID=248.

Rainie, L. (2005, January). The state of blogging (data memo). Retrieved April 25, 2008, from http://www.pewinternet.org/pdfs/PIP_blogging_data.pdf

Wanta, W., & Hu, Y.-W. (1994). The effects of credibility, reliance and exposure on media agenda-setting: A path-analysis model. *Journalism Quarterly, 71*(1), 90–98.

White, H. A., & Andsager, J. L. (1991). Newspaper column readers' gender bias: Perceived interest and credibility. *Journalism Quarterly, 68*(4), 709–718.

2.5   VIDEO GAME DESIGN AND ACCEPTANCE OF HATE SPEECH IN ONLINE GAMING

Ryan Rogers

> *You might think the greatest perils of signing online to play a video game would be dodging digital bullets or saving the universe from a fictional alien race. However, as this reading argues, there are other, real-world, concerns for our society—such as how game design can influence the acceptance of hate speech.*

Bigotry and hate thrive in online gaming; hateful comments are almost constant while playing games (Meunier, 2010), and gamers say they often encounter varied forms of hate speech in games (Rogers, 2010). To play an online game, you log on via a video game console or computer connected to the Internet, then play game sessions with others where avatars (graphical representations of the players) interact. Normally, gamers interact via headset chat or by exchanging typed messages in addition to playing together. The lack of content regulation in online gaming and the flexibility for users to leave sessions freely do little to discourage antisocial behaviors (Rajagopal & Bojin, 2002). Indeed, the anonymous nature of the Internet may encourage users to say things they wouldn't say in real-life situations (Li, 2006). People are more tolerant of hateful online content than in other contexts (Leets, 2001).

Some 60% of Americans play video games (Pratt, 2008), for an average of 7 hours a week (Vorderer & Ritterfeld, 2009). Video games are powerful tools that can teach gamers how to do many things (Gee, 2003). Traditional media effects research states that individuals can learn from and be influenced by media, and as Zillmann and Weaver (1999) argue, the learning and cues involved in video games may extend beyond the actual time spent playing. Thus, an understanding of video game effects—including priming—is important. Priming refers to how exposure to media content might influence people's later judgments (Roskos-Ewoldsen, Roskos-Ewoldsen, & Dillman Carpentier, 2002). Studying priming effects is important because they can occur subtly, and unnoticed information can influence behavior (Van den Bussche, Van den Noortgate, & Reynvoet, 2009). As such, minor, imperceptible changes to a game's design may have profound yet undetected effects on gamers in and outside of gaming. In light of this, I set out to analyze how aspects of a game's design might influence gamers' acceptance of hate speech among the gaming community.

I define hate speech as words motivated by group prejudice, intended to physically or psychologically harm someone based on their race, religion, gender, or sexual orientation. Hate speech in video games may be an example of modern prejudice. Modern prejudice is subtle, and thus more acceptable, prejudice against specific groups.

Hate speech in video games is most often directed at individuals who do not fit the stereotype of the heterosexual, adolescent, white male (Meunier, 2010; Rogers, 2010). Video game content may contribute to hateful messages by fostering racial and gender stereotypes (Glaubke, Miller, Parker, & Espejo, 2001) and narrow value systems (Soukup, 2007).

POSSIBLE EFFECTS OF VIDEO GAME DESIGN ON HATE SPEECH

Different game designs may cause different behaviors; for example, fighting games provoke more hostility than shooter games (Eastin & Griffiths, 2006). Even small alterations within the same game can produce different effects on gamers (Barlett, Harris, & Bruey, 2008). Level of *competition* may be one key variable. Research has shown that gamers primed with competition are more aggressive than those primed with cooperation (Anderson & Morrow, 1995), and that aggressive competition such as found in online gaming enforces patriarchal norms (Soukup, 2007). By their very design, video games require different levels of competition; they can promote cooperation or head-to-head competition. Therefore, it is possible that more competition in a game would result in more acceptance of hate speech.

A second key variable is *fragmentation*, or a programmed divide in gamer interaction. Such interruptions may be the result of loading times, changes in a game's flow, or software or hardware malfunction. This divide creates a psychological distinction between online gaming and real world interactions, such that gamers become more aware of online gaming mediation. Gamers view mediated online gaming as distinct from real-life experiences and interactions. Gamers experience fragmentation and a heightened awareness of mediation when they perceive distance between one another over the Internet due to the anonymous nature and the global stage of the medium (Li, 2005; Rajagopal & Bojin, 2002; Williams & Clippinger, 2002). Another important result of fragmentation is frustration, which can elicit more intense reactions (Bandura, Ross, & Ross, 1963). The more a game is interrupted and fragmented, the more mediated it feels and the more frustrated a gamer will become. Likewise, games by nature can be frustrating when a gamer loses, gets killed, or is outmatched. This frustration can manifest itself in the same way that a football player may lose his temper and commit a foul. These interruptions themselves contribute to fragmentation, which may make gamers feel more distanced from hate speech, making it more acceptable.

HYPOTHESES AND THE EXPERIMENT

To test the relationships between competition, fragmentation, and the acceptance of hate speech during gaming, I designed an experimental study in which participants viewed a 15-minute video segment of recorded game play, in which actors played *Gears of War 2* and followed a script. The recorded game play was manipulated to operationalize the variables of interest.

Participants in the experiment were between the ages 18 and 54 but were mostly white men between 18 and 24. One group of participants (n = 19) was exposed to a high competitive game mode and a second group (n = 22) to a low competitive game mode. Both game modes incorporated two levels of fragmentation (low and high), and seven instances of hate speech (thrice faggot, thrice bitch, and once nigger). A brief analysis prior to the experiment revealed that "faggot" and "bitch" are used most frequently while "nigger" is used less frequently in online gaming. Notably, hateful comments in the script were directed at groups that do not fit the gamer stereotype—racial minorities, homosexuals, and females. In the high competition game mode, two teams of five killed one another until one team was eliminated or time ran out. The low competition game mode forced two teams of five to control an area of a map for a predetermined period of time. Both modes feature similar cycles of low and high fragmentation as the players chatted, undistracted, before the game (low), only teammates chatted in-game with distractions (high) and, again, everyone chatted undistracted after the game (low). Other breaks in online gaming etiquette/code of conduct were included on the tapes, so I could measure acceptance of interactions and behaviors beyond hate speech. Breaks in etiquette included: disruptive communication (noise, singing), unsporting behavior (team killing, showing off), lack of skill/unfamiliarity with the game, and cheating.

As participants viewed the recording, they rated the acceptability of the in-game actions and behaviors with a MS Interactive Perception Analyzer dial. They had continuous control of the dial and adjusted it to reflect their acceptance of the gamers' behavior in real time as they watched the taped game session. The acceptance scale ranged from 0 (least acceptance) to 100 (high acceptance). Finally, subjects filled out a survey assessing demographic information, prior gaming experience, feelings about hate speech (nigger, faggot, and bitch) in and outside of gaming, enjoyment of the game, attitudes toward violations of game etiquette, how realistic the sessions were, and how communication differs between online gaming and face-to-face interactions.

On the basis of the aforementioned above procedure, I examined the following hypotheses. A one-way analysis of variance test was used for H1, and a mixed multifactorial analysis of variance test was used for H2.

H1:   The higher the intensity of competition in the game design, the more acceptable hate speech is to gamers.

H2:   The higher the fragmentation in game design, the more acceptable hate speech is to gamers.

Two research questions provide an exploratory measure of how sensitive the online gaming community is to hate speech as opposed to other breaks in online gaming etiquette, and explore gamers' perceptions of hate speech in the venue of online gaming. Paired t-tests were used on both RQs.

RQ1:   How does the acceptance of hate speech compare to acceptance of other etiquette violations in online gaming?

RQ2:   Is hate speech more acceptable while playing games than when used elsewhere?

HOW HATE SPEECH IS INFLUENCED BY GAME DESIGN

Participants watching the high competition game mode gave higher ratings for the overall acceptability of hate speech (M = 51.34, SD = 12.60) compared to participants in the low competition condition (M = 45.17, SD = 10.81), although the difference did not reach the level of statistical significance. Participants watching the high competition game mode were significantly more accepting of multiple uses of the term "bitch" than were participants watching the low competition game mode [F(1,39) = 4.43, p = .05]. There were no significant differences between conditions for acceptability of multiple uses of the term "faggot" and one occurrence of the term "nigger". Notably, "faggot" was deemed acceptable in game modes with high competition but not in the low competition condition. "Nigger" was never viewed as acceptable although lower competition featured a stronger disapproval than the high competition game mode.

There was a significant difference in acceptance of hate speech between low fragmentation and high fragmentation stages [F (1,40) = 9.60, p = .004, η^2_p = .94]. In the low fragmentation stage, the mean acceptance of hate speech (M = 46.20, SD = 12.54) was lower than the mean acceptance of hate speech in the high fragmentation stage (M = 52.78, SD = 16.69).

Significant differences suggest that overall hate speech is less acceptable than other etiquette breaks [t(40) = 8.14, p < .001]. However, when analyzing etiquette violations and hate speech occurrences individually some etiquette violations are less acceptable than certain hate speech terms. The term "faggot" was found to be more acceptable than body humping [t(40) = 2.01, p = .05]. Overall, participants in the low competition condition were less likely to accept breaks in etiquette than those in the high competition condition [F(1,39) = 12.20, p = .001].

There was also a significant difference between participants' overall acceptance of hate speech when responding to the survey and while watching the game session. Overall, hate speech was more acceptable while watching the game session than in the survey [t(39) = 2.33, p = .02]. According to the survey, paired t-tests indicated that the most acceptable form of hate speech is "bitch" [t(40) = 7.11, p < .001] when compared to the term "faggot," and "nigger" is the least acceptable [t(40) = 5.09, p < .001] when compared with the term "faggot." There were no significant differences in acceptance levels between types of hate speech while watching the game session. Participants were also more likely to accept etiquette violations while watching the game session than during the survey [t(38) = 6.51, p < .001].

WHAT DOES THIS ALL MEAN?

The limited support for H1 suggests that acceptance of hate speech is influenced by competitive game design. Competition may increase aggression and hostility (Anderson & Morrow, 1995; Soukup, 2007), and it may also increase acceptance of aggressive and hostile actions, such as hate speech. This finding expands Eastin and Griffith's (2006) study that showed different game types result in different hostility levels in users, implying that exposure to competitive game genres can influence an individual, specifically in regards to hate speech.

Perhaps when a game is competitive, gamers do not feel obliged to be respectful or make concessions for female gamers. The presentation, or lack thereof, of female avatars likely contributes to gamers' perceptions that a term such as "bitch" would be acceptable (Dill & Thill, 2007). Gamers may perceive that there are not many female gamers playing online or that those who are playing online are stereotypical, so the term "bitch" is more acceptable. This acceptance indicates a culture of male dominance and female exclusion, and it bolsters Soukup's (2007) claim that competition in video games enforces patriarchal norms.

Gamers must be aware of how their attitudes may change in the face of competition, specifically, that their acceptance of hate speech related to women might increase, and misogynistic tendencies may arise from that acceptance. Furthermore, if game designers would like to encourage more diverse demographics, they should diversify game content. There are ways to soften competition or create more welcoming environments for female gamers; perhaps, this environment could be achieved by including assertive female avatars, encouraging female participation or more strict retribution against misogyny in the community.

Game design that fragments gamer interactions will increase a gamer's acceptance of hate speech. This expands Leets' (2001) finding that hateful content is more acceptable online than offline. This suggests that gamers don't necessarily feel distance between one another because they're playing an online game; rather, gamers feel distance between one another because of interruptions presented by the specific interface they are using. When gamers' interactions are fragmented by the interface, the experience seems more mediated and less "real," and hate speech becomes more acceptable. Creating more meaningful interactions by allowing gamers to feel less distanced from one another could influence the gaming community to be less accepting of hate speech. Gamers and game designers alike should be aware of how each small change to an interface can contribute to their feelings and behaviors, even within the same game.

The data from the research questions suggest that hate speech is less acceptable than are other etiquette violations, indicating that the online gaming community is more sensitive to issues of hate speech than they are to other breaches of etiquette. As such, gamers may be sensitive to issues of race, sexual orientation, and gender in their online community, but specific game designs can hinder that sensitivity.

Gamers are most sensitive to race hate speech and least sensitive to gender hate speech while gaming, and more sensitive when they are not viewing a game session. This suggests that engagement with online gaming increases acceptance of hate speech (Leets, 2001). Someone who may take exception to the terms "faggot" or "nigger" in real life might be more accepting of those terms while playing online games. Likewise, gamers were more likely to disapprove of etiquette violations when filling out a survey than when watching a game session. Gamers may be more forgiving of transgressions against their community while they are in-game than when asked about it after the fact.

The acceptance of hate speech in online gaming can be influenced by high competition and high fragmentation. Hate speech in online gaming can be tempered by video game design, and as such, gamers and designers alike should be cognizant of this finding. With this heightened awareness and more diverse video game content, gamers can get back to dodging digital bullets and fighting fictional aliens.

IT'S YOUR TURN: WHAT DO YOU THINK? WHAT WILL YOU FIND?

1. Look at video game advertisements and Web sites. How might these outlets contribute to the use and acceptance of hate speech in online gaming? Who are video games marketed toward?

2. If you were producing a new video game, what steps would you take to appeal to a variety of gamers and how would you try to address the issue of hate speech in your game?

3. How would you deal with hate speech in a video game? Is this different than how you might act in another setting?

4. Consider the price of video games and video game consoles. How might social class influence the use, type, and acceptance of hate speech in online gaming?

REFERENCES

Anderson, C., & Morrow, M. (1995, October). Competitive aggression without interaction: Effects of competitive versus cooperative instructions on aggressive behavior in video games. *Personality and Social Psychology Bulletin, 21*(10), 1020–1030.

Bandura, A., Ross, D., & Ross, S. (1963). Imitation of film-mediated aggressive models. *The Journal of Abnormal and Social Psychology, 66*(1), 3–11.

Barlett, C. P., Harris, R. J., & Bruey, C. (2008). The effect of the amount of blood in a violent video game on aggression, hostility, and arousal. *Journal of Experimental Social Psychology, 44*(3), 539–546.

Dill, K., & Thill, K. (2007). Video game characters and the socialization of gender roles: Young people's perceptions mirror sexist media depictions. *Sex Roles, 57*(11/12), 851–864.

Eastin, M., & Griffiths, R. (2006). Beyond the shooter game. *Communication Research, 33*(6), 448–466.

Gee, J. P. (2003). *What video games teach us about learning and literacy.* New York: Palgrave/Macmillan.

Glaubke, C. R., Miller, P., Parker, M. A., & Espejo, E. (2001). *Fair play? Violence, gender and race in video games.* Oakland, CA: Children Now. Retrieved March 28, 2011, from http://gamedev.cs.cmu.edu/spring2004/handouts/ChildrenNow_report.pdf

Leets, L. (2001). Responses to Internet hate sites: Is speech too free in cyberspace? *Communication Law & Policy. 6*(2), 287–317.

Li, Q. (2006). Cyberbullying in schools: A research of gender differences. *School Psychology International, 27*, 157–170.

Meunier, N. (2010). Homophobia and harassment in the online gaming age. Retrieved September 22, 2011, from http://xboxlive.ign.com/articles/106/1060720p1.html

Pratt, B. (2008). The demographics of video game players. Retrieved September 22, 2011, from http://ezine-articles.com/?The-Demographics-of-Video-Game-Players&id=1111304

Rajagopal, I., & Bojin, N. (2002). Digital representation: Racism on the World Wide Web. *First Monday, 7* (10).

Rogers, R. (2010, April). *The virtual locker room: Hate speech and online gaming.* Paper presented at the annual conference of the Eastern Communication Association.

Roskos-Ewoldsen, D., Roskos-Ewoldsen, B., & Dillman Carpentier, F. R. (2002). Media priming: A synthesis. In J. Bryant & D. Zillmann (Eds.), *Media effects: Advances in theory and research* (pp. 97–120). Mahwah, NJ: Lawrence Erlbaum Associates.

Soukup, C. (2007). Mastering the game: Gender and the entelechial motivational system of video games. *Women's Studies in Communication, 30*(2), 157–178.

Van den Bussche, E., Van den Noortgate, W., & Reynvoet, B. (2009, May). Mechanisms of masked priming: A meta-analysis. *Psychological Bulletin, 135*(3), 452–477.

Vorderer, P., & Ritterfeld, U. (2009). Digital games. In R. Nabi & M. B. Oliver (Eds.), *The SAGE handbook of media processes and effects* (pp. 455–468). Thousand Oaks, CA: Sage.

Williams, R., & Clippinger, C. (2002, September). Aggression, competition and computer games: Computer and human opponents. *Computers in Human Behavior, 18*(5), 495–506.

Zillmann, D., & Weaver, J. (1999). Effects of prolonged exposure to gratuitous media violence on provoked and unprovoked hostile behavior. *Journal of Applied Social Psychology, 29*(1), 145–165.

Audience Studies

3.1 WOMEN WITH PHYSICAL DISABILITIES, BODY IMAGE, MEDIA, AND SELF-CONCEPTION

Michelle A. Wolf, Melinda S. Krakow, and Rebecca Taff[1]

This reading reports the results of focus groups with women who have physical disabilities. The women explored how messages from media and people around them shaped their thoughts and feelings about themselves and their bodies.

When you think about your body, you are engaging in a process of self-conception, a subjective, fluid practice shaped by messages from other people and media. How people respond to you affects how you think and feel about yourself (Kinch, 1963). This thinking takes place in a body-conscious culture that is saturated with media images of "ideal" bodies. Gerbner and his colleagues have been arguing for decades that television plays a significant role in cultivating a shared reality. Television is an important force in the self-conception process because it distributes a continuous, repetitive system of images and messages, and the more time people spend "'living' in the world of television," the more likely they are to "report perceptions of social reality which can be traced to (or are congruent with) television's most persistent representations of life and society" (Gerbner, Gross, Signorielli, Morgan, & Jackson-Beck, 1979, p. 14). As reminders of what is "right" and as sources of cultural ideals of beauty and bodies, television circulates cultural standards that shape how we come to see ourselves.

This reading is designed to deepen your understanding of how women with physical disabilities think and feel about media representations of women's bodies and their own bodies. We conducted four focus groups with 16 women with physical disabilities ranging in age from 23 to 67 years. We asked participants to think about media messages while we posed questions about culturally ideal bodies, whether they saw themselves represented on television, how they felt about their own bodies, and the sources of their body image.

MEDIA AND CULTURAL IDEALS

The focus groups began with a discussion of how women are represented in media and the cultural ideals of the female body. Most participants easily recalled images of women who are young; have perfect skin; and are wrinkle-free, tall, thin, and glamorous. Some described the cultural ideal as sexual, powerful, strong, and confident; others compared her to Barbie, a Playboy Bunny, and a "calendar girl."

When discussing examples of the cultural ideal, an overarching variable—generation—emerged and continued as a thread throughout the discussions. Because the participants ranged from 23 to 67 years old, their experiences of growing up and using media varied. For this reason, we identify the participants by "P" and age, for example P30.

Several participants recalled women in media who began acting decades ago. P43 described them as having a "motif of class and beauty," such as Sophia Loren, Joan Collins, and Linda Evans from the TV series *Dynasty*. More current and common examples of "ideal" women included Angelina Jolie, Kim Kardashian, Heidi Klum, The Suicide Girls, Jennifer Aniston, Kate Winslet, Drew Barrymore, Jennifer Lopez, and Michelle Obama.

Although recalling these media images was easy, reconciling this cultural ideal with the participants' own ideas about ideal bodies was difficult. Some denied the existence of a cultural ideal: "I don't think there is a cultural ideal. I think we like to pretend and make Barbie into an ideal and then berate people when they try to be that person" (P23). For P40, a single body type did not come to mind when she envisioned the cultural ideal: "But I definitely [don't] think I have a sense of there being one ideal, or even an approximation because so many of my friends don't fit any of those ideas. Like, if you don't happen to have legs, immediately any sort of BMI [body mass index] things kind of fall off the cliff." P55 introduced another variable, sexual orientation, to acknowledge that lesbians "look at concepts of beauty in a different kind of way . . . there's more room for being fat . . . you don't have to put on make-up." The contrast between the culturally ideal body and the participants' experiences of their own bodies became more significant when the conversation transitioned to media representation and exclusion.

MEDIA REPRESENTATION AND EXCLUSION

Discussions of cultural ideals shifted to concerns about the paucity of televised women with physical disabilities. Most participants struggled to identify media representations of their own bodies, but some recalled specific, isolated examples. P43 mentioned two men from her youth: "Chester, who walked with a limp on *Gunsmoke*," and Mr. Magoo, a visually impaired cartoon character who was ridiculed because he "bumped into everything." Others remembered Dr. Kerry Weaver from the TV series *ER* and Abbey Curran, the woman with cerebral palsy who was crowned Miss USA 2008. P23 applauded *The L Word* for presenting "the best disabled person I've ever seen on television . . . she's deaf and it's obvious, and they sign and then she talks . . . they put it at the bottom like subtitles."

Some participants were disturbed by poor representations in reality television. P35, for example, criticized the TV's *Extreme Home Makeover* for being "paternalistic" and focusing on people trying to "overcome" their disabilities. The word "overcome" can be offensive to people with physical disabilities because "[d]isabled people do not succeed 'in spite of' their disabilities as much as they succeed 'in spite of' an inaccessible and discriminatory society. They do not 'overcome' their handicaps so much as 'overcome' prejudice" (Ragged Edge Online, 1992).

When asked if they saw themselves represented on television, most participants responded with a resounding "no" because they did not see women with physical disabilities. P40 said she would be astonished to see her body on television. She related more to the diversity she sought out in programming, "not just in terms of disability but also in terms of ethnicity, in terms of gender orientation." P35 was disappointed that she never saw anyone she could relate to in a dramatic setting. P42 mentioned actress Geri Jewell from *Facts of Life* and *Deadwood* because she had a similar type of cerebral palsy. Interestingly, she found reflections of herself in both female and male characters. For instance, she related to "my male version of myself," Josh Blue, who won the *Last Comic Standing* in 2007, and two characters with physical disabilities (a man and a woman) who were played by non-disabled actors. P43 was frustrated by the lack of sexuality in representations of women with physical disabilities. P42 was also disappointed by such limited representation, particularly in "any kind of romantic, sexy kind of way."

Regrettably, most of the participants only "saw" themselves if they carved their bodies into parts or spoke of body types. Some participants noticed their large breasts. Others recognized physical shape, as when P57 mentioned women who were "big and kind of hefty." P23 identified two women who were shaped like her, in *Numb3rs* and *The Mentalist*. P40 described her experience as finding "traces of difference," for example, coroner Al Robbins on *CSI* and attorney Emily Resnick on *Boston Legal*. Even with these examples, the participants could not relate because they experienced their bodies as whole bodies. This stands in sharp contrast to previous research on non-disabled heterosexual women who easily carved their bodies into fragmented body parts (Wolf, Nichols, & Decelle, 2009).

Because women with physical disabilities are virtually excluded from mainstream media, they experience what Gerbner and Gross (1976) and Tuchman (1978) refer to as symbolic annihilation. Being represented in media—positively or negatively—is a form of power because at least you exist. Exclusion is tantamount to being symbolically annihilated from the cultural conversation. In the absence of fair, diverse media representation, the participants expressed concerns about other people's susceptibility to media messages, and the profound impact this had on how others saw them.

Nevertheless, 11 of the participants said they felt good about their bodies. Perhaps the most striking here is that so many participants expressed positive body image feelings. For some, this varied with their pain level, but not with their body image satisfaction. These positive feelings are especially significant because the questions the participants discussed have been posed to hundreds of non-disabled students in classrooms and to non-disabled men and women in more than 20 focus groups, and the overwhelming conclusion from this research is that most of those questioned said they did not feel good about their bodies (Wolf, Krakow, & Morahan, 2010).

The participants' positive feelings, however, were challenged by how other people responded to them. Because other people could not see them without first seeing their disability, their disability *was* their "body image" to others. Some wished they could be inconspicuous, and many recalled onlookers who could not separate the participants' disability from them as people. Distinguishing between her body and her "body presented to the world in a wheelchair," P56 said that using a wheelchair "obviously changes everything, and there are lots of times I hate it that people are noticing it." To negotiate their own self-conceptions, the participants found ways to deal with people who stared at them, as P39 explained: "My disability being so visible, no arms and legs. I don't feel bad all the time because of my disability, but there's definitely a constant feeling of most people who don't know me think I look like a freak. The biggest way to deal with people staring is I just don't look. I don't notice it so that it doesn't bother me."

Some participants said that attention from strangers made them hesitant to enter social situations because other people can be condescending and some treat them like children. Others recalled strangers who tried to assist them when no assistance was requested or needed. As a result, the participants experienced two levels of thought about their bodies and their body image: their own feelings and the perceptions of others. P57 said she became "more visible" when she began using a cane: "People go out of their way to open doors for me when it's really not necessary." P56 exclaimed: "People talk to me all the time like I'm a child. Or they 'honey' me." P56 disliked being in crowded social settings and going to parties because she was very uncomfortable. She described "the kind of setting where the whole point is to present yourself socially to strangers" and said: "It's very difficult to do that from a wheelchair. And I also can't move around. If I'm over here and the room is crowded and I really would like to be over there, I can't get there."

Some participants shared painful feelings about their bodies and how others reacted to them. P58 thought she was too heavy: "I'm embarrassed. I'm ashamed. And I keep envisioning that it's going to change, that I won't feel pain, and that I'm going to look a certain way." Even when participants tried to "blend in," their disability drew unwanted attention. P34 dressed more conservatively because "I have an awkward gait. I walk with a cane, which tends to end up being a conversation starter." Sometimes this annoyed her, but sometimes she "worked it out:" They'll be like "oh why have a cane?" And I'll say "because I'm a pimp." P27 wore loose clothing because her knees were "stuck in like a bent angle." If she wore "jeans or anything that's tight," she was "more noticeable." This had a downside, though: "Some people don't understand when I say 'oh, I need to take the elevator instead of the stairs.' . . . They see me and they don't understand; this girl, she's young, there's nothing wrong with her."

Interactions with others shaped the participants' life choices, and for those with jobs, the workplace was a positive source of social interaction. The participants felt confident because people appreciated them for their job performance. Being at work was better than being in public because coworkers came to know the participants as people, and body image was not at the forefront of these social interactions. P56 explained: "Everybody knows me, and the people that don't know me, I'm like the unquestioned expert about certain things that I do." She said this is where she comes across "the best . . . when you are just presenting yourself with complete comfort about yourself because work is not about 'are you pretty.'"

The participants who were most comfortable with their bodies found communities of support, and many were involved in disability communities. P35 knew a lot of activists with disabilities and spoke to other women with disabilities, which helped her to develop a sense of her community. P56 found community support and "gained a lot of my confidence from that." Over time she "reached a point, where I had a job that was related to that." P25 was involved in a few disability communities and sat on a youth advisory council: "I have a group of people that I see in the summertime at the youth leadership forum. And we keep in contact as friends . . . And it's amazing. It is empowering. It's great to meet these new young people and see what they're going through now, or what they're not going through."

BEING BORN WITH A DISABILITY VS. HAVING AN ACQUIRED DISABILITY

For some participants, physical changes such as weight gain were sources of body image dissatisfaction. This was especially true for those who acquired disabilities. For example, P57 began to struggle with her weight as a child. When she started using a wheelchair after a car accident in her teens, weight became an even greater challenge. Again, generation was part of the conversation, as when participants who felt good about their bodies also experienced the trials that come with aging and loss of function. P63 felt good about her recent weight loss because it was easier to move about. However, this was hard to maintain, given the increased pain she experienced over time, a conflict that became more complex when she explained the impact of a lifetime of exposure to cultural ideals, giving testimony to cultivation theory: "I guess it's embossed in my brain what the ideal body is. And now you can't even say I'm middle-aged anymore. The other side of middle age, and I take a shower, and I look at my bulging middle and I go 'Oh, I want to liposuction.' . . . And I guess I have taken it along with me for a long time, and I have embraced that image of not having the middle fat."

The participants spoke at length about differences between being born with a disability and having an acquired disability, and how this contributed to their body image over time. In one group, two participants observed such a distinction when P27 expressed surprise to hear that P67 did not want to use crutches as a youth because she "didn't want to look like an old lady." P27 responded: "It's so funny that you felt like you'd feel like an old woman because when I got my crutches, the doctors were like "you can start using them now or you can start using them later." And I got them because they're purple and I thought they were cool, and my friends all thought they were cool. I never felt like maybe that's a generational thing. I never felt like they would make me look old."

Older participants also recalled the difficulty in finding people with disabilities who shared their experiences before the disability rights movement was established. Younger participants were surprised to hear about this. P63 said she was so focused "on the negative" that she forgot that "in P23's generation, there is a young woman with a disability who has the self-image to go up and compete in a beauty pageant . . . growing up like some of us in the '50s [that] never would have crossed my mind. Ever." P58 reflected on her struggle to reconcile her pre-accident body image from her youth with her current body: "Everything changes. And you think it's over, and it's only begun, and then 20-something years pass." P23 observed significant differences, "a whole different mindset," in comparison to P34, who said she knew where she stood because she "was born into it." For several participants, acquiring a disability brought about a process of self-acceptance, as P58 explained: "It's like being any minority, that you can't change who you are. You are you who are, dynamic as you are. And that's part of it. But when you are not born into it, you have to become it and work with it, and you don't understand because you were on the other side."

Other participants also came to feel good about their bodies after they acquired their disability. P25 expressed the positive feelings that emerged 5 years after she became disabled. It took her a year to "realize that one of the things that had happened to me was that my body image had plummeted. That I would look in the mirror and hate the way I looked, even though nothing visible has changed about me." For a long time, P25 felt "hatred toward my body because it had stopped working for me and I was in pain." She worked on her self-image and was pleased to say, "I feel much better about my body now than I did before I was injured."

THINKING ABOUT DISABILITY IN EVERYDAY LIFE

One in five Americans has a disability (Centers for Disease Control and Prevention, 2008; U.S. Census Bureau, 2010). Although the general population sees disability as an exception to life, in fact it is a natural and normal part of life. Tragically, media exclusion, combined with the minimal contact that most people have with men and women with physical disabilities, encourages a very narrow way thinking about disability in our culture. The problem is that disability is far from being normalized. P58 captured this well: "That's the sad part, nobody's been taught that a disabled person is normal, that we can have passion and have the same feelings inside." As a result, and in important ways, the body image of women with physical disabilities is more complex than non-disabled women who think about their body image. And because, as Kinch (1963) reports, other people's responses to us are powerful, they affect how we think and feel about ourselves. For many of us, this is a lifelong struggle.

NOTE

1. The authors thank Suzanne Levine for her outstanding service as the disability consultant for this research.

IT'S YOUR TURN: WHAT DO YOU THINK? WHAT WILL YOU FIND?

1. You are the producer of a five-character TV series like *Friends* that includes a woman with physical disabilities. Given what you've read here, create a list of bullet points for your writers to help them create diverse, fair, and socially responsible portrayals of *all* five friends on the show.

2. View *Hollywood Images of Disability* (http://vimeo.com/16733842). Prepare for a group discussion of the video and the concept "symbolic annihilation" described in this chapter. Where did the women in the video find themselves represented in media? Where did they see themselves excluded?

3. Visit the National Center for Disability and Journalism's homepage at www.ncdj.org. Review the links and then read the *Disability Style Guide* and the *Tip Sheets for Reporters*. Then read *Beyond the AP stylebook: Language and usage guide for reporters and editors* at http://www.ragged-edge-mag.com/media-circus/styleguide.htm. Considering this information and what you read here, imagine you're a journalist preparing to interview and write a news feature about Kathleen Martinez, Assistant Secretary for Disability Employment Policy (http://www.dol.gov/odep/welcome/AssistantSecretary.htm). Develop a set of at least five interview questions for Martinez.

REFERENCES

Centers for Disease Control and Prevention. (2008). *Disability and health: Data and statistics*. Retrieved September 25, 2011, from http://www.cdc.gov/ncbddd/disabilityandhealth/data.html

Gerbner, G., & Gross, L. (1976). Living with television: The violence profile. *Journal of Communication, 26,* 173–199.

Gerbner, G., Gross, L., Morgan, M., & Signorielli, N. (1979). The "mainstreaming" of America: Violence profile no. 11. *Journal of Communication, 30,* 10–29.

Kinch, J. W. A. (1963). A formalized theory of the self-concept. *The American Journal of Sociology, 68,* 481–486.

Ragged Edge Online. (1992). *Beyond the AP stylebook: Language and usage guide for reporters and editors.*

Retrieved September 25, 2011, from http://www.
ragged-edge-mag.com/mediacircus/styleguide.htm

Tuchman, G. (1978). Introduction: The symbolic annihilation
of women by the mass media. In G. Tuchman, A. K.
Daniels, & J. Benét (Eds.), *Hearth and home: Images
of women in the mass media* (pp. 3–38). New York:
Oxford University Press.

U.S. Census Bureau. (2010). *Census bureau releases 2009
American community survey data.* Retrieved September 25, 2011, from http://www.census.gov/newsroom/
releases/archives/american_community_survey_acs/
cb10-cn78.html

Wolf, M. A., Decelle, D., & Nichols, S. (2009). Body image, mass media, self-concept. In R. A. Lind (Ed.),
*Race/gender/media: Considering diversity across au-
diences, content and producers* (2nd ed., pp. 36–44).
Boston: Allyn & Bacon.

Wolf, M. A., Krakow, M. S., & Morahan, T. (2010,
November). *Television, media representation and
self-conception: How gay, bisexual, and heterosexual men talk about television's construction of
body.* Paper presented at the National Communication Association 96th Annual Convention, San
Francisco, CA.

3.2   NEGOTIATING THE MEDIASCAPE: ASIAN AMERICAN MEN AND AMERICAN MASS MEDIA

Helen K. Ho

> *The last decade has seen interest groups and film and television studios attempt to increase
> diversity in the entertainment industry. Television has recently presented audiences with
> more multicultural ensemble casts and Asian American male lead actors than ever before.
> But, how might Asian American men bring their understandings of what it is to be Asian
> American to these representations?*

The role of American mass media and its portrayals of Asians in the formation of Asian
American identity has been largely overlooked in Asian American studies. Yet, some studies
have shown that stereotyped opinions of what it means to be American, as well as Asian, are
reinforced by media representations of "Fresh-off-the-boat" (FOB) immigrants or model minorities (Danico, 2004; Kim, 1999). These bimodal stereotypes can influence Asian American men's
self-concepts, as well as interpretations of other Asian Americans.

I conducted in-depth interviews with 27 self-identified Asian American men at a Midwestern
university. Men were asked for their general impressions and specific recollections of Asian American
men in the media, then were asked to respond to photos of contemporary leading Asian American
actors: Jackie Chan, John Cho, Masi Oka, and Daniel Dae Kim. Interviewees, whose names I have
altered here, ranged from 18 to 41 years in age, were asked for opinions and reactions to these pictures.
There were 8 Korean Americans (Alex, Andrew, Dan, David, Jae-Sun, Josh, Tom, Young Min); 11
Chinese Americans (Aaron, Avery, Bobby, Brad, Jimmy, Edison, Francis, Gary, Hugh, Nick, Oliver);
2 Japanese Americans (Hiroki, Randy); 3 Indian Americans (Ekram, Fred, Partha); 1 Vietnamese
American (Jonathan); 1 Filipino-American (Dean); and 1 bi-ethnic Asian American (Ben).

WHAT IS ASIAN AMERICAN?

Broadly, there were two main themes which emerged from interviewees' definitions of what it
means to be Asian American. One was rooted in race and ethnicity, and one in class and culture.

Race/Ethnicity-Based Definitions

With their stories of growing up in predominantly white neighborhoods and schools, it became clear that interviewees demarcated "Asian American" by the stereotypes—FOBs, model minorities—found in society writ large. "Someone who has black hair, yellow skin, and kind of black eyes. I look at people . . . Asian, not Asian, it's clear" (David, Korean-American). Most interviewees used David's definition for Asian American, which focused on phenotype or biological difference. This approach narrowed "Asian American" down to include specific "Oriental" ethnicities, explained by Korean American Jae-Sun: "I think it's Japanese, Korean, Chinese. . . . If you think about Asian American, that's the Oriental Asian. . . . Like a white person, I don't think they'd think of Vietnamese or Thai." Vietnamese American Jonathan agreed, sharing that most people guessed him to be "Chinese, Japanese, or Korean." All interviewees said that they had been mistaken as an ethnicity other than their own.

While men disliked how this "Oriental" formulation promoted interchangeability by erasing ethnic difference, they also found it helpful in defining what it means to be Asian American. For example, it helped some men justify the exclusion of Indian Americans from "Asian American." Indian American Ekram explained how he understood himself using this definition: "For demographic purposes, I identify as Asian American . . . [but] people who are "Oriental" looking are distinctly thought of as one group and South Asians [as another]." Ekram is also aware of the Black/white racial framework that shapes him (Tuan, 1998; Kim, 1999), stressing, "Because of my dark skin, I identify more as a person of color." Ekram understands his racial positioning as a dark-skinned minority, but is also aware of that the privileges of class and education make him a model minority (Ekram is an academic in a technological field). The position of Indian Americans in the larger framework of Asian America offers a site where the nuances of race and class are augmented (Prashad, 2000).

Class-Based Definitions

Some men offered cultural, classed definitions of "Asian American," which reinforced the assumption that Asian Americans are an upwardly mobile, model minority. Josh (Korean American) said: "I think there are really two categories: People that are really Americanized, and people that have a really strong connection back to [Asia]. They're kind of two different species." According to Hugh (Chinese American): "Asian American is someone who's not . . . FOBby. I think there's a clear distinction between those who seem to accept or embrace American culture and those who haven't." Overall, this cultural—and generational—approach trumped racial distinctions. Many times, interviewees declared they did not consider themselves wholly "Asian." Using cultural distinctions allowed interviewees to set themselves apart from unassimilated FOB Asians. Josh confessed, "I don't give off the vibe of being really *Asian*." In defining FOB, men cited fashion choices, English-speaking abilities, and American cultural competency.

Because all of my interviewees were upwardly mobile men in college, their concepts of Asian American involved a particular experience of educational accumulation, cultural assimilation, and cosmopolitanism. This distinction secured the role of class in understanding Asian America.

ASIAN AMERICAN MEDIA VISIBILITY

Interviewees were asked to discuss four Asian American lead actors: Jackie Chan, John Cho, Daniel Dae Kim, and Masi Oka. The actors were chosen based on a set of pilot conversations in which people of all races were asked to name contemporary Asian Americans still on screens in the early to mid-2000s. Actors who had not produced any memorable mainstream recent texts, such as Jet Li, were not presented to interviewees.

The four stars presented in this study have increased the visibility of Asian American men in American popular culture. Daniel Dae Kim was featured as one of *People* magazine's "Sexiest Men Alive" (2005), and John Cho was featured on the list two times (2006, 2009). Although Masi Oka did not make the official list, he was featured as a "Chic Geek" in the 2006 issue. *People* is certainly not the golden standard of popularity in America, but the rise of Asian Americans to celebrity standing suggests that Asian Americans have made gains in a cultural arena mainly populated by white men. Understanding these characters and their narratives provides insight into how texts, readers, and communities engage in discursive relationships about race and ethnicity (Shohat & Stam, 1994).

Exit the Dragon

Most interviewees cited Jackie Chan, most known for his work in the *Rush Hour* (1998–2007) and *Shanghai Noon* (2000–2003) franchises, as the first memorable Asian they saw on screen. Many of the Asian stereotypes they knew of seemed to have roots in Chan's portrayals. Korean American Tom explained, "He's the reason why . . . everybody thinks that we do kung fu." "It fits the public's stereotype [of Asian Americans]," Indian American Fred explained. "You take *Rush Hour*–Jackie Chan is Asian. That's why kung fu is associated with [being Asian]."

Despite the stereotypes associated with Chan, Chinese American Edison saw Chan's career as inspirational: Chan's success in America mirrored Edison's own experience as a Chinese immigrant. Now that Edison identifies more with American culture, he believes that Chan perpetuates stereotypes: "How can you as an Asian really relate to Jackie Chan? . . . He's ridiculous." Others described Chan as, "for better or worse," a core reference for understanding Asian Americans. Today, Edison sees hope in new Asian characters on screen.

Moving beyond Jackie Chan toward a new generation of actors was a common topic of discussion. Filipino American Dean explained: "Jackie, he's maybe the last line of some of the older archetypes of his generation, like Bruce Lee, Jet Li." Although Bruce Lee's visibility in American popular media is also linked to this stereotype, this generation of Asian American interviewees found Jackie Chan's portrayals more relevant to how Asian American men are understood in their daily lives. Yet, while Chan was named as a prominent Asian on screen, interviewees dismissed him as irrelevant to contemporary Asian America.

For Japanese American Hiroki, Chan's films are no longer "really Chinese" and instead are more "Asian American." For Hiroki, this mirrors Asian Americans' transnational ties and assimilation into American culture. However, Hiroki stood alone in this interpretation of Chan as an Asian American figure. While Chan's global status may be seen as Americanized, most interpreted the actor as purely Asian. Indian American Partha asserted, "He's in the mainstream but. . . . He's an Asian guy." Bi racial Ben agreed, using a nationalist definition of Asian American: "I guess you could go with media power. But he's not [Asian American]. He's a Chinese national."

Others, using their own definitions of Asian America, failed to identify with Chan. Chinese American Oliver explained, "He's always been more associated with China, and not just himself being that way, [but also] perceptions of him." To Oliver, Chan is someone who engages in Asian performance, but is also widely interpreted by mainstream audiences as Asian. Chinese American Brad's description of Chan ultimately mirrors how men described FOBs on the college campus: "There's always this thing where he's foreign . . . people don't really accept him as American." Interviewees understood Chan as a foreigner unable to fit into American social settings; he represents the FOB image that they identified against.

Entering the *White Castle*

Interviewees identified Korean American John Cho as distinctly opposite to Jackie Chan. Interviewees knew Cho from his mainstream success as Sulu in 2009's *Star Trek*, but mostly as Harold Lee in the *Harold and Kumar* films (2004, 2009, 2011). Interviewees thought the films' portrayals perpetuated prototypical images of Asians in the United States. Critiques of Cho showed how men bring negotiations of their own minority status to reading minority characters: "Harold [is] what people stereotype Asian Americans as. He's this overly hard-working guy who's underappreciated and goes unnoticed by everyone. . . . he's this stereotypical Asian guy" (Avery, Chinese-American). This highlights the difficulties Asian Americans feel as stereotyped model minorities. Even Dean, who saw Cho as leading a new generation of representations, labeled Harold as a typical "smart, nerdy guy." Despite the progress of Harold being a lead character, it is negated by the fact that he is still presented as a model minority.

Yet, most men, like Josh, admired Cho's work as an Asian American actor: "He's kind of just like a regular guy in his movies. . . . The humor behind [them] is that he's actually pretty American, but everyone that the two confront in the movie goes, 'Ching chong ching chong, your dad runs a gas station.'" This theme of "being a regular guy" was echoed across interviews: "[Harold is] more of a fun-loving, regular American kind of guy" (Brad). "He's cool, he's just another guy, he just happens to be Asian" (Aaron, Chinese American). When asked if being an American who "just happens to be Asian" is something with which he identifies, Aaron agreed: "I want to avoid it having it be, 'This is the Asian guy.'. . . I don't want it to be something that makes me stand out." Most men joined Aaron in his ideal to be seen foremost as someone whose race is not the first marker of their identity—just as regular guys with many qualities, including a racial designation. In this way, Cho is admired because his race is not as visible: his performance is American, not necessarily rooted to being Asian American. "He can be an average person," Ben concluded, "but it's pretty clear that you don't have to be Asian American to enjoy watching [him]."

Some saw Asian Americans in media as commodities consumed by mainstream audiences. This nuanced reading points to the ways in which men believed they are defined as Asian Americans by others. "These characters are fairly representative of a middle-class, easily-consumable-by-White-culture reality of many educated second-generation Asian Americans," said Jimmy (Chinese American). Many like Jimmy defined "Asian American" by performance and appearance, but also by how this performance is consumed and re interpreted by others.

Cho was seen a more palatable commodity than Jackie Chan. If Chan portrayed the kung fu-fighting FOB, Cho portrayed the modern-day Asian American. Both portrayed characters in American situations, but Cho's unaccented English and ability to be a "regular guy" marked him as Asian American, while Chan's broken English and foreign portrayals marked him as FOB. Identifying differences between the actors, Hugh reinforced the idea that Asian American can be defined by a performance of dress, mannerisms, and stature: "[Cho] even *looks* the most American."

From Zeroes to *Heroes*

How do interviewees negotiate Asian American actors who play foreign nationals? Masi Oka became a mainstream celebrity in 2006 when NBC launched *Heroes*, a new ensemble show featuring a global cast of characters coming to terms with superhuman abilities. The multi layered storyline centered on Hiro Nakamura, a Japanese man with the power of time travel uniting the show's characters in a mission to save the world. Ben had the most nuanced negotiation of Oka's performance: "Quite a few people don't like him because he plays the stereotypical Asian. . . . [But] he's Asian American. . . . he has to put the accent on and play this game, even though he's American. . . . It's not really any kind of awesome, positive portrayal."

For Ben, there is some dissonance about an American actor playing a FOB: Oka's Asian American status seems to make his portrayal of an Asian particularly conspicuous.

The Hiro character prompted the most negative comments, mostly on his outward appearance. Compare Hugh's response to his comment that John Cho "looks American": "Hiro looks like one of my dad's friends! Again, the weak, small guy with the glasses and bad hair!" Josh labeled Hiro "a token Asian . . . chirpy and small," and both Jonathan and Korean American Dan described his outfit as a "Japanese schoolboy uniform" despite knowing that Hiro is an adult businessman. Here, the visibility of an Asian American male lead on television is complicated, even negated, by this stereotypical portrayal. Brad expressed his dissatisfaction: "Hiro just gives me that sense that he's that little, shrewd Asian who . . . isn't very outspoken. I'm sure he has those moments where he breaks out of that stereotype, but the mere fact that they show it to begin with is enough." Hiro's mere appearance elicited for a very specific and negative stereotype for Brad, suggesting how much outward appearances are implicated in Asian American men's negotiations of race and performance.

Aaron explained how Hiro's FOB status, linked in his mind to Jackie Chan, prevented any positive reading: " [Hiro] encapsulates everything that Jackie Chan started. He is a short, nerdy, comic book geek who can't pronounce his R's right." The "foreign Oriental" stereotype has played such a key role in forming the "popular" idea of what Asian American is, and is so pervasive, a character like Hiro cannot be separated from it. Oka's Asian American background was eclipsed by his Asian performance. As Avery explained, "The fact that he's Asian American doesn't really matter to most people because they see him and they just think, Asian."

Men's reactions to the character involved how they believed others saw the character. For Dean, Hiro was a problematic stereotype precisely because "of the way he looks . . . and the way he fits into society and how people react to him. So, I guess my definition of Asian American is really based on how people react to us." Tom was the only one who saw potential for Hiro, only because he knew whites who viewed him positively: "He's really cute in the way that he acts . . . these are white people that say this. So, that has a lasting impression."

The issue of Asian American attractiveness threaded through each of my conversations. When interviewees labeled an actor attractive, they used white standards of masculine attractiveness, such as a rugged physique. For Dan, a white actor's popularity is based on theatrical ability and attractiveness, but different standards apply to Asian American actors. The belief that Asians are not good looking, he explained, is why "they don't make it quite on top as the other actors who have both [good skills and attractiveness]."

Finding a *Lost* Masculinity

The last actor discussed was Daniel Dae Kim, another Asian American actor playing a foreign national on primetime television. Kim is mostly known for his work on ABC's *Lost* (2004–2010) and as Detective Chin Ho Kelly in the 2010 TV remake of *Hawaii Five-O.*

Interviewees rarely recalled Kim in their lists of Asians on screen, but had the most to say about his character, Jin-Soo Kwon, on *Lost*. Jin was discussed with some ambivalence as interviewees worked through how he straddled the line between Asian and American. Japanese American Randy identified Jin as a "typical stoic, quiet, minor-role character"; finding similarities with Hiro, many cited Jin's lack of English-speaking skills and traditional Korean values on the show. Yet, the negativity surrounding the portrayal of *Heroes*' Hiro was not expressed in discussions of *Lost*'s Jin. Avery identified Jin as "still foreign, but [with] a more American feel than Hiro." Again, men used standards of appearance, along with the show's narrative, to make sense of Kim's character.

This was particularly the case when men thought of Jin and other *Lost* characters, often shirtless on the beach. Edison claimed this as a new representation: an Asian American being "very manly." Kim's portrayal was pleasurable in a way that Oka's was not; Kim's body, fitting standards of Western physique, could be objectified. Oliver linked Jin's image with "typical" masculine portrayals, taking into account others' perceptions: "It's not a very common portrayal," he mused. "It's kind of funny that objectifying him is positive." The image of the muscular Asian body—but not the hyper-muscular, kung fu body—was seen as a media exception, and men linked Kim's body to the representational space typically given to white television heroes. "He looks semi-between Asian and American. *[Can you explain that?]* I think it's an image you'll find in America, of portraying something Asian, but packaging it into an American product" (Francis, Chinese American). Tom said: "The body he has right now is not really the common Korean body . . . he's not like the typical Korean. He's more American. *[A Korean in an American body?]* Exactly." Here, masculinity is manifested in the American body. Saying "it's good to see the Asian American man as not so effeminate," Jimmy points to a binary that positions white as masculine and Asian as feminine (Said, 1978). This stereotyped dynamic, long perpetuated by media representations, is ruptured by Kim's image.

Interviewees focused on Jin as the best example of "Asian American" precisely because his racial difference was so visible at the beginning of *Lost*. For Oliver and others, the amount of narrative focus given to Jin placed him on the same playing field as other *Lost* characters. The visibility of Jin's story, along with Kim's visibility in Hollywood, lent to the credibility of his Asian American identity. Men spoke the most eloquently about Jin, the Asian character's interactions with American characters, and his character development. According to Andrew (Korean American): "He has a very strong Korean character, very stern. He begins to open up later; you see it in his relationship with his wife at the beginning. He's very, 'You listen to me and me only, it's just me and you and we're gonna get off this island.' But later he opens up . . . actually I like his character the most, because he has . . . a lot of heart." Men of all backgrounds appreciated Jin's character and the transformations he made on *Lost*. Says David, "I could really trust this guy. He's very humble. . . . He's a respectable character."

For men of all backgrounds, Jin's story shows a pathway to assimilation and respect. "I feel like he represents the general Asian population just because. . . . he's trying to change from being Asian. . . . It's how he takes his background and uses it in a new setting, which is what an Asian American pretty much has to do, when they come from whatever country to another country to live, how they change. I feel like Jin does that on the island, so you can connect to him a lot more, and gives a better representation of Asian-Americans," said Fred. Dean also identified with the character: "[He's] the ideal Asian American because he is very unapologetic for who he is. He is very individual in the sense that he retains his traditions in spite of those around him or what may be going on around him." For Dean, seeing Jin enabled a sense of self-pride in being Asian American.

Seeing these Asian Americans negotiate white social settings on screen seemed to provide interviewees with a realistic account of what it means to be a racial minority in a white culture. Just as interviewees bring their understandings of Asian America to their negotiations of TV characters, they believe that narratives of Asian America define them. Identifying the stereotypes that inform narratives of Asian Americans, interviewees admired Daniel Dae Kim and John Cho more than Jackie Chan and Masi Oka, not only for their non FOB portrayals but also for breaking into a predominantly white entertainment industry. In addition, both Cho and Kim are seen as sexually desirable to some degree. In this context, their racial difference is also rendered invisible as their bodies become "consumable" by conforming to dominant masculine types.

IT'S YOUR TURN: WHAT DO YOU THINK? WHAT WILL YOU FIND?

1. Why might the "Oriental" definition of Asian American be so prevalent? Can you find parallels to other definitions of other racial or ethnic minorities?

2. When describing what it means to be Asian American, interviewees used, broadly, race-based and class-based definitions. How do these definitions change, stay the same, or intersect with other notions,

such as gender, age, or appearance, when regarding Asian American actors?

3. What are some qualities that come to mind when you think of "masculine"? How might these qualities shift by culture, race, or even class?

4. Debate: Is minority visibility in the media a good thing, even if it promotes stereotypes?

REFERENCES

Danico, M.Y. (2004). *The 1.5 generation*. Honolulu: University of Hawai'i Press.

Kim, C.J. (1999). The racial triangulation of Asian Americans. *Politics and Society, 27*(1), 105–138.

Prashad, V. (2000). *The karma of brown folk*. Minneapolis, MN: University of Minneapolis Press.

Said, E.W. (1978). *Orientalism*. New York: Random House.

Shohat, E., & Stam, R. (1994). *Unthinking Eurocentrism: Multiculturalism and the media*. London: Routledge.

Tuan, M. (1998). *Forever foreigners or honorary whites?: The Asian ethnic experience today*. New Brunswick, NJ: Rutgers University Press.

3.3 MAN UP: VIEWER RESPONSES TO IMAGES OF LESS THAN IDEAL MALES IN ADVERTISING

Neil Alperstein

Because women have often been depicted in advertising as objects instead of people, critics are concerned about the emulation of ultra-thin models used in advertising and the potential promotion of eating disorders such as anorexia. But what about men? And what if the images are not of the unattainable ideal? The author studies men's responses to less-than-ideal male images in ads.

Feminist author and speaker Jean Kilbourne (see Reading 5.9) argues that there is long-term harm in exposing young girls and women to the unattainable ideals presented in advertising. However, only recently has the concern for the depiction of men in advertising started to emerge as researchers and critics have come to understand that advertising may have broad social consequences that go beyond the intended outcome of selling a product or service. That concern has focused on ideal body images and the ways in which men compare themselves to advertising's depictions of masculinity.

Sociologist Michael Kimmel (1996) has declared that masculinity proceeds from men's bodies. The ideal male image in advertising and other media portrayals, according to Kimmel, includes standards of power and independence as well as qualities such as rugged individualism, adventurous spirit, risk taking, displays of physical prowess, and having a high degree of personal autonomy. But what happens when the average guy confronts idealized images in advertising and perhaps realizes that he cannot live up to such expectations? Many men may become depressed and dissatisfied with their bodies (Gulas & McKeage, 2000).

In this reading, however, I raise a different question: what happens when male viewers are presented with less-than-ideal images, such as the cavemen who appear in a long-running U.S. advertising campaign for GEICO auto insurance? In other words, if looking at unattainable idealized images is depressing, might looking at less-than-ideal images be uplifting, or at least provide relief regarding the feeling of having to live up to the idealized other?

DIVERSE REPRESENTATIONS OF MASCULINE GENDER IDENTITY

Along with ideal images of masculinity, advertisements beginning in the mid-1990s began to include less-than-ideal images of men, a trend that may be rooted in societal changes regarding men's roles. Traditional masculinity, represented by images of muscularity and strength, gave way to a more volatile gender identity that wavers between the traditional and the new. Barbara Ehrenreich (1984) describes how beliefs about men as family breadwinner shifted toward a newer consumer role. Similarly, Susan Faludi (1999) writes about how men's roles shifted from what she labeled the functional or breadwinner to the decorative or ornamental. In the early 1990s when Faludi began writing her book, the U.S. economy was in a recession. She claimed that traditional men felt emasculated when their lives as wage earners were threatened, and their functional roles such as family breadwinner were replaced with decorative or consumer roles. When the economy improved, Faludi, still working on the book, noted that "the men I was talking to were still stricken with a sense that they had been betrayed, and that the betrayal went much deeper than a paycheck" (Halpern, 1999, p.37).

SOCIAL COMPARISON OF LESS-THAN-IDEAL IMAGES IN ADVERTISING

This reading is based on my research into how male consumers of advertising compare themselves to less-than-ideal images of masculinity, those images that are consistent with their changing social role. In 1954, the social psychologist Leon Festinger developed the theory of social comparison that described comparing oneself to another as a basic human need. Over the years, the theory has been expanded and revised to consider issues relating to the individual's social environment, for example, when someone makes comparisons upward (someone who is better off), downward (someone is worse off), or lateral (someone is like me). Comparisons to an idealized image, based on Festinger's original concept, would be made in the upward direction (emulation of the celebrity or sports figure in the ad). Viewing images of those less fortunate, however, may direct the comparison downward, leading consumers to feel superior to others. Therefore, the ways in which we compare ourselves to others are more complex than originally thought. Although this research focuses on how men compare themselves to less-than-ideal images of other men, social comparison theory could easily be applied to how women compare themselves with other women and to cross-gender comparisons.

Specifically, what I have set out to do is to consider how men compare themselves with less-than-ideal images in television advertising, particularly when they are portrayed as cavemen, wolves, or in other socially embarrassing ways, and how male viewers negotiate the meanings of those less-than-ideal images. To investigate this, I showed a series of six commercials that included ideal and less-than-ideal images to a dozen young men (aged 18 to 24), and then I conducted in-depth interviews with each. The advertisements targeted men and featured products that ranged from auto insurance (GEICO) and fast food (Quiznos) to beer (Budweiser) and soft drinks (Pepsi). I asked these young men for their general reactions to the commercials in order to elicit their understanding of the advertiser's message and their interpretation of the message, with particular interest in the ways in which those young men compared themselves to the key images in the commercials. I was also interested in their self-perception with particular regard for body consciousness.

THREE EMERGENT THEMES

I discovered three recurring themes and emergent patterns in the male viewer's responses that help to explain the ways in which men compare themselves to others, especially those depictions in advertising of characters who are less than ideal.

Awareness of the "Everyman" or Average Quality of the Key Figure

The young men who viewed the six advertisements overwhelmingly expressed their awareness and understanding of the key figure's average middle-class qualities, which was something to be celebrated and appreciated. This reaction was apparent in a Pepsi commercial featuring comedian Dave Chappelle, who in the context of the commercial, is an average guy about to embark on an average date, except with a comedic twist in which he is stripped of his pants by a runaway robotic vacuum cleaner. The contradiction between the character's average physical qualities and his social status or class in the commercial became the point of comparison, as related by one young man: "I wouldn't say he's muscular (speaking of Dave Chappelle). He's relatively skinny and he looked like he's about average height. He's not like a completely attractive person. And he's not handsome the way a male model would be. He looks like he's in an everyday situation. For a lot of commercials there are super models and you're sitting there saying 'Oh, not everybody looks like that,' so it's good to see a normal average looking guy drinking Pepsi, so people can relate to his situation."

Similarly, in a long-running campaign for GEICO auto insurance featuring cavemen to illustrate how easy their online service is to use, the following comment was offered: "Other than their faces, I'd say they looked like normal males. They looked lean and average size, around 6 ft. I'd say. I think the fact that from the neck down they looked completely normal, like a normal man, and then up there was the really ugly face . . . the beards and really long hair."

In addition to cavemen, men are depicted in the advertisements as lower animals such as wolves, as in an ad for the Honda Pilot. As with the other advertisements of less-than-ideal images, this one elicited responses regarding the average qualities of the wolf-man and his middle-class lifestyle. One participant noted: "The man in the Honda commercial looked average . . . flabby. I wouldn't say his body mass index is over 30, not obese. He's bald. I remember that. He was out of the shower shaking water off his head. He had a little bit of a gut, but nothing you can't hide underneath two shirts . . . just the average middle-aged father with a family of four."

He later said: "He has a good family. A nice house. A great car—a Honda. A reliable car. He didn't have rippling muscles. He didn't have a six pack of abs. It's a nice change, because I don't have to be reminded like every time I buy underwear that I don't look like that. I think it makes me more acceptable."

In describing the average qualities of the character in the Honda commercial, one young man reflects on social class cues: "The family goes camping every weekend. That's not something an upper class family would likely do. Middle of the road as they come. Just Johnny next door. Let's call him 'Joe the Plumber'. Very middle America. I'm as middle of the road as they come. So, I guess I do relate to the guy in that way.

Identification with Aspects of the Key Figure's Lifestyle – "Breaking Free."

Although men may not have the desire to look like the less-than-ideal images displayed in the commercials, in appreciation of their middle-class status, male viewers also point to particular aspects of the key figure's lifestyle: eating in restaurants and dressing in nice clothing. Most prominent, however, was the male viewers' appreciation for the freedom to act with unrestrained behavior, like a wild animal. In particular, the notion of breaking free repeatedly came up in responses to the commercial for the Honda Pilot briefly identified above. As stated by one participant: "It does show that middle class is cool or okay. Acceptable. But the chance to break free, to be wild. . . . It was almost as if Honda Pilot was an escape route from living your life." He went on to say:

> I think it all comes back to that guy letting loose. Although we may have the nine to five job. Because we have medical and dental benefits. Because he has a wife and two kids to take care of. Responsibilities like that. There's always a part of you that is relieved when you have the chance to break free.

Let loose. Not be confined. I look back at my nieces and see they don't have a care in the world and that guy in the commercial [wolf-man] he didn't have a care in the world, which is awesome. I wish everybody could be like that. At the same time, I don't want to be bald. I don't want to have a gut. I don't want to have to be taken care of exclusively by my wife because I don't know how to interact with people. The carefree attitude is kind of nice though.

Additionally as one young man noted in response to viewing the GEICO cavemen: "I may not want to look like him, but I sure would like to dress like him, live like him and date girls like him."

Downward Comparison to the Key Image in the Commercial

On the surface, it might be assumed that a soccer icon such as David Beckham would be counted among idealized images, but in a commercial that is part of Adidas' "Impossible is Nothing" campaign, Beckham represents an everyman character, a late bloomer who suffered greatly prior to his emergence as a world-class footballer. While the men I spoke with were quite aware of Beckham, his prowess on the field and his antics off the field, they appreciated his average size and the casual apparel he was wearing. They said he was the most normal looking of the key images from the advertisements. In this way, the Adidas commercial served as a safe harbor for men who did not want to, at least initially and of their own accord, compare themselves with the other less-than-ideal images of wolf-men, cavemen, and images of social embarrassment.

While the men I interviewed wanted to disassociate themselves from particular physical attributes of several of the key characters in the commercials they viewed of less-than-ideal males, they do not necessarily want to distance themselves from aspects of their lifestyle and social class. As the physical attributes were so closely connected to the lifestyle depicted, it was evident that a more complex process of interpreting the mixed signals the advertisements sent was being utilized. For example, as was the case of the GEICO cavemen, the men I interviewed could appreciate their stylish clothing, but not their facial features that were incongruent with the former. In comparison, one young man said in reference to the caveman, "I'm a hairy person. But I wouldn't want to be like him."

In reference to the Honda commercial, one interviewee said: "I suppose there's not much he can do about it (his looks). I don't know how much judgment I can pass on how satisfied he is with his looks. If I were him, I would not be satisfied."

The men I interviewed consistently employed downward comparisons of the cavemen, wolves, and images of humiliated males, describing them as dumb or stupid, unlike themselves. Although they may have found appreciation in some particular aspect of the key image's lifestyle, respondents often asserted that they would not want to be in that physical position, look like that, or be as irrational in their own behavior. In other words, while a male viewer might report that he is attracted to the opposite sex and therefore can appreciate how in the Budweiser beer commercial featuring a caveman that the caveman "gets the girl," and because the male viewer likes to drink beer, he can appreciate the attraction to the beverage being advertised, the men interviewed consistently said, "I'm glad I'm not like him." Except for the image of David Beckham, these images are perceived by male viewers to be physically unattractive. There is no desire to be physically like the key figures in the commercials and little desire to emulate those key figures in most respects, except when it comes to particular aspects of the middle-class lifestyle portrayed in the commercials. It is through the food the key figures in the advertisements eat, the girls who are attracted to them, the clothes they wear, and the freedom to which they aspire that male viewers find meaningful; otherwise, the young men I interviewed employed downward comparison, distancing themselves from their physical attributes and lack of public manners.

VIEWING LESS-THAN-IDEAL IMAGES MAKES US FEEL BETTER ABOUT OURSELVES

Men who view advertisements in which they confront images of less-than-ideal men seem to feel that things could be much worse. In other words, the key figures in the commercials set the bar so low as to create a social environment in which men find comfort. When compared with the physical grotesqueness, public exposure, and lack of manners portrayed by key figures in some advertising, men feel a sense of relief that this was happening to them, not me. Not only do such advertisements provide a comic relief for the viewer, those depictions are a form of recompense—a payoff by the advertiser—for what may be lacking in men's lives. Male viewers may not "get the girl" or have big muscles, but they can laugh at those on the screen or page who have even less. Social comparison theory is helpful in explaining the self-enhancement that men experience as they encounter advertisements that feature less-than-ideal men. The three themes I present here suggest that the route to self-enhancement once associated with emulating others is not straightforward; men interpret less-than-ideal images and the social situations depicted in the advertisements in a complex manner. Men may not want to look like those less-than-ideal men in advertising, but they may evaluate the advertisement based on social status cues like eating well and enjoying the fantasy of uninhibited freedom that beckons them.

Less-than-ideal images in advertising counter-balance traditional constructions of masculinity that are part of our everyday cultural referent system. In order to make sense of a less-than-ideal image, the viewer must understand the implausibility of the image of men as cavemen or men as wolves. Images of less-than-ideal males provide an opportunity for further thinking in which the viewer replaces the simplistic, perhaps stereotypical, meaning conventionally linked to the visual/verbal expression—men lack intelligence or men have not evolved—with a complex meaning that is more in comparison with the individual's own evaluation of himself and his social environment. Therefore, male consumers must work to find the meaning in the advertisements. The consumer can move in the direction of the less-than-ideal image, for example, empathizing with the key figure's low status and lack of respect; isolate and identify with only one aspect of the less-than-ideal image, such as his clothing, discarding or partially disassociating himself from that aspect of the image he finds distasteful; or reject the image as the viewer finds comfort in the fact that the image and the situation in which the less-than-ideal character finds himself is not "me".

My research suggests that in addition to focusing on qualities associated with traditional masculinity, male viewers evaluate advertisements based on portrayals of social class. When it comes to advertised products for whom men make up the dominant market segment—beer, soft drinks, auto insurance, sports equipment, fast food, and trucks—the utilization of a less-than- ideal image may serve the purpose of metaphorically "spreading the word" about a new or emergent less-than-ideal masculinity—an unintended consequence of advertising. The multiple ways in which advertising depicts both traditional and non-traditional males is a function of product categories being advertised. Mixing idealized images and less-than-ideal images, along with other representations, opens up masculinity to multiple pathways in which male viewers subjectively interpret and thus compare themselves to images depicted in advertising. The category, masculinity, is not one entity. As is the case with race and class, masculine gender identity takes on various cultural meanings and significance.

IT'S YOUR TURN: WHAT DO YOU THINK? WHAT WILL YOU FIND?

1. All of the commercials identified in this research may be accessed online. View them with your friends or fellow students. What themes come up as you discuss these ads?

2. This chapter focused on how white men compare themselves to images in advertising. Would you expect social comparisons to be different based on race or ethnicity? Would you expect women to employ different strategies of social comparison when evaluating advertisements?

3. Advertising has both intended effects, namely selling a product or service, as well as unintended social consequences, like the use of stereotypes. How should advertisers and their agencies consider the

potential ethical dilemmas posed by those unintended social consequences of advertising? In other words, how can advertisers avoid the use of stereotypes?

4. It was pointed out in this chapter that the depiction of less-than-ideal images in advertising follows the changes that have taken place in the social environment of middle-class males. Do you think advertising accurately reflects those societal changes, or do you feel it paints a distorted picture of society?

5. Social comparison works for cross-gender comparisons too. If you're male, look at advertisements featuring women, and if you're female, look at ads featuring men. In what ways, do you find comparisons between yourself and the images in those advertisements?

REFERENCES

Ehrenreich, B. (1984). *The hearts of men: American dreams and the flight from commitment.* Garden City, NJ: Anchor Press/Doubleday.

Faludi, S. (1999). *Stiffed: The betrayal of the American man.* New York: William Morrow & Company.

Festinger, L. (1954). A theory of social comparison processes. *Human Relations, 7,* 117–140.

Gulas, C., & McKeage, K. (2000). Extending social comparison: An examination of the unintended consequences of idealized advertising imagery." *Journal of Advertising, 29*(2), 17–28.

Halpern, S. (1999). Susan Faludi: the *Mother Jones* interview. The Pulitzer Prize-winner who identified the backlash against feminism turns her attention to the next oppressed class men. *Mother Jones, 24*(5). 36–39.

Kimmel, M. (1996). *Manhood in America: A cultural history.* New York: Free Press.

3.4 HOW TV NEWS MAKES ARABS AND MUSLIMS FEEL ABOUT THEMSELVES

Dina Ibrahim and Aymen Abdel Halim

This reading investigates how young Arab Americans and Muslims think and feel about the images and stories presented by the media about their culture and faith. Participants in a focus group explained how they think the news programming makes them feel about themselves and their sense of identity.

Arabs and Muslims in America often find themselves in the awkward position of defending their faith and culture, in part due to news coverage and how it is interpreted by the audience. This reading focuses not on whether news stories contain stereotypes and negative images of Arabs and Muslims, but on Arabs' and Muslims' personal interpretations of news content, and the impact of those interpretations on self-conception and public displays of identity. We use cultivation theory to elucidate the cultural framework in which religious identity and self-conception develop.

The central principle of cultivation theory is that people learn much of what they know from television. Electronic media, including the Internet and social networking, provide information we use to shape our social realities. Even with the increasing popularity of the Internet as a news source (61% of Americans report accessing their news online), TV news reaches 78% of Americans (Purcell, Rainie, Mitchell, Rosenstiel, & Olmstead, 2010). Television is considered a ubiquitous environment for learning in American culture (Morgan & Signorielli, 1990, p. 13).

Gerbner, Gross, Morgan, and Signorielli (1980) argue that the cultivation process is one in which electronic media play a major role in how audiences achieve a common understanding of issues. Television in particular shapes how people from diverse ethnic backgrounds are portrayed and perceived by society. Media scholars have argued that by simply watching television, an act that seems inherently passive as we stare at the screen, we are in fact actively creating and interpreting meaning from the stories we see and hear (Morley, 1986). The impressions we have about people and places are often constructed using information we get from television. Although reporters create the narratives, they don't actually control what those stories mean to the audience. It is the viewers who actively create meaning, and that interpretation can vary widely depending on their individual backgrounds.

Other researchers studying how television affects viewers' values and attitudes find that exposure to television messages affects audiences' perceptions of reality (Greenwald, 1968; Hawkins & Pingree, 1980). Kinch's theory of the self-concept (1972) also helps us understand how television audiences feel about themselves. Self-concept, or how people perceive themselves, is the result of how other people perceive them, and their opinion and evaluation of those external appraisals.

To see how media coverage of Muslims and Arabs makes them feel about themselves and their sense of identity, we conducted a focus group in San Francisco with 13 Muslim American men and women of varied ethnicities, between the ages of 18 and 32. Nine were Arab, three were Pakistani American, and one was Vietnamese American. They described how they feel, where they get their news, and what they think of it. We also asked them to offer recommendations on how to improve news coverage of Arabs and Islam. We identify participants by speaker number, gender, and age: for example (#3, M, 29).

ANGER AND FRUSTRATION

Most of the Muslims we spoke to expressed disappointment with the mainstream news industry in the United States, which perpetuates images that lead to a feeling of frustration, anger, and disgust. Part of the frustration for these young Muslims is because they often feel helpless to respond to criticism of their faith in electronic news discourse, particularly cable news stations such as CNN and FOX News, which rely heavily on the talk show format and often hire commentators they deem experts. The Muslims in our focus group did not consider the guests or commentators credible.

> (#3, M, 29) It makes me feel mad, and pissed off. They're on a TV station like CNN, these people they're supposedly experts and they have no clue about what they're talking about. It makes me sick turning on the TV, flipping through channels and finding these people on TV talking. It makes me feel like what can we do or how can we counteract that?

One young man was particularly annoyed with the way that cable news conducts interviews and discussions when it comes to issues in the Middle East. He noticed a systematic pattern of demeaning the Arab viewpoint that is manifested by interrupting or abruptly ending a conversation. He finds this technique particularly disturbing to watch and also expresses feeling powerless to participate and engage in the public dialogue of cable television news channels.

> (#2, M, 21) I can't stand to watch certain stations like Fox News. And if you turn it off, you're just going to be mad, and you want to see how it ends out. It always ends out bad. I get so pissed off, so angry, I start talking to the TV.

These feelings of anger and frustration were articulated by more of the men than the women in the group. The men were more expressive about their anger, whereas the women seemed to be more contained. A woman said that she channels her anger at the news into being a better person and ambassador for her faith. Other participants, who felt it was counterproductive to get upset with people who misunderstand their faith and culture, said that ignoring society's negative attitude toward Islam was their preferred coping mechanism.

> (#1, F, 20) It's frustrating but a lot of the time I just brush it off. I want people not consider me for my race first. So I try to be more educated. I read more, I try to excel in school better, so I kind of have to prove to the world that you're not the negative, and you're not whatever the news tries to say you are.
> (#2, M, 21) I can't be bad, I can't be like other kids and misbehave because I feel like if I do that people will be like "oh, he's that way because he's an Arab" or "he's just that way because he's a Muslim," "he's just an angry Arab like we see in the news."

The participants described how their feelings and self-conception evolved over time. A few of them said that even before they followed the news, as children in middle school and high school, the influence of the news images on their peers had a much stronger impact than now, in their 20s. The male participants said they were more physically and verbally aggressive in middle and high school, but now they have a better grip on handling the fear of being different, and that fear has developed into pride in their faith and culture.

> (#4, F, 19) You're afraid, but it makes you more powerful in a way, because during 9/11 everybody used to say racist things to you, but it makes you want to defend yourself more, it makes you stand up, and be proud that you're a Muslim.

Because these Muslims know the difference between news images of their faith and how Islam is practiced and taught within their families and communities, it is frustrating for them to watch the news and hear from people who support Quran burning or oppose building Islamic community centers or mosques around the country. Many Muslims may feel rejected by American society, but those we spoke to felt it was important to strive for a better, more inclusive image of Islam that would be slowly constructed through their social interactions.

ISLAMOPHOBIA

The young Muslims in this group had plenty of stories to tell when we asked how others' perceptions of them, acquired through the news, affected their lives. Descriptions of harassment and abuse came pouring out. As these stories illustrate, their anger and frustration were not only directed at electronic news sources, but also at the messages being sent to mainstream audiences.

> (#12, M, 21) My sister wears the hijab [head veil], we used to go to the same high school, and people wouldn't stop talking. People were calling her names, saying "go back to your country." She used to go home crying every day. She had to drop out of school and move [back to Yemen]. She was a 4.0 student. I think the news just puts Muslims in the worst picture ever. Like, especially FOX News, they have no limit. They'll just go all out.
> (#8, F, 19) People would come up to me and be like "are you Iraqi? Are you Afghan?" They always said those two races. I'm from Vietnam. A lot of people were really ignorant. They really didn't know anything about the whole religion, even the basics. Then a few years ago, someone tried to burn the masjid [mosque] out there [in Antioch, California].

Burning mosques and various other incidences of hate crimes against Muslims are well documented after 9/11 (CAIR, 2006). But in 2010, when the anti-Islamic rhetoric escalated in the news, Muslims in California and around the country were on high alert for hostility directed at their communities. The focus group participants regarded these verbal and physical attacks on Muslims as a by-product of news images and stories that fuel hatred and suspicion of Islam.

SOURCES OF NEWS

The majority of the participants reported frequently augmenting television news content by visiting news Web sites. They use Facebook and Twitter to stay updated on current events. They had strong praise for the Internet, because they perceived that it promoted diversity of opinion more effectively than television did. The group had divergent views on the value of news consumption, and a few of them were simply tuned out to American news.

> (#9, M, 20) Recently, I kind of barely watch the news now, American news. I'm usually just watching Al Jazeera. That's where I get most of my news from.

Some of the group did not watch much television news, preferring to access their news online, where they have the freedom to pursue their own research and cross-reference multiple sources to arrive at an informed conclusion. Others praised the control that the Internet gives them, a stark contrast with the helplessness they feel when they watch cable television news. The Internet provides them with a way to personally navigate and have a stronger sense of dominating the news discourse.

> (#11, F, 21) We don't have time to sit there and watch TV, so a lot of us, including myself, watch things online. So the time that we have, we're gonna sit there and watch what we like to watch, rather than whatever's on.

Even the students who rely on Facebook as a news source recognized that there were limitations to exclusively relying on people you know for news. There was a strong sense of independence when it came to seeking electronic news sources. One of the participants, a 19-year-old veiled and outspoken female, felt it was imperative to pursue diverse news perspectives, and used Twitter to stay informed.

(#4, F, 19) A lot of people get their information on Facebook. I'm obsessed with Twitter. I don't just follow Muslim bloggers, I follow Christian bloggers and Jewish bloggers. When they have blog posts, they tweet about it, and you can read it right then and there. Twitter has trending topics, the key words that are being said at a certain time. I was really happy because on Eid [Muslim holiday], "Eid Mubarak" was a trending topic. One day, I logged on to Twitter, and it said "Quran burning," and I was like "Hold up. What is this?" and I had to click on it, and it's cool because you get to see a live stream of what people are saying, and how they're using that key word at the same time. I follow Anderson Cooper on Twitter and different journalists, but I try to follow independent media on there as well, because independent media tends to be more active on Twitter.

IMPACT OF NEWS IMAGES ON IDENTITY

The group expressed the significance of having an Arabic or Muslim name as an expression of self-identification. Participants were proud of their names and believed the names were of central importance not only to their identities as Arabs and Muslims, but also as tools to challenge negative stereotypes and perceptions. Many Muslims named Osama or Jihad were constantly made fun of, but in this group, there was a strong disapproval for people who change their names to more Western-sounding ones. They believe that in the context of negative news coverage relating to Arabs or Muslims, it is important to take pride in their Arab and Muslim names.

(#2, M, 21) My dad is very proud of who he his because of the way he named me and my siblings after Quranic verses, great names, but a with lot of my uncles, a select few don't like their name. They'd be called Sam, instead of like Samir, or Mike instead of Mahmoud.

The Muslim men in this group expressed that they had a fairly easier time than Muslim women did in evading the negative effects of news coverage regarding Muslims. Due to the negative attention Muslims receive, they considered Muslim women exceptionally courageous for wearing the hijab and admirably respect their decision to do so, especially after 9/11.

(#12, M, 21) It's easier for a guy to dress a certain way. Usually on Eid or on Ramadan holiday, I wear traditional Arab clothing. And you know walking in the street, going to the mosque, I see those weird stares that you get from people, walking down the street, but not every day like Muslim women.
(#2, M, 21) It's much harder for Muslim women. When a woman is wearing the hijab, she could be any culture, any race, wearing hijab, you're considered an Arab, you're considered a Muslim, based on what they've seen in the media. I can wash my face and put the flag in my room, and walk out and I'm just like everybody else. But they have to deal with it on a daily basis. They have to deal with the constant harassment everywhere they go. I definitely give the respect due to them because they can handle it.

The women in the group said they had become immune to people staring at their head-scarves, and were always happy to explain to non-Muslims that they choose to wear it as an expression of modesty. They admitted it was not always fun to be so easily identified as a Muslim but that they were proud of their faith and being different made them feel stronger. They noted that news images tended to portray Muslim women as weak and oppressed, but to them that was a misconception. The veiled women we spoke to had vibrant career aspirations and were assertive about changing the way the news depicts them.

PART OF THE SOLUTION: RECOMMENDATIONS

What do these young men and women intend to do about what they perceive as misperceptions and stereotypes of Islam and Arabs in the news? One might expect them to disengage with the news and simply tune out. However, the participants want to remain informed with the latest news to engage others in an ongoing dialogue and debate of perspectives.

> (#13, F, 22) I don't want to tune it [the news] out because as Muslims living here, and wearing the hijab, you stand out, so people are going to ask me about those issues. I try to make myself prepared and actually know about the issue beforehand.

One participant recommended examining alternative news sources, particularly international news station Web sites to better understand Muslim and Arab perspectives.

> (#2, M, 21) Al Jazeera has an English page. I tell them "You want to know what's going on? Uncensored?" And people will go on there and be like "Oh my God, wow, they show dead bodies?"

The participants agree that the electronic news industry needs to change its tone of coverage and treat people of all faiths with respect and dignity. Descriptors such as "terrorist" need to be universally applied, not just to people of their faith and culture. They said that when terrorism is in the news, the default assumption is that an Arab or Muslim is responsible. They cited the story of a Caucasian man who crashed a plane into an IRS building in February 2010. News organizations did not refer to him as a terrorist.

> (#2, M, 21) "Terrorist" is now the derogatory term for Arab or Muslim, it's not used for any other purpose. Right now, you can't call a white man a terrorist. It's against the rules and confusing your viewers. They called him an "angry tax agent." He's terrorizing people, right? And he's not called a terrorist, that word is reserved for Arabs.

Despite their harsh criticism of television and electronic news sources, there were still participants who expressed a desire to work for television stations. Their objective is to change the industry from within; and with a wider range of diversity in newsrooms that includes more Arabs and Muslims, the hope for these participants is that they can improve the quality of news themselves.

> (#4, F, 19) It really makes me sad because I know they're working hard to be good journalists, and it sucks that these big name corporations that I'd one day like to work for, like CNN seem lazy in my eyes that they couldn't go out and find a better person to interview. Or they couldn't go out and properly research their story.
>
> (#11, F, 21) It makes me feel outraged, but when I step outside, and when I talk to Americans, normal people, just as ourselves, I feel better. I'm changing one step at a time with the people that are fed this biased news.

Through sharing their opinions on news images and stories about Arabs and Muslims, the group agreed that TV news programming cultivates narrow and limited perceptions of their people. These young men and women believe that this cultivated imagery is directly responsible for how other people perceive them, and consequently, how they feel about themselves.

Ultimately, they believed that these news images and stories contributed to their desire to educate society and become positive, articulate role models who would eventually change social perceptions of their faith and culture. The participants expressed hope that they could change social perceptions of their faith and culture by augmenting news reports with their own interactions with their fellow Americans. Staying informed by continuing to consume the news with which they don't necessarily agree is important to these young Muslims and Arabs, but so is reaching out to people, answering their questions patiently, and excelling academically and professionally in order to counteract the news images.

IT'S YOUR TURN: WHAT DO YOU THINK? WHAT WILL YOU FIND?

1. Check out some of the media outlets mentioned by the focus group participants. Do you see some of the same things they discussed? Why do you think the coverage is as it is?

2. If you are not Muslim, talk to Muslim friends and ask them about their interpretations of and opinions about coverage of Islam in the media. To what extent do they think the news contributes to Islamophobia? If you are Muslim, talk with friends who are members of other minority groups (e.g., African Americans or Latinos), and ask the same sorts of questions. Then, talk to white friends about the same issues. What differences do you see, and why?

3. Imagine you're a TV news producer and wanted your newscast to be as neutral as possible on these issues. What would you tell the journalists to do, when covering stories about Islam?

REFERENCES

Council on American Islamic Relations (CAIR). (2006). *American public opinion about Islam and Muslims.* Retrieved September 24, 2011, from http://www.cair.com/Portals/0/pdf/american_public_opinion_on_muslims_islam_2006.pdf

Gerbner, G., Gross, L., Morgan, M., & Signorielli, N. (1980). The "mainstreaming" of America: Violence profile #11. *Journal of Communication, 30*(3), 10–29.

Greenwald, A. G. (1968). Cognitive learning, cognitive response to persuasion, and attitude change. In A. G. Greenwald, T. C. Brock, & T. M. Ostrom (Eds.), *Psychological foundations of attitudes* (pp. 147–170). New York: Academic Press.

Hawkins, R. P., & Pingree, S. (1980). Some processes in the cultivation effect. *Communication Research, 7*(2), 193–226.

Kinch, J. W. (1972). A formalized theory of the self-concept. In J. Manis & B. Meltzer (Eds.), *Symbolic interaction: A reader in social psychology* (pp. 245–261). Boston: Allyn & Bacon.

Morgan, M., & Signorielli, N. (1990). Cultivation analysis: Conceptualization and methodology. In N. Signorielli & M. Morgan (Eds.), *Cultivation analysis: New directions in media effects research* (pp. 13–34). Newbury Park, CA: Sage.

Morley, D. (1986). *Family television: Cultural power and domestic leisure.* London: Comedia.

Purcell, K., Rainie, L., Mitchell, A. Rosenstiel, T., & Olmstead, K. (2010). *Understanding the participatory news consumer: How Internet and cell phone users have turned news into social experience.* Pew Internet & American Life Project. Retrieved September 24, 2011, from http://www.pewinternet.org/Reports/2010/Online-News.aspx

3.5 FINDING HOME IN A SONG AND A DANCE: NATION, CULTURE, BOLLYWOOD

Sheena Malhotra

In this piece, the author considers issues of ethnic, gender, and class identities as she reflects on how Bollywood films can evoke "home" for members of the South Asian diaspora (displaced or dispersed people). Bollywood (a contraction of "Bombay" and "Hollywood") produces commercial Hindi films. It is the largest film industry in the world, producing more than twice the number of films that Hollywood produces annually.

A diasporic community consists of people displaced from their homeland through voluntary or forced migrations. The struggles of diasporic populations center around two ongoing issues: the transmission of cultural values/norms to future generations and coming to terms with multiple home spaces. But what is home? And how do cultural values get transmitted? Chandra Mohanty (1993) reminds us home is not necessarily a physical space, but rather can be a space where we create a sense of belonging emotionally, politically, and through our ideas and beliefs. This sense of belonging is actually created through various sites of influence—our families, friends, school, media, power structures in society, and all the various communities in which we are involved. In this essay[1], I focus on one of these sites (media) for one particular community (South Asian diaspora) and their negotiations with "home." I write from the perspective of a participant observer, someone who is both a participant and researcher within a community. I am a first-generation Indian woman, currently living in Los Angeles. First coming to the United States at 18, I have gone back and forth between India and the United States, looking for home in different spaces. My family lives in India; I work and live in the United States. Like Mohanty, the more I traverse the globe, the more I too believe that home really is an ideological space. Or as they might say in the movies, "Home is where the heart is."

In this chapter, I unpack how Hindi films and the Bollywood dream machine come to symbolize home, and occupy an increasingly powerful role of transmitting cultural norms within the South Asian community, particularly for first-generation immigrants. Yet, there are many different negotiations of home depending on one's subjectivity, or how one is positioned within society. For example, Gayathri Gopinath (2003) has written about the complicated relationships queer subjects have with "home" and "nation" because of their outsider status to "home" within a social system where men dominate, and which assumes and enforces heterosexuality as the norm (heteropatriarchy).

So when diasporic populations evoke "home," it is important to ask how exactly home is construed and how it gets conflated with nation. What notions of the nation get reproduced in our imaginary? What are the omissions of class in these reproductions? What equations of gender do these films champion? What notions of "home" are reproduced, by and for different diasporic subjects? Can we complicate those readings?

Some crucial information to our discussion is that India opened up its economy in 1991 and global flows of people, culture, and capital became vital to its accomplishments (Joshi, 1998). Additionally, the success of Bollywood films in the "overseas" markets post-1990 translated into efforts to be more inclusive of the diasporic experience, which was imagined (and portrayed) as primarily wealthy and educated in Bollywood. Framed through the *mediascapes* Appadurai (1996/2000) theorized, which refer to the images of the world created by the media and their global distribution, the diasporic Indian was increasingly represented as crucial to the Indian economy and nation-state (Mankekar, 1999). The effort to appeal to this group has produced representations in many Bollywood films of Indian identity that are no longer necessarily tied to the homeland. Post-1990, Bollywood notions of identity are based on cultural values, religious customs, even celebrations of wealth that are associated with the diaspora (Malhotra & Alagh, 2004). So increasingly, "home" is located in values, practices, and customs, which can be anywhere physically or literally (although we mostly see it being located in the United States or Western Europe). Bollywood speaks to and draws in the diaspora, and increasingly, the diaspora looks to Bollywood to find "home."

This chapter focuses on two instances of diasporic audiences using Bollywood in various ways to construct home. First, I read the documentary film *Bollywood Crossings,* as an ethnographic study of diasporic audiences who engage (and struggle) with Bollywood films in their quest for home. Second, I write about an eventful evening with a queer diasporic community and its use of a particular film to re-imagine home. Both instances focus on audiences of Bollywood films in global contexts and show us the power of Bollywood to insert itself into their imaginaries. I find that Hindi films are a powerful vehicle for evoking "home" for diasporic populations. Additionally, they are utilized by otherwise potentially disenfranchised populations to imagine themselves into the nation, even as the nation gets increasingly narrowly re imagined by Bollywood films.

BOLLYWOOD CROSSINGS: **CULTURE IN THE MOVIES**

When heterosexual, upper middle-class, diasporic audiences use Bollywood films to cultivate relationships with home, those relationships often become an uncontested acceptance of the nation and its norms. But what aspects of the nation get erased in this easy acceptance? I come to these questions and discussion through *Bollywood Crossings,* a documentary directed by Tavishi Alagh (2008), which follows several diasporic subjects as they make sense of their lives and search for cultural roots in Bollywood-style filmic representations. The film is an ethnographic study filmed over 3 years. (I worked on *Bollywood Crossings* as a consultant; I viewed and worked with the approximately 90 hours of raw footage shot for the film.) The film interweaves dialogues with more than 150 audience members, organizers, and performers involved with, and excited about, Bollywood shows and films touring the United States. It charts diasporic audiences' close relationships with Bollywood films and music by focusing on the lives of five central characters. Three of the main protagonists are friends living in New York. Each has a different and complicated relationship with Bollywood, India's dream industry. The three men, Sanjay, Ashwini, and Zulfi, come to represent three viewpoints of diasporic use of media to connect with home.

The first of the friends is Sanjay. For Sanjay, Bollywood *is* India. He is a working-class boy who has "made it" in the technology industry in America and now lives in a large suburban house. He argues that he has the best of both worlds, dancing with his wife Bollywood-style for the viewer. He spends upwards of $200 per ticket on the Bollywood star shows he attends with his friends and is very impressed with himself for being in the second or third row, so close to the stars he loves and admires. Ironically for him, it is by being in the United States that he can "almost touch" the Indian stars. He is earnest in his embodiment of the Bollywood dream. It is a recreated nostalgic space that, in effect, exists only in his head and eclipses his lack of access back home. But it is powerful enough to sustain him. In fact, it is a home where he has affluence, control, and access. He no longer wants to make the distinctions between Bollywood and India.

The second friend is Ashwini. For Ashwini, Bollywood is a bridge, an educational tool. It is a bridge to connect him back to his roots, through the songs he shares with other diasporic friends. Bollywood is considered "cool" and hip these days, and so makes him feel valued in mixed (American and Indian) social spaces. And it is an educational tool for his future children. He is a second-generation immigrant, having spent much of his formative years in Africa and Europe, being an outsider, constantly trying to "blend in." Now a proud New Yorker, Ashwini's voiceover is intercut between shots of him driving the streets, taking a ferry ride with the backdrop of New York City's skyline, and prepping for a party at his house. As he reveals stories about learning Swahili as a boy, and then finding himself in Paris with no French language skills as a teenager, we see visuals of Ashwini in multiple intercuts of the spaces he inhabits in the present day. Form begins to mirror content as we realize that his grounding is never in one physical space. It is found instead through the imaginary bridge of Bollywood films. In fact, he no longer needs to return "home" to the physical space of India, partially because India is bridged for him culturally in the media products he consumes. Overlayed on visuals of a Thanksgiving feast at Ashwini's home where wine glasses clink to cheers of "Happy Thanksgiving," we hear him say, "I enjoy a fusion lifestyle. I enjoy being an Indian and being a New Yorker at the same time." Another cut shows him walking in an Indian "Independence Day" parade waving an Indian flag on the streets of New York. He concludes, "I would even go so far as to say I'm *more* comfortable being an Indian in New York, than being an Indian in India." For Ashwani, fusing the two worlds through the easy appeal of the love stories and songs, the mix of high fashion, Bollywood style, and designer rituals creates an accessible way for him to participate in nostalgia for a home, a culture, an India that he never knew, except through films. Perhaps, is it partially the bridge of Bollywood that has made that hybrid world possible for him?

And then there is Zulfi, born to Hindu-Muslim parents, who occupies a third diasporic relationship with Bollywood. For Zulfi, Bollywood remains a contested space, one that struggles to represent "India" through a certain lens, and one that he continually struggles with. He loves the old classic Bollywood films of bygone eras that evoke nostalgia for a time when his family had the elite lifestyle of the colonial Raj. His nostalgia for India and a lost world, a different era, is so palpable that it coats his voice as he sings about a land he can never quite return to. He wrestles with the cultural loss he fears is inevitable for his daughter and argues that Bollywood cannot recreate India, "It's one thing to be nostalgic about films and film music, but what troubles me is the fact that Indian culture and Bollywood culture have become synonymous. And that, in a sense, is tragic."

As the film progresses, Zulfi journeys back to India, visiting old haunts and relatives, searching for home in different ways. But at his core, he continues to be a traveler torn between worlds. At the end of the film, Zulfi, probably with the most privileged heritage of the three friends, returns to India to work. In the last few sequences, Zulfi talks about the reasons people come to America, how this way of life becomes a part of who you are and yet you are confronted with the constant dilemma of whether to return home or not. We see Zulfi in the foreground; New York city lights in the distance. As we leave him sitting on a park bench watching the lights, there is a loneliness that seeps through his quintessential immigrant's dilemma. We end with him driving toward the airport. A poignant overlay of his voice singing an old Hindi song translates as, "These strangers are kind enough, I know. But they are still strangers in the end. Today, in a land of strangers, I'm craving the land that is home."

All three diasporic audience positions—the first that conflates Bollywood with India, the second that uses Bollywood as a bridge to create a hybrid world, and the third that sees Bollywood as a contested space that can never quite capture India—give us insights into how powerful the engagement with media can be for a diasporic audience looking for home. These deterritorialized subjects seem to find home in the mediated worlds of their imagination. In fact that link is so powerful that even though they are outside the nation, they do not have the crucial distance to critique the Bollywood-produced discourses of the nation. Instead, they continually reproduce and glorify these discourses. The sexist gender portrayals in Bollywood films, and the disappearance of the working and poor classes, go without interrogation. What gets foregrounded is a search for home, which is squarely equated with nation and brought that much closer in their imaginaries through the mediation of Bollywood.

QUEERING THE NATION, CREATING HOME THROUGH BOLLYWOOD

In this section, I write about an evening spent with a queer diasporic group reclaiming Bollywood in ways that might open up the exclusions inherent in its representations. Gayatri Gopinath (2003) has written convincingly about how the desire to belong to a home or nation is framed through our particular lens of gender and sexuality. She argues that a traditionally invisible queer subjectivity within the nation might be able to negotiate alternative modes of belonging to the nation. My evening with *Satrang* illustrates her point.

It's a chilly Los Angeles night when I make my way to the BeverlyWoods home where I'm told that *Satrang*, the Southern California-based South Asian Queer group, is hosting a *Sholay* night. It is my first time meeting the folks at *Satrang*. I am awkward. But they are welcoming. Hindi and English with varying accents fill the room as I enter its warmth. The latest Bollywood hit songs play in the background and at first, everyone mills about, eating, drinking, and reminiscing about their relationship with the film, *Sholay* (which roughly translates as "Embers" or "Flames"). *Sholay* is a film released in 1975, which became one of the highest grossing and longest running films in India. Many people watched the film repeatedly, and it became an instant cult classic of sorts. I overhear conversations comparing notes on how many times they'd seen the film "back home." The invitation had encouraged attendees to come dressed as their favorite *Sholay* character, and as I look around the room I see various characters from the film, some of whom are in drag. I watch a beautiful "woman" twirl with her many layered skirt and ask, "How do you like my *Basanti*?" (Basanti is the film's heroine). Most exclaim that the twirler, Salim (I have not used people's real names in this section), makes a beautiful Bollywood heroine. Someone teases him about the hours he must have spent on his stunning makeup. Soon, the hardwood floor in the living room is cleared as the call goes out to start the film. The gigantic television takes center stage. The film begins. Some are viewing it casually, popping in and out of the room during their favorite scenes, socializing in the next room when not watching. There are a select few though, who are fully committed to the viewing experience and interacting with it.

Roshini has donned the garb of the bandit in the film, *Gabbar Singh,* and is thoroughly enjoying saying his lines a split second before the actor. "*Kitne aadmi thay?*" ("How many men were there?") she bellows, complete with gestures, almost drowning out the onscreen bandit. Some of the other audience members shush her; others join her in the dialogue. Almost everyone in the room knows these lines by heart. In fact most of the dialogue is lip synced by the entire audience. Entire decades and continents are spanned in their sing-along to one of the film's popular songs, "*Yeh dosti*" or "This friendship." There is particular pleasure taken in this song and the bond between the two male protagonists, because it is one that has been subversively read by critics (Ghosh, 2002) as signifying a possibly gay relationship. When done by this audience, performing the various characters, and the speaking aloud of the lines takes on an embodied intensity because they are inserting themselves into a heterosexually normative script, reading against the grain, finding pleasure in their subversive readings and side comments about what might "actually" be going on between the onscreen friends.

As the film approaches its climax, the heroine, Basanti, begins singing her last song on screen. Salim, who has spent painstaking hours practicing this song in his twirly skirts, begins to mirror her every move in the center of the living room. Her song declares that she will dance as long as she breathes, dancing on broken glass to save the life of her lover (over-the-top drama being essential to the Bollywood formula). Salim puts all the tragedy, the angst, and the grace into his strangely mirror-like dance. She twirls with a flourish. He twirls with a flourish. She glares down the villain bandit. He glares down the world that would judge him by staring down the lifesize bright screen image. In the spinning of his skirts, he embodies her. And in his embodiment of the classic film heroine, he produces a space where the queer South Asian diasporic community finally gets to go home. To a home where they are seen in their fullness, both South Asian and queer, where they are viewed as desirable subjects and are not relegated to the shadows or the sidelines. They return to a home where their queer embodiments of characters reclaim and re imagine films that evoke the nostalgia of their teenage years. It is a home that exists only in the interstices of fantasy and reality, of here and there, of queer and straight. Yet it is an important home. "For those who live on the borders," Hegde (2002, p. 264) argues, "home is an imaginary construct that shifts between all these (geographical, historical, emotional, sensory spaces."

Salim, Roshni, and other members of *Satrang* have formulated alternative modes of belonging to a nation that is not able to embrace their subjectivities in all their fullness. Their gender-queer performances have subverted and rewritten conventional gender norms within these films. There was obviously nostalgia for a film that represented their childhood. But they opened up new interpretations and new spaces for themselves in how they interacted with the film. Nostalgia, Gopinath (2003) reminds us, is a powerful mode strategically deployed to imagine new belongings even as queer South Asian subjects balance a complicated and sometimes contested relationship with their national identities and home. And so it was on that chilly Los Angeles night. Nostalgia met embodied performance to bring the *Satrang* folks home on their own terms.

IMAGINARY HOMES, LOST AND FOUND

By looking at the diasporic audiences in two ways, both as presented in *Bollywood Crossings* and as evoked by the *Sholay* night with *Satrang*, I have argued that when diasporic audiences engage with Bollywood, it can be a powerful way to evoke "home." However, one's relationship with that home is dependent on one's subject position. If one is from a more dominant group, the relationship with home and nation is one of acceptance and even celebration, where Bollywood is seen as equivalent to India, or as a bridge to the culture. However, there are many questions one can ask about the home that gets re created through Bollywood films. When Bollywood becomes the medium through which one gets to "go home," it is crucial to ask about the "homes" that get erased or are no longer portrayed. I have previously argued (Malhotra & Alagh, 2004) that one of the trends in post-1990 Hindi cinema is a move away from films that deal with poverty and the "common" person to films that often glorify wealth. There are numerous gender critiques of Bollywood as well. Therefore, conflating Bollywood with the nation reproduces a nationalist, sexist, and classist discourse. When Bollywood becomes the primary framework through which one connects to India, the potential disconnects are many.

However, there may be ways to reclaim Bollywood, to subvert its dominant discourses, and to recuperate a sense of home and belonging. If one's subject position is marginalized, the relationships among home, nation, and Bollywood films can be a complicated and contested one. First, from a marginal position, the conflation of Bollywood and India is contested as hegemonic discourses about gender and sexuality are performed. Furthermore, in their embodied engagement with Bollywood, the marginalized find spaces not only to rewrite themselves but perhaps to re script the imaginary discourses of the nation.

NOTE

1. I want to acknowledge and thank Tavishi Alagh for permitting me to use her film and footage for this paper. I also thank Kathryn Sorrells and Aimee Carrillo Rowe for their dialogue and editing help.

IT'S YOUR TURN: WHAT DO YOU THINK? WHAT WILL YOU FIND?

1. This chapter focused on diasporic audiences and their negotiations of home. Diasporic populations are people living away from their homeland. We encountered examples of how they might occupy more than one cultural space in their imaginary. Think about how you negotiate moving between different cultural spaces to which you belong (perhaps between your family home and your college room). What are the tools you utilize to create a sense of home where you are? What are the tools you use to bridge these different spaces?

2. Think of a media text or music genre that evokes a sense of "home" for you. What aspect of home does it evoke and why? Is there a sense of nostalgia for a past, or is it a new construction of home that is born in your imaginary through this text? Is this "pull" stronger when traveling away from home?

3. Of all the "characters" you met in this chapter, is there one whose use of media and home you can identify with? What are the parallels you might draw with Sanjay, Ashwini, or Zulfi and your own relationship with certain films or songs? Have you ever found yourself reading "against the grain" when watching popular films or television series?

4. The queer reading of Bollywood was an alternative reading of mainstream texts. It was a reading that created a more inclusive space for queer subject positions. Working in small groups with your classmates, choose a film you like, and try to create an alternative reading of that text. Rework its storyline in a way that it is more inclusive of your own subject positions, so you can see yourselves in the film. Or, rework the film to construct an alternative reading that disrupts mainstream ideas about gender, sexuality, race, or class. Be creative. Share your reworked story ideas so that the class can discuss how it imagined an alternative, inclusive reality.

REFERENCES

Alagh, T. (Director) (2008). *Bollywood Crossings*. In A Drink With Jam & Bread Productions (Producer). India.

Appadurai, A. (1996/2000). *Modernity at large. Cultural dimensions of globalization*. Minneapolis: University of Minnesota.

Ghosh, S. (2002). Queer pleasures for queer people: Film, television and sexuality in India. In R. Vanita (Ed.), *Queering India: Same sex love and eroticism in Indian culture and society* (pp. 207–221). New York and London: Routledge.

Gopinath, G. (2003). Nostalgia, desire, diaspora: South Asian sexualities in motion. In J. E. Braziel & A. Mannur (Eds.), *Theorizing diaspora* (pp. 261–279). Malden, MA: Blackwell.

Hegde, R. S. (1998/2002). Translated enactments: The relational configurations of the Asian Indian immigrant experience. In J. N. Martin, T. K. Nakayama, & L. A. Flores (Eds.), *Readings in intercultural communication: Experiences and contexts* (pp. 259–266). Boston: McGraw-Hill.

Joshi, V. (1998). India's economic reforms: Progress, problems, prospects. *Oxford Development Studies, 26*(3), 333–350.

Malhotra, S., & Alagh, T. (2004). Dreaming the nation: Domestic dramas in Hindi films post-1990. *South Asian Popular Culture, 2*(1), 19–37.

Mankekar, P. (1999). Brides who travel: Gender, transnationalism, and nationalism in Hindi Film. *Positions: East Asia Cultures Critique, 7*(3), 731–761.

Mohanty, C. T. (1993). Defining geneologies: Feminist reflections on being South Asian in North America. In Women of South Asian Decent Collective (Ed.), *Our feet walk the sky: Women of the South Asian diaspora* (pp. 351–358). San Francisco: Aunt Lute.

3.6 "WHY DON'T YOU ACT YOUR COLOR?": PRE TEEN GIRLS, IDENTITY, AND POPULAR MUSIC

Pamela J. Tracy

This reading presents part of a larger qualitative study concentrating on social and cultural dimensions of pre teen girls' popular music experiences. One dimension of the study was the ways that racial and gendered identities as well as friendship histories affect and are affected by the girls' uses of popular music. The reading focuses specifically on one phenomenon the author calls "why don't you act your color?" Explore with the author the relationships among identity, race, being a girl/boy, popular music use, and what these categories mean in terms of social interaction and constructions of difference.

Emily: They like listen to this kind of music [R&B, hip-hop, rap] and we listen to it sometimes. Once I was singing a song and I was singing The Thong Song and Vanecia and Teresa were like, "Emily, you're not Black, why do you act like a Black person."

Vanecia: When we do this [pretend to be TLC] and stuff, we do dance clubs and all of that other junk and then Emily, she goes, "okay, like you know" and she be acting all Black and all hard like this [Vanecia is snapping her fingers and moving her head back and forth] . . . And I be like "Emily, don't be acting our color, act your color." And, she's like "okay, then whatever." And, then on the next day she be acting our color and I tell her again and she gets real smart with me and we get into fights . . . what I'm trying to say is I can't see why White people don't act White, Black people act Black.

After spending several months with Emily and Vanecia and their fourth-grade classmates—I'll call them the Central girls—it became apparent that popular music was omnipresent and integral to their everyday lives. More specifically, as illustrated in the quotes above, listening, dancing, and singing to music meant more than entertainment. When they talked about popular music, sang and danced in the school lunchroom and on the playground, and acted out Destiny's Child and TLC in their bedrooms and basements, these girls communicated not only pleasure, but also their racial and gendered identities. The type of music they listened to, how they listened to this music, and who they listened with mattered in terms of how they organized their friendships, how they expressed their identities, and how they negotiated their place in their social and cultural worlds. The girls' frustrations with each other and their struggles to understand what it means to "act your color" are an important part of their experience with popular music.

I argue that when they engaged with music, the Central girls constructed a sense of self and other that was tied to contextual conditions (e.g., where they were and who they were with), their understandings of social and cultural relations, and their interpretation of what it means to be "me" and "you." Of course, this reading doesn't tell the whole story. While the girls negotiated their own identities when engaging with music in the lunch room and/or in their dance groups, dominant racial and gendered belief systems continued to affect their ways of seeing and being with others in other school-and home-based contexts.

I conducted research with the Central girls at their urban elementary school in a large Midwestern city. The participants were fourth grade girls ranging in age from 9 to 11 years old. In terms of race and ethnicity, five girls including Emily and April described themselves as white/Caucasian, five girls including Tracey named themselves African American/Black, Teresa said that she was African American/American Indian/white, one girl described herself as American Indian/white, one said that she was Malaysian, and Maria named herself Hawaiian. I spent approximately 10 months and on average 3–4 days a week with the girls in their school. In addition to individual and peer group interviewing, administering questionnaires, and asking the girls to keep a media journal, I observed and participated regularly during recess, lunch, free time, literature, dance, and art classes. I also participated in a school-wide roller-skating party, clean-up event, read-a-thon, and spring concert. During all of these events, I took notes, asked the girls questions, and participated in their activities.

Before I begin, I want to briefly highlight the theoretical assumptions that guide my interpretations of the Central girls' popular music experiences. Cultural studies audience scholars are interested in understanding how people make sense of media and how media experiences affect everyday life. This scholarship is grounded in the assumption that media and popular culture experiences are important socialization practices that both negatively and positively influence how we construct a sense of self and others. While media and popular culture texts (e.g., movies, TV shows, songs, and fashion) are understood as potentially powerful influences, these scholars argue that audiences actively construct meaning when they interpret media images, sounds, and forms. In fact, sometimes people use media products to construct identities, to resist authority, and to build knowledge.

Nevertheless, meaning construction is understood to be a social process influenced by a variety of contextual conditions, including audiences' day-to-day interactions with others, societal belief systems, economic relations, cultural experiences, other media texts, and familial practices. Some of these social practices, such as working, schooling, and advertising, function ideologically. That is, they work to create belief systems that are taken for granted as "the way things are." These belief systems, more often than not, serve to privilege some people and ways of being over others. For example, the Central girls frequently made connections between their everyday experiences with boys and the music lyrics about heterosexual dating. As they interpreted the texts, they reflected on their direct knowledge about relationships. At the same time, many of the lyrics referenced sexual relations that the girls described as "about older girls" and "stuff we don't know about." Despite the fact that they had no direct experience, they accepted the lyrical messages—messages privileging heterosexuality and warning them about boys/men—as valid and important for future reference. In doing so, they relied on social and cultural belief systems about heterosexual relationships and particular gender behaviors to interpret media content.

In terms of research, a variety of scholars emphasize the value of ethnographic study for investigating how audiences engage with media (see, for example, Ang, 1996; Bennett, 2000). Ethnographic research allows us to understand how the construction of meaning depends on a variety of social relations, practices, and situations. Through observation, participation, and interviewing, we can gain a better understanding of how day-to-day interactions and different contexts affect media experiences. In reference to the Central girls' study, the ethnographic methods I used enabled a closer investigation into their popular music experiences particularly in terms of understanding more fully how they enacted their identities. By spending more time with them and expressing my interest in their lives, we were able to create some space for discussing difficult and seemingly taboo topics.

In addition to valuing context and the social aspect of media use, Cultural studies scholars also focus on the process of identity construction. Feminist scholars argue that identity (or how we understand and enact a sense of self and other) is "communicated" and "practiced" rather than predetermined by race, gender, class, age, sexuality, ability, and ethnicity. For example, Vanecia, one of the Central girls, defines herself as an African American/Black and "half white" girl. She explained, "When I am with my mom's family, they are White, I feel different than when I am with my dad's family." As you will read later, Vanecia identified quite strongly with other African American/Black girls when they talked about whites listening to hip-hop and "acting Black," and, at other moments, she danced to this music with her white friends. How she understands her place in her social and cultural world is complicated and enriched by her many multiple and layered identities. Vanecia's interpretations of her immediate experiences, what might be required of her at any given moment, and her readings of larger social and ideological systems such as media influence the ways she communicates her identities. If we were to judge Vanecia on the basis of her skin color or gender alone, we would most likely make assumptions that don't fully represent her day-to-day experiences.

In reference to their popular music experiences, the Central girls communicated their identities in a variety of ways. For example, the girls listened to particular types of music because they identified with certain lyrics, rhythms, and related fashion and dance styles—their lived experiences were reflected in the music form and content. Some girls listened to learn more about what "will happen in the future"—projecting ahead to a particular way of being a woman. Heather listened to Macy Gray because she liked the music, but also because she wanted to communicate that she had different tastes than her classmates and, more importantly, that she was different than others. Maria listened to TLC because she felt that the song *UnPretty* and its message about "being yourself and not listening to others" verified her beliefs. And, some of the girls sang and danced to certain genres during lunchtime because this communicated that they knew the music, which helped them achieve a certain social status.

In addition, as the girls and boys listened, danced, and sang to particular songs, others around them were constructing perceptions about them. Because Kathleen, a white girl, didn't like rap or hip-hop, she was described as being "all that" or thinking that she was better than others. Conversely, when Marcus, an African American boy, listened to rap music with "cussing" in it, he was constructed as a potential troublemaker. The Central girls' experiences illustrate the relationship between music and identity and highlight that identity is simultaneously how we communicate a sense of self to others and how we are constructed by the world around us.

"WHY DON'T YOU ACT YOUR COLOR?"

Emily, April, and Maria on "Acting Black"

During their peer group interview, this group of girls discussed why they felt that African American girls might connect to Destiny's Child music more than they (read: non-Black girls) did. This discussion slowly evolved into several stories about their experiences with being told to "act their own color."

Emily: They [African-American/Black girls] like listen to this kind of music [R&B, hip-hop] and we [non-Black girls] listen to it sometimes. Once I was singing a song and I was singing The Thong Song and Vanecia and Teresa were like, "Emily, you're not Black, why do you act like a Black person."

April: Like a lot of Black people like White things and White people never say anything bad about Black people . . .

Emily: Yeah. We all like Britney Spears . . .

Maria: Like at my birthday party . . . Remember at my birthday party, Chelsea just started dancing and Shaquilla and Vanecia were playing together and they just went, "Oh no, you're White Chelsea. Listen to something else."

Pam: Does this affect your friendships?

Maria: Kind of.

Maria: Me, Emily, and April don't even listen to some of the music around them when we want to because we are their friends.

Emily: We know what they are going to say . . .

Maria: Yeah.

Pam: What kind of music? Like Destiny's Child?

Maria: Like even Destiny's Child they go, like Shaquilla goes "Oh, no, don't do that."

Emily: Me and April were singing it once and she's like "No Emily, no April."

Maria: And Tiffany, remember when they said that about Tiffany. They're not Tiffany's friend even though last year Shaquilla and them were Tiffany's friend. They're not her friend this year because they think she acts like she's Black.

Tracey, Vanecia, and Teresa on "Acting Black"

While they were discussing how they came to know poppin' (a dance move), Teresa, Tracey, and Vanecia started making fun of the boys in their class who have tried to make this move. In doing so, they told stories about one white boy, Kyle, who tried to "act Black." This conversation led to a more serious discussion about their frustrations with white girls who sang and danced in particular ways that, according to this trio, mirrored Black dance and communication styles. First, they explained that they liked to form dance groups during recess to act out their favorite singers, particularly TLC.

Pam: Okay, the other girls that you do this with, Shaquilla, Emily, April, Maria . . . you do the same thing. They say who they are [which singer they are] . . .

Vanecia: They say who they are. When we do this and stuff, we do clubs and all of that other junk and then Emily, she goes, "okay like you know" and she be acting all Black and all hard like [Vanecia is snapping her fingers and moving her head back and forth] this no offense, Tracey [I think she said this because she knows they are Tracey's friends], but she acting all Black and hard and other things like that. And I be like "Emily, no," and she be like, "oh no," and sometimes I be playing with her and I be acting like I'm a different color . . .

Tracey: And then she go out and get a attitude.

Vanecia: I say, "Emily, don't be acting our color, act your color." And she's like, "okay then whatever." And then on the next day she be acting our color and I tell her again and she gets real smart with me and we get into fights . . . I end up punching her and she end up running off crying and they end up coming back punching me back and I end up . . .

Pam: What bothers you about Emily acting your color?

Teresa: Cause it's like . . .

Tracey: It's annoying . . .

Vanecia: Well, what I'm trying to say is I can't see why White people act White, Black people act Black, it would be fine.

Teresa: I know. When White people try to act like Black people, it seems like they're not happy with their own color. Or when they try to be like Black . . .

Vanecia: So people will let them fit in.

Pam: So you do listen to this song with other girls. What happens when you are listening to it and Emily is trying to act Black, do you still keep on listening to it? Do you stop?

Vanecia: I listen to it and I tell her to stop.

Teresa: I know, because it gets on my nerves when she tries to act like Black people. Because it's like, why can't they just be happy with their color? Don't try to be like other people. If you don't fit into something, just let somebody know . . .

Friendship Histories

During the interviews, both groups of girls were very passionate about how they each conceptualized the relationship between music and identities. At those moments when they wanted to communicate racial unity, Vanecia, Teresa, and Tracey established a firm connection between skin color and who can listen to particular musical genres. However, the concepts of "acting Black" or more broadly, "acting your color" continued to be more complex when enacted in everyday life. In this case, cross-cultural friendship histories and gendered relationships significantly affected how girls performed and thought about racial identities. For example, Kyle, a middle-class white boy who doesn't "act his color," represented for these girls (Teresa, Vanecia, Tracey, and Maria) the most visible "acting Black" case. They spoke frequently about Kyle's attempts to act like his Black friend, Nate. According to Teresa, "Kyle tries to be a Black boy . . . listening to our music and saying 'hey, what's up my homie'. . . this is annoying and I tell him to stop." While it "annoyed" Teresa, she also explained that she doesn't think it bothered Nate because he and Kyle have been friends for a long time. Maria and Emily also made the same assessment. Tracey made the comment that "yo, those are my sisters" indicating that while she didn't like them "acting Black," Emily, April, and Maria were her friends. Emily's comment that it was hard to talk about "acting your own color" because "one of her best friends is African-American" may also indicate the ways in which friendship histories complicate these identity conflicts. Friendship histories in relationship to racial identities were important in terms of understanding how both girls and boys negotiated their differences.

Gendered Allegiances

Girls' accusations about "acting your color" only reveal part of their musical story. While racial alliances were forged at these moments, on other occasions, girls publicly relied on each other in their journey to "get the boys out of their face." Their gendered allegiance in this quest was evident in their collaborative attempts to make sure that "their music" (not the boy's music) was played during lunch and free time in the classroom. In their mutual attempts to unite, Tracey, Vanecia, Teresa, Maria, Emily, and April formed a dancing/singing group.

> We do it outside on the playground. We can't find no hang out, but the one hang out is over here in a small corner we really like, when we get over there if it's cold or when we get over there, like, anyone will bring snacks for our group . . . the teachers don't know about the group . . . we make up our own songs . . . and, we only let boys who are nice to us be in the group.

While they occasionally let boys in, they did so only if the boys would let them be the leaders. According to Tracey,

> Like Mark, he's the boy you have to watch out for. Like all the girls we're controlling him . . . we have to work hard to keep him away from the girls. We got him in check.

This girl-dominated group provided an opportunity for them to act out their favorite singers and bands, and "to teach other girls who don't know how to dance our moves that we learned . . .so that others won't make fun of them." In addition, they often engaged in public scrutiny of boys who made fun of their music especially when these same boys sang and danced to TLC and N'Sync at other times. Their connections to each other through their shared gendered experiences with boys reveal the necessarily unfixed nature of identity.

The Central girls also used their music to build and maintain their friendships. Tracey described the ways in which popular music helped her to "make up" with other girls after a playground fight. She explained,

> Like we were mad because we were outside and everything went wrong. Then during lunch, someone will go up and ask Isabella and Pete [teachers] to turn on Destiny's Child. So they play it and all the girls [who have been fighting] they like get back together once they get back in the class . . . because right when they say the words . . . you can picture your group together . . . when you get together, it makes you end up happy and makes you want to dance and stuff like that.

In this context, after a fight and in the lunchroom—a space that they associated with listening to "their music," the meaning of Destiny's Child music and the relationship once established between genre and identity changed. For these girls, their relationships and the context of their interactions and engagement with music mattered in terms of how they expressed who they were and how they perceived others. While their racial and gendered identities were always present, these girls shifted their identification with others, at times, based on the exigency of the moment. The girls' experiences illustrate that identities are enacted, that we actively communicate who we are and use media to do so, and that our media consumption is always tied to social and cultural issues.

IT'S YOUR TURN: WHAT DO YOU THINK? WHAT WILL YOU FIND?

1. In reference to the concept of "acting Black," Williams (2000, p. 6) argued "it is sad to see rap music eviscerated of its passion and pathos and appropriated by the mainstream . . . [E]ven though I have never enjoyed rap as an art form, I could always at least appreciate it as an authentic outlet of expression for poor, inner city Black youths. Madison Avenue has gotten into the act, with ads like William Shatner's ('*Star Trek's*' Capt. Kirk) on behalf of Priceline. com. To the beat of Young MC's hit tune 'Bust a Move,' Shatner raps his way through an ebonics-laced pitch for airline tickets . . . Why is African

Americana always fair game for such appropriation and ridicule? Is nothing Black sacred? Why is Black dialect considered comical in the mouths of whites? . . ." (p. A6)

What do you think are the key elements of Williams' statement? What do you think about it? How does this relate to the Central Girls' popular music experiences?

2. While conducting research, I witnessed several moments when students and teachers made assumptions about people based on their music preferences. What kinds of connections have you made or witnessed between identity and music taste? What are the potential social implications?

3. Interview a friend about a song he/she likes. Listen to the song together, and try to understand how she/he interprets and experiences this song. Consider

what practices, people, and/or beliefs influence your friend's musical experiences. What did you learn about this person? About music?

Possible questions you could ask include: Why did you choose this song to bring in today? What is it about it that you like? Dislike? What does this song make you think and feel? What do the lyrics mean to you? Are they connected to your life? When, where, and with whom do you usually listen/sing/dance to this song? Is there anytime, place, or person that you would not listen/sing/dance to this song? Is there any music that you do not listen to?

4. Search the Internet for the phrase "acting Black" or "wannabe." What claims are made? By whom? What is being said about identity, race, culture, politics, media, etc? Do you agree or disagree with what is being said? Why? How is this connected to your experiences?

REFERENCES

Ang, I. (1996). Ethnography and radical contextualism in audience studies. In J. Hay, L. Grossberg, & E. Wartella (Eds.), *The audience and its landscape* (pp. 247–264). Boulder, CO: Westview Press.

Bennett, A. (2000). *Popular music and youth culture: Music, identity, place.* New York: St. Martin's Press.
Williams, L. (2000). Commentary: Whites' entertainment is black's irritainment. *New Pittsburgh Courier, 91(76)*, A6.

3.7 ARGUING OVER IMAGES: NATIVE AMERICAN MASCOTS AND RACE

C. Richard King

The author claims that arguments about Native American mascots (such as the Cleveland Indians' Chief Wahoo) are actually arguments about race, and hence a barometer of race relations in our society. To see these arguments in action, he analyzed statements USA Weekend *audiences posted in response to a Web poll asking: "What is your opinion about changing a sports team's mascot because it offends Native Americans?"*
Before reading this essay, see the first "It's Your Turn" activity.

Native American mascots, once accepted icons, have become controversial symbols over the past quarter century. Increasingly, they raise troubling questions. Does the continued use of American Indian symbols and nicknames in sports honor or insult Native Americans? Do mascots like Chief Wahoo of the Cleveland Indians perpetuate racist stereotypes? Does it matter whether the Washington Redskins team name is intentionally offensive or merely happens to offend many Native Americans? Answers to these queries have much to tell us about race. Indeed arguments over Native American mascots are ultimately arguments about race. In obvious and invisible ways, critics and defenders invariably speak about race relations and ethnic identity when they speak about the use of Indian nicknames and images in sports.

An impressive literature has emerged discussing the racial politics of Native American mascots (see Churchill, 1994, especially pp. 65–72; Connolly, 2000; Davis, 1993; King & Springwood, 2001; Pewewardy, 1991; Spindel, 2000; Vanderford, 1996). It directs our attention to the ways individuals understand and construct race: *identity*, or how they imagine themselves; *imagination*, or how they perceive others; and *representation*, or how they give life to social categories (such as bravery, physicality, and masculinity) through cultural difference. Scholars and activists have contended that the creation and more recent contentiousness of mascots illuminate the stereotypical images central to whites' interpretations of Native Americans, the centrality of Indianness to the formulation of whiteness in the United States, and the changing place of Native Americans in American society.

In what follows, building on these discussions, I will not trace the evolution of specific mascots, nor unpack the meaning of Indian imagery. Rather, after a brief overview of some of the common stereotypes, I propose to make sense of mascots by listening to the unfolding dialogues about these sports symbols in an effort to grasp the place of race in popular interpretations of them. Moreover, to hear the positions advanced in these debates most clearly, I avoid rehearsed defenses, press releases, and official accounts orchestrated by institutions; instead, I concentrate on the ways in which citizens, consumers, and fans interpret Native American nicknames and symbols. Throughout, I make sense of how media consumers talk about Indians images in sports, asking what arguments do they advance to defend and criticize mascots.

Although elsewhere I have openly criticized mascots (see Springwood & King, 2001), here, I want to step back and analyze the positions of supporters and opponents. I focus my attention on one representative case, an electronic forum hosted by *USA Weekend* in 1997. After briefly reviewing the historical uses of Indian symbols and nicknames in American athletics, I detail the various arguments. On this foundation, I touch on the implications of the mascot controversy for our understanding of race and the media.

BACKGROUND

For much of the past century, Indian symbols and nicknames have been a common, if increasingly contested, part of American sports. Today, numerous secondary schools across the country, more than 80 colleges and universities, and dozens of professional and semi-professional sports teams have Native American mascots. The origins, popularity, and problems posed by these athletic icons offer a useful foundation for a fuller consideration of ongoing arguments about them.

Euro-Americans have selected and supported Native American mascots for a number of reasons. Some schools, such as Dartmouth College, have historically defined themselves through a specific relationship with American Indians. More often, especially at public universities, regional history and local pride have inspired students, coaches, and administrators to adopt Indian mascots. The University of Utah Running Utes provide a prominent example of this tradition. Elsewhere, historical accident, coincidence, or circumstance gave rise to mascots. For instance, St. John's University was known as the Redmen initially because their uniforms were all red, and only later, did fans and alumni create fuller traditions of playing Indian.

Whatever the specific origins of individual icons, Euro-Americans were able to fabricate Native Americans as mascots precisely because of prevailing sociohistorical conditions. That is, a set of social relations and cultural categories made it possible, pleasurable, and powerful for Euro-Americans to elaborate images of Indians in athletic contexts. First, Euro-Americans have always fashioned individual and collective identities for themselves by playing Indian. Native American mascots were an extension of this long tradition (Deloria, 1998). Second, the conquest of Native America simultaneously empowered Euro-Americans to appropriate, invent, and otherwise represent Native Americans and to long for aspects of indigenous cultures destroyed by conquest. Third, with the rise of public culture, the production of Indianness in spectacles, exhibitions, and other sundry entertainments proliferated, offering templates for elaborations in sporting contexts.

Given this history, it is not surprising that Native American mascots have relied on stereotypical images of Indians. Accentuating physical features (nose, skin color, or hair), material culture (buckskin, feathers, headdress), expressive forms (dance, face painting), or other attributes (stoicism or bravery) associated with the native nations of North America, they reduce past and present Native Americans to well-worn clichés derived from dime novels, Wild West shows, movies, scouting, and advertising. More often than not, such renderings have more to do with Euro-American interpretations and preoccupations than with indigenous cultures. Indian imagery in sport tends to be frozen in the past (romanticized representatives from a golden age), cluster around the peoples of Plains (the Lakota and other nomadic horse cultures principally), and elude to, if not emphasize, cultural conflicts between Euro- and Native Americans. In the process, generic Indians emerge, which cannot be faithful to native histories and tradition, precisely because their invention depends on decontextualization. These invented Indians that dance at half-time, mark the stationery of educational institutions, and appear on baseball caps and T-shirts, are of two types: the warrior and the clown, mirroring the historic bifurcation of indigenous people into two types of savages—noble and ignoble. The warrior aspires to honor. Stressing bravery and bellicosity, the warrior exudes character traits Euro-Americans have long prized: individuality, perseverance, pride, fidelity, and excellence. Numerous high schools, colleges, and professional teams have seized upon the warrior, real (Chief Osecola at Florida State University) and imagined (the former Chief Illiniwek at the University of Illinois). In contrast, the less common clown mocks, making Indians a joke, a sideshow burlesque. The Cleveland Indians' Chief Wahoo is perhaps the most recognizable clown. (For a fuller discussion of the portrayal of Native Americans, see King & Springwood, 2001; Pewewardy, 1991; Spindel, 2000.)

Despite, or perhaps because, of the imagery associated with them, Native American mascots increasingly have become contentious. More than three decades ago, amidst the civil rights movement and a cultural resurgence throughout Native America, Indians began questioning mascots, forcing both Dartmouth College and Stanford University to change their mascots. More recently, while some institutions, including St. John's University and the University of Miami (Ohio), have *retired* their mascots, a smaller number, including, the University of Utah and Bradley University, have *revised* their use of imagery. Other schools without Native American mascots, such as the University of Wisconsin and the University of Minnesota, have instituted policies prohibiting their athletic departments from scheduling games against institutions with Indian mascots. At the same time, countless communities and boards of education have confronted the issue. Many have deemed such mascots to be discriminatory, requiring (as did the Minnesota and New York State Boards of Education and the Los Angeles and Dallas School Districts) that schools change them. In the wake of these events, numerous individuals and organizations have challenged the persistence of such icons. Nationally, numerous organizations, ranging from the National Congress of American Indians and the National Education Association to the United Methodist Church and the National Association for the Advancement of Colored People, have taken positions against the continued use of Indian images in sports. Finally, the media have taken a leading role in modifying public perceptions of mascots, as when the *Portland Oregonian* changed its editorial policy and refused to print derogatory team names.

ARGUMENTS

In July 1997, the *USA Weekend* Web site (http://www.usaweekend.com/quick/results/chief_wa-hoo_qp_results.html) asked its visitors, "What is your opinion about changing a sports team's mascot because it offends Native Americans?" Visitors could vote in support of changing or keeping such mascots and submit a reaction to the ongoing controversy. Of those who came to the site, 2,419 participated in the quick poll with 42% voting to change and 58% voting to retain mascots. In turn, 299 visitors (124 opponents and 175 supporters) offered a fuller opinion. These opinions form the basis of my analysis. The comments will be reproduced exactly as they were written, typos and all, and people are identified here the same way they identified themselves online.

In Defense of Mascots

Supporters of mascots offer a number of interconnected arguments that collectively labor to make such images acceptable and to defuse the controversy. They stress respect, intention, fairness, and common sense notions of symbols, play, and politics.

　　To many who support mascots, the use of Native American symbols and nicknames honors Indians. Michelle from College Station, Texas, gave clear voice to this perspective, "Team masots are adopted to reflect positively on a team, to symbolize an image of bravery, agility, tenacity, and strength. Native Americans should view this as a compliment rather than an insult." Likewise, A. McClung suggests, "The naming of teams . . . whether it be Braves, Warriors, Indians, Cherokees, etc. have been a thing of honor, prestige and recognition . . . [It] conjures up images that are in my opinion, positive and wholesome to our Native Americans." And, Bob Dunwoody asserted, "Native Americans or American Indians whatever they wish to be know as today should be PROUD that they have been selected as a name because it their ancestors Pride, Honor, Bravery, and Physical Prowess and Endurance." More hypothetically, Rick Bartholomew, a staunch Cleveland fan, remarks, "If I was an Indian, I would be as proud as pie to have a team named after my heritage." And, Bee from Maine exclaims, "YOU PEOPLE SHOULD LIGHTEN UP!!!!!!!!!!!!!! IT'S JUST THE NAME OF A BASEBALL TEAM. IT'S NOT EVEN MAKING FUN OF NATIVE AMERICANS. THEY SHOULD TAKE IT AS A COMPLIMENT." Finally, Jimmy Conn overtly mixes insult and honor, "I feel that native americans should take it as a compliment and have better things to complain about like america being stolen from them, but i guess alcohol does bad things to your train of thought."

　　Supporters often couple arguments about honor and respect with discussions of intentionality. Scott from Port Huron, Michigan, succinctly presents this position, "I DON'T THINK THE NAMES WERE MEANT TO HURT ANYONE. THEY WERE PICKED OUT RESPECT IF

ANYTHING." Similarly, Hector Cadena notes, "If the team nicknames were meant to intentionally be derogatory, then I could understand someone taking umbridge with them. But in reality, the names are meant as a salute to the fierceness and bravery." And according to Terri McDowell, "PEOPLE NEED TO FIND BETTER THINGS TO DO WITH THEIR TIME! THESE NAMES WEREN'T MEANT TO BE OBJECTIONABLE."

Arguments in support of mascots on occasion speak about race through analogies between Native Americans and other ethnic groups. Many, like Betty from Albert Lea, Minnesota, are proud to see "their heritage" displayed in an athletic context: "I am Norwegian. I am happy to have the Vikings use this Scandinavian heritage as their team name." Jon from Apple Creek, Ohio, wonders, "Why isn't someone complaining about Notre Dame?" Similarly, Jenni from South Dakota asks: " My husband's family is of Norwegian heritage. Does this mean we should start a campaign to dump the Vikings?" Perhaps, she continues, those offended "should consider the advantages of the perpetual mass marketing campaign that rides along with these mascots . . . It isn't all bad!" Kim Stevens encourages critics "to lighten up. Don't take things so personal. Scandanvian people aren't up in arms about Minnesota using the name 'Vikings' . . . Take it with a grain of salt."

Many defenders of mascots like Terri McDowell and Bee from Maine cannot grasp the importance of mascots and resort to dismissive comments. They dub it "silliness" or "a waste of time" because other problems (usually unnamed) deserve attention. They encourage detractors to "lighten up," "to get over it," "to grow up," "to get a life," "to get a grip," and "to get real." In part, this derives from a collective sense of sport as playful, frivolous diversion. As Ralph W. Sullivan asserts, "Sports is entertainment, anybody who takes it seriously enough to get upset over a name, a score, or whose on first needs help. How about putting first things first. There are other priorities." Moreover, this refusal to take mascot seriously arises from a folk understanding of symbols. Richard from Salem, Oregon, argues against changing the nicknames because "After all it is just a name!" And Brookie from Birmingham, Alabama, does not understand "what the big deal is . . . A name is just a name, nothing else."

Not all arguments in support of mascots lean on honor, intention, or analogy. In fact, some proudly flaunt their intolerance, overtly advancing racist claims. Rick from Las Vegas opined, "The native Americans are mostly peaceable. Some need to be reminded who won the wars." And Bill Smith from El Paso added, "I tend to think that all of this noise about mascots offending certain groups of peoples is taking up valuable time and effort that could be directed at solving important issues. And besides the Indians lost the war and therefore it is our right to make fun of them (at least we give them welfare and a place to live)."

Taken together, arguments in defense of mascots take five key positions. First, they refuse to engage or take seriously the concerns of living Native Americans in their defenses of "their" imagined Indians. Second, they exhibit a propensity to tell Native Americans how it is or how they should feel (namely respected and honored). Third, their arguments question the grounding of critics, enjoining them to "get real" or " get a life," precisely as they infantalize them through demands that opponents "grow up." Fourth, supporters display an inability and unwillingness to see or talk about race. When race does enter into their discussions, moreover, they qualify and constrain it. One the one hand, they suggest that racism is meaningful only when it is intentional, guided by ill-will, and truly significant (that is in the real world). On the other hand, many supporters claim parity between their ethnic heritage and racial condition and that of Native Americans, arguing that Irishness, for instance, is equivalent to Indianness in terms of the privileges, possibilities, and histories.

In Opposition to Mascots

Opponents of mascots advance a set of overlapping arguments. Throughout, they foreground race, history, and power.

Not surprisingly, opponents of mascots devote great energy to challenging the arguments advanced in defense of such symbols and nicknames. In the *USA Weekend* forum, opponents frequently underscored the ignorance of supporters. In playful and pejorative terms, they questioned supporters' familiarity with Native American cultures and their knowledge of American history and the English language. With almost equal frequency, opponents dispute assertions that macots honor Native Americans. Jay Rosenstein asks, "Why do people continue to insist these nicknames honor American Indians when the people you claim to be honoring tell that it's not? You honor and respect someone by listening to them." Jim Northrup, an Anishinaabe, has never felt honored by mascots; and more, he continues, "Someone telling me I should feel honored does not feel the same as being honored." As Arek Dreyer suggests, "It is pretty arrogant to dictate what someone else should be honored by."

Arguments against mascots pivot around race. Some note with sadness that Native Americans still lack parity with other ethnic groups. Elaine Flattery remarks, "Other races simply aren't subjected to this sort of racial stereotype propaganda. Native American images and names should not be the 'property' of corporate American exploit and merchandize." Similarly, Beth from Alstead, New Hampshire, argues:

> The fact that caricatures of American Indian people exist with the consent from white people means that the race isn't take seriously in this country and they are being "used" for the entertainment and contrived message that white people get from them. You don't see these kinds of mascots of other races . . . Because American Indian Nations have been stuffed into third world roles for the past three centuries, they are being denied the voice to have white America listen to them.

Others question the racial content of names and symbols. "Using Native Americans as mascots," Danielle N'Dhighe asserts, "is racist and should be stopped immediately. After all we don't see teams like the Washington Blackskins . . . or the San Francisco Slant Eyes. Almost everyone would agree that such things would be racist and denigrating. Why then do we allow Redskins and Chief Wahoo?" And John Whalen asks, "How can 'redskins' be interpreted as anything other than blatant racism? How can any ridiculous charicature such as Chief Wahoo be seen as anything other than demeaning?"

Opponents of mascots do not simply highlight racism, they also actively strive to make the racial content of mascots tangible, linking them to more palpable and familiar version of race. For some, the historic tradition of Black face is a striking parallel. Nota Bell, for instance, finds mascots "no less distasteful than shuck & jive antics in black face is to Black Americans." More commonly, opponents offer racial analogies, comparing Native Americans with other racial groups. Frequently, they invent new and intentionally provocative team names. These include "New York Niggers," "Jersey Jewboys," "Washington Wops," "Mississippi Blackies," "Atlanta Rednecks," "Washington Palefaces," "Los Angeles Spics," "Chicago Pollacks," and "Cleveland Honkies."

In contrast with supporters, opponents of mascots stress history and power, situating nicknames and symbols in a broader context of oppression. Dolores Jones, for instance, suggests that "Native Americans have always been oppressed peoples . . . They DESERVE some RESPECT!!! What is being done by sports teams is mockery." Eric Anderson, in turn, asserts,

> This whole deal is a 'controversy' only because non-Natives with power continue to show disrespect for Native peoples and cultures. You might think that five hundred years of genocide has been enough, but corporate greed and the longstanding tradition of racism in America just won't let go. If

Native peoples are offended by these mascots – and they are – then the mascots should be changed. It is a matter of courtesy and respect.

Likewise, Bolaji from Pasadena, California, laments "the past of the USA continues to haunt it." Despite heartfelt claims to honor or respect indigenous peoples through mascots, he continues, "the bloodiness and hate of the country's history inevitably taints whatever good intentions there might be in [these] positive gestures." A. T. Lang pushes this thinking even further, "The problem with this country now and in the past is they want to sweep 'THE INDIAN ISSUE' UNDER THE RUG! Over 60 million Indians were slaughtered, raped, enslaved, and [had] their land stolen. The 'Indian Holocaust' was one of the cornerstones behind Hitler's slaughter of 6 million Jews. It is long past due for this country to show respect for the rights of the FIRST AMERICANS. That includes not using them for 'mascots' AND NOT sweeping Indian issues under the rug any longer!!!!" Undoing this history and respecting Native Americans as equals, Andrew Jackson concludes, demands not only that mascots be retired but also that "THIS COUNTRY HONOR THE TREATIES THAT WERE SIGNED WITH THE NATIVE PEOPLES."

Arguments advanced against Native American mascots display four key features. First, they overtly engage with and challenge supporters' knowledge and understanding. Second, they direct attention to race and its effects. Third, they actively racialize the debate over mascots, making analogies between the experience and condition of Native Americans and those of other racial groups, particularly African Americans. Fourth, they historicize the use of American Indian nicknames and symbols, connecting them with broader patterns of discrimination and oppression.

INTERPRETATION OF THE ARGUMENTS

The arguments over the continued use of American Indian nicknames and symbols have much to teach us about race and the media. They remind us of the creativity and situated agency of media consumers. Texts, images, and performances do not have fixed meanings but rather audiences actively interpret them, negotiating and literally creating their significance. The critique and defense of mascots, along with the efforts (successful or not) to retire and retain them underscore, moreover, that these processes are not singular. Rather, audiences struggle with one another, and often with social institutions, including the media, to give meaning to signs (mascots); their worlds of experience and collective heritage (identity); and their positions, perspectives, and possibilities.

Supporters and defenders of mascots clearly disagree about the significance of mascots. Whereas supporters insist that mascots foster respect and are meant to honor Native Americans, opponents assert that they denigrate Native Americans, perpetuating historical patterns of discrimination and dispossession. The distinct positions advanced in the unfolding debates point to deeper differences: supporters stress text (honor, intention), while opponents emphasize context (history and racism). Supporters isolate; opponents make connections. Supporters argue for intent; opponents argue for effect. Supporters consider symbols and names flat and more or less unimportant; opponents think of symbols as powerful cultural forms that reflect social relations and reinforce historical inequalities. Supporters deflect and deny the import of race; opponents highlight the centrality of race.

In effect, supporters and opponents occupy, what Prochaska (2001, p.175) dubbed "mutually exclusive communicative communities" informed by distinct interpretive frameworks. To my mind, something fundamental is discernible in the arguments advanced and their "communities" of origin. That is, they advance competing visions of race. Supporters, who might be described as advocates of a more-or-less dominant, if not reactionary, notion, hold that "we are all more or less equal," that the ill intentions of prejudiced individuals produce racism, and that discussions of discrimination should be confined to "real" and "important" social domains. In contrast, opponents advance an emergent, counter-hegemonic perspective—that is, an interpretation reading the social relations and cultural categories against the grain, exposing the power and meaning embedded within accepted norms, ideologies, and behaviors. Opponents argue that race and racism are central to the American experience, that the effects of racial hierarchy cannot be ignored, and that symbols such as mascots—far from being frivolous—are significant measures of race relations. In this light, the ongoing controversy over mascots is as much about conflicting interpretations of race as it is a series of arguments over the appropriateness of Native American images in popular culture.

IT'S YOUR TURN: WHAT DO YOU THINK? WHAT WILL YOU FIND?

1. Before reading this essay, write down every word, image, or sentiment that comes to mind when thinking about Native American mascots (e.g., the Cleveland Indians' Chief Wahoo or the Washington Redskins). Then, after reading the essay, individually analyze your earlier responses. As a class, identify and interpret themes and patterns that emerged from this exercise.

2. Compare and contrast mascots that represent ethnic groups. How is using names such as the Vikings or Fighting Irish (un)like using names such as the Redskins, Savages, and Fighting Illini? What do these differences suggest about how Americans have understood race and ethnicity? What do they tell us about racial identity, privilege, and relations in the contemporary United States?

3. Why are there no African American mascots? What does the prevalence of Indian symbols and nicknames paired with the absence of Black symbols and nicknames suggest about ethnic identity, racial stereotyping, and respect?

4. Visit one of the following Web sites. Study the tone, presentation, arguments, content, and effectiveness. Think critically about how the authors talk about mascots, Native Americans, race, symbols, and history. Consider, moreover, how they use the electronic medium and what the Web site suggests about audience involvement in cultural politics. To foster greater insight, visit one site in support and one site in opposition to mascots. PRO: *http://www.studentsforchief.com/* CON: *http://www.retirethechief.org/*

REFERENCES

Churchill, W. (1994). Indians are us? Culture and genocide in Native North America. Monroe, ME: Common Courage Press.

Connolly, M.R. (2000). What is in a name? A historical look at Native American–related nicknames and symbols at three U.S. universities. Journal of Higher Education 71(5), 515–547.

Davis, L. (1993). Protest against the use of Native American mascots: A challenge to traditional, American identity. Journal of Sport and Social Issues, 17(1), 9–22.

Deloria, P. (1998). Playing Indian. New Haven: Yale University Press.

King, C. R., & Springwood, C. F., (Eds). (2001). Team spirits: Essays on the history and significance of Native American mascots. Lincoln: University of Nebraska Press.

Pewewardy, C. D. (1991). Native American mascots and imagery: The struggle of unlearning Indian stereotypes. Journal of Navaho Education, 9(1), 19–23.

Prochaska, D. (2001). At home in Illinois: Presence of Chief Illiniwek, absence of Native Americans. In C. R. King & C. F. Springwood (Eds.), Team spirits: Essays on the history and significance of Native American mascots (pp.157–185). Lincoln: University of Nebraska Press.

Spindel, C. (2000). Dancing at halftime: Sports and the controversy over American Indian mascots. New York: New York University Press.

Springwood, C. F., & King, C. R. (2001). "Playing Indian": Why Mascots Must End. Chronicle of Higher Education. Nov. 9, 2001. B13–B14

Vanderford, H. (1996). What's in a name? Heritage or hatred: The school mascot controversy. Journal of Law and Education, 25, 381–388.

Produsage

4.1 DREAMING IN COLOUR: FAN FICTION AS CRITICAL RECEPTION

andré m. carrington

Media audiences have long used the means of distribution available to them to respond to popular narratives in print, television, and film—from circulating reviews among their friends to producing stories of their own. This reading draws attention to the global frame of reference in which audience members situate themselves as fan writers in increasingly transnational media marketplaces.

Fan fiction, a form of creative response to media that originated with amateur publishing in print through mimeographs and photocopying machines and now circulates online through tradi-tional Web sites and social networks, provides evidence of how audiences make popular media their own (Bacon-Smith, 1989). Yet fan fiction also enables amateur authors to act as critics. By considering the questions about identity, belonging, and desire that fans bring to their creative portrayals of the Black and female characters who occupy minor roles in popular films, books, and television series, particularly when those works involve settings that are predominantly white and part of the "first world," I look to fan fiction as a critical form of reception. Seeing how fans employ critical thinking enhances the currency of our scholarly theories of globalization, gender, reception, and the circulation of media. This perspective on media fandom also expands our ideas of where audiences fit into the study of contemporary culture by considering the negotiations that fans undertake to help them determine what meanings they see—and would like to see— in the representation of racialized, gendered, and diasporic identities.

Race, diaspora, class, gender, and sexuality all exert influences on reception and audience response, and this is particularly evident in works of fan fiction that portray characters of color. The disproportionate attention devoted to minor characters in the respective texts of origin lets us observe audiences participating in the critique of how minority status is represented in popu-lar media. As is the case in most narrative media, plots are driven by the title characters of the two popular fantasy series I examine—*Buffy the Vampire Slayer* and *Harry Potter*. Developing the fictional biographies of these characters is the prerogative of the professionals who produce books, films, and TV series about them. Minor characters get secondary attention. When it comes to reception, however, minor figures' marginal status allows fans with to flesh out the background stories and imagine the characters' interior lives. A benefit of looking to fan fiction to understand the representation of race, class, gender, and sexuality is that although colored and queer characters are represented narrowly (usually as supporting characters) in dominant media, they garner greater attention among fan writers precisely because of their relative obscurity. They give fans more to work and play with when writing for other fans (Gleason, 2006). At the "Remember Us" online archive for fan fiction featuring characters of color (http://www.dreaming-in-color.net), fans can read and contribute their own stories exploring these possibilities. The fan-authored stories that I selected from the archive to demonstrate how fans think critically about race, diaspora, class, gender, and sexuality in this essay reimagine the British and American settings of the texts on which they are based by focusing on female characters from the Anglophone African diaspora.

The United Kingdom functions in the *Buffy the Vampire Slayer* television series as an alternative national context against which to juxtapose conventional assumptions about the United States, particularly with respect to gender- and class-specific attitudes toward tradition and propriety. The vampire slayer fantasy at the center of *Buffy* is an ersatz horror narrative turned humorous counter-myth in which the blonde, doe-eyed heroine gains the power to vanquish supernatural evildoers instead of playing the helpless victim. The character embodying Britain in the series is the heroine's mentor, the "Watcher" Rupert Giles, and the romanticized history of the vampire slayer tradition positions Britain as the headquarters of a "Watchers Council" peopled by men steeped in tea and the supernatural. In the second and fourth seasons of *Buffy*, however, Black British/diasporic characters named Kendra and Olivia, respectively, appear to complicate the idea that a white, male Briton can represent the singular manifestation of the British touch in the vampire slayer tradition. Fan fictions featuring these two characters present alternative roots for the vampire slayer fantasy, including a more skeptical attitude toward the fantastic element in the series that sheds light on how audiences approach genre from different perspectives.

The Olivia character allowed *Buffy* fans to confront the tensions of race, nation, gender, and genre at work in the series. In the fourth season, Buffy discovers her staid British mentor's personal life in a direct way when she walks into his home and is greeted by a woman wearing one of his shirts—and little else. Olivia, as portrayed by Phina Oruche, cuts a striking figure of Black womanhood. She upsets the expectations about sexuality that are set in place by Giles's character. She enters into the series to rekindle a romance that predates Buffy's adventures, suggesting that sexuality is something hidden, rather than absent, for the British characters' roles in the series. More important, Olivia reacts with surprise and displeasure when she learns that Buffy is a vampire slayer and Giles is her Watcher; from her point of view, the fantastic world of magic and monsters is the hidden aspect of Giles's identity. Thus, Olivia was positioned to offer an alternative perspective on *Buffy the Vampire Slayer*'s gender and genre politics. While her shared gender identity and racial difference set her up as Buffy's rival for the forms of affection they both sought from Giles, her gendered and racial difference from Giles marked her as his appropriate counterpart. Olivia's Britishness called attention to the European mythology of swords and sorcery at the center of the series even as she shied away from them. On screen, her apparent rejection of Giles left the supernatural as something for the upstart American woman and the European male figure for mastery to share, tidily binding together the meanings of the differently gendered but commonly white identities of the principal characters who represented the national frames of reference in the series.

Lost in this equation, however, was the diasporic quality that brought together Olivia's Britishness, her femininity, and her Blackness. A fan-authored story called "Home" (Lindamarie, n.d.) invokes not only British elements familiar to *Buffy* viewers, but also fantastic elements from an African diasporic tradition, giving Olivia a racially specific point of entry into the peculiarly gendered and sexual intervention in the fantasy and horror genres that characterize *Buffy*. If *Buffy the Vampire Slayer* writ large is a story that revises gendered notions to allow a white, blonde victim to become a heroine, "Home" is a story allowing a Black British ingénue to become a participant, instead of a sideliner, in the unfolding of a fantasy narrative.

In "Home," a trope (or literary/rhetorical device) for the supernatural of West African origin (specifically, the deity referred to as Oya among the Yoruba peoples of contemporary Nigeria and Benin and their diasporic relations) is the touchstone for Olivia's belonging in the fantastic milieu of *Buffy*. Throughout the short duration of the story, Giles and another British man chant Olivia's name and the name of the deity together:

> "Olivia. Oya. Olivia. Olivia. Oya."
>
> The power rises inside her like water, like that from which she's just stepped. Shivery, chilling—exciting. A burning, bittersweet feeling almost like pain, but more like freedom. It starts down at her toes, ankles. But rises.

The use of this particular trope signals a number of critical gestures on the part of the fan writer. First, it demonstrates a substantive effort to find and use relevant information about the national, racial, and diasporic spaces that are already part of the series in a way that lends nuance, depth, and specificity to the representation of Blackness on television. The deity whose name the story invokes is one of several orishas, divine figures who are associated with aspects of the world and wider cosmology of Yoruba peoples. It is significant that Oya is the orisha who personifies a river. When Olivia emerges from water in the story, the immediately preceding reference to Oya negates another possible allusion: to Christian baptism in a European or African American context. Thus, the story builds an empowering experience for a Black character through a decisively Black diasporic system of meaning.

Essentially, however, the plausible allusion to Olivia's fictionalized African diasporic background represents an attempt to revise the story told on screen in a way that would extend, rather than constrain, the role of a Black female character in television. Although the frustration of Olivia's desires was a key element in her episode, her role in a work of fan fiction is not bound to the same limitations. Fan fiction thus demonstrates how different stakeholders in the production of a media text such as a television show bring different priorities to their viewing practices. Thus, a character such as Olivia can move to a central position. The narration in "Home" takes place from Olivia's point of view. Its plot fantasizes a situation in which Olivia gains mastery over the secret elements of Rupert Giles's world and inspires him to return to England.

> She left him two years ago, and then there were no more visits. She went back to London, back to safety, but it didn't matter. She already knew, knew the world she lived in and the things she'd been taught weren't the half of it. She'd seen through a crack in the facade, and now the whole wall was crumbling.
>
> "Oya. Olivia. Oya. Oya. Oya." She can feel it swelling through her chest, her heart aching so hard she feels it might burst.

As it turns out, the "Home" of the title is not the London that offers familiarity and safety. Instead, Olivia has found a new place for herself within the hidden world of her love interest. Olivia's heartache represents her attempt to reconcile her desire for Giles with the disturbing revelation of his supernatural qualities, a resolution she is never offered on-screen but one that was fascinating enough for a fan writer to share her vision of it with other *Buffy* viewers.

Fan fiction affords readers and viewers a transformative space in more ways than one when it comes to issues of race, gender, diaspora, class, and national identity. As the story above indicates, fans can use their own writing to open up the repertoire of genre tropes and plot developments that are otherwise foreclosed for characters of color in their favorite narratives. A TV series characterized by the tropes of fantasy in white European and North American traditions can draw on African diasporic sources, instead. This kind of imaginative space has implications for the way media audiences bring considerations of geographic and political spaces into their reading and viewing practices. When fans encounter the way *Buffy* invokes a romanticized Britain to gesture toward a fantastic tradition longer than the history of the United States but linked to it via their Anglophone lexicon, they might also imagine Britain's colonial legacy that gives a character like Olivia recourse to Yoruba traditions within an otherwise predominantly white space. A similar idea animates the work of *Harry Potter* fan fiction that I consider below.

Rather than presenting one character at a time as singular exceptions to an all-white corps of actors representing the United Kingdom, J.K. Rowling's series of young adult novels and the films adapted from them admirably portray contemporary Britain as the crisscrossed diasporic space that it is. The *Potter* books and films explicitly identify Black, South Asian, and East Asian people as Harry Potter's classmates at his wizarding school, offering fans a glimpse of a white hero character's coming-of-age in a context that reflects the demographics of a real multiracial world and reproduces it on the film set through casting. However, in the same way that the aforementioned story complicates the Olivia character in *Buffy* through references to the cultural specificity through which a woman like her might experience being Black and British, the following example of fan fiction about *Harry Potter* further transforms its setting by conceptualizing a life-changing event that might take place in the young adult world of *Harry Potter* from a Black British woman's point of view. In so doing, it takes advantage of a medium with no particular target market, no age-appropriate boundaries on sexual content and violence, and no bottom line—in short, the peculiar circumstances of writing as an amateur for an audience of one's peers—to address all-too-common problems of sex and violence among contemporary youth. The story does so while remaining firmly grounded in the issues of race and class that characterize the backgrounds of people such as *Harry Potter*'s Black British and diasporic characters.

"The Broken Wall, The Burning Roof and Tower," a story by a fan who uses the pseudonym dangerous_angel, focuses on Angelina Johnson, a Black student older than Harry Potter who attends his wizarding school. While the books and films never acknowledge multiracial Britain as a space in which real conflicts and divergences over belonging and desire would emerge for Black British characters such as Angelina Johnson in *Harry Potter*, the fan fiction delivers a complex treatment of these issues in order to lend depth to an original plot. The story implies that an unseen antagonist has raped the Angelina Johnson character, and she recovers from the trauma with the aid of another minor character. In the process, both the recovering protagonist and her caring new friend form a bond that requires them to question the conventions of the young adult fantasy narrative and its British context in specifically racialized, class-inflected terms.

The author describes Angelina feeling removed from herself in terms familiar to readers of the *Harry Potter* novels: "Being a Gryffindor was supposed to be about victories, the bright and the bold, and shouting what had to be said. But now she knew that was not all there was to her. Being her meant losses, dark shadows, and things that could not be said." Angelina's pain jeopardizes her sense of belonging. She feels doubly betrayed—the rapist was one of her Gryffindor housemates. She feels shut out from the discourse of heroism and, furthermore, disconnected from her role as a feminine love interest. By setting up the traumatic event of rape as the occasion for a character's return to a gender-specific role, the fan writer underscores the tendencies of women's roles in young adult fiction, making explicit the sexual and power relations that drive those roles. This character's racial identity, however, multiplies the attention a fan reader must devote to her femininity and victimized status. While women and men of all ages and all racial backgrounds can be targets of sexual violence, perpetrators of such crimes against women of color are historically less likely to be treated with the same severity as those who enact violence against white women. Furthermore, women of color are typically more vulnerable to the kind of misogynist victim-blaming that occurs when they are victims of sexual violence. In a sense, this story provides a vital check on the gendered and age-specific assumptions, along with racial prejudices, that allow sexual violence to go largely unnoticed in mainstream media.

In addition to feeling excluded from the meaning of Gryffindor identity, Angelina feels alienated from a particular meaning of virginity. In part two of the story, dangerous_angel writes:

> [H]er mother had given her much more freedom compared to her cousins and other girls of her status. "Do what you must, but keep your dignity," she'd always said. Her dignity being her virginity. Her mother had hopes of marrying her into one of the old families from the Caribbean or Africa, who were rooted in a history that involved more than European wand waving.

Deviating from the terms in which most *Harry Potter* characters pursue status, which involve aspiring to become great wizards, this anomalous story sets "European wand waving" and a racialized economy of social capital ("old families from the Caribbean or Africa") at opposite poles. Angelina's predicament casts a gender and class fantasy about marrying well, within the context of diasporic Blackness, in relief against the genre-specific fantasy of wizardry. The denigrating term "European wand-waving" reflects the distortion wrought by Angelina's traumatic experience. She is so thoroughly disenchanted that she identifies with a family and diasporic community made up of people for whom the *Harry Potter* fictions have their own charged term, "Muggles," which matches "European wand-waving" for its distancing effect. Yet instead of simply reconnecting the Angelina character to wizardry or relegating her to the magical world's fictitious hierarchy in which identification with Muggles is denigrating, the fan author portrays her remembering her mother's words in familial advice and racially coded language. "Dem no see time like we," Angelina remembers her mother saying, echoing a Black diasporic accent and grammar to remind us of Angelina Johnson's racially specific way of perceiving the world.

A young white student named Montague, a minor villain in the *Potter* books, arrives to comfort Angelina. His decisive act as her newfound ally comes when he confronts her antagonist, requiring Montague to interrogate his own identity as a white Englishman and, importantly, as a wizard. Just as the term "European wand-waving" highlights the conflation of whiteness and the fantasy genre, and just as the use of culturally specific fantastic ideas from an African frame of reference breaks apart that conflation in the *Buffy the Vampire Slayer* fan fiction, the confrontation between Montague and the perpetrator shows a fan writer recognizing how Blackness and whiteness are represented with a problematic lack of depth even in the multiracial United Kingdom imagined by *Harry Potter*. Angelina's heritage again provides the language in which to understand her trauma.

Fred Weasley, Angelina's erstwhile boyfriend in the story, becomes the object of Montague's ire as Montague learns that he was the rapist. Montague questions him heatedly, but he responds:

> 'You don't know anything, Montague. Angelina would've never married me.' Montague turned back to him, his confusion evident . . . 'You think you Slytherins are the only ones obsessed with bloodlines. You can trace your history back to Merlin's time. She can do it back to tribes that existed before all the supposed great civilizations. Her parents would've never let her marry me. My family has no money. I'm nobody except another Englishman who knows nothing except what's going on in his own garden.'

This leaves us with an intriguing set of questions. Can a Black British character such as Angelina Johnson inhabit both the fantasy genre and a rich, perhaps equally mythological idiom of Blackness at the same time? Do the whiteness, heterosexuality, and normative gender of most characters in the fantasy, horror, and science fiction genres that are so popular among media fans give them limited appeal, compared with the sparsely detailed and mystified backgrounds of Black, diasporic, and female minor characters that beg to be fleshed out by attentive amateurs? Or, can media audiences rethink the settings and histories attributed to whiteness, Blackness, and national spaces in their favorite narratives by considering phenomena such as diaspora in ways that enrich their experiences with the representation of minor and principal characters alike? Finishing the story is one way to find out one fan's take on these questions, but to read and write fan fiction is to consider the implications of more than one possible ending to any story.

All these questions leave aside the possibility of casting people of color and women in more central roles in media content, reflecting the diversity and interconnectedness of the world. Fan fiction offers another kind of reflection, however: a reminder that readers and viewers can and perhaps should think critically about race, gender, and class in entertainment media despite their obvious limits. Pleasure is one goal of the creative impulse that gives rise to fan fiction, but critical thinking as a means to that end, and as an end in itself, displays another way in which readers and viewers are invested in what they receive from popular media.

IT'S YOUR TURN: WHAT DO YOU THINK? WHAT WILL YOU FIND?

1. Think of a person of color who plays a minor role in a TV series, comic book, or film you've enjoyed, and write a fictitious biographical sketch for that character, taking into account how people with this character's racial background and gender identity are situated in their national context.

2. Read some fan fiction of a media text with which you're familiar (*Star Trek*, *Buffy*, etc.) by visiting a Web site such as *fanfiction.net*. How do these writings reflect the issues I've discussed here?

3. Think about how social class might factor into audience members' interest in and ability to join the fan fiction community. Does the content you found while considering the above activity seem to reflect the breadth of social strata? Or, did it seem like there was a digital divide? What role do you think computer/Internet access plays in people's participation in practices such as reading and writing fan fiction online?

REFERENCES

Bacon-Smith, C. (1989). *Enterprising women: Television fandom and the creation of popular myth*. Philadelphia: Temple University Press.

dangerous_angel. (2005). "The broken wall, the burning roof and tower, part 1: Change (in the house of flies)." Retrieved October 6, 2011, from http://luckybrans.livejournal.com/26057.html

dangerous_angel. (2005). "The broken wall, The burning roof and tower, part 5: Release." Retrieved October 6, 2011, from http://luckybrans.livejournal.com/28620.html

Gleason, D. (2006). Why people tend not to favor main characters. *The fanfic symposium*. Retrieved October 6, 2011, from http://www.trickster.org/symposium/symp192.htm

Lindamarie, "Home." (n.d.). Retrieved October 6, 2011, from http://web.archive.org/web/20040428134913/www.panavatar.net/luminescent/fanfiction/home.htm.

4.2 CRANK DAT BARACK OBAMA! SOCIAL MEDIA AND THE 2008 PRESIDENTIAL ELECTION

Travis L. Gosa

This reading examines the use of social media in the 2008 presidential election. During the election of the first African American president, YouTube and social media Web sites were flooded with Obama-inspired dances, video mash-ups, and tribute songs. The author argues that user-generated Internet content has become an important aspect of political discourse, and asks whether Obama helped close the "participation gap" that has existed among Black and poor youth.

The year 2008 is now remembered for the historic election of Barack Obama as the first African American president of the United States. Given the country's long struggle with racial discrimination and exclusion, the Obama election represents an important milestone toward achieving social equality. Obama is also the first "digital" president; the 2008 presidential election was the first in which political participation and civic engagement moved to online communities, such as Facebook and YouTube.

Online politics represent a potential civil rights dilemma of the early twenty-first century. Citizens with Internet access and computer skills will get to participate in "digital democracy," while others could find themselves left without a voice. People from disadvantaged backgrounds often lack the money, equipment, and skills needed to access the Internet (Kress, 2008). My research deals with Black adolescents, a subgroup at risk of being left behind in the shifting winds of technological change due to racial and social class disadvantage. Like other researchers, I am concerned that Black and/or poor youth *with* Internet access are not blogging, uploading digital photos, or sharing their own media creations online (Hargittai & Walejko, 2008; Jenkins, Clinton, Purushotma, Robison, & Weigel, 2009).

This reading presents a case study of social media participation in the 2008 presidential election. A case study is one way that social scientists develop an in-depth understanding of a single event. As you read about the election, I want you to consider how social media blur the conventional lines between media producer and consumer, and even the division between politics and entertainment. My goal is to show you how Black youth became active participants in the election by "cranking dat Obama." That is, by uploading Obama-inspired dances, video mash-ups, and tribute songs to social media Web sites. In the vernacular of hip-hop culture, "cranking dat" refers both to an impromptu dance style and the practice of playing really loud music. As the following narrative shows, one way Black youth participated in the election was by dancing and rapping about politics on the Internet. This "Obama Effect," I believe, helped Black and poor youth become a powerful political constituency and close the participation gap on social media Web sites.

THE IMPORTANCE OF SOCIAL MEDIA LITERACY AND PARTICIPATION

Society is in the midst of a media revolution. Within the last two decades, computer and Internet technologies have dramatically altered the ways in which we communicate and experience entertainment. Before the advent of Twitter micro blogging and YouTube videos, media were heavily centralized and controlled by old media companies, such as cable television networks, music studios, and newspapers. In old media, popular music was produced by professional musicians and record labels, and multi-track albums were sold in brick-and-mortar record stores. There was a clear distinction between you, the audience, and the performer or artist on the radio.

The decline of old media began with the popularization of the Internet in the 1990s. On the original information superhighway, you could send an instant electronic letter (e-mail) to a friend without going to the post office. This was like a futuristic science fiction movie. But by modern standards, the superhighway was just an expensive and slow toll-road. In 1990, Internet access cost approximately $20 *per hour* (adjusted for inflation in 2010 dollars). With the fastest connection available, it would have taken about 2 days to download a 3 minute video from the Internet. It also would have cost $1,000 in access fees.[1] Only the most privileged members of society could afford computers and Internet, or had the skills and leisure time necessary to be online. This is what researchers call the digital divide. As technology has gotten cheaper, the digital divide has shrunk along the lines of social class (rich/poor) and race (white/Black), but some differences remain (Kress, 2008).

According to the U.S. Department of Commerce, 94% of households with income over $100,000 subscribed to broadband Internet in 2009 compared with 35% of households earning less than $25,000. We also live in a racially stratified society. Members of racial minority groups are more likely to experience poverty, and have fewer household or educational resources. As a result, racial minorities are also less likely to be connected to the Internet. Seventy percent of white households have high-speed access, but only half of Black, Native American, or Latino households subscribe (Blank & Strickling, 2010).

It is important to have Internet access because society is moving online. In the era of social media or new media, we use Internet-connected gizmos to express ourselves, manage interpersonal relationships, and seek out information. Unlike old media, there is now an emphasis on user-generated content produced and distributed by amateurs. The idea is that anyone can contribute knowledge to encyclopedias (via Wikipedia), become a singer and movie director (via YouTube), or publish his or her own photography magazine (via Flickr). As such, social media blur the traditional line between producer and consumer, artist and audience.

You probably already know about social media's impact on the entertainment industry. "Sharing" (or "stealing") music has been a favorite pastime of college students since the advent of Napster in 1999. I am interested in social media because it involves the larger issue of digital stratification or virtual inequality. Online participatory culture now impacts society's haves and have-nots. Those who participate develop computer and communication skills needed to compete in a globalized, information-based economy. Social media literacy represents a type of hidden curriculum, beyond formal schooling, which will determine who is deemed desirable to employers and who has access to information about job openings on social networks like LinkedIn. Disadvantaged groups may be shut off from these opportunities, thereby reinforcing their lower standing in society.

In addition to economics, civic engagement has moved to online communities. The 2008 presidential election was the beginning of digital democracy. Wikis, blogs, text messages, and YouTube became sources of political power for organizations and individual citizens. Influence was wielded by candidates through e-mails and text messages. Barack Obama was especially savvy in his use of social media networks. He "friended" more than 5 million voters on the Internet, and collected millions of donations through his MyBarackObama.com Web site.

These economic and political functions of social media have led researchers to become concerned about the possibility of a participation gap due to racial and social class disadvantage. Because Black youth are, on average, less affluent, this subgroup is the least likely to participate in social media. Previous studies on middle school, high school, and college students show that Black youth have the lowest levels of computer and Internet use, and are less likely to produce music and videos online than their affluent white peers (Hargittai & Walejko, 2008; Jenkins et. al, 2009).

The participation gap is disheartening because we want all young people to develop the skills needed to become active participants in the new digital world. Two individuals may have already helped Black youth gain ground in social media participation. The story involves two very different, though equally charismatic personalities: the teen rap sensation Soulja Boy (Tell'Em) and President Barack Obama. For the remainder of the chapter, I want you to consider how "cranking dat" became a form of social media entertainment and political expression. While reading the case study, keep in mind the questions about race and social class disadvantage.

CRANK DAT BARACK OBAMA

The entree of Black youth into social media spaces involved the rise of popular ("viral") dances, songs, and video mash-ups about Barack Obama. To better understand how race and social class might be affecting social media participation during the election, I listened to over 600 unique rap songs about Barack Obama, watched a few hundred Obama-inspired music videos, and collected more than 90 full-length Obama "mixtapes."

During the presidential election, it seemed like Black youth were everywhere on the Internet. The plausibility of helping elect the first president who looked like us (relatively young and Black) caused Black youth to develop a grassroots Internet blitzkrieg never before seen in political history. On social media Web sites such as MySpace and YouTube, Black youth pioneered "cranking dat Obama" during the 2008 election. This referred both to creating funny Obama dances and making up clever rap songs. It involved rapping "Barack The Vote" or yelling "*My* President Is *Black*!" The latter refrain came from the Obama tribute song by superstar rappers Young Jeezy and Nas. Black youth downloaded the instrumentals, developed their own lyrics to the song, and then uploaded the remixes declaring Obama to be their favorite candidate. Using smartphones and webcams, they uploaded hundreds of dance videos in support of Barack Obama.

What was all this "cranking dat" about? Well, the cranking of Obama overlapped with a popular culture craze started by one of my favorite rappers, Soulja Boy (Tell'Em). Right before the election, in 2007, a 17-year-old high school dropout began uploading homemade tracks to his YouTube and MySpace accounts. One track by Soulja Boy entitled "Crank Dat Soulja Boy" consisted of only the default beats that come prepackaged on FruityLoops music editing software. Over an infectious steel drum loop, Soulja Boy provided sparse rhymes about gun-play and not-so-subtle allusions to sex, though pretty tame by today's rap standards. Notably, "Crank Dat" also contained instructions to a corresponding line dance. The dance involved a simple leaning and rocking technique, followed by a flying Superman (the superhero) dive, all finished by a back-and-forth motorcycle gesture (like you're cranking the accelerator).

Within months of its release, YouTube enthusiasts flooded the Internet with thousands of "Crank Dat" dance responses and reinterpretations, including "Crank Dat Batman" and "Spiderman." In addition to placing Black kids at the helm of viral dance crazes, "Crank Dat" also popularized the art of the video "mash-up"—the digital media practice of blending multiple media sources to create a seamless new production. Important in mash-up culture is the splicing of conflicting material for humorous and satirical effect. In the Soulja Boy mash-up movement, children's cartoon videos were "remixed" with the song so that *SpongeBobSquarePants*, *Dora The Explorer*, *Lion King*, and *Winnie the Pooh* all appeared to be cranking dat. The result was a hilarious parody of innocent children characters mimicking the urban, hip-hop dance.

Following the Soulja Boy craze, Obama became the next mash-up dance sensation on the Internet. In early November of 2007, the first "Crank Dat Obama" mash-up featured Obama sharing his stiff and off-rhythm dance moves on the *Ellen DeGeneres Show*. The clip was re-edited to make it seem as if Obama was cranking dat, on beat to the Soulja Boy tune. Over a million viewers clicked on the YouTube link to watch the would-be president crank dat and do the Superman.

Within the week, amateur rappers uploaded full-length rap songs to match the new Obama dance. For example, Phokuzd (pronounced "Focused"), an underground emcee from Michigan, instructed everybody to "Crank Dat Obama." Snap your fingers, throw your hands in the air, and wiggle down to the floor—all while standing in line to vote for Obama. According to the video, doing the dance would show all the Obama "haters" (opponents) that you supported Obama's "swagger" (style and personality). Likewise, a young man calling himself "Smokin' Jo Beats" choreographed his Obama dance as a southern snap dance. In his online videos, he instructed everyone to snap their fingers, crank left to right, and scream the campaign slogan "Yes We Can!" In many variations of dance, "Crank Dat Obama" took on the dual meaning of dancing and pulling the lever for Obama in the voting booth.

For those exhausted from snapping and cranking, the Internet was also populated with Obama tribute slide dances. Slide dances, like the "Electric Slide" or "Cha-Cha Slide," are popular at wedding receptions and parties due to their easy-to-learn steps and repetitive nature. Some of the most popular Obama slide dances included "The Obama Hustle" and "The Obama Shuffle."[2] The virtual dances crossed over into real-life political meetings. Obama supporters could be found performing the slide dances at traditional political spaces such as community centers and voter registration rallies.

The Obama dance craze was not a case of amateurs dancing alone in their bedrooms. Young people organized themselves into political dance mobs, virtual break dancing competitions in which teams attempted to out-dance each other. In a typical dance mob, the winner is decided by the popular online vote. In the election year, the crews attempted to motivate viewers to vote for their team and presidential candidate. The largest dance mob competition took place on IbeatYou and YouTube between the "Obaminators," composed of dancing Obama supporters; the "McCainiacs," a dance squad endeared to Republican candidate John McCain; and the

"Palinistas," an all-female dance squad for vice presidential candidate Sarah Palin. The competition yielded hundreds of amateur dancers doing back flips and line dances for their favorite candidate. Noting the popularity of the dance mob movement and the talented dancers involved, Jon M. Chu, the director of Hollywood dance films such as *Step Up 2* and *Step Up 3D*, attempted to organize the rival crews into an "official" dance off.

Besides dance, cranking dat also included creating Obama music mash-ups. The audio software known as "Pro-Tools" allowed amateurs to remix Obama's campaign speeches with the hottest club beats. The result was Obama's message of "hope" and "change" layered over beats by Jay-Z or Lil' Wayne. In fact, one popular strategy during the election was to develop lyrics about Obama to the beat of Lil' Wayne's smash hit "A-Milli." One mix by rapper APT, called "Obama-A-Milli," garnered over 10 million hits on YouTube. Rhyming over instrumental beats downloaded from the Internet, aspiring emcees declared that real gangstas were down with Obama, the Electoral College, and political participation. To emphasize the historical significance of electing a Black president, another trend was to create mixes of Obama speeches with iconic songs from the Civil Rights era. Mixes with Sam Cooke's "A Change Gonna Come" or James Brown's "I'm Black and I'm Proud" provided an oratory link to the past.

CRANKING OBAMA IN SOCIAL CLASS AND RACIAL CONTEXT

In the emerging era of digital democracy, producing and distributing new dances and songs became a novel way to endorse presidential nominees. The phenomenon provides some clues about social class and racial dynamics in social media participation. Although the dance mobs eventually consisted of people of all backgrounds, Black youth possessed an advantage in the creation of this social media fad. The notion of ownership and racial pride proved to be an important motive for logging on and getting involved. The possibility of helping elect the first Black president meant that Black youth were very excited, and willing to use all their creative energies to help "Barack the Vote." For this generation, the "Obama Effect" turned dancing into an historical imperative.

Beyond a basic Internet connection and a computer, this type of social media required few financial resources. Thus, the digital divide did not result in a participation gap during the election. Black youth were able to become active participants because they could draw on the cultural resources of hip-hop culture in order to dance, rap, and remix Obama's campaign. The dances and styles of inner-city Black youth have flowed into the mainstream via rap music since the 1980s. The "Crank Dat" phenomenon amplified this process using social media. New media technology allowed unknown Black kids to start a popular culture fad without the intervention of multinational corporations or record executives. Instead of a top–down defining of tastes, "Crank Dat" provided an example of an organic, multidirectional creation of popular culture. Anyone, rich or poor, could participate by taking the basic beat, adding their own moves, and uploading the results to the Internet.

The user-generated dances generated millions of clicks on YouTube, but isn't dancing and rapping about Obama just entertainment? Not completely. These materials helped make the Obama election seem like a populist social movement, not just a presidential election. Some observers have referred to the ubiquity of Obama's image as "Obama-mania." Supporters weren't just wearing Obama T-shirts; they were dancing, singing, and yelling about the virtues of Obama. The media creations of youth described in this chapter contributed to this movement.

The amazing thing is that social media may affect how people behave in real life. In the 2008 presidential election, YouTube dancing was accompanied by political activism, voter registration rallies, and voter turnout. Youth voters, those under age 30, typically have the lowest rates of turnout. However, in the Obama election, youth turnout was the highest since 1972. Importantly, the numbers indicate that the Black and white youth vote provided the margin of victory for the Obama campaign. Obama lost to John McCain by large margins among the majority of white voters, white men, and white women. It was only the white "Obama Youth" subgroup, those 18 to 29 years of age, who actually supported Obama in majority numbers. It is difficult to know if the songs and dancing caused youth to turnout in record numbers. At minimum, we can say that Black youth were part of the digital and real change that took place during the election.

NOTES

1. These estimates are based on average 2,400 bits-per-second dial-up modem access to early Internet providers like CompuServe and America Online. Today, access speeds are typically measured in millions of bits-per-second (mbps). Thus, high-speed broadband refers to 1 mbps access or faster.

2. Step-by-step tutorials for these dances can found on YouTube.

IT'S YOUR TURN: WHAT DO YOU THINK? WHAT WILL YOU FIND?

1. The social media participation of Black youth during the Obama campaign relied heavily on hip-hop music and dance. Do you believe that hip-hop is "political"? Why or why not? Locate other examples of rap songs or videos that relate to civic engagement.

2. I've described several positive uses of social media. Can you think of any negative consequences of social media technology? If you wanted to teach young people how to use social media in a responsible manner, what would you tell them?

3. One of the main arguments of this chapter is that dancing and singing can blur the line between entertainment and political activity. Do you agree? What other examples of this trend can be found in the news media or on television?

4. The digital divide can make economic and political participation difficult for lower income people who are less likely to have a dedicated broadband connection at home. Besides accessing the Internet from a home computer, where else can people go online? How might that affect their knowledge of, interest in, and ability to participate in the type of political activity described here?

REFERENCES

Blank, R. M., & Strickling, L. E. (2010). *Exploring the digital nation: Home broadband Internet adoption in the United States*. Washington, DC: U.S. Department of Commerce. Retrieved December 2, 2010, from http://www.esa.doc.gov/DN/

Hargittai, E., & Walejko, G. (2008). The participation divide: Content creation and sharing in the digital age. *Information, Communication & Society, 11(2)*, 239–256.

Jenkins, H., Clinton, K., Purushotma, R., Robison, A. J., & Weigel, M. (2009). *Confronting the Challenges of Participatory Culture: Media Education for the 21st Century*. Massachusetts Institute of Technology Press: The John D. and Catherine T. MacArthur Foundation Reports on Digital Media and Learning. Retrieved September 25, 2011, from http://digitallearning.macfound.org/atf/cf/%7B7E45C7E0-A3E0-4B89-AC9C-E807E1B0AE4E%7D/JENKINS_WHITE_PAPER.PDF

Kress, T. M. (2008). In the shadow of whiteness: (Re)Exploring connections between history, enacted culture, and identity in a digital divide initiative. *Cultural Studies of Science Education, 4(1)*, 41–49.

4.3 HOW COLLEGE STUDENTS DISPLAY ETHNIC IDENTITY ON FACEBOOK

Sitthivorada Boupha,[1] *Ashley D. Grisso, John Morris, Lynne M. Webb, and Monica Zakeri*

The authors conducted a content analysis of a national sample of college students' open Facebook home pages to discover how they enacted ethnic identities via Facebook.

Mead (1934) posited that the self could only be created through interaction with others. He viewed the interplay between self and society as dynamic, with both the self and society mutually influencing one another. Goffman (1959) applied Shakespeare's notion that "all the world is a stage" to everyday social life, extending the drama metaphor to view interactants as performers, audience members, and outsiders. For Mead and Goffman, the self is created and enacted via conversation in face-to-face interpersonal interactions. Today, interpersonal communication often takes place through computer-mediated communication, often via social networking sites such as Facebook. Given that identity construction is enhanced when self-presentation is conducted publicly (Kelly & Rodriguez, 2006), and in non-anonymous relationships (Zhao, 2008), users can construct the presentation of self and communicate their identities online. We extend Mead's and Goffman's concepts of self and self-presentation to examine college students' presentations of ethnic identity on Facebook.

Ethnicity is a social-constructed phenomenon—learned, enacted, and brought into being via the exchange of messages. Studying messages can reveal normative communication practices in a given interaction context, such as Facebook, including the enactment of ethnic identity.

Stephens (2007) described *social networking* as interactions that allow people to share themselves with others. College students, often away from home for the first time, form social networks for many reasons, including finding a sense of connectedness or belonging in the college community. Many of the interactions in college networks take place face-to-face. However, Walther et al. (2008) noted, "Even when previously unacquainted individuals meet offline at college, they check the other's Facebook profile to learn more about that person and whether there are any common friends or experiences" (p. 31).

Facebook is the most popular social networking Web site among U.S. university students. The site provides uniformity across users' home pages; users are prompted to provide demographic information, including gender, birthday, hometown, as well as political and religious beliefs. Choices are made from drop-down menus (e.g., gender) or open fields (e.g., hometown). No obvious opportunities to indicate race or ethnicity appear under the information tab. Therefore, if users wish to indicate ethnicity, they must do so in an open field or in venues beyond the information page.

Previous research on Facebook has examined various issues from gender differences in Facebook behaviors (Taraszow, Aristodemou, Shitta, Laouris, & Arsoy, 2010) to the ritualized use of Facebook (Debatin, Lovejoy, Horn, & Hughes, 2009) to the narrative potential of status updates (Page, 2010). However, we located only three previously published research reports examining issues of ethnicity related to Facebook (DeAndrea, Shaw, & Levine, 2010; Grasmuck,

Martin, & Zhao, 2009; Wasike & Cook, 2010); these authors do not discuss college students' displays of ethnic identity on Facebook. The purpose of our study was to examine how college students display ethnic identity on Facebook. To this end, we posed two research questions:

RQ1. To what extent, if any, do college students display ethnicity on Facebook?

RQ2. What Facebook venues, if any, do college students use to display ethnic identity?

DATA COLLECTION AND CODING

Given that Facebook users who wish to indicate ethnicity must do so in an open field or in areas beyond the information page, we initially examined Facebook home pages to discover where users displayed ethnicity. Our three coders each independently examined all sections and tabs among five randomly selected home pages of college students in a national sample ($N = 15$). The coders detected evidence of ethnicity in the following venues: about me, applications, groups, interests, name representation, pages, quotes, status, and wall postings. As a second pre-test, each coder independently searched for ethnicity displays in 10 additional randomly selected home pages ($N = 30$). The coders met and discussed their findings, resulting in the inclusion of only the five following venues: (a) applications, (b) groups, (c) interests, (d) quotes, and (e) wall postings.

We found no or very limited evidence of ethnic displays in additional venues, such as notes, status updates, and pages the users liked. Of course, such venues may contain ethnic displays from time to time, but not in great enough numbers to emerge at least twice among our random selection of 45 college students' open home pages. Furthermore, we acknowledge that we did not examine pictures. We were interested in examining ethnicity as a socially constructed phenomenon. In contrast, considering pictures presumes ethnicity is biological or genetically based. We also elected not to examine musical preferences, reasoning that music typically has mass appeal beyond any one ethnic group, especially among college students. For example, many college students who identify as European Americans enjoy rap and salsa music.

We coded information from the previously identified five venues. *Applications* included software programs listed as applications on the home page. *Groups* were memberships in Facebook groups. *Interests* and *Quotes* were collected from the "info" tab. Users can post comments on the "wall" of other Facebook "friends." The three most recent postings on the home pages' walls by a user other than the owner of the home page were analyzed as *wall postings*. For each home page and each venue, the coders simply counted the number of displays as well as noted the exact text (e.g., a group titled "Token Black People at [X University]")[2].

We sampled 50 college networks on Facebook by randomly selecting .001% of users' open home pages on 50 campus networks, one network for each U.S. state, yielding a sample of 488 home pages. We sampled the Facebook home pages of users, hereafter called simply pages, who held membership in a college network, either as an undergraduate, graduate, or alumni who graduated within the last 10 years. Although we collected data from all 50 states using random sampling, we collected data only from college students and recent alumni *with open pages*. Thus, our results may not be typical of all college students.

To pilot test our procedures, we coded 60 pages (20 per coder) randomly selected from the research sample and found no flaws in our data collection system. Then, three coders (two males and one female, all MA students in Communication) individually counted the displays of ethnicity on each page for one third of the research sample. All data were collected within a 2-week period in the Fall of 2008. To assess inter-coder reliability, each coder recoded a randomly selected 10% of another coders' previously coded pages; intercoder agreement was 94%.

WHAT WE FOUND

As described above, only five Facebook venues emerged as sites of ethnic displays in at least two student pages from our randomly selected sample of 45 pages. Our content analysis examined only these five venues across the 488 pages in our research sample.

RQ1: To What Extent, If Any, Do College Students Display Ethnicity on Facebook?

We coded 511 displays of ethnicity across the 488 sampled pages. The number of displays per page ranged from 0 to 23, with a mean of 0.84 ($SD = 2.50$). Only 142 (29.10% of the total sample) pages contained ethnic displays. Among these 142 pages, the number of displays ranged from 1 to 23, with a mean of 3.60 ($SD = 3.95$). The frequency distribution of the 142 pages subsample revealed that most pages contained only a few displays, as 80.28% ($n = 114$) of the pages contained only one, two, or three displays. The remaining pages ($n = 28$; 19.72%) contained multiple displays (4–23). Only a very few pages ($n = 8$; 5.63%) contained a great many displays (11–23).

RQ 2: What Facebook Venues, If Any, Do College Students Use to Display Ethnic Identity?

The analysis revealed that, among the five examined venues, the most frequently employed venues for displaying ethnicity were in ascending order *wall postings* ($M = 00.06$, $SD = 0.34$), *quotations* ($M = 0.08$, $SD = 0.44$), *interests* ($M = 0.09$, $SD = 0.55$), *applications* ($M = 0.15$, $SD = 0.79$), and *groups* ($M = 0.46$, $SD = 1.83$). Across the five venues, the number of displays in individual venues ranged from 0 to 23. Table 1 provides a telescoped view of the findings by

TABLE 1   Displays of Ethnic Identity per Venue among Pages Containing Displays ($n = 142$)

	NUMBER OF PAGES	NUMBER OF DISPLAYS	MEAN	SD	RANGE
Wall Postings	13	31	0.22	0.61	0–3
Quotations	25	39	0.27	0.78	0–6
Interests	20	42	0.30	0.99	0–7
Applications	31	76	0.53	1.40	0–11
Groups	79	224	1.58	3.13	0–23
Total across Subsample	142	411	3.60	3.95	1–23

displaying the data for the subsample of 142 pages that contained at least one display of ethnic identity. Findings from each venue are discussed below in detail.

Groups.   We identified groups ($N = 227$) of the following self-described ethnicities: Black ($n = 69$), Caucasian ($n = 64$), Asian ($n = 48$), Middle Eastern ($n = 16$), Hispanic ($n = 8$), and others ($n = 22$). Many groups were defined via explicit language, such as "*I'm Black (Facebook Global Group)*," "*White people,*" "*tha real N.I.G.G.A.S. of tha U.S.,*" and "*The light skin nation.*" However, others employed more subtle representations, such as "*being black is a blessing,*" "*Dora the Explorer is so an Illegal Immigrant...,*" and "*the* [sic] *National Asian-American Association Program.*"

Applications.   The venue with the second highest number of ethnic displays was applications ($N = 76$). The most frequently used application, Bumper Stickers ($n = 48$), often displayed a combination of a pictures and words, typically intended to be humorous (e.g., "*I'm Asian, be jealous*" and "*I wasn't sleeping, I'm Asian,*" accompanied by pictures depicting the pun). Other applications employed to display ethnic identity included Chinese Astrology, My Heritage ("Italian American"), Quizzes ("You Are a Canadian"), Flair ("WARNING! Latinas make better lovers"), and Super Wall ("Chinese new year").

Unlike groups and applications that may be created by another user and that additional users simply join, messages containing ethnic displays on the remaining three venues (interests, quotes, and wall postings) were original and unique to each user. The latter three venues are discussed below in descending order of frequency in our sample.

Interests included quite diverse displays, such as "Canadian Pride," "European Culture," "Hispanic Culture," "Italy," "Germany," "Thai food," and "Kung Fu." Some pages contained personal information under interests, such as "Chennai, India (hometown)." Other items referenced ethnic media, such as "Anime," an animation originating in Japan; sometimes such items were listed in isolation, but other times in combination, such as "Anime, Manga, Anime Club, Okami Japanese." Finally, a few users elected to employ complex lists of ethnic interests, such as "New Zealand; French electronic scene; Deutsche Fußball-Bund, India," and "*Fútbol (just to watch), la tele, Corona, Dos Equis, chicas, Mexico, España.*"

Quotations included "לארשי תא בהוא ינא!" [Israel!]," "Viva la revolution! [Long live the Revolution!]," and "La belleza esta en los ojos del observador [Beauty is in the eyes of the beholder]," as well as confusing quotations such as "I was just thinking about Japanese things … like my boyfriend in 8th Grade. He was Ukrainian." However, most pages containing ethnic displays in the quotations venue employed straightforward messages about ethnicity: "Nigga b 4 real," "Italian Unite or those who love anything about Italians," "hot ass squinty jew boy," and "Everyone ♥'s an Asian Boy."

Finally, *wall postings* are posts left by friends. Users can easily delete such text; however, if users allow comments to remain on their pages, we reasoned they find the comments a desirable addition to the page. Ethnic displays on wall posts included long rambling statements, such as "*I think it would fall more along the lines of german occupation on france. Still have a few kinks to work out. But you can be the namby pamby french guy, and ill be the cold blooded german guy, and we live in Russia. I swear, this is comedic gold my friend*" as well as short sentences such as "*Happy birthday da machi . . . .*", "*chinaaa ingrataaaa*", and "*Mah nigga . . . u work 2day?!*" A few posts were literally unreadable to the coders, such as this post in Korean, "다들 반가운 얼굴이오~ㅋㅋㅋ," and this one in German, "Hey honey! Scho was vor des weekend? Ich hab wahrscheinlich sturmfrei! Also könnten wir bei mir was machen!"

WHAT DOES IT ALL MEAN?

Our results document three important ways that Facebook serves as a viable means for college students to display ethnic identity: (a) Although Facebook clearly offers no designated or intended venue for users to display ethnic identity, nonetheless college student users employ a variety of Facebook venues to display ethnicity. (b) Users from numerous ethnic backgrounds display ethnic identity via Facebook venues—so the venues must be "workable" for displaying ethnic identity. (c) The venues provide rhetorical tools and communication channels to create messages diverse in both form and content that communicate ethnic identities.

We did not include pictures or music as potential venues of ethnic displays. However, among the remaining possibilities, we discovered that college students use primarily five specific Facebook venues to display ethnicity: groups, applications, interests, quotations, and wall postings. Of these, three typically involve adopting displays created by others (groups, applications, quotations). The other options involve using displays created by friends (wall postings) or self-created to develop original enactment of identity (interests).

Given the participatory nature of social networking, users may be helping others display their ethnic identities via the creation and display of applications, groups, and quotations. These three venues offer opportunities for additional users to enact ethnic identity simply by re-displaying an ethnic display previously created by another. For example, if Anna creates a Flair button that says "Latina woman are hot!" that button becomes available to other Facebook users. Thus, simply by creating the button to display on her own page, Anna helps other Latinas enact ethnic identity by displaying the same button. Expanding on Goffman's premise of presenting the self in everyday life and Mead's theory of the self and society, Facebook users may influence their Facebook networks via displays of ethnic identity, and in turn influence both their sense of self and others' notions of self.

Several of the sampled pages displayed ethnic identity by calling forth ethnic stereotypes, such as using African American dialect in a quotation. Observers may interpret such open displays of stereotypic behaviors as the page creators "owning" the stereotype and claiming stereotypic ethnic behaviors as part of their self-identity.

Among the pages containing ethnic displays, most contained only a few (1–3), and very few pages (under 6%) contained a great many displays. Perhaps ethnicity is a small part of many users' identity but a larger part of just a few users' identity. Future research examining additional social networking Web sites may provide further insights into how users employ pages as sites of casual or concentrated enactment of ethnic identity. As we continue to examine sites that allow users to establish, change, and maintain displays of ethnic identity, we will understand more about the presentation of self, including ethnic identity, and the means by which the self can be constructed and enacted online.

NOTES

1. The authors acknowledge equal contribution to this research project. For a more detailed description of the study's methodology, contact Lynne M. Webb at LynneWebb320@cs.com.

2. Our codes followed these procedures: A zero represented no displays of ethnicity in a venue. An ethnic display was represented by a 1 and a notation of the text itself was recorded (e.g., a group titled "Token Black People

at [X University]"). If text was unavailable for some data points (e.g., a Bumper Stickers application image without text), a description of the image was recorded. For each additional display per user, we added one; scores in indi-

vidual venues ranged from 0 to 23. The coders entered data into an Excel spreadsheet, recording both the quantitative value and the qualitative responses (i.e., exact text or description of images on the page).

IT'S YOUR TURN: WHAT DO YOU THINK? WHAT WILL YOU FIND?

1. Facebook does not prompt new users to display ethnicity as they do biological sex, religion, and politics. Does this lack of attention to ethnicity depict Facebook as nondiscriminatory, conflict-adverse, clueless, attempting to develop software with mass appeal, and/or viewing ethnicity as unimportant to Facebook "friendships"?

2. Given that a Facebook page represents both a presentation of public self and a display of private identity, list three reasons why a college student may elect to display ethic identity "in a big way" as well as three reasons why a student may elect *not* to do so.

3. Examine your friends' Facebook pages. Look at every fifth page from your friends list, until you have examined at least 10 pages. In what venues do your friends display ethnicity? Can you find some venues that we did not find in our research? Consistent with our sample, do about one third of your friends' pages contain at least one display of ethnic identity? If not, what do you think this says about your friendship group, given that they are above or below our sample's average in the extent of displays of ethnic identity?

REFERENCES

DeAndrea, D. C., Shaw, A. S., & Levine, T. R. (2010). Online language: The role of culture in self-expression and self-construal on Facebook. *Journal of Language and Social Psychology, 29,* 425–442.

Debatin, B., Lovejoy, J. P., Horn, A. K., & Hughes, B. N. (2009). Facebook and online privacy: Attitudes, behaviors, and unintended consequences. *Journal of Computer-Mediated Communication, 15,* 83–108.

Goffman, E. (1959). *Presentation of self in everyday life.* New York: Anchor.

Grasmuck, S., Martin, J., & Zhao, S. (2009). Ethno-racial identity displays on Facebook. *Journal of Computer-Mediated Communication, 15,* 158–188.

Kelly, A. E., & Rodriguez, R. R. (2006). Publicly committing oneself to an identity. *Basic and Applied Social Psychology, 28,* 185–191.

Mead, G. H. (1934). 1927 class lectures in social psychology. In D. L. Miller (Ed.), *The Individual and Social Self* (pp. 106–175). Chicago: University of Chicago Press.

Page, R. (2010). Re-examining narrativity: Small stories in status updates. *Text & Talk, 30,* 423–444.

Stephens, K. K. (2007). The successive use of information and communication technologies at work. *Communication Theory, 17,* 486–507.

Taraszow, T., Aristodemou, E., Shitta, G., Laouris, Y., & Arsoy, A. (2010). Disclosure of personal and contact information by young people in social networking sites: An analysis using Facebook profiles as an example. *International Journal of Media and Cultural Politics, 6,* 81–102.

Walther, J. B., Van der Heide, B., Kim, S. Y., Westerman, D., & Tong, S. T. (2008). The role of friends' appearance and behavior on evaluations of individuals on Facebook: Are we known by the company we keep? *Human Communication Research, 34,* 28–49.

Wasike, B., & Cook, J. A. (2010). Hispanic students and social networking. *Web Journal of Mass Communication, 25,* 1.

Zhao, S. (2008). Identity construction of Facebook: Digital empowerment in anchored relationships. *Computers in Human Behavior, 24,* 1816–1836.

4.4   "WALKING IN THE CITY" IN AN AGE OF MOBILE TECHNOLOGIES

Robert Mejia

The author contends that mobile technologies can reconfigure our experience of public places, and can be used to "purify" public places of "undesirable" elements. This reading discusses movement as a productive practice, explores the historical relationship between technology and mobility, provides a theory of mobile practices, and considers the implications of mobile technologies for experiences of race, class, and gender.

Chicago is a fascinating mixture of people and institutions: hot dog stands, street performers, state of the art museums, tourists, posh hotels, business elite, and more. I have visited many of these places and bumped shoulders with a wide array of people. But, I have never actually *met* anyone in the city, nor have I wanted to do so. Sure, I remember the face of the attractive bookstore employee and have had polite conversations with museum staff regarding their collection, but these were all understood as byproducts of the primary experience: I went to the museum to see the collection; I went to the bookstore to look at the books. One day was different, however. I brought my Nintendo DS, and found myself eager to meet someone.

My experience is not unique: mobile information and communication technologies (mICTs), such as cell phones, global positioning devices, and mobile video game systems, have become increasingly important means of navigating contemporary society. Indeed, it is not uncommon to feel naked or lost upon leaving one's home without such a device. This dependency is not abnormal; for even those who have not yet bought into the system, the pressure to do so is immense. As modern society increasingly demands consistent access to communication networks for everyday functioning, the cost of being offline, even temporarily, rises (Horrigan, 2009).

Increasing mICT access in and of itself, however, is not necessarily the solution, because doing so ignores the problem of how mICTs function to reconfigure our experience of reality itself. As Lev Manovich (2001) warns, ICTs work to configure a particular relation to the everyday, and ask us, the user, "to mistake the structure of somebody's else [experience] for our own" (p. 61).[1] As more of our communication takes place via ICTs, we find that what was once thought to be a supplemental communication device becomes the primary point of engagement. To the extent that this is true, then at least a portion of our communication is structured by an (online) environment in which we cannot be present; we can only engage with an interface, which then communicates with others on our behalf.

RHETORICS OF SPACE

Movement is a means of arranging a social reality, insofar as choosing to walk down one path as opposed to another adds both a content and a form to that choice which would not have existed otherwise. Some of the most recognizable city spaces, such as the Magnificent Mile in Chicago, are given their significance precisely because of the masses that occupy these places. Because movement matters, modes of governance have coalesced around its regulation; movement can disrupt social norms, thereby causing panic in others who occupy that given space. That said, the management of movement is not a neutral phenomenon, but rather resonates with questions of power.

To understand how power is intrinsic within movement, I distinguish between four theoretical concepts: place and space; strategies and tactics. Place and space mark distinctions between the stability and instability of a given area. *Place* refers to the established formation of a particular area. This spatial arrangement has the backing of a combination of tradition, legality, and mere presence that grant it the status of the normal (de Certeau, 1984/1988). Places function to create and shape subjects who enter their terrain. The university is one such locale in that an assortment of individuals, upon entering the campus, are divvied up into teachers and students (and others), with their own corresponding sets of functions, according to each individual's proximity to the legitimating institutions that uphold this particular field. *Space* refers to the practices that exist within a given place that work to create, shape, modify, and/or destroy that particular spatial reality (de Certeau, 1984/1988). Places come into existence only to the extent that they are practiced (i.e., spaces); but in order to retain the status of the normal, this fact of creation must be suppressed. Should this secret be acknowledged, the sanctity of the place would be undermined by the possibility of equally legitimate alternative spatial practices.

To ensure the continuation of a particular mode of spatial arrangement, the underwriting institution and/or individual "with will and power" has at their disposal an array of resources, such as money (de Certeau, 1984/1988, pp. 35-36). The deployment of these resources constitutes *strategies* that by either incentive or threat compel individuals within a place to behave in a particular fashion. Tactics, in contrast, are further removed from such resources. As such, *tactics* do not create places, but rather work to exploit existing spatial structures in order to create contingent, livable spaces (de Certeau, 1984/1988, p. xix).

This difference in function is not a matter of chance—strategies are not sexier than tactics and therefore more intimate with power, and if only power would give tactics a chance it would see he or she has a nice personality. Strategies create place because they possess the resources necessary to automate desires via the implementation of technology. Tactics create space because, lacking such resources, they are dependent upon operating within that selfsame technological environment— thereby necessarily reproducing aspects of the existent system. To better illustrate this point, a brief history of technology and its relationship to walking practices is offered in the following section.

TECHNOLOGY AND WALKING RHETORICS

The advent and adoption of mICTs has marked a historic transformation from a strategy of mobile privatization to that of mobile systemization. The era of mobile privatization began when regular access to mobility, enabled by the automobile and demanded by industrial capital, converged in the 1920s with new communications technologies, such as the telephone and radio, to create a new social unit that was increasingly isolated from its neighbors (Lynd & Lynd, 1929; Williams, 1974/2005). As automobiles and radios became more popular, "not only [did] walking for pleasure become practically extinct, but the occasional event such as a parade on a holiday attract[ed] far less attention" (Lynd & Lynd, 1929, p. 260). Walking ceased to be a social, communal affair, and henceforth became a public and thus, ironically, private practice. Hence, *mobile privatization* is the name given to that period of technology "which served an at-once mobile and home-centered way of living" (Williams, 1974/2005, p. 19).

Walking did not die in the 1920s. Instead, walking practices were reconfigured to adhere to new public interests. The cityscape was transformed with new technologies meant to govern mobile practices: signage designating proper walkways (e.g., crosswalks), movements (e.g., speed limits), and impasses (e.g., stoplights). People continued to walk; however, some practices, such as cutting across a street, became "illegitimate acts" within the established walking regime. The shift in walking practices was not to be found in whether people cut across lawns and/or streets on their way to an event, but rather with what incentive and authority they now did so.

The change brought about by mobile privatization is that a new notion of public space has forced older mobile practices to rely on tactics, as opposed to strategies, when its desires are not fulfilled by the existing system. This outcome, however, is not necessarily to be mourned. Nostalgia for the "America that walked as a community," Lynd and Lynd's (1929) old Middletown, America, must always be tempered by recognition of the illegitimate figures of its own spatial strategies: sundown towns, segregation, and so on.[2] The point of this brief history has not been to necessarily elevate one mode of spatial organization above another, but rather to provide a context in which to understand the new shift in mobility coalescing around the mass adoption of mICTs.

TOWARD A THEORY OF MOBILE SYSTEMIZATION

Mobile gadgets have long been considered masturbatory devices due to what is believed to be their exclusionary functions (Gunn & Hall, 2008). The advent of mICTs complicates this picture, however, as these devices are increasingly meant to be used in conjunction with the existing spatial arrangement. Unlike the iPod and earlier Sony Walkman that were meant to move the user from an undesirable place (e.g., crowded bus) to a preconfigured, exclusive, pleasurable space (e.g., the playlist), mICTs are increasingly meant to engage with the present spatial arrangement (e.g., Google Maps). For spatiality to become the object of ICT engagement, however, it must be capable of being subjected to numerical representation; and that which can be converted into digital code is that which can be programmed (Manovich, 2001).

Making space programmable allows for the implementation of a new set of spatial strategies. In this new regime, what I call mobile systemization, mICT users and non-users alike are converted into *avatars* so that they can become present in virtual space. People are transformed into avatars precisely because the conversion of physical place into programmable space makes life increasingly unlivable without ICTs. For instance, as more of our everyday experience occurs in virtual space, as opposed to physical place, many of us have become familiar with creating user profiles for social networking Web sites. These profiles are not innocent traces of our offline self, but rather carefully crafted avatars created for the sole purpose of facilitating online social engagement. In this regard, avatars differ from other representational figures, such as the signature, in that they are utilized to move through space rather than merely mark one's prior presence. The question then remains, what does it mean that the avatar is increasingly becoming necessary for navigating everyday place and space?

The existence of the avatar is contingent upon the acceptance of digitization by the user. In order for an avatar to be used, the user must accept the basic premise that the use of another body (i.e., the avatar) is capable of fulfilling one's desire. As more of our livelihood appears to be dependent upon ICT engagement, avatars become a convenient means by which to manage our simultaneous movement through multiple social spaces: need help keeping in touch with friends? Make a Facebook profile. Having trouble finding a date? Set up an eHarmony account. Maintain business contacts?

LinkedIn is for you. These Web accounts function as avatars in that they operate as a primary point of engagement for the user. Consistent access to these and other avatars has become such a compelling force, in and of itself, that movement through mICT dead-zones is actively avoided. The avatar has become necessary for maintaining one's presence within an increasingly virtual society.

The problem, however, is that all too often it is assumed that the Web account is a reflection of an authentic user who stands behind the technology. In actuality, the avatar works to open up the user to mathematical manipulation. As Lev Manovich (2001) argues, the new media object, in this case the user, "*becomes programmable*" ([Italics in original] p. 27). mICTs convert the user into numerical code for the sake of representing the user in virtual space; and since this space is programmable, so too is the user's movement transformed according to the logic of the mathematical code. *Mobile systemization*, hence, refers to the conversion of individuals into avatars for the sake of making movement programmable.

MOBILE SYSTEMIZATION AND EXPERIENCES OF RACE, CLASS, AND GENDER

The avatar became a part of mobile systemization at that moment in which the ideal city begun to transition from being an industrial and administrative center (e.g., Old Detroit) to a technological center driven by finance capital, tourism, and gentrification (e.g., Contemporary Chicago) (see McCarthy, 2011). Mobile systemization facilitates this transformation in that it serves an at-once fragmented and evermore interdependent way of living. Participation within mobile systemization promises to create a spatial arrangement in which anything one could need is already carefully mapped out for one's enjoyment. Being connected, however, is not merely a one-way street of data flow, from environment to user, but simultaneously converts the user into a source of information as well. It is the effects of this conversion upon notions of class, gender, and race that I now turn my attention: the automation of social presence and the historical flattening of identity.

Digitization results in the creation of an avatar that comes to stand in for and speak on behalf of the user. Here, presence becomes automated because upon creation of a virtual self, the avatar is invested with the authority to operate apart from the user, as if it were the user. The Facebook profile, for instance, maintains an online presence regardless of user intervention and transforms the nature of all subsequent communication. This is amplified in terms of mobile practices, in that mICTs are capable of converting physical place into digital space as one walks through an environment. To the extent that online spaces are coded with cultural logics (boyd, Forthcoming), the mobilization of these virtual environments makes it possible to radically reconfigure the city to allow for users to ignore undesirable subjects. This demand is already being requested as a Google Search for "avoid ghetto" paired with "Google Maps" reveals 49,800 results; search for "avoid ghetto" without the quotes, and 15 of the top 20 are requests for GPS implementation of that function. In essence, mICTs convert populations into avatars for the sake of managing one's movement through space; and if my mICT does not recognize your avatar or designates it as undesirable, then you are to be avoided.

Another effect of mobile systemization is that identity itself may no longer have any purchase in the conventional sense. If the avatar is linked to the possession of particular mICTs and/ or software, then the digitized self functions as a commodity to be exchanged for social capital. This is because the avatar is a digital thing that is not bound to conventional human constraints, and hence can be (theoretically) manipulated to take on any shape or form. Black, brown, white, male, female, intersex, and so on, all elements of identity are open to manipulation and/or transgression in digital space: you can be whomever or whatever you want to be. Yet, as noted earlier, there just remains the pesky little problem of the physical body that is left behind. This is the raced, classed, and gendered body, which is marked as a threat to be avoided.

Because our primary point of engagement is increasingly that of the avatar, the body that is left behind is reduced in its authority to speak legitimately from its lived experience. When all identity is merely that of an aesthetic choice, then the answer to experiences of racism, classism, or sexism is to just "be something else." This is what Cameron McCarthy (2011) means when he writes that culture has been reduced to an aesthetic experience. The strategy of mobile systemization is to purify space by separating desirable subjects from undesirable ones. When identity becomes an aesthetic preference, rather than a historical construction, then discrimination becomes the fault of the one who is different; they should just choose a different avatar.

BE YOURSELF, BE YOUR AVATAR

The appeal of mobile systemization is that it promises a framework for maintaining an ever greater presence within the world. Relationships, travel plans, finances, everything can more easily be maintained through participation within online space. Thanks to the ability for ICTs to become mICTs, that system can now be carried with us wherever we may go. As appealing as this system may be, however, the cost of online participation is that of sacrificing the self for that of the avatar. We may stand behind the screen, thinking we are commanding the screen, but increasingly the screen is commanding us; participation requires that *we* adhere to its rules and regulations, not the other way around. One such rule is that identity is erased from that of a historical thing toward that of an aesthetic preference.

The implications of this shift for walking practices are that place is increasingly becoming programmable. It may soon no longer be enough to maintain a physical presence in a particular place, but also possess the corresponding avatar to remain recognizable. mICTs, which promise to grant us ever greater social presence, may also be the means to enact an ever more rigid form of social exclusion; but when identity via the avatar becomes a matter of aesthetic preference, then such discrimination will also remain just that—a matter of taste. As I walked through the city of Chicago (at the beginning of this reading), my aesthetic preference was only for those who owned the very same game I was playing. To the extent that taste is a cultural construct, marked by a history of race, gender, and class, my aesthetic preference foreclosed the possibility of meeting a vast array of social subjects. As I write, this concern may seem relatively innocent; but tomorrow, when the city is reconfigured along the lines of Facebook, LinkedIn, MySpace, eHarmony, etc., such choices will no longer be so benign.

NOTES

1. I use "mICT" to speak only of mobile information and communication technologies, and instead use the more general ICT when I am speaking of the larger mobile and non-mobile infrastructure.

2. Sundown towns are cities with explicit policies that prohibit people of color from living within it. While the city of Lynd and Lynd's study, Muncie, Indiana, was not a sundown town, the practice was widespread in Indiana, and representative of the heartland more generally (Loewen, 2005).

IT'S YOUR TURN: WHAT DO YOU THINK? WHAT WILL YOU FIND?

1. In what ways have mICTs (cell phone, GPS, or mobile video game system) changed how you move through your everyday spaces? For instance, how is your daily walk to class different or similar when you are on your cell phone?

2. How does the participation in a particular social networking site or ownership of a certain mICT affect your identity? Do you use MySpace, Facebook, or other social networking site? How are your conversations different across those particular sites? How are online conversations different or similar to your offline conversations?

3. How would you communicate with others if you could not use ICTs, mobile or otherwise? For instance, if your cell phone broke, would you drive to a friend's house to see if he or she wanted to hang out?

4. How many friends do you have who do *not* have access to ICTs or mICTs? How does this affect your ability, and even your willingness, to communicate with them? What might this tell you about social class in our society?

REFERENCES

boyd, d. (Forthcoming). White flight in networked publics? How race and class shaped American teen engagement with Myspace and Facebook. In L. Nakamura & P. Chow-White (Eds.), *Digital race anthology*. New York: Routledge.

de Certeau, M. (1984/1988). *The practice of everyday life*. Berkeley: University of California.

Gunn, J., & Hall, M. M. (2008). Stick it in your ear: The psychodynamics of iPod enjoyment. *Communication and Critical/Cultural Studies, 5*(2), 135–157.

Horrigan, J. B. (2009). *The mobile difference*. Washington, DC: Pew Research Center.

Loewen, J. W. (2005). *Sundown towns: A hidden dimension of American racism*. New York: The New Press.

Lynd, R. S., & Lynd, H. M. (1929). *Middletown: A study in American culture*. New York: Harcourt, Brace, and Company.

Manovich, L. (2001). *The language of new media*. Cambridge, MA: MIT Press.

McCarthy, C. (2011). Reconstructing race and education in the class conquest of the city and the university in the era of neoliberalism and globalization. In C. McCarthy, H. Greenhalgh-Spencer & R. Mejia (Eds.), *New times: making sense of critical/cultural theory in a digital age* (pp. 86–103). New York: Peter Lang.

Williams, R. (1974/2005). *Television: Technology and cultural form*. New York: Routledge.

4.5   BECOMING MODULAR: THE (RE-)ASSEMBLED QUEER "MALE" BODY AND ITS DIGITALLY ENABLED SEXUAL ECONOMY

Diego Costa

> *The author argues that heterosexual desire has always been embedded in the fabric of everyday life; that everyday life (from the architecture of a city to the language of a people) is precisely what guarantees the constant rearticulation of heterosexual desire and the ideologies that undergird it. The very world around us has been set up in a way that enables, and encourages, straight people to meet, greet, and possibly engage in romantic and/or sexual experiences. But what about queers?*

In everyday life, there is a sense that a man and a woman's chance encounter (at work, at the bank, at church, at a club) that leads to dating, marriage, or a one-night stand is a "natural" part of life, if not its main purpose. But what about subjects whose desire do not coincide perfectly with the heterosexual mandate (that men must desire women and women alone, and vice-versa)? What about those whom we have come to call gays, lesbians, bisexuals, transsexuals, et al? What about queers? Unable to take the same smooth roads toward a heterosexually tailored sense of future, even if sharing similar goals, what other pathways might queers create in order to make sense of "the world"?

VOCAB

In order to help you with the jargon inevitable in academic texts, here is a brief description of key terms you will encounter. They will help you gain the kind of basic literacy in Queer Theory and psychoanalytical theory that help shape this essay:

Subject: a helpful stand-in for "man" or "woman" that works to speak of humans without necessarily gendering them.

Queer/Queerable/Queering: one of the fundamental concepts of Queer Theory is that the gay-straight binary is a heterosexist fiction that we are better off not rearticulating. Since it is unproductive and homogenizing, even if convenient, to think of all people who do not identify as straight as "gay," I will use the term **queer** when speaking of the subjects I take on in the essay (men who have, or fantasize about, having sex with men utilizing new media technologies as a mediator). In a sense, all men are **queerable**, considering their only sanctioned option has been the non-option of compulsory heterosexuality. With the Internet, new kinds of sexual objects, practices, fantasies, and subjects become available, which also make possible the **queering** of men who were previously just queerable— and can now be, with the help of digital technology, queer (if not in identity, at least, in practice).

Desire: borrowing from the symbolic language of psychoanalysis, I use desire to mean the basic psychic structure of the subject that drives them toward certain objects (of desire). A queer object, for example, would be one that escapes the clear-cut dictatorship of heterosexist relations such as "men desire women" and "women desire men," which turns the subject into a function, stripping her/him of a desire that is her/his own.

WHAT ABOUT QUEERS?

Until the 1990s, with the popularization of the Internet in a great part of the developed and developing world, the history of queer sex and romance was a history of psychological and physical struggle. In several contexts, even to this day, including in certain areas in the United States, it still is. The very naturalized fabric of life that provides and promotes a mold and a narrative for heterosexual sex works as a policing roadblock for all other desires that do not qualify as legitimate, or 100% straight. Those who managed to be conscious of their queer desires, once in a while or consistently, had to either repress them, channel them elsewhere, or pursue sex partners in a clandestine way, risking their well-being. We, of course, found ways of making contact with one another: for sexual pleasure for exchange of knowledge, and what queer studies scholars call *world-making*. The ways queers managed to find one another, in bars, city squares, parks, public bathrooms, and the like, however, tended to involve a high degree of risk before the Law (both de facto and symbolic), public opinion, harassment, and physical violence from strangers serving as soldiers of a State bent on suppressing and punishing anything queer. The subjects willing to take the risk posed by all of these agents of repression (fleshly and internalized ones) in order to find partners had to, necessarily, put their own *bodies* on the line.

The advent of the Internet, however, made it possible for (some) queers, for the first time in history, to bypass a lot of the risks posed by public cruising in our quest for love, friendship, sex, a sense of kinship, and other fundamental pleasures. It is important to note that this new prospect for contact was, and remains, often limited to and/or experienced rather unevenly by certain groups of people depending on geographical location, economic status, class, race, and religious background, among other variables. So while we can claim a kind of democratic impossibility for sexual contact to all queer(able) subjects born into a system whose only legitimate desire was heterosexual desire, the ubiquity of the Internet introduces a great divide between those who can, those who can't, and those who are seldom able to make queer sexual contact happen easily. There is a new cost, along with the new possibilities, to turning queer desire into pleasurable experience.

While queers may still engage in what Tim Dean (2009) calls "aimless cruising," carefully, and skillfully, turning public spaces into possible conduit and stage for pleasure, digital technology creates an alternative to that necessary risk-exposure from the pre-Internet days. One is now able to reduce public space as the mere link between two, or more, desiring subjects. Without having to cruise around the city until laying eyes on another subject wandering around the same physical space, queers can create an online network for contact that, provided at least one of the parties has the proper living arrangements, makes it possible for queer sex to happen in the shadow of the surveilling heterosexual gaze. Of course, it is part of the structure of the human psyche to internalize this gaze, in what psychoanalytical theory calls the "superego," but provided the queer subject is able to negotiate with this psychic entity its sexual encounter, the external roadblocks aren't an inextricable part of his narrative anymore.

According to Shaka McGlotten (2001, p. 72), "Once upon a time, bodies in Real Space risked everything for the big time sensualities of queer touch (. . .) Now, in the space of the screens, where possibilities of encounter and sex seem limitless, and where the dangers of infection and exposure to the Law appear minimal, tactility is the first thing to go."

Queers can use Web sites such as *Adam4Adam*, *Manhunt* and *Craigslist* to set up descriptive and photographic profiles of themselves that are perpetually available for browsing, gawking, enticement, consideration, and invitation for a physical sexual encounter. These digital spaces, however, lend themselves to a kind of play that may lead to its own authentic ends, doing away with the physicality of sex altogether—or turning the fleshly contact into a mere supplement of the sexual experience. Both McGlotten (2001) and Dean (2009), among others, have criticized "digital cruising" for the elitism behind the infinitude of potentiality that it seemingly offers to those who can afford it.

This new economy of queer bodies puts forth a queer latency in all bodies, but the degree to which these bodies can advance, and author, the script of their desired encounter varies widely. The copious rhetoric and photographic depictions of fantasies, along with pleas for subjects willing to play a role in them, expose anyone looking (no matter how they may identify to themselves and society at large) to other kinds of sexualities and sexual practices previously unfathomable—or repressed before even being considered. It also allows for the male body to become an "object," in the psychoanalytic sense of the word (an object of someone's desire, and with its own desire). When queer men were cruising in quiet parks in the wee hours, or etching notes on public restroom stall doors, they weren't exactly able to gaze at their object of desire in the way that, for example, women's bodies have been displayed for consumption so prevalently in popular culture (guaranteeing a sexual economy, even if paralyzing them into oppression). This inability to properly look at and (re-) discover one's own object of desire has always been a strategy from the heterosexist regime to make queer pleasure hard to revel in, or to even be considered. By coming out of the darkness of dangerous public cruising places into the potential freedoms of digital intimacy, the male body is able to enjoy its position as a "thing" (a thing to be fashioned by himself and a thing to be offered to the other) and be properly invested as a possible site for desirability. Between the mid-1990s and the early 2000s, the queer(able) male body went from ineffable to obsessively (self-) represented, almost omnipresent. The sexual economy fueling its unstoppable production also drove queer(able) men's bodies from the parallel or underground world of the alleys to digital everyday-ness (or, at least, to the possibility of both): We can construct our bodies, probe the body of others, and schedule to meet them as we cross the street using our mobile devices, as we multitask at the office, shop, or chat with our mothers on Facebook. The sexual economy of queer(able) male bodies today can possibly run together with all other non-queer economies.

But as Dean (2009) would argue, this possibility for a non-paranoid, brightly lit, and easily accessible sexual *happening* is laden with problems regarding difference and alterity. At the same time that cruising sites may do away with some of the property of *chance* in the encounter between strangers (one can list thorough descriptions of the kind of "other" that one wants), digital technology also widens the gap between the haves and have-nots in the realm of sexual experiences—in the flesh and in digitally assisted fantasy.

For Dean, pre-Internet cruising constituted a healthy way for queer men to go about being in the world, as it exposed them to *strangeness* in a way that heterosexual folk may have avoided at all costs. The need to have sexual contact with other bodies—along with a lack of ready-made social routes for sublimation—drove queer men into meeting all sorts of people that they would normally never have crossed paths with, privileging them with the possibility for what psychoanalyst Lucien Israël (1996) calls "transnarcissistic love" (p. 191), an openness to an object previously unaccounted and unimagined by the subject. The potential for a transnarcissistic love is one borne out of the respect of the other as other, including all the surprises and risks that might entail for the subject. This willingness to create contact and hope for an exchange in which nothing guaranteed is, for Dean, a positive (in the '80s, literally positive, with AIDS) aspect of "aimless cruising" because, unlike online cruising, one never knows what one is going to get. One is susceptible to lose control, to lose oneself, in the encounter with the other's strangeness. This openness to what we could call the trauma of the enigma of the other is for psychoanalyst Jean Laplanche (cited by Fletcher, 2002-2003) necessarily linked to "being available to the other who comes to surprise me" (p. 16).

When gays cruise digitally, to Dean's chagrin, they shield themselves from strangeness by filtering out certain kinds of strangers they assume not to desire: it becomes a game of pre-determined exclusion. Digital cruising entails a privatization of public life that Dean finds homogenizes pleasure, limiting its breadth, "even as it may seem to increase its available quantity." (p. 193).

It is common to browse *Craigslist* personal advertisements or the profiles on cruising sites that not only paint a very specific picture of the ideal stranger one would like to meet, but also script in minute detail the sexual acts that are supposed to take place. Anyone who has engaged in e-mail correspondence back and forth with online sex-partners-to-be knows the tendency for a pre-emptive scripting of the sexual encounter. There are directions, rules, suggestions, and cues, much as in a film script or stage directions for a play. One might argue that this is a great accomplishment for queer sexuality: we can now seek, if not actually find, precisely what we would like to get. However, as in the movie business, the scriptwriter is normally not the actor. The actors' lines and context are dictated by the writer. There is clearly a power play at work in both situations. And when it comes to online cruising, the script-writing tends to come from the party who can afford to "host" the sexual act.

This predetermination echoes the dynamics at work in heterosexuality's unquestionable readymade narrative and its history of males as the ones who can afford to script it. In today's queer(able) context, being able to *host* involves a series of privileges that rig the cruising and sexual experiences from the get-go. The host is most likely someone who can afford to live by himself, in a neighborhood that potential partners are willing to visit and in a setup where receiving strangers at home will not pose risks. Of course, there is a cost to hosting, as in being vulnerable to gossip, violence, or robbery. But there are also perks: the host is more likely to decide the duration of the sexual encounter, to stage it based on his previous knowledge of the physical space, and to script it according to his likes and dislikes. As most cruising subjects may not have the ideal situation for hosting the encounter, a willing host is something to prize, which gives him a lot of leverage to turn the *travelling* partner(s) into an instrument for his own fantasy.

If we think about who, in the context of the United States, is more likely to possess the attributes of a host, we quickly realize how this power setup plays out not only in terms of class, but also race. If the host is likely someone living by himself in a safe and convenient neighborhood that guarantees some kind of anonymity, and holds the kind of job that grants him free time to cruise before, after or during work hours, he is more likely to be white.

The ubiquity of digital technology, acquired by some but whose affects are felt by all, brings more than shifts in the social landscape of queer(able) *world-making*. Yes, digital cruising may re-produce elitist practices making actual queer contact less likely than what Dean calls (queer) networking. As queer men flock to Web sites that charge for services, or apps that require expensive gadgets and monthly plans, and as they feel compelled to script sexual practices and partners into fantastic ideals, they lose the kind of "openness to the other without the necessity of having a particular object of seduction," as Dean (2009, p. 195) puts it. Minorities are, evidently, the first to get ruled out (see the common belting out of "no asians!," "whites only, sorry!," and the like in personal ads and profiles), or fetishized, turned into exotic instruments (as in ads that may read "looking for hung black thug tops" or "Where is my Latin Papi?"). This "instrumentalization of the other as an object of use" (Dean, 2009, p. 194), which white privileged men do not completely escape but may have more control over, may help all queer(able) men with an Internet connection to engage in sex practices they may not otherwise—even if in an unbalanced way.

There is much more at stake in this new sexual economy than just the social realities that it seizes and helps perpetuate. Since queer(able) men are, at last, able to become objects of desire to be gazed at, considered, lusted over, and consumed, that changes the relationship they have with their own bodies—widening the possibilities for what they can accomplish, psychologically, between their sense of self and the physical representation of their self(ves).

When looking at the profiles and ads, it is evident that queer(able) men depict their bodies through fragmentation. Under the justification of a quest for anonymity, these bodies are cropped, cut out, blurred, re-framed, re-arranged, and detached from their presumed original whole. They, most importantly, become faceless. The headlessness of these bodies, turned into a collection of limbs, helps them fit in with the presumed fantasy of the other, whom they are trying to seduce (into objects of their own fantasy). As psychoanalyst Jacques Lacan (2006) reminds us, the fantasy of the self is always the fantasy of the other. This newly acquired ability to fragment one's body, turning it into a modular *thing*, works to phenomenologically and psychologically divorce queer(able) men's bodies from the notion of the always already heterosexual(ized) body of the mythic straight men (impenetrable and made to act, not to be displayed).

This is a symbolic intervention with tremendous consequences for a society that may, through the digital, finally see its strict codes of sexual conduct become more flexible and modular—if not increasingly debunked. It is also an important intervention in the individual psyche of queer(able) men to be able to look at their bodies and the bodies that they desire, to look at them repetitively, in a way, deconstructing and reconstructing them. For queers whose demand for love may have always been undermined by the limits of a historically abject queer body (or a body made abject through queerness), this ability to reconfigure one's materiality-for-the-Other may not only diminish the signifying force of the material itself but also engage the male Subject in a queering practice of self-display otherwise reserved to female bodies. Except here the doing is made combinatory as in a dynamic open system.

We could say that before this digital sexual economy the male body was, ultimately, only imaginable as a properly heterosexual(ized) body (or its botched queer likeness), desiring of a properly heterosexual(ized) female body. Queer desires felt invariably, well, *queer* in the chasms between their different objects of desire and the body that served as fleshly tool to engage with them. That old body, always already heterosexual, can now travel along with a different tune of queer desire, finding different fantasies to fit, different angles to display and different ways of being in the world that may escape what used to be the inherent abjection of a male body not one-hundred-percent heterosexualized.

The fragmentation of the male body into modular parts that is involved in the process of representing one's body online, to package it into fragments, is akin to the early childhood developmental process Lacan famously refers to as the mirror stage. It has to do with the moment the child realizes, through looking in the mirror, or her caretaker's face, that she is an agent independent from her caretaker and the objects around her. Most notably, the child in the mirror stage accepts the impression that she is not just a collection of limbs, but a coherent whole as the image in the mirror, as true. This is, as Lacan is quick to point out, a *misrecognition*, since the image in the mirror is, like the pixels on the screen, just that – an image.

Such a fundamental process in the psychic life of the human infant is here, in a way, relived in reverse as the queer adult "male" (to the extent that we all agree on the flimsy premise that all humans with penises are unquestionably "males") finds himself before his mirror image (webcam photos are *literally* mirrored) only to break its misrecognized cohesive whole into pieces. The fact that he will do that in the name of queer desire reveals an agency that places the queer(able) subject in a position astoundingly *other* than the one he was forced to occupy before appropriating the Internet for his own pleasure. Yet, the wider the digital divide between those who can host and those who must travel, those who are connected and those who aren't, the more we will be creating different classes of queers. If the digital enables a certain kind of queer authentication, we are sure to be left with a hierarchy of authenticity.

IT'S YOUR TURN: WHAT DO YOU THINK? WHAT WILL YOU FIND?

1. Search for personal ads online, looking for some of the points presented here. What other aspects do you consider relevant about what you see in the ads' text and images?

2. How may some ways the issues surrounding queer(able) cruising apply and differ from a heterosexual economy of contact? What other roles may race play in these economies? And what about women?

REFERENCES

Dean, T. (2009). *Unlimited intimacy: Reflections on the subculture of barebacking*. Chicago: The University of Chicago Press.

Fletcher, J. (2002–2003). Recent developments in the general theory of primal seduction. *New Formations, 48*, 5–25.

Israël, L. (1996). *La Jouissance de L'Hystérique*. Paris: Éditions Arcanes.

Lacan, J. (2006). *Écrits*. (B. Fink, Trans.). New York: W. W. Norton & Company.

McGlotten, S. (2001). Queerspace is the space of the screen. *Text, Practice, Performance, 3*, 54–89.

CONTENT

When most people think about the media, they think about media content—a particular film or magazine, a treasured book, their must-see sitcoms, a helpful Web site, favorite songs, video games, or music videos, and so forth. Unfortunately, however, many people don't think critically about media texts. What do these mediated messages say about our social world? Some people may quickly respond "nothing!"—but that's not so. The media content we use is part of our popular culture, and it says a great deal about our world.

And what that media content says about our world matters a great deal to audiences, even if we don't know it. If we don't have firsthand experience with certain aspects of our world, and if we don't know certain types of people, then what we know about that part of the world and those types of people comes from the mass media. Sometimes the media actively and even overtly try to teach us something, as when the Count on *Sesame Street* starts doing his thing or when a popular show features a story line designed to combat bullying or illiteracy. Many of us can sing "Conjunction Junction" from *School House Rock*. It's easy to see that audiences can indeed learn from the media. But the fact is, we learn even when the media don't intentionally set out to teach us—the content of media consistently (if implicitly) demonstrates who matters and who doesn't, who is taken seriously and who isn't, who is feared and who is trusted, and who is best suited to perform certain roles or functions in our society. If you have any doubts as to whether we're affected by the media content we consume, turn to Bradley Gorham's piece (Reading 2.1) at the start of the Audience section. He reviews the social scientific evidence demonstrating how stereotypical images in the media affect audiences.

The readings in the Content section critically examine the texts presented by the mass media for our consumption—everything from Disney films to video games and beyond. There are 27 readings, divided into three chapters. The alternative tables of contents indicates which readings address issues of class.

Chapter 5 presents *Journalism, Advertising, and Public Relations*. Some of its nine readings use content analyses, a method rooted in the social sciences that involves counting each occurrence of whatever is being studied. Other readings use more qualitative methods such as textual analysis or rhetorical analysis to highlight and interpret the dominant themes found in media content. The first five readings are rooted in news media. In Reading 5.1, Christine McKenna Lok and Lauren Chartier examine the differences in media attention to and coverage of two young people (one

Black male, one white female) who committed suicide after being bullied at school. Patti Brown (Reading 5.2) discusses how media have framed the coverage of people who have either entered the United States without the permission of the government or stayed in the country after their visas have expired. Reading 5.3, by Rebecca Lind and Colleen Salo Aravena, shows how feminism has been framed in U.S. electronic news and public affairs content. Chiung Hwang Chen (Reading 5.4) looks at what some have considered a "positive" stereotype, though any stereotype is limiting: Asian Americans as a "model minority." Reading 5.5 presents Xiaomei Cai and Cynthia Lont's analysis of the representation of race and gender on online news site home pages.

The next four readings focus on advertising and public relations. In Reading 5.6, Susan Dente Ross and David Cuillier examine how American Indian tribes represent themselves on their own official Web sites, comparing tribes that operate casinos to those that do not. Becca Gercken (Reading 5.7) analyzes how Native Americans have been presented in the promotional trailers for films produced by Native Americans. Reading 5.8, by John Rodriguez, argues that advertisers wishing to target Hispanics effectively must consider what he calls the "triptych of Hispanic-targeted advertising." The chapter ends with Reading 5.9, in Jean Kilbourne addresses the representation of women in advertising. She argues that women and girls are "cut down to size" in a variety of ways, which has significant ramifications for our society.

Chapter 6, *Film and Entertainment Television*, contains 10 readings, focusing on specific films and TV shows. Race and ethnicity are included in the first four readings, and gender in the last six, although there is often an intersection across race, gender, and/or social class. In Reading 6.1, Jonathan Rossing investigates how Stephen Colbert's recurring critique of "colorblindness" encourages us to consider the complex realities of race and racial privilege. Naomi Rockler-Gladen (Reading 6.2) looks at how *The Lion King* encourages and justifies racial separatism and hierarchy. Reading 6.3, by Leslie Grinner, applies the *SCWAMP* tool—which can help identify whether media content reinforces dominant ideologies by favoring certain social groups—to *The Twilight Saga*. John Sanchez, in Reading 6.4, turns to the representation of Native Americans, discussing how American Indian identity began in the media, and how it continues to be shaped by today's media.

The collection of readings grouped together by a gender focus begins in Reading 6.5 with Jennifer Kramer's look at how *The Bachelor* perpetuates an image of catty women who will go to great lengths to beat other women to win their man. Terri Russ (Reading 6.6) analyzes MTV's *My Super Sweet 16* and concludes that the series reinforces traditional gender roles of girls as nothing more than spoiled consumerist Daddy's Little Girls. In Reading 6.7, Gust Yep and Allen Conkle interrogate how gay domesticity is constructed in *Brothers and Sisters*, and present the implications thereof, for both the U.S. mainstream culture and the U.S. gay subculture. The chapter ends with three readings about motherhood. Katherine Lehman, in Reading 6.8, considers complex representations of motherhood on TV programs featuring women with multiple personality disorder: *United States of Tara*, *Desperate Housewives*, and *Weeds*. Stacey Irwin (Reading 6.9) takes a more global, more personal look at representations of motherhood in the media, which she argues are often more caricature than stereotype. Lea Popielinski (Reading 6.10) argues that *The Devil Wears Prada* and *The Nanny Diaries* represent the evolution of a familiar type of fairy tale: a maiden overcomes the subjugation of a more powerful older woman (the wicked stepmother) to gain freedom and happiness.

Chapter 7 presents eight readings addressing *Music and New Media*. It begins with works focusing more on gender, and then moves to readings which are more focused on race. In Reading 7.1, Cynthia Cooper analyzes hate speech on the Internet, finding, among other things, that the sites focus on sexual themes to such an extent that political and social issues involving gay rights and the gay community were ignored. Inas Mahfouz (Reading 7.2) uses computational analysis to study the posts to *Global Pulse 2010*, a 3-day online collaborative jam designed to bring together socially engaged participants from all over the globe. She focuses on the most active forum, "Empowering Women and Girls." Jody Morrison (Reading 7.3) looks at the *PostSecret* blog, investigating the role of blogging in identity and relationship maintenance. Reading 7.4 is an analysis of Eminem's *Love the Way You Lie* by Rachel Griffin and Joshua Phillips, who argue that the song strengthens cultural myths about domestic violence and normalizes men's violence against women.

Thuc Doan Nguyen, in Reading 7.5, evaluates *AudreyMagazine.com*, which explicitly targets Asian American women, and concludes that the magazine reinforces an assimilationist ideal. Kiana Cox's (Reading 7.6) close reading of the lyrics of the "Hot Rap Singles" for 2005–2010 reveals (and discusses the implications of her findings) that most African American women in rap are depicted as a source of sexual spectacle and fulfillment. Kanye West's *Diamonds from Sierra Leone* is the subject of Reading 7.7, by Michael Adorjan and Athena Elafros. The authors address how West examines several interrelated issues in the song, including the relationship between diamonds, Black masculinity, and social status. Finally, in Reading 7.8, Eric Freedman tackles the question of whether *Resident Evil 5* is racist—challenging us to look for the answer not only in the game's images but also in the very industry creating the game. Videogame design limits players' interactions; the game engine shapes the discourse; commercial imperatives, market forces, political economies, all rule our play and shape our response.

Journalism, Advertising, and Public Relations

5.1 WHY ARE SOME BULLYING VICTIMS MORE NEWSWORTHY THAN OTHERS?

Christine McKenna Lok and Lauren Chartier

The authors conducted a content analysis study of newspaper coverage within Massachusetts of two bullying victims known to have committed suicide, looking at the differences in coverage of the two young people. The results inform us not only about media practices, but also about the framing of the social issue of bullying as debated in the legislature.

Living in Massachusetts in 2010, the media attention devoted to bullying was hard to miss. In January, teenager Phoebe Prince took her own life after being bullied at her high school in Western Massachusetts. Within months of her death, bullying legislation was proposed, debated, and passed at the State House. During deliberations, another young Massachusetts resident, Carl Walker-Hoover, was mentioned occasionally as he had committed suicide the previous April after facing bullying at school.

WHO WERE PHOEBE AND CARL?

Phoebe Nora Mary Prince, 15 years old at the time of her death, had moved from Ireland with her mother and younger sister to spend the school year with her aunt, uncle, and cousins. Phoebe had a difficult transition to the United States. She briefly dated a senior football player, only to face months of harassment afterward from him and some of his popular female friends. Phoebe later dated for a short time another senior athlete, whose ex-girlfriend and other female friends would call Phoebe names such as Irish slut and whore. After a day in which students yelled at her in the library and threw an empty beverage can at her as she walked home, Phoebe killed herself. Her family remembered her in her obituary as bright, artistic, enthusiastic, and beautiful.

Carl Joseph Walker-Hoover, 11 years old at the time of his death, was in the sixth grade at a college-preparatory charter school for sixth through twelfth graders. From the start of the school year, classmates teased him for acting like a girl and being gay, though Carl did not identify as gay. Despite ongoing intervention with the school from his mother, the bullying continued. On the day of his death, Carl's backpack bumped into a TV, which then bumped into a classmate. She threatened to beat and kill Carl, and both students were disciplined. The directive was to have lunch together for the rest of the week to get to know one another. Instead, that evening Carl killed himself. His obituary described a caring young man who attended church weekly, participated in sports and Boy Scouts, loved to read, and was devoted to his younger brother.

PRIOR STUDIES OF NEWS COVERAGE OF VICTIMS

Race, ethnicity, class, sexual orientation, age, class, and beauty are pivotal variables for understanding the newsworthiness of victims. An intersectional approach to analysis understands that for each individual, these aspects of identity build upon one another (Barnum & Zajicek, 2008; Shields, 2008). Phoebe experienced life not only as a teenager, but as a white teenage girl in a suburban high school where status comes from being connected to popular boys. Carl was a sensitive African American boy in a uniform-enforcing charter school in a declining city. Reporters saw not just race or gender or class, but multiple identities simultaneously.

In the popular press, editorials have identified and criticized the media fascination with white, middle-class, attractive victims like JonBenet Ramsey, Laci Peterson, and Natalee Holloway while other equally tragic disappearances and murders are not reported widely (Foreman, 2006; Hutchinson, 1998; Robinson, 2005). Academic studies have shown that covers of news magazines over-represent white female children among crime victims (Gonzales & Eschholz, 2002). Local television news broadcasters focus disproportionately on suburban crime and are much more likely to interview neighbors and personalize the story in suburban regions (Yanich, 2004). Disparities even extend into crime fiction. The program *Law & Order: Special Victims Unit* features significantly more child victims and white victims than Manhattan actually experiences (Britto, Hughes, Saltzmann, & Stroh, 2007).

In general, stories are likely to gain momentum if they align with the American mainstream culture of heteronormativity, an assumption that all individuals are straight and conform to the masculine or feminine ideals appropriate to their sex. In recent years, the image of affluent white "mean girls" has taken center stage (Brown & Tappan, 2008; Ringrose, 2006). Anti-gay bulling also has become a common trope, often leaving the impression that gay-bashing is normal and to be expected (Padva, 2007).

OUR STUDY

This content analysis focused on newspapers in Massachusetts. Although national and European news media did cover these stories, generating a complete list of such print and video features would have been impossible. Deliberate attention to our state alone also helped us contextualize Massachusetts' legislative efforts to reduce bullying. As our local television stations are inconsistent in their archiving of videos, we excluded them from analysis.

Two local databases provided full coverage of daily papers in Massachusetts' largest cities along with many weekly papers from smaller communities. We researched the period from April 6,

2009 (Carl's suicide) through May 6, 2010 (three days after the Governor signed a new anti-bullying law). Using the search terms "Phoebe Prince" and "Walker-Hoover," we found 40 stories featuring both children. Over three times as many articles focused on Phoebe alone (292) as for Carl alone (84). To some extent, greater coverage for Phoebe may have been expected simply because she was seen as the latest in a troubling new trend. If that were the case, however, one also would expect that Carl's death would be referenced in most of those stories about Phoebe. Clearly it was not.

We did notice more equal treatment in their hometown newspaper *The Springfield Republican*. There, Phoebe was featured alone in 79 stories, Carl alone in 45 stories, and both together in 21 stories. While the ratio remained at nearly two to one, it was a significant improvement from the statewide coverage. Much of that local coverage for Carl stemmed from his mother's race for School Committee after her son's death in an effort to make bullying a higher priority for the district.

For the analysis of the content of the articles, we eliminated letters to the editor, opinion pieces, duplicate AP wire stories, and references to online features. What remained were 247 articles. We assessed all of these articles (86) that included Carl, all of the *Springfield Republican* articles (98) that included Phoebe, and a nonchronological convenience sample (62) of articles with Phoebe in the remaining statewide papers.

MEDIA BIAS

We used OpenCode software to help us identify themes, or similar characteristics in the articles. We discovered the following five themes.

Sexualizing Teenage Girls

Much of the coverage of Phoebe touched on the topic of dating. One reporter made note of the fact that Phoebe's suicide happened only days before a school dance, as if such events should be the main focus of teenage girls' lives. Twenty writers mentioned Phoebe's romantic relationships. Authors used language that simultaneously trivialized her emotions and suggested great drama: Phoebe variously flirted with boys, had crushes, stole other people's boyfriends, and made female classmates jealous.

One fascinating aspect of the coverage of Phoebe was the choice of photographs. While she was described on the one hand as sexually assertive, the visual images suggested a bashful and conservatively dressing young woman. Not selected were images available on Irish social media sites that showed a more glamorous Phoebe with makeup and close-fitting outfits. We make note of this fact not to argue that one image is necessarily more accurate than another, but to question whether the Massachusetts reporters felt they needed to portray an entirely innocent victim (Christie, 1986). Teenage girls in the United States have a difficult balancing act: they are encouraged simultaneously to present themselves provocatively and to remain chaste (England, Shafer, & Fogarty, 2007).

The Penalty for Gender Non-Conformity

At 11 years old, Carl had not publicly or privately declared that he was gay or straight, but he none-theless was subjected to homophobic name-calling throughout the school year. For young people, calling a male classmate "gay" can have less to do with sexual orientation than with holding him accountable for not fulfilling the expectations of masculinity (Pascoe, 2007). Twenty-one articles reference the gay teasing directed at Carl, and two clarify that Carl did not self-identify as gay. The articles typically included comments that children ridiculed Carl for his clothing and told him he acted like a girl. A few articles recounted a teacher's fond memory of Carl singing along with Rihanna. Several mentioned that Carl had grown up with a single mother and kissed his grandmother before bed each night. One column even identified a favorite book *Diary of a Wimpy Kid* (Abraham, 2010). While we can find stories here and there of Carl's carrying a hammer around his house or planning to be a businessman, the overarching image was of an effeminate young man. Somehow he seemed to merit less concern than the feminine young woman who died months later.

Hesitancy to Accept Allegations of Bullying against Carl

In stark contrast to the immediate connection of Phoebe's death to mean girl behavior from classmates, initial stories about Carl's suicide were very cautious about pointing to bullying as the motivation for the child's final act. Reporters tended to specify that Carl's mother was the one describing the ongoing bullying at school, or that Carl had told her that bullying was happening, or that he had killed himself after *alleged* incidents of bullying. For the most part, the passage of the anti-bullying legislation equalized the language between the two children's stories. However, even then, the openness was not universal. For example, in describing the prospects of the anti-bullying bill in April, Chabot's (2010) language distinguished between the alleged bullying of Carl and the actual bullying of Phoebe, as attested by criminal charges against several of her classmates. This difference cannot be attributed solely to race, as we will see later that reporters had greater access to corroborating witnesses of Phoebe's treatment.

More Graphic Descriptions of Carl's Death

News media widely reported that both young people hung themselves. However, descriptions varied a great deal. Stories of Carl's death were much more graphic. Sixteen articles explained he used an extension cord and that his mother found him hanging on the second floor. In stark contrast, Phoebe's death by hanging was merely alluded to at first. Eventually, a few articles did mention where she was found and by whom, but none of the Massachusetts newspapers in our time period mentioned that Phoebe had hung herself with a scarf.

We fear that many reporters and readers have become desensitized to the tragedy of the loss of young Black lives, particularly young men living in urban areas. Editors felt comfortable revealing details about Carl's last moments while shielding that information about Phoebe. Their lack of surprise at the death of a Springfield youth contributed as well to the judgment that his case was less newsworthy than Phoebe's.

Differential Uses of Adjectives

We do not have access to the report cards of Phoebe and Carl, nor to standardized test results or teacher assessments. For that reason, we cannot know whether the young people were vastly different in terms of academic potential and performance. What we do know is that Carl was not described as intelligent. He merited descriptions as a student of promise and a voracious reader, but not as smart. We wonder the extent to which white privilege may have made it more likely for Phoebe to receive her public labels of intelligent and bright.

We are fairly confident that white privilege along with gender helps to explain why Phoebe was described as attractive while Carl was not. Despite his good looks, the most flattering adjective that Carl garnered was "sweet-faced" (Hyde, 2009, p. A13). We hypothesize that similarly accurate words like handsome and beautiful did not occur to reporters attuned to Eurocentric standards of beauty (Robinson-Moore, 2008).

SOCIAL POLICY IMPLICATIONS

Questions of disparities in news coverage are of utmost importance if we are to ensure fair representation of experiences and ideas in the public sphere. The contrast specifically related to Phoebe and Carl has generated interest beyond our project. Bergman (2010) conducted interviews with stakeholders about the media stories and discovered an important element: social capital. Phoebe had classmates with a father who was a colleague of a *Boston Globe* columnist. That Irish American columnist, in turn, had been stationed in the past in the paper's Ireland bureau and felt solidarity with the child. With help from contacts provided by the high school students, the reporter wrote seven columns and contributed to at least six news stories about Phoebe (Bergman, 2010).

That Phoebe's classmates had connections to bring the story to wider attention highlights the differences in social capital between residents of many suburban and urban schools. While Phoebe's parents did not appear in any interviews, nor did they seem to be advocating for attention for the case, their daughter became a national headline. Carl's mother, on the other hand, became her son's champion but without the same results. She did not have the same connections as the people involved in bringing Phoebe's case to light.

What gets covered, and how the stories are covered, have important implications for the development of social policy. In developing anti-crime legislation, for example, high-profile cases of white middle-class girls and young women often hijack attention from much more common forms of crime. If news coverage does not reflect accurate crime statistics, the public and policy makers may be motivated to fix the wrong problems. The publicity surrounding Phoebe and Carl provides an unfortunate example of such shaping of legislative debate.

Because the problem of bullying was framed as attitudinal—mean suburban girls—the gendered structure of American schooling was rendered invisible. Even after two teenage boys were charged with statutory rape for their relations with Phoebe, reporters failed to ask questions about gender dynamics in high school dating. Left unexplored were the influence and power that popular senior athletes have over freshman girls, the double standard labeling sexually active teenage girls as whores and boys as studs, and the need to hold men as accountable for dating transgressions (like cheating) as women. As a result, the new anti-bullying law has no provisions to deal with gender inequality. Also, the attention to suburban mean girls has narrowed the legislature's gaze from broader school violence initiatives working across urban, suburban, and rural school districts.

Sadly, homophobia was left unaddressed in the anti-bullying legislation. Reporters did not question Carl's reaction to being called gay. Stories took for granted that anyone would be horrified to be labeled a homosexual. Such a response should not be typical. Even religious traditions that deny gay marriage recognize the inherent dignity and worth of all individuals, including gays and lesbians. Massachusetts' law recognizes the action of bullying but does nothing to minimize the biases that lead to the targeting of particular groups. Nor does the law do anything to promote expanded gender roles for girls and boys. Carl was teased for not complying fully enough with expectations of masculinity. Reporters could have explored further what behaviors Carl's classmates had identified as feminine. By taking for granted that some activities are inherently more masculine than others, newspapers and policy makers missed the opportunity to challenge cultural norms of gender performance.

IT'S YOUR TURN: WHAT DO YOU THINK? WHAT WILL YOU FIND?

1. Track the race and gender of crime victims and perpetrators for a week on the evening news on a local television station. Compare your findings against regional population demographics on the U.S. Census Web site at *http://quickfacts.census.gov/qfd/index.html*. What did you find? Now, go beyond the numbers and compare the content of the coverage. What themes do you find, and how do they differ across victims or perpetrators of different demographic groups?

2. Learn about anti-bullying legislation in your own state. Visit your state legislature's Web page and/or watch the National Conference of State Legislatures' webinar on state anti-bullying policies at *http://www.ncsl.org/default.aspx?tabid=21807*. Send a letter to your state senator and representative sharing your own experience and analysis of bullying.

3. Write your own content analysis of recent episodes of a television series focused on young people. Programs such as *Everybody Hates Chris, Friday Night Lights, Gilmore Girls, Glee,* and *Huge* often feature tensions between popular and unpopular students. How often are characteristics like income/social class, ethnicity, sexual orientation, and interests used to marginalize cast members? Is bullying used as a humorous plot device meant simply to entertain the audience, or does the program feature a satisfying challenge to a bully and his/her message?

4. Visit and/or post to one of the following campaigns' Web sites. The *It Gets Better* campaign features videos from a wide range of adults offering messages to gay, lesbian, bisexual, questioning, and transgendered young people that adolescent bullying is temporary and a fulfilling adulthood awaits. The *Make It Better* campaign offers tools to students to create change in their own high schools now.

5. Become familiar with suicide prevention services in your area and consider volunteering. Befrienders Worldwide offers contact information for hotlines internationally at *http://www.befrienders.org/*.

REFERENCES

Abraham, Y. (2010, April 8). Two deaths too many. *Boston Globe,* B1.

Barnum, A.J., & Zajicek, A.M. (2008). An intersectional analysis of visual media: A case of Diesel advertisements. *Social Thought and Research, 29.* 105–128.

Bergman, S. (2010, June 9). Words of their passing: Why was one local teen suicide national news and another relatively unnoticed? *Daily Hampshire Gazette.* Retrieved October 6, 2011, from http://www.gazettenet.com/2010/06/09/words-of-their-passing

Britto, S., Hughes, T., Saltzmann, K., & Stroh, C. (2007). Does "special" mean young, white, and female? Deconstructing the meaning of "special" in *Law & Order: Special Victims Unit. Journal of Criminal Justice and Popular Culture, 14*(1), 39–57.

Brown, L.M., & Tappan, M.B. (2008). Fighting like a girl, fighting like a guy: Gender identity, ideology, and girls at early adolescence. *New Directions for Child and Adolescent Development, 120,* 47–59.

Chabot, H. (2010, April 13). Casinos curb bully bill progress. *Boston Herald,* 6.

Christie, N. (1986). The ideal victim. In Fattah, E.A. (Ed.), *From crime policy to victim policy: Reorienting the criminal justice system* (pp. 17–30). New York: St. Martin's Press.

England, P., Shafer, E.F., & Fogarty, A.C.K. (2007). Hooking up and forming romantic relationships on today's college campuses. In Kimmel, M.S. (Ed.), *The gendered society reader* (pp. 531–547). New York: Oxford University Press.

Foreman, T. (2006, March 14). *Diagnosing "Missing White Woman Syndrome."* Anderson Cooper 360° Blog. Retrieved October 6, 2011, from http://www.cnn.com/CNN/Programs/anderson.cooper.360/blog/2006/03/diagnosing-missing-white-woman.html

Gonzales, C., & Eschholz, S. (2002, November). *A picture is worth a thousand words: Newsmagazine cover photos of children as ideology.* Paper presented at the American Society of Criminology Annual Meeting, Chicago, IL.

Hutchinson, E.O. (1998, August 13). Devaluing black life: The Sherrice Iverson murder. *Los Angeles Sentinel*, A6.

Hyde, S. (2009, April 18). Breaking the silence around bullying. *Boston Globe*, A13.

Padva, G. (2007). Media and popular culture representation of LGBT bullying. *Journal of Gay and Lesbian Social Services, 19*(3/4), 105–118.

Pascoe, C.J. (2007). *Dude, you're a fag: Masculinity and sexuality in high school.* Los Angeles: University of California Press.

Ringrose, J. (2006). A new universal mean girl: Examining the discursive construction and social regulation of a new feminine pathology. *Feminism & Psychology, 16*(4), 405–424.

Robinson, E. (2005, June 10). (White) women we love. *Washington Post*, A23.

Robinson-Moore, C.L. (2008). Beauty standards reflect Eurocentric paradigms—So what? Skin color, identity, and black female beauty. *Journal of Race and Policy, 4*(1), 66–85.

Shields, S. (2008). Gender: An intersectionality approach. *Sex Roles, 59*(5/6), 301–311.

Yanich, D. (2004). Crime creep: Urban and suburban crime on local TV news. *Journal of Urban Affairs, 26*(5), 535–563.

5.2   WHAT'S IN A NAME?: FRAMING THE IMMIGRATION STORY

Patti Brown

> *This reading explores how media have framed the immigration story and, in the process, how the media have shaped both the story and public opinion.*

Immigration is among the most important media stories of our day. Actually there are two different immigration stories. One deals with those who enter the United States through official immigration channels seeking legal permanent residence (LPR) status. This group annually includes some 463,000 people "new arrivals" as well as more than 667,000 who are already living in the United States and whose status is legally adjusted from a category such as refugee, temporary worker, foreign student, family member, or undocumented immigrant. In 2009, 1.1 million people were granted LPR status bringing the total number of people with "green cards" in the United States to 12.5 million, many of whom—7.9 million—are eligible to apply for citizenship.

The other story concerns an estimated 800,000 to 1 million people per year who enter by crossing the U.S. border without government permission or who remain here after their visa has expired. The Department of Homeland Security estimates that there are 10.8 million people living in the United States today whose immigration status is unauthorized.

Both of these are important stories, and often the stories get intertwined, but the media's spotlight has been focused primarily on the conflict surrounding what is called "illegal immigration."

The Dallas Morning News named the Illegal Immigrant its 2007 Texan of the Year. "He is at the heart of a great culture war in Texas – and the nation, credited with bringing us prosperity and blamed for abusing our resources. How should we deal with this stranger among us?" (DMN, 2007).

Why does this matter? Because there is a strong correlation between the amount of coverage the media give to stories such as immigration and the salience or importance the public ascribes to those issues (McCombs & Shaw, 1972). Newspapers, television, radio, online blogs, and news services tell us not just *what* to think about (called agenda setting), but they also can influence *how* we think about these issues (known as priming). By leading a news broadcast with a story on illegal immigration, or placing the story on the front page, the media let us know that immigration is an important issue. The way the media report on immigration—from the frequency, quantity, and angle of coverage to the sources quoted—influences how we think about and make judgments regarding the issue.

A ROSE BY ANY OTHER NAME

The words we use to describe someone or something frame the situation in a positive, negative, or neutral light and say as much about us as they do about the person or thing being described. The media face challenges in describing those who have either entered the United States without the permission of the government or who have stayed in the country after their visas have expired. How do the media frame the stories they present about these people? Are these people presented as "illegal aliens" or "undocumented migrants?"

Frames are central organizing themes used in the narrative of a story. Entman (1991, p.7) says frames "are constructed from and embodied in the keywords, metaphors, concepts, symbols, and visual images emphasized in the news narrative." Frames present a certain view of a story in much the same way a picture frame or a window frame limits what a viewer sees.

Media struggle to choose the right words to use when covering the immigration story which are both unbiased and accurate. For example, *The Minnesota Daily* made a conscious decision to use "undocumented immigrant." Editor in Chief Anna Weggel (2006) wrote, "We wanted to find a phrase that in part names the people being referred to, but also describes the action that is making them the subject of a story." Many of the paper's readers saw the term "illegal immigrant" as "dehumanizing," and the paper acknowledged that the term "could have negative connotations that sway the way readers think about an entire group of people."

"Hearing a group of people referred to over and over as 'illegal' can drill into readers' minds that these are bad, reckless individuals that do not deserve to be in our country"; recognizing that "undocumented immigrant" is not perfect, Weggel wrote, "Our goal is to create a level of understanding and fairness for all of our readers."

Language is organic; it evolves over time with culture and use. Fifty years from now, people will look back at how the keywords, metaphors, concepts, symbols, and visual images used today—such as illegal, amnesty, undocumented, or aliens—not only shaped how audiences viewed the policies and the people who were at the center of the debate, but also how the words themselves shaped the very tenor of the discourse in the public square.

FRAMING IMMIGRATION

Dominant frames in the immigration story include national security; border control; population; human rights; and immigration reform frames, which will all be discussed here, as well as other frames such as crime; amnesty and guest worker; sanctuary city; documentation and credentialing; language; economic; educational and health; and diversity.

The National Security and Border Control Frames

The national security frame deals with the government's role in protecting the United States from foreign and domestic threats. The border control frame is intrinsically linked to national security but deals more precisely with the nearly 1 million people who enter and leave the United States every single day.

Over the past decade, stories about immigration have been tied to coverage of homeland security. In the aftermath of the terrorist attacks on September 11, serious questions were raised about how the terrorists were allowed into the United States in the first place. When *The 9-11 Commission Report* was issued, *The New York Times* (Shenon, Jehl, & Johnston, 2004) covered its release, "Correcting the Record on Sept. 11, in Great Detail," and reported, "The commission's report found that the hijackers had repeatedly broken the law in entering the United States."

In a story "Are We Safer?," *The Miami Herald* (Gordon, Taylor, & Hutcheson, 2006) reported, "A close examination of the federal government's homeland security effort shows there have been major accomplishments since the attacks on Sept. 11, 2001. But it also reveals how vulnerable to a catastrophe the nation remains."

Under the headline "America must secure its borders now," the *Erie Times-News* ran an opinion editorial by a Pennsylvania congressional representative (Peterson, 2007) reinforcing the concern about how "vulnerable we still are as a nation" 6 years after Sept. 11 and how important border security is to prevent "terrorists, drug traffickers and violent gang members from entering our country and harming America."

In January 2011, the U.S. Border Patrol captured Said Jaziri, an Islamic cleric from Tunisia who gained notoriety when he called for the death of a Danish cartoonist who had drawn the Prophet Muhammad. In an article headlined "Radicals lay siege to our borders," the conservative *Washington Times* reported that Jaziri, who was discovered hiding in the trunk of a car some 50 miles outside San Diego, paid a Mexican human trafficking cartel $5,000 to smuggle him into the United States (Swain & Sharad, 2011). Although the numbers of individuals apprehended along the Mexican border who originate from countries identified by the United States as sponsoring terror have jumped in the past decade, hyperbole about "radicals" "laying siege" frames the topic in polarizing discourse.

However, some claim that how the United States controls the flow of immigrants has more to do with racial prejudice, ethnic bigotry, or xenophobia than national security. *Los Angeles Times* columnist Gregory Rodriguez (2008) expressed frustration with "ongoing strains of xenophobia and racism in U.S. society."

In September 2005, *The Arizona Republic* used the headline, "Hayworth bill tackles 'invasion'" (Coomes, 2005). Defending his position, U. S. Representative J. D. Hayworth said, "This is not xenophobia. This is not racism. This is national security."

A frame such as national security can be used to report a story in either a positive or a negative way, and over time, the frame can change in tone. Public support of airport travel security measures was high right after the 2001 terrorist attacks, but people have grown weary of the hassles and view the precautions as discriminatory to certain groups. When the TSA rolled out full-body scanning machines and more invasive body pat-downs in 2010, one traveler armed with an iPhone recorded his encounter with a security screener, protesting, "Don't touch my junk, and don't touch my kid's junk either." The video went viral on YouTube, and news outlets across the country ran stories about the updated "don't tread on me" motto highlighting travelers' increasing frustration with the inconveniences and indignities of airport security done in the name of homeland security.

The (Over) Population Frame

The population frame is concerned with people and numbers. The frame focuses on the number of people who presently live in the country, who immigrate through official channels, who are denied visas, and who arrive without visas. One of the many challenges with reporting the immigration story today is the sheer number of people involved. The U.S. Census Bureau projects that by 2050 the U.S. population will be 420 million, 24% of which will be immigrants. Among those here today, 53.3% are from Latin America—more than one third of the total foreign-born population and nearly half of those here illegally.

The crux of what the media call "the immigration debate" is about how many people are allowed to immigrate to the United States, from which countries, what education, job skills, or family ties are required, and how those decisions are made. Countless numbers of individuals and special interest groups hold vastly differing views on U.S. immigration laws and on proposed reforms. The tenor of this public discourse has become particularly contentious during the past decade.

Using terms such as "flood" or "invasion" to describe the number of immigrants frames immigration as a serious problem needing a drastic solution. Some have called for revisions of how the U.S. Constitution provides for birthright citizenship. *The New York Times* reported that "the next big immigration battle centers on illegal immigrants' offspring, who are granted automatic citizenship like all other babies born on American soil. Arguing for an end to the policy, which is rooted in the 14th Amendment of the Constitution, immigration hard-liners describe a wave of migrants . . . stepping across the border in the advanced stages of pregnancy to have what are dismissively called 'anchor babies'" (Lacey, 2011).

Readers are also likely to see the immigrants themselves as the root of the problem instead of looking at other factors, such as employers who willingly hire undocumented individuals to save money. *The Salt Lake Tribune* quoted a source who said Arizona would not be a "sanctuary state for illegal employers or illegal aliens" (Carlisle, 2008). Should the media frame businesses hiring undocumented workers as "illegal employers," public attention could shift from the immigrant to corporations that drive down wages among the working class and create a voiceless underclass of immigrants who number in the millions.

The Human Rights Frame

The human rights frame concerns the fundamental rights of every human being to dignity, freedom, justice, and peace. It is one of the most compelling frames; immigrants are frequently a disadvantaged and vulnerable population who lack the language skills, financial security, and employment opportunities enjoyed by native-born people.

Immigrants entering the United States illegally often do so with the aid of human smugglers called coyotes who charge as much as $2,500 or more to walk people across the border and hook them up with transportation, drop houses, and employment. The *Chicago Tribune* (Spagat, 2006) reported that "while most smugglers walk their customers several nights across the deserts that dominate the frontier's nearly 2,000 miles, others take frightening risks." A National Public Radio report detailed some of the grim statistics: "Over the past nine years in Arizona, Border Patrol agents and others have discovered more than 1,800 bodies — all remains of people who died trying to get into the United States" (Robbins, 2010).

Open-border advocates who view U.S. immigration policy as biased against people of color point to stories about people literally dying to come to America and question the moral compass of a nation that could allow such a thing. Mike King, an editorial writer for *The Atlanta Journal-Constitution*, addressed conflicts between the national security and human rights frames, "A true test of our feelings about race, the economy and the role low-wage earners play in it awaits. Indeed, the conversation will reflect the core values that move our moral compass as a nation" (King, 2006).

Large-scale workplace immigration raids provide evocative images of arrests, detentions, and court proceedings. Pictures of people crying as their loved ones are led away in handcuffs, or of protestors waving American or other national flags, or holding signs saying "no human being is illegal" or "what part of 'illegal' don't you understand," fan the flames on both sides of the issue. How the media frame the story can influence not only the direction of the public debate but also how individual human beings are treated in their interactions with others.

Immigration Reform

The immigration reform frame deals with attempts to retool legislation governing U.S. immigration policy. This political frame includes the positions and opinions of lawmakers, political candidates, policy advisors, lobbyists, commentators, and citizens.

A bipartisan immigration reform bill, the Comprehensive Immigration Reform Act of 2007, included provisions for increased border security, including a fence along the nearly 2000 miles of the U.S.-Mexican border and an expanded guest worker program. The bill was controversial to many groups. Restrictions in the bill on family reunification were decried by immigrant advocates. Labor unions and others saw the guest worker provision as creating an economic underclass. A significant factor in its defeat was conservative talk radio, which *The Washington Post* credited with mobilizing listeners across the country to put pressure on their legislators to squash the bill (Weisman & Murray, 2007).

Another legislative attempt at immigration reform —the Dream Act (Development, Relief, Education for Alien Minors)—has received a great deal of attention. If passed, the Dream Act would allow a path to citizenship for children brought to the United States through unauthorized channels by their parents. President Obama spoke of this in his 2011 State of the Union address just a month after a U.S. Senate filibuster blocked the bill from moving forward. "Today, there are hundreds of thousands of students excelling in our schools who are not American citizens. Some are the children of undocumented workers, who had nothing to do with the actions of their parents. They grew up as Americans and pledge allegiance to our flag, and yet live every day with the threat of deportation. Others come here from abroad to study in our colleges and universities. But as soon as they obtain advanced degrees, we send them back home to compete against us. It makes no sense." (Obama, 2011).

In April 2010, the governor of Arizona signed the nation's toughest state immigration bill into law. People on both sides of the divide were quick to provide the media with new sound bites and headlines. *The New York Times* ran a statement issued by the Mexican American Legal Defense and Educational Fund saying Governor Brewer had "caved to the radical fringe" and predicted that the law would create "a spiral of pervasive fear, community distrust, increased crime and costly litigation, with nationwide repercussions" (Archibold, 2010). Dozens of cities, businesses, and organizations across the country cancelled contracts with Arizona businesses, restricted employee travel to the state, or held symbolic boycotts. However, imitations of the legislation have appeared in many other city councils and state legislatures attempting to address economic and social problems associated with the unauthorized migration of foreign nationals.

REFRAMING, REFOCUSING, AND REPORTING

How media select and report stories is driven largely by factors attributed to dominant class biases inherent within the media. Mainstream media are largely owned by corporate conglomerates and run almost exclusively by educated, upper-income white men. Newsrooms are staffed overwhelmingly by people who are part of the dominant class and share certain class biases influencing how stories are selected and edited.

The dominant class has a vested interest in maintaining the status quo to insure its position of hegemonic power. Research has shown that the media often perpetuate racial stereotypes and increase racial conflict which serves to further the status quo—even though, as a group, journalists are more likely to support progressive political causes that may serve to advance the agenda of immigration reform.

The media have an enormous challenge to report complex and controversial stories such as the contemporary immigration story well. *The Dallas Morning News* was criticized by readers for the choice of the illegal immigrant as the 2007 Texan of the Year. Some readers thought the paper was bestowing an honor on the illegal immigrant. Far from it, the paper was acknowledging the reality of a phenomenon that is part of the public discourse. The paper concluded the editorial by saying, "What you think of the illegal immigrant says a lot about what you think of America, and what vision of her you are willing to defend. How we deal with the stranger among us says not only who we Americans are today but determines who we will become tomorrow."

IT'S YOUR TURN: WHAT DO YOU THINK? WHAT WILL YOU FIND?

1. Review a few editions of your local newspaper, a national newspaper, or find newspapers from Texas, New Mexico, Arizona, or California. Look for stories about immigration, and count how many times you find the frames listed earlier. What other frames do you find? What do these frames tell you about the people who are here without permission? What do these frames tell you about the reporters and newspapers that published these stories?

2. Look for two sets of stories, one about immigrants from Central America and one about immigrants from Asia, Africa, and Europe. Try to find at least three articles for each set. Compare the framing of immigrant groups from Central America to those from other parts of the world. Are the stories about certain immigrants framed more positively than the stories about others? What are keywords and frames used by the media in reporting on different immigrant populations? Which groups are treated more sympathetically by the media? Which groups get the most negative coverage?

3. Compare the difference between how mainstream and alternative media cover immigration in terms of both keywords and frames. Find a conservative paper, a liberal paper, a conservative news blog, and a liberal news blog. What differences do you see in the way each addresses the topic of immigration? How do the different media use photos and graphics in reporting on immigrants?

4. Interview a member of the media who is identified as a member of an immigrant community. Ask your interviewee what insights he or she has into the unique challenges of reporting on news about immigrant groups. What biases has she or he personally encountered from the "dominant" community?

REFERENCES

Archibold, R. (2010, April 24). Arizona enacts stringent law on immigration. *New York Time*, A1.

Carlisle, N. (2008, February 18). Arizona crackdown could add to Utah's illegal immigration woes. *The Salt Lake Tribune*, 1A.

Coomes, J. (2005, September 1). Hayworth bill tackles 'invasion.' *Arizona Republic*, SRN1.

Entman, R. (1991). Framing U.S. coverage of international news: Contrasts in narratives of the KAL and Iran Air incidents. *Journal of Communication, 41*(4), 6–27.

Gordon, G., Taylor, M., & Hutcheson, R. (2006, September 10). Are we safer? *The Miami Herald*, 1A.

King, M. (2006, March 30). Finally U.S. tackles illegal immigration. *The Atlanta Journal-Constitution*, 15A.

Lacey, M. (2011, January 5). Birthright citizenship looms as next immigration battle. *New York Times*, A1.

McCombs, M., & Shaw, D. L. (1972). The agenda-setting function of mass media. *Public Opinion Quarterly, 36*, 176–187.

Obama, B. (January 25, 2011). State of the Union Address. Speech presented at Washington, D.C.

Peterson, J. (2007, June 29). America must secure its borders now. *Erie Times-News*, 1F.

Robbins, T. (2010, October 6). Illegal immigrant deaths set record in Arizona. *Morning Edition. National Public Radio*.

Rodriguez, G. (2008, April 6). A 670-miles-long shrine to American insecurity. *Los Angeles Times*, 1O.

Shenon, P. Jehl, D., & Johnston, D. (2004, July 24). Correcting the record on Sept. 11, in great detail. *New York Times*, 1A.

Spagat, E. (2006, December 31). Border smugglers in demand—heightened security creates a boom. *Chicago Tribune*, 4B.

Swain, C., & Sharad, S. (2011, February 18). Radicals lay siege to our border; Illegal immigration is declining but not from terrorist countries. *The Washington Times*, B1.

The Illegal Immigrant. (2007, December 30). *Dallas Morning News*, 1P.

Weggel, A. (2006, November 13). An evolving language. *The Minnesota Daily*, A7.

Weisman, J., & Murray, S. (2007, June 20). Republicans hearing static form conservative radio hosts. *The Washington Post*, 1C.

5.3   FRAMING FEMINISM

Rebecca Ann Lind and Colleen Salo Aravena

An analysis of news and public affairs content reveals that "women" and "feminists" are portrayed in very different ways. The authors argue that, ultimately, feminists are presented as out of the ordinary, and not quite "normal."

To "frame" something is to make sense of it. According to Gamson (1989, p. 157), "facts have no intrinsic meaning. They take on their meaning by being embedded in a frame or story line that organizes them and gives them coherence, selecting certain ones to emphasize while ignoring others." News stories include factual elements, but as Gitlin's (1980, p. 29) analysis revealed "the media were far from mirrors passively reflecting facts found in the real world. The facts reported were out there in the real world, true: out there *among others*. The media reflection was more the active, patterned remaking performed by mirrors in a fun house." Roeh further argued very the process of selecting the words to describe an event is value-laden: "no author or speaker is free of the necessity to choose words, syntax, and order of presentation. It does make a difference if 'friction' and not 'dispute' is chosen" (1981, p. 78). Such differences are important because research has shown that people's attitudes and judgments can be affected by the media's framing of issues,[1] especially when people lack firsthand knowledge of an issue (Gitlin, 1980).

So, what about feminism? How do the media frame feminism? Do the media even pay attention to feminism?

Reprinted and adapted from Rebecca Ann Lind & Colleen Salo, "The Framing of Feminists and Feminism in News and Public Affairs Programs in U. S. Electronic Media." *Journal of Communication, 52(1)*, pages 211–228, by permission of OXFORD UNIVERSITY PRESS. Reproduced with permission of OXFORD UNIVERSITY PRESS in the format Journal via Copyright Clearance Center.

SEARCHING FOR THE FRAMES

Wordlink is a form of computerized network analysis (Danowski, 1993)[2] which maps the relationships among words within messages. Because Wordlink can compute the frequency with which certain words, terms, concepts, attitudes, and values are associated with feminists, it helps identify the frames used to represent feminists. By also looking at how often those same words are associated with women in general, we can more fully understand the framing of feminism and feminists.

Our unit of analysis is the word pair. Because "you shall know the meaning of a word by the company it keeps," we can infer the meanings of particular words (e.g., "feminism" and "feminists") by investigating their surrounding word context. Using Wordlink, we sifted through the text and found all words appearing within seven words before or after our target words "feminism," "feminist," "feminists," "women," and "woman." Wordlink recorded and counted all of the word pairs, which we then compared with the media frames being investigated in this study.

The body of text we studied was two and a half years' worth of transcripts of news and public affairs programs aired from May 1993 through January 1996 on ABC, CNN, NPR, and PBS.[3] We analyzed every word in every story on every news and public affairs program, for a total of 135,759,087 words.

SIX GUIDING FRAMES

Our investigation of prior research helped us create a set of six frames that guided our analysis. We searched the text for evidence of DEMONIZATION in which feminism and feminists are framed as deviant. We looked for a PERSONALIZATION AND TRIVIALIZATION frame—focusing on appearance, style, or personal qualities. A GOALS frame reflects attention to civil rights, reproductive rights, workplace rights, and the goals for equality generally held by feminists. Fourth, the VICTIMIZATION frame reveals feminists as weak and vulnerable; while (fifth) the AGENCY frame represents feminists as strong and capable. The SITE OF STRUGGLE is the sixth frame, reflecting the variety of locations (home, school, religion, work, etc.) of feminist activities.[4]

THE FRAMES REVEALED

Before addressing the framing of feminists and women, we first consider a relatively common complaint that women and women's issues in general are neglected in the mass media. We analyzed 135,759,087 words. The target words "woman" and "women" appeared 1,158,756 times, or 0.85% of all words. The target words "feminist," "feminists," and "feminism" appeared 25,139 times, or 0.02% of all words. Clearly, feminism continues to receive relatively little attention in the media.

The Demonization Frame

Critics claim feminists are demonized when portrayed in the media as crazy, ill-tempered, ugly, man-hating, family-wrecking, hairy-legged, bra-burning radical lesbians. We looked through the text for the co-occurrence of such words with our target words. Women/woman co-occurred with demonizing words 3,287 times, meaning that 0.28% of all references to women/an appeared in a demonizing frame. (Table 1 presents an overview of the results for the first

Table 1   Five Main Frames for Representing Women and Feminism

	DEMONIZATION		PERSONALIZATION & TRIVIALIZATION		GOALS OF MOVEMENT		VICTIMIZATION		AGENCY	
	#	%	#	%	#	%	#	%	#	%
Women	3,287	0.28	40,148	3.46	26,770	2.31	13,756	1.19	6,920	0.59
Feminists	507	2.02	733	2.92	1,302	5.18	252	1.00	295	1.17

five frames.) Some of the most common co-occurrences were women-bad (202 appearances), women/an-lesbian/s (184), women/an-jerk/s (89), and women/an-bitch/y/es (87). Feminist/s/ism co-occurred with demonizing words 507 times, or 2.02% of all references. The most common co-occurrence was feminist/s/ism-radical (57 times), followed by militant (13), lesbian/s (12), amuck/amok (12), raging (6), and masculine (6). Thus, feminists are demonized more often in the media than are women.

The Personalization and Trivialization Frame

This frame includes attention to personal attributes—appearance, marital status, personal habits, or personal style. A focus on style over substance trivializes people and their positions. Rhode (1997) argued that a focus on feminists' appearance is particularly troublesome, because feminists who reject traditional standards of femininity are ridiculed, while those who do not are deemed vain and perhaps even hypocritical.

Our analysis revealed 40,148 co-occurrences between women/an and personalizing words (3.46% of all woman/en references), which seemed to emphasize romance and marital status, clothing and appearance, motherhood, sex, and body parts. The media paid a great deal of attention to women's romantic and marital status. For example, the word pair women/an-married appeared 1,217 times, while women/an-divorce appeared 98 times. Other common word pairs included women-single (291), women-marriage (215), woman-husband (528), woman-wife (252), and woman-mrs (106). Women's clothing and appearance were also of interest, with woman-beautiful co-occurring 299 times, women/an-attractive (266), women/an-hair/ed (215), women/an-clothes/ing (208), women-fat (74), women-thin (41), women/an-fashion (88), and woman-ugly (17). Motherhood was also a great concern to the media. References to children and babies abounded, with woman-child co-occurring 519 times, woman-children 473 times, women/an-kids 322 times, woman-pregnant 332 times, and women-pregnancy 125 times. An emphasis on sex is revealed by the co-occurrence of woman/en and lexical variants of sex (491 co-occurrences), women-erotic (65), and women-lovers (60). Women's body parts also received extensive attention in the media; woman/en-breasts co-occurred 161 times, women/an-eyes appeared 123 times, woman-leg/s/ged appeared 41 times, and women-hands appeared 81 times.

Our target feminist words co-occurred with personalizing words 733 times, or in 2.92% of feminist/s/ism references. Attention to marital status was reflected in word pairs, such as feminist-marriage (15 co-occurrences), feminist-wedding (4), and feminist/s-single (4). Clothing and appearance were reflected in word pairs, such as feminist/s-fashion/ed (9), feminist/m-bras (8), and feminism-ugly (1). Feminists' maternal status was shown by the co-occurrence of feminist/

ism-mother (9), feminist-child (8), feminist-kids (3), and feminist/s/ism-baby/ies (6). Media attention to sex, when considering feminists, focuses on "deviant" sex. There were 13 co-occurrences of the words feminist/s/ism and sex/sexual, but this is overshadowed by 8 co-occurrences with homosexuals/ity, 12 with lesbian/s, and 19 with gay/s. The personalization of feminists didn't seem to extend to body parts; there were very few word pairs associating feminists with legs, breasts, etc. Surprisingly (given the findings of prior research), feminists are personalized and trivialized by the media less often than are women.

The Goals Frame

Many people argue that when feminists or women are personalized and trivialized, media provide less attention to substance (e.g., the issues, goals, or agenda of the women's movement). While there is no single agenda or set of goals on which all feminists agree, we define the goals frame as concerned with civil, workplace, and reproductive rights, preventing violence toward women, and improving general conditions for women. Our target women/an words co-occurred with goals words 26,770 times, or 2.31% of references to women. Workplace issues were prevalent; for example, the word pair women/an-work/ing appeared 2,236 times, and woman/en-pay co-occurred 341 times. Words reflecting general improvements also received heavy attention, as seen by the word pairs women/an-rights (715), women-help (631), women-better (498), women/an-equal/ly/lity (410), women-change (334), and women/an-sexist/ism (56). In terms of civil rights, women/an co-occurred with lexical variants of discrimination 333 times. Reproductive rights are linked with women through the word pairs women/an-abort/s/ion/ions (686), women/an-choice/s (537), and women/an-contraceptive/ion (42). Attention to issues of violence toward woman is evident through word pairs, such as women/an-violence (941 co-occurrences), women/an-abuse (452), women/an-harassment (364), and women/an with lexical variants of rape (773).

The words feminist, feminists, and feminism appeared with goals words 1,302 times, or 5.18% of all feminist/s/ism references. Concern for improving general conditions for women, and for the women's movement in general, was more evident than a concern for the workplace. Feminist/s/ism co-occurred with movement 107 times and with agenda 14 times, feminists-beliefs co-occurred 10 times, feminist/ism-revolution co-occurred 12 times, and feminist/ism-sisterhood co-occurred 5 times. The feminist target words co-occurred with lexical variants of sexism 6 times, and with equity/equal 15 times. Workplace-oriented words were much less commonly linked to feminists, with feminist/s/ism-work co-occurring 21 times, and feminist/s/ism-working 5 times. In terms of civil rights, no lexical variants of discrimination co-occurred with the feminist target words. Reproductive rights issues appeared in word pairs such as feminist/s/ism-abortion/s/ist (27 co-occurrences) and feminist/s-choice (7). The most common co-occurrences of words representing concerns with violence toward women were feminist/s-violence (32) and feminist/s with lexical variants of rape (10). Thus, feminists are more closely associated with the (general) women's movement's goals than women are.

The Victimization Frame

Women and feminists are portrayed in a victimization frame when their representation refers to weakness, vulnerability, mental illness, crime, fear, dysfunctionality, and so forth. Our target words women and woman co-occurred with victimization words 13,756 times, representing 1.19% of all women/an references. The most commonly occurring victimization word pairs were associated with crime: women/an and variations of abuse (1,078), rape (773), victim (477), and fear (456). Women/an-vulnerable co-occurred 80 times, and women/an-wounded co-occurred 65 times.

Feminists were presented in a victimization frame in 1.00% of references to feminist/s/ism, for a total of 252 times. The leading word pairs were feminist/s-violence (32) and feminist/s-violence (31), feminist/s with lexical variants of rape (10), and feminist/s/ism with victim (8). Although critics have decried the media's tendency to portray feminists as victims, we found that women are portrayed as victims more than feminists are.

The Agency Frame

This frame reflects an active individual having strength, capability, voice, leadership, power, etc. The words women and woman appeared in an agency frame 6,920 times, or in 0.59% of all references. The most common word pairs were women/an and lexical variants of power (861), strong (822), respect (274), leader (266), advocate (132), and activist (118). Feminist words co-occurred with agency words 295 times, or 1.17% of all feminist references. The most common word pairs were feminist/s/ism and variants of activist (38), leader (34), power (28), voices (10), advocate (8), victory (6), and won (6). Thus, while neither group is strongly framed as having agency, feminists appear within an agency frame more than women do.

The Site of Struggle Frame

Our work with the text led us to wonder, "where are feminist ideas and actions located?" We identified 10 sites, each of which will be discussed briefly: home, geographic location, health, media and the arts, workplace, court/law, education, politics, sports and leisure, and religion. Table 2 presents more detail.

TABLE 2   The Site of Struggle for Women and Feminists

	WOMEN		FEMINISTS	
	#	%	#	%
Home	20,101	1.73	220	0.88
Location	17,709	1.53	292	1.16
Health	16,829	1.45	129	0.51
Media/Arts	14,272	1.23	432	1.71
Workplace	12,245	1.06	138	0.55
Courts/Law	11,754	1.01	166	0.66
Education	10,094	0.87	203	0.81
Politics	7,468	0.64	402	1.60
Sports/Leisure	4,985	0.43	36	0.14
Religion	3,944	0.34	156	0.62

Home words orient the subject to the family, home, house, marriage, furniture, guests, kitchen, patio, apartment, and so forth. Our target women words co-occurred with home words in 1.73% of all references, while our target feminist words co-occurred with home words in 0.88% of references. Thus, women were significantly more likely to be linked with home than feminists were. Geographic Location words link our target words to some actual city, state, or country. Women/an co-occurred with geographic location words in 1.53% of references; feminists in 1.16%. Women were significantly more likely to be oriented to a specific location than feminists were. Health words reflect states of illness and wellness (such as disease, health, cancer, doctor, etc). Such words co-occurred with women/an in 1.45% of references, and with feminist/s/ism in 0.51%. While issues of health and reproductive care may be feminist concerns, they're more closely associated with women.

Media and the Arts words include audience, theatre, television, book, magazine, author, radio, movies, painting, song, etc. Of all references to women/an, 1.23% were media and the arts words, as were 1.71% of all references to feminist/s/ism. Feminists are more likely to be framed in terms of media than women are. Workplace references include jobs, working, management, labor, and careers. Women/an co-occurred with workplace words 1.06% of the time, while feminist/s/ism did so in 0.55% of all cases. Although work issues are part of the feminist agenda, women are more likely to be framed in terms of work than are feminists. Court/Law words include all references to the legal system, such as judge, jury, lawyer, attorney, lawsuit, police, crime, and trial. Of all references to women/en, 1.01% co-occurred with court/law words, while 0.66% of references to feminist/s/ism did so. Thus, women are more likely to be framed in terms of the legal system than feminists are. Education words address concerns of teaching, learning, studying, school, colleges, universities, etc. They were applied about equally to the two groups: 0.87% of references to women/an and 0.81% of references to feminist/s/ism.

Politics words deal with the political system, and include government, congress, senate, senator, elections, voters, politicians, etc. Politics words occurred in 0.64% of woman/en references, and in 1.60% of feminist/s/ism references. Our target feminist words were more likely to co-occur with politics words than our target women words were. Sports and Leisure words include recreational activities of all types, such as play, sports, baseball, team, exercise, aerobics, and jogging. They appeared in 0.43% of all references to women/an, and in 0.14% of all references to feminist/s/ism. Women were more likely to be associated with sports and leisure than were feminists. Religion words address religious beliefs of all types: god, catholic, muslim, bible, religious, etc. They appeared in 0.34% of all references to women/an, and in 0.62% of all references to feminist/s/ism; feminists were more likely to be associated with religion than women were.

WHAT DO THE FRAMES REVEAL?

We found that feminists are portrayed in a remarkably different fashion than "regular" women are, but that isn't necessarily bad. While many people have argued that feminists are portrayed negatively, we found feminists are in many ways portrayed more positively than "regular" women are. Feminists are less often framed in a personalized and trivialized fashion than women are. Feminists are less often framed as victims, and more often as having agency, than women are. The goals of the women's movement are more closely associated with feminists than with women.

However, the picture of feminism and feminists in the media isn't all good, either. As Tuchman (1978) argued, symbolic annihilation occurs when social groups (such as feminists) are absent from, condemned by, or trivialized in, the media. Our research shows that feminists are not subjected to trivialization to the same extent as women in general, but feminists are personalized and trivialized in a substantial proportion of all references—the media clearly consider information such as a feminists' appearance and marital status important.

In terms of presence, feminists are relatively absent from the news and public affairs programs analyzed for this study. "Woman" or "women" appear more than 40 times as often as the words "feminist/s/ism," indicating that feminism is still routinely ignored by the media. We argue that by failing to attend to feminists and feminism, the media frame feminism as unimportant. After all, if feminism were of value, it would receive media attention. (Wouldn't it?) Whereas the six main frames we investigate in this research function actively (through word choice and word association), inattention passively (via silence) frames feminism as unimportant.

Feminists are also condemned in the media; we found feminists and feminism are significantly more likely to be demonized than women are. Feminists are nearly 10 times as likely to be associated with words such as jerks, bitches, radical, or bad than women are. Of all the frames, demonization is the third most common for feminists, which becomes even more striking in light of the fact that demonization is the frame *least* commonly applied to women.

In analyzing the site of the struggle, we found feminists less likely to appear in the context of a home or in any specific geographic location, less likely to participate in the legal system, or the workplace, less likely to be engaged in issues of health and well-being, or sports or leisure activities, than "regular" women are. The sites where feminists appear more often than women include media and the arts, politics, and religion.

The media's presentation of the domain in which feminism and feminists operate is important for several reasons. First, it implicitly informs the audience as to the appropriateness of feminist concerns—and hence a feminist perspective—in these domains. The media present a vision of a social world in which feminism doesn't really belong in the home, or the workplace, or the legal system. Feminism doesn't seem, at least according to the media, to function within the private sphere—it is more often found in the public sphere (media and the arts, politics, religion). This may reinforce the perception that feminism is neither relevant nor particularly applicable to the bulk of daily life for the majority of citizens.

The pattern of mediated representation of the site of feminist struggles also implies that feminists are not quite "normal," not quite "regular." "Real" women have homes, live in real places, and engage in regular day-to-day work and leisure activities. "Real" women do the types of things we (audience members) do—but feminists are much less likely to be portrayed in such situations than "regular" women are. Instead, feminists are involved with the types of things that most of us will never become active in—politics, and media and the arts. To the extent that feminists don't do the same things as "regular" women, audiences could easily assume that feminism and its concerns are not relevant to regular people, and perhaps are actually abnormal.

NOTES

1. See, for example, Gamson, 1992; Iyengar, 1991; McLeod, 1995; Price, Tewksbury, & Powers, 1996; Shoemaker, 1982; Terkildsen & Schnell, 1997.

2. We thank James Danowski of the University of Illinois at Chicago for his assistance in collecting and analyzing the data.

3. All segments of these programs aired between May 1993 and January 1996 were analyzed: ABC: *Breaking News, Good Morning America, News Special, Nightline, Prime Time Live, This Week with David Brinkley, Turning Point, World News Saturday, World News Sunday, World News Tonight, 20/20.* CNN: *Both Sides with Jesse Jackson; Capital Gang, Crossfire, Diplomatic License, Evans & Novak, Future Watch, Health Week, Health Works, Inside Business, Inside Politics, Larry King Live, Moneyline, Moneyweek, News, Newsmaker Saturday; Pinnacle, Reliable Sources, Science and Technology Week, Showbiz Today, Special Assignment, Talkback Live, Your Money.* NPR: *All Things Considered, Morning Edition, Weekend Edition.* PBS: *American Experience, Charlie Rose, Frontline, Nova, Wall Street Journal Report, Washington Week in Review.*

4. As you read this, you may have a sense that you want more detail about the words, that you'd like to read some of the sentences in which they appeared so that you can see the words in context. However, to computational linguistics researchers, the collocated word pair *is* the context. Collocation is a widely accepted contextualizing device, especially when analyzing large bodies of text as we do here. Even though it may initially seem unusual that we don't provide any exemplar sentences, we are following accepted practice for this methodology.

IT'S YOUR TURN: WHAT DO YOU THINK? WHAT WILL YOU FIND?

1. What does it mean to you when someone is a "feminist?" Where did you get those ideas? Have you ever said or heard anything like, "Well, I'm not really a feminist or anything, but I think it's unfair that Catholic women aren't allowed to serve as Priests just because they're female"? Why do you think people might frame their statements about the role of women in such a manner?

2. Why do you think the media present feminism and feminists so differently than "regular" women are presented?

3. Investigate your local newspaper for references to women and to feminists, and compare what you find to the findings presented here.

4. We'd expect *Ms. Magazine* to frame feminists at least as positively—if not the same as—as it frames women. Read a few issues of *Ms.*, make the comparison, and find out for sure. Are you surprised at what you found? Why do you think *Ms.* frames these two groups as it does?

REFERENCES

Danowski, J. A. (1993). Network analysis of message content. In W. D. Richards Jr., & G. A. Barnett (Eds.), *Progress in communication sciences, Vol XII* (pp 197–221). Norwood, NJ: Ablex.

Gamson, W. A. (1992). The social psychology of collective action. In A. D. Morris & C. M. Mueller (Eds.), *Frontiers in social movement theory.* New Haven: Yale University Press.

Gamson, W. A. (1989). News as framing: Comments on Graber. *American Behavioral Scientist, 33*(2), 157–161.

Gitlin, T. (1980). *The whole world is watching: Mass media in the making and unmaking of the New Left.* Berkeley, CA: University of California Press.

Iyengar, S. (1991). *Is anyone responsible?: How television frames political issues.* Chicago: The University of Chicago Press.

McLeod, D. M. (1995). Communicating deviance: The effects of television news coverage of social protest. *Journal of Broadcasting and Electronic Media, 39,* 4–19.

Price, V., Tewksbury, D., & Powers, E. (1996). *Switching trains of thought: The impact of news frames on readers' cognitive responses.* Paper presented at the annual convention of the International Communication Association, Chicago.

Rhode, D. L. (1997). Media images/feminist issues. In M. A. Fineman & M. T. McCluskey (Eds.), *Feminism, media and the law.* (pp. 8–21). New York: Oxford University Press.

Roeh, I. (1981). Israel in Lebanon: Language and images of storytelling. In W. C. Adams (Ed.), *Television coverage of the Middle East* (pp. 76–88). Norwood, NJ: Ablex.

Shoemaker, P. (1982). The perceived legitimacy of deviant political groups: Two experiments on media effects. *Communication Research, 9,* 249–286.

Terkildsen, N., & Schnell, F. (1997). How media frames public opinion: An analysis of the women's movement. *Political Research Quarterly, 50,* 879–900.

Tuchman, G. (1978). Introduction: The symbolic annihilation of women by the mass media. In G. Tuchman, A. K. Daniels, & J. W. Benet (Eds)., *Hearth and home: Images of women in the mass media.* (pp. 3–38). New York: Oxford University Press.

5.4   "OUTWHITING THE WHITES": AN EXAMINATION OF THE PERSISTENCE OF ASIAN AMERICAN MODEL MINORITY DISCOURSE

Chiung Hwang Chen

> *If a stereotype reflects positive attributes, it's still a stereotype, and it still presents a group of people in a simplistic and hence inaccurate fashion. The author examines the persistence of one such stereotype: Asian Americans as a "model minority."*

THE MODEL IMAGE OF ASIAN AMERICANS

You've heard about it before. Perhaps your parents warned you about it. You might have discussed it with your classmates. You may even believe it. There's a group of people who are smarter, who study harder, and have more success than the rest of us. These people are Asian Americans.

At least that's the stereotype. Of course, reality is much more complex. But people act on these stereotypes. On campuses all over America, students warn one another to stay out of classes where there are too many Asian faces. "Asian Americans are curve wreckers, grade grinds," they say. This stereotype of academic success is part of a larger stereotype of general Asian American success. Asian Americans are called the "model minority" because many Americans think that Asian Americans have succeeded in American society when other minority groups have not.

Where did this stereotype come from? The American mass media helped create and perpetuate it.

Before World War II, the stereotype of Asian Americans was negative: we were the "Yellow Peril." Large numbers of Asians immigrated to America during the nineteenth-century gold rush. Cultural and racial differences made Asian Americans odd to white eyes. Asian population growth in the American West also made white workers insecure about their jobs. A fear of Asian Americans taking power in America produced the Yellow Peril stereotype. But as World War II ended, the dominant media image began to shift.

The media began praising Asian Americans, especially because during World War II Japanese Americans had endured the confiscation of their homes, land, and property as well as their imprisonment in internment camps with apparently little complaint. After the war, many Japanese Americans quickly recovered economically. The national news and popular magazines[1] noticed, and began to publish "positive" stories of how Asian American culture produced success.

In the 1950s, the media focused on the lack of crime in Asian American communities. In the 1960s, the media wrote about Asian American economic success. The media tried to explain why Asian Americans succeeded when other minority groups apparently did not. Since then, the trend has continued; the media focused on Asian American economic success, reporting that this minority group was "outwhiting the Whites" ("Success story," 1971, p. 24) in both economic and academic terms. These media portrayals helped to create a model minority stereotype: Asian Americans were successful, smart, and patriotic. They worked hard, didn't break the law, and had stable families. They epitomized American success. In other words, they apparently showed what people willing to work hard in America can achieve.

Unsurprisingly, this stereotype led to a backlash against Asian Americans. Other Americans began to wonder how they could compete against Asian Americans. If Asian Americans were highly represented at America's best universities, for example, some people began to think that their numbers should be limited so that more whites and others could attend. Asian Americans suffered socially and even economically when people characterized them as one-dimensional academic nerds. We were supposed to lack communication skills and thus were sometimes not promoted to leadership and management positions. Asian Americans even suffered violence from people who resented their supposed success. This stereotype also gave the mistaken impression that Asian Americans didn't suffer from discrimination because they seemed to succeed. In its extreme form, it led people to assume that discrimination no longer existed at all in America; the logic suggested that any unsuccessful group fails because of its own shortcomings.

In the past few decades, people began questioning the accuracy of the model minority stereotype. In fact, the stereotype misleads because Asian Americans are not as one-dimensional as the stereotype has it. Not only that, but Asian Americans may not actually be as successful as the stereotype suggests. At the very least, the truth is more complex. Asian Americans seem economically successful partly because so many live in California where the cost of living and salaries are higher than in much of the country. But salaries and job levels of Asian Americans are lower than those of whites with similar education. Asian Americans do face discrimination. There is an Asian American underclass. In these and other ways, reality is more complex than the stereotype suggests. We all would be better off if we thought of Asian Americans in non-stereotypical ways.

ON STEREOTYPES

Yet the model minority stereotype remains strong in America. Why is it so hard to get rid of stereotypes? One reason is because stereotypes utilize simple forms of thinking and save us from more complex thinking. In fact, we probably can't get beyond stereotypes altogether. Long ago the famous journalist Walter Lippman (1922, p. 16) said that "the real environment is altogether too big, too complex, and too fleeting for direct acquaintance. We are not equipped to deal with so much subtlety, so much variety, so many permutations and combinations. Although we have to act in that environment, we have to reconstruct it on a simpler model before we can manage with it." We create simplified pictures of the way the world works—stereotypes—to operate efficiently in the world.

These simplified pictures are not altogether false, often, though they are misleadingly incomplete. But stereotypes are more than just any simplified pictures or ideas. These simplified pictures insist that other groups differ from "us" in fundamental and even dangerous ways. So even though we always have a tendency to stereotype, because it makes life more manageable, stereotyping is harmful because it unnecessarily separates different groups of people. Thus, we might suggest, stereotypes may always exist, but we should also always fight against them.

Journalism can prompt people to look beyond simplified notions to what is really happening in the world. Journalism can be a tool to fight stereotypes. At least it can be if journalists are aware of the harm that stereotypes cause and consciously fight the stereotypes. If they aren't aware, journalists tend to repeat—or *reproduce*—stereotypes.

In the 1950s, 1960s, and 1970s, news magazine journalists writing about Asian Americans seemed unaware that they were creating and repeating a stereotype. Their efforts strengthened the model minority stereotype. But by the 1980s and the 1990s, journalists knew that this stereotype existed. They also knew that many people thought it was harmful, despite its seemingly positive nature. Some journalists chose to perpetuate the stereotype; after all, it seems to compliment Asian Americans, and it apparently coincides with some facts. Others agreed with the critique of the stereotype, however, and pointed out how the stereotype fooled people.

These latter efforts to fight the stereotype were not as successful as journalists probably intended them to be. In spite of calling the stereotype into question, parts of their stories strengthened the stereotype. This happened, I believe, because most journalists continued to write within a model minority *discourse*. Even while they claimed that the stereotype was misleading, much within their stories continued to support the stereotype.

ON DISCOURSE

Before showing how these stories reproduced the stereotype, we need to understand the term "discourse." Discourse can be a complex concept, but here I simply use it to mean a particular way of writing about a particular subject. Writing within a particular discourse means that we ask the same types of questions as others who have written about the subject; we also find the same kinds of answers. The questions and answers may not be identical for everyone writing within the discourse—people may even strongly disagree with one another—but they are similar enough that people have a hard time thinking of other questions and answers.

Let's take an example—one that a key scholar of discourse used (Foucault, 1990): homosexuality. Historically, there has been a medical discourse about homosexuality. The discourse assumed that homosexuality is abnormal. It also assumed that a biological explanation must lie behind this "abnormality." Once people made these assumptions, the key question became why some people are homosexual. Other possible questions, such as why only one form of expressing sexuality is regarded as normal, were ignored. While many answers were given to the former question, political, cultural, and social answers were largely disregarded, at least by those operating within the discourse.

A discourse is not a stereotype. But it can support stereotypes by causing people to look for answers only to certain types of questions. In the case of the model minority discourse, I believe that is exactly what happened. The primary problem with the model minority discourse is that those writing within the discourse fixate upon a single question: Why are Asian Americans so successful? This isn't a bad question if journalists also ask other questions. But for journalists writing about Asian Americans, it became virtually the only question. Consequently, despite efforts to show how the model minority stereotype simplifies and misleads, journalists in the 1980s and 1990s kept reproducing important aspects of the stereotype.

MEDIA EXAMPLES OF MODEL MINORITY DISCOURSE

My argument stems from analysis of news magazines' stories on Asian American from the 1950s to 1990s. I concentrate on the 1980s and the 1990s, and provide typical examples from these years, because this is a key period for journalists' awareness of the stereotype. A 1984 story in *U.S. News & World Report* noted that being Asian American doesn't automatically mean success; large numbers of Asian Americans live in poverty or barely scrape along. Thus, it demonstrated awareness that the model minority stereotype, like all stereotypes, obscures wide variations among a group of people. The story also noted that many Asian American scholars disliked the stereotype. But it also quickly stated that "success stories abound" within the Asian American community, with poor Asian Americans "climbing out of poverty." In spite of concerns about the stereotype, the article stated that "there's no denying that Asians, especially the long-established families and the new immigrants with education and skills, have done well" (Asian Americans, 1984, p. 47). This same pattern of mentioning potential problems with the model minority stereotype, only to quickly reaffirm the importance of Asian American success, occurred often throughout the 1980s (see also "Asian Americans," 1982; "A formula," 1984; "Do colleges," 1987; Bell, 1985; Brand, 1987; Doerner, 1985).

A problem with the model minority stereotype is that it doesn't differ as completely from the Yellow Peril stereotype as it seems to on the surface. Gary Okihiro (1994) and others argued that both stereotypes depend on an underlying prejudicial fear of conquest from Asia. The Yellow Peril represented military and physical conquest, while the model minority represents more purely economic conquest of America (as if Asian Americans are not real Americans). The model minority represents a fear that Asian Americans work too hard and study too much, and will thus assume power within America.

Some journalists recognized that the model minority stereotype held connections to the Yellow Peril stereotype through a common underlying fear. But because reporters were also so concerned to explain Asian American success, they ended up reinforcing the fear upon which both stereotypes depended.

Why did Asian Americans succeed? In the *New Republic*, Bell said it was because they "consistently worked 15 to 18 hours a day" (1985, p. 30). A *Newsweek* story quoted a Vietnamese immigrant: "Some of the kids only study, study, study, and don't enjoy the normal activities of high school" ("A formula," 1984, p. 78); according to Brand in *Time*, they became "relentless book-worms" (1987, p. 46). Zinsmeister (1987) found that Asian American workers and students were able to maintain themselves at little expense and were almost robot-like; they labored and studied for hours on end without filling their human needs for relaxation, fun, and pleasure. Many articles (especially those by Brand and Zinsmeister) accurately recognized that Asian Americans were seen as an "updated yellow peril"; however, they gave readers little reason to seriously question the stereotype. They were more concerned that their readers understood Asian American success. Thus, because they continued to write within model minority *discourse,* they could not effectively counteract the model minority *stereotype.*

In the 1990s, journalists continued to recognize that the model minority stereotype was problematic. Some tried to dispel its misleading images. Still, many struggled to produce non-stereotypical images because they continued to center above all else the question of why Asian Americans succeed. A 1993 article in *Time* is one example. The author, James Walsh, featured a young Asian American, Took Took Thongthiraj, as "the personification of American promise" (p. 55). With a perfect grade-point average at UCLA, Thongthiraj intended to get a Ph.D. and teach women's and Asian American studies at the university level. Her story, according to Walsh, was "hardly unique," because Asian Americans approximated Garrison Keillor's Lake Wobegon "where all the children are above average." Walsh commented that Asian Americans reflected their cultures (he meant Asian, not American) "extremely well, especially those who have drawn from the wellsprings of the older civilizations of India, China, Japan and Korea" (p. 55). These cultures, he suggested, produced the "outstanding success stories" of Asian Americans.

Like many journalists of the 1980s, Walsh noted problems with the model minority stereotype. He explained that although Asian Americans enjoyed material success, they bore "resentment, envy, even backlashes of violence from such other subnationalities as blacks and Latinos" (he could also have mentioned whites) (p. 55). He also helpfully suggested that Asian American experiences do not constitute a single story. Many from less economically developed backgrounds in Asia have a difficult time in America getting beyond dead-end jobs or reliance on government handouts. In such communities, delinquency and gangs are major problems, he reported. The Asian American story isn't just one of uninterrupted success. But despite these helpful moves toward questioning the stereotype, Asian American success continued to be Walsh's major focus. He cited additional Asian American success stories to show that hard work and sacrifice are the dominant theme of this group's experiences.

Another *Time* story (Allis, 1991) tried to deconstruct the stereotype of the Asian American "science geek." It partially succeeded, but reinforced other aspects of the model minority image at the same time. Allis reported that many young Asian Americans were "chafing at the model minority myth," and turning instead to fields in social sciences and liberal arts. For example, Tohoru Masamune, an MIT graduate, gave up his high-paying job with a computer company to become an actor. The story quoted Masamune: "It was a huge risk, but it is also a huge risk going into something your heart's not into" (p. 64). David Shin, likewise, scored 1,580 out of 1,600 on his college boards but consciously chose to leave science behind, rejecting MIT and attending Harvard to study government.

Although well-intentioned, and while undercutting one aspect of the stereotype, Allis didn't quite debunk the model minority image. By interviewing only students from prestigious schools, he did little to lead his readers to believe anything other than that Asian Americans still flooded into Ivy League schools. Asian Americans remained unchallenged as a natural model minority; Asian Americans who succeeded still garnered all the attention.

Thus in the 1980s and 1990s, some journalists recognized problems with the model minority stereotype and tried to show how it was misleading. But, I believe their efforts weren't entirely successful, largely because they continued to insist that Asian American success was the most important attribute of the Asian American community—they continued to write within the model minority discourse. So most emphasized the same question in their articles: Why do Asian Americans succeed? And they continued to find similar answers to those who had earlier helped create the model minority stereotype. Therefore, these articles didn't effectively confront the fear that rests behind the model minority stereotype: Asian Americans will wrest power from "real" Americans.

A MOVE AWAY FROM MODEL MINORITY DISCOURSE

One article, however, more effectively moved away from the model minority stereotype. It did so by writing outside of model minority discourse. It didn't ignore the fact or question of Asian American success, but it didn't center it as the most important issue. In this 1990 *Time* article,

Howard G. Chua-eoan wrote about problems with the model minority image and the painful struggles of Asian Americans in their American "paradise."

Chua-eoan didn't deny that many Asian Americans found success in America, but he also pointed out that "there is no pan-Asian prosperity, just as there is no such thing as an 'Asian American'" (p. 33); it's more accurate to speak of Chinese Americans, Japanese Americans, and Thai Americans than Asian Americans. It is also more accurate to distinguish between new immigrants and those who have lived several generations in America. Although there were middle-class fourth-generation Japanese Americans and prospering new immigrants from Taiwan and South Korea, there were also matriarchally organized Filipinos and Hmong tribesmen who depended on government assistance. He used "the most troubled Asian Americans"—refugees from Indochina—as examples to show that many in the Asian American community lived with little hope. These Cambodians had few marketable skills and entered the workforce at the lowest levels. Survivors of a genocidal war, these people felt the warfare had followed them across the ocean. They lived where walls were painted "GOOKS GO HOME." Chua-eoan quoted a mother who said, "My daughter was shot, my son stabbed. I used to be happy here. Now all I do is worry. I worry all the time" (p. 34). The reality, according to the article, was often disguised by the model minority image; reality seemed a "strange notion" to those who were bombarded by the media's stories of Asian American whiz kids and professional success.

In Chua-eoan's view, the model minority stereotype implied that all was well in the Asian American community and blinded people to the needs of individual Asian Americans. Like other articles, the story also noted that the stereotype had triggered a backlash from both whites and other minorities. But it dissected this backlash more carefully than other articles did. Chua-eoan pointed out that until recently Canadian businesses owned more of California than Japanese did; it was the Japanese, however, who were deemed encroachers by the media. The story also pointed more carefully to how Asian Americans remain discriminated against, no matter how much assimilation and success they achieve, simply because so many Americans refuse to regard someone with an Asian face as anything but an outsider. It told, for example, of how medical school graduates emigrating from India found it almost impossible to get residencies in Los Angeles area hospitals. They have little choice except to take lower paying jobs as hospital orderlies or lab technicians.

In essence, Chua-eoan moved the center of attention from why so many Asian Americans succeed to how the model minority stereotype causes problems for Asian Americans and misleads others about Asian American experiences. Chua-eoan did not deny that many Asian Americans succeed. But he seemed to recognize that reproducing the model minority stereotype yet another time, by focusing our attention on success, causes more harm than good. He saw that America has important problems that the model minority stereotype encourages us to overlook. He portrayed Asian Americans as real people with real aspirations and problems, and not as the one-dimensional, success-at-all-cost creatures of the model minority stereotype. He did not contribute to fear of Asian Americans. In essence, he counteracted the model minority stereotype by leaving the model minority discourse.

UNDERSTANDING THE POWER OF DISCOURSE

This reading reviews one racial stereotype the American news media help create and reproduce—the model minority stereotype of Asian Americans. Although the stereotype seems positive, it carries harmful effects. Most particularly, it remains close to the negative Yellow

Peril stereotype; both appeal to a racist fear that Asians might illegitimately take power within America. News magazines unselfconsciously produced and perpetuated this stereotype from about the 1940s to the 1970s. In the 1980s and 1990s, journalists became aware that this stereotype produced harmful effects. Some journalists wrote about how the stereotype was misleading. But they didn't altogether succeed at counteracting the stereotype because they continued to write within model minority discourse—a discourse centrally concerned with explaining Asian American success.

I believe that journalists can effectively combat the stereotype only by writing from outside the model minority discourse. Journalists are aware of many minority stereotypes; however, most do not understand the power of discourse. If journalists keep asking the same questions about particular minority groups, they will likely reproduce the same stereotypes, even if inadvertently. Journalists need to pay more attention to discourses in order to write fair and balanced stories about minorities.

NOTE

1. This reading is drawn from a larger project (Chen, 2000). The primary sources for that project were mainstream news magazines (i.e., *Time*, *Newsweek*, *U.S. News & World Report*) and popular magazines (i.e., *New Republic*, *Nation*, *People*). The time period covered was from 1942 (the beginning of U.S. involvement in WWII) to the end of 1999. There I used discourse analysis to examine stories dealing with some aspects of Asian American success.

IT'S YOUR TURN: WHAT DO YOU THINK? WHAT WILL YOU FIND?

1. As small groups, analyze four or five of the articles on Asian Americans listed as references. Do you think the articles end up perpetuating or combating the model minority stereotype? Which aspects support and which counteract the stereotype?

2. What types of discourses do the news media utilize in stories about other minority groups? What are the most common stereotypes about other minority groups within America? What do you think the relationship is between these stereotypes and media discourses?

3. Many people think that "positive" stereotypes cause no harm. What do you think? Why? Do the media have a role, or even an obligation, to fight against stereotypes that are harmful? Why or why not? What about when the stereotype and its harms are more controversial?

4. Does it violate journalistic values of neutrality and objectivity when journalists consciously fight against harmful stereotypes? Does it violate journalistic values of neutrality and objectivity when journalists inadvertently reproduce harmful stereotypes? Is it possible to write about minorities in ways that neither fight against stereotypes nor reproduce stereotypes, given that so many people are already aware of (and perhaps believe) such stereotypes? Discuss these three questions in relationship to each other.

REFERENCES

Allis, S. (1991, March 25). Kicking the nerd syndrome. *Time*, pp. 64–66.

Asian-Americans: A "model minority." (1982, December 6). *Newsweek*, pp. 39–42, 51.

Asian-Americans: Are they making the grade? (1984, April 2). *U.S. News & World Report*, pp. 41–47.

Bell, D. A. (1985, July 15/22). The triumph of Asian-Americans. *New Republic*, pp. 24–31.

Brand, D. (1987, August 31). The new whiz kids. *Time*, pp. 46–51.

Chen, C. H. (2000). *From pariah to paragon: Mormon and Asian America model minority discourse in news and popular magazines.* Unpublished dissertation: University of Iowa.

Chua-eoan, H. G. (1990, April 9). Strangers in paradise. *Time*, pp. 32–35.

Do colleges set Asian quotas? (1987, February 9). *Newsweek*, pp. 60.

Doerner, W. R. (1985, July 8). To America with skills. *Time*, pp. 42–44.

A formula for success. (1984, April 23). *Newsweek*, pp. 77–78.

Foucault, M. (1990). *The history of sexuality: An introduction*, Vol. 1. New York: Vintage Books.

Lippmann, W. (1922). *Public opinion*. New York: Harcourt, Brace.

Okihiro, G. Y. (1994). *Margins and mainstreams: Asians in American history and culture.* Seattle: University of Washington Press.

Success story: Outwhiting the Whites. (1971, June 21). *Newsweek*, pp. 24–25.

Walsh, J. (1993, Fall Special Issue). The perils of success. *Time*, pp. 55–56.

Zinsmeister, K. (1987, November). Prejudice against Asians: Anxiety and acceptance. *Current*, pp. 37–40.

5.5 THE UNCHANGING FACE OF THE NEWS: A CONTENT ANALYSIS OF ONLINE NEWS SITES

Xiaomei Cai and Cynthia Lont

The authors analyzed photos on the homepages of five major news Web sites to uncover how gender and race were portrayed. The results were compared to prior work analyzing how the front pages of print newspapers portrayed women between 1989 and 2007.

Until a few years ago, the "important" news was on the front pages of print newspapers. Whether a small community paper or the national press, the stories on the front pages announced to the readers this is *the news* of the day. It is reasonable then to expect that those who were seen on the front-page photos were *the most important people* of the day.

With the decline of print newspaper readership and the increase in readership of online news by 18–24 years old readers (Zickuhr, 2010), the home pages of online news sites replaced the front page as the door to the inside news. Are these home pages merely electronic replacements of print newspapers' front pages, with the same content, or do they differ in significant ways including the way they portray different groups?

Prior research found newspapers under-represented women in front page stories. Even when women were featured, they were more likely to appear in crime, accident, or feature stories than in hard news, political, or business stories (Potter, 1985). Men were three to five times more likely than women to appear in front page photos (Blackwood, 1983).

One longitudinal study, presented by Lont & Bridge in earlier editions of this book, focused on a sample of the front pages of newspapers across the United States over an 18-year period (Bridge, 1989, 1992, 1994, 1995a, 1995b, 1996, 2000; Lont & Bridge, 2008). These content analyses examined the roles assigned to women and men on the front pages. What is compelling about Lont and Bridges' work is the study of the same variables in the same medium, over a long period of time.

The studies are easy to understand, identifying the number of women and men shown in front-page photographs, quoted as experts in the stories (references), and writing the articles (bylines). Although other factors were added or deleted over the 18-year span of these studies, these three elements remained constant.

156   PART TWO   CONTENT

TABLE 1   Percentage of Women on the Front Page of U.S. Newspapers 1989–2007

	1989	1992	1994	1995	1996	2000	2007
Photos	24%	32%	39%	33%	33%	32%	31%
References	11%	13%	25%	19%	15%	17%	21%
Bylines	27%	34%	33%	34%	34%	28%	34%

All percentages are rounded.

Table 1 shows that women were in the front-page news between 11% and 39% of the time, and, therefore, men were in the front-page news between 61% and 76% of the time. In the 1989 study, women were 24% of those portrayed in the photographs, 11% of the references, and 27% of the bylines. The all-time high for women was in 1994 (39% in photographs, 25% of references, and 33% of bylines). By 2007, the numbers had fallen with women portrayed 31% (photographs), 21% (references), and 34% (bylines).

Although women are 50.7% of the population in the United States, continue to earn more money each year, are a large part of purchase decisions (whether they provide all or part of the income), are more educated, live longer than men, and are the head of more households than ever before in U.S. history, their numbers as reflected on the front pages of U.S. newspapers in 2007 were not equal to those of men, nor had they been over the past 18 years.

OUR STUDY OF ONLINE NEWS SITES

Perhaps women and men are portrayed more equitably in online news. To test this, we analyzed the home pages of five online news sites, representing a more international perspective than the prior studies of U.S. newspapers referenced above.

Just as print newspapers have front pages, Internet news sites have home pages, pulling readers deeper into stories within the site. Each home page we analyzed had a similar format, although they differed in the number and placement of photos and stories. Unlike the front pages of newspapers, there are few bylines presented on the home page stories. The home page often has a photo with only one or two lines about each story; bylines, if any, usually appear only after clicking through to the full story (which was not part of our data collection method described below). We couldn't replicate Bridge's analysis of bylines or references on the home pages, but we studied how the photos portrayed women and men, and added the variable of race.

The questions we asked were: How is gender represented on the home page photos of the most popular news sites? Are women and men equally portrayed within the photos within the same types of news? How does this compare to the front pages of print newspapers between 1989 and 2007? How is race portrayed on the most popular news sites home page photos?

We used Alexa.com to identify the top 20 most viewed news Web sites. Alexa.com is the leading company providing reliable online traffic data (Williams, 1998). Of the Web sites listed in the top 20 in September 2009, we selected five (excluding news aggregators such as *Yahoo! News* and *Digg* because they do not generate original news reports). The Web sites we analyzed were: *CNN.com, nytimes.com, bbc.co.uk, usatoday.com,* and *reuters.com.*

Unlike print newspapers, online news sites change throughout the day. What days and times of day would we capture and examine on the front home page news? From October 2009 through November 2010, we randomly selected two constructed weeks and using the software Snagit we "snagged" the front page of each news site. Based on Nielsen NetRatings data (T. Gontek, personal communication, June 10, 2009), we found three times a day when the most people were online: between 9:00 and 11:00 a.m. (74% of the online population is online during this time), between 2:00 and 4:00 p.m. (80%), and between 6:00 and 8:00 p.m. (81%). We captured the entire homepage of each news site three times a day during each of the pre-selected 14 days over a 6-month period. Because we were studying gender and race, we only examined photos that featured at least one human being, excluding photos without people and nonphotographic illustrations. The 210 home pages analyzed contained a total of 2,091 people in 1,652 photos. On average, each page contained eight photos of people. Ultimately, our sample included 321 photos from *cnn.com*, 299 photos from *nytimes.com*, 412 from *usatoday.com*, 371 from *bbcnews.co.uk*, and 249 from *reuters.com*.

We coded each of the 2,091 people for *gender* (male; female; unknown), *race* (Black, white, Asian, other), and *Hispanic ethnicity* (yes, no) based on physical characteristics. Ordinarily, we would use terms such as "African American" instead of "Black"; but due to the international nature of our sample, the term "African American" did not fit. We coded type of news coverage as *soft* or *hard* news. Hard news is the coverage of events which are factual and need immediate reporting; soft news does not have a short shelf life. *Story topic* was coded using 12 categories, such as domestic politics, military activities, defense and terrorism, living, style, entertainment, arts and travel, and sports *Name identification* of the person in the photo reflected whether the individual's name was written out in the caption or the story. Based on the 2010 Standard Occupational Classification published by the Bureau of Labor Statistics (2010), *occupation* was coded according to 15 categories which ranged from politician to spouse.

Four coders went through 20 hours of training, practicing on Web sites which were not part of our study. Intercoder reliability was between 71% and 91%.

THE REPRESENTATION OF GENDER AND RACE ON THE ONLINE NEWS SITES

What did we find out about the portrayal of the 2,091 people in the photos? At 32% female (68% male), the ratio of women to men isn't all that different from most of the photograph-related findings presented in Table 1. Whites represented 69% of the sample; 19% were Black, 5% Asian, and 3% Hispanic. Of the whites, 69% were male and 30% were female; of Blacks, the numbers were 77% and 23% ; of Asians, 51% and 49%; and of Hispanics, 77% and 23%. With the exception of Asians, a small percent of the overall sample, men significantly outnumbered women.

With regard to gender and type of the news, 40% of the women appeared in the living/style/entertainment and arts category; 25% of the men appeared in this category. Only 16% of the women, in contrast to 31% of the men, appeared in photos dealing with hard news. In general, this tells the reader that women are not part of the factual, "needs-to-be reported now" news but in the softer area of entertainment and lifestyle. Some might argue that soft news is not as important as hard news and, hence, that women's contributions are not as important.

Additional analysis found that 24% of all men, but only 20% of all women, were identified by name. Fewer than half of the sample was identified by occupation, but of these more than half (53%) of the men and only 33% of women were so identified. Once again, men are identified by name and occupation, which connects them to the important news area of work. Women are less likely to be identified by name or occupation, and may be seen as less important if the reader neither knows her name nor what she does for a living.

SO WHAT?

Our students often ask, "Who cares if women and men, and people of color, are not seen within the news sites?" Good question. There are several answers.

If women and men are each roughly half the population, then one would think that each gender should be represented in the news about half of the time, but that is not reflected in our data. Some journalism scholars argue there are fewer women and people of color reporting the news, therefore, fewer to write stories which portray these groups. While this might have been true in the 1970s and 1980s, the number of women and people of color in the field of journalism has risen dramatically since the 1970 Equal Employment Opportunity Commission (EEOC) mandate that women and minorities be included in the field of journalism. So why don't we see more equitable representation in the online news?

Some argue women don't make enough "important" news to be covered and, hence, they are not shown as often as men. Once again, we found that the news on the home page is often connected to war and politics and men are prominent in these areas. The argument can be made as to whether this news is more important than health care, environmental issues, or education where we see a higher representation of women, but does not explain why fewer men of color are also portrayed on the home pages of these online news sites.

The most important question is how the media affect our perception of ourselves. Some mass media studies and theories indicate the media affect us in multiple ways (Gerbner & Gross, 1976). If females are portrayed in the Style and Entertainment section and males are on the seen as leaders on the home pages, what does that tell the women and men, girls and boys of color who read the news? Most of us decide what we want and can be based on the role models we see. The more we see women and people of color in diverse and nonstereotypical roles, the more possibilities open up for all.

Gender representation in media has been studied from a variety of perspectives (e.g., Morgan, 1982, 1987; Potter, 1985; Signorielli & Kahlenberg, 2001). The Cultural Indicators Project tracked the gender representation on prime time television for decades (Shanahan, Signorielli, & Morgan, 2008). Until the 1980s, men outnumbered women by two or three to one on prime time television. Women were less likely to be portrayed as working outside the home and were significantly younger than their male counterparts (Signorielli, 1989). Unlike entertainment content, news reports are meant to reflect the real world, so it is conceivable that news portrayals of gender have longer lasting effects on the audience.

Gaye Tuchman (1978) referred to the absence of a specific group in the media as "Symbolic Annihilation"—the idea that if a group is not represented in the media, then that group does not exist in the minds of the audience. Our study of photos on Internet news sites reveals that the term is still appropriate 30 years later. Certain groups are portrayed more in the news; others are not. The issue of how it affects those who read the news remains important.

IT'S YOUR TURN: WHAT DO YOU THINK? WHAT WILL YOU FIND?

1. Many students believe the roles assigned to women or people of color in the media are less stereotypical and more diverse than they were 20 years ago. Do you agree or disagree? What examples can you give to support your opinion?

2. If there are more female and minority journalists than there were 20 years ago, why do you think Internet news sites continue to represent white men more often than women and people of color?

3. Conduct a content analysis. Randomly capture three days of an Internet news site home page or newspaper front page. Count how many times you see women, men, and people of different races in the

photos. How do these percentages compare to the population? Then, do the same with the Sports or Style sections. Are these section percentages different from the home page? Why do they differ? Next, write down what males are identified as doing and what females are identified as doing. What percentage of female and males are identified by their relationship to another human being (spouse, sibling, parent)? Do the percentages differ across sections? Finally, write down what people of different races are doing in the photos. Who are the leaders, the followers, the celebrities, the victims, or the criminals? What do these roles say about these groups in our culture or your local community?

REFERENCES

Blackwood, R. E. (1983). The content of news photos: Roles portrayed by men and women. *Journalism Quarterly, 60,* 710–714.

Bridge, M. J. (1989). *The big stories: A woman's voice is rarely heard.* Published report. Alexandria, VA: Unabridged Communication.

Bridge, M. J. (1992). *The news, as if all people mattered.* Published report. Alexandria, VA: Unabridged Communication.

Bridge, M. J. (1994). *Arriving on the scene: Women's growing presence in the newsroom.* Published report. Alexandria, VA: Unabridged Communication.

Bridge, M. J. (1995a). *Slipping from the scene: News coverage of females drops.* Published report. Alexandria, VA: Unabridged Communication.

Bridge, M. J. (1995b). What's next? In C. M. Lont (Ed.), *Women in the media: Content, careers, and criticism* (pp. 15–28). Belmont, CA: Wadsworth Press.

Bridge, M. J. (1996). *Marginalizing women: Front-page news coverage of females declines in 1996.* Published report. Alexandria, VA: Unabridged Communications.

Bridge, M. J. (2000). *Sidelining women: A Fact Sheet.* Unpublished paper.

Bureau of Labor Statistics. (2010). *2010 standard occupational classification.* Retrieved October 6, 2011, from http://www.bls.gov/soc/soc_structure_2010.pdf

Gerbner, G., & Gross, L. (1976). Living with television: The violence profile. *Journal of Communication, 26,* 173–179.

Lont, C.M., & Bridge, M.J. (2008). Confronting the front pages: A content analysis. In R. A. Lind, *Race/gender/media: Considering diversity across audiences,* content, and producers (2nd ed, pp. 128–135). Boston: Allyn & Bacon.

Morgan, M. (1982). Television and adolescents' sex role stereotypes: A longitudinal study. *Journal of Personality and Social Psychology, 43,* 947–955.

Morgan, M. (1987). Television, sex-role attitudes and behavior. *Journal of Early Adolescence, 7,* 269–282.

Potter, J. (1985). Gender representation in elite newspapers. *Journalism Quarterly, 62,* 636–640.

Shanahan, J., Signorielli, N., & Morgan, M. (2008, May). *Television and sex roles 30 years hence: A retrospective and current look from a cultural indicators perspective.* Paper presented at the International Communication Association.

Signorielli, N. (1989). Television and conceptions about sex roles: Maintaining conventionality and the status quo. *Sex Roles, 21,* 341–360.

Signorielli, N., & Kahlenberg, S. (2001). Television's world of work in the nineties. *Journal of Broadcasting & Electronic Media, 45,* 1–19.

Tuchman, G. (1978). The symbolic annihilation of women by the mass media. In G. Tuchman, A. Daniels, & S. Benet (Eds.), *Hearth and home: Images of women in the mass media* (pp. 5–38), New York: Oxford University Press.

Williams, M. (1998, September 28). Alexa makes sense out of the chaos that tangles the Web. *The Washington Post,* F23.

Zickuhr, K. (2010). *Generations 2010.* Retrieved October 6, 2011, from http://www.pewinternet.org/~/media//Files/Reports/2010/PIP_Generations_and_Tech10.pdf

5.6 GAMBLING WITH IDENTITY: AMERICAN INDIAN SELF-REPRESENTATIONS ON TRIBAL WEB SITES

Susan Dente Ross and David Cuillier

The authors examine how American Indian tribes represent themselves on their own official Web sites, comparing tribes that operate casinos to those that do not. They find that tribes with casinos tend to play up Indian stereotypes, such as teepees, demure maidens, connection with nature, feather headdresses, and savage braves. This might attract more non-Indian tourists, but at what price?

What if you went online to gather information for a research paper on American Indians and ran across a Web page displaying teepees, feathered headdresses, and savage braves with chopping tomahawks yelling "whoo-whoo-whoo-whoo!" Did you stumble across the homepage for the Cleveland Indians or Atlanta Braves? Or maybe you came upon a promo for a new stereotype-laden Disney movie, *Pocahontas and Sacajawea Weave Baskets*? Or maybe you accidentally typed in "Aryan Nation" in your Google search?

Or you might simply have landed on the official Web site of an American Indian tribe.

What? How can that be? How could an American Indian tribe represent itself on its own official Web site in ways that would surely offend some people or, at minimum, perpetuate stereotypes? Well, the results—and implications—of our study might surprise you. When we delved into the self-representation of American Indians on official tribal Web sites, we discovered a world of familiar stereotypes.

IDENTITY AND REPRESENTATION

Before discussing the findings of our study, we should talk a little about identity and self-representation, something we all do individually and as members of the different groups to which we belong. Social scientists argue that identity is a process, not a fixed thing. Identity is the solidarity that arises from recognition of a common origin or shared characteristic with another person, group, or ideal (Weaver, 2001). In this sense, identity is constructed in and through interactions with others.

Power also plays a role in identity formation because those with power have greater influence over social and communication processes and, therefore, greater ability to shape the situations in which identities are formed and re-formed. The media, which dominate so much social communication, play a significant role in the social construction of identity. Media stories and images provide handy and salient information, which we sort through and organize to help categorize people and things. Particularly when we have little or no direct knowledge, media content provides the building blocks with which we form our perception of others' iden-

Cuillier, David and Ross, Susan Dente "Gambling with Identity: Self-Representation of American Indians on Official Tribal Websites," Howard Journal of Communications 18:3 197-219.

tity. All of this is important because the ability to construct identities can be a tool for power and prejudice.

Native American Identity

In the United States, historical representation of the Indian as "other," outside the mainstream, has established cultural boundaries of difference to justify occupation of Indian land and annihilation of tribes (Hanson & Rouse, 1987). The dominant Anglo culture has represented American Indian identity as nonhuman and savage (Said, 1979). Several scholars have called this destructive identity the "White man's Indian," built upon a number of stereotypes, including the stoic chief adorned in a headdress, the noble savage, the demure Indian maiden, and the spiritual soul connected to nature.

Whereas some of these images appear benign or even benevolent, the White man's Indian perpetuates "acceptable racism" and objectification of the American Indian throughout Euro-American popular culture—sports and school mascots like the Atlanta Braves, films including Disney's *Pocahontas*, advertising such as Land O'Lakes butter, and a stream of popular images, Web sites, and even news reports (Miller & Ross, 2004).

Yet identities are not constructed solely by the media or the powerful. Even the most disenfranchised members of society participate in their identity construction and may engage in practices of resistance to exert influence over their social identity. Many scholars have examined how identity is contested, negotiated, and adapted to resist those in power or to gain power by those who are subjugated. Vulnerable members of society may adopt explicit political and social positions to oppose dominant messages that manipulate or marginalize them.

Far from being seen as negative incidents to be avoided, moments of tension thus may provide opportunities to challenge dominant truth claims and to reshape information and images perceived as relevant and significant (Fairclough, 1992). For example, to diffuse the negative connotation of the term "queer" as used in the dominant culture, gays and lesbians have reappropriated the term to affirm their self-identity (Henderson, 2001).

Similarly, indigenous peoples can negotiate Anglo-imposed identity to their own advantage. American Indians may adapt the White man's Indian identity to attract non-Indian patrons and increase economic gain. Navajo and Pueblo artists, for example, learned tourists purchased more wares that conformed to the non-Indians' stereotyped image of what Indian art *should* look like, an artifact of the past (Sorrells, 2003).

The identity adaptation central to such ethnic tourism also has been noted in the Indian gaming world. To promote and foster the success of tribal casinos, the facilities often appeal to non-Indian tourists by adapting the image of the White man's image of the exotic Indian "other" (Cooks, 1998). The décor and advertising of successful casinos represent a one-size-fits-all pantribal identity for the Indian who represents a horse-culture plains tribe, even though many Indian nations do not share the dress or traditions of this culture. Some tribes have even patterned their casino decorations after tips from Disney marketing specialists.

The financial outcome can be positive for indigenous peoples. By attracting more tourists, tribes increase economic power and, therefore, are better positioned to break cycles of poverty and subjugation. Indian gaming revenues, which increased from $500 million in 1988 to $25 billion in 2006, have provided a variety of benefits for tribes, including the building of roads, schools, utilities, and housing, a drop in mortality rates, and the ability to provide college scholarships for their members.

Framing Identity

Scholars have long studied texts to examine identity. Framing scholars, for example, examine the overt images, language, and structure of messages to identify the imbedded, culturally resonant, covert meanings that influence audience understanding of reality, including issues of race and self-identity (Goffman, 1974). Frames are unconsciously embedded in visual and verbal messages, and they call upon familiar and durable cultural values, ideologies, and narratives to establish relatively stable connections between familiar signifiers—even stereotypes—and new information.

In framing theory, meaning is socially constructed through a reciprocal, interactive cycle of communication. Framing theory acknowledges the creative ability of communicators to generate original meanings, their desire for efficiency, and their tendency to use shortcuts. It also recognizes the ability of audience members to reshape and recode the messages they receive. The key to understanding frames is to recognize that they can communicate only those meanings that the receivers already recognize, regardless of the intent of the senders.

Framing theory also recognizes that dominant messages in a given society tend to be the products of elite individuals and social institutions and to project the views and values of these elites. Accordingly, frames tend to reinforce the status quo and to be ethnocentric and pro-establishment. Thus, the use of old frames (such as the White man's Indian) in new ways (such as to attract tourism) may be fraught with the potential for misinterpretation by receivers who misconstrue the distinct or resistive intent.

At the same time, communicators may strategically adopt nondominant frames. Therefore, tribes targeting the dominant society (non-Indians) through their Web sites might be expected to employ dominant cultural frames that reinforce the status quo. Tribes directing their Web sites toward their own community might employ frames that diverge from the elite consensus to challenge the status quo of negative stereotypes.

Studies have identified a variety of frames of American Indians communicated through the media. The frame of Indians as "historic relics" describes what scholars call the White man's Indian identity, encompassing elements of the three dominant media frames: the generic Indian, the Indian as the other, and good–bad Indian frames. The historic relic frame presents Indians as remnants of a mythical, colonial era. Historic relic Indians can display good traits, such as nobility and stoicism, or bad traits, such as savagery. Either way, the frame situates Indians in the past, fixed in the world of the Pilgrims and up to the end of the 1800s. Historic relic Indians are obsolete in the contemporary world and therefore easier for the dominant society to ignore or subjugate.

In contrast, the frame of "voiced participant" Indian emerged from a recent study (Miller & Ross, 2004). Voiced participants are whole people who function fully within modern mainstream society either with or without embracing traditional aspects of Indian culture. Voiced participants are self-actualized individuals who speak for themselves with credibility on issues of significance if and when they adopt the perspective of the mainstream.

EXAMINING INDIAN IDENTITY ON TRIBAL WEB SITES

While many tribes appropriate the White man's Indian identity for casino marketing as an effective strategy to attract tourists and maximize profit, this represented identity may spread (intentionally or not) beyond the casinos themselves into other realms of tribal communications with non-Indians. In recent years, Indian nations throughout North America have expanded their online presence, with official tribal Web sites surging from about a dozen in 1995 to literally hundreds by 2003 (Mitten, 2003). These Web sites provide Indian nations the opportunity to communicate to millions of people in their own words and images.

This reading reports the results of our study of 224 official American Indian Web sites. Did Indian nations with the incentive to attract tourists to casino gambling challenge or perpetuate negative stereotypes?

We employed both framing and critical discourse analysis (CDA) to analyze how American Indians used their online spaces strategically to adopt, adapt, or resist the dominant Euro-American representation of American Indian identity. We coded each homepage as evoking one of three frames: the Informational frame, the Historic Relic (White man's Indian) frame, and the Voiced Participant frame.

Informational sites provided primarily text and graphics, such as lists of tribal officers or programs, or basic tribal demographics. These data-driven pages typically presented very few, if any, graphic images. *Historic relic (White man's Indian)* sites relied predominantly on "conventional images" of the noble savage existing in a romantic natural state and embodying stoic, chiefly virtue. Images of teepees, warbonnets, fierce braves, demure Indian maidens, and other stereotypical images dominated, and text described tribal peoples as fixtures of another time, with little or no sovereignty or autonomy. *Voiced Participant* sites included portrayals of modern life in the tribe and described a community that had emerged from any mythical past to function within mainstream society (Miller & Ross, 2004). The tribes speak for themselves and participate in Anglo-European systems. The sites provide a complex set of both traditional and modern images, such as photos from powwows alongside images of tribal members dressed in Western shirts or suits, engaged in sports and community activities. The text might include assertions of sovereignty, challenges to the dominant culture, and discussion about contemporary tribal issues.

Besides coding the homepages of these sites, we also used CDA to capture nuance and meaning that would be missed by our broad-based frame analysis. A primary goal of CDA is to make visible how a variety of players deliberately employ symbolic practices (images as well as words) to advance their own agendas within the complex societal play of differences of power and reach, and with both intended and unexpected results.

RESULTS

We found that most of the tribal Web sites provided genealogy, history, language, tribal government information, and community events. Overall, the informational frame was the most common on the Web sites, accounting for 57% (127) of all sites. The second most prevalent frame was historic relic at 26% (59). Voiced participant frames accounted for 17% (38).

Nearly two thirds of the Web sites were produced by nations that have casinos. A few clusters of tribes shared similar informational homepage templates, usually provided by a coordinating regional agency. As shown in Table 1, more than a third of the casino-tribe Web sites represented their identity within the historic relic frame. In contrast, only about 1 in 10 non-casino tribes represented the historic relic frame. Therefore, casino tribes were nearly four times more likely than non-casino tribes to represent their identities within a historic relic frame.

The voiced participant frame was employed by 20% of the non-casino tribes but only 15% of the casino-tribe Web sites. Therefore, casino tribes are both more likely to represent themselves

TABLE 1   Frames for Casino- and Non-Casino Tribe Sites

FRAME	CASINO TRIBES		NON-CASINO TRIBES	
	N	%	N	%
Historic relic	50	36	9	10
Informational	67	49	60	70
Voiced participant	21	15	17	20
Total (total N = 224)	138		86	

on their Web sites as historic relics and somewhat less likely to represent themselves as voiced participants than non-casino tribes.

Casino Tribes' Historic Relics

Many of the photographs on casino-tribe Web sites were dominated by feathers, war paint, young braves, eagles, and other stereotypical images. The Warm Springs Web site (www.warmsprings. com), which prominently displayed the image of a stoic Indian brave in a traditional headdress, was typical of casino tribes that represented the historic relic frame. Secondary images included an Indian mask, Indian blanket, eagle, teepees, Indians on horses, and three Indian women in traditional dress. No images depicted modern scenes of the reservation or members performing everyday activities.

The text on the homepage included a description of the reservation as a place where "time turns to the pace of a culture that has been thousands of years in the making." The text also focuses on connection to nature, reminding viewers that Indians are different and have a mystical connection to nature, land "stretching from the snowcapped summit of the Cascade Mountains to the palisaded cliffs of the Deschutes River in Central Oregon." The paragraph ends by differentiating the Warm Springs tribe from the dominant culture by inviting readers to "escape to another nation." This text delivers the message that non-Indians should view tribal enterprises as an escape to the exotic, the pastoral, carefree, natural world of the noble savage.

The Mashantucket Pequots of Connecticut, operators of the largest casino in the country, also have a homepage that represents the tribe as a historic relic (http://www.foxwoods. com/TheMashantucketPequots/Home). The page begins with this text: "The symbol of the Mashantucket Pequot Tribal Nation is a reflection of the past. The tree, perched on a rocky knoll and framed against a clear sky, represents Mashantucket, the 'much wooded land' where the people hunted and prospered." This statement embodies the tribe's expressed connection with nature (trees, rocky knolls, and clear skies), traditional cultural practices (hunting), and an idyllic peaceful life in the past (reflection of the past and "prospered"). Furthermore, the background is a picture of a forest, and the Web site displays no modern images. The focus is on the past, of Indians hunting and being one with nature. Pictures on the site focus on Indian warriors with painted faces.

Yet the Web page speaks from the White man's position. The language is self-distancing; the authors are not, evidently, "the people." This symbolic displacement and identification with the reader recurs across Web pages that adopt the historic relic frame, where the tribe is often described as "they" rather than "we." For example, the Lac Vieux Desert Tribe of Michigan represented its noble identity on its homepage: "They are a nation of wise and intelligent leaders, non-obtrusive, talkative and happy people" (http://www.lvdtribal.com/). Within the historic relic frame, there is no discussion about discrimination, oppression, or problems on the reservation.

Nearly two thirds of the casino tribes, however, did not represent their identity as the White man's Indian. Nearly half of these sites (49%) were informational, and some 15% included a variety of images from the past and present that demonstrated a voiced participant frame. In the latter group, the Cabazon Band of Mission Indians in southern California included photographs of tribal members in modern clothes working on federal issues to identify and protect sacred sites as well as stories and photographs of tribal leaders discussing legislation with members of Congress (http://www.cabazonIndians-nsn.gov/). The Hoopa Valley Indian Tribe, also of California (http://www.hoopa-nsn.gov/), demonstrated some of the most voiced language and images of all tribes, including a photo of tribal members protesting dams.

Non-Casino Tribal Identity: Voiced Participants

Web sites for non-casino tribes were less likely to adopt the White man's Indian frame. Instead, these sites employed a greater proportion of modern images, focused on individual tribal attributes rather than a generic pan-tribal identity, explained the context and meaning of historical photos, and asserted tribal sovereignty. A significant proportion of the non-casino Web sites served as little more than online placeholders for the tribe, comprises mainly generic text. Given the general economic disparity between casino and non-casino tribes (National Gambling Impact Study Commission, 1999), perhaps these tribes could not afford the more elaborate Web designs of casino-tribe Web sites that conveyed the stereotypical Indian symbols.

Despite reliance on text-heavy designs, non-casino tribes tended to picture local Indians in everyday life. For example, the Alabama-Coushatta Tribe of Texas pictured members in street clothes and baseball hats accompanying text that emphasized current tribal issues (www. alabama-coushatta.com). The Quinault tribe in Washington state pictured its leaders in modern dress as well as canoeing tribal members wearing orange life jackets—a mix of the old and new (www.quinaultIndiannation.com).

Sometimes non-casino tribes included historical photos, but they generally did so differently than casino tribes. Whereas casino tribes typically provided photos of chiefs and teepees without contextual explanation, non-casino tribes tended to explain the photos and provide less stereotypical images. For example, the Delaware Tribe of Eastern Oklahoma (www.delaware-tribeofIndians.nsn.us) included images of their specific tribal heritage and decorated the page with a pattern described as a traditional Delaware ribbon pattern, but the text emphasized current affairs and events.

Textual assertions of sovereignty and resistance were strong on voiced participant non-casino tribal sites. The Delaware tribal homepage is composed mainly of an essay written by the chief describing the history of the tribe, including how the tribe was subjugated and persecuted by European Americans. The essay states, "Nevertheless, through war and peace, our ancestors had to continue to give up their lands and move westward." The site uses such words as "trickery" to describe Anglo-Americans.

The Skull Valley Goshutes tribe in Grantsville, Utah, also expressed resistance by focusing its Web site (www.skullvalleygoshutes.org, which has since been removed) on the nuclear waste and chemical weapons stored on and near the reservation. The homepage described the pollution and problems brought to the area, including a coal-fired power plant and the world's largest nerve gas incinerator. This site offered no images of braves or eagles. Instead, the tribe's homepage was dominated by a photo-collage of nuclear power plants, newspaper articles, a scientist, a pencil, and the planet Earth. The collage bore this quote from scientist Marie Curie: "Nothing in life is to be feared. It is only to be understood."

MAKING SENSE OF IT ALL

So what does all this mean? This analysis of tribal Web sites suggests that casino tribes are more likely to adopt the historic relic frame to strategically represent their identity as the White man's Indian than non-casino tribes. In line with prior research and theories, Web sites of casino tribes appear to seek to maximize their appeal to non-Indian audiences by relying on stereotypical images of the noble and ignoble savage and failing to assert sovereignty or to challenge oppression in other ways. We cannot identify intent, but it is possible casino tribes appropriate the dominant group's identity as a branding strategy to increase their own economic power.

Another explanation may be simply that tribes with casinos may have more financial resources to produce more elaborate, image-heavy Web sites. Such sites may use more stereotypical images in part because they emphasize colorful, striking visuals. In contrast, many non-casino tribal Web sites were outdated and of poor technical quality, lacking graphic art and timely information. Or, it is possible that non-Indian consultants or Web designers hired by the more affluent casino tribes may have influenced the design and content toward greater reliance on frames that resonated with the dominant Anglo culture.

Regardless of *why* casino tribes—and some non-casino tribes—adopted the historic relic frame on their Web sites, the fact that they do has important ramifications for American Indian identity and positioning in relationship to the dominant culture of Euro-Americans. New technologies such as the Internet have been heralded as a way for oppressed groups to voice resistance, but our study suggests tribal Web pages instead may reinforce existing power inequities. Although casino gambling has allowed many tribes to increase economic power, the images portrayed for tourists online could perpetuate stereotypes. The White man's Indian, created through language and visuals, exemplifies an ideology of exclusion, difference, and racism.

Any short-term increases in casino revenues stimulated by the adoption of the historic relic frame should be weighed against the harm such continued stereotyping inflicts upon all American Indians. While entrenched stereotypes are evident in the media, the impact of these stereotypes is magnified through their adoption in official tribal communications. When non-Indians see American Indians represent themselves as historic relics, that identity may be more readily and less critically adopted and reinforced among non-Indians.

If American Indians are to achieve equality in U.S. society, then the entrenched stereotypes and Anglo-imposed identity of Indians must be shed from discourse, popular culture, and official tribal Web sites. Some tribes might benefit financially in the short term by displaying for the world an exotic representation of themselves as the other, but in the long term such gambling with identity likely perpetuates injustices against American Indians.

IT'S YOUR TURN: WHAT DO YOU THINK? WHAT WILL YOU FIND?

1. Go online and check out official Native American Web sites. You can find a list at www.indiancircle.com or at www.nativeculturelinks.com/nations.html. Look at the pictures they have on their Web. How many represent stereotypes? How many depict modern images of everyday life?

2. Read the text of Native American Web sites. How many integrate "nature" and tradition, as if they tribe is locked in the past? In contrast, look for examples of resistance, challenging the non-Indian establishment.

3. Go online and find Native American tribe casino Web sites. Are the images different from the official tribal Web sites? Who are they targeting?

4. Get into discussion groups and search online for examples of Web sites created by subjugated people in society. How do those groups represent themselves to the rest of the world?

5. Visit or talk with members of a Native American student club on campus, and ask them what they think about tribal Web sites and the images you find on them. What are their feelings about it?

REFERENCES

Cooks, L. M. (1998). *Warriors, wampum, gaming, and glitter: Foxwoods Casino and the re-representation of (post) modern Native identity.* Mountain View, CA: Mayfield.

Fairclough, N. (1992). *Discourse and social change.* Cambridge, MA: Polity Press.

Goffman, E. (1974). *Frame analysis: An essay on the organization of experiences.* New York: Harper & Row.

Hanson, J., & Rouse, L. (1987). Dimensions of Native American stereotyping. *American Indian Culture and Research Journal, 11*(4), 33–58.

Henderson, L. (2001). Queer communication studies. *Communication Yearbook, 24,* 465–484.

Miller, A., & Ross, S. D. (2004). They are not us: Framing of American Indians by the Boston Globe. *The Howard Journal of Communication, 15,* 245–259.

Mitten, L. (2003). Indians on the Internet—Selected Native American Web sites. *The Electronic Library, 21,* 443–449.

National Gambling Impact Study Commission. (1999). *Final report on national gambling impact.* Retrieved October 6, 2011, from http://govinfo.library.unt.edu/ngisc/

Said, E. W. (1979). *Orientalism.* New York: Vintage.

Sorrells, K. (2003). Embodied negotiation: Commodification and cultural representation in the U.S. Southwest. In M. J. Collier (Ed.), *Intercultural alliances: Critical transformation* (pp. 17–47). Thousand Oaks, CA: Sage.

Weaver, H. N. (2001). Indigenous identity: What is it, and who really has it? *American Indian Quarterly, 25,* 240–255.

5.7 MARKETING AUTHENTICITY: "REAL INDIANS" AS COMING ATTRACTIONS IN CONTEMPORARY HOLLYWOOD

Becca Gercken

This reading looks at the marketing of Native films, noting the media's manipulation of race as a promotional device to sell movies and its molding of the narrative of what "Indian" means in America.

Smoke Signals (1998) marked a crucial turning point in Hollywood's representations of American Indians. Hailed as the first Indian movie, its release transformed the artistic and critical guidelines for cinematic representations of indigenous peoples. Before *Smoke Signals*, movies offered a fixed and often inaccurate narrative of Indian identity; after *Smoke Signals*, movies offered a dynamic and more complete narrative of Indian identity, and authenticity became a marketing strategy.

This reading will consider what Hollywood is presenting to audiences as "authentically Indian." To understand the work of contemporary Native filmmakers, work that frequently references, re-frames, and undermines traditional Hollywood portrayals, we must first be aware of the pre-defined Indian identities established by popular culture such as those found in *The Searchers* and *Dances With Wolves*. Native-made movies are working to re-write these portrayals, and yet the *marketing* of Native-made films frequently relies on established portrayals. In examining the promotional packaging of these films, we'll see how the media manipulate race as a promotional device, and mold the narrative of what "Indian" means in America. In particular, we'll examine the trailers (previews) for *Smoke Signals*, *The Doe Boy*, and *Skins* to see how they were marketed as "authentic Native products" and what sort of movement or transformation there has been in the marketing of Native films since the release of *Smoke Signals*. What do these trailers tell us about how the dominant culture understands Indians? What level of familiarity does the trailer assume regarding American Indian cultures? American Indian histories? What stereotypes do the trailers reinforce? What stereotypes do they disrupt? What—according to the trailers—makes these films "real Indian" movies? This question is crucial because the answer reveals both what the popular media has constructed to be "authentically Indian" and why, after 60 years of inaccurate portrayals of Indians, there is now value in "authentic" representations.

Movies are fun; we go to the movie theatre or put in a DVD because we want to be entertained. But movies can also teach us about American culture, about how we imagine ourselves and our history. Movies create narratives about this country and its people, and thus by studying movies, especially multiple movies about a topic, we can learn much about how Americans feel about the time, the people, and the cultures represented in them. You're probably familiar with Westerns, a genre popular since movies began. The cinematic narrative of American Indians is well-established: white settlers move into "unoccupied land" and have to defend that land, often with the help of the cavalry, from the Indians—who are shown as murderous savages rather than as a people protecting their own property. Given the popularity and longevity of Westerns, it is not surprising that most analyses of Indians in movies are about these types of films; critics (e.g. Bird, 1996; Kilpatrick, 1999; Rollins & O'Connor, 1998) have analyzed Westerns to understand what they teach us about American perceptions of Indian-ness and how Indians fit into the stories America creates for itself. And what can we learn about Indians from the movies?

John Ford's 1956 movie *The Searchers* is widely considered the best American Western. Ethan Edwards (John Wayne) spends years searching for his niece Debbie, who was captured by Comanche Indians in a raid that left most of her family dead. Ethan's plan is not to rescue Debbie, however; it is to kill her because, as the movie tells us over and over again, it is better to be dead than to be Indian, and the longer Debbie is with the Comanche, the more Indian she becomes. Although Ford intended this movie as a critique of America's racism toward Indians, contemporary critics still find the film's portrayal of Indians problematic. Westerns were revived in the 1990s. *Dances with Wolves* (1990) and *The Last of the Mohicans* (1992) offered a new type of Western, one more sympathetic to American Indians. However, even in these more positive portrayals, Indian characters remain marginalized; both stories are told not by Indians, but by white men choosing to live as Indians. Moreover, the Indians in both tribes are "vanishing": Chingachgook is the *last* of the Mohicans, and *Dances with Wolves* ends with a voice-over explanation that within a few years, the Lakota people would be contained within reservations, their once-great nomadic horse culture destroyed by the U.S. government. These movies, like most Westerns, teach us that Indians' stories are told by whites not by Indians (in the movies themselves and in their production). They also teach us that Indians—or at least their traditional cultures—disappeared over 100 years ago. This narrative of Indian identity remained in place until the release of Chris Eyre's *Smoke Signals* in 1998.

The promotional trailer for *Smoke Signals* informs audiences that it is the first totally Native American-made (produced, directed, written) feature film, but much of the trailer seems designed to appeal to a Euro-American audience. The trailer's voice-over tells viewers that Victor (the 20-something protagonist) is making his initial foray off reservation land and searching for his tribe's cultural practices. This language marginalizes Victor both in the United States, where he is a foreigner, and on his reservation, where his culture is foreign to him. It also reinforces the notion that America has "given" Indians their cultures, since Victor can only find his by leaving the reservation. This excerpt, in its reliance on familiar dominant culture narratives of Indians, is grounded in generalized beliefs about Natives. Other portions of the trailer, however, appeal to an Indian audience with references to reservation cars, barter, and Hollywood Indians. It is especially interesting to note that while the appeal to the white audience is grounded in generalized beliefs about Natives (they are isolated on the rez, they have lost their cultural practices), the appeal to the American Indian audience is grounded in cinematic stereotypes: by alluding to *Dances with Wolves* and *The Lone Ranger and Tonto*, the trailer appropriates existing Hollywood narratives of America and Indians to communicate with its Indian audience.

The trailer for *The Doe Boy* (2001) largely resists the direct appeal to cinematic stereotypes found in the *Smoke Signals* trailer just as it resists positioning itself as an "Indian movie." The trailer instead subtly indicates its subject through the physical appearance of the film's characters, a sharp contrast to *Smoke Signals*, which overtly identifies the Indian subject matter through voice-over. Virtually all of the characters shown in *The Doe Boy* trailer are easily recognizable as Indian through phenotype: dark skin, dark, straight (and often long) hair. Thus, the trailer meets audience expectation of "what Indians look like" while offering a realistic depiction of contemporary Indian peoples. The film is promoted as a coming-of-age story with clearly Indian overtones that hint at the notion of a vision quest, a strategy that in its allusion to actual traditional indigenous cultural practices also meets audience expectation in regards to American Indian traditions as they have been portrayed by Hollywood.

As the trailer progresses, there are more stereotypical descriptions of Indians as one with nature via frequent hunting sequences and dramatic shots of a deer—and Indians—running through woods, stereotypes that escalate dramatically as the trailer comes to a close. Suddenly the audience sees Hunter, the protagonist, wearing a feather and war paint and carrying a bow and arrow as he hunts a deer. This hunt is characterized by a voice-over as Hunter bringing about his destiny. Audiences learn with this sequence that contemporary Indians maintain traditional practices, but those practices appear static: there is no indication in the trailer that in the larger context of the film, this scene resists rather than reinforces Hollywood's historicizing impulse.

Randy Redroad, director of *The Doe Boy*, created his own trailer for the film which makes an interesting comparison as audiences can directly contrast directorial intent with studio marketing. The director's trailer opens with a shot of a buck running through the woods. Shots of key characters are intercut with scenic shots, and contemporary "Indian" music provides atmosphere. There is no dialogue, although "life" and "blood" are briefly mentioned in text appearing near the end of the trailer, which also references searching for a beast of mythic origin. Viewers get few cues other than actor phenotypes and music that this film is "Indian," although the use of the word "blood" hints at identity questions. The concept of blood in the movie is much more complex than the trailer implies, but because the trailer doesn't provide context, viewers are likely to interpret the line as a standard reference to anxieties about authentic blood identity. Unlike the studio trailer, the director's trailer makes no appeal to existing Hollywood narratives of Indian-ness or a coming-of-age plot structure. Like the best and most traditional Native stories, audiences are left to construct the meaning for themselves.

Made 4 years after *Smoke Signals* and 1 year after *The Doe Boy*, *Skins* reflects a shift in the promotion of "authentic Indian-ness" and assumes a more culturally informed and diverse audience. The trailer immediately locates viewers in Indian country and culture, opening with contemporary indigenous music (untranslated), and a reference to the Lakota nation, an invocation of indigenous sovereignty. It also mentions Mount Rushmore, a national landmark carved into the highly contested Black Hills, and the 1890 massacre of Lakota at Wounded Knee. In the clip, Rudy uses the Lakota word *tiospaye* when explaining his actions to his brother Mogie. Viewers are told that the film is about the search for justice being undertaken by the two brothers, a clear invocation of the past mistreatment of Indians, mistreatment already established by the trailer through its reference to Wounded Knee and Mount Rushmore. The trailer ends with a shot of the movie's title centered on a traditional drum. These elements of the trailer demonstrate that in the four short years between *Smoke Signals* and *Skins*, Hollywood Studios believe that Americans are more informed—or at least want to be more informed—about both contemporary Indian lives and Indian history. The trailer appears to credit Hollywood itself—specifically Chris Eyre, the movie's director—for America's recent familiarity with Native Americans when it tells the audience that *Skins* is made by the director of *Smoke Signals*. Thus, the trailer reinforces the notion that movies are the source for America's narrative of Indian identity, a narrative which this trailer seems to be transforming.

However, while the references to indigenous sovereignty and history and the use of Lakota do indeed mark transformations in the cinematic promotion of American Indians, the trailer for *Skins* also risks falling into familiar Hollywood patterns of Indian representation, including the notions that Indians are vanishing or drunk (or even worse, vanishing *and* drunk). After its initial invocation of the indigenous sovereignty of the Lakota nation, the trailer refers to Pine Ridge as having been forgotten by America, and then turns its focus to the alcoholism of Mogie, a central character, and Indians in general, with references to drunken brawls and the liquor industry in White Clay, Nebraska. Alcohol abuse is central to the film and thus must be part of the promotion of the film; moreover, alcohol abuse is a widespread and serious issue among Native peoples, and so we cannot conclude that the trailer is playing to stereotypes. In fact, the trailer does some work unraveling stereotypes of drunken Indians by treating it both as a family matter—indicating that not all Indians are drunk and that action against substance abuse is taken within the community—and as a serious news matter worthy of the attention of the larger population. These serious overtones are balanced by some humorous images of Mogie's alcoholism, but these images can be read as a culturally typical treatment of a serious matter, an Indian way of telling the story of alcoholism.

Because the trailer's portrayal of alcoholism is nuanced and compassionate, we can turn to more subtle invocations of Indian stereotypes, most notably the allusion to blood which is so central to how non-Indians—and often Indian themselves—understand American Indian identity. The movie's promotion does not simply describe the movie as being concerned with blood, something viewers would probably interpret as a reference to the fraternal relationship of the movie's two central characters. Instead, the reference to blood is immediately followed by the word "brothers," phrasing which separates the notion of blood from the relationship of Rudy and Mogie and thus invokes legislative understandings of Indian identity. This reference plays directly to a foundational element of the dominant culture's perceptions of Indian peoples: that Indian identity is measured not through cultural practices or life ways, but through blood quantum. Clearly, although the trailer has disrupted notions of Indians' place in American history and altered portrayals of drunk Indians, it reinforces the notion that blood is the primary signifier of Indian-ness, a damaging message that puts the determination of Indian identity in legislative control.

Each of these three movie trailers draws on similar, if slightly varied, signifiers of authentic Indian-ness while reimagining indigenous cultural practices in a contemporary setting that resists the static, historicizing impulse for which Hollywood depictions of Indians are known. The films are also marked as "authentically Indian" through their titles, which offer viewers a clear and immediate indication that they are about Indians through an interesting mix of dominant culture/ Hollywood stereotypes and representations of Indian cultures. *Smoke Signals* clearly plays to Hollywood notions of early Indian communication methods to "signal" to the viewing audience that the film is about Indians. This choice is underscored when comparing the movie's title to that of the short story on which it is based: "This Is What It Means to Say Phoenix, Arizona." *The Doe Boy* offers a more subtle indication of "real Indian-ness" with a reference to American Indian naming customs that accurately reflects both cultural practices and their Hollywood representations. *Skins* offers a potentially controversial title indicating the movie's subjects: "skins" is a word that has been used for centuries as a racial slur against Indians but is also used by Indians themselves as a positive self-descriptor. The title, then, reminds viewers of racist attitudes toward American Indians while presenting a positive representation of contemporary indigenous peoples, a clear disruption in the typical Hollywood narrative of historicized, marauding Indians.

Although the release of *Smoke Signals* was a transformative moment in the Hollywood narrative of Indians in America, key cinematic markers of Indian-ness—phenotype, material culture, naming practices—remain largely static, fixed as identifiers of "authentic Indian identity." Contemporary indigenous filmmakers model these cinematic identity politics, acknowledging the narrative reality of Hollywood Indian-ness through complex and sometimes contradictory stories that both repudiate and reinforce existing cinematic portrayals of American Indians. We must be aware not only of the larger rhetorical field in which these films have come to signify, but of the fact that these predefined Indian identities established by popular culture play out on the bodies of real people.

IT'S YOUR TURN: WHAT DO YOU THINK? WHAT WILL YOU FIND?

1. Identify which elements of the trailers for *Smoke Signals*, *The Doe Boy*, or *Skins* target a European-American audience and which target an American Indian audience. Next, imagine that you are creating two separate trailers, one designed to draw a white audience and the other to draw a Native audience. What pre-existing notions about Indians exist in both groups that you can use to appeal to your audiences? What scenes from the movie would best illustrate these preexisting notions? After you have created your trailers, discuss which problems of racialized promotion this strategy solves and which

problems it compounds. Finally, how has this exercise affected your awareness of the racial stereotyping used in film promotion?

2. Watch the trailer for a traditional Western (*Stagecoach*, *Broken Arrow*, etc.). What do you learn about how Hollywood imagines America's western history? American Indians? The fight for resources on the American frontier? Consider which elements of this trailer would still resonate with a contemporary audience and which elements might alienate the audience or seem outdated.

3. Many people think that we should not be concerned with racism in American movies either because films are "entertainment" or, especially in the case of classic Westerns, because the movies are "too old" and thus no longer relevant to our lives or our current understanding of race and ethnicity. Do you agree? What would we miss if we did not examine the depictions of Indians in American movies? Why should popular culture be considered important in helping us understand American notions of identity, especially as they relate to race?

4. Other racial and ethnic groups have been frequently—and stereotypically—portrayed in American movies. Consider the implications of these representations. If you were to watch trailers for movies about the mafia, for example, what would you learn about Italian Americans? What stereotypes do the trailers rely on and reinforce? How different, if at all, are these kinds of stereotypes from those of American Indians found in Westerns?

REFERENCES

Bird, E. S. (1996). *Dressing in feathers: The construction of the Indian in American popular culture*. Boulder, CO: Westview.

Kilpatrick, J. (1999). *Celluloid Indians: Native Americans and film*. Lincoln: University of Nebraska Press.

Rollins, P. C., & Connor, J.E. (1998). *Hollywood's Indians: The portrayal of the Native American in film*. Lexington: University of Kentucky Press.

5.8   ADVERTISING AND HISPANIC CULTURE

John R. Rodriguez

> *Advertising has long addressed consumers' interests and appealing to their values, but has not always reflected the values of the Hispanic culture positively. This reading provides an overview of negative and positive advertising models which both government and private agencies have adopted concerning Hispanics.*

The Hispanic population in the United States is a quickly growing demographic—estimated at about 14.8% of the total population (U.S. Census Bureau, 2006). This 14.8% is, in fact, a gold-mine of barely tapped potential consumers whom many advertising agencies are beginning to target. Because of such of a large percentage, we can assume that the goal of any advertising agency is to maximize profitably.

To understand how to maximize profitability, an agency may look at data about the specific buyers. Some questions that might be asked include: What is important to a Hispanic family? To a Hispanic individual? What do Hispanics eat? Wear? What are the most important tenets in Hispanic culture? What types of television, radio, and Web sites do Hispanics turn to?

Following such a general line of questioning, we can consider that some of the main media outlets for advertising include television, the Internet, radio, and print. Specific methods may then be devised for compiling data which in turn can help construct specific advertisements targeting Hispanics.

DOMINANT VALUES IN HISPANIC CULTURE

I believe there are three main values in Hispanic culture that come together to form a triptych: language, family, and food.

Language Is Key

The most important factor that one needs to understand about the Hispanic culture, which ties ALL Hispanic cultures together, is the importance of language. The label "Hispanic" does not define a race of individuals, but a culture of individuals from various Spanish origins (not limited to those from Latin countries, as implied by "Latino/a"). Hispanic culture is based on many different figures—food, religion, language, clothing, and traditions—but language is key.

As a child, I understood my father when he would speak to me in his native dialect. However, years later in college, I was completely unfamiliar with the "Spanish" which was taught from academic text books. The disparity between what I understood as a child as the proper "Spanish" language would be challenged in this classroom setting. Later, I learned that many Hispanic communities have many different dialects. A Hispanic from Cuba will have a different dialect than a Hispanic from Mexico. Many words may be different or infer different things, but the fact remains—language is the foundation by which each Hispanic community is solidified.

In considering language, advertising agencies must figure out which dialect is the most prevalent and how an advertisement might appeal to Hispanics. Below, I discuss a few of the advertising campaigns which directly targeted Hispanics on the basis of language, family, or traditional cuisine. Here's a sneak preview: "*Yo quiero* Taco Bell?"

The Family Element

Not only is language an important factor in targeting Hispanics as a potential consumer interest, but family is also crucial. Family is one of the most structurally solid entities in the Hispanic culture. When my father would use the word *familia,* he did not just mean my mother and me; he meant our entire extended family, an important factor when targeting advertising to Hispanics. For example, if a product that my father purchased was satisfactory, he would inform of the rest of our kin. Advertising agencies understand the power of word-of-mouth endorsement. This type of low-key advertising is especially important in Hispanic culture. It is my experience, being from a Hispanic family, that the husband or eldest male is considered the authority figure of the family. The lesson, then, for the advertising agency is that if you can sell the head-of-household, not only have you reached the essential nuclear family, but the rest of the blood relations, also.

Food Is Essential

When thinking of language and family as important tenets of Hispanic culture, one must consider cuisine. Traditional food goes hand-in-hand with Hispanic language and family values. Dishes such as *menudo, barbacoa, tortillas, frijoles,* and *arroz* come to mind. These are common dishes of the American Hispanic diet. Factoring in cuisine is also a way in which many advertising agencies have targeted the Hispanic demographic. Consider Taco Bell: almost all meals include *frijoles* and *arroz* (beans and rice). This is no coincidence: beans, rice, and tortillas are staples of most Hispanic diets. In order to appear as an authentic Mexican food establishment, a business *must* include these items. Leaving out such culinary components would not be good for business—especially if traditional Hispanic individuals or families are a part of the target demographic.

The Triptych of Hispanic-Targeted Advertising

Language, family, and cuisine create a triptych of Hispanic advertising. Language is the foundation by which all Hispanic culture is built. Family is the center around which most Hispanic culture revolves, and a traditional cuisine provides the staple by which almost all Hispanic families survive. If an advertising agency targets at least two of the three, the chances for success are probably greatly increased. So what does this triptych look like in practice? In the next section, I discuss several ad campaigns in which I have identified these three tenets of advertising targeting the Hispanic demographic.

HISPANIC-TARGETED ADVERTISING STRATEGIES

Advertising's engagement with the Hispanic culture has not always been positive. In fact, during the Great Depression, campaigns were launched by states that resulted in the deportation and forced repatriation of Mexicans back to their native lands. A name synonymous with anti-Hispanic fervor during this era was Harry J. Anslinger, who said, " . . . the primary reason to outlaw marijuana is its effect on the degenerate races" (Lurigio, Rabinowitz, & Lenik, 2009). This marketing diatribe was directed toward people of color: African Americans, Asians, and especially Hispanics from Mexico. This anti-Hispanic campaign stated that Mexicans would bring cannabis across the border and "infect" white women with their satanic drug (Yaroschuk, 2000). However, as Yaroschuk argues, this campaign to export Mexicans was based on the perceived need to provide jobs to "white" Americans—jobs which had been held by Hispanics. The anti-marijuana campaign of the late 1920s, then, could be considered a way to legitimize directing anger and hostile feelings toward anyone who wasn't white. As a result, many people of color, including Hispanics, were forced to vacate their positions in order to provide work for unemployed white Americans.

Amidst all of the hostilities generated because of the anti-marijuana laws which were in fact aimed at Mexican laborers, a new law was created in 1931. This law, known as the *Mexican Repatriation*, would force Hispanics out of the United States and back to their native countries. According to Yaroschuk, some Hispanics who would not leave were harassed and incarcerated. In some states such as Texas, laws were so harsh for marijuana possession that a person could end up with life in prison or even worse—death. It was also seen that this was a way to deal with the "colored" population, and that the majority of law breakers fit stereotypical profiles (Yaroschuk, 2000).

We can see in this early example of anti-Hispanic campaigning that advertising can be used for both positive and negative promotion. Diversity and multiculturalism have not always been the top priority. Today, we can see advertising appeal to diverse audiences for products from companies, such as McDonalds, Taco Bell, State Farm, and Microsoft. In fact, many TV commercials use one tenet of our triptych: language. For example, in the State Farm ad titled "*Barista*," a Hispanic man uses the term "*la familia*." Other examples include the "I'm loving it" campaign by McDonald's (family and food), the "*Yo quiero* Taco Bell?" commercials (language and food), and some advertising advice given out by Microsoft (2009) aimed at helping companies hoping to target Latinos/Hispanics.

The Acculturated Hispanic

Hispanics who are born in the States tend to adopt many behaviors considered inherent to American culture. However, these same Hispanics may still keep their language, food, family values, and other pieces of Hispanic doctrine intact. This coexistence of American culture and Hispanic traditions is *acculturation*. Acculturation occurs when specific familial beliefs are nurtured to cohabitate with other national or regional behaviors and beliefs (Devito, 2009). For example, a Hispanic man may feel that his family is the most important aspect of his life; however, he may want to enlist in a branch of the Armed Services because of patriotic *and* personal axioms. The need to protect both family and country could be seen as acceptance of both cultures.

Because of acculturation, advertising agencies cannot use rote formulas, as they can in appealing to white communities. Marketing companies must find out how to reach a whole population of people who keep both immigrant and native cultural values intact (Sonderup, 2004). Enter the world of bilingual and bicultural advertising. As mentioned previously, a number of campaigns are now taking a multicultural approach.

Multiculturalism must not be confused with diversity. *Multiculturalism* can be defined as appreciating and embodying values from more than just one culture, whether as an individual or a community (Samovar & Porter, 1982). *Diversity*, on the other hand, can be seen as trying to identify differences in persons or communities, such as race, sex, and culture (Samovar & Porter, 1982). It may sound confusing, but multiculturalism can be observed in a Hispanic family which still keeps all of its immigrant values intact while adopting American values. Diversity comes in when a line can be drawn between what defines an American Hispanic community and an American Asian community. Considering communities as both diverse and multicultural is the key when brainstorming what advertising campaigns might appeal to groups. Multiculturalism is apparent when commercials deliver some or their entire message in more than one language. Such bilingual advertising tries to appeal not only to multicultural Hispanics but also to non-Hispanics.

The Assimilated Hispanic

Assimilation occurs when people interpret what they hear or see based on their own experiences, biases, etc. (Devito, 2009). For example, an individual born into a Hispanic family in which a native language is spoken, certain cultural values observed, and certain cultural food are prepared, may deny this family culture and instead fully adopt whatever national behavior and values are considered the norm, because they may believe this is the RIGHT thing to do as a reaction to these societal conditions (based on their personal interpretation). In America, which is largely considered a melting pot, this "norm" could take on different qualities. However, in countries such as Japan, certain customs, foods, and especially language are considered an absolute or complete culture.

So, is assimilation a good thing or a bad thing? If one completely sheds his or her immigrant culture, is he or she shedding heterogeneous identity? Or is that person creating a new identity for him or herself, one that is not based on immigrant perceptions, but based on personal understanding. Assimilation and acculturation lead us into a whole new path of issues, one where personal identity and cultural identity can be looked at as conflicting intrapersonal struggle. If this type of intrapersonal conflict between identities assumed from heritage and identities assimilated from cultural adaptation does exist, how can marketing firms appeal to groups in both camps? The answer is *bilingual advertisement.*

TARGET HISPANIC DEMOGRAPHIC

We have all seen commercials that include a white man or woman saying a phrase such as "we can help." Then, in the same commercial, a Hispanic man or woman will repeat the phrase in Spanish: "*podemos ayudar.*" In fact, most printed products come with directions, warning labels, and even other advertisements presenting content in English and in Spanish.

What does all of this mean? It means that America's Hispanic population is beginning to matter. It is one of the largest in the world, and it keeps growing. According to Microsoft's Web site for Latino advertising information, Hispanics in the United States comprise a larger consumer base than in Argentina, Spain, or even Canada (Microsoft, 2009). Considering this, it is safe to assume that marketers spend millions on efforts to find best practices to appeal to America's quickly growing Hispanic demographic.

This type of advertising strategy characterizes population segments in which all of the collective members share similar interests, heritage, etc. Recall the triptych of Hispanic-targeted advertising: food, language, and family. Advertising firms and marketing companies striving to be successful must know that these values are important to Hispanic families and individuals, and must emphasize either parts of the triptych or all of it in campaigns. Even something as simple as the word *gracias* in a majority English advertisement has effectively targeted the Hispanic audience.

To see how important the Hispanic population in the United States is to marketers, just search online for the phrase "bilingual advertisement." You will find a plethora of companies who specialize in Hispanic marketing strategies.

Considering the Ethical Boundary

The potential for any company to increase its consumer base by adding the large Hispanic demographic can be very tempting, and the rush to turn a profit can often lead down another unpleasant path. Does the campaign have racist overtones? Are the advertisements tasteful? Do the advertisements single out people based on skin color, race, or ethnicity? What would be considered offensive to the target audiences?

The most basic definition of racism is that one group of people or an individual consider that they are superior to others, basing their judgment on race (Devito, 2009). A slogan as innocuous as "*Yo quiero* Taco Bell" can be seen as racist. So let us apply our definition of racism to the commercial. My first observation was that a domesticated dog that is indigenous to Mexico was personified and used as the spokesperson for the commercial. Part of me feels as though they are using an animal that is considered "man's best friend" instead of an actual Hispanic, because people would more easily relate to owning a dog than identify with an actual person of Hispanic culture. This also brings me to reflect on the notion of ownership. One of the reasons early societies had slaves is because the owners felt vastly superior to those who were owned. Also, in today's society many Hispanics are employed, for very low wages, in roles that used to be the job of a slave: maid, gardener, field worker, etc. Not only is the food cheap but also the labor used to make it. However, we don't want to see the actual people who make the food or are associated with it; instead, we will use an icon that is cute and identifiable.

Acknowledging all that I have just pointed out in the Taco Bell commercial, here are a few conclusions that could possibly be derived from the content:

A culturally adapted perception: There are white and Hispanic people in the commercial; both the English and Spanish languages are spoken; people see that there is a balance to the content. The marketing is effective in that it has appealed to the heritage, language, and food of the Hispanic demographic, as well as the English-speaking populace.

A culturally assimilated perception: Hispanics have been assimilated into the English-speaking population of the United States. Yes, the commercial's content may pay homage to Hispanic heritage, but it assumes that all Hispanics living in America speak English. Thus, it does not have all of the dialogue in both Spanish and English—mostly just English.

A culturally insensitive perception: Mexican food is cheap, disgusting, and makes people fat and lazy. The language is spoken too fast, and it sounds like gibberish. People who buy this food are also stupid, lazy, and fat. The only thing good about this commercial is the cute dog.

The question of stereotypes and racism aside, let's apply our triptych concept and consider some of the imagery and language used in the TV commercial. First, we have a Chihuahua who speaks both in English and Spanish. Thus, the advertisement is bilingual, connecting to the language component of Hispanic culture. Because the ad promotes an establishment specializing in Mexican-esque fast food, we have a connection to the traditional Hispanic foods. The advertisement surely seems to hit on many of the divisions which Hispanics would either find important or at least relate to. Or would they?

To fully interpret Hispanic-targeted advertising, we must also look at the moral implications surrounding target marketing or marketing segmentation. Marketing segmentation divides groups of people into target audiences, based on a number of criteria. These criteria include but are not limited to *age, gender, race, similar interests, etc.* The groups of people are divided even further into what is called customer segments.

By separating consumers into columns, based on measures such as "race" and "gender", do marketing firms effectively *segregate* us? Marketing segmentation can be controversial, in part because it so often targets lower socioeconomic classes for products deemed unsafe or harmful (Rittenburg & Parthasarathy, 1997). There is much suggestive imagery at work in fast-food, tobacco, and even alcohol advertisement: if you buy the product, you will be happy, become more sociable, and may even become rich. So, are the *Yo quiero* Taco Bell TV commercials still as innocent?

However, some of the more controversial campaigns aside, marketing segmentation can also be seen as reflecting sensitivity to the target demographics' interests. If conducted properly, consumer segmentation marketing can effectively reach Hispanics who may otherwise not attend to an ad directed at whites. That Taco Bell commercial could be perceived as a whimsical comment on the liveliness and rich cultural history of Hispanic audiences. By using such Hispanic icons, Taco Bell appeals to the immigrant heritage paradigm.

The new advertising model for targeting the Hispanic demographic is still in an evolutionary state. However, as our society grows in its diversity, hopefully our sensitivity to diverse cultural opinion will also.

IT'S YOUR TURN: WHAT DO YOU THINK? WHAT WILL YOU FIND?

1. I believe that diversity is an important part of our national heritage. Being both of Hispanic culture and a native-born American, I can identify with target demographic advertisements. What is your culture? Are there any TV commercials or other types of advertising media that you find particularly appealing?

2. Consider the Mexican Repatriation Act of the 1930s, and today's advertising models aimed at Hispanics, specifically marketing segmentation. How ethical are today's standards? Can you think of any advertisements that may "cross the line?" If any are available online, show them to your classmates, and discuss.

3. Find other examples of bilingual advertisements, and consider where they might fit in terms of the three cultural perceptions presented when discussing interpretations of the Taco Bell ad. Show them to your friends, especially those of different demographic groups, and see what they think.

4. Form groups of three in class, trying to create groups of similar demographic characteristics. Each group should identify a demographic group that is different from itself, and interview members of that other group. Ask about topics such as heritage, age, and cultural observances. (Find the information online if representatives of that group are unavailable.) Then, each group should devise a culturally sensitive ad (print, radio, TV, or online) promoting a product based on what they've learned. Present the ads to the class for discussion of the ads' strengths and how some of the weaknesses might be overcome.

REFERENCES

Devito, J. (2009). *The interpersonal communication book* (12th ed.). New York: Pearson.

U.S. Census Bureau. (2006). *Hispanics in the United States.* Retrieved October 2, 2011, from http://www.census.gov/population/www/socdemo/hispanic/files/Internet_Hispanic_in_US_2006.pdf

Lurigio, A. J., Rabinowitz, M., & Lenik, J. (2009). A century of losing battles: The costly and ill-advised war on drugs in the United States. *Justice Policy Journal, 6*(2). Retrieved October 2, 2011, from http://www.cjcj.org/files/a_century.pdf

Microsoft. (2009). *Reach your target audience - Latinos.* Retrieved April 10, 2011, from http://advertising.microsoft.com/ad-network/audience/latinos

Rittenburg, T., & Parthasarathy, M. (1997). Ethical implications of target market selection. *Journal of Macromarketing, 17*(2). Retrieved April 10, 2011, from http://jmk.sagepub.com/content/17/2/49.full.pdf+html

Samovar, L., & Porter, R (1982). *Intercultural communication: A reader* (3rd ed.). Belmont, CA: Wadsworth.

Sonderup, L. (2004, April). Ad Market Review *Hispanic marketing: a critical market segment.* Retrieved October 2, 2011, from http://www.admarketreview.com/public_html/docs/fs075.html

Yaroschuk, T (Director). (2000). *Hooked: Illegal drugs & how they got that way–marijuana, assassin of youth* [Television series episode]. Boston: Tera Media.

5.9 "THE MORE YOU SUBTRACT, THE MORE YOU ADD": CUTTING GIRLS DOWN TO SIZE IN ADVERTISING

Jean Kilbourne

The author discusses how girls and women are portrayed in advertising. She argues that we are relentlessly exposed to unattainable ideals of physical perfection and that women are portrayed as less powerful than men. She also considers the ramifications of such representations.

"The more you subtract, the more you add," says an ad that ran in several women's and teen magazines in 1997. Surprisingly, it is an ad for clothing, not for a diet product. Perhaps it is overtly a statement about minimalism in fashion. However, the fact that the girl in the ad is very young and very thin reinforces another message, a message that an adolescent girl constantly gets from advertising and throughout the popular culture, the message that she should diminish herself, she should be *less* than she is.

On the most obvious and familiar level, this refers to her body. However, the loss, the subtraction, and the cutting down to size also refer to her sense of her self, her sexuality, her need for authentic connection, and her longing for power and freedom. I certainly don't think that the creators of this particular ad had all this in mind. And it wouldn't be important at all were there not so many other ads that reinforce this message and did it not coincide with the current cultural crisis for adolescent girls.

When a girl enters adolescence, she faces a series of losses—loss of self-confidence, loss of a sense of efficacy and ambition, and the loss of her "voice," the sense of being a unique and powerful self that she had in childhood. Girls who were active, confident, feisty at the ages of 8 and 9 and 10 often become hesitant, insecure, self-doubting at 11. Their self-esteem plummets. As Carol Gilligan, Mary Pipher, and other social critics have pointed out in recent years, adolescent girls in America are afflicted with a range of problems, including low self-esteem, eating disorders, binge drinking, date rape and other dating violence, teen pregnancy, and a rise in cigarette smoking. Teenage women today are engaging in far riskier health behaviors and in greater numbers than any prior generation.

It is important to understand that these problems go way beyond individual psychological development. Even girls who are raised in loving homes by supportive parents grow up in a culture—both reflected and reinforced by advertising—that urges girls to adopt a false self, to become "feminine," which means to be nice and kind and sweet, to compete with other girls for the attention of boys, and to value romantic relationships with boys above all else. Girls are put into a terrible double bind. They are supposed to repress their power, their anger, their exuberance and be simply "nice," although they also eventually must compete with men in the business world and be successful. They must be overtly sexy and attractive but essentially passive and virginal. How can we resist these destructive messages and images? The first step, as always, is to become as conscious of them as possible, to deconstruct them.

Regardless of the intent of the advertisers, what messages are girls getting? What are they told? Primarily girls are told by advertisers that what is most important about them is their perfume, their clothing, their bodies, their beauty. Their "essence" is their underwear. "He says the first thing he noticed about you is your great personality," says an ad featuring a very young woman in tight jeans. The copy continues, "He lies." "If this is your idea of a great catch," says an ad for a cosmetic kit from a teen magazine featuring a cute boy, "this is your tackle box." Even very little girls are offered makeup and toys like Special Night Barbie, which shows them how to dress up for a night out. Girls of all ages get the message that they must be flawlessly beautiful and, above all these days, they must be thin.

Adolescent girls are especially vulnerable to the obsession with thinness, for many reasons. One is the ominous peer pressure on young people. Adolescence is a time of self-consciousness and terror of shame and humiliation. Boys are shamed for being too small, too weak, too soft, too sensitive. And girls are shamed for being too sexual, too loud, too boisterous, too big (in any sense of the word), having too hearty an appetite. Many young women have told me that their boyfriends wanted them to lose weight. One said that her boyfriend had threatened to leave her if she didn't lose five pounds. "Why don't you leave him," I asked, "and lose 160?"

The situation is very different for men. The double standard is reflected in an ad for a low-fat pizza: "He eats a brownie . . . you eat a rice cake. He eats a juicy burger . . . you eat a low-fat entree. He eats pizza . . . you eat pizza. Finally, life is fair." Although some men develop eating problems, the predominant cultural message remains that a hearty appetite and a large size is desirable in a man, but not so in a woman.

The obsession starts early. Today at least one-third of 12- to13-year-old girls are actively trying to lose weight, by dieting, vomiting, and/or taking pills. Some studies have found that nearly 80% of fourth-grade girls are dieting. And a survey in Massachusetts found that the single largest group of high school students considering or attempting suicide is girls who feel they are overweight. Imagine. Girls made to feel so terrible about themselves that they would rather be dead than fat.

No wonder it is hard to find a woman, especially a young woman, in America today who has a truly healthy attitude toward her body and toward food. Bulimia and anorexia are the extreme results of an obsession with eating and weight control that grips many young women with serious and potentially very dangerous results. Although eating problems are often thought to result from vanity, the truth is that they, like other addictions and compulsive behavior, usually have deeper roots.

Advertising doesn't cause eating problems, of course. However, these images certainly contribute to the body-hatred so many young women feel and to some of the resulting eating problems, which range from bulimia to compulsive overeating to simply being obsessed with controlling one's appetite. Advertising does promote abusive and abnormal attitudes about eating, drinking, and thinness.

Being obsessed about one's weight is made to seem normal and even appealing in ads for unrelated products, such as the British watch ad featuring an extremely thin young woman and proclaiming "Put some weight on." The additional weight is the watch. The woman is so thin she can wear the watch on her upper arm.

The magazines and the ads deliberately *create* and *intensify* anxiety about weight because it is so profitable. On a deeper level, however, they *reflect* cultural concerns and conflicts about women's power. Real freedom for women would change the very basis of our male-dominated society. It is not surprising that many men (and women) fear this.

"We cut Judy down to size," says an ad for a health club. "Soon, you'll both be taking up less space," says an ad for a collapsible treadmill, referring both to the product and the young woman exercising on it. *The obsession with thinness is most deeply about cutting girls and women down to size.* Some argue that it is men's awareness of just how powerful women can be that has created the attempts to keep women small. Indeed, thinness as an ideal has always accompanied periods of greater freedom for women—as soon as we got the vote, boyish flapper bodies came into vogue. No wonder there is such pressure on young women today to be thin, to shrink, to be like little girls, not to take up too much space, literally or figuratively.

At the same time there is relentless pressure on women to be small, there is also pressure on us to succeed, to achieve, to "have it all." We can be successful as long as we stay "feminine" (i.e., powerless enough not to be truly threatening). One way to do this is to present an image of fragility, to look like a waif. This demonstrates that one is both in control and still very "feminine."

The changing roles and greater opportunities for women promised by the women's movement are trivialized, reduced to the private search for the slimmest body. In one commercial, three skinny young women dance and sing about the "taste of freedom." They are feeling free because they can now eat bread, thanks to a low-calorie version. A commercial for a fast-food chain features a very slim young woman who announces, "I have a license to eat." The salad bar and lighter fare have given her freedom to eat (as if eating for women were a privilege rather than a need).

Most of us know by now about the damage done to girls by the tyranny of the ideal image and the obsession with thinness. But girls get other messages too that "cut them down to size" more subtly. In ad after ad girls are urged to be "barely there"—beautiful but silent.

"Make a statement without saying a word," says an ad for perfume. And indeed this is one of the primary messages of the culture to adolescent girls. "The silence of a look can reveal more than words," says another perfume ad. "More than words can say," says another. A lipstick ad says, "Watch your mouth, young lady," while one for nail polish says, "Let your fingers do the talking," and one for hairspray promises "hair that speaks volumes."

An Italian ad features a very thin young woman in an elegant coat sitting on a window seat. The copy says, "This woman is silent. This coat talks." Girls, seeing these images of women, are encouraged to be silent, mysterious, not to talk too much or too loudly. In so many different ways, they are told "the more you subtract, the more you add."

It is impossible to know how much of this message is intended by the advertisers. Is it harmless wordplay, or is it a sophisticated and clever marketing ploy based on research about the silencing of girls, deliberately designed to attract them with the promise of at least some form of self-expression? I don't know. Advertisers certainly spend a lot of money on psychological research and focus groups. They usually know what they are doing. But sometimes, they are just reflecting common cultural beliefs and concerns. It doesn't matter whether it is intended or not. What matters is the effect. And I contend that the cumulative effect of these images and words urging girls to express themselves through their bodies and through products is serious and harmful.

As Erving Goffman (1978) pointed out in *Gender Advertisements*, we learn a great deal about the disparate power of males and females simply through the body language and poses of advertising. Women, especially young women, are generally subservient to men in ads, both through size and position. Sometimes it is as blatant as a woman serving as a footrest in an ad for Think Skateboards.

Other times, it is more subtle but quite striking (once one becomes aware of it). A double-paged spread for Calvin Klein's clothing for kids conveys a world of information about the relative power of boys and girls. One of the boys seems to be in the act of speaking, expressing himself, while the girl has her hand over her mouth.

Girls are often shown as playful clowns in these ads, perpetuating the attitude that girls and women are childish and cannot be taken seriously, whereas even very young men are generally portrayed as secure, powerful, and serious. People in control of their lives stand upright, alert, and ready to meet the world. In contrast, females often appear off-balance, insecure, and weak. Often our body parts are bent, conveying unpreparedness, submissiveness, and appeasement.

We cover our faces with our hair or our hands, conveying shame or embarrassment. And, no matter what happens, we keep on smiling. "Just smiling the bothers away," as one ad says.

An ad for vodka features a woman in the water and the copy, "In a past life I was a mermaid who fell in love with an ancient mariner. I pulled him into the sea to be my husband. I didn't know he couldn't breathe underwater." Of course, she can't breathe underwater either.

Breathe underwater. As girls come of age sexually, the culture gives them impossibly contradictory messages. Advertising slogans such as "because innocence is sexier than you think" and "nothing so sensual was ever so innocent" place them in a double bind. "Only something so pure could inspire such unspeakable passion, " declares an ad for Jovan musk. And a very sexy ad features a couple making love while the woman is wearing a bra called "Pure." Somehow girls are supposed to be both innocent and seductive, virginal and experienced, all at the same time. As they quickly learn, this is tricky.

Females have long been divided into virgins and whores, of course. What is new is that girls are now supposed to embody both within themselves.

This is symbolic of the central contradiction of the culture—we must work hard and produce and achieve success and yet, at the same time, we are encouraged to live impulsively, spend a lot of money, and be constantly and immediately gratified. This tension is reflected in our attitudes toward many things, including sex and eating. Girls are promised fulfillment both through being thin and through eating rich foods, just as they are promised fulfillment through being innocent and virginal and through wild and impulsive sex.

Advertisers are aware of their role and do not hesitate to take advantage of the insecurities and anxieties of young people, usually in the guise of offering solutions. A cigarette provides a symbol of independence. A pair of designer jeans or sneakers conveys status. The right perfume or beer resolves doubts about femininity or masculinity. Because so many anxieties have to do with sexuality and intimacy and because advertising so often offers products as the answers and uses sex to sell, it is perhaps the concept of sexuality that is most deeply affected.

"You can learn more about anatomy after school," says an ad for jeans, which manages to trivialize sex, relationships, and education all in one sentence. Magazines targeting girls and young women are filled with ads and articles on how to be beautiful and sexy and appealing to boys—all in service of the advertisers, of course, who sell their wares on almost every page. "How Smart Girls Flirt," "Sex to Write Home About," "15 Ways Sex Makes You Prettier," and "Are You Good in Bed?" are some of the recent cover stories for *Jane* magazine.

The emphasis for girls and women is always on being desirable, not on experiencing desire. Girls who want to be sexually *active* instead of simply being the objects of male desire are given only one model to follow, that of exploitive male sexuality. It seems that advertisers can't conceive of a kind of power that isn't manipulative and exploitive or a way that women can be actively sexual without being like traditional men.

Women who are "powerful" in advertising are uncommitted. They treat men like sex objects: "If I want a man to see my bra, I take him home," says an androgynous young woman. They are elusive and distant: "She's the first woman who refused to take your phone calls," says one ad. As if it were a good thing to be rude and inconsiderate.

Mostly though, girls are not supposed to have sexual agency. They are supposed to be passive, swept away, overpowered. "See where it takes you," says a perfume ad featuring a couple passionately embracing. "Unleash your fantasies," says another. "A force of nature." This contributes to the strange and damaging concept of the "good girl" as the one who is swept away, unprepared for sex, versus the "bad girl" as the one who plans for sex, uses contraception, and is generally responsible. A young woman can manage to have sex and yet in some sense maintain her virginity by being "out of control," drunk, and/or deep in denial about the entire experience.

In adolescence, girls are told that they have to give up so much of what they *know* about relationships and intimacy if they want to attract men. Most tragically, they are told they have to give up each other. The truth is that one of the most powerful antidotes to destructive cultural messages is close and supportive female friendships. But girls are often encouraged by the culture to sacrifice their relationships with each other and to enter into hostile competition for the attention of boys and men. "What the bitch who's about to steal your man wears," says one ad.

Of course, some girls do resist and rebel. Some are encouraged (by someone—a loving parent, a supportive teacher) to see the cultural contradictions clearly and to break free in a healthy and positive way. Others rebel in ways that damage themselves. A young woman seems to have only two choices: she can bury her sexual self, be a "good girl," give in to what Carol Gilligan (Brown & Gilligan, 1992, p. 53) terms "the tyranny of kind and nice" (and numb the pain by overeating or starving or cutting herself or drinking herself into a stupor). Or she can become a rebel—flout her sexuality, seduce inappropriate partners, seduce everyone, smoke, drink flamboyantly, use other drugs. Both of these responses are self-destructive, but they begin as an attempt to survive, not to self-destruct.

Many girls become women who split themselves in two and do both—have a double life, a secret life—a good girl in public, out of control in private. A feminist in public, involved in an abusive relationship or lost in sadomasochistic fantasies in private. A lawyer by day, a barfly by night. Raiding the refrigerator or drinking themselves into a stupor alone in their kitchens at night, after the children are in bed, the laundry done. Doing well in school, but smoking in order to have a sexier, cooler image. Being sexual only when drunk.

There are few healthy alternatives for girls who want to truly rebel against restrictive gender roles and stereotypes. What they are offered by the popular culture is a superficial toughness, an "attitude," exemplified by smoking, drinking, and engaging in casual sex—all harmful behaviors. In 1990, Virginia Slims offered girls a T-shirt that said, "Sugar and spice and everything nice? Get real."

In 1997, Winston used the same theme in an ad featuring a tough young woman shooting pool and saying, "I'm not all sugar & spice. And neither are my smokes." As if the alternative to the feminine stereotype was sarcasm and toughness, and as if smoking was somehow an expression of one's authentic self ("get real").

Of course, the readers and viewers of these ads don't take them literally. But we do take them in—each is another grain of sand in a slowly accumulating and vast sand pile. If we entirely enter the world of ads, imagine them to be real for a moment, we find that the sandpile has entirely closed us in, and there's only one escape route—buy something. "Get the power," says an ad featuring a woman showing off her bicep. "The power to clean anything," the ad continues.

"Hey girls, you've got the power of control," says an ad for hairspray. "You never had this much control when you were on your own" (hair gel). "Exceptional character" (a watch). "An enlightening experience" (face powder). "Inner strength" (vitamins). "Stronger longer" (shampoo). Of course, the empowerment, the enlightenment, is as impossible to get through products as is anything else—love, security, romance, passion. On one level, we know this. On another, we keep buying and hoping.

Other ads go further and offer products as a way to rebel, to be a real individual. "Live outside the lines," says a clothing ad featuring a young woman walking out of a men's room. This kind of rebellion isn't going to rock the world. And, no surprise, the young woman is very thin and conventionally pretty.

"Think for yourself," says yet another hollow-cheeked young woman, demonstrating her individuality via an expensive and fashionable sweater. "Be amazing" (cosmetics). "If you're going to create electricity, use it" (watches).

"Break the rules," says a perfume ad. It goes on to give the confusing advice, "Stand apart, keep your head, go with your heart." The thin and pretty young woman featured with her boyfriend is a perfect example of conventional "femininity." As is the young woman in the Halston perfume ad that says, "And when she was bad she wore Halston." What kind of "bad" is this?

"Nude with attitude" features a Black woman in a powerful pose, completely undercut by the brevity of her dress and the focus on her long legs. Her "attitude" is nothing to fear—she's just another sex object. Good thing, because a lot of people are especially scared of powerful Black women.

The British ad "For girls with plenty of balls" is insulting in ways too numerous to count, beginning with the equation of strength and courage and fiery passion with testicles. What the ad offers these girls is body lotion.

Some ads do feature women who seem really angry and rebellious, but the final message always is the same. "Today, I indulge my dark side," says an ad featuring a fierce young woman tearing at what seems to be a net. "Got a problem with that?" The slogan is "be extraordinary not ordinary." The product which promises to free this girl from the net that imprisons her? Black nail polish.

Nail polish. Such a trivial solution to such an enormous dilemma. But such triviality and superficiality is common in advertising. How could it be otherwise? The solution to any problem always has to be a product. Change, transformation, is thus inevitably shallow and moronic, rather than meaningful and transcendent. These days, self-improvement seems to have more to do with calories than with character, with abdomens rather than absolutes, with nail polish than with ethics.

This relentless trivialization of her hopes and dreams, her expectations for herself, cuts to the quick of a young girl's soul. Just as she is entering womanhood, eager to spread her wings, to become more sexual, more empowered, more independent—the culture moves in to *cut her down to size.*

Black nail polish isn't going to help. But it probably won't hurt either. What hurts are some of the other products offered to girls as a way to rebel and to cope—especially our deadliest drugs, alcohol, and nicotine. These drugs are cynically and deliberately offered by advertisers to girls as a way to numb the pain of disconnection, to maintain the illusion of some kind of relationship, to be more appealing to men, to be both "liberated" and "feminine," and, perhaps most tragically, to subvert their rebellious spirits, the very spark within that could, if not coopted, empower them to change their lives.

IT'S YOUR TURN: WHAT DO YOU THINK? WHAT WILL YOU FIND?

1. Look through the advertisements in a magazines catering to a diverse range of female readers (*Cosmopolitan*; *Ladies' Home Journal*; *O, The Oprah Magazine*; *Marie Claire*; etc.) To what extent do the ads reflect the types of images discussed here? Do the different magazines represent women and girls differently? How?

2. Work together in small groups to conceptualize a magazine ad for a new line called "Vocal" jeans. Be sure the copy and artwork make the product appealing to consumers, but take care not to "cut girls down to size."

3. If you were the producer of a teen-oriented TV program and an advertiser submitted a commercial demeaning overweight girls (and threatening their already fragile self-esteem), would you air it? Why or why not? Whose responsibility is it to make sure that ads are appropriate for the audiences?

4. Although the representation of men was mentioned, the focus of this chapter is on women. Look through popular magazines to see how men are represented in advertising. What do these images tell us about what it means to be a man in today's society?

REFERENCES

Brown, L. M., & Gilligan, C. (1992). *Meeting at the crossroads: Women's psychology and girls' development.* New York: Ballantine.

Goffman, E. (1978). *Gender advertisements.* Cambridge, MA: Harvard University Press.

Film and Entertainment Television

6.1 "PEOPLE TELL ME I'M WHITE": STEPHEN COLBERT AND COMIC DECONSTRUCTION OF COLORBLINDNESS

Jonathan P. Rossing

The author analyzes Stephen Colbert's humorous deconstruction of "colorblindness," a complex sub-section of racial discourse. Colbert's critique of colorblindness through humor urges the audience to reflect on the realities of race consciousness, racism, and racial privilege.

Topical political humor typically evokes one of two reactions. First, for centuries people have dismissed and trivialized comic texts: "It's *merely* entertainment." "What could we possibly learn from comedy?" The implication is that serious topics may never be treated with levity or light-heartedness. Fun cannot be educational. Second, people criticize humor for violating social norms and appropriate boundaries. For some, humor "goes too far" and offends, particularly when it addresses topics such as race, gender, sexual orientation, and religion. Suddenly that which was easily dismissed becomes a lightning rod of controversy as an errant joke mobilizes protests, boycotts, or heated debate. Both positions reject humor as a serious subject worthy of careful consideration. Given these rejections, how can humor positively impact our understanding of important social political issues such as race or gender? For a topic as serious as racism, why study humor?

I present another perspective on humor that treats the play and fun with appropriate seriousness. Humor deserves serious study because it directs important attention to often overlooked features of everyday life such as common cultural assumptions. Humor yields new perspectives on familiar habits and shines light on the contradictions of society. Jon Stewart highlights the shortcomings of politicians on *The Daily Show*. Sacha Baron Cohen highlighted homophobia, racism, and anti-Semitism when he assumed multiple exaggerated characters such as Borat or Ali G. Comedians such as Dave Chappelle, Russell Peters, and Wanda Sykes regularly call out instances of everyday racism. By holding a funhouse mirror to contemporary culture, humor reflects recognizable practices, but distorts and exaggerates these everyday realities in ways that make audiences see themselves and their society from new vantage points (Boskin, 1997; Critchley, 2002). Humor on race in particular presents an important reflection of the ways race matters and how people make sense of race.

One of today's most effective exemplars of topical critical humor is Stephen Colbert of Comedy Central's *The Colbert Report*. Colbert gained popularity as a mock-commentator on *The Daily Show with Jon Stewart* before launching his own fake-news program in a parody of conservative news programs such as Fox News' *The O'Reilly Factor*. An expert with the funhouse mirror, Colbert uses distortion and hyperbole to defamiliarize everyday realities, such as debates over gay marriage, barriers to women in politics, or conversations about race and racism.

THE PROBLEM OF COLORBLINDNESS

Over 400 years of racialized thinking, decision making, and actions have created privileges and oppression that continue to influence social opportunities, identities, resource distribution, ways of thinking, and much more (Vera & Feagin, 2007; Hartigan, 2010). Yet despite abundant evidence for the ongoing significance of race, many people claim that race is irrelevant and position racialized thinking as a thing of the past. This colorblind worldview denies the importance of racial identity and ignores the persistence of racial injustice. From this vantage point, society and culture have moved "beyond race" while only a handful of exceptional bigots clench tightly to outdated, racist thinking. From this colorblind perspective, anyone who "sees" or "talks" about race becomes complicit with "racism."

Ignoring race, however, carries significant consequences. Removing race from public conversations and erasing its social political salience enables people to deny the consequences of racial thinking and action. For example, people can easily dismiss continued segregation in housing and school systems as natural patterns that are based solely on economics or living preferences. Worse, colorblindness eliminates race as a viable explanation for social injustices. For example when racialized thinking and practices no longer appear as plausible factors, people turn to individual blame and failure as explanations for racial disparities in incarceration rates, health care access, or wealth distribution (Bonilla-Silva, 2010. In these instances, deliberately avoiding any discussion of racism in its many forms allows racial privilege and oppression to continue unchecked. Arguably of greatest concern is the way colorblind discourses enable "whiteness" to remain invisible. When we ignore white as a significant racial marker, we can neither question nor challenge the privileges, power, and implied value of white identity (Kendall, 2006; Tochluk, 2010). Patricia Williams describes colorblindness as a tension between everyday realities and "what one is cultured to see or not see—the dilemma of the emperor's new clothes" (1991, p. 5). Like the emperor in the fairy tale, unaware of his nudity, colorblindness enables people to remain ignorant of the complex realities of race.

COMIC DECONSTRUCTION OF COLORBLINDNESS

Stephen Colbert's satire of colorblindness on Comedy Central's *The Colbert Report* presents an illustrative case study of humor's critical possibilities[1]. Although his satirical news program addresses politics and culture broadly, he comments on racial matters with regularity. His persona embraces a colorblind existence. Colbert repeatedly denies the significance and reality of race, including his own white racial identity. In this way, he plays the foolish emperor, unaware of racial realities in U. S. culture and too proud to admit he may be wrong. But Colbert's satire is significant because he also critiques and deconstructs colorblindness. With almost every rejection of race, Colbert uses humor to undermine his colorblind attitudes and highlight the limitations of these ways of thinking. Like the child in the fairy tale crying "The emperor *is* naked!" Colbert ironically draws attention to the blatantly ignored realities of race in U.S. culture, thereby highlighting both the unsupportable claim of colorblindness and the inescapable role of racialized thinking in everyday life.

"I Don't See Race" (but It's Everywhere)

In almost every report on race or every interview where race emerges as a salient issue, Stephen Colbert openly asserts his colorblindness. "I don't see race," he insists. "I'm colorblind." However, his exaggerated naiveté pushes this colorblind position toward absurdity and reveals the limitations of this mindset. Discussing the 2008 Democratic primaries with political strategist and news analyst Donna Brazile, a Black female, Colbert claimed, "I don't see race. I've—I've evolved beyond that. By the way, are—you said you were a black woman. Um, can you—do you have anything to prove that? Because I don't see race" (April 30, 2008). His exaggeration gestures to the reality that people almost never have difficulty reaching conclusions about race. His request for proof of Black femininity cues the audience to consider the relative ease with which people classify racial identities. The joke works because no one in the audience would seriously request such evidence. We have already, unwittingly, made determinations about Brazile's racial identity. Moreover, pairing race with gender Colbert strengthens his critique of colorblindness. We do not claim to be "gender blind" in relation to phenotypic markers and recognizable performances; how do we claim to be colorblind? He repeats this subtle critique in an interview with Cornel West, a professor at Princeton University, when he points to obvious phenotypic markers long used to identify race. Colbert explained to West, "I don't see race. I've evolved beyond that." West, a Black man, pushed back, "But when you see me what do you see?" Colbert replied, "I see a big, bushy beard and hair. I have no idea what race you are" (September 24, 2008). These parodies of colorblindness highlight the hypocrisies and impossibilities of ignoring race.

Colbert issued one of his strongest challenges to the logic of colorblindness on the evening of President Obama's inauguration: "I never empathize with people who are not like me. So the reaction I had to Obama's inauguration must logically mean that I am a black man. I had no idea, because I don't see race" (January 20, 2009). He claims not to see race, but he betrays his own "logic" as he easily recognizes Obama as a Black man. Furthermore, the comedic implausibility of a white man claiming to "logically" be a black man, or vice versa, highlights the carefully patrolled and readily recognized lines of racial identity and performance. This lesson also illustrates that when people deny their race-consciousness, they more firmly mark themselves as players in a racial culture. The claim to colorblindness does not make sense outside of a context or framework where race undeniably exists.

Paradoxically, colorblindness often results in heightened race-consciousness, particularly in discourses of reactionary colorblindness that identify race as they condemn race-consciousness. This contradictory position often emerges amidst complaints of alleged white disenfranchisement and alienation (Winant, 1997). For example, an *Esquire* magazine cover story about Senator John Edwards in August 2007 asked, "Can a white man still be elected president?" The accompanying story described Senator Edwards as "the white man out, talking about issues that hearken back to the days when a women president or a black president were gauzy, aspirational fantasies" (Pierce, 2007, p. 64). At first this reaction seems to fall outside a discussion of colorblindness because it demonstrates race consciousness. But only if one ignores racial realities from the outset can a person believe that white men, especially those in middle- and upper-class economic situations, are marginalized and oppressed. For example, complaining that white men cannot hold powerful positions ignores the reality that whites have had access to seats of power since the formation of the country. Every U.S. election represents a validation of whiteness. A biracial president does not negate the reality that the vast majority of Congress, the Supreme Court, and other powerful decision makers are white and male. Claiming that white people are systematically disadvantaged not only ignores racial inequalities, but also diverts attention from persistent racial inequities and privileges (Bonilla-Silva, 2010).

Early in the 2008 presidential primaries, Colbert parodied this reactionary colorblind discourse and revealed the cracks in its logic. Colbert advised Senator John Edwards to declare himself a Black woman in order to gain advantage in the polls. "Think about it, Senator," he urged. "There is no downside, unless America isn't ready for a black, female president. Of course, if that happens, you've got a great fall back. You're a white guy. And they usually get elected" (August 13, 2007). His professed colorblindness (and gender-blindness) enables both this preposterous advice and an unfounded belief in reverse discrimination against white men. It betrays a strongly self-interested race-consciousness even as the advice implies a longing for a race-neutral world. However, Colbert once again disrupts this position of reverse discrimination. First, the caveat about America's readiness to elect a woman of color as president highlights the race-consciousness that pervades U.S. culture. This statement parodies the questions that pundits and journalists posed throughout Barack Obama's campaign: "Is America ready for a black president?" and the follow-ups: "Is Senator Obama too black? Not black enough?" Slipping this "downside" into his advice hints at the cultural and institutional barriers that remain in place for some citizens. Moreover, even though his shtick bemoans the lost opportunities for white men, his closing comment prominently highlights the power and privileges of whiteness. The "fall back" position of being a white man who typically wins elections brings to the foreground the racial realities that colorblind positions ignore.

"Racism Is Over!"(Some Exceptions Apply)

A proclaimed commitment to colorblindness also enables people to declare racism dead and consequently to explain persistent racial inequalities in non-racial terms. In other words, colorblindness rewrites history in a way that sections off the evils of racial oppression into discrete, neat packages so that they appear as isolated moments of the past with little connection to the present. Such "rhetorical containment" eliminates race as an explanation for ongoing injustices and privileges and allows people to eliminate any responsibility or guilt we might have for the ongoing role of race in U.S. culture (Flores, Moon, & Nakayama, 2006). Media texts contribute to this containment. The stories of television and film in particular tend to bracket racism and racial discord as disconnected events of the past, detached from the present.

Colbert critiques this corollary to colorblind discourses when he openly declares the "End of Racism." In one instance, he apologized for slavery and instructed citizens to stop looking to the past in a performance that mimicked the way people frame racism as an isolated incident of another time. A video montage, however, ironically undermined his proclamation. The montage included symbols of racial oppression from both past and present: for example, blackface performers, racist cartoons of the early twentieth century, and a reminder of comedian Michael Richards' epithet-laden performance only 3 months prior to this proclamation (February 1, 2007)[2]. These images gesture to the mass media's role in shaping public conceptions about and attitudes toward race. The montage suggests that a simple declaration will neither end racism nor eliminate these deeply held patterns of racial thought and action.

Furthermore, the montage on the death of racism marked its life span as the length of human history—from 4004 B.C. to February 1, 2007 (the date of the episode). An existence of over 6,000 years frames racism as an ongoing problem that could not possibly end overnight with one election or one apology. Both the enduring presence and the multiple manifestations of racism reveal that racism is not easily declared dead. Colbert's comic juxtaposition between a claim that racism is over and the reality of long-standing racialized practices makes it difficult for the audience to accept comfortably his colorblind position. The ironic context in which he situates his "End of Racism" declaration refutes racism as a distant or isolated evil and frames it an ongoing fact of history.

Exposing Privilege

Perhaps his strongest counter-punch to colorblindness is a recurring joke that prominently foregrounds whiteness as a privileged and empowered position in which citizens are heavily invested. Frequently, after proclaiming his colorblindness, Colbert offers the caveat, "People tell me I'm white, and I believe them because . . . " The evidence he cites in every instance directs attention to racial privilege and disparity. For example, as he proclaims ignorance of race, he brings to light injustices such as power relationships and racial profiling in the criminal justice system: " . . . and I believe them because police call me 'Sir.'" Likewise, Colbert tweeted to his followers on Twitter, "people tell me i'm white, and i believe them because i've never been arrested in my foyer" (@StephenAtHome, July 23, 2009)[3]. He calls attention to institutional and cultural exclusion of people of color in the television industry: " . . . and I believe them because I have a late night talk show." He showcases ongoing patterns of community segregation and "white flight": " . . . and I believe them because I belong to an all-white country club." Similarly in an installment of his mock-editorial segment "The Word" titled "Black and White," he explained, "I'm not talking about seeing races as black and white. I don't see skin color." But the side bar offering comic commentary undercuts his claim: "'Lucked Into' All-White Gated Community" (April 10, 2008). He even calls attention to instances of everyday racism and privilege as he explains, " . . . and I believe them because I have no trouble catching a cab." After Barack Obama's election, he extended this pointed criticism by claiming of President Obama: "People tell me he's black and I believe them because I don't trust him." In each instance, his quick comic reversal uncovers overlooked practices and ideologies that sustain racial privilege and oppression. Marking these ideologies forces the audience to confront these realities and invites the audience to change or challenge them.

TAKING HUMOR (AND RACE) SERIOUSLY

Like any media text and art, humor and its meaning will be continually negotiated in complex social environments. One must be careful not to standardize its message or reject the possibility that others will approach the text from another vantage point that yields a different response.

Nevertheless, the serious messages in some comic texts cannot be ignored. Critical attention to discourses some might initially consider "trivial" may yield important insights for conversations on race and racism. Humor deserves serious attention, particularly the humor that addresses social identities and constructions, such as race, gender, sexuality, or socioeconomic status.

In Colbert's case, his commentary on race calls attention to colorblindness as an untenable position riddled with contradictions. Espousing an unwavering commitment to race-neutrality and post-racialism, Colbert employs ironic shifts to undermine the logic of this belief system and invite the audience to account for the inescapable role race plays in everyday life. Specifically, Colbert highlights unavoidable race-consciousness that surfaces in colorblind discourses. Colbert's exaggerated performances also make visible white racial identity and privilege. He foregrounds the often unexamined ways that white racial identity emerges in everyday interactions, and these unexpected comic ruptures may help people recognize the privileges and injustices we overlook. The harder individuals try to ignore the realities of racial disparities and injustices and identities, the more we recreate and perpetuate the racial lines we claim not to see. In short, with every joke about colorblindness and a post-race society, Colbert reminds his audience that race matters.

NOTES

1. All episodes of *The Colbert Report* are available at http://www.colbernation.com/. The book *I am America (And So Can You!)* (2007) also typifies his satirical style. It includes a chapter dedicated to race that provides additional examples of the material in this chapter.

2. Michael Richards, known for his role as Cosmo Kramer on *Seinfeld*, unleashed a tirade of epithets and racial, verbal assaults at a pair of audience members during his performance at the Los Angeles Laugh Factory in November 2006.

3. Colbert was commenting on Harvard professor Henry Louis Gates Jr., who was arrested at his home in Cambridge, Massachusetts, in July 2009.

IT'S YOUR TURN: WHAT DO YOU THINK? WHAT WILL YOU FIND?

1. Colbert wrote a mock-editorial for *Esquire* magazine in August 2008 titled "Stephen Colbert's Guide to White Male Oppression" (available at http://www.esquire.com). Read this satirical complaint about the plight of white males. What is his point in this article? Who is his target audience? After reading the editorial, consider the title again: Does it take on a different meaning than you originally assumed?

2. Visit the Web sites for *The Colbert Report* (http://www.colbertnation.com) and *The Daily Show with Jon Stewart* (http://www.thedailyshow.com). Search for additional clips that address either race or gender (keyword suggestions: African American, racism, race, sexism). What comedic strategies do Colbert and Stewart use to provoke their audiences to reflect on issues of race and gender?

3. In what ways is Colbert limited as a white man in his comedic engagement with race and gender? What are the opportunities and advantages of his identity position? Can you think of other comedians of different racial backgrounds who address some of these same issues through humor?

4. Humor frequently provokes audiences to think about topics they might otherwise ignore, and it confronts audiences with significant controversial issues. But humor rarely provides a concrete solution to the problems is presents. Would you consider "proposing a solution" to be the responsibility of humor? What can audiences do to follow up on comic provocations?

REFERENCES

Bonilla-Silva, E. (2010). *Racism without racists: Color-blind racism and the persistence of racial inequality in the United States* (3rd ed.). Lanham, MD: Rowman and Littlefield.

Boskin, J. (Ed.). (1997). *The humor prism in 20th–century America.* Detroit, MI: Wayne State University Press.

Colbert, S., Dahm, R., Dinello, P., & Silverman, A. (Eds.). (2007). *I am America (And so can you!* New York: Grand Central Publishing.

Critchley, S. (2002). *On humour.* New York: Routledge.

Flores, L.A., Moon, D. G., & Nakayama, T. K. (2006). Dynamic rhetorics of race: California's Racial Privacy Initiative and the shifting grounds of racial politics. *Communication and Critical/Cultural Studies, 3,* 181–210.

Hartigan, J. (2010). *What can you say? America's national conversation on race.* Stanford, CA: Stanford University Press.

Kendall F. (2006). *Understanding white privilege: Creating pathways to authentic relationships across race.* New York: Routledge.

Pierce, C. P. (2007, August). The beauty contest. *Esquire, 148,* 64–65, 122.

Tochluk, S. (2010). *Witnessing whiteness: The need to talk about race and how to do it.* Lanham, MD: Rowman & Littlefield.

Vera, H., & Feagin, J. R. (Eds.). (2007). *Handbook of the sociology of racial and ethnic relations.* New York: Springer.

Williams, P. J. (1991). *Seeing a color-blind future: The paradox of race.* New York: Noonday Press.

Winant, H. (1997). Behind blue eyes: Whiteness and contemporary U.S. racial politics. In M. Fine (Ed.), *Off white: Readings on race, power, and society* (pp. 40–53). New York: Routledge.

6.2 RACE, HIERARCHY, AND HYENAPHOBIA IN *THE LION KING*

Naomi Rockler-Gladen

> *This textual analysis of Disney's* The Lion King *argues that the film reinforces the concept of a hierarchical society in which it is "only natural" that one social group (in this case the hyenas, whose portrayal echoes stereotypes of African Americans) is outcast and doesn't receive adequate resources.*

If you're like many of my students, you might be puzzled by the title of this chapter. Race and hierarchy in *The Lion King*? Why would anyone think about a children's movie in such a manner? After all, if you're like my students, you love *The Lion King*. In my public speaking classes, I ask my students to give an introductory speech about three objects that represent their past, present, and future. One semester, three different students brought in a copy of *The Lion King* as the object to represent their past. People love this film. *The Lion King* is a hugely popular, Academy Award-winning film. It spawned a landmark Tony Award-winning stage show. So why take such a lovable, popular film and think about what it has to say about race?

Many people are quite reticent to analyze Disney films critically. In 1995, several professors edited a collection of critical essays about Disney films. They gave some of the essays to their students, and this is what they found:

> Even our own students, occupying a halfway house between film critic and mass audience, are extremely resistant to the critique of Disney film . . . [O]ur students commonly complained, "You're reading too much into this film!" and "You can't say that about Walt Disney!" These students consistently cite four easy pardons for their pleasurable participation in Disney films and its apolitical agendas: it's only for children, it's only fantasy, it's only a cartoon, and it's just good business. These

four naturalizations create a Disney text exempt from material, historical, and political influences . . . .Our students' attitudes suggest that Disney successfully invites mass audiences to set aside critical faculties. (Bells, Haas, & Sells, 1995, p. 4)

You may feel the same way, or perhaps you've never given much thought to what the "messages" of a Disney film might be. I invite you to put your skepticism on hold for a few pages and think critically with me about *The Lion King*. Here, I argue that *The Lion King* makes the concept of societal hierarchies seem natural and desirable, especially in relationship to race.

This is a textual analysis of *The Lion King*. As with all textual analyses, it's important that you understand that I'm not looking for "hidden" or "subliminal" meanings in *The Lion King*, nor am I arguing that I am telling you the "correct" meaning of the film. Rather, I am offering my interpretation of what I think this film says about race and hierarchy. I doubt very much that Disney intended the film to be interpreted in this way, and I doubt your average 4-year-old viewer even knows what a racial hierarchy is. However, when a critic analyzes a film textually, it doesn't matter whether the producer intended the film to mean something in particular, or whether a viewer interprets the film in a similar way. Textual critics operate under the assumption that films are one of the places where members of a culture learn implicitly about the rules, norm, and power structures of their cultures. In other words, the media are one of the places where people learn about their culture's *ideology*—just as we also learn about a culture's ideological rules, norms, and power structures from our parents, peers, teachers, and clergy.

The Lion King is one of many places where a child might learn implicitly about how race and hierarchy function in his or her culture. For this reason, I believe it's important for us to think critically about what we're watching.

HIERARCHY AND *THE LION KING*

A hierarchy is a system in which some members of a culture have more privilege, economic resources, status, or other form of power than other members of a culture. Your classroom is a hierarchy. The instructor has more power than you and the other students. He or she decides what you will do in class every day and has the power to assign you a grade. You are expected to sit in your desk and do as the instructor asks.

Hierarchies usually are shaped like triangles. In a hierarchical system, usually only a few people have power, while many people have little power. In your school, the students outnumber the instructors, and yet the instructors have all the power. There are even fewer deans and administrators in your school, and yet they have even more power than the instructors.

Most important, hierarchies are *naturalized*. That is, they seem normal and typical to many or most members of the hierarchy, even to the people without the power. You have spent many years of your life in a classroom, and it seems normal and typical to you that the instructor has more power. You've probably never seriously questioned this. Because hierarchies often remain unchallenged, the powerful people stay in power.

There are many hierarchies within societies. In U.S. culture, for example, we have a gender hierarchy. Although there are many individual exceptions to this statement, in general men have more power than women. Similarly, although there are many individual exceptions to this statement, we also have a racial hierarchy in the United States As sociologist George Lipsitz (1998) argued, minorities in the United States disproportionately live in toxically polluted environments, are more likely to receive longer prison terms than whites for the same crimes, and receive inferior health care. Unlike many minorities in the United States, most whites have never been pulled over unfairly by police officers, followed around a store, or otherwise experienced "racial profiling." Unlike minorities, whites can turn on a television set and see many people who look like them.

The Lion King is about a lion cub named Simba who is heir to the throne of the Pridelands, a fictitious animal jungle society. Scar, the brother of King Mufasa, longs to become king himself. He enlists the help of the hyenas, a group of outcast animals who live outside the Pridelands, to help him kill the king and usurp the throne. After murdering Mufasa, Scar persuades Simba that he's to blame for his father's death. Simba goes into exile, and Scar assumes the throne, telling the other lions that Simba is dead. In exile, Simba is befriended by a warthog and meerkat who teach him to live the carefree life of "hakuna matata." Meanwhile, the Pridelands fall apart under Scar's rule, largely because the hyenas have been allowed to move in and have depleted all the resources. Simba's childhood friend Nala finds Simba, now grown, and urges him to dispense with his "hakuna matata" lifestyle and claim responsibility for the throne. After seeing an image of his father from the heavens, Simba goes home, defeats Scar, and becomes the rightful king. Order and beauty is restored to the Pridelands.

The Lion King contains a society in which power is in the hands of a few, and in which this hierarchy is naturalized and deemed desirable to all. In the Pridelands, the lions are the most powerful members of society, while all the other animals are hierarchically inferior. This is demonstrated visibly at the beginning of the film, when the newborn cub Simba is presented to the Pridelands as the future king. All of the animals of the kingdom gather around Pride Rock, the lions' den which, physically, is high above them, to watch the Simba's presentation. As Rafiki, a monkey and spiritual figure, presents the cub to the Pridelands, a beam of light illuminates the cub, a Christian allusion suggesting divine sanction of the cub's predestination to power. As Simba is presented, the other animals in the kingdom bow and applaud wildly.

In an early scene, King Mufasa justifies the hierarchical society to young Simba, referring to the hierarchy as the "circle of life," which he claims must not be violated for fear of chaos. However, the "circle of life" operates clearly in the interests of the lions, who thrive at the top of the hierarchy as the dominant elite. Mufasa justifies the inequality of the hierarchy by arguing that it's beneficial to all. None of the other animals in the Pridelands question their inferior status, despite the fact that sometimes the lions eat them. No revolutionary antelope group is shown plotting to demand more equitable conditions. Even Zazu, a dodo who is the king's servant, doesn't question the hierarchy, although he is humiliated repeatedly by Simba and by Mufasa, who uses Zazu as a subject of a "pouncing lesson" for Simba. In fact, the only resident of the Pridelands who questions the societal hierarchy is Scar, the film's villain. Thus, the hierarchy is *naturalized*; it's made to look normal, desirable, and necessary for the good of all.

RACE AND HYENAPHOBIA IN *THE LION KING*

The Lion King contains a number of hierarchies. For example, *The Lion King* naturalizes a gender hierarchy. The lions clearly have more power than the lionesses. Although Nala is shown to be physically stronger than Simba, it is Simba who is predestined to be the leader. Power is passed in the kingdom from male to male, even though in the case of Scar, the kingdom falls apart under male leadership, and the Pridelands would have been better off with a female leader such as Nala. But here, I'll focus specifically on the topic of race, and what I believe *The Lion King* says about race and hierarchy.

Historically, racial hierarchies often involve segregation of hierarchically "inferior" groups, who are separated from the rest of society and forced to live with inadequate resources and few opportunities. In Nazi-occupied Poland, for example, Jews were removed from society and forced to live in desolate ghettos, where they eventually were murdered. In South Africa, through the system of apartheid, the indigenous African population was segregated from the more affluent white population and forced into inadequate living conditions with inadequate schooling. Similarly, in the Southern United States until the 1960s, "Jim Crow" laws legally separated African Americans from whites and forced them into inadequate housing, schools, and economic situations. In the United States today, de facto segregation and "White flight" make segregation a continuing reality; as of 1993, 70% of all Latino and African American children attended predominantly minority schools (Lipsitz, 1998, p. 38). In California and Texas, angry public sentiment struggles to keep "illegal" immigrants out and to make English the official U.S. language; and throughout the Midwest, Native Americans for years have lived on reservations where they suffer some of the highest poverty rates in the country.

In *The Lion King*, the segregated group is the hyenas. The hyenas don't necessarily represent any *particular* group (although as I argue below, their portrayal echoes derogatory stereotypes of African Americans) but rather might represent any hated group of outsiders throughout history—Native Americans, Mexican Americans, immigrants, and so forth. They represent the *concept* of the feared and hatred outsider whom the mainstream culture fights to keep out. The order of the circle of life depends on the hyenas staying outside the lush Pridelands. When hyenas wander into the Pridelands, King Mufasa chases them out. When hyenas are integrated into the Pridelands, the Pridelands disintegrate.

Similar to other segregated groups throughout history, the hyenas live in a poverty-stricken land. Unlike the lush Pridelands, the hyenas' land is barren. They don't have enough food. Unlike beautiful Pride Rock, where the lions live, the hyenas live in caves and amongst elephant skeletons that are the *Lion King* housing equivalent of dilapidated projects in the inner cities. Although they're wealthy, the lions feel no obligation to help the hyenas overcome their poverty. In fact, when the hungry hyenas venture into the Pridelands in search of food, Mufasa chases them out.

At no time in *The Lion King* do we learn that segregation is not a good thing and that lions ought to learn to overcome their "hyenaphobia" and create a more multicultural society. Quite the opposite is true. Hyenaphobia is never proven irrational. When King Scar invites the hyenas to move into the Pridelands, all of the lions' worst fears are realized. After a period of time, the Pridelands are as barren as the hyena lands, and the food supply has run out. In response to the decay of the Pridelands, the lionesses encourage Scar to desert the Pridelands and move on. It is the story of white America's flight to the suburbs. As the old unspoken fear goes, if minorities are integrated into mainstream culture, everything will fall apart. *The Lion King* creates a situation where these fears are justified and naturalized. Some creatures, *The Lion King* tells us, really do deserve to live in poverty and be segregated.

The Lion King does contain some positive nods to African Americans. Two well-known African Americans provide the voices of prominent characters: James Earl Jones as Mufasa and Whoopi Goldberg as one of the hyenas. Many African Americans and Africans were involved in the production of the film, and the film contains a good deal of African music (both of these trends continue to an even larger degree in the theatrical version of *The Lion King*). However, although these inclusions shouldn't be dismissed, they don't mask the negative stereotypes of African Americans that surface in *The Lion King*.

The hyenas signify the stereotypical caricature of the African American welfare recipient. Popularized by President Ronald Reagan in the 1980s, the legendary "welfare queen," who "poached" the taxpayers' money by having babies out of wedlock, became the scapegoat for the nation's economic problems. Like the "welfare queen," the hyenas are the villains in this individualistic tale because they are "scavengers" taking resources they haven't earned. They aren't self-sufficient; they sneak into the Pridelands and poach food. No explanation is ever given as to why the hyenas aren't entitled to share the resources of the Pridelands, just as no clear explanation is given as to why the Pridelands disintegrate when the hyenas are integrated. The needy hyenas simply are assumed to be unworthy scavengers.

Physically, the hyenas resemble the post-slavery "Black Sambo" stereotype that was prevalent in U.S. popular culture for many years, including in the popular radio and television series *Amos 'n' Andy*. This stereotype emerged from the traditional minstrel show, in which African American or white men would mock African Americans by covering their faces with unnaturally dark blackface, exaggerating common African American physical features, and acting comically inarticulate and insipid. The hyenas resemble this stereotype. They have bulging eyes, protruding lips, and as Scar describes them, "vacant expressions." They laugh hysterically and loudly all the time. Two of the main character hyenas show some intelligence, but the hyena Ed is the ultimate Sambo. He never speaks; he just laughs and laughs, and wags his protruding tongue like a rabid dog.

The hyenas represent an odd, contradictory mix of racial phobias. They are violent, and the lions' stereotypes of the violent hyenas are justified throughout the hyenas' actions. At the same time, the hyenas who are feared for their violence are helplessly buffoon-like—especially Ed. They are at the bottom of the food chain and scarcely can find enough food to eat to stay alive. When Scar instructs the hyenas to kill young Simba, they fail miserably, instead falling into a pile of thorns as they run after the cub. In accordance with their dishonest nature, they lie to Scar and claim they have killed Simba. This is similar to stereotypes of minorities throughout history, including African Americans, who contradictorily are considered by many to be ignorant, yet somehow frighteningly violent. In addition, the hyenas roam together like gang members, representing stereotypical fears and of minority gangs.

Scar's use of the hyenas to usurp the throne reflects the fear that minorities might be mobilized to overthrow the powers that be, reminiscent of *Birth of a Nation* (Griffin, 1915), the epic Ku Klux Klan propaganda film in which Northern outsiders mobilize evil, stereotypical former slaves to wreak havoc upon the South. In addition, "Be Prepared," the musical sequence in which Scar invites the hyenas to support his coup, alludes visually to Hitler's propaganda film *Triumph of the Will* (Riefenstahl, 1935). The hyenas march in perfect procession, their forms emphasized by tall, looming shadows, a scene that echoes the high-stepping, redundant marching scenes from *Triumph of the Will*. Scar, through this analogy, is like Hitler. "Stick with me and you'll never go hungry again!" he roars throughout the canyon, a promise similar to Hitler's promise in the skeletal remains of post–World War I Germany. The analogy between the hyenas and the Nazis is evidence of the film's justification of the race hierarchy. The Nazis, after all, are widely understood as racial *oppressors*, not as victims of an unjust racial hierarchy; and by comparing the hyenas to Nazis, the film shows no sympathy for the hyenas' plight.

The hyenas, as it turns out, fight miserably in the final race battle between the lions and hyenas. The race hierarchy is restored at the conclusion of *The Lion King*. The surviving hyenas presumably are sent back to the shadowy place, and the Pridelands are once again idyllic. The circle of life is restored—and part of that circle of life includes the exclusion of the outsider hyenas.

RECONSIDERING THE CIRCLE OF LIFE

We live in an unjust, hierarchical world. A relatively small number of people have access to wealth, privilege, and opportunity, while millions and even billions of others live in poverty and have little access to resources. In the United States, we live in a nation where equality and justice are valued highly, and yet our nation is filled with economic, gender, and racial hierarchies.

One might say that this is just the way the world works. Some people will always have more money, status, freedom, and resources than other people. However, the fact that hierarchies *do* seem like "the way the world works" is evidence that hierarchies have become naturalized to us. It seems natural, normal, and perhaps even desirable that some people are more powerful than other people.

But it's just a children's film, you might say. How can a children's film have such impact? It is precisely because *The Lion King* is seen as "just entertainment" and "just a children's film" that it does have impact. Viewers don't take it seriously. People assume that as a popular, lovable Disney film, its message must be positive. The film's larger ideological implications remain unchallenged.

The Lion King is by no means the only example of media content that teaches us about concepts, such as race, segregation, and hierarchy. As you read this book, you'll find other discussions of media texts that reinforce similar lessons. As I noted earlier, an assumption of textual media analysis is that through the media, members of a culture learn implicitly what the rules, norms, and power structure of their culture ought to be—the *ideology* of their culture. Certainly *The Lion King* does not turn children into racists. However, when members of a culture view many messages such as *The Lion King*, the ways in which we as a culture view ideological concepts such as race, segregation, and hierarchy are shaped.

IT'S YOUR TURN: WHAT DO YOU THINK? WHAT WILL YOU FIND?

1. I believe that media texts are one of the places where members of a culture learn about the rules, norms, and power structures of our culture—that is, our *ideology*. Think about other Disney films that you seen. What do you think are the ideological lessons of these Disney films? Are there other Disney films that you feel have an ideological message about race, hierarchy, or segregation?

2. I've found that many people don't think Disney films ought to be analyzed critically. Do you agree that many people feel that way? Why or why not? If people don't think that Disney films ought to be analyzed critically, what (if any) might be some negative consequences of this?

3. Sometimes, the ideological nature of a media text can be made more visible if viewers try to understand the text from a different point of view. To do this, conduct a mock *Lion King* debate on this topic: "Should the hyenas be integrated into the Pridelands?"

Divide the classroom into four groups: Hyenas; Lions, the "Circle of Life Party" (a political party of Pridelands animals who firmly believe every animal should behave in accordance with their place in the "circle of life," and that the lions are benevolent rulers), and the "Progressive Jungle Democratic Alliance" (a political party consisting of Pridelands animals who want to create a more democratic system where all animals govern the Pridelands equally). Each group should create a statement and debate each other on the topic. Afterward, discuss the exercise and the film. Has your perspective on *The Lion King* changed after this activity? Do you agree with me that *The Lion King* promotes segregation?

4. Imagine you wanted to create a film like *The Lion King* but that didn't promote segregation. Could you tell the same story in a different (more inclusive) way? How? Using the same characters, what other stories could you tell that would be compelling but not exclusionary?

REFERENCES

Bell, E., Haas, L., & Sells, L. (Eds.). (1995). *From mouse to mermaid: The politics of film, gender, and culture.* Bloomington: University of Indiana Press.

Griffin, D.W. (Director). (1915). *Birth of a nation* [Motion picture].

Lipsitz, G. (1998). *The possessive investment in Whiteness: How White people profit from identity politics.* Philadelphia: Temple University Press.

Riefenstahl, L. (Director). (1935). *Triumph of the will* [Motion picture].

6.3 BELLA'S CHOICE: DECONSTRUCTING IDEOLOGY AND POWER IN *THE TWILIGHT SAGA*

Leslie A. Grinner

> *The author presents a framework— applicable to any text— that you can use to help determine the extent to which media content perpetuates dominant ideologies. Using the* SCWAMP *framework, the author concludes that* The Twilight Saga *film series reinforces dominant ideologies.*

The cinematic version of *The Twilight Saga* is a series of films, starting with *Twilight* (2008). Based on a popular book series by Stephanie Meyer, the films have become a global box office bonanza. The three young lead actors—Kristen Stewart, Robert Pattinson, and Taylor Lautner—provide major star power and, with the two male leads especially, sex appeal. With all the hype around these films and actors, it is easy to overlook some of the ideological messages being transmitted to the audiences who engage with them.

The Twilight Saga introduces us to Bella Swan, a 17-year-old, middle-class white girl who moves from Phoenix, Arizona, to Forks, Washington, to live with her father Charlie after her mother's remarriage. Bella becomes reacquainted with Charlie's best friend Billy Black and his son Jacob, Quileute Indians from the neighboring reservation. Although Bella is introverted and awkward, she is easily accepted by her high school peers; she quickly becomes the romantic interest of several male characters while being embraced as a confidant and counselor to several female characters. But Bella is most attracted to the odd and aloof Cullen family and the four Cullen siblings. The cultural stories of forbidden love, teen angst, vampires versus werewolves, and good versus evil are told with all of the drama, action, suspense, and intrigue one would expect from a major Hollywood franchise.

It may seem that I'm "overanalyzing" these films, that they are less harmful than I am making it out to be. Certainly, *The Twilight Saga* follows the same formula as so many teen romance films before it, using rites of passage such as prom and graduation to maintain the focus on youth culture. Furthermore, the pervasive cultural story of "Forbidden Love" stands as the foundation for these films. But there's something else—an invisible set of ideals that guides this film and others. We need to make these ideals visible, and in doing so we can become a more media-literate population. I refer to this set of ideals as *ideology*.

Ideology can be defined as a set of beliefs that guide a culture—the most commonly known and understood values and mores. However, the role of ideology is much more complex than this. Ideology tells us who or what is *most valued* in our culture (and by extension, what is *least valued*). It's so pervasive that it lies at the very foundation of our society. Media can reinforce or resist ideology. In order to analyze how *The Twilight Saga* reinforces the U.S. culture's dominant ideologies, we must first identify what they are. I've developed a framework to help assess the dominant ideological positions at work in media/popular culture texts, and to explore what the material consequences of these may be. I call this tool *SCWAMP*.

SCWAMP, which stands for *Straight, Christian, White, Able-Bodied, Male, and Property Holding,* is an intersectional framework. Intersectional analysis explains that ideological positions are interconnected and relational. These relationships are shaped and impacted by the society in which they're embedded. Being able to identify the dominant ideologies present in media, and the ways in which we buy into those ideologies, provides us with a way to either consciously conform to or actively resist them. We can become a culture that is more media literate, which will allow us to be more educated and informed consumers of media.

I'll use *The Twilight Saga* to demonstrate how the *SCWAMP* framework operates. The series is well-suited for this type of analysis, because it reinforces dominant ideologies yet obscures this by placing them within a discourse of teen romance. Once you learn to use *SCWAMP*, you can apply it to any media text.

APPLYING THE *SCWAMP* FRAMEWORK

How can we discern whether or not the components of *SCWAMP* are at work in *The Twilight Saga*, and in society at large? The components can be easily tested by investigating the privileges and benefits connected to them, the ways in which they constitute societal norms, and the consequences associated with deviance from those norms.

Straightness/Heterosexuality

How do we know that straightness/heterosexuality is most valued in our culture? Evidence of this can be found in the treatment that lesbian, gay, bisexual, and transgender people encounter on a daily basis, such as gay-bashing and other forms of discrimination. In contrast, heterosexuality is taken for granted as a normal, natural part of humanity. Adrienne Rich (1994) refers to this phenomenon as *compulsory heterosexuality*. When we meet people, we often assume that they are heterosexual, and treat them accordingly.

Heterosexuality is the hegemonic norm in *The Twilight Saga* (as it is in so many films), with the primary relational focus being on the forbidden love between Bella and Edward. But these films also convey compulsory heterosexuality by having every primary character either involved with, pursuing, or avenging the death of a heterosexual partner. Although vampires have long been conceptualized as having bisexual identities, the vampires in these films are definitely heterosexual. The Cullen family is a nuclear unit with a mother, a father, and five kids. Four of the kids are involved in heterosexual couplings with one another—Emmett with Rosalie, and Jasper with Alice. The audience is asked to overlook the incestuous nature of these relationships because all of the Cullen children are "adopted." Bella's new peers are also preoccupied with heterosexual desire. In fact, when Bella realizes that every man in her peer group is romantically interested in her, she becomes a matchmaker, setting up male–female partnerships between her friends. Bella chooses to live with her father so that her mother can focus on her new marriage, and in *Eclipse* Bella questions her father about his status as a single man. Jacob is pursuing Bella, and explains the concept of "imprinting" to her—an involuntary mechanism by which shape shifters find their soul mates. Apparently imprinting can transcend species but not sexual orientation. And the vampire Victoria is obsessed with avenging the death of her heterosexual partner, James.

Christianity

In a society founded in part on the premise of religious freedom, how is it that *Christianity* may be considered a dominant ideology? Certainly there are numerous ideological positions rooted in non-Christian religious beliefs. However, we continue to conduct life in the United States according to the Christian calendar, where even in public schools and government institutions, breaks correspond to Christmas and Easter. Christian-based discourse—phrases such as "sacrificial lamb" and "prodigal son"—pervades our language. In film, Christian-based moral tales underpin almost every narrative. The consequences for not conforming to a Christian ideology can include living with a poor reputation because of sexual practices or other choices of individual morality. In most Hollywood films, people who don't prescribe to the dominant Christian ethos are often punished in some way, such as experiencing illness, financial hardship, or unhappiness.

In *The Twilight Saga*, the Christian ethos is best embodied by Edward Cullen. This is ironic, since vampires are soulless—and, by Edward's own admission—*damned* creatures. But strangely, this damned creature provides a moral compass for Bella, especially around issues of sexuality. *Eclipse* begins with Edward asking Bella to marry him, and her refusing. Later, shortly after telling her father she is a virgin, Bella tells Edward that she desires to have sex with him. When he rejects her advances, asserting that he fears he might hurt her, she begins to bargain with him: she appeals to his class status by stating that she will allow him to pay for an expensive college or car, that she *will* marry him. Edward finally admits that his rejection of her advances is rooted in his concern for her soul. He has agreed to transform her into a vampire—which would render her soulless—but he will not have sex with her before marriage. Thus, her virginal status is held in higher moral regard than her status as a human being. Bella stands in direct contrast to Edward; she has no concern whatsoever for her own soul, and is represented as being largely nonspiritual. It is the men in her life, both human and not, who keep her morally sound.

Whiteness

How can we be sure that *whiteness* is most valued in our culture? There are numerous examples demonstrating this. Most positions of political and financial power in our country are held by white men, and people of color still hold very few positions of power. Specific racial and ethnic minorities continue to be racially profiled, and are often prohibited from obtaining employment, housing, and other resources. Like all components of *SCWAMP*, whiteness is an attribute that is taken for granted such that it is almost invisible. In media, we refer to certain television shows, types of music, and films as "Black," though it is almost never heard that a film is "white"—even though many are written, directed, and produced by white people and contain an entirely white cast. There are also myriad images of whiteness in media, and very few depictions of other racial and ethnic groups.

Although it contains a somewhat "multicultural" cast, *The Twilight Saga* also reinforces whiteness as a standard of superiority. *Twilight* introduces us to Bella's peer group: an Asian male and female, a white male and female, and a Black male. This peer group appears throughout the films; the exception is Tyler, a Black male who loses control of his van and almost kills Bella, and who has only appeared in some of the *Twilight* films. Bella is literally the whitest human being in this film. She's as pale as the vampires in the area, and she is desired by boys from every racial group. The vampires in this series are almost entirely white, except for Laurent (who is Black) and several nameless, lineless members of Victoria's newborn army. Although all of the other vampires in the United States are represented as "American," Laurent has an accent which distinguishes him as a foreigner. He is also represented as a Trickster, as he at times harms and at other times seems to help the Cullen family. The Volturi—or Vampire Royalty, the most powerful vampires in the world—reside in Italy and are all white.

Native Americans, on the other hand, are represented in stereotypical ways: they are "closer to nature," and some of them are even animals. References to the treaty between the Quileute People and the Cullen ancestors invoke a history of broken treaties between indigenous and white people in the United States. Bella becomes the first outsider at a Quileute Council meeting; her status as a "paleface" is overlooked, even though it is well known that she is dating the "natural enemy" of the Quileutes—a vampire. When given a choice between a boy of color who is at least half-human and completely alive and a white boy who is both inhuman and dead, Bella chooses the white boy.

Able-Bodiedness

How do we know that *able-bodiedness* is most valued in our culture? To be blind or deaf, to read/write/comprehend differently, to have autism or some other intellectual disability, to be in a wheelchair or to walk differently—in short to be differently abled—in our culture is to be devalued. Those who are differently abled continue to struggle against debilitating stereotypes, and must fight to maintain basic rights to access, agency, and resources. Mainstream culture continues to covertly add more attributes to the "disabled" list; people who are overweight, don't speak English, or don't fit into the dominant beauty standard of our culture are often treated as if they are not capable—as if they are disabled. In media, differently abled people are often portrayed as villains (think of Darth Vader with his disfigured face) or as comic relief (think of Mary's brother Warren in the popular film *There's Something About Mary*). They are often placed in media to be pitied, laughed at, or despised.

Physical ability is highly valued in a film dedicated (at least in part) to showcasing creatures with super powers. In *Eclipse,* when Jacob and the werewolves decide to unite with the Cullen family to save Bella from Victoria, Bella expresses concern that the wolves will not be fast or strong enough to fight Victoria's army. She has these doubts despite the fact that in *New Moon* she learned that werewolves are faster than vampires, and indeed are destined to kill them. The one physically disabled character in the films—Jacob's father Billy Black, who uses a wheelchair—is also a man of color. Edward emerges as the most able-bodied of the *Saga*; he saves Bella by killing Victoria and her protégé, while Jacob is injured by a vampire. In this way, Bella's choice of Edward over Jacob as a mate is justified in part by physical ability.

Male

Are *men* truly more valued than women in society? Examples of this can be found in everything from language to economics. When either women or men perform a courageous act, it is often said that they "have balls" (referring to testicles). People never say that someone "has ovaries" when they've taken a risk or shown bravery. The common belief in U.S. culture is that anything associated with the feminine is weak, while masculine traits are deemed stronger and more valuable to society. A material consequence of this belief is that women are paid less than men for performing the same work, and work perceived as feminine—parenting, nursing, teaching, and the like—remains completely undervalued in our culture. In media, women are often relegated to inferior status.

Gender is written on *The Twilight Saga* in a variety of ways, including the men's policing of Bella's sexuality and her choice to forsake everything and everyone she knows and loves to become a vampire and be with Edward for eternity. During a conversation about the new boy in her life, Bella's mother expresses an assumption that Bella is already sexually active by telling her to "Be safe." Conversely, three men—Bella's father, Jacob, and Edward—place themselves as the keepers and protectors of her sexuality by insisting that she not indulge her desire to engage in sexual intercourse with Edward. Unlike Shakespeare's *Romeo & Juliet*, where both characters end their lives rather than live without the other, Bella is the only partner who must give up *everything* in order to be in a relationship. Edward can remain in his nuclear family unit, and is not required to sacrifice family, lifestyle, or his very soul as Bella must do to be with him. In *New Moon* we are introduced to Emily, a Quileute woman who is the mate of Sam, leader of the wolf pack. Emily's face is disfigured; Bella learns that in a fit of anger, Sam became a wolf and mauled her. Like Bella, Emily is willing to overlook and endure the inner beast of her male partner and place herself in harm's way to be with him.

Property Holder

Finally, what does it mean to be a *property holder*, and how can we know that this is most valued in U.S. culture? The term as I use it refers not only to land as property, but also to capital in its many forms: economic, intellectual, and cultural. Economic capital includes cash, credit, and other material possessions. Intellectual capital consists of a level of education deemed most valuable by society. Cultural capital often includes both economic and intellectual capital, but can also include athletics and other accepted forms of "coolness" or "street credibility." In media, material wealth and social status are presented repeatedly, which reinforces audience members' desire for them. Lower class or unpopular people are often presented as despicable characters, and the emphasis is often on either their transformation into more socially acceptable human beings or their demise.

The Twilight Saga is heavily inscribed with issues of class. Although her father is working class, Bella is most drawn to the wealthy Cullen family. Carlisle, the Cullen patriarch, claimed the top spot in Forbes Magazine's 2009 *Fictional 15* list of the wealthiest fictional characters. The Cullen children exhibit obvious wealth: all possess expensive cars, clothing, live in a luxurious home, and are lavishly groomed. Edward exhibits his former and present high class position by listening to classical music and reciting Shakespeare verbatim, engagements with so-called "high" culture. By contrast, Jacob Black lives on the dingy and dilapidated Quileute reservation.

His mother is never mentioned or shown, and he exhibits his low class position by working with his hands. While Bella insists throughout the series that she is not materialistic, she is clearly impressed by the trappings of wealth enjoyed by the Cullens. Thus, she chooses a damned but wealthy creature over one who is mortal but working class.

MEDIA LITERACY: A STRATEGY TO END OPPRESSION

With *SCWAMP* as a supplemental framework, we can begin to understand the multiple and sometimes hidden messages that exist in media. They may not otherwise be obvious to us, for good reason. The more comfortable we are with our media experiences, the less we question them; we dutifully support existing structures that are oppressive to ourselves and others. We don't often think about ideology, because it has been normalized and naturalized to the point that it's no longer visible to us. It is the air we breathe and the food that we eat. Identifying ideology is the first step in becoming a media-literate society. We must take this step in order to work on ending oppression in our culture.

IT'S YOUR TURN: WHAT DO YOU THINK? WHAT WILL YOU FIND?

1. Choose several different texts and apply *SCWAMP* to each of them. If one or more of the *SCWAMP* elements doesn't apply, explain why.

2. We all buy into the dominant ideologies of our culture (*SCWAMP*) at some level, even if we don't fit into one or all of the *SCWAMP* elements. With a partner, list some of the ways your beliefs and actions might reflect the dominant ideology.

3. Identify some popular culture texts that have helped you buy into *SCWAMP*, and some that have helped you resist it. Explain how the texts support each position.

4. If you were going to retell *The Twilight Saga* in such a way that the *SCWAMP* elements wouldn't be found, or would be contradicted, what would you change?

REFERENCES

Rich, A. (1994). Compulsory heterosexuality and Lesbian Existence. In A. Rich (Ed.), *Blood, Bread, and Poetry: Selected Prose* (pp. 23–75). New York: Norton Paperback.

6.4 MASS MEDIA, MASS MEDIA INDIANS AND AMERICAN INDIANS

John Philip Sanchez

American Indians[1] have been a part of the American Mass Media since the very first newspaper was published in Boston, in 1620. Newspapers have evolved, but have media frames of American Indians? The author examines how American Indian identity began in the American media and how it continues to be shaped by the American media today.

At the beginning of the twenty-first century, American Indians and the American public are still wondering about each other. American Indians wonder why they are thought of as a people that are mystic with secret healing powers or as a culture that has not evolved beyond the ethnocentric perceptions of Indians in the eighteenth century with brightly colored beads, buckskin clothes, and feather headdresses. The American public wonders why real American Indians are not like those media images they see on television, on the Internet, or at the movies. The American public also wonders why so many American Indians are unhappy about and do not feel honored by the high school, college, and professional sporting teams that use American Indian imagery as mascots for their teams. While most people in the United States may say they've heard about American Indians, not many can say they really know even just one American Indian person.

Today most Americans will say that they know something about American Indians or American Indian cultures primarily because of the American mass media. But what is the American public really learning about American Indians and American Indian cultures as seen through the frames of the American mass media?

Publick Occurrences Both Forreign and Domestick, published in Boston in 1690, is recognized as the first newspaper in America. It introduced some of the most uncomplimentary stereotypical ethnocentric perceptions of American Indians into the American mass media, and stands at the beginning of mass media news frames in America. The first news story is actually a story about American Indians and the observance of a day of Thanksgiving. However, the second news story about American Indians reports that two boys are missing and thought to be hurt by the *barbarous Indians* lurking about, which represents the first appearance of the uncomplimentary media frame describing American Indians as *savages*. This label became an identifier for American Indians that continues even today (Sanchez, in press).

The framing of American Indians in uncomplimentary, stereotypical, less than human ways has also been a common practice in books, magazines, movies, radio and television programming. This practice continues today even in news media, as I found when studying 10 years of network evening news programs from 1990-2000 on ABC, CBS, and NBC (Sanchez, 2010). My analysis revealed that the news frame used most when portraying American Indians showed American Indians dressed in beads and feathers, and portrayed as a people who have not progressed beyond the eighteenth century (Sanchez, 2010). Even as many people turn to the network news programs for the truth and for accurate news reporting, the commonplace stereotypical representations of American Indians continue to reinforce a limited set of insensitive perceptions.

Print journalism also continues to produce news stories about American Indians in stereotypical ways. Recently at a seminar on news media ethics, I asked a group of working newspaper journalists what was the first thing they thought of when asked to think about American Indians. "Poverty and third world like conditions for American Indians" was the most common answer from this group, with "images of eighteenth-century American Indian stereotypes" being second most common. One newspaper editor with 25 years of experience as a newspaper journalist mentioned that I was the first American Indian she had ever met, although she had written stories for her newspaper about American Indians (Sanchez, 2009).

Film as a medium has portrayed insensitive American Indian stereotypes from its beginnings. From the initial years of cinema until relatively recent times, most American Indian characters were played by non-Indian actors with spray painted Indian red tans. Today many of the leading roles of American Indian characters are performed by American Indian actors who are tribally enrolled and speak in authentic tribal languages. Employing American Indian actors who look and sound like the American Indian characters they are supposed to represent is a positive step for the American cinema. However, the old Hollywood Indian stereotypes persist. Today, most of the more recent films continue to use early contact American frontier settings and the old Hollywood Indian stereotypical image of beads, buckskins and feathers, war bonnets, bows and arrows. Mysticism still prevails. There are, however, some exceptions that have opened a space for more complex and authentic portrayals.

In most Hollywood films, there is a clear "good Indian"/"bad Indian" dichotomy. The "good" Indians are those who chose to leave their own people and traditional way of life, assimilate into the dominant culture, and conform to the social mores of the dominant culture—the American way of life. Many times the "good Indians" are those who help the cavalry hunt down and kill the "bad Indians." The "bad Indians" are those that hold on to the old ways of their culture and choose to fight for their right to roam free, live in their own land, speak their own languages, and make their own decisions. Since the good guys always win in typical Hollywood films, the perception of assimilation as continued existence and tradition as extinction is reinforced through the direct contrast of these character tropes (literary/rhetorical devices).

The Last of the Mohicans (1992), based on a novel originally published in 1826, is filled with American Indian actors and utilizes the good/bad Indian motif. Magua, played by Wes Studi (Cherokee), is portrayed as a "bad" or hostile savage, a perspective shared by the "good" Indian characters in the film, such as Uncas, played by Russell Means (Lakota), who is sympathetic to the Caucasians. The hostile Magua is the foil to the good Uncas. The climactic scene is a violent struggle between the two Indian characters, representing civilization and savagery. To many American Indians, both in the period in which the film was set and today, Magua is not "bad" but a warrior hero who fights to the end against the unwelcome changes imposed upon his traditional culture by European contact, and Uncas, the "good" Indian, has been corrupted by allowing the values of the white culture to take precedence over his own traditional ways. "Good" and "bad" are determined in terms of the ethnocentric stereotypes imposed upon the interpretation, and "good" (friend to the white culture) is offered survival while "bad" (friend to Native culture) must perish.

In November 2003, *The Missing* resurrected the old Hollywood ethnocentric perceptions of the 1950s Westerns with a story set in 1885 and using the good/bad Indian motif. This time the leading white character, played by Tommy Lee Jones, adopts an Apache Indian identity and becomes the "good" Apache Indian; the conflict is with the "bad" or hostile psychotic Apache Indians who have just escaped from the reservation. In the end, Jones' character is portrayed as more Indian than the actual Apache Indians. He wins the day, reinforcing the notion that white values are superior and that Natives are doomed.

Inglourious Basterds (2009), set in WWII Germany, features a half-breed Apache Indian character played by Brad Pitt, which re-introduces, with the nauseating sounds of ripping skin being pulled from the skull, the graphic violence of American Indian scalping to yet another audience of media consumers. Here the "good" and "bad" are facets of the same character, with the brutal savagery of the character's actions somehow being for the greater good of the Basterds' subversive mission against the Nazis.

In addition to the good Indian/bad Indian stereotype, there are many more examples of uncomplimentary or insensitive framing of American Indians in the media today, even when intentions are good.

Dances with Wolves uses American Indian actors and indigenous language and went to great efforts to portray Indian country[2] as it may have been in the American 1800s prior to first contact with Euro-Americans. However, it is actually a film about a White Union soldier who comes into contact with an American Indian culture, learns about the Lakota Indian ways, adopts an American Indian identity, and in the end, when the Lakota are being hunted down by the cavalry, is the only person who is able to ride off into the sunset with his new wife, also a white person adopted into the tribe. Again, it is the white characters who are able to survive while the Natives are being annihilated.

The *Twilight* series is set in contemporary times in the State of Washington, but depicts Native characters in distinctly stereotypical ways. With little knowledge of the Quileute Indian Tribe that lives in Washington State, the author, when inventing the Jacob character, conflated the European werewolf tradition onto the Quileute tribal origin stories which involved wolves. In these films, stereotypes of mysticism, animalism, and shape-shifting abilities by the American Indian characters are perpetuated to yet another generation of enthusiastic young fans.

Avatar is set in the future, in a utopian society where first contact can be re-enacted. The lead white male character is disabled and an outcast in his everyday life, but as an avatar, or facsimile of the native beings he encounters, he is fully abled and accepted. This leads him to eventually "go native" and save the day, fighting against the colonists, ultimately becoming a leader because of his bicultural insight. Again, even though the ostensive message of the film is one of respect for indigenous culture and resources, there is an implied stereotype that the Native peoples are not sophisticated and capable enough on their own to produce a leader or to save themselves and that they must be saved by the white lead character.

In contrast, some films have featured Native characters who are more complex and less stereotypical. The first Native film character to move beyond the Hollywood Indian beads and feathers image was Chief Bromden, played by the late Will Sampson (Oklahoma Creek), in the 1975 film *One Flew Over the Cuckoo's Nest*. This character opened a new opportunity for American Indians to be portrayed with a more realistic contemporary identity and had perhaps the greatest positive impact on American Indian identity in film.

In 1990, CBS introduced the *Northern Exposure* television series. Focusing on a transplanted New York doctor and the townspeople of Cicely, Alaska, the interaction between the doctor and the American Indian population is one of the first on television where American Indian characters are not dependant on stereotype. They own successful businesses and participate in the daily life of a contemporary American society. At the same time, they are traditionalists and the keepers of sacred and revered Native culture.

In 2003, ABC Hallmark Entertainment took another new step with *The Dreamkeeper* mini-series. Here, ABC Hallmark presents both traditional American Indian imagery and the contemporary, clearly distinguishing between them. *The Dreamkeeper* is about a young Lakota teenager living on a South Dakota reservation and his very old Grandfather who happens to be an elder storyteller for the Lakota people. As they face the real-life struggles of Native peoples in contemporary times, the grandfather's traditional stories provide insight and reinforce continuation of identity. This film very nicely addresses some of the ethnostress issues that American Indians must deal with every day in the United States and grapples with where American Indians may actually fit in this tableau.

Each day millions of households in the United States turn on their televisions for news and entertainment. Television perhaps becomes the most convenient and most available means of sending information into the homes of children, both Native and non-Native. What non-Native people of any age remember from consuming these mass media images of American Indians will help them identify what they come to believe as American Indians and American Indian cultures. What American Indian people remember from these same media perceptions will leave them confused about who they are as a people and as dignified indigenous cultures. American Indian people today in reality are rarely as they appear in the American mass media.

NOTES

1. I use the terms "American Indian," "Indians," and "Native American" interchangeably to reference the Indigenous peoples/cultures of North America.

2. Indian country refers to American Indian communities, American Indian reservations/lands, or large or small groups of American Indians throughout the United States.

IT'S YOUR TURN: WHAT DO YOU THINK? WHAT WILL YOU FIND?

1. How many American Indian individuals do you know personally? When was the last time you invited one over for dinner or did some other activity together? In what ways do the Indian people you know resemble or not resemble Indian characters you've seen in movies and television shows?

2. Ask your friends and relatives to draw a picture of an Indian family. How are the characters in the family depicted? Do they carry tomahawks, bows, and arrows; dress in buckskins and moccasins; have painted faces; and live in a tipi with a fire pit and a horse nearby? Or, do they look more like the family that lives next door to you?

3. Most films that have American Indians in them present the "good Indian bad Indian" theme. Discuss the characteristics of each in films you have seen that have American Indian characters. Do you agree or disagree with the ideas in this essay?

4. Discuss several things that you can do as a journalist that would begin to change how American Indians are covered in the news media.

REFERENCES

Federal Register / Vol. 75, No. 190 / Friday, October 1, 2010 / Notices. Retrieved from http://www.fcnl.org/pdfs/fedtribalrecognitionlist2010.pdf

Indian rodeo news.com. (2004). *American Indian Film Institute announces new Will Sampson documentary feature film.* Retrieved April 14, 2011, from http://indianrodeonews.com/news.asp?ID=67

Sanchez, J. P. (in press). American Indian news frames in America's first newspaper, *Publick Occurrences Both Forreign and Domestic*. In M. G. Carstarphen & J. P. Sanchez (Eds.), *American Indians and the mass media*. Norman. University of Oklahoma Press.

Sanchez, J. (2010). *News media framing of American Indians: A ten year study of American Indian news reports from the big three evening network news programs.* Unpublished manuscript.

Sanchez, J. (2009). Unpublished raw data.

6.5   IT'S OKAY THAT WE BACKSTAB EACH OTHER: CULTURAL MYTHS THAT FUEL THE BATTLING FEMALE IN *THE BACHELOR*

Jennifer S. Kramer

The Bachelor *has been a fixture on ABC since 2001, and in each season eligible bachelors (tall, dark [but not too dark; as of 2010 all the bachelors have been white], handsome, and rich) sift through a harem of 25 women. The Cinderella format is common in many reality shows (Pozner, 2009), but what is largely ignored—and what this reading addresses— is how* The Bachelor *perpetuates an image of catty women who will go to great lengths to beat other women to win their man.*

When I was in high school, my ex-boyfriend's sister and I were interested in the same boy. We battled for him. I won. It was not pretty. She and I sparred, and eventually I broke up with the guy to get back together with my ex-boyfriend. She dated the object of our once joint affection for years, eventually marrying someone else, as did I. I often thought about how much I was in the wrong for hating her so much for having the same good taste in boys. Why did I do this? I'd never fought over a male before or after this. The foundation to fight for my man was set in motion long before my interlude with the claws. Fighting for your man is seen as necessary for many women, particularly in order to earn that brass (diamond) ring. It's one of the few scenarios in which women are required to be aggressive. Just watch *The Bachelor*, you'll see. The story of women desperate to find a man in *The Bachelor* for their Cinderella happily-ever-afters includes mythic battles between women to win the man.

Entwined within the story of Cinderella are American cultural myths that perpetuate the normalcy of women fighting each other. Those myths include "the possibility of success," "the value of a challenge," and being a "woman's woman" (Larson, 2004, p. 222, 229). These myths can be found in Cinderella imitators such as *The Bachelor* and serve as powerful persuasive forces because they are valued by the culture. This reading examines the myths that fuel the success of *The Bachelor*, not only in its popularity, but more important, for the lack of critical analysis that sheds light on the weekly battles among the gaggle of women vying for the bachelor. This battleground is a uniquely feminine one where the women's aggressive style is acceptable because their stake as desirable women is challenged.

CINDERELLA MYTH IN *THE BACHELOR*

The Cinderella fairy tale as told today depicts a beautiful young woman forced to be a slave for her stepfamily after her father dies. The local prince searches for a wife by hosting a ball, which Cinderella attends through the magic of her fairy godmother. However, the magic disappears at midnight causing Cinderella to lose a glass slipper which eventually leads the prince to her. He delivers her from slavery into a happily ever after. Tannenbaum (2002) sums up the message from Cinderella as "To get the prince, a woman must (a) be beautiful and (b) compete with the evil Other Women" (p. 140). *The Bachelor* lives up to this simplistic Cinderella plot quite nicely and is regularly touted as a Cinderella story. The premise of the show is that one desirable and eligible man has 25 available women and can choose one for the happily ever after. The series rarely creates a lasting relationship, though there have been a few exceptions. However, the draw of the Cinderella myth is so powerful that the ratings for *The Bachelor* have remained remarkably strong, despite the format's repetitiveness.

Each season proceeds with the bachelor progressively whittling down his choices by offering roses to women he'd like to continue dating. The first night consists of the bachelor meeting 25 model-thin and perfectly coiffed, dressed, and stilleto'd women over much alcohol. At the end of the evening, 25 women are winnowed to 15. During the next episode, the harem participates in fantasy group dates (often requiring as little clothing as possible), after which the group is reduced to 10. The following episode usually includes group fantasy dates, but a select few go on (often extravagant) one-on-one dates, and then the lot is almost halved to five or six. Another episode involves even more fantasy one-on-one dates and one group date, and the group is cut to four. At that point, the bachelor visits the four women's families, followed by another cut. Finally, the bachelor spends more significant overnight time with the remaining three women in exotic locales, leading to another elimination. The remaining two women meet the bachelor's family; and after a more "realistic" date at the bachelor's mansion, the bachelor chooses his princess in a dramatic final rose ceremony where the one left standing receives not only the final rose, but also a large diamond ring and, ostensibly, the bachelor's heart.

The women claim the opportunity to meet the bachelor is like being in a fairy tale and that they really do believe their foray into reality dating television is a viable way to find the perfect husband. For example, in the first episodes the women label the bachelor as prince charming and that they literally are "Cinderella." In season nine, ABC tried to make the fairytale even more "real" and procured an Italian prince as the bachelor. The stakes were clearly higher in this season because the women no longer were just fighting for their man, but for the position of real princess. Often the viewers heard the women discussing who is and isn't princess material.

WHY THE MYTHS WORK SO WELL

We need to take a more critical gaze at the dating reality television genre because as Kavka claims, it "works at the level of *feeling* rather than cognitive content" (2008, p. x) and viewers are enthralled by watching the *performance* of love since love is too difficult to describe. Viewers suspend belief watching these shows because they feel a sense of intimacy with the contestants. The intimacy is heightened by contestants' true emotion confessions one-on-one with the camera (Aslama & Pantti, 2006). The result is as if the contestant's confession is not about the "we" of television talking to the "us" of viewers, but rather "individuals addressing individuals" (p. 179) in the privacy of one's home. The hook of feeling intimacy sneaks in cultural messages, as reality television "circulates informal 'guidelines for living' that we are all (at times) called upon to learn from and follow. These are not abstract ideologies imposed from above, but . . . practical techniques for reflecting on, managing, and improving . . . our personal lives with the resources available to us" (Ouellette & Hay, 2008, p. 2).

Reality television then serves to reinforce many of the taken-for-granted ideological discourses found within popular cultural myths such as Cinderella. Fiske (1987, as cited in Ouellette, 2003) explains that ideological discourse stems from those who are in power who work to naturalize meanings "about an important topic area . . . [to the point that the meanings seem like] common sense" (p. 117). The ideological discourse for women is based upon economic social power relationships which work to keep women in submissive roles (Cupaiuolo, 2004); therefore, dating reality television "drive[s] home the notion that no emotional, professional or political accomplishment can be possibly compared with the twin vocations of beauty and marriage" (Pozner, 2004).

Tannenbaum (2002) explains that the socialized role of being feminine forces women into a double bind because women need to be able to show others that they are independent, yet they still need a man to complete them. Mingling the myth of Cinderella with its supporting myths has thus created an ideological discourse: "Being competitive, catty, and cunning are part of the stereotype of femininity" (p. 27). We have come to expect and desire such depictions of women who backstab each other in their quest to win the bachelor's love. Larson (2004) argues that the power of such myths is rooted in their ability to become shorthand for persuasion because those who believe in them are emotionally attached to the myths. These myths work to support the belief in a happily-ever-after derived from a man whisking a woman off into the fairytale while the remaining women fight one another.

POSSIBILITY OF SUCCESS (THROUGH) VALUING CHALLENGES

The *possibility of success* myth explains that "through hard work, ethics, and future orientation, [one] will succeed and succeed very well" (Larson, 2004, pp. 220–221). We feel a strong sense of sympathy for Cinderella because she is in a situation that will not afford her the ability to rise above her slavery circumstances through her hard work. The *myth of valuing challenges* comes through to save Cinderella because she is put through a horrible situation. In the valuing challenges myth, we believe that there will be great rewards one day for those who struggle, almost as if it is a "right of passage or initiation" (Larson, 2004, p. 222). Wisdom comes from surviving the challenge, and the survivor has "a sense of something good coming out of the suffering" (Larson, 2004, p. 223).

These myths are intertwined within *The Bachelor.* The future orientation of the success of winning the bachelor's heart is stressed repeatedly by the contestants. Throughout the first few episodes of each season, the women talk to the camera claiming how ready they are for this challenge and what they bring to the competition to overcome the challenge (i.e., other women). For example, the women claim their competitive prowess, as when Lindsay (fighting for bachelor Bob's affection) tells the camera that she is accustomed to competing with women because of her background in cheerleading. Then her demeanor drastically changes from smiling to sneering as she warns the audience that she must *always* win. Likewise, Rhonda from season one is clearly proud of the fact that she is fighting for the possibility of success in the bachelor, rather than make friends with the other women. She is baffled that any woman would be hurt when not liked by the other women. Even after the competition is over, the valuing challenge myth is reinforced when the runner-up for Andy's heart, Beavin, (bawling in the back seat of the limo taking her away from her love), states that this will not destroy her, but rather will make her more resilient.

Valuing the challenge of winning results in the women directing their competitiveness toward one another through aggression, which even they describe as catfights. The producers play up the catfight spectacle through promos before commercial breaks such as in season 13 when Molly and Jillian tell one another they will kick one another's ass over Jason. At the rose ceremony in the third week the same season, the host asks the women if they need to tell the bachelor anything before he makes his decision. What follows is a verbal group catfight that centers on the most malicious of the women, Megan. The catfight is broken up when Shannon leaves the rose ceremony formation for the bathroom. Once there, her microphone clearly picks up the sound of vomiting. The camera cuts to Megan demeaning Shannon with a storm of epithets because Shannon simply is not strong enough.

WOMAN'S WOMAN MYTH

Larson describes the *woman's woman* as "soft spoken, kind, and nurturing. She may work, but she is also the perfect wife and mother, and is immaculately groomed. However she is also vain, rarely has meaningful thoughts, and never wastes time on serious things" (2004, p. 229). By depicting women solely as physical objects, we rarely see them as powerful. Women have often seen each other as competition in many realms of their lives and so have become adept at quickly sizing up their female competition as to what makes a woman's woman (Russ, 2008; Tannenbaum, 2002). In season four, Estella tells the camera during her first group date that she hopes Misty is sent home because of her voluptuous body; meanwhile, the camera captures Bob's lecherous grin as Misty dives into the pool. The women's nurturer capabilities are also up for evaluation as Jillian demonstrates in season 13 during a group date to a radio studio. She tells the DJ she is jealous of the connection Stephanie has with Jason because they both have a child.

The Bachelor women's stake in being seen as desirable, acceptable women is constantly in question throughout the show, fostering whirlwinds of insults. Comments made behind each other's back are rampant, criticizing one another's adequacy for the bachelor, decency as a woman, and even their human decency. Sometimes these criticisms are shared with the bachelor. In season 10, Stephanie gives Andy an earful during their one-on-one time, telling him that there are women he should cut because they lack independence and she knows he desires such a woman. Next, Stephanie is shown telling the camera that Amber is the woman Andy needs to cut. Finally we see a camera confessional from Stephanie exclaiming she has no problem sabotaging any other woman who gets in her way. Stephanie receives a taste of her own backstabbing medicine when during the same group date Kate tells Andy he shouldn't trust Stephanie because she is obsessed with him.

Any woman who is assertive in gaining the bachelor's attention will be criticized by the other women for not demonstrating woman's woman characteristics. While women are just as aggressive as men, they are more likely to express their aggression in a passive aggressive, or indirect, manner (Richardson, 2005). As the prior examples demonstrate, *The Bachelor* highlights the plight of women in the woman's woman double bind, as they clearly are supposed to be putting themselves out there for the bachelor to make *his* choice, but in doing so the cultural myth of the woman's woman forces them to be competitive. They need to hide their aggression so as to still be seen as feminine and because of "fear of physical, economic, or emotional retaliation if they openly expressed overt opposition to someone more physically or socially powerful" (Tannenbaum, 2002, p. 63). Women's fear of negative consequences is confirmed through *The Bachelor* when Stephanie and Kate are cut by bachelor Andy at the rose ceremony directly following their criticisms to him about other women.

Pozner (2009) points out that in reality television romance, "Only the prettiest, most passive girls without agency or voice, without ambition or individuality were rewarded with love, financial success, and the ultimate prize: being picked by the prince" (p. 58). The only exception to this rule is in season 16 of *The Bachelor* when Jake chooses Vienna, despite the other women regaling him with tales of her bitchiness. However, even this exception is short lived, as within a mere 3 months of the show ending, they engaged in a tabloid-war breakup.

AND THE BACK STABBING CONTINUES . . .

It's easier to resort to following cultural plotlines in our lives when faced with difficult situations such as looking for love. And *The Bachelor* serves them up for us on a silver platter laden with a rose. Perpetuation of the cultural myths of Cinderella, the possibility of success, valuing challenges, and being a woman's woman has helped put women in a double bind, as women "can be successful [only] as long as [they] stay 'feminine' (i.e., powerless enough not to be truly threatening) . . . . Powerful women are seen by many people (women as well as men) as inherently destructive and dangerous. Some argue that it is men's awareness of just how powerful women can be that has created the attempts to keep women small" (Kilbourne, 1999, p. 137, 262). Because the women are all dating the same man, they end up being forced to spend more time with one another than the bachelor. The way out of this situation requires one to be partnered because this means a woman "has attained a measure of power" (Tannenbaum, 2002, p. 169). So the women fight one another in the manner through which they've been socialized—by stabbing one another in the back.

In American society, the richest, most powerful people are still white men (Wood, 2009). As a result, it makes sense that shows such as *The Bachelor* are desirable to the predominantly male television executives—these shows preserve the cultural plotlines that have kept them in power. In addition, if enough women watch the show, they perpetuate the myths that keep women backstabbing each other instead of challenging the man who is cheating on them and the double bind that continues to limit their power.

IT'S YOUR TURN: WHAT DO YOU THINK? WHAT WILL YOU FIND?

1. You are part of the casting team for *The Bachelor*. What socioeconomic backgrounds would you look for in the female contestants? Compare your list to the women's backgrounds given in episodes of *The Bachelor*, or through online biographies. Determine what class cultural myths related to gender are communicated through *The Bachelor*.

2. In small groups, produce a proposal for a romance reality television show that would not rely on the cultural myths presented here, or other cultural myths that position men or women as superior to the other. How likely is your show to succeed, and why?

3. Watch the credits (or check online) to determine whether the producers of other reality romance shows are male or female. Compare shows produced by women to shows produced by men. Are the cultural myths perpetuated different in these shows? Why or why not?

4. Examine the communication of your friends and family. In what ways are the cultural myths discussed in this chapter present in your everyday communication? How are these myths harmful and/or beneficial?

REFERENCES

Aslama, M., & Pantti, M. (2006). Talking alone: Reality TV, emotions and authenticity. *European Journal of Cultural Studies, 9*, 167–184.

Cupaiuolo, C. (2004). Arts & culture. *Ms. Magazine*. Retrieved April 17, 2011, from http://www.msmagazine.com/arts/2004-07-02-orenstein.asp.

Kavka, M. (2008). *Reality television, affect and intimacy: Reality matters*. New York: Palgrave Macmillan.

Kilbourne, J. (1999). *Can't buy my love: How advertising changes the way we think and feel*. New York: Touchstone.

Larson, C. U. (2004). *Persuasion: Reception and responsibility* (10th ed.). Belmont, CA: Thomson/Wadsworth.

Ouellette, L. (2003). Inventing the Cosmo girl: Class identity and girl-style American dreams. In G. Dines & J. M. Humez (Eds.), *Gender, race, and class in media: A text reader* (2nd ed., pp. 116–128.). Thousand Oaks, CA: Sage.

Ouellette, L., & Hay, J. (2008). *Better living through reality TV: Television and post-welfare citizenship*. Malden, MA: Blackwell Publishing.

Pozner, J. (2004, Fall). The unreal world: Why women on "reality TV" have to be hot, desperate and dumb. *MS Magazine*. Retrieved March 25, 2011, from http://www.msmagazine.com/fall2004/unreal-world.asp.

Pozner, J. (2009). Unraveling reality TV's twisted fairytales. *Bitch: Feminist Response to Pop Culture*, Spring (43), 52–59.

Richardson, D. S. (2005). The myth of female passivity: Thirty years of revelations about female aggression. *Psychology of Women Quarterly, 29*, 238–247.

Russ, T. L. (2008). *Bitchin' bodies: Young women talk about body dissatisfaction*. Chicago: Stepsister Press.

Tannenbaum, L. (2002). *Catfight: Rivalries among women—from diets to dating, from the boardroom to the delivery room*. New York: Perennial.

Wood, J. T. (2009). *Gendered lives: Communication, gender, and culture* (8th ed.). Boston: Wadsworth.

6.6   IS DADDY'S LITTLE GIRL A BITCH OR A PRINCESS?: NARRATIVES OF FEMALE IDENTITY ON *MY SUPER SWEET 16*

Terri L. Russ

The author turns a feminist lens on the narratives of My Super Sweet 16 *and argues that the intertwining individual stories—coupled with the overriding narrative of the show—work to reinforce traditional gender roles of girls as nothing more than spoiled consumerist daddy's girls.*

Once upon a time, there was a beautiful little girl who lived a privileged existence where everything she wanted magically came to her. She had all the best toys and shiniest jewels. Her closet overflowed with the latest high fashion clothes and shoes. Sometimes when the beautiful little girl wished for something it wouldn't come to her; however, all she needed to do was cry a few tears, remind everyone how much she deserved the item, and it was hers.

Fairy tale existences like this have long been a staple of fiction from children's stories to romantic comedies. We turn to them as momentary distractions wherein we are able to suspend our less than ideal lives where everything we want is not magically given to us, even when we deserve it. In 2005, MTV introduced to a new addition to this genre—*My Super Sweet 16*.

According to the MTV Web site, *My Super Sweet 16* takes viewers "behind the scenes for all the drama, surprises and over-the-top fun as teens prepare for their most important coming of age celebration."

The opening sequence of each episode introduces audiences to the underlying premise with the catchphrase, "Sometimes 16 ain't so sweet." The narrative begins with the introduction of the individual whose quest for the perfect party is being chronicled. The birthday girl introduces herself, talks about her family, and then moves into a discussion of how rich *she* is, even though *her* wealth is actually her parents'. The extent of this wealth becomes increasingly apparent as the narrative switches to party planning.

NARRATIVES WITHIN NARRATIVES

Most of us probably don't think about the role stories play in our daily lives; however, narrative theory presents a way for us to step back and consider how important stories are to us. The physical world may be out there in existence, but it doesn't begin to make sense until we narratize it. In story form, we speak the events of life: "The world of communication is not a world that speaks for itself, all attempts to represent this world must involve transforming a speechless reality into a discursive form that makes sense" (Bochner, 1994, p. 26). We can define narrative then as "the stories people tell about their lives [it] is both a means of 'knowing' and a way of 'telling'" (Bochner, 1994, p. 30).

Narratives are not just the stories we tell about life, though. Because we understand our existence through the stories we tell about it, narratives become intricately intertwined with our experience. We don't just tell stories; we live them. Arthur Frank (1995) explains, "The truth of stories is not only what *was* experienced, but equally what *becomes* experience in the telling and its reception" (p. 22, emphasis in original). The experience becomes real for us when we tell another about it. Stories, then, "are told in being lived and lived in being told" (Carr, 1986, p. 61).

Working in conjunction with our individual narratives are master narratives helping guide our lives and create meaning. Maines (1996 p. 92) clarifies that these "are forms of collective stories that are implicit or embedded in a culture or group and have some kind of structure." Acting as paradigms, master narratives have a "prefiguring effect" through which we construct what we see based on what we *expect* to see. We use master narratives to help us make sense, but at the same time we use them, they limit us.

It could be argued that there is a symbiotic chicken and egg type relationship between gender roles and narrative. Do narratives dictate the roles, or do we use our roles to construct narratives? As we are living the stories of our life, we enact our identity through the gender roles we take on. However, these roles are to some extent predetermined by gender narratives permeating society. Our individual narrative, therefore, becomes woven through with vestiges of these larger gender narratives.

This interweaving of narratives becomes clear when we examine how they play out in *My Super Sweet 16*. Cultural expectations and norms of genderized roles are demonstrated through the narratives the "characters" on the show embody as they live out their birthday quest narrative.

SWEET, SPOILED, SASSY

Narratives provide multilayered and powerful frameworks of meaning "within which lives are configured" (Maines, 1996, p. 93). What is or is not accepted as "normal" depends upon the strictures created by the narrative. With this in mind, I examine the impact of master narratives of gender on the individual narratives of the show. I divide my analysis into three parts: (1) Narratives as paradigms of gender roles, (2) Narrative establishment of normal and acceptable behavior, and (3) Narrative limitations of existence. Although I separate these into individual categories, each aspect is inherently implicated by and involved with the others.

"I Deserve This!" Narratives as Paradigms of Gender Roles

Gender roles are those behaviors and attitudes expected by virtue of our gender. We are immersed in gender roles from the moment of our birth. The expected delicacy of little girls is reflected in the pastel colors dominating their nurseries, while the expected hardiness of boys is reflected in the bright colors of their nurseries.

Gender roles are expressed in various cultural maxims assumed to be accurate without critical examination or questioning. A prime example is the maxim "Daddy's Little Girl," thought to epitomize the ideal father–daughter relationship. In this relationship, the little girl is the perfect daughter while daddy is the ultimate ever-loving and forgiving parent. When mommy says no, daddy says yes. In daddy's eyes, his little girl can do no wrong, even when he faces evidence indicating otherwise. The phrase Daddy's Little Girl creates a box all little girls are put into. To play the Daddy's Little Girl role, a girl must be pretty, quiet, and submissive, a thing to be admired.

The Daddy's Little Girl role appears throughout most episodes of *My Super Sweet 16* and is apparent from the opening biographical segment. In describing themselves, many of the birthday girls openly refer to themselves as a Daddy's Little Girl. Sisters Priya and Divya present a textbook example of this narrative. Their role as spoiled Daddy's Little Girls is apparent when we see their cars, a Mercedes for Priya and a Bentley for Divya. Neither girl has a driver's license, but they own the title to their respective vehicles. Their Daddy Little Girl status is locked in when they are looking at purses, and Priya dismisses an otherwise cute purse for *only* costing $275. Priya seems to be implying that for a princess like her, such a purse is an insult. Priya's comment represents a significant portion of the Daddy's Little Girl role—it signifies and is signified by what products she owns.

The Daddy's Little Girl narrative on *My Super Sweet 16* revolves around being the spoiled little girl who daddy dotes on and showers with anything she wants. Individual birthday girl narratives such as those of Priya and Divya reiterate this master narrative. If we were to summarize the master Daddy's Little Girl narrative, it would read much like the story of the beautiful little girl I presented earlier. When it comes to the party for Daddy's Little Girl, there is no question of what kind of party she will have—the biggest and best party of the year where money is no object, and no request is too far-fetched. The girl will be presented with an equally big gift, her dream car or perhaps a piece of expensive jewelry. As Daddy's Little Girls, the *My Super Sweet 16* girls know they are loved through these tangible things.

Completing the Daddy's Little Girl family is mom. If we see mom on individual episodes, she is a tangential figure. Within the master Daddy's Little Girl narrative depicted on *My Super Sweet 16*, mothers are one-dimensional characters cast in one of two roles—another giver of gifts or the control freak-out to ruin the life of Daddy's Little Girl. In either role, mom is reduced to a servant running around waiting on Daddy's Little Girl. Priya and Divya's mom embodies the gift-giver role as she buys them whatever they want. As the episode progresses, we see mom standing in the background on a few occasions, yet we learn nothing else about her. She remains just another giver of gifts that demonstrate daddy's love for his little girls. Even though mom gives the gifts, it is made clear that they are really from daddy.

Representing the other mom role is 15-year-old Alexa's mother. During Alexa's biographical recitation, we are told her mom is a control freak. Alexa, however, makes it clear that her party is not a democracy, and she is the dictator in charge. Although we see glimpses of Alexa and her mother disagreeing on elements of the party planning, the ultimate feud occurs on the day of the actual party. Looking over the party room, Alexa throws a fit over the centerpieces that her mom preferred. When her mom tries to explain that the centerpieces netted a $3,000 savings in the overall party costs, Alexa demands to be given the $3,000—and her car, a black fully loaded Infiniti Q45 with a sticker price of $41,000. Running to daddy, Alexa gets her wish, and by the end of the episode she gets her car as well.

The beginning of any narrative introduces us to the main characters and sets forth the plot of what will happen, along with the tone of how it will happen. Coming into the *My Super Sweet 16* narrative, we already know that the main character will be the birthday girl through the use of "my" in the show's title. What the show develops for us, though, is the depth of her deservingness as translated into how much she is loved as demonstrated through the extravaganza of a party her daddy throws for her. In the show, there are numerous other characters—friends, classmates, party planners, and others. However, the key supporting character is daddy, or perhaps more accurately, daddy's wallet. Their roles are clear—the little girl dreams and the daddy makes her dreams come true. More than just dreaming, though, the little girl mandates that she is entitled to all she desires. As we analyze the narrative deeper, we learn that what she desires most is more.

"I Want More!" Narrative Establishment of
Normal and Acceptable Behavior

A significant aspect of the Daddy's Little Girl narrative involves the continual spoiling of Daddy's Little Girl. While the individual specifics vary, the overall theme remains the same—in the world of *My Super Sweet 16*, what is normal and acceptable is: anything. If it exists and daddy's little girl wants it, daddy will make it happen.

Gifts such as Alexa's car are just one aspect of the master *My Super Sweet 16* narrative. The party itself acts as a performance of the Daddy's Little Girl status for everyone. Like any performance, it is well-planned and comprises multiple acts. The performance opens with the choosing of a theme, usually done outside of the narrative framework of the show. What we see in the show is a brief allusion to the theme and how it will be represented through sets, props, and supporting bit players. What strikes me as significant in these parties is not that there is a theme other than Sweet 16. After all, many children's birthday parties are guided by a theme. For my daughter's seventh birthday, we had a carnival theme to guide the festivities. We set up a few game booths, and her grandmother dressed up as a fortune teller. The key difference between my daughter's party and those seen on *My Super Sweet 16* is the extravagance and expense involved with the theme acting as a framing device to showcase Daddy's Little Girl's wealth.

The public nature of the performance is established with the handing out of invitations. Not all episodes of *My Super Sweet 16* highlight the actual invitations; however, when we do see them it is clear that they were not purchased at the local drug store. Most birthday girls do more than simply pass the invitations out at school, making the giving of the invitation an event in-itself, a type of party before the party. Many ask; only a lucky few will receive one.

The birthday girl's final performance is her appearance at the party we have been watching her plan and argue about throughout the episode. For this final performance, the girl's hair and makeup is professionally done, and she is sheathed in an expensive party dress. The quest for the perfect dress begins when the birthday girl jets off to some far-away city to find a dress un-like any available in her city. While such a trip may result in the perfect dress, usually it merely causes more reasons to have a tantrum. Despite flying to Paris, one of the fashion capitals of the world, Ava fails to find even one dress special enough for her party. Faced with the need to have just the right dress, Ava chooses a custom-designed dress. At the very least, the birthday girl will opt for a dress that is custom enhanced. For example, Meleny's dress cost $3,000 before being enhanced with $4,000 of Swarovski crystals. When the dress arrives not reflecting Meleny's vision for the perfect dress, it is sent back for further customization.

Once the birthday girl is fully outfitted to reflect her wealth and beauty, she is ready to be whisked off to the party like a princess—in a special vehicle. Cindy arrives in a horse-drawn carriage befitting her Cinderella theme. Priya and Divya arrive by limousine. Like Priya and Divya, most birthday girls opt for some sort of chauffeur-driven vehicle, with the oversized Hummer as the vehicle of choice. For Amanda, even a chauffeur-driven limousine is not sufficient once she learns that the car's air-conditioning is broken. Being a good daddy and fulfilling his role, Amanda's daddy drives her in his Acura.

The party itself, though the stated theme of the show, seems to be a minor aspect of the master *My Super Sweet 16* narrative. Rarely do we see the birthday girls' arrival, unless there is a problem, such as Carlysia arriving to walk down the red carpet amongst her admiring fans who have already been admitted to the party. Instead of seeing the party narrative in full, we are instead treated to a montage of clips from the party. We see snippets of the birthday girl dancing and perhaps having one last temper tantrum or blurbs of people raving how this is the best party of the year.

This final act of the birthday quest seems to indicate that the performance isn't about the party but about getting to the party. The focus is on the trials and tribulations the birthday girl must endure. As we watch her narrative unfold, we are entertained. Many of us shake our heads in amazement. We wonder when Sweet 16 became the Spectacle of 16. As a form of entertainment, the master *My Super Sweet 16* narrative and individual narratives achieve their goal of entertainment. However, as with other media messages, the show also creates a standard. Presented without critical commentary, the extravagant parties of *My Super Sweet 16* become the new norm of Sweet 16 parties and have been co-opted by other television shows. For example, episode 79 of the sitcom *Still Standing*, entitled "Still Sweet," focused on 15-year-old Lauren's quest for an extravagant Sweet 16 party. The episode featured many of the same themes highlighted in the MTV show, such as choosing a theme, buying a dress, arranging the proper arrival, and hiring the right entertainment.

Overall *My Super Sweet 16* does more than merely push the boundaries of what is normal and acceptable. I would argue that it removes the boundaries altogether. In the post-*My Super Sweet 16*-world, not only ain't 16 so sweet, it's also a spectacle. As the show continues to air new episodes and the spectacle of sweet 16 parties continues to trickle into mainstream society, it will be interesting to see what boundaries are pushed next.

"I'm Daddy's Little Girl, Forever." Narrative Limitations of Existence

As a defining narrative, Sweet 16 is a one-shot deal—you only have one 16th birthday. Likewise, as a life-defining narrative Daddy's Little Girl has a built-in limitation—the girl grows up. However, in actually living out the narrative, something happens to these Daddy's Little Girls—the aging process is stopped or even reversed. The temper tantrums portrayed on *My Super Sweet 16* look like those of toddlers. When these teenage girls don't get their way, they stomp their feet, cry, and scream until daddy appears to save the day. In part, the problem arises from the use of the diminutive *little*. In order to be Daddy's Little Girl, the girl must stay little. She may age and mature physically, but as demonstrated repeatedly throughout the various *My Super Sweet 16* narratives, her mental and emotional maturation seems to be stunted. The built-in limitation of the Daddy's Little Girl narrative then becomes a limitation of her complete existence.

I have to wonder what is at the bottom of this slippery slope of extravagant sweet 16 parties. If a girl's parents spend $200,000 on a sweet 16, such as Nicole's parents did for her French-themed extravaganza, what will she expect for her high school graduation? Her college graduation? Her wedding? And what happens when those major life-defining moments we celebrate with big parties are over? Where will the little girl go, and what will she do? Will she be trapped forever as Daddy's Little Girl, or will she find out who she is outside of this defining role?

The love between a father and a daughter can be a special type of love; however, within the Daddy's Little Girl narrative, this love seems skewed. As illustrated throughout the series, this love seems to require that the girl remain little. In *My Super Sweet 16*, although it looks like the girls have control, they really don't. Sure they get more stuff and the party they want, but in the end they must acquiesce to daddy's demands for them. Instead of learning how to care for themselves or gain the power to purchase their own items, they remain in a vicious circle of adolescence. Both the daddy and the girl are complicit in maintaining this illusion of love through infantalization.

As *My Super Sweet 16* makes clear, the fairy tale existence of the beautiful girl we met at the beginning of this reading is a reality for some little girls. However, it is an existence of illusions. The birthday girls' beauty is enhanced through a special dress, expensive jewelry, and professional hair and makeup. She presents the appearance of living the perfect life, but is she happy? Based on the numerous tantrums and myriad tears seen throughout the show, the answer seems to be no.

IT'S YOUR TURN: WHAT DO YOU THINK? WHAT WILL YOU FIND?

1. The parties portrayed on *My Super Sweet 16* are extravagant and expensive spectacles unavailable to most teens. Discuss the narrative these parties create about socioeconomic class and class differences.

2. *My Super Sweet 16* occasionally features males as the central figure. Watch at least one such episode, and analyze the narrative. Pay attention to ways that it differs or reflects the narratives of females.

3. Using what you now know about narrative theory, pick one of our favorite shows and determine the specific and master narratives it presents.

REFERENCES

Bochner, A.P. (1994). Perspective on inquiry II: Theories and stories. In M.L. Knapp & G. R. Miller (Eds.), *The handbook of interpersonal communication* (2nd ed., pp. 21–44). Thousand Oaks, CA: Sage.

Carr, D. (1986). *Time, narrative, and history*. Bloomington: Indiana University Press.

Frank, A. W. (1995). *The wounded storyteller: Body, illness, and ethics*. Chicago: University of Chicago.

Maines, D. (1996). Gender, narrative and the problematics of role. *Michigan Sociological Review, 10*, 87–107.

6.7 THE NEW GAY DOMESTICITY: HOMONORMATIVITY IN ABC'S *BROTHERS AND SISTERS*

Gust A. Yep and Allen Conkle

> *This reading examines the construction of gay domesticity in a mainstream U.S. television show, by analyzing the portrayal of "homemaking" and family life and their associated gender dynamics, and discussing the implications of such representations in U.S. mainstream culture in general and U.S. gay culture in particular.*

Throughout its first four decades [in U.S. living rooms], television virtually denied the existence of homosexuality. The families, workplaces, and communities depicted in most network programming were exclusively heterosexual. As recently as the early 1990s, in fact, even the most astute viewers could likely spot only a handful of openly lesbian, gay, and bisexual characters in an entire year of network television. After only a few television seasons, however, gay-themed episodes and references to homosexuality were everywhere . . . American television [now seems] obsessed with gayness.

—Becker (2006, p. 3)

The simple visibility of gay people and the concomitant steps toward assimilation are not . . . solely beneficent. [For gays and lesbians] to finally see [themselves] and be *seen* publicly is exhilarating . . . To be *seen*, [however], is not necessarily to be *known*. Indeed, media saturation of a previously invisible group can perpetuate a new set of pernicious fictions, subduing dissent by touting visibility as the equivalence of knowledge.

—Walters (2001, p. 12, emphasis in original)

Offering the viewer the opportunity to see—and the potential to know—gay men through the relationship between Kevin Walker and Scotty Wandell, a male couple, *Brothers and Sisters* is the first major network show to feature a same-sex wedding and commitment ceremony between two regular gay characters on prime-time television in the United States (Keck, 2008). With an international distribution and an average of 11.9 million viewers in the United States alone (Armstrong, 2009), the show features an all-star cast that includes Academy and Emmy Award winner Sally Field, Golden Globe winners Rachel Griffiths and Calista Flockhart, and Emmy and Golden Globe winner Patricia Wettig. *Brothers and Sisters* is an American Broadcasting Company (ABC) dramatic series that features the lives of the Walker family. The Walkers run Ojai Industries, a family-owned produce distributor and wine producer. Set in Pasadena, California, and in the greater Los Angeles area, the show focuses on the dynamics and relationships of the Walker family: father William (deceased), mother Nora, their five children, and Nora's brother.

Since their wedding and commitment ceremony in the finale of the second season, the prime-time series has continued to bring to U.S. and international audiences details of the new domestic life of Kevin and Scotty and their decision to raise a child as a gay couple.

KEVIN AND SCOTTY: THE CONSTRUCTION OF A GAY ROMANCE

In the second episode of the season opener, Kevin Walker meets Scotty Wandell. Scotty is a somewhat flamboyant gay man who quickly surmises that Kevin is also gay after a few minutes of initial interaction. Scotty, as the more "out" character, was quite open about his attraction to Kevin. Their interactions consisted of a mixture of flirtation and apprehension, playfulness and seriousness, excitement and fear as Scotty made observations about Kevin's internalized homophobia and his desire to "pass" as a heterosexual man, comments that aggravated Kevin. On their first date, Scotty impulsively kisses Kevin, which is received negatively. This leads Scotty to confront Kevin about his shame around two men kissing in public, capturing some of the tension they experience in the early stages of their relationship.

Kevin invites Scotty into his family and after a series of conflicts related to Kevin's class status and internalized homophobia, as well as Scotty's flamboyance and lower class status (at several points Scotty was homeless), they break up. Eventually, after another legal problem, Scotty hires Kevin to represent him and the two are reunited. Their romance begins to blossom.

After Saul, Kevin's gay uncle, despondently shared, while inebriated, the sadness and loneliness in his life, Kevin begins to appreciate his relationship with Scotty. This leads him to propose to Scotty. Scotty accepts. The second season finale features their elaborate same-sex wedding and commitment ceremony[1].

KEVIN AND SCOTTY: THE CONSTRUCTION OF GAY DOMESTICITY

Beginning with the third season, Kevin and Scotty start their lives as a committed male couple, giving viewers a detailed perspective of gay domesticity in U.S. prime-time television. According to Gorman-Murray (2006), gay domesticity refers "to the diverse ways in which gay men [and lesbians] design, create and use domestic spaces, and how these constructions articulate, or challenge, the dominant understanding of home in [western cultures] as a heterosexualized family space" (p. 228). In other words, gay domesticity is about the process by which gays and lesbians engage in "homemaking" and the creation and maintenance of family life within the context of heteronormativity. A heteronormative culture, such as the United States, is one that elevates and normalizes heterosexuality while making other sexual expressions and relationships deviant and abnormal (Yep, 2003). Gay domesticity has the potential to challenge ideas of home and family life as exclusively heterosexual as well as create news forms of homonormativity. The "new homonormativity," according to Duggan (2003, p. 50), refers to a new form of normalization of gay and lesbian relationships that upholds and sustains heteronormative assumptions (e.g., gendered division of labor in a household) and institutions (e.g., marriage) and produces and reinforces a privatized and depoliticized gay culture based on domesticity and consumption.

Through our analysis of the show, we argue that gay domesticity, in this representation, is characterized by acquisition and consumption and heteropatriarchal family dynamics. While Kevin and Scotty, as a male couple, challenge conceptions of home as a heterosexualized space, they also (re)produce a new form of homonormativity.

More Acquisition and Consumption, Less Politics

As Kevin and Scotty begin their domestic lives together, their relationship as a gay couple becomes increasingly apolitical in favor of a focus on acquisition and consumption. While the portrayal of gay domesticity on prime-time television may destabilize the assumed heterosexuality of the home (e.g., father, mother, and children), this association also provides a way to normalize and sanitize a nonconforming sexuality linking gay masculinity with values and moralities associated with heteronormative domestic family life (e.g., having children) that is acceptable to the U.S. mainstream.

In the first episode of the third season, newlywed Kevin strives to attain partnership in his law firm. When he is offered keys to the vacation mansion of the head of the firm, Kevin and Scotty experience wealth and luxury: pools, fine art, Baccarat crystal glasses, a crystal whale that costs more than Kevin's car. He tells Scotty that he will buy him two whales when he becomes partner. As Scotty willingly accepts Kevin's promise of such extravagant gifts, he seems to gladly abandon his humble beginnings as a poor and, at various points, homeless, gay man. The episode constructs a gay male domestic culture centered on acquisition of luxury goods that might be seen as trophies that symbolize power and respect. Scotty appears to be "redeemed" from being poor, and goes from being a homeless queer—degenerate and dangerous—to becoming a member of a middle/upper class couple—safe and wholesome. In the process, Scotty has been transformed from a character that challenged the status quo into a character with a depoliticized point of view centered on consumption and the pursuit of a culturally acceptable form of gay domesticity.

In the eighth episode of the third season, Scotty makes the cover of a Los Angeles magazine as an upcoming culinary star, gets promoted to head chef at his restaurant, and receives a substantial pay raise. Although their current home is less spacious and inviting than the homes of Kevin's heterosexual siblings, it is nevertheless filled with objects, acquisitions, and multiple home computers. After receiving Scotty's good news, the couple immediately discusses plans for a new home complete with a deck, a Jacuzzi, and hardwood floors. This suggests that gay domesticity is about upward social mobility.

Throughout Kevin and Scotty's dialogue, there are allusions to what might imply a more radical and "queer" domesticity—they mention group sex, parties, online hook-ups. These are all tongue-in-cheek comments that diminish alternative methods of "home" construction. These jokes undermine potentially queer—and more radical—family organizations and reinforce the existing norms, while contributing to the construction of new gay norms based on a politics of acceptability and assimilation, which is based on the existing structures of heteronormativity. The politics of acceptability and assimilation suggest that as long as gays and lesbians form families using existing "time tested" (i.e., heteronormative) formulas of family construction, gays and lesbians will gain social and cultural acceptance (Yep, Lovaas, & Elia, 2003). With these normative standards of gay domesticity, the gay male subject is acceptable only if he is monogamous, economically productive, and ultimately pursues the goal of the traditional family. This heteronormative system marginalizes many individuals who are not conforming to these prescribed standards of living, loving, and participating in the "economy" of gay domesticity.

By the end of the third season, Kevin and Scotty decide to have a child and begin to consider adoption and surrogacy. The focus of Kevin's character throughout the unfolding plot of the fourth season and continuing into the fifth is centered on the acquisition and the incurred debt necessary to procure a surrogate. Although ultimately unsuccessful to bring a child into their lives, the plot concentrates on the couple spending more than $100,000 in this pursuit. It appears that the ideal of gay domesticity is to have children. Given the tremendous financial cost involved in this process, the form of gay domesticity represented in *Brothers and Sisters* is definitely associated with middle/upper class values.

More Heteropatriarchal Family Dynamics, Less Equality

Heteropatriarchy, according to Yep (2003), refers to "an overarching system of male dominance through the institution of compulsory heterosexuality" (p. 31). This system of male dominance is manifested and reinforced in various social institutions, including the family. Family dynamics, such as parental roles and gendered divisions of labor, tend to reinforce heterosexuality and patriarchy—heteropatriarchy (Gorman-Murray, 2006). These dynamics produce uneven power relations that are associated with gender, and they are evident in the ways that Kevin and Scotty construct their family life.

Since the beginning of their relationship, Kevin always had more power than Scotty. This is manifested financially, professionally, and emotionally. Kevin comes from an upper class family—the owners of Ojai Industries, several homes, and various properties north of Los Angeles. In contrast, Scotty comes from a lower class standing and, as mentioned earlier, was homeless at various points in his life. In the early stages of the relationship, Scotty acknowledges that Kevin is "out of his league." In the third season, Kevin is not offered partnership at his firm and subsequently resigns to accept a lower paying position with his brother-in-law, a California senator. This salary shift disturbs the balance of Kevin's upper class status and provider role and Scotty's lower standing and earning power in the relationship. Such a loss of balance is further exacerbated by Scotty's ascending status—he is promoted to head chef of a restaurant. Although the situation presents a possibility for greater financial equality between the two men, Kevin "resolves" it, in the eight episode of the third season, by buying a $725,000 home as a symbolic gesture of his ability to provide for Scotty. In the fourth season, it is Kevin who is in charge of talking to bankers and taking care of the debt they incur to find a surrogate for their child. Even when the couple decides to open joint accounts, Kevin takes the lead. In their relationship, it appears that Kevin is always financially in charge.

Kevin is a successful and ambitious attorney with a fully staffed office in a high-rise building complete with panoramic views of the city. Scotty, on the other hand, is a worker in the service industry, including insurance, catering and food services. In the sixth episode of the first season, Kevin asks Scotty to be his date for a fundraiser, which Scotty politely turns down because he had to work. Kevin offends Scotty when he offers to pay for his wages. As the story unfolds, it turns out that Scotty was a waiter at Kevin's fundraiser, thus making their differences in status even more evident. As their relationship evolves, Scotty finds a clear career focus in the restaurant industry. He becomes a successful chef and later decides to partner with Saul, Kevin's gay uncle, to open a restaurant offering "comfort organic food" at the end of the fourth season. However, when Kevin and Scotty decide to have a child, Scotty confesses to Nora, Kevin's mother, that he recognizes that his career is not as important as Kevin's. Interestingly, Scotty's confession is one of acceptance—and not even resignation—of his lower professional status in the relationship.

Kevin is more emotionally distant in the relationship, which appears to give him more power. By withholding his feelings, Kevin seemingly maintains a sense of control. When Kevin finds out from the fertility clinic, in the twelfth episode of the fourth season, that he is much less likely to be the biological father of their child—four (out of five) of his embryos were unsuccessful—he refuses to talk about his disappointment and hurt, even after Scotty begs him to do so. In contrast, Scotty is much more emotionally expressive. This is exemplified in the first episode of the fourth season when he admits to Kevin that he feels unsure and scared about having a child or in the second episode of the same season when he tells Nora about his fears and apprehension about taking care of a baby. Kevin's emotional distance and Scotty's emotional expressiveness not only create tension in their domestic lives but also maintain a gendered dynamic in which Kevin and Scotty reproduced heteronormativity: Kevin becomes the symbolic "man," while Scotty becomes the symbolic "woman" in their relationship.

The gendered dynamics of the gay domesticity portrayed in the show clearly presents Kevin as the traditional husband and breadwinner in the family. Throughout the series, Kevin is characterized as someone who "lives for his work," earns more money than Scotty, loves to provide for the family, and takes charge of decisions in their relationship. Kevin controls the decisions about having a child by being more dominant than Scotty with the staff at the fertility clinic and more controlling than Scotty with Michelle, the eventual surrogate and Scotty's best friend. Kevin is extremely competitive—even with Scotty. These traits make him the more traditional husband in the family. Kevin's role as the "man" in the relationship becomes more obvious in the fifth episode of the fourth season when he and Scotty attempt to dance the tango that eventually ends up in an argument after Kevin refuses to relinquish the lead (and play the female role) in the dance.

Scotty, on the other hand, is presented as the feminized partner in the relationship and becomes a more traditional "wife." His career is secondary to Kevin's in spite of his own successes. Throughout the series, Scotty is found engaging in more traditionally feminine activities. For example, he is always cooking—for Kevin and Kevin's family. When the Walkers get together for dinner, which occur frequently in the show, Scotty is either cooking or helping Nora in the kitchen. Even Nora prefers to cook with Scotty more than with the other women in the family. In the tenth episode of the fourth season, Scotty makes leis, tropical drinks, and dinner for Justin's (Kevin's younger brother) wedding rehearsal. Scotty is shown as a "natural" caretaker—he is apparently the only person who could put Evan, Nora's grandson, to sleep after Nora's futile attempts in the second episode of the fourth season. In many ways, Scotty becomes Nora's "daughter-in-law." Scotty even suggests he will bring their child to work with him, solidifying his symbolic role as the "mother," whose work is less valued. Through this process of feminization, the gay domesticity presented in the show reinforces heteropatriarchal family dynamics and perpetuates relational inequalities.

IMPLICATIONS

The depiction of the details of the relationship between Kevin and Scotty in *Brothers and Sisters* offers the viewers—heterosexual, gay, lesbian, bisexual—an unprecedented opportunity to not only to see but to know gay men in their relationships on prime-time television. Episode after episode, the viewer is invited to learn the particulars of gay domesticity.

What are the implications of these representations in U.S. mainstream culture in general and U.S. gay culture in particular? A closer examination of such representations suggests that gay domesticity is a paradox (Gorman-Murray, 2006). One the one hand, gay domesticity can challenge the normalization of heterosexuality associated with the concept of home. This is evident as Kevin and Scotty, two men in a committed relationship, share a life and a home together and create a family by attempting to bring a child into their unit. By showing gay men in family and "homemaking" activities, they call into question the idea of home as an exclusively and unquestionably heterosexual domain. On the other hand, gay domesticity can reinforce heteronormative arrangements. This is also evident in our analysis as Kevin and Scotty create a form of gay domesticity characterized by acquisition, consumption, and heteropatriarchal family dynamics. The new gay domesticity is homonormative; it upholds and sustains heteronormative values and ideals, whiteness and the view that gay men are white, and middle-class aspirations in U.S. culture. This new visibility, in the end, can open up new spaces in U.S. mainstream culture to imagine, see, and know different ways of living and loving. While this might be welcome in U.S. gay culture, the new gay domesticity also reinforces and perpetuates heteropatriarchy and its underlying inequalities.

NOTE

1. As of 2010, gays and lesbians are not allowed to marry in California and many other states in the United States. Their wedding, in this sense, was technically a commitment ceremony that simultaneously highlights the need of gays and lesbians to have their relationships publicly recognized and the oppression and differential treatment they experience in the United States.

IT'S YOUR TURN: WHAT DO YOU THINK? WHAT WILL YOU FIND?

1. When thinking about the ways that Kevin and Scotty's relationship was portrayed, what assumptions might a straight audience ascertain about gay relationships? What might a gay audience member assume?

2. How does this portrayal serve as a tool that liberates? How does this characterization police gay men in the ways they construct relationships?

3. How does the portrayal of class struggle throughout Kevin and Scotty's relationship paint a certain image of what the appropriate social status is for gay men? Who is left out of this picture? How might this impact the views of someone watching the show?

4. Why might the writers of *Brothers and Sisters* create a relationship that does not threaten the existing heteropatriarchal order of relationships, through reinforcing stereotypically gendered behaviors and power dynamics? If you were to write a gay couple for a new television show, how might you create a "gay male couple" that challenges existing norms and illustrates a more "radical" relationship structure?

REFERENCES

Armstrong, J. (2009, March 2). *Ratings: 'Brothers & Sisters' strong, though no match for 'Jesse Stone.'* Retrieved September 17, 2010, from http://hollywoodinsider. ew.com/2009/03/02/ratings-brother/.

Becker, R. (2006). *Gay TV and straight America*. New Brunswick, NJ: Rutgers University Press.

Duggan, L. (2003). *The twilight of equality? Neoliberalism, cultural politics, and the attack on democracy*. Boston: Beacon Press.

Gorman-Murray, A. (2006). Queering home or domesticating deviance? Interrogating gay domesticity through lifestyle television. *International Journal of Cultural Studies, 9*(2), 227–247.

Keck, W. (2008, May 11). *Top this: A gay ceremony on ABC's 'Brothers & Sisters.'* Retrieved September 17, 2010, from http://abcnews.go.com/Entertainment/ story?id=4824155&page=1.

Walters, S. D. (2001). *All the rage: The story of gay visibility in America*. Chicago: University of Chicago Press.

Yep, G. A. (2003). The violence of heteronormativity in communication studies: Notes on injury, healing, and queer world-making. In G. A. Yep, K. E. Lovaas, & J. P. Elia (Eds.), *Queer theory and communication: From disciplining queers to queering the discipline(s)* (pp. 11–59). Binghamton, NY: Harrington Park Press.

Yep, G. A., Lovaas, K. E., & Elia, J. P. (2003). A critical appraisal of assimilationist and radical ideologies underlying same-sex marriage in LGBT communities in the United States. *Journal of Homosexuality, 45*(1), 45–64.

6.8 FRAGMENTED FEMININITY: POSTFEMINISM, MOTHERHOOD AND MULTIPLE PERSONALITIES ON PRIME-TIME TELEVISION

Katherine J. Lehman[1]

This reading considers innovative television comedies that provide complex heroines and enable networks to appeal to diverse viewing audiences. However, these dark comedies may also convey harmful messages about motherhood.

Showtime's *United States of Tara* offers a domestic comedy with a twist. Tara (Toni Collette) is a suburban mom with a multiple personality disorder. One moment she's Alice, a perpetually perky homemaker. Next, she's "T," a crass, gum-cracking teen. By nightfall she often transforms into Buck, a boorish man who prowls bars in search of excitement. Between transformations,

Tara tries to connect with her exasperated husband and parent two rebellious teenagers, who are going through identity crises of their own.

Tara's multiple personalities provide us with an unusually multifaceted heroine—and a clever commentary on modern women's roles. *United States of Tara* was created by Diablo Cody, who penned the independent film *Juno*. Cody claims that *Tara* provides fresh perspectives on mental illness and motherhood in general (Showtime, 2008).

However, *Tara* is not the only series to feature heroines with multiple and often conflicting personalities. ABC's *Desperate Housewives* ended its fourth season by catapulting characters 5 years into the future, transforming glamorous, self-centered model Gabrielle (Eva Longoria) into a frumpy, harried mother. Series creator Marc Cherry claimed the change made the housewives' problems more "relatable" to viewers (Dawidziak, 2008). Similarly, Showtime's popular series *Weeds* capitalized on the concept of a suburban mom (Mary-Louise Parker) living a double life as a drug dealer.

From its beginnings, television has both signaled changes in American families and conveyed moral messages about how proper mothers and wives should behave. Accordingly, if these contemporary series claim to speak to challenges facing modern women, what do these multifaceted characters tell us about motherhood? Characters such as Tara and Gabrielle transcend boundaries of space and time, exercising choices and mobility denied to less privileged women. Yet, assuming one identity often means renouncing others: Tara cannot simultaneously be sexy and strong, and Gabrielle sheds her glamour upon becoming a mother. These series tend to undermine feminist gains by characterizing personal ambition as damaging to family life and relationships. Ultimately, these tales reinforce boundaries between private and public spheres and box characters into predictable roles: mother *or* careerist, protector *or* seductress. Furthermore, they support cultural ideologies that criticize working mothers, blaming individual women rather than inflexible social structures for their inability to balance roles and create a coherent self.

SETTING THE STAGE: CLASS, RACE, AND DISABILITY

Tara is perhaps the most daring of these series, as it places a comedic spin on a serious condition. Tara suffers from dissociative identity disorder, stemming from sexual abuse and parental neglect as a child. Although she seeks to achieve wholeness—or integration of her personalities—through talk therapy, she chooses not to take medication, because she says the drugs have a deadening effect. Even as the series makes light of Tara's character changes, it empathetically portrays the effects of mental illness on her family. Cody admits to using Tara's personalities as a metaphor for the multiple roles that mothers assume, and to sneaking subversive cultural commentary into the series. She feels that Tara offers a unique take on mental illness: although such disorders typically isolate characters from their families, this series depicts a family weathering the turmoil together (Showtime, 2010).

Cody also enhanced Tara's "everywoman" qualities by placing the series in a Kansas suburb. She describes the family as working-class, which may be accurate if we measure class status based on the husband's landscaping job (Showtime, 2008). However, class status in media is conveyed through not only careers and income level, but also material possessions, speech, and behavior. Scholars note that television tends to overrepresent the middle class: Butsch's (2003) comprehensive survey of domestic sitcoms from 1946 to 2000 identified nearly 70% of television families as solidly middle class. Because television rarely depicts working-class families, it tends to ignore financial struggles that many families face and to promote the idea that women can choose to prioritize motherhood over work.

Accordingly, Tara's lifestyle and possessions reflect middle-class norms. Tara's decision to decline medication and her self-employed status as an artist mark her as financially secure. (The series makes no mention of her receiving disability benefits or of struggling to afford therapy.) The series also boasts sleek set designs and a plot in which Tara's husband purchases a second house on a whim. Tara's alter personalities also define her class status: although Alice the homemaker is emblematic of upper-middle-class domestic perfection, Buck's preference for beer, bowling, crude jokes, and flannel shirts contrasts with Tara's more refined tastes.

Desperate Housewives and *Weeds* both emphasize the luxuries and social conventions of suburban life. On *Desperate Housewives*, Gabrielle's material fortune rises and falls, but her character is marked as upper middle class through her expensive consumer tastes and reliance on her husband's income. *Weeds* is set in an upper-middle-class California community and often mocks suburban mores. Although Nancy, the mother in *Weeds*, rebels against conformity, she nevertheless fights to preserve her family's class standing by resorting to an illicit career after her husband dies.

In addition to presenting middle-class life as the norm, characters in all three series occupy a largely white world. This is typical for television. In 2010–2011, whites comprised 77% of regular characters on scripted network series, and Showtime drew criticism for airing multiple series with all-white casts (GLAAD, 2010; Hernandez, 2010).Gabrielle's Mexican heritage makes her one of few minorities on *Housewives*' Wisteria Lane. Although Gaby generally fits in with her white neighbors, her fiery temper, heightened sexuality, and old-world relatives promote familiar media stereotypes of Latinas (Merskin, 2007). Tara and Nancy are both white and typically socialize in homogenous circles. However, Nancy associates with Mexican drug dealers, and both characters develop friendships and working relationships with African American characters who offer creative inspiration and parenting advice. These secondary characters may add racial diversity to these series, but they primarily serve to further white heroines' self-discovery.

POSTFEMINISM IN POPULAR MEDIA

In addition to reinforcing white middle-class norms, all three series offer postfeminist portrayals of women. The term *feminism,* in its basic definition, refers to a social movement and philosophy that advocates the social, political, and economic equality of women and men (Hex, 2000). In American culture, the feminist movement is credited with opening new educational and career opportunities for women—and is often blamed for creating a society in which women feel they must "have it all." *Postfeminism* can refer to the time period following feminist activism of the late 1960s and 1970s, or it can describe the commonly held idea that feminism is unnecessary or harmful because women have already achieved equality with men (Press, 1991).

Scholars have detected a strong postfeminist trend in contemporary media. Press (1991) writes that many television programs depict working women in a way that downplays their career ambitions. Characters are shown in the home more often than the workplace, and they seamlessly blend work and family life—in contrast to real-life women's struggle to combine the two roles. Negra (2009) has identified characters' ambivalence about career ambition as a form of postfeminism. She notes that in many popular films, characters magically regress to childhood or escape to time periods before feminism existed, firmly choosing to be traditional wives rather than single career women.

The ambivalence and time travel Negra describes is demonstrated strongly in *Desperate Housewives*. Between seasons four and five, the characters age 5 years. Former fashion model Gaby is suddenly stripped of her wealth and exceptional beauty due to her husband's temporary disability and, apparently, her decision to have children. Gaby wears smocks and capris (over a fat suit) instead of designer dresses; she trades her long tresses for a short, unkempt hairdo and constantly chases after her unruly daughters. The character strives to regain her image and claw her way back into elite social circles. While the narration laments that Gaby no longer recognizes herself, husband Carlos continually emphasizes that these years have been the happiest of his life and reminds her that family is more fulfilling than material possessions or their past life as a corporate power couple.

Although the heroine of *United States of Tara* does not literally time travel, her multiple personalities regress to earlier stages in her life—and in women's lives more broadly. Two of her alter egos are children: when feeling insecure, she becomes "Chicken," a child who desires protection. Her teenage personality, "T," enables her to evade adult responsibilities and act provocative. However, Tara also reverts to earlier points in American women's history. Her alter ego Alice, who does housework in high heels and pearls, is a clear allusion to the middle-class housewife ideal of the 1950s and 1960s. As Haralovich (2002) argues, early sitcoms often relegated women to the feminine sphere of the kitchen and showed them mediating family conflicts with civility and grace.

In one episode, Tara feels unable to live up to fellow mothers' expectations and to solve her son's problems at school. She transforms into Alice and saves the day, whipping up an elaborately decorated cake for the school bake sale and then smoothing over a conflict with her son's teacher. As Alice, she evokes an imagined past in which domestic perfection was the true measure of femininity and conflicts were sweetly resolved. However, we are not encouraged to see Alice as a proper role model. While Tara's family enjoys Alice's gourmet cooking, they seem frightened by her forced cheerfulness and claim to moral authority.

Sometimes Tara's alter ego is male. Buck, a working-class Vietnam vet, dons an undershirt and heavy boots, speaks with a drawl, and walks with a swagger. Buck often serves as the family's protector who can hold his own in a fistfight. However, he is also a nurturer who uses his feminine side to lure women. Tara as Buck brings comedic relief to the series and lends it sexual allure, as Buck pursues other women. Yet, Buck also contributes to the series' postfeminist sensibility. Often aggressive and sexist in the ways he talks about women, Buck contradicts feminist ideals of equality. Yet the series' creators speak fondly of the character, and credit him with holding the family together (Showtime, 2009). Buck provides a macho counterpart to Tara's husband, who is more passive and accommodating, and Buck often inspires the men to assume more masculine behavior.

LIKE MOTHER, LIKE CHILD: PARENTING MISHAPS

Although Tara's mental illness sets her apart from most viewers, she faces the same question that haunts many real-life women: Am I a bad mother? In *The Mommy Myth*, Douglas and Michaels (2004) argue that popular media promote unrealistic standards of perfection for American mothers, including the idea that parenting should be central to women's identity. By blaming individual women for their failings, media distract attention from the material struggles of family life, such as inadequate social support for childcare and education.

Programs such as *Tara* and *Weeds* contribute to this "mommy myth" by continually pointing out parents' successes and failures. These stories of middle-class moms struggling to keep it all together—and falling short—could be comforting to some viewers seeking commiseration for their own imperfect mothering. However, these images also tap into cultural conversations that blame women rather than inflexible social structures for their failures at parenting, and judge mothers for prioritizing personal ambitions over their children.

Weeds is rife with judgments about Nancy's parenting. Nancy's family has all the right foundations: they live an orderly suburb with good schools, and an uncle moves in to fill the fatherly role vacated by Nancy's husband. However, Nancy's growing sons are damaged by her high-strung personality, irregular working hours, and inability to keep pot dealing separate from family life. Her love for her children is palpable, and she attends to their lives through PTA meetings and family dinners. However, her failure to set a maternal role model leads her sons down paths of alienation and criminality. In one episode, she takes her sick infant to a doctor who lectures her on the importance of a stable home environment. The doctor's voice becomes muted and distant as the camera focuses on Nancy's shamed expression. When Nancy's son Silas turns 18, she sends him a gift basket as an apology, with a card congratulating him on raising himself. On one level, this dialogue suggests that crime doesn't pay—Nancy, after all, is a drug dealer. Yet the series revolves around her mismanagement of her parenting responsibilities and the risks she takes for her homegrown business rather than the ravaging effects of drugs themselves. (Nancy doesn't use drugs.)

Desperate Housewives also presents Gabrielle as a dysfunctional parent, although references to her own sad childhood encourage us to have sympathy for her character. Gaby's daughter Juanita is ill-mannered and obese, spurring criticism from neighbors. Gaby attempts unorthodox methods to get her child to lose weight—including inventing a game in which her chubby child chases the family car to get exercise. Gaby insists on perfection, even pulling her daughter out of a school talent show for fear of embarrassment.

In one episode, Gaby is ostracized by fellow mothers for failing to supervise her daughters' play dates. She attempts to clear her name by throwing Juanita a fancy birthday party—but implicates herself when the party ends in injury and mayhem. Although such episodes typically close with characters reassuring Gaby that she is a good (enough) mother, we are privy to many moments in which Gaby selfishly sips cocktails and hollers at her children in the other room. These plotlines suggest that Gaby is not naturally maternal—that her previous life of vanity and entitlement has ill-equipped her to raise a healthy, socially adjusted child.

The specter of bad motherhood also hangs over *Tara*'s home. The pilot episode revolves around Tara's conflicts with daughter Kate. In her opening monologue, Tara laments that she can keep track of clients' needs as a freelance artist, but she can't manage her daughter's sexual proclivities. Unsure how to approach her daughter, she veers wildly from one personality to the next. As "T," she becomes her daughter's friend and helps her secure a prescription for morning-after pills. As Alice, she overreacts and washes out her daughter's foul mouth with soap. As Buck, she roughs up her daughter's boyfriend at school. When she returns to her old self, Tara tries to talk rationally to her daughter about sex but is rebuffed. In other episodes, Tara accepts her son's disclosure that he is gay, but "T" interferes by making out with one of his crushes. Tara's attempt to protect her son from hurt and rejection leads to greater distance between them.

In addition to displaying parenting mishaps, all three series suggest that mothers are solely responsible for how their children turn out. The teenagers in *Weeds* follow in mom's footsteps by turning to drug dealing and violence—their deceased father, in comparison, is remembered as a stabilizing influence. Tara's multiple personalities and sexual confusion influence her daughter, who at 17 creates a fictional alter ego and dabbles in sex work. In *Desperate Housewives*, Gaby's husband Carlos often serves as the voice of reason, explaining how Gaby's parenting is damaging their daughter.

Significantly, these women lack a wider supportive community of other mothers. *Weeds'* Nancy has an antagonistic relationship with fellow mother Celia, and her career places her outside the privileged circle of suburban motherhood. Tara's closest confidante is her sister, initially a childless single woman, and Tara's own mother undermines her parental authority. Although *Desperate Housewives* featured candid conversations about parenthood in its early seasons, Gaby's entrance into motherhood is an isolating one, separating her from coveted social circles and placing her in competition with neighbors who deem her a "bad mom." This individualist thread denies characters the opportunity to learn from collective wisdom and places the burden and the blame on their shoulders.

These series also present women's personal ambition as a force that endangers the family. When Gaby fails as a parent, it is usually due to attempts to bolster her own ego or social standing above the needs of her daughter. Tara's choice to experience her personalities rather than taking medication causes her children continual embarrassment and anger, and prevents her from being truly present in their lives. In *Weeds'* third season, Nancy's bad business decisions spark a fire that destroys her suburb, and we watch her family's home go up in flames.

MULTIPLE PERSONALITIES AND THE MODERN WOMAN

While these characters' lives are more chaotic than the average woman's, they reflect contemporary viewers' concerns. Many modern women feel their energies and identities are divided between private and public life, and some, like Gabrielle, might long for the person they were prior to having children. Many viewers can relate to Tara's earnest attempts to be best friend, nurturer, and protector to her children, or to Nancy's desire for adventure.

However, we should question the meanings these series give to these complex characters. Rather than celebrating imperfect parenting, these series often judge mothers for their inability to achieve balance and for placing their personal needs and ambitions above their children's. These messages may resonate strongly with working mothers, who must continually juggle responsibilities and priorities.

Perhaps most harmful, these series hold individual women fully accountable for their children's development rather than implicating other family members or social structures. By making light of Tara's struggles with parenting, *Tara* fails to consider the broader effects of sexual violence and inadequate mental health care. By crediting Juanita's weight to permissive parenting, *Desperate Housewives* fails to consider corporate and social influences contributing to widespread childhood obesity. *Weeds* could comment on the struggles of single parents reentering the workforce—and the poverty that makes illicit careers so alluring—but instead it emphasizes one mother's crimes.

Of course, these are dark comedies designed to entertain us, and we can't expect fictional television to fully reflect reality. But writers could easily inject greater realism into the scripts— for example, Tara could gripe about therapy bills, Gaby's husband could step up to shoulder parental responsibility, and Nancy could moonlight as a low-wage worker.

Modern mothers are rewriting societal scripts every day, as they balance multiple roles and strive for wholeness and recognition. Tara and her comrades are fun to watch, and they provide a welcome change from the idealized TV housewife of yesteryear. However, domestic comedies can and should do much more to challenge conventional myths about motherhood.

NOTE

1. The author would like to acknowledge Sarah Bruno for contributing ideas to this essay.

IT'S YOUR TURN: WHAT DO YOU THINK? WHAT WILL YOU FIND?

1. What messages do these programs convey about motherhood, and why are they potentially harmful? How could scripted television represent mothers more fairly?

2. What is postfeminism, and how is it reflected in media? Do you think programs such as *Desperate Housewives* present women as already equal to men and desiring more traditional roles? Why or why not?

3. What aspects determine characters' class status in television? How can we tell if a family is comfort-ably middle class, rather than rich or poor? Why does it matter that the vast majority of TV families are middle class?

4. Choose a television series that features a mother, and analyze one or two episodes closely. What is the family structure (two-parent, single parent, etc.), and what roles does the mother assume at home and at work? What ethnic and economic groups does the family represent? How are conflicts resolved? What morals or messages does this program convey about motherhood?

REFERENCES

Butsch, R. (2003). A half century of class and gender in American TV domestic sitcoms. *Cercles, 8,* 16–34.

Dawidziak, M. (2008, September 25). *Desperate Housewives* hits fast-forward buttons on characters' lives. *Cleveland Plain Dealer.* Retrieved October 6, 2011, from http://www.cleveland.com/tv/index.ssf/2008/09/desperate_housewives_hits_fast.html

Douglas, S., & Michaels, M. W. (2004). *The mommy myth: The idealization of motherhood and how it has undermined all women.* New York: Free Press.

The Gay and Lesbian Alliance Against Defamation. (2010). *Where we are on TV report: 2010–2011 season.* Retrieved April 27, 2011, from http://www.glaad.org/publications/tvreport10/diversity

Haralovich, M. (1992). Sitcoms and suburbs: Positioning the 1950s homemaker. In L. Spigel & D. Mann (Eds.), *Private screenings: Television and the female consumer* (pp. 111–142). Minneapolis: University of Minnesota Press.

Hernandez, L. (2010). Diversity report card: Showtime. *Latina.* Retrieved April 27, 2011, from http://www.latina.com/entertainment/tv/diversity-report-card-showtime

Hex, C. (2000). Fierce, funny feminists. *Bust, 16,* 52–56.

Merskin, D. (2007). The three faces of Eva: Perpetuation of the hot-Latina stereotype in 'Desperate Housewives'. *The Howard Journal of Communications, 18,* 133–151.

Negra, D. (2009). *What a girl wants?: Fantasizing the reclamation of self in postfeminism.* New York: Routledge.

Press, A. (1991). *Women watching television: Gender, class and generation in the American television experience.* Philadelphia: University of Pennsylvania Press.

Showtime Networks. (2008). *Diablo Cody discusses Tara's alters.* Retrieved April 27, 2011, from http://www.sho.com/site/tara/video.sho?bclid=5253538001

Showtime Networks. (2009). Meet Buck. In *United States of Tara: Season One,* DVD (Hollywood: Paramount).

Showtime Networks. (2010). Chats with the cast. In *United States of Tara: Season Two,* DVD (Hollywood: Paramount).

6.9   MOTHERS IN MEDIA

Stacey Irwin

> *TV characters such as June Cleaver, Clair Huxtable, Rosanne Connor, Carol Brady, Marge Simpson, Angie Lopez, Marie Barone, Lorelai Gilmore, and Lois Griffin have laughed and cried with us as they reveal motherhood in a variety of ways. This reading considers the media's image of motherhood.*

For me, becoming a mother was like striking gold three times. I feel blessed to be a mother, and excited and perplexed by this experience. Yes, I thought about having children from the time I was small, but I never really, I mean really, thought about what it was going to look like and how it might affect the life I was planning. I was going to have it all. I would have the "him" time, the "them" time, the "me" time, and the "we" time. I was feeling so empowered to reach for my dreams by my family and mentors that the idea of how I was going to do it ALL was not even a thought. I needed a bit of reality to firmly plant my feet on the ground. And I did not have that.

When people said I could have my cake and eat it too, I believed them. And then it came down to figuring it all out. Our decision was that my husband was to be the primary home-based parent, and I was to be the breadwinner. This made financial sense. I was more established in my career. After a short maternity leave, I was back to teaching and my husband was trying to get our 4-week-old baby to take a bottle of expressed breast milk. The roller coaster was only beginning.

I can't say it has been an easy ride. I love my kids, and I am happy that my chosen career has given us modest financial security. I set out to make it work. I hit the books to learn how other moms do this thing called motherhood. I read reports about consumer goods I might need for this new resident. I read parenting magazines and talked to random pregnant mothers I met in the doctor's office. I wanted to be an educated mother. I fully invested in breastfeeding, attachment parenting, and wearing my baby, sometimes more than one at a time, and embraced every moment as I worked full time, went to graduate school, and tried to be a wife. My husband and I were a team—an exhausted team.

It wasn't easy when my daughter's first instinct was to cry out for "Daddy" when she woke up in the middle of the night. It was tough to watch my son go to Daddy when he got hurt on the swing. It is the way it is. The home-based parent is usually the parent children count on most. But that doesn't mean that mixing up the roles has not been tough. We often think about the notion that it really is the "role," and not the "gender," that defines our parenting experiences.

I am the one racing to school from work to catch the classroom play or to chaperone a field trip. He fills out the excuse cards, packs the lunches, deals with mounds of laundry, and makes up car games so that the kids don't get bored with errands. It is an interesting life we lead. I am thankful and grateful that the kids know that he is securely there for them at a moment's notice. I am happy that they are learning about a strong work ethic from me. I try to share these experiences in my Media and Women's Culture class. Many of our conversations center around the ways mothers are portrayed in the media. I hope to give my students that dose of reality that I missed.

As someone schooled in the ways of the media, I have often been taken off guard by the way the media address me, the participant, the audience, the viewer (Ellsworth, 1997). I wonder if the media makers, some who are women, know the moms I know or understand the way I feel about things. But of course theirs is an economic model, not an educational one. Still, much can be learned from the media. I marvel at the ways they "get it wrong" on talk shows and sitcoms. Yes, my mom friends and I laugh about the way media portray us, but we also seriously consider the consequences of consistent saturation of the "Media Mom." The mothering role is so much more multifaceted and rich than it is shown in magazines and on television and film.

I wonder how the media affected my sense of what a mother was, and the kind of mother I was going to be. My mother was home full time with me until high school. I am not cut from that same cloth. I can say that I feel strongly for my counterparts who are home with children. Their choices and feelings matter greatly to me. There are times when I yearn for that role. And there are times when they wish they had my role. There is something about being a mother, to me, that is constantly unresolved. What I do know is that careful study of media moms can open our eyes to new and different ways of thinking about motherhood, so we can think about our mutual goals on this earth instead of our differences.

Mothers in media are designed as *caricatures*, because they present a satirical picture or an exaggeration of something that we can easily remember. I don't call these "stereotypes" because although the media do tend to perpetuate preconceived and oversimplified notions of motherhood, the portrayals are varied enough that they seem not to rely on only a few typical characteristics.

The mother experience is constructed by culture, and media culture is an important and all-consuming part of life. This is one reason why notions of mother, motherhood, and mothering find themselves squarely in the midst of media fire. Mother Goose, angry stepmothers, and Mother Nature abound in our media culture. Commercial mothers tell us to brush our teeth, wash our hands, and eat healthy nutritious meals. Cartooned mothers stand many mothering notions upside down and push them to the extreme. Talk show moms scrutinize mom jeans and discuss how we can lose those circles under our eyes.

Media consumers base the things they care about and are concerned with on the content they see in the media (Brooks & Hebert, 2006). When the caricatures of mothers are viewed as good or bad or not seen at all, the shift of care and concern is also altered. This kind of scrutiny occurs in the fictional and nonfictional media world.

Etymologically, the word mother stems from the notion of caring for. Mother*hood* increases the notion to the guarder or protector of care. When the root of mother is juxtaposed or cast onto the mediated notion of mother, interesting caricatures, both exaggerated and satirical, can be more closely studied. This reading is by no means an exhaustive look, but a reflective study of mothers in the media across a variety of media platforms and genres, in several different broad categories, to better understand the media mother. To explore this further, I identify four main themes surrounding the mediated depiction of motherhood.

THE POLITICS OF MOTHERHOOD

On television, in print, in film, and on the Internet, political mothers take a stand. In some cases, the view we see is a faint caricature of the real motivation. In other cases, it is pure satire. And in still other cases, mothers are harnessing the media and creating their own stories.

Mothers in political circles have been a focus of media attention as far back as the first First Lady, Martha Washington. In the last 40 years, the media have focused on different aspects of women associated with politics. We read about who made the best chocolate chip cookie (Barbara Bush or Hillary Clinton), saw Laura Bush scrutinized for her twin daughters' choices, and watched *Saturday Night Live* parody Hillary Clinton and Sarah Palin. Michelle Obama became "Super Woman" for the front cover of a regional magazine. In all cases, these women's roles as a mother, whether it be Sarah Palin in the reality show *Sarah Palin's Alaska*, Hillary Clinton's *It Take A Village*, or Laura Bush's *Spoken from the Heart*, shed light on motherhood in the political arena and the ways that media play with the motherhood identity.

Other books about mothers have shifted the line from political Mom to activist Mom. *Not One More Mother's Child* and *Peace Mom: A Mother's Journey through Heartache to Activism* by Cindy Sheehan and *American Mourning* by Catherine Moy and Melanie Morgan shared differing views about war and motherhood, and became the focus of negative media attention (Knudson, 2009; Slattery & Garner, 2007). In films such as *Erin Brockovich,* social class also becomes an issue. Brockovich was an unemployed single mother who became an activist to help her children grow up in a cleaner environment; she was later scrutinized when her daughter struggled with drug abuse.

GOOD/BAD MOTHERING

Mothers in the media are often defined based on how well they fit into society's definition of mothering. In TV crime shows such as *Law and Order: Special Victims Unit,* mothers are often seen as criminals or causing their children to commit crimes. Media moms are overwhelmingly portrayed as weak, silly, stupid, or deranged (*Malcolm in the Middle, Desperate Housewives, South Park*), and bad mothering is more central to plot themes than bad fathering (Cuklanz & Moorti, 2006). In rap music, misogynistic lyrics illustrate a female dichotomy. Rappers often talk about their children's mothers (baby mamas) in derogatory ways, but in the same song have high regard for their own mothers (Tyree, 2010). Rap singers often praise their mothers for putting up with them and sacrificing for them, while stating that their baby mamas were unworthy of love, care, protection, or financial help.

Reality television also shows mothering in the extreme. Families become a spectacle where caricature mothers are spun as the center of conflict: they are exchanged (*Wife Swap*), reprogrammed (*Super Nanny*), and scrutinized (*Kate Plus 8*). It seems as if bad mothering, or bad mothering in light of some alternative sense of "good mothering," sells in the media.

The good/bad mothering theme is also evident in parenting magazines, frequent sources of information about breastfeeding and hand feeding (formula) a newborn. The rhetorical debate of "breast or bottle" in these magazines is focused on a mother's choice, and not on the human rights issue of being able breastfeed one's child, or the public health benefit of children who have been nursed (Foss & Southwell, 2006). In many cases, magazines note that "breast is best" but then focus on the difficulty, time demands, or mother's potential inability to produce milk. A 2006 issue of the free mainstream parenting publication *Babytalk* received ridicule for showing a nursing baby on the magazine's cover. Because popular culture shows the breast as erotic rather than functional, mediated images of breastfeeding mothers and babies are considered negative (Brown & Peuchaud, 2008).

The good/bad mother conversation shifts the decision from a choice perspective to a health perspective, when the American Association of Pediatrics (2005) clearly recommends exclusive breastfeeding for the first 6 months of a babies life. Advertisements for formula are important to the bottom line of many parenting magazines, so pro-breastfeeding articles are less frequent and rarely contain clear and insightful information. Breastfeeding, a free endeavor, needs to gain momentum as a public health initiatives like the anti-smoking campaign and the Mothers against Drunk Driving campaign, and increase media awareness as a health initiative.

THE MOM CLASS

Research notes a disparity between the way upper and middle-class mothers are represented in the media, in contrast to lower income mothers. Most lower income women are not positively portrayed. Caricatures of middle and upper class mothers on television are often seen as passive, self-absorbed, and concerned with superficial things, but lower income mothers are concerned with obtaining minimal health care, nutrition, and basic needs for children. This story is not being told through mainstream entertainment media.

Socioeconomic status and race differences are also highlighted in the reality genre. Long work hours, insufficient finances, and poor childcare are family problems that cause social anxiety, so scrutiny of the family and mothering skills is increased for these populations (Brancato, 2007.) Children learn about gender differences on television, and lower minority families are watching more television programming than middle and upper class families. Lower income television viewers also tend to watch television in real time, so they cannot fast-forward through commercials. Girls learn to act like women and mothers through media portrayals of gender roles, and mainstream media devalue girls. What are young girls learning about being a Mom from Disney and MTV? The Special Supplemental Nutrition Program for Women, Infants and Children (WIC) started a media campaign aimed at reaching women of lower socioeconomic status to educate about breastfeeding. They have taken an advocacy approach and seek out the lower socioeconomic population through movies and music, to educate and advocate breastfeeding (Jenkins, 2009). The news focus on multiples births is more prominently and negatively reported when the mother is considered working poor or on welfare, and more acutely during an economic recession (Charles & Shivas, 2002). The rhetorical use of concern for children in the news is often highlighted with stories about poor and minority women framed as bad mothers (Springer, 2010).

THE LABOR OF MOTHER LOVE

Much can be noted about media caricatures of mothers who either choose to work outside the home, or "stay at home" with children. These representations rarely explore the vast ranges of reasons why women live these roles, and often portray these choices as opposite poles in the spectrum of opportunities, choices, and needs for women and their families. Sometimes demonized, other times praised, mothers who works full time and mothers who are home with children are cast in extremes. TV news stories describe moms who work outside the home as "seeking balance," and mothers who don't work outside the home as "opting out." Shows such as *The Good Wife*, *New Adventures of Old Christine*, *Parenthood*, *Teen Mom,* and *Real Housewives of Ocean County* use fictional and reality genres to explore a mother's choice to enter, re-enter, or leave the workforce.

In striving for balance, a working mother spends hours on different tasks associated with working and mothering. Television shows discuss quick and nutritional meals moms can make, and techniques to organize her life so she can get it all in. What most advertisements don't show is that many home-based mothers are also running between sporting events and are also making the quick meals. So much media content about and for mothers tells us that life can be balanced, that homes with children can be clean and decorated, and that moms can have time for themselves. And we buy into this. According to Collett (2005), many moms strive to cultivate this impression, an image they think others might want to see or they themselves think they should be. The problem with this kind of content is that it suggests that if mom were just a little bit better at juggling all of the elements of her life, things would be perfect. And she might even be able to look like one of those women on Wisteria Lane. Additional research sheds light on women's feelings of the need to airbrush the motherhood body away, as if a post-pregnancy body is a negative body (D'Enbeau & Buzzanell, 2010). Representations of mothers who have to do it all, and have to look good doing it, are unrealistic and perpetuate concerns about body image and growing older, but are the mainstay of the fashion and cosmetic industries.

THE BOTTOM LINE

Robinson and Hunter (2008) argue that magazine content is shifting, from presenting caricatures of the housewife and supermom to a more gender-neutral presentation emphasizing the family. On the one hand, this reflects the changing nature of a mother's role and the family structure, which seems positive; but on the other hand, moms are being removed from the equation all together. Women and girls are a driving force in the economy, receive a post high school education in greater numbers than men, are avid consumers of media, and make up more than half of the American population. And a bit more than half of that population are mothers. Media represent mothers as mere caricatures and shadows of their true selves. Yes, there are very good mothers, and some not so good ones. So what? Take back the power to make your own choices about motherhood. The mainstream media, both news and entertainment, air what sells—women's issues, though they are often everybody's issues, are rarely the top priority. The media can both limit and empower you. Use it to your full advantage. There is a reason why everyone always says "Hi mom" into the camera when they are on TV.

IT'S YOUR TURN: WHAT DO YOU THINK? WHAT WILL YOU FIND?

1. My students often hold strong convictions regarding mothering choices, including choices about breastfeeding, vaccinations, work and home aspirations, large families versus small families, blended families, and adoption. How do you feel about these issues? Have you ever reflected on them? How are these choices portrayed in the television shows you watch?

2. Interview your mother or another woman about her caregiving experiences. Record it if possible. Why she made the choices she did? What themes do you notice in her responses? Were things different for her than you thought they were?

3. Write a letter to yourself. In your letter, talk about your thoughts about becoming a parent. Put your letter in an envelope, seal it, and put it somewhere safe until you become a parent (or for 10 years), so you can open it and see what you were thinking about.

4. Travel through the city on public transportation, or sit in an airport or mall and watch mothers in action. Look at the objects they are using such as strollers, backpacks, front carriers, and other consumer goods. What might you surmise about a mother based on the items she uses in public? How are these the same or different from the mothers you see on television or film or in magazines? What class differences do you see?

REFERENCES

American Academy of Pediatrics. (2005). Policy statement. Organizational principles to guide and define the child health care system and/or improve the health of all children. Section on breastfeeding: Breastfeeding and the use of human milk. *Pediatrics, 115* (2), 496–506.

Brancato, J. (2007). Domesticating politics: The representation of wives and mothers in American reality television. *Film & History, 37*(2), 49–56.

Brooks, D.E., & Hebert, L.P. (2006). Gender, race and media representation. *The Sage handbook of gender and communication*. Thousand Oaks, CA: Sage.

Brown, J. D., & Peuchaud, S. R. (2008). Media and breastfeeding: Friend or foe? *International Breastfeeding Journal, 3*(15).

Charles, S., & Shivas, T. (2002). Mothers in the media: Blamed and celebrated—an examination of drug abuse and multiple births. *Pediatric Nursing, 28*(2), 42–145.

Collett, J. (2005). What kind of mother am I? Impression management and the social construction of motherhood. *Symbolic Interaction, 3*(28), 327–347.

Cuklanz, L. M., & Moorti, S. (2006). Television's 'new' feminism: Prime-time representations of women and victimization. *Critical Studies in Media Communication, 23*(4), 302–321.

D'Enbeau, S., & Buzzanell, P. M. (2010, Spring). Caregiving and female embodiment: Scrutinizing (professional) female bodies in media, academe, and the neighborhood bar. *Women & Language, 33*(1), 29–52.

Ellsworth, E. (1997). *Teaching positions: Difference, pedagogy, and the power of address*. New York: Teachers College Press.

Foss, K. A., & Southwell, B. G. (2006). Infant feeding and the media: The relationship between *Parents' Magazine* content and breastfeeding, 1972–2000. *International Breastfeeding Journal, 1*(10).

Jenkin, C. (2009). Health, science and the media. *Breastfeeding Medicine, 4*(1), S71–S72.

Knudson, L. (2009, April). Cindy Sheehan and the rhetoric of motherhood: A textual analysis. *Peace & Change, 34*(2), 164–183.

Robinson, B. K., & Hunter, E. (2008). Is mom still doing it all? Reexamining depictions of family work in popular advertising. *Journal of Family Issues, 29*(4), 465–486.

Slattery, K., & Garner, A. (2007). Mothers of soldiers in wartime: A national news narrative. *Critical Studies in Media Communication, 24*(5), 429–445.

Springer, K. W. (2010). The race and class privilege of motherhood: *New York Times* presentations of pregnant drug-using women. *Sociological Forum, 25*(3), 476–499.

Tyree, T. C. M. (2009). Lovin' Momma and hatin' on Baby Mama: A comparison of misogynistic and stereotypical representations in songs about rappers' mothers and baby mamas. *Women and Language, 32*(2), 50–58.

6.10 WICKED STEPMOTHERS WEAR DIOR: HOLLYWOOD'S MODERN FAIRY TALES

Lea M. Popielinski

> *The author argues that* The Devil Wears Prada *and* The Nanny Diaries *represent the evolution of a familiar type of fairy tale: a maiden overcomes subjugation by a more powerful older woman to gain freedom and happiness.*

A young woman gazes up from the foot of a Manhattan skyscraper, awed by its power to dwarf her and excited by the challenge it represents. She's just finished college and is about to enter another world that promises to transform her and deliver her into the professional life of her dreams. She's no Rapunzel, waiting inside a tower for a dashing hero to whisk her away, but an adventurer in her own right, prepared to scale the tower herself. With an ambitiousness as inspired as it is naïve, our young woman is about to become the heroine of the modern-day fairy tale.

Recent films *The Devil Wears Prada* (2006) and *The Nanny Diaries* (2007) follow protagonists much like this young lady as they begin jobs they consider transitional but necessary trials toward their ultimate aspirations. The only obstacles confronting *Devil*'s Andrea "Andy" Sachs and *Diaries*' Annie Braddock in attaining their career goals, ironically, are their employers. This chapter will discuss the evolution of a familiar subset of fairy tales: the story of a maiden overcoming subjugation by a more powerful older woman to gain freedom and happiness. Once upon a time, this antagonist was often a witch or a wicked stepmother motivated by jealousy, greed, or fear of being dethroned; but in contemporary films targeting an adult audience, she appears as a wealthy woman whose status affords her the ability to make the rules. I will address how Miranda Priestly and Mrs. X, the characters who take on this role in these movies, carry on the wicked stepmother model in updated variations. Andy and Annie, meanwhile, are hardly Snow White and Cinderella, but the spirit of the character type is maintained in a form relatable to young twenty-first century women.

This reading deals with archetypes, classic models of a person or concept that take a consistent form by appearing repeatedly within a cultural genre. The wicked stepmother and the innocent, persecuted heroine are major fairy tale archetypes. Psychoanalysts have interpreted the use of archetypes in storytelling as symbolic of the beliefs of a culture's collective unconscious (Franz, 1973). Other authors focus on the archetypes' social context to examine how they reflect their cultures (Zipes, 1993). I use a combination of the two methods, in using *Devil* and *Diaries* to explore how the two archetypes have changed in some ways but are still recognizable in others, in relation to women's changing roles and concerns. I suggest that North American culture is conflicted about how contemporary women's roles diverge from fairy tale ideals, proud of the independence and ambition of young women with no real influence yet more ambivalent about women who are aged and/or successful enough to wield social and economic power, and that the race, sexuality, and class status of the women in these films are significant to the reproduction of these archetypes.

THE MOVIES

In *Devil*, Andy Sachs has moved to New York seeking work in her dream profession of journalism. She procures a position that "a million girls would kill for," as junior assistant to *Runway* fashion magazine's notoriously patronizing editor in chief, Miranda Priestly. Although her frumpy style indicates to Miranda a lack of credibility, Andy is determined to persevere because the experience will open all the doors in Manhattan's journalistic offices to her. Eventually, with help from coworker Nigel, she adapts to her circumstances and the workplace's standards of appearance while developing the business contacts and self-confidence that boost her job performance and Miranda's approval. As she grows devoted to her job, however, she loses touch with her boyfriend and friends. When she becomes party to politics and backstabbing, she finally wants out, unwilling to sacrifice her ethics. As the movie ends, Andy's boyfriend is moving away, and she goes to work at a more modestly run newspaper, on Miranda's favorable recommendation.

Meanwhile, Annie Braddock is less certain about her ambitions. After failing a job interview, she saves a child named Grayer from an accident and is invited by his wealthy mother, Mrs. X, to become his nanny. Believing that the work will be a good source of income while she figures out her life, Annie accepts. She finds herself performing all the parental duties for a socialite mother and philandering father. She finds support from her friends and from a studly neighbor in the Xes' building, whom she calls "Harvard Hottie." Annie's affection for Grayer balances her growing frustration until Mr. X makes an unwanted pass at her, which Mrs. X uses as an excuse to fire her. She vents her anger on a teddy bear outfitted with a "nannycam;" the resulting video, in which Annie pleads that the Xes become more active parents, shames Mrs. X in front of a seminar, though she later learns that Mrs. X has taken her advice. Meanwhile, she applies to graduate programs in anthropology, and her romance with Harvard Hottie appears to be underway.

THE INNOCENT PERSECUTED HEROINE

I have used the phrase "innocent persecuted heroine" several times already because it is a standard way of describing this character type among fairy tale theorists (see *Western Folklore,* vol. 52, no. 1, 1993). It should be immediately apparent that in the present-day fairy tale, this figure has undergone dramatic transformations, not least of which is the fact that Andy and Annie are not persecuted in any traditional sense, having freely accepted their jobs. Although surface details have changed quite substantially, the changes are consistent with the innocent persecuted heroine's (hereafter, IPH's) history as an archetype and the core elements to the narrative structure and positioning of the IPH tale. Andy and Annie are not actual IPHs, but their films belong to a related subgenre.

It's essential to see the development of archetypes within their historical contexts. Many European fairy tales began as products of oral folklore before being published (Franz, 1973; Tatar, 2002), often existing in multiple forms in different periods and locales. Publication and distribution, however, caused particular versions, such as the Grimm brothers' adaptations, to become more widely accepted. These privileged versions obscure the diversity of the previous contexts in which the stories appeared.

Even within the IPH subgenre, the heroines have not always been innocent and persecuted but often became so when their stories were adapted for wide appeal. *Little Red Riding Hood* gives us one fascinating example: in "an oral version of the tale recorded in France at the end of the nineteenth century, Little Red Riding Hood performs a striptease before the wolf, then ends the litany of questions about the wolf's body parts by asking if she can go outside to relieve herself" (Tatar, 2002, p. 17), thus outwitting the wolf and escaping, rather than being saved by a hunter. Other heroines are innocent throughout the story but allow brutal violence to occur once they've attained higher status: the Grimms' Cinderella invites her stepsisters to her wedding, where birds peck out their eyes, and Snow White allows her stepmother to be placed in red-hot iron shoes that cause her to dance herself to death. The idealistically innocent heroine did appear in earlier eras, but she was not as monolithic as she gradually became.

Since the 1930s, probably the most influential transcriber of fairy tales has been Disney. Their animated feature film versions of IPH tales are so iconic that many in recent generations regard them as the gold standard and may not be familiar with earlier versions. It may be worth considering why the IPH archetype proliferated at this time. The construction of morality and femininity in twentieth-century North America may have demanded less ambiguity than Europeans of earlier periods were comfortable with.

Things became more complicated with the emergence of the women's movement, beginning in the 1960s. The first feminist engagements with fairy tales appeared in the early 1970s (Lieberman, 1972; Lurie, 1970; Rowe, 1979), and even nonfeminists in the present day recognize feminist objections to the archetypes. Some latter-day Disney films feature noticeably more active or intelligent heroines, and parodies such as *Shrek* defy the archetype altogether.

Likely because of feminist influence and the sense that the archetype has become cliché, it has become difficult to produce straightforward IPHs. A fairy tale meant to be relevant to contemporary women must be more complex. Thus, the fact that the goals and concerns of the heroines of *Devil* and *Diaries* diverge dramatically from those of Disney's mid-century prototypes does not necessarily exclude them from being kin to the IPH subgenre. In some ways, the stories and their protagonists conform to the conventions of standard IPH narratives, such as in the heroines' solitude and in their search for identity.

Michael Mendelson (1997) observes that while male heroes and wicked women in *Grimms' Fairy Tales* occasionally collaborate with one another, young, virtuous women seldom work together in a similar fashion. Although Andy and Annie have friends and boyfriends outside of their workplaces, their social lives conflict with their jobs. While Annie has no peer coworkers at all, Andy begins her job as an outcast among her colleagues. The nearest that women in the Grimms' tales come to a collaborative relationship, Mendelson suggests, is when a fairy godmother or similar figure arrives to offer brief and temporary assistance to a heroine. Andy has a helper of this sort in Nigel: the scene in which he brings her to *Runway*'s castoffs closet and dresses her, Cinderella-like, in designer garments, marks the turning point in the film, after which she becomes a model employee and eventually impresses Miranda.

Mendelson also focuses on "the coming into selfhood" and how "[i]n this singular process of psychological individuation, the solitary figure takes center stage" (1997, p. 120). Andy has chosen her future identity, and her time at *Runway* is her journey toward self-realization. In *Diaries*, this process is even more transparent. In an early scene, a job interviewer asks our heroine, "Who is Annie Braddock?" Annie's inability to answer this question leads her to take the job she believes will help her find herself. That she expects to find self-discovery through nannying makes most sense with respect to her relationship with Mrs. X: having one's very own wicked stepmother becomes a rite of passage toward adulthood.

THE WICKED STEPMOTHER

The stepmother is so important to the Western coming-of-age story that now that she is no longer a domestic terrorist infiltrating the heroine's home; the young women must seek her out on her own territory. Andy would not have the credentials, the recommendation, or the first-rate experience to compete for her dream job, and Annie might still be taking ill-fated interviews at business offices, if they had not first passed through gauntlets conceived by Miranda and Mrs. X. Besides the workplace taking on a familial quality in both films, both films include the motif of parental replacement. In *Devil*, Andy's father visits, but she is continually interrupted by telephone calls from Miranda and her impossibly urgent demands. The evening grows increasingly frustrating, peaking when the distracted Andy shuts a taxi door on her father, literally and painfully. In *Diaries*, the mother substitution is more overt. Annie has been raised by a single mother and nurse, whom she doesn't want to disappoint. When she takes the nanny job, she lies to her mother and says she was offered a financial position. The ruse falls apart in a tense confrontation between Mrs. X and Mrs. Braddock, in which the former seems surprised to learn that Annie has a mother.

Compared to Andy and Annie as IPHs, Miranda and Mrs. X retain more traditional characteristics relating to the wicked stepmother, most visibly in their dictatorial styles. Steven Swann Jones (1993, p. 28) regards the "jealous stepmother who favors her own daughter and forces the heroine to perform disagreeable, dangerous, or impossible chores" to be a staple of the IPH genre. Miranda reduces Andy to running errands and performing menial tasks, culminating in an ultimatum for Andy to find an unpublished *Harry Potter* manuscript; Mrs. X's to-do list for Annie is less demanding but more degrading, frequently designed to emphasize their difference in status. Although danger is not a theme in either movie, disagreeable and impossible chores certainly are.

IN A LAND NOT SO FAR AWAY

The release of two very similar films that reinvent these archetypes in more familiar guises suggests that there's a social need or desire for such images to be reproduced in this way. The critical questions are: "What do *Devil* and *Diaries* say about their social context?" and "Why are the symbols packaged the way they are?"

We must view these symbols in terms of how we understand race, gender, class, and sexuality in our cultural context. In some respects, the archetypes are still strongly bound to the correct combination of these four dimensions. More marginal archetypes, like the fairy godmother, may be flexible. Others, like Prince Charming, are optional. The heroine and the stepmother, however, might not be recognizable as such were they not both white, heterosexual women of the economic classes appropriate to their character types.

Archetypes must appear to represent the broadest range of subjectivity possible. The cultural separation of social categories into One and Other, in which One is not merely the dominant of the two but the standard, neutral, and default category, casts Othered categories as marked identities, seen in terms of their difference from the "norm." Using the example of sex/gender, Simone de Beauvoir (1989 [1949], p. xxi) writes, "Man represents both the positive and the neutral, as is indicated by the common use of *man* to designate human beings in general; whereas woman represents only the negative, defined by limiting criteria, without reciprocity." Applying the concept to race, then, a Black heroine would be able to stand as an archetype for all Black women, but only a white heroine is constructed to stand for all women: whiteness, unlike other(ed) races, does not need to be articulated. Only whiteness, in de Beauvoir's terms, is neutral.

Similarly, a version of *Devil* with Andy as a lesbian would probably not allow her to "just happen to be" a lesbian. Rather, her inevitable tomboyishness might be used comically as she fumbles with feminine clothing, or she might grapple with homophobic parents. While there's nothing wrong with producing a film about a straight, white woman, we can't assume that her race and sexuality are therefore any less important to her character development than for those with more marked identities. Whiteness and heterosexuality are just as central to constructing these characters as class and gender.

The centrality of Andy and Annie's whiteness is actively reinforced by the fact that each one's closest female friend is Black. Annie's friend Lynnette directly emphasizes that Annie's choice to enter domestic servitude is made from a position of racial privilege when she points out that generations of women in her own family have worked hard not to perform that labor again. Annie can *only* submit herself to it knowing that her racial privilege grants her other options. She herself acknowledges that her race, citizenship, and English language fluency make her "the Chanel bag of nannies." Andy and her best friend Lily never talk about race as overtly, but the absence of other white women in Andy's social circle highlights her dyadic relationship with the older white mother-substitute.

Andy and Annie's heterosexuality is also reinforced by those around them; Lynnette's roommate Calvin is openly gay, while Nigel is depicted using stereotypically gay mannerisms. The deflection of homosexuality away from the main characters renders gayness as a marked identity, so that any character not "read" as gay will appear to a heterosexist audience as straight. The heroines' heterosexuality is not incidental: it's necessary to maintain the characters as archetypes, not only because of heterosexuality's default status but also because it leaves open the possibility of a Prince Charming, necessary for the fairy tale framework, even if that possibility does not come to fruition. Straight womanhood must be opposed to straight manhood, without all of the complicated ambiguities that lesbian and bisexual identities and nonconformist gender expressions introduce.

Class advancement has always been a central theme of fairy tales, especially IPH tales (Panttaja, 1993). Andy and Annie frame their ambitions as paths to careers rather than wealth, but the economic disparity between the heroines and their employers underlines a direct correlation between money and power. Reading the films side-by-side illustrates that the differences between women who marry into money, like Mrs. X, and women who earn it themselves, like Miranda, are not necessarily significant to archetypal readings. Andy and Annie's seemingly humble approach to money is necessary to further contribute to their neo-IPH profile to the extent that standard IPHs are often rewarded specifically for not seeking a reward. The connections among power, money, and a lack of ethics demonstrate why the wicked stepmother archetype has been revived in this form at this time: contemporary North American culture feels very differently about young women who work hard to achieve all the hallmarks of middle-class female success than it feels about older women who have actually attained positions of power.

"Women's liberation" of the 1970s gave way to "girl power" by the 1990s. Girls of the current generation are often taught they can do anything. North American culture is proud of young women earning college degrees and entering the job market because it exemplifies cultural progress and open-mindedness. Critically, this pride only lasts while these women have little social power. Our culture feels much more ambivalent toward older women who are succeeding, as is reflected empirically by research suggesting that workplace advancement grows increasingly more difficult for women than for men (and more difficult for Black men than for white men) over the course of their careers (Maume, 2004). The face of *new* employees is diverse in many fields, but our culture is still most comfortable with white men in the *most elite* positions. Although many claim to support the advancement of women and people of color to powerful positions, there may still be an unconscious cultural anxiety about this ideal's realization. Because it is inappropriate to admit this anxiety, it emerges in our cultural products through the use of archetypes embedded in the collective unconscious.

For example, Miranda acts as both Andy's challenger and her mentor. She considers Andy, on some level, a successor. But Miranda is not depicted as a strong executive who takes employees under her wing to groom them, a character type more strongly associated with men; she's depicted in a gendered manner, insofar as terms like "shrew," "ice queen," and "dragon lady" only exist at the intersection of femaleness and class power. Movies about this type of powerful woman give voice to otherwise suppressed cultural fears about giving women "too much" power. Andy's refusal to be seduced into this role is crucial to the archetype she continues to embody.

What's more, these fears are not restricted to the office setting. Mrs. X obtained her power by marrying a rich man. The differences and similarities to Miranda are notable. On the one hand, her power is much more limited, and working for her does not provide upward mobility. She restricts her nannies from dating out of concern that the nanny will be less devoted to her work;

but when she learns of Annie's relationship with a young man in their own building, the offense is doubly threatening for the transgression of class boundaries. Mrs. X thus exhibits more of the classic wicked stepmother's characteristics of jealousy and fear of losing her privilege. The gulf between her and Annie is much smaller than the gulf between Miranda and Andy. The former is a question of whose wedding band lands on one's finger; the latter is a matter of years of experience and ladder-climbing.

On the other hand, all of the emblematic terms I listed earlier—"shrew," etc.—are similarly applicable to Mrs. X. Bestowing economic power on a woman, according to these narratives, transforms her from naïf to harpy. Both films give their stepmothers a personal edge but do so through tumult in their marriages. The only person who has the power to hurt each of these women is her husband. The circumstances under which the divorces loom and the impact they have on the two women are very different, but it is intriguing how the same device is used in both to create chinks in the stepmothers' armor.

HAPPILY EVER AFTER?

This discussion of *Devil* and *Diaries* suggests that contemporary North American culture strongly values progressive gender politics to the extent that it results in young, educated, unmarried women joining the workforce with great ambition but modest goals. It also suggests, meanwhile, that this same culture is simultaneously ambivalent about women gaining a surplus of power within the same context. I call this "ambivalence" because there does not seem to be an outright objection to women holding positions of power so much as a sense that women who hold these positions fit a certain—and not always complimentary—category of womanhood. On this note, it is important to end by observing that neither film completely demonizes its wicked stepmother. In the transition from fairy tale archetype to contemporary social construction, this character type has grown more complex, appropriately so, for her relevance in an increasingly complex society.

IT'S YOUR TURN: WHAT DO YOU THINK? WHAT WILL YOU FIND?

1. With a partner, choose a different film genre—action, romance, science fiction, etc.—and discuss the types of female characters who appear in it. What patterns can you recognize in their depiction? What cultural beliefs about womanhood or femininity seem to be illustrated in these character types? How do race, sexuality, age, and dis/ability (even if they are unmarked) contribute to creating these character types?

2. Find a book containing fairy tales you've never read or heard before, perhaps from a non-European culture. Choose one and imagine what would change or remain the same if it were made into a movie. Which themes or characters seem to fit easily into contemporary scripts, and which don't? Thinking about elements like violence, morals, and characters'

objectives, what aspects of twenty-first century culture, possibly aspects we usually take for granted, make an adaptation of the story difficult?

3. Look for articles in news magazines about women and men in powerful positions, such as politicians and business leaders. Compare the way the authors describe their subjects. To what extent do they discuss their subjects' family lives, career histories, appearance, and professional success? How positive or negative do they sound? What similarities and differences are there in the articles and any accompanying photography? If you can, find news magazines from 10, 20, and 30 years ago to see if, and how, profiles of female and male professionals have changed.

REFERENCES

de Beauvoir, Simone. (1989 [1949]). *The second sex*. New York: Vintage Books.

Franz, M. L. (1973). *An introduction to the psychology of fairy tales*. Zurich: Spring Publications.

Jones, S. S. (1993). The innocent persecuted heroine genre: An analysis of its structure and themes. *Western Folklore*, *52*(1), 13–41.

Lieberman, M. (1972). "Some day my prince will come:" Female acculturation through the fairy tale. *College English*, *34*, 383–95.

Lurie, A. (1970, December 17). Fairy tale liberation. *New York Review of Books*. Retrieved October 6, 2011, from http://www.nybooks.com/articles/archives/1970/dec/17/fairy-tale-liberation/

Maume, D. (2004). Wage discrimination over the life course: A comparison of explanations. *Social Problems*, *51*(4), 505–527.

Mendelson, M. (1997). Forever acting alone: The absence of female collaboration in *Grimms' Fairy Tales*. *Children's Literature in Education*, *28*(3), 111–25.

Panttaja, E. (1993). Going up in the world: Class in "Cinderella." *Western Folklore*, *52*(1), 85–104.

Rowe, K. E. (1979). Feminism and fairy tales. *Women's Studies*, *6*, 237–57.

Tatar, M. (2002). *The annotated classic fairy tales*. New York: W. W. Norton & Company.

Zipes, J. (1993). Spinning with fate: Rumpelstiltskin and the decline of female productivity. *Western Folklore*, *52*(1), 43–60.

Music and New Media

7.1 ANTI-GAY SPEECH ON THE INTERNET AND THE MOVEMENT TO COUNTERACT CYBER HATE

Cynthia A. Cooper

A Web site allows you to create your own racist avatar, choosing from swastikas, crosses, machine guns, even a cartoon image of Hitler killing a young man wearing a pink triangle. Another site enshrines Matthew Shepard in flames counting up the days he's "spent in hell" since his 1998 murder. You can hear Matthew's screams and his pleas for you to repent, before it's too late for you too. Welcome to the world of cyber hate. This reading discusses the main themes of anti-gay hate speech on the Internet.

The two instances described above are among the most extreme examples of anti-gay imagery on the Web, but they certainly are not alone. Internet sites advocating hate against gays, Jews, African Americans, and immigrants have grown so fast in recent years that getting an accurate count of their number is nearly impossible. A 2010 report by the Southern Poverty Law Center reported 932 identifiable hate groups in the United States, most with active Internet sites or links to sites of a national organizing group (SPLC, 2010a), up from 844 in 2009. This suggests a steady increase in the creation of new groups dedicated to spreading hateful rhetoric based on race, ethnicity, religion, or sexual orientation. The growth of hate group Web sites also coincides with an increase in reported hate crimes. The Hate Crime Statistics Act of 1990 mandates the compilation of an annual report on crimes motivated by a bias against persons based on race, religion, sexual orientation, and ethnicity/national origin. The most recent Uniform Crime Report (U. S. Department of Justice, 2009) found that 18.5% percent of all hate crimes were linked to sexual orientation bias with the most common being assault, intimidation, and property destruction or vandalism (Table 4). The 1,436 sexual orientation offenses reported in 2009 represented a 4% increase from 2005, and a long-term analysis of hate crimes data shows that gays are the victim of violent crimes twice as often as African Americans and Jews, and 14 times more often than Latinos (SPLC, 2010b). Although no direct correlation can be made between the increase in Internet hate group sites and bias crimes against the LGBT community, it is clear that both are on the rise.

Most hate group sites offer information about the organization's ideology and solicit memberships and donations but may also sell merchandise such as books, T-shirts, and music. Some even boast dating forums for like-minded singles. Don Black, former KKK Grand Dragon and creator of *Stormfront*, claimed the site was the point of first contact for most new Klan members after it launched in 1995 (Marriott, 1999, p. 4). In 2002, *Stormfront* reportedly attracted 2,000 hits a day, but that exploded to more than 40,000 unique visitors daily after Barack Obama became a frontrunner in the U.S. presidential race (Saslow, 2008). Today the organization has expanded worldwide with *Stormfront* sites for members across Europe and 15 countries, including Canada, Croatia, Ireland, South Africa, and Portugal. The reduced expense of online communications is key to the rapid expansion of hate groups because traditional print media such as newsletters, newspapers, and brochures are expensive to produce and distribute. In addition, hate groups don't always have open access to traditional communication channels, so the Internet has become the most powerful and economical tool in the hatemonger's arsenal of communication devices. The anonymous access, sophisticated Web design with video and audio capabilities, and relative lack of regulation make it the perfect medium to reach the masses.

Of course, anti-gay rhetoric is nothing new, and Internet hate speech directed at gays and lesbians is simply an outgrowth of hate against other identifiable groups. The Christian Identity Movement and Aryan Nation traditionally promote the belief that whites are the Bible's chosen people with their primary enemies being Jews—often dubbed the "Agents of Satan." In recent years, however, as mainstream media and legislative initiatives have lent more exposure to gay community issues, many of these groups have expanded their focus to include hate against gays and lesbians. Each new television show such as *Glee* or *Modern Family* that features positive portrayals of gays and lesbians is met with an equally prominent anti-gay voice. In the past, extremist organizations were often dismissed as disorganized fanatical fringe groups preaching to a relatively small and geographically dispersed congregation. Today, the Internet provides a centralized information center uniting followers of the Christian Identity, Aryan Nation, and KKK movements across economic and geographic boundaries, with increased numbers of followers linked via the Internet.

I became interested in the growth of Internet hate speech and began a series of studies accounting for much of what I discuss here. Over a 12-year period, I've studied Web sites of hate groups for form and content. By coding the content of these sites (content analysis) and exploring the texts and messages on these sites (textual analysis), I gained greater understanding of the meanings behind the messages and the motivations of anti-gay groups. While there are some differences among sites in content and presentation, most anti-gay groups share some basic characteristics. First, the major theme is to speak out against the gay lifestyle, although discussion of other groups (Jews and African Americans) or social concerns (abortion, Affirmative Action) may also occur. Little attention is given to bisexuals, transgender individuals, or people with other sexual orientations; the focus is mostly on gay men and lesbians. Second, the sponsoring organization typically identifies itself with Christian, family-oriented values. Groups including Watchmen on the Wall, The Christian Gallery, and Focus of the Family all rely heavily on Bible scripture to justify their anti-gay views. In fact, another report by the Southern Poverty Law Center also noted that "anti-gay sentiment is exploited by Christian white supremacists to organize the bigoted. Neo-Nazis, Skinheads, Christian Identity followers, white robed cross burners and talk show circuit 'racialists' may be divided over tactics, but they agree on who their enemies are. And gays, like Blacks and Jews, are categorically hated" (Berrill, 1992, p. 31).

One note of warning: Many of the sites discussed here track visitors and post the comments and e-mail addresses of anyone who criticizes their organizations. You should consider this before deciding whether you want to view any Internet sites of hate groups.

THE ANATOMY AND COMMUNICATION OF HATE

Explaining why people hate others is a monumental, if not impossible, task. It is hard to find anyone who is completely without prejudice or dislike of some person or group. But *hate*, repulsion and justification of violence or oppression against those different from us, is a completely different level of behavior altogether. Hate has been the subject of research for years, much focusing on its genetic and psychological underpinnings. Biologists often describe hate as an adaptive biological mechanism, an outgrowth of the fight or flight reflex. Psychologists study manifestations of hate as culturally created attitudes, especially in the form of prejudice against groups deemed threats to one's own identity. Social scientist Zillah Eisenstein stated that hate is a learned trait; it "seeks safety and self-protection on one hand, destruction and annihilation on the next" (2000, p. 93). This involves not merely disliking others but supporting (through words or actions) attempts to cause them harm. Such attitudes often result from complex interaction among societal, political, and religious institutions.

Politically, hate defines communities exclusively by race, religion, ethnicity, or sexual orientation. This results in the isolation of those groups and continues the cycle of prejudice, discrimination, even violence. People who aren't members of a targeted group often turn a blind eye to hateful rhetoric but silence can equal complicity. Unwillingness to speak out against those who exhibit hateful speech and action allows the hate to flourish.

Hate also has a religious component. Virtually all identifiable hate groups root their beliefs in the Bible, which they believe justifies their actions against others. The use of Christian ideology and dogma can be a powerful ally when trying to convince others of the validity of a viewpoint.

The most extreme manifestation of hate is the hate crime but a far more common form of expressing bigotry is through hate speech. Hate speech denounces whole groups of people solely because of their race, ethnicity, religion, or sexual orientation. It can be delivered through a variety of communication channels, whether printed in brochures or newsletters, recorded on audio or videotape, or delivered interpersonally through intimate conversations or to larger audiences at rallies, revivals, and meetings. Hate crimes are illegal, but hate speech, generally protected by the First Amendment, is not.

To understand anti-gay hate speech on the Internet is to consider the union of basic human instincts with advancing technologies, the clash of protected rights with concerns for social responsibility, and the evolving distinctions between traditional and changing meanings of community. There is little doubt that the development of the Internet has changed the way in which people communicate and form communities. Some have envisioned the Internet as the ultimate public sphere where individuals define themselves by choosing which communities to join. Thus, the potential for individual empowerment is deemed a major benefit of Internet communities. Indeed, gay and lesbian advocates have long argued against Internet filtering systems that block community health and education sites because this deprives users, particularly gay youth, of essential resources. Linking to PFLAG (Parents and Friends of Lesbians and Gays), The Trevor Project, or AfterEllen.com may be the only source of information and belonging for an isolated youth struggling with his or her sexuality.

But the Internet's empowering force can't be restricted only to so-called positive purposes. If the Internet has the potential to bring together people to enlighten, educate, and form communities, it may also be used by groups to defame, misinform, or even harm others. In fact, the Internet is a perfect meeting hall for hate groups.

Likewise, the anonymity provided by the Internet often fuels more aggressive behavior than people would express in traditional social situations, especially if their beliefs are not supported. The disinhibiting effects of the Internet can easily turn aggression into cyber violence, causing Internet users to feel free to express anger and hatred they'd censor in a more public, and accountable, setting. Anonymity allows us to set aside our cultural filters because we can't be directly linked to our words and actions. Vanderbilt (2008) analogizes the same anonymity afforded while driving our cars in traffic in an experiment where a stopped driver intentionally didn't move when a traffic light turned green. Drivers in convertibles waited longer to honk, and honked fewer times, than those whose identity was cloaked within a closed car. Imagine in your own life a situation in which you felt comfortable giving someone a real piece of your mind because your identity was masked behind a fake username or an avatar. Could you have been as candid in person? The same may be true of the hatemonger who proudly spouts hate in the relative anonymity of an Internet chat room but would think twice before walking down Main Street displaying a white hood or a swastika.

ANTI-GAY SPEECH ON THE INTERNET

As stated before, the anti-gay Web sites I studied certainly have some differences in content and format, but there are many shared themes and tactics. Many narratives misrepresent the gay lifestyle to create a basis for hatred as well as implicit and explicit calls to action against gays. In recent years, many of the anti-gay groups have expanded their focus to include commentary on political and social issues involving the gay community. For instance, the American Guardian site is devoted entirely to what it identifies as the growing and evolving threat of child molestation, which it concludes is perpetrated solely by gay men. Ignoring government statistics proving otherwise, gays are shown to prey on young boys as a way to recruit and perpetuate the "species." When hate groups do address the political issue of gay rights, it too is typically reduced to terms of sexuality and disease. For example, conservative talk-show host Bob Enyart has labeled AIDS prevention advocates as people who actually work to spread AIDS, and the Family Research Council (FRC) once posted that the real goal of the gay rights movement is to legitimize pedophilia. FRC's chairman, Paul Cameron, is notorious for misrepresenting other researchers' work to falsely claim that homosexuals are more likely than heterosexuals to be mentally unstable, to commit crimes, to drive while drunk, and to miss days at work.

Most disturbing is the recent rise of the Christian organization named Watchmen on the Walls whose Web site declares that homosexuality is the chief enemy of a natural family and that same-sex marriage will lead to the degradation of society. Watchmen now boasts a global coalition of believers, but its U.S. membership had its roots in the Russian and Ukrainian immigrant communities living in northwestern states. One of the original leaders was Scott Lively, co-author of *The Pink Swastika*, which claims that Hitler was gay and that fascist gays were the masterminds behind the rise of Nazism and the systematic murder of millions of Jews, gays, and gypsies during the Holocaust. Lively's book has been routinely dismissed by Holocaust scholars as full of inaccurate, revisionist history, and despite his declaration that he does not promote violence, several former Watchmen members were also linked to assaults at gay-pride events throughout the western United States. In 2007, several members were charged in the death of Satender Singh, a 26-year-old man picnicking with friends when self-identified church members attacked him because they thought he was gay (Sanchez, 2007). Singh, who was not gay, died from his injuries.

Although the representation of gays on these sites is disturbing, the techniques employed are rather commonplace. Reducing individuals to a singular trait, particularly an undesirable one, lays the groundwork for hate against them. Representing any individual as a single-dimension being, especially through a representation as contentious as "deviant," "predatory," or "pedophile" begins the process of dehumanizing them. And once a person is seen as less than human, targeting him for verbal or physical violence becomes much more acceptable.

Another shared characteristic of anti-gay Web sites is the encouragement of some type of call to action or advocacy. While most anti-gay sites are steeped in Christian dogma, some also encourage participation in the "fight" to stop gays and lesbians. The Westboro Baptist Church (WBC), through its site *Godhatesfags.com*, promotes pickets against popular community, business, and civic leaders whom they believe support gay rights initiatives. Most recently, the WBC has catapulted itself into the worldwide spotlight by protesting at the funerals of fallen service men and women because it believes that God is punishing America for its tolerance of gays and lesbians by killing soldiers in Iraq and Afghanistan. The group often shows up at funerals with signs reading "God Loves Crippled Soldiers" and "Thank God for Dead Soldiers." The WBC's efforts have resulted in a federal law and several state laws banning protests within certain distances of cemeteries. And when in 2011 it posted its plans to protest the funeral of a 9-year-old girl killed during a shooting spree at a meeting with Arizona Representative Gabrielle Giffords, the outcry was immediate. Among those was Angel Action, a group of individuals sporting giant angel wings that block any view of WBC's offensive protest signs. The tactic was first used 10 years earlier when friends of murdered Wyoming college student Matthew Shepard encircled WBC protestors to protect his family. Still, WBC boasts on its Web site of having staged more than 45,000 protests and features hundreds of photos to memorialize its efforts.

Finally, it is worth noting that all anti-gay Web sites share two other common elements: justification of their hatred rooted in biblical teachings and use of American patriotism to promote the virtues of hating gays and lesbians. The use of the Bible as authority is a staple throughout, reinforcing the divine justification for hatred and bigotry against gays and lesbians. Absent any scientific, legal, or statistical evidence to support their claims, these groups rely on their interpretation and enforcement of God's word as their sole authority. After all, there's no need to defend one's position when it has been ordained by God.

A second characteristic is the representation of anti-gay imagery in terms of American patriotism and symbols. Many sites include American flags, songs, and strong patriotic images such as the bald eagle to imply that homosexuality is un-American, and that it is a citizen's responsibility to combat homosexuality. One cartoon features Uncle Sam in his typical finger-pointing stance proclaiming "I WANT YOU - TO HATE FAGS."

COMBATING ANTI-GAY SPEECH AND CYBER HATE

When the polarizing and disinhibiting effects of cyber communities lead to the spread of hate, questions often arise as to whether these expressions are protected speech under the First Amendment. Throughout our nation's history, the concept of free speech has been valued, and is typically questioned only when it conflicts with other universally acknowledged values such as national security and public safety. Supreme Court rulings historically have extended Constitutional protection to all speech unless such speech encourages imminent incitement to violence or serves as *fighting words*—words which by their very utterance inflict injury or tend to incite violence. As evidenced by the federal and state laws aimed at WBC's funeral protests, jurisdictions can establish reasonable buffer zones to narrowly restrict such protests for privacy and public safety reasons. But the speech itself, whether verbal or visual, may not be banned.

So what's to be done to combat the hatred and violence advocated on anti-gay Internet sites? Until such speech crosses the line into advocacy of imminent criminal behavior against gays and lesbians, it's protected by the very same laws that prohibit censorship of Web sites providing useful resources to gay and lesbian youth.

The answer is more speech, not less. Undesirable (even bad) ideas are best countered not by censorship but by better, more enlightened speech. Although it may not be comforting to those who find themselves targets of hateful rhetoric, it is best when hate speech is out in the open. Without their protected right to expose themselves and their rhetoric, the messages of anti-gay groups would flourish in an underworld of hate never subjected to public scrutiny. WBC's funeral protests are now met with peaceful counter-protests by Angel Action, and by the United Protectors and the Patriot Guard, motorcyclist groups that assure a soldier's family will never hear WBC's hate-filled rhetoric. It represents the root value of the First Amendment and the best of our humanity as undesirable speech is countered with better speech and not with violence.

IT'S YOUR TURN: WHAT DO YOU THINK? WHAT WILL YOU FIND?

1. The author claims that "the answer is more speech, not less." Divide into groups representing various sides of this issue. Debate the topic: "Should hate speech on the Internet be allowed?"

2. What, if anything, do you think should be done about hate speech on the Internet? Should it be banned? Require that users be 18-years or older? Given a rating so that parents can block access from their children? What are some other options?

3. Imagine you're designing a system to prevent hate speech from being posted on the Internet. How might you accomplish this task? Who might determine what should or shouldn't be allowed? On what grounds might the decisions be based—in other words, what would be okay, what wouldn't, and why?

4. Log onto a Web site of a group working to combat Internet hate. You can do a search to find one or look at those of these advocacy groups: Southern Poverty Law Center (*www.splcenter.org or www. tolerance.org*), Anti-Defamation League (*www. adl.org*), or Patriot Guard Riders (*http:// patriotguard.org*).

   What group(s) does this organization identify as spreading hate on the Internet? How do they define hate speech and determine that a group should be identified as a hate group? Do you agree/disagree with these definitions? How does the organization combat hate speech on the Internet? What approach or strategy does it take to counter those who spread hate? What can you do?

REFERENCES

Berrill, K.T. (1992). Anti-gay violence and victimization in the United States: An overview. In G. Herek & K. Berrill (Eds.), *Hate crimes: Confronting violence against lesbians and gay men* (p. 31). Newbury Park, CA: Sage.

U. S. Department of Justice. (2009). Federal Bureau of Investigation. *Hate crimes statistics, uniform crime report.* Retrieved October 9, 2011, from www2.fbi.gov/ucr/hc2009/index.html

Eisenstein, Z. (2000). The politics of hate. In R. Gottesman (Ed.), *Violence in America: An encyclopedia* (Vol. 2, pp. 93–94). New York: Charles Scribner's Sons.

Marriott, M. (1999, April 6). Extremists find open forum on the Internet. *The San Diego Union-Tribune*, 6–7.

Sanchez, C. (2007). *The Latvian connection.* Southern Poverty Law Center, August, 1–7.

Saslow, E. (2008, June 22). Hate groups' newest target. *The Washington Post*, A3.

Southern Poverty Law Center (2010a). *Hate map.* Montgomery, AL: Simon Wiesenthal Center.

Southern Poverty Law Center (2010b). Anti-gay hate crimes: Doing the math. *Intelligence Report*, Winter, Issue 140. Montgomery, AL.

Vanderbilt, T. (2008). *Traffic: Why we drive the way we do and what it says about us.* New York: Vintage Books.

7.2   MINING THE OPINION OF THE GLOBE

Inas Y. Mahfouz

> *This reading is an example of computational analysis of opinions in human-generated online texts. The corpus under study is part of the* Global Pulse 2010, *a 3-day online jam discussing the hot issues that occupy people around the globe. The author focuses on the forum* "Empowering Women and Girls."

Do you consult online reviews before buying a product or watching a movie in the theatres? Have you ever voted in an online poll or considered the ratings of any product before obtaining it? Have you ever participated in online debates, discussion forums, and jams? If so, then you have probably used one of the Online Social Interactive Media (OSIM). OSIM facilitate the creation and exchange of user-generated content. They appeared in the 1990s because of the advent of several Internet-based applications. The appearance of OSIM has provided users with a new source of information that has never been available before. People can learn about others' opinions of products, politics, or any possible topic simply by surfing the Net to consult such opinionated sites. This in turn has called for a faster means for analyzing such opinionated documents; consequently, a new field of study, whose prime concern is the analysis of subjectivity in texts, emerged. The computational analysis of opinion in texts is usually referred to as Opinion Mining (OM) or Sentiment Analysis (SA).

OPINION MINING: WHAT, WHY, AND HOW

Opinion mining is "the quantitative and qualitative analysis of text for the purpose of determining its opinion-related properties (ORPs)" (Esuli & Sebastiani, 2007, p. 424). The objective of OM technologies is to extract opinions from unstructured human-authored documents. The computational treatment of opinion has been called brand monitoring, market analytics, online anthropology, opinion mining, sentiment analysis, and subjectivity analysis (Pang & Lee, 2008).

OM appeared in the first decade of the third millennium as a natural response to the ever-increasing amount of online opinionated documents and the users' need to analyze these documents to reach decisions about various issues, including politics, goods and services, movies, etc. Pang and Lee (2008) mention various possible applications of OM, including reputation management, public relations, trend prediction in sales, government intelligence (by monitoring sources of hostile communications), politics (to understand the opinion of voters or unravel the opinions of politicians to provide more information about them), and sociology (to analyze how new ideas spread). In fact OM has become an integral part of all aspects of everyday life. OM serves a wide range of purposes in almost all domains. It influences politics in two ways. First, politicians depend on OM to gather information about public opinion. Second, many people, especially younger generations, rely on the Internet for political news. According to a report published by Pew Research Center (2008), the Internet and specifically social networking sites played a clear role in the 2008 American Presidential elections as "more than a quarter of those younger than age 30 (27%) . . . have gotten campaign information from social networking sites" (2008, p. 2). And 27% of Americans aged 18–24 rely on social networking sites for information about candidates. Moreover, OM plays an influential role in marketing; before buying any product, consumers likely consult online reviews. The influence of social networking on marketing is "20 times higher than that for marketing events and 30 times that of media appearances" (Trusov, Bucklin, & Pauwels, 2009, p. 98). The influence of OM also extends to entertainment sites such as *Tomatometer* (www.rottentomatoes.com) and *Metacritic* (www.metacritic.com) which compile reviews of music albums, movies, games, etc. and give their users a final judgment.

OM is conducted on either word level or sentence and document level. The first approach is the semantic- or lexicon-based approach. It determines whether a certain word or phrase has positive or negative associations. The second approach is context based, investigating how the structure of a document and its domain affect its polarity.

Lexicon-based approaches usually concentrate on adjectives and adverbs, whereas document-based approaches have investigated sentence or document polarity. Today, several sites analyze online opinionated documents and provide users with final results. Tweetminster organizes Web content and messages posted to Twitter to create news and form opinion analysis. Sysomos provides two SA tools, namely: MAP (Media Analysis Platform) and Heartbeat. MAP analyzes online conversations, whereas Heartbeat provides this analysis in the form of user-friendly graphs.

OPINION MINING AND INTENSIFIERS

The present study examines intensifiers as a potential subjective element. An intensifier can be defined as "a point on an abstractly conceived intensity scale; and the point indicated may be relatively low or relatively high" (Quirk, Greenbaum, Leech, & Svartvik, 1985, p. 589). The reason for studying intensifiers in relation to OM is that they reflect some sort of subjectivity on part of the conceptualizers; "the conceptualizers are very much involved in projecting their own perspective on an entity" (Athanasiadou, 2007, p. 555). Although much OM study has concentrated on adjectives and adverbs as potential subjectivity elements, intensifiers have not attracted much attention from researchers, which makes this study an important step.

Intensifiers have a fuzzy and complicated nature that renders them difficult to understand and analyze. Some linguists refer to intensifiers as degree adverbs, subjuncts, mood adjuncts, or degree intensifiers. I use the term "intensifier" throughout this reading.

The present study depends on Paradis' (1997) categorization which divides intensifiers into five paradigms according to their degree. These paradigms are: maximizers, boosters, approximators, moderators, and diminishers. Members of the same paradigm have almost the same degree. However, it should be noted that the five paradigms form a continuum from maximum to minimum; maximizers such as *quite, absolutely, completely, perfectly, totally, entirely, utterly,* and *dead* have more reinforcing power than approximators such as *almost.* Similarly, moderators such as *quite, rather, pretty,* and *fairly* have more attenuating power than diminishers such as *a (little) bit, slightly, a little,* and *somewhat.* You will notice that *"quite"* can perform two different roles, depending on context, but such difference is ignored in this study because it does not affect the final results.

Paradis' (1997) model is very similar to Quirk et al's (1985) system, but it adds two important dimensions: totality and scaling. Some intensifiers reflect totality such as *completely, absolutely,* and *utterly,* while others express a degree on a scale like *somewhat, a bit,* and *very.* This perspective has not been tackled by any other model of intensifiers, and it makes Paradis' categorization more appropriate for studying subjectivity in documents. According to Paradis (1997; 2000), both "totality" and "scalar" intensifiers can reinforce or attenuate the modified adjective or adverb. Maximizers are reinforcing totality intensifiers, whereas approximators are attenuating totality modifiers.

The corpus used here is the participants' posted contributions of *Global Pulse 2010.* This is a 3-day online collaborative jam organized by the U.S. government to bring together nearly 7,000 socially engaged participants from different corners of the world. The aim of the jam was to learn the opinions of thousands of participants about 10 key issues, such as empowering women, education, and democracy. Because all posts represent opinionated documents, *Global Pulse 2010* provides an excellent corpus for this type of analysis.

Furthermore, by focusing on a forum called "Empowering Women and Girls," I am able to understand the participants' opinions about how to accomplish such empowerment. This was the most active forum of the 10 in the event, with 1,620 postings representing a corpus of 191,495 words. Females contributed 77% of the content of this forum; males and participants who did not reveal their gender posted the rest. According to the Global Pulse 2010 (2010) content and analysis report, the postings have touched upon various topics, such as "women & technology, the meaning of empowerment, the use of media and empowerment, and improving education and training for women."

I used *Oxford Wordsmith Tools 5.0* (English Language Teaching Worldwide, 2010) to search for intensifiers and determine their role in OM. This tool is commonly used for analyzing texts, and allowed me to examine the frequency of intensifiers and the contexts in which they occur, so I could estimate their role as potential subjectivity clues.

USING INTENSIFIERS TO MINE THE OPINION OF THE GLOBE

Mining opinions concerning the empowerment of girls and women required two preparatory steps. The fuzzy nature of intensifiers and the different roles they perform necessitate establishing a syntactic constraint on the study. The analysis has been restricted to intensifiers of adjectives for two main reasons: subjectivity is commonly expressed through adjectives, and second because "degree is commonly associated with the class of adjectives" (Paradis, 1997, p. 19). Before conducting the analysis, I divided the corpus into three subcorpora: one for postings by females, another for postings by males, and a third for postings by those who didn't report their gender. This division facilitates the comparison between males' and females' use of intensifiers.

The subcorpora were analyzed in three stages. First, the overall frequency of each of the items under investigation was calculated; second, the frequency of each was calculated for each of the three subcorpora; lastly, the syntactic constraint was applied to determine whether it is followed by an adjective or is used in any other context. Table 1 sums up the results of the analysis;

TABLE 1   The Distribution of Intensifiers over the Corpus and the Three Subcorpora

INTENSIFIER	TOTAL FREQ.	MALE	FEMALE	GENDER UNKNOWN	EXAMPLE
Most	347	26	100	4	Markets should have little government intervention so as they can work most efficiently
Very	329	71	247	11	Fighting battles with women can be very difficult and sad.
Well	212	9	27	1	These are traits that are particularly well suited to women, and from my experience as educator, with great success.
Enough	84	3	3	0	They are not enough informed about their rights, but I am convinced that it is not only a legal problem.
Rather	60	0	4	1	Dear Gillian My opinion of single-sex schools is rather short. To me they are just a means to separate males from females.
Totally	50	2	10	0	Both are totally unacceptable in today's world.
Quite	40	3	24	0	I think the program is very meaningful. It shows win-win benefits. Indeed I am quite interested in your program.
Completely	33	1	5	0	Such low awareness prevents them from realizing that they live in a parallel world, completely disconnected from ours (that of the educated lot).
Almost	29	1	3	0	So she grows up almost 'empty-headed' and follows all forms of ideas in the form of tradition.
Highly	24	6	15	0	Money is highly valued, and much status and power are attached to this.
Absolutely	21	2	6	0	Jennifer, You're absolutely right.
Extremely	19	4	14	0	In the whole of Morocco, there is an extremely high illiteracy rate, especially in the countryside.
A little	11	0	6	1	Would you be able to expand on what you meant when you said (in your earlier post) that it was a little more controversial in Azerbaijan?

the first column gives the intensifier; the second states its total frequency in the three subcorpora; and the third, fourth, and fifth columns provide the frequency of the intensifier in each subcorpus after applying the syntactic constraint. It should be noted that intensifiers whose overall frequency is less than 10 (e.g. *slightly, somewhat,* and *fairly*) have been ignored. Other intensifiers such as *jolly* and *dead* did not appear in the corpus at all.

One of the most important observations about the corpora is that 100% of "intensifier plus adjective" occurrences express clear subjective opinions, which support the assumption that intensifiers can easily be used as subjectivity clues. Furthermore, the frequency of scaling intensifiers is much higher than that of totality intensifiers. The most frequent scaling intensifier is *most*, while the most frequent totality intensifier is *totally*. Attenuators are less frequent than reinforcers; only three attenuators appear in the corpus, and their frequency is not very high. Moreover, females tend to use intensifiers more than males do. The frequency of each intensifier in the postings by females is three times or more that in the postings by males. Females make excessive use of the intensifier *very*, and sometimes even it is repeated for emphasis, for example, "However, even though governments may claim about doing a lot from women, still there are very very few examples of gender positive policies." Finally, some intensifiers such as *very* and *extremely* are always followed by adjectives.

EMPOWERING WOMEN AND GIRLS: FIVE MAIN THEMES REVEALED

My focus on the "Empowering Women and Girls" forum was not only because it was the largest forum, but also because the forum specifically addresses equality for a subset of the world's population that is often oppressed. My analysis of the intensifiers revealed five main themes in the corpus. The themes were identified through the use of intensifiers, as each of these opinions appeared over and over again throughout the forum. Participants of both genders relied extensively on intensifiers to express their strong attitude regarding these themes.

One theme raised by participants is *the importance of education for women*; several participants expressed their concern about the high levels of illiteracy especially among women: "there is an extremely high illiteracy rate, especially in the countryside, and especially among women." Consequently, education plays a very important role in empowering women. "Education is paramount! It is the single most important tool to [e]nhance women's self-worth." Discussions also touched upon ways of improving education and the influence this would have on women: "What kind/style/type of education is most important for empowering women and girls?" "Quality of education is definitely very important."

A second theme is *the necessity of including men in any attempt to empower women*. This can take place through one of two ways. The first is to educate young boys about positive gender norms. For example: "We need to be promoting equity and positive gender norms (and modeling this behavior) with very young children to enable future social change that transform social gender norms for the future." The second technique is to encourage men and boys to engage in conversation about women and raise their awareness of the role of women in societies and the necessity of appreciating it: "There is some very innovative work coming out of Africa, emerging GBV strategies which engage men and boys." "The most effective approach tends to bring men and boys into the conversation. Ask them how they think about their mothers and sisters."

Third, the intensifiers used by participants revealed the theme of *the value of economic empowerment of women*. Postings pointed out that governments should devise programs that help women develop financially. Eventually, economic empowerment of women would facilitate attaining political power: "It is very important for governments to develop strategies to create a platform where women are empowered to realize their full potential. Women must be provided with enterprise development training and access to technology skills." "When they [women] are powerful economically, they can influence not only young girls but they can start a tribe and this will make the famous ""butterfly effect"" . . . by starting a new trend and they will be enough powerful to convince their political leaders."

Satirizing patriarchal practices is the fourth theme that emerged in women's use of intensifiers. Women stated that in several societies men dominate women completely; they get all the benefits and sometimes even use violence against women: "That is quite . . . pathetic. And we can see that although females can be more independent now, many males still don't want to admit this fact." "Nigeria is a highly patriarchal society, where men dominate all spheres of women's lives, both public and private." "How does a society/country change its values so that violence against women is totally unacceptable and punished?"

Finally, intensifiers also revealed *the image of women in media,* and participants evaluate the influence of this on the status of women in their societies: "Otherwise our children see the proof on TV that mums are totally right at their workplace in a kitchen. And men earning the money." "Thanks for the sharing. You are totally right. You just hit the core of media business towards women. I call it 'business' because media make women a product for selling."

Some participants suggested that media should play a clear role in empowering women: "I agree media is an extremely powerful tool to advance any cause, especially when the strategy behind the project is well researched and implemented." "Amy, your presentation is quite fantastic using the media as a form of empowerment of women."

EMPOWERING WOMEN AND INTENSIFIERS: A FINAL NOTE

Global Pulse 2010 facilitated a global conversation about problems that worry citizens in different parts of the globe. The fact that "Empowering Women and Girls" became the largest forum in this global conversation reflects the importance of the topic. Participants of both genders manipulated intensifiers to voice their concerns about the status quo of women and the challenges they face. Postings addressed a range of themes pertaining to the topic of the forum, including the importance of educating women and how to develop education, the role of men in empowering women and how to change old-fashioned patriarchal stereotypes, economic empowerment of women, and finally the role of media in empowering women. This proves that this forum not only revealed the problems but also pinpointed solutions.

IT'S YOUR TURN: WHAT DO YOU THINK? WHAT WILL YOU FIND?

1. Log on to *Tomatometer (rottentomatoes.com)* and see the ratings of a movie that you have recently watched. Decide if you agree or not with this rating and add your own.

2. Visit *tweetsentiments.com* and analyze tweets pertaining to a topic of your interest. Compare the value of positive, negative, and neutral sentiment. Are these values similar to your expectations?

3. WebCONC is a free online concordancer that generates concordances (a list of words in a text along with their immediate context) of Web pages. Use WebCONC to obtain a concordance of all the

words of an online product review. You should focus on intensifiers and their role in the detection of subjectivity.

4. Of the five main themes revealed by the sentiment analysis, which do you think is the most important in empowering women and girls? Why?

REFERENCES

Athanasiadou, A. (2007). On the subjectivity of intensifiers. *Language Sciences, 29,* 554–565.

English Language Teaching Worldwide. (2010). Retrieved October 5, 2010, from http://www.oup.com/elt/catalogue/guidance_articles/ws_form?cc=global

Esuli, A., & Sebastiani, F. (2007). PageRanking WordNet synsets: An application to opinion mining. *Proceedings of the 45th Annual Meeting of the Association for Computational Linguistics (ACL'07),* (pp. 424–431).

Global Pulse 2010 (2010, September 2). *Analysis Forum: Empowering Women and Girls.* Retrieved November 5, 2010, from http://www.globalpulse2010.gov/topic2.pdf

Pew Research Center for the People and the Press. (2008). *Social networking and online sources take off: Internet's broader role in campaign 2008.* Retrieved October 8, 2011, from http://people-press.org/reports/pdf/384.pdf

Pang, B., & Lee, L. (2008). *Opinion mining and sentiment analysis.* Retrieved October 8, 2011, from http://www.cs.cornell.edu/home/llee/omsa/omsa.pdf

Paradis, C. (1997). *Degree modifiers of adjectives in spoken British English.* Lund: Lund University Press.

Paradis, C. (2000). It's well weird. Degree modifiers of adjectives revisited: The nineties. In J. M. Kirk (Ed.), *Corpora galore: analyses and techniques in describing English* (pp. 147–160). Amesterdam: Radopi.

Quirk, R., Greenbaum, S., Leech, G., & Svartvik, J. (1985). *A comprehensive grammar of the English language.* London: Longman.

Trusov, M., Bucklin, R. E., & Pauwels, K. (2009, September). Effects of word-of-mouth versus traditional marketing: Findings from an Internet social networking site. *Journal of Marketing, 73,* 90–102.

7.3   COMMUNITY BLOGGING AS RELATIONAL AND IDENTITY RESOLUTION: GENDER, RACE, AND THE *POSTSECRET* PHENOMENON

Jody D. Morrison

This reading looks at the PostSecret *blog—a site where people's secrets are publicly posted. The author investigates the role of blogging in identity and relationship maintenance, and argues that blogging can provide a unique forum for the potential resolution of issues pertinent to men, women, and their relationships.*

"When I fight with my Marine Corps father . . . I feel like describing all the gay sex I've had."

This message was typed on white paper, cut into pieces, and glued to a postcard adhered with the image of the award-winning photograph, Raising the Flag on Iwo Jima. The postcard was anonymously sent to the home of Frank Warren in Germantown, Maryland, and then appeared on Warren's blog, *postsecret.blogspot.com* on February 3, 2008. This postcard might also eventually appear in one of Warren's books, in a slideshow at one of his lectures, or as part of a national or international art gallery exhibit.

Why would this person choose to self-disclose by creating and mailing a postcard to a stranger? Why would people want to share a secret knowing it might appear in a public forum like a blog? This reading addresses a unique and popular community blog designed to showcase people's anonymous secrets artfully constructed on postcards and mailed to a stranger who requested them. After describing the history of Warren's project, an analysis of the *PostSecret* phenomenon will shed light on the role of blogging in identity and relationship maintenance. Blogging also provides a unique forum for the potential resolution of issues pertinent to men, women, and their relationships.

THE HISTORY OF *POSTSECRET*

While vacationing in Paris, France, in 2003, small businessman and "accidental artist" (Gammage, 2005, E6) Frank Warren bought three postcards of Antoine de Saint Exupery's *The Little Prince*. Before bed that night, he put the cards in the nightstand drawer, went to sleep, and had a vivid dream about the cards. He dreamt that he opened that very drawer and found the cards with messages written on their backs. One of the cards read, "You will find your answers in the secrets of strangers." The next Sunday, Warren began thinking about an art project involving postcards and secrets, which became *PostSecret*.

Starting in November 2004, Warren distributed 3,000 postcards inviting people to share anonymous secrets. One side of the postcard was his home address, as well as directions to transform the other side of the postcard from a blank canvas so that it could become part of a community art project. Messages were to be legible, brief, creative, and to reveal anything truthful that had never been shared with anyone. Warren distributed the cards on the street, in the library, in metro stations, left them in art galleries—and people started mailing them back. The cards often address provocative topics like marriage, parenting, abortion, infidelity, repressed fantasies, coming out, office romances, and incest. As he received them, he exhibited them in Washington, D.C.'s annual Artomatic multimedia arts event. After the exhibit closed and he had stopped passing out the cards, people kept sending him cards, but not the ones he had distributed. People created their own cards and "somehow the idea of *PostSecrets* spread virally in the real world" (Warren, 2008).

Warren wanted to keep sharing the cards that came in, so he created a blog, now the largest advertisement-free blog on the Web, where he displays a selection of the cards and viewer responses, updating the blog every Sunday by replacing the old cards with the new (they are not archived). Every Saturday night, Warren selects cards for the blog from about 1,000 secrets he receives during the week. He thinks of himself "almost like a film editor, taking these little visions of people's lives and connecting them together to tell this narrative" (Warren, 2008).

Over 150,000 postcards later, the cards have been featured in a popular music video (*My Dirty Little Secret* by The All-American Rejects). Warren has published four books and appeared on most major news broadcasts. Selected cards are displayed in traveling art exhibits and numerous art gallery shows in the United States and abroad. In January 2005, when federal funds ended for the 1-800-SUICIDE hotline, Warren's plea for funds on his site resurrected it. Warren also recently started *PostSecret* blogs in France (postsecretfrance.blogspot.com) and Germany (postsecretdeutsch.blogspot.com).

WHY SELF-DISCLOSE ON A POSTCARD?

The choice to self-disclose, revealing information about yourself that is unknown to others, is a decision everyone faces in the course of relationships. As part of deciding whether to disclose, we weigh the perceived risks and rewards by considering the topic of the disclosure, characteristics of the intended recipient, the context, and most important, the perceived impact on the relationship. Although we certainly do self-disclose at times without giving it much thought (oftentimes with regret), we also do approach disclosing as an important relational turning point. Sometimes though, as a result of considering the costs and benefits, we also choose not to self-disclose (Thibaut & Kelley, 1959).

Given the decision not to self-disclose, we are faced with the challenge of private rumination about the issue we once considered sharing. For some people, this is comforting; for others, it is quite painful.

Given these options, the choice to self-disclose by creating and mailing a postcard to a stranger is an interesting phenomenon. The fashioning of the secret on a small canvas like a card gives people the opportunity to visually represent what they may not be able to share with someone face-to-face. They can depict on the card what they cannot put into words. Perhaps through the creation of the card, people are able to work through the issue represented in the secret.

The small size of the typical card, 4x6 inches, might matter as well. Maybe people feel like their secret is more manageable if it can fit on a postcard. The small size might also make it possible for people who are not generally creative to have confidence in some artistic ability. The visual elements are usually quite compelling and help portray the message. As you can see from the selection of cards if you check out the blog, some people spend a great deal of time selecting the images to complement what they write. Many of the visual elements are clipped or altered images from other sources. Some appear to be unique works of art and graphic design. Sometimes it's hard to tell what is unique and what is re-appropriated. Some cards are, indeed, just writing, but very few cards have no writing whatsoever.

WHY SELF-DISCLOSE ON A POSTCARD AND SEND IT TO A STRANGER. . . ?

Creating a postcard is but one part of this process—self-disclosing on a card that you keep to yourself is not as beneficial as mailing it to a stranger. At least that is what my students tell me. For 2 years, I engaged my interpersonal communication undergraduates in a classroom activity that involved students researching, creating, and exchanging anonymous postcard secrets and writing an essay about the process. My students revealed that creating the postcard is insufficient, and the real benefit comes from mailing it in so that it is shared. You get to self-disclose, but not to the involved recipient, thus eliminating any potential perceived relational fallout. In their essays, some students admitted to not participating in the exchange part of the activity (which intended to simulate the "mailing" of the cards), and some confessed to not putting a lot of effort into creating their card. They admitted feeling left out, since after seeing the number and quality of other student cards, they believed they missed out on the benefits others had received. They felt that they had not fully self-disclosed. So, what then is the benefit of mailing the postcard to Warren? It is the "unburdening of the secret to the world," one student wrote, "it doesn't feel as heavy inside knowing that someone else knows."

Warren is often asked why he thinks people mail in the postcards and confess their secrets. At a lecture he gave at my university, he said: "If you look at the cards you know that some people just want to share a funny story or talk about a sexual taboo, but other people in other cards, they are so painstakingly made and they have such detail and the secrets are complex, and I think other people might be sharing secrets in order to search for grace or authenticity or maybe to understand their secret in a new way, maybe to redefine a part of their past in a more empowering way" (2008, January 31).

. . . WHO POSTS IT ON HIS BLOG?

Students also report they like the idea of sending a card to Warren, not just because he is a stranger, but specifically because they know that it might appear on the blog. Students who submit postcards tell me that they get caught up in monitoring the site to see if their card is selected. Many report feelings of excitement, relief, and resolution about the shared issue when their card is posted on the blog—even if it is only displayed for a week. The blog is a unique forum, unlike the experience of, for example, writing a secret on a bathroom stall. If your card appears on the blog, it has a (perceived) large audience who can choose to give anonymous feedback. This is what in part makes the *PostSecret* blogs unique—not only do people contribute to the blog by sending in cards, but they can also post comments—it truly is a "community" blog. So for the *PostSecret* artist who cannot discuss issues of sexuality with his/her Marine-Corps father, one can imagine that perhaps he/she has gained some strength or clarity about his/her sexual identity knowing that blog viewers have read the secret. Perhaps the sender envisions compassion from this blog audience, maybe even a response submitted to the site, such that the problems apparent in this parent-child relationship will be assuaged.

Sharing a secret on the blog might also be a way to help others. Knowing the large viewership, perhaps submitting a secret is a way to "give back" to a community of like-minded people. Warren suggests that sharing secrets are "cathartic and therapeutic" and can "bring a sense of healing" not only to your own life but to the community (Warren, 2008).

In addition to facilitating identity issue resolution or giving back to the community, my students have told me that the blog is a perfect forum for sharing things they otherwise cannot reveal in their relationships, especially their most intimate ones. Gammage suggests that people view the blog "as the Internet version of a confessional, a kind of virtual therapist's couch" (2005, p. E6).

Communication scholars, especially Sandra Petronio (2000), argue that the viability of a relationship is dependent upon one's ability to manage disclosures in a relationship. Her theory of privacy management is centrally concerned with the inevitable tensions, or "relational dialectics," we face between privacy and openness, between being private and being public (Baxter & Montgomery, 1996). In relationships we are constantly managing these boundaries—navigating what we want to share and what we do not. Sometimes the boundary is permeable, and sometimes it's not. The permeability of a boundary will change over time and depending on the circumstance. A closed boundary can provide safety and autonomy, whereas an open boundary can promote intimacy, but with greater vulnerability. This theory suggests that the public self-disclosures on *PostSecret* postcards help people balance the tensions they experience in their relationships so that the relationships can be maintained.

The *PostSecret* blog is really then a conversation between strangers, with text and pictures instead of talk and nonverbal cues, about things we cannot share within our relationships. The individual secrets are not necessarily what draw people to the blog, rather their desire to make connections. Although the first connection is between the postcard creator and Warren, Warren then has the choice to expand the connection to the online community worldwide. Warren helps people connect, as McLuhan (1964) posits, by providing the medium for a global village, extending our senses, bodies, and minds through the blog.

Warren also started a *PostSecret* chatroom space on the U.S. blog (in English and French), called "PostSecret Community," which further facilitates these connections. The English "Community" is divided into 10 different forums, including "ages 20 and over," "ages 35 and over," "the LGBT community," and "advice."

WHAT SECRETS ARE PEOPLE SHARING?

So now that we know a little about *why* people are disclosing on a postcard (to a stranger hoping it might appear on a blog), you might be wondering just *what* people are sharing. According to Warren, the most common secret submitted is not that lofty. Warren receives the secret, "I pee in the shower," artistically rendered in many different ways at least two times a week (Warren, 2008). However, other patterns and trends have also emerged. He reports receiving a "surprisingly large number of secrets" dealing with issues related to body image, eating disorders, self-harm, and suicide. Here are a few examples:

- *Sometimes I wish that I was blind, just so I wouldn't have to look at myself everyday in the mirror* (2005).
- *I can't pee with someone next to me . . . I fear someone will see my small penis* (2006).
- *When I eat, I feel like a failure* (2005).
- *For years I tried to hurt myself so that he'd notice me* (2005).
- *I've stopped cutting myself but started plucking my pubic hair with tweezers instead* (2005).
- *I was seven years old the first time I attempted suicide* (2005).
- *Every time I approach an overpass, I think how easy it would be to simply turn the wheel ever so slightly to the left and find peace, at long last . . .* (2005).

Another common theme in the cards is "longing for intimacy – which can also be seen as frustrations with a boyfriend or girlfriend - not wanting to be alone" (Hiaasen, 2007, p. 3E). Here are some selections from the *PostSecret* blog on February 11, 2008 (just before St. Valentine's Day) that exemplify this theme:

- *I wish you still loved me the way you did when we drove down this road in Montauk.*
- *If I could only fall out of love with you I would.*
- *I still don't believe you love me.*
- *The only thing worse than being single on St. Valentine's day is wishing you were single.*

He has also received secrets on more than just 4x6 postcards, including on parking tickets, report cards, yearbook pages, maps, sonograms, photographs, napkins, CDs, hotel card keys, and even on a one-pound bag of coffee. It appears as if people select a particular correspondence format to become part of the message. For example, the following secret was submitted on a cracked and damaged video tape: *I destroy videos of myself as a child because it pains me to see a time before I ruined my innocence* (Warren, 2007b). This message was typed on a part of a death certificate: *I never kissed my son after he was born because he was sick and I was scared. He died 2 hours later . . .* (Warren, 2007b).

GENDER AND RACE ON *POSTSECRET*

Although Warren has identified some patterns and themes suggesting that many of us struggle with common problems, he also acknowledges noticing a subtle gender difference among post-card creators. "Even though men and women both keep secrets, women keep the best secrets. Women have these rich, creative, interior lives" exposed in these cards (Warren, 2008). He suggests that perhaps part of it has to do with social power, in that men still have more power than women and may feel more freedom to express emotions. Perhaps this is why postcard senders are mostly women (Zayas, 2005, p. 1). Although women may be more emotionally expressive, they may not have as many outlets as men in which to share. *PostSecret* might thus be especially valuable to women. In addition, Warren said that a recent survey indicated that "among college women, *PostSecret* is viewed more often than eBay, Amazon or Yahoo" (Hiassen, 2007, p. 3E).

According to Warren, of his four books, *The Secret Lives of Men and Women* (2007a) primarily represents issues relevant to both genders. He contrasts secrets from men and women, but also shows their similarities. Key themes include issues related to choice of partner, sex (fantasies, sexual identity, promiscuity), parenting, infidelity, divorce, and pregnancy (birth control, miscarriage, abortion). Here are a few examples:

- *I often wonder what it would have been like if I chose the "other man" instead of my husband.*
- *Sorry that I'm a horny bastard and wouldn't let you sleep last night. I suck, I know. Have a good day babe.*
- *To save time in the morning I always put my kids to bed with clothes, shoes and socks on!*
- *My wife is having an affair with my neighbor's wife. They don't know that I know.*
- *I knew I was gay on my wedding day but wanted children and feared aids* (sic)
- *It's not his baby.*
- *I will never forgive myself for letting my girlfriend get an abortion.*
- *Sometimes I feel like I lied to you when I said I was ok with not having children . . .*

It is important to note that the gender of the postcard creator in many of the cards is not always evident, unless as a specific part of the verbal message or visual element. My students told me that if the gender of the sender wasn't obvious, they tried to figure it out by analyzing handwriting style ("too puffy for a guy"), colors used ("no guy would own a sparkly marker"), and sometimes the amount of effort put into creating the card (the more effort, the more likely it was perceived to be created by a woman).

Although Warren doesn't seem to have explicitly referred to race on *PostSecret*, my review of the cards he's posted since the start of the blog suggests a couple of interesting findings. The books and the site seem to be a neutral, racially level playing field for those with secrets to share. Racial identity has all but vanished on the blog, or at least has been rendered invisible (either by postcard creators or by the selection process). When race is revealed, although not a common theme, it is only as part of an "issue" disclosed or as part of the visual on a card, and is usually about a mixed-race relationship, prejudice, or someone coming to terms with racial identity. Here are ALL the *PostSecret* messages in Warren's four books (2005, 2006, 2007a, 2007b) that I could easily identify as overtly dealing with race. Interestingly, in the first *PostSecret* book, cards specifically dealing with race were placed together.

- *I use the word nigger* (2005).
- *I love black girls and I am white* (2005).

- *I wish I was white* (2005).
- *I feel ugly because I'm half-black, half-white* (2005).
- *My boss is Black, I've dated Black men, I have friends of all ethnic backgrounds and I am a minority, too . . . but I'm still a racist* (2005).
- *I'm extra nice to blacks to show them that I am nothing like my forefathers* (2006).

IF YOU SHARE A SECRET, IS IT STILL A SECRET?

My students thoroughly enjoyed discussing the *PostSecret* phenomenon, and I'd like to report one final question we pondered. We wondered whether this self-disclosure process changes the nature of secrets—is it no longer a secret if you share it, even if you don't know the recipient? The responses were mixed, but most believed that in sharing the secret, the secret and the person disclosing it are changed. Warren, however, has a different perspective. He says that his blog contains "living secrets," especially since he has more freedom to post offensive, obscene, violent, and sexual comments (Warren, 2008).

So what changes about the secret varies, perhaps depending on whether you are the postcard artist, or the blog viewer. I believe the answer lies in the double meaning of *PostSecret*, it's not just a secret one posts in the mail, but in posting the secret, you are now beyond its hold.

IT'S YOUR TURN: WHAT DO YOU THINK? WHAT WILL YOU FIND?

1. Visit the *PostSecret* blog and read the cards and feedback submitted to the site for the week. What strikes you the most about what you see?

2. While viewing the cards on the blog, do you find that you are attempting to identify the race and/or gender of the postcard creator? How is race and gender signified? How is it meaningful to be able to identify race or gender?

3. Would you consider creating and sending a card to the site? What kinds of issues would you need to consider to make your decision?

4. How do you feel about self-disclosing via postcard to Warren, fully aware of the potential for the card to be published in a book for profit?

REFERENCES

Baxter, L.A., & Montgomery, B.M. (1996). *Relating: Dialogues and dialectics*. New York: Guilford.

Gammage, J. (2005, July 7). A secret service. *The Philadelphia Inquirer*, E1, E6.

Hiaasen, R. (2007, December 30). Gathering and sharing secrets. *The Baltimore Sun*, p. 3E.

McLuhan, M. (1964). *Understanding media: The extensions of man*. New York: McGraw Hill.

Petronio, S. (2000). *Balancing the secrets of private disclosures*. Mahwah, NJ: Lawrence Erlbaum Associates.

Thibaut, J., & Kelley, H. (1959). *The social psychology of groups*. New York: Wiley.

Warren, F. (2005). *PostSecret*. New York: Harper Collins.

Warren, F. (2006). *My secret*. New York: Harper Collins.

Warren, F. (2007a). *The secret lives of men and women*. New York: Harper Collins.

Warren, F. (2007b). *A lifetime of secrets*. New York: Harper Collins.

Warren, F. (2008, January 31). Lecture at Salisbury University.

Zayas, A. (2005, July 19). Artist's blog shares secrets with the world. *Chicago Tribune*. Retrieved July 27, 2005, from *http://www.chicagotribune.com*

7.4 EMINEM'S *LOVE THE WAY YOU LIE* AND THE NORMALIZATION OF MEN'S VIOLENCE AGAINST WOMEN

Rachel Alicia Griffin and Joshua Daniel Phillips

> *The authors analyze* Love the Way You Lie *from a rhetorical feminist perspective and illuminate how the song strengthens cultural myths about domestic violence and subsequently normalizes men's violence against women. Before continuing, we urge you to go online to read the lyrics and watch the music video.*

Come inside, pick up your bags off the sidewalk
Don't you hear sincerity in my voice when I talk?
Told you this is my fault, look me in the eyeball
Next time I'm pissed, I'll aim my fist at the drywall
Next time? There won't be no next time
I apologize, even though I know it's lies
I'm tired of the games, I just want her back. I know I'm a liar
If she ever tries to fuckin' leave again,
I'ma tie her to the bed and set this house on fire.[1]

This is the final verse of Eminem's *Love the Way You Lie*, released in June 2010, and featuring pop/R&B singer Rihanna. The song was number one on the *Billboard* Hot 100 Chart for 11 weeks, and the music video premiered on MTV during the hit reality show *Jersey Shore*. Soon thereafter, Eminem, who has rapped about his violent behavior toward women, and Rihanna, who is publicly recognized as a survivor of intimate partner violence (often called domestic violence), performed live at the 2010 MTV Video Music Awards which had an estimated audience of 11.4 million (Carter, 2010).

We argue that the song's lyrics and video imagery reproduce cultural myths about domestic violence, including notions that: (1) men and women are equally responsible for perpetuating violence in relationships, (2) women "ask" to be abused, and (3) violence is a means to ignite sexual arousal.

Highlighting the prevalence of violence against women, Alhabib, Nur, and Jones (2010) assert, "Worldwide, domestic violence is as serious a cause of death and incapacity among women aged 15–49 years as cancer, and a greater cause of ill health than traffic accidents and malaria combined" (p. 370). With regard to teenage girls and young women in particular, approximately 20% have experienced dating violence (Silverman, Raj, Mucci, & Hathaway, 2001); those at the highest risk to be victimized are females aged 16–24 (Rennison & Welchans, 2000). We recognize that males can be abused by female partners, but statistics show (Bureau of Justice Statistics, 2006; Tjaden & Thoennes, 2000) that women are close to three times more likely to experience domestic violence than men. Therefore through a feminist lens, we position intimate partner violence as a cultural epidemic that renders females systemically vulnerable to male aggression.

To critique *Love the Way You Lie*, we use a rhetorical feminist perspective (Hart & Daughton, 2005) to deconstruct the lived experiences the artists represent and the gendered implications of the song. A feminist critique promotes critical consumption of popular culture (Sellnow, 2010) which necessitates mindfulness toward the covert ways that sexism and patriarchy infiltrate our everyday lives. According to Johnson (2004), a society is patriarchal when it is dominated by males, identified according to masculine norms, and centered upon male interests. A feminist perspective also recognizes popular culture as far more than just entertainment; rather, popular culture is positioned as pedagogical (Brummett, 2011; Sellnow, 2010) which highlights the ways that audiences learn from what they see and hear via popular culture (Sandlin, 2007). Therefore, it is important to critique popular culture because mediated messages are capable of furthering the dehumanization and commodification of women (hooks, 1996; Kirk & Okazawa-Rey, 2010).

THE NORMALIZATION OF MEN'S VIOLENCE AGAINST WOMEN

Our analysis revealed three cultural myths depicted in *Love the Way You Lie* that function to normalize men's violence against women.

Men and Women Are Equally Responsible

The first cultural myth perpetuated by the song is that men and women are equally responsible for intimate partner violence. However, as noted earlier, although females can be violent toward male partners, the opposite (men attacking women) is the norm. Representations negating this reality rigorously reduce perceptions of male accountability. Consider Eminem's lyrics which continuously bring attention to the violent behavior of both partners. For example, during an abusive scene in the music video between Megan Fox[2] (the female partner) and Dominic Monaghan (the male partner), Eminem raps about how *both* Fox and Monaghan are enraged, and links their behaviors to their state of mind. He indicates that neither partner has a handle on their emotions, and therefore the collective and impersonal "rage" of the situation is at fault.

Later Eminem indicates that the two people have equally bad tempers. He compares one to a tornado and the other to a volcano. Referencing the partners as equally fierce natural disasters leads the audience to understand that men's and women's tempers in a violent relationship are comparable. This interpretation is problematic; it does not account for cultural systems privileging men through oppressing women. To symbolically depict men and women as equally sharing the blame in a violent relationship grossly undermines the social reality that men are more likely to be the cause of the violence. In the event that a female does engage in violence toward her male partner, she most likely does so to protect herself and/or her children (Campbell, Rose, Kub, & Nedd, 1998).

Because Fox and Monaghan are depicted as equally violent toward each other, it also becomes easy to dismiss their violence at the micro level without noting the epidemic prevalence of violence in heterosexual partnerships at the macro level. Representing both partners as violent excuses society's culpability because the issue is presented without the consideration of the systemic legacies of hegemonic masculinity and female oppression. The audience, especially males, can identify with Eminem's lyrics and the video's visual narrative which voice their frustrations with women and subsequently mark them as helpless men who become violent only when pushed over the edge by women. This interpretation, in accordance with dominant patriarchal ideologies, exonerates abusive males from responsibility for their choices and positions them as victims rather than frightening mirrors of society.

Women "Ask" to Be Abused

The second cultural myth, that women "ask" to be abused, beaten, and raped, is rooted in our patriarchal culture as a means to hold women responsible for the acts of violence perpetrated against them. This myth justifies men hurting women as an acceptable means to discipline and punish those who are not in alignment with patriarchal expectations of femininity. Despite the efforts of anti-gender violence activists to uproot this myth, it remains highly visible in cultural texts such as *Love the Way You Lie*.

A specific point of concern is Monaghan's character who is lyrically and visually represented as being *driven* to batter Fox's character. This idea surfaces during the music video when Monaghan violently slams Fox onto their bed after she slaps him on the chest. The audience witnesses Fox "enticing" him to beat her even to the point of engaging in violence herself.[3] Because Fox is depicted as the partner who gets physical first, the audience is given the perception that the woman is responsible for starting the violence. In this vein, it becomes possible to read the bruises on her face as justifiable. With that, the song reinforces the dominant ideological tendency to "blame the victim" which positions women at fault for the choices that their male counterparts make to hurt them (Kirk & Okazawa-Rey, 2010).

After this fight scene, Fox attempts to leave the house and presumably the relationship. As she approaches the front door, Monaghan grabs her shoulder bag causing her to spin around and the couple's fighting resumes. The imagery and lyrics offer two conclusions. First, if Fox had not hit Monaghan, he would not have been *forced* to use physical violence against her. Second, if Fox had not tried to leave, Monaghan would not have been *forced* to physically stop her. In both instances, we are beckoned to view Fox as the instigator and consequently view Monaghan's behavior as a reaction to that behavior.

The culmination of Fox's attempt to leave the relationship is summarized in Eminem's final lyrics of the song. The last three lines of the third verse present a musical narrative of what domestic violence looks like—corroborating the notion that the violence men inflict on women is only in response to the actions of women. Therefore, we can assume that if Fox would have "acted right" (i.e., in accordance with patriarchy), she would not have been physically abused, verbally abused, and eventually threatened with being burned alive. This logic not only assumes that men cannot control their anger, but also reinforces the idea that women, not men, need to change their behavior if they wish to end the cycle of domestic violence.

Violence Ignites Sexual Arousal

The third myth involves blurring the distinctions between violence and sex. We see this each time Rihanna sings:

> Just gonna stand there and watch me burn
> Well that's all right because I like the way it hurts.

Domestic violence is thus described as a passionate exchange between two lovers. By alluding to the idea that being abused is enjoyable because the pain is desirable, Rihanna encourages the audience to believe that women not only ask to be abused, but that they also take pleasure in being abused. The four times Rihanna mentions her enjoyment of the torment, her lips curl, she licks her fingers, and the audience is invited to extract sexualized meanings that directly correlate pain and pleasure. We read the lyrics coupled with Rihanna's lip curl as an enticing moment of audience appeal. Every close-up of Rihanna's voluptuous red lips becomes a sexualized symbol of how violence may be transformed into enticing lust. She appears to crave sexual contact overlapping with gratifying pain, which, in accordance with cultural myths about sex and love, allows violence to be misinterpreted as unbridled passion.

Coupled with Rihanna's lyrics are the images of Fox and Monaghan's characters living out the cycle of domestic violence. Throughout the video, the audience is bombarded with quick-cutting scenes illustrating their relationship as violent one moment and passionate the next. For example, after Fox has attempted to leave the house, Monaghan throws her against a wall and ferociously punches his hand through the drywall next to her head. After a quick cut to a remorseful Monaghan regretfully bowing his head, the two lovers instantaneously engage in hot passionate kissing, standing upright against the damaged wall.

The hypersexualized pushing, shoving, and punching between Fox and Monaghan are accompanied by Eminem's lyrics delivered with a tangible intensity:

> Got that warm fuzzy feeling, yeah, them chills, used to get 'em
> Now you gettin' fuckin' sick of lookin' at 'em
> You swore you'd never hit 'em, never do nothing to hurt 'em
> Now you're in each other's face spewing venom in your words when you spit 'em
> You push, pull each other's hair, scratch, claw, bit 'em
> Throw 'em down, pin 'em, so lost in the moments when you're with 'em.

This aggressive imagery coupled with the lyrics discursively invites the audience to blur the lines between romantic intimacy and domestic violence.

The repetitive cycles oscillating between violence and sex provide the foundational narrative for Fox and Monaghan's relationship throughout the music video. This oscillation subjects the audience to Monaghan and Fox's reconciliation represented as kissing, sex, and other forms of intimacy only to be thrown back into acts of physical and verbal abuse. Alarmingly, when the conflation of sex, passion, and violence in *Love the Way You Lie* is read from a feminist rhetorical standpoint, we bear witness to the ways that men's violence against a woman can be misinterpreted as sexual rather than criminal. At the end of the music video, the audience leaves these two intimate partners where we first encountered them: peacefully asleep in their bed, limbs harmoniously entangled.

THE POWER OF POPULAR CULTURE

The greatest danger of this song is the subtlety of the dominant messages imparted to casual listeners—so subtle that perhaps even Rihanna and Eminem genuinely believe that the song serves as a warning of the dangers of intimate partner violence. Yet, we must recognize that even if the song is intended and/or interpreted as a "warning" about the cycle of domestic violence, it serves as a warning to the women who are beaten rather than the men who choose to beat them. Therefore, men's violence against women is discursively positioned as a women's issue despite the overwhelming research and advocacy that positions violence against women as an issue caused by men (at the micro level) and patriarchy (at the macro level) (Kirk & Okazawa-Rey, 2010; Tjaden & Thoennes, 2000).

Incredibly indicative of the re-centering of male privilege, despite the song's depiction of the cycle of domestic violence, is Eminem's placement at the core of the song not only as the main artist but also as the perpetrator who sings being an abuser. In this context, Eminem's real-life persona as a musician who has rapped about his abuse of women in such songs as *Kim* and *My Mom* coupled with his role as the primary artist positions him at the center of attention. In contrast, Rihanna as the survivor (both in real life and in the song) is rendered to the periphery by way of singing the chorus and being the guest artist featured on Eminem's album.

To be fair, it is also important to mark this rhetorical text as a site of struggle. Borrowing from Brummett (2011), the song might be positioned as a "battlefield" of social and political forces where the line between healthy and unhealthy relationships is a struggle, the cycle of intimate partner violence is a struggle, and Fox and Monaghan literally struggle with each other. Likewise, the song lyrics and music video visibly position domestic violence in mainstream culture and accurately mark the cyclic nature of intimate partner violence. For instance, Eminem raps:

> Here we go again, it's so insane
> 'Cause when it's going good, it's going great
> I'm Superman with the wind in his back
> She's Lois Lane, but when it's bad, it's awful.

In addition, Fox is shown in the video attempting to leave the violent relationship three times, but is emotionally drawn (Monaghan offers her a teddy bear) and physically dragged (Monaghan grabs her shoulder bag) back despite her desire to break free. This specific representation mirrors the reality that most battered women attempt to leave several times before they leave for good or are murdered (Jenkins & Davidson, 2001). The final verse unequivocally marks the omnipresence of danger in violent intimate relationships. Thus, as Eminem indicates, false promises of changed behavior will not protect women.

Love the Way You Lie should be understood as a pedagogical rhetorical text that illustrates and reproduces cultural myths about domestic violence. Shockingly, "[m]ost women . . . experience a certain amount of what could be defined as sexual violence as part of daily life" (Kirk & Okazawa-Rey, 2010, p. 257). Naming this reality, Jensen (2009) offers "sexual intrusion" meaning the everyday nature of patriarchy that degrades female intellect, invades female bodies with unsolicited commentary, and imposes an omnipresent sense of fear. Deconstructed from a rhetorical feminist standpoint, *Love the Way You Lie* is exemplary of sexual intrusion as a pervasive popular culture text that perpetuates dangerous cultural myths about domestic violence and subsequently dehumanizes women as survivors and victims of gender violence. Although the intent of the artists may have been to shock their audience with images of burning homes and "private" moments, the results of their efforts clearly reproduce damaging messages concerning gender violence. Such reproductions unmistakably contribute to the normalization of men's violence against women.

NOTES

1. Words and Music by Alexander Grant, Marshall Mathers and Holly Haferman Copyright (c) 2010 Songs of Universal, Inc., Shroom Shady Music, Universal Music - Z Songs, Hotel Bravo Music and M Shop Publishing. All Rights for Shroom Shady Music Controlled and Administered by Songs of Universal, Inc.

All Rights for Hotel Bravo Music and M Shop Publishing Controlled and Administered by Universal Music- Z Songs. All Rights Reserved used by Permission.

2. Fox donated her appearance fee to a shelter for abused women (Dinh, 2010). Although this gesture was noteworthy and admirable, it did not receive nearly as much coverage as did her role in the video.

3. Our argument here is not to excuse or minimize the ways that Fox engages in violent behavior but rather to contextualize the differences between this representation of domestic violence and the realities of most battered women.

IT'S YOUR TURN: WHAT DO YOU THINK? WHAT WILL YOU FIND?

1. From your perspective, does *Love the Way You Lie* affirm and/or contest the normalization of men's violence against women? Which aspects of the authors' argument do you agree and/or disagree with?

2. Other singers, including Ludacris and Mary J. Blige (*Runaway Love*) and the Dixie Chicks (*Goodbye Earl*), have released songs about violence against women and girls. After listening to these songs, how are the messages that Eminem and Rihanna send in *Love the Way You Lie* similar and/or different?

3. Using clippings from magazines and newspapers, create a collage that resists the reproduction of cultural myths about intimate partner violence in *Love the Way You Lie*. Be sure to include words and images that communicate the messages that you feel are missing from the lyrics and/or music video.

4. Think about the lyrics and music video of your favorite song about relationships. What messages does that song send about gender identities, love, and intimacy?

5. Look at how the popular media cover domestic violence. Compare how women who represent different identity groups such as sexual orientation, race, and class are represented. What differences do you notice?

REFERENCES

Alhabib, S., Nur, U., & Jones, R. (2010). Domestic violence against women: Systematic review of prevalence studies. *Journal of Family Violence, 25*, 369–382.

Brummett, B. (2011). *Rhetoric in popular culture.* (3rd ed.). Los Angeles: Sage.

Bureau of Justice Statistics. (2006). *Intimate partner violence in the U.S. 1993–2004.* Retrieved October 7, 2011, from http://bjs.ojp.usdoj.gov/content/pub/pdf/ipvus.pdf

Campbell, J., Rose, L., Kub, J., & Nedd, D. (1998). Voices of strength and resistance: A contextual and longitudinal analysis of women's responses to battering. *Journal of Interpersonal Violence, 13*, 743–762.

Carter, K. L. (2010). *2010 VMAs nab MTV's biggest ratings since 2002.* Retrieved October 7, 2011, from http://www.mtv.com/news/articles/1647778/20100913/story.jhtml

Dinh, J. (2010). Megan Fox donates her "Love the Way You Lie" fee to women's shelter. *MTV.* Retrieved October 7, 2011, from http://www.mtv.com/news/articles/1645119/20100805/eminem.jhtml

Hart, R. P., & Daughton, S. M. (2005). *Modern rhetorical criticism.* (3rd ed.). Boston: Pearson.

hooks, b. (1996). *Reel to real: Race, sex, and class at the movies.* New York: Routledge.

Jenkins, P. J., & Davidson, B. P. (2001). *Stopping domestic violence: How a community can prevent spousal abuse.* New York: Kluwer Academic/Plenum.

Jensen, R. (2009, June). *Beyond multiculturalism: Taking power and privilege seriously in teaching diversity.* Keynote delivered at The Pedagogy of Privilege: Teaching, Learning, and Praxis Conference, Denver, CO.

Johnson, A. (2004). Patriarchy. In P. S. Rothenburg (Ed.), *Race, class and gender in the United States.* (6th ed., pp. 165–174). New York: Worth.

Kirk, G., & Okazawa-Rey, M. (2010). *Women's lives: Multicultural perspectives.* (5th ed.). Boston: McGraw-Hill.

Rennison, C. M., & Welchans, S. (2000). *Bureau of Justice Statistics special report: Intimate partner violence.* Retrieved October 7, 2011, from http://www.popcenter.org/problems/domestic_violence/PDFs/Rennison&Welchans_2000.pdf

Sandlin, J. A. (2007). Popular culture, cultural resistance, and anticonsumption activism: An explanation of culture jamming as critical adult education. *New Directions for Adult and Continuing Adult Education, 115*, 73–82.

Sellnow, D. (2010). *The rhetorical power of popular culture: Considering mediated texts.* Thousand Oaks, CA: Sage.

Silverman, J. G., Raj, A., Mucci, L. A., & Hathaway, J. E. (2001). Dating violence against adolescent girls and associated substance use, unhealthy weight control, sexual risk behavior, pregnancy, and suicidality. *Journal of the American Medical Association, 286*(5), 572–579.

Tjaden, P., & Thoennes, N. (2000). *Extent, nature, and consequences of intimate partner violence: Findings from the National Violence against Women Survey.* U.S. Department of Justice, Office of Justice Programs. Retrieved October 7, 2011, from http://www.ojp.usdoj.gov/nij/pubs-sum/181867.htm

7.5 *AUDREYMAGAZINE.COM*: PORTRAYALS OF ASIAN AMERICAN WOMEN ONLINE BY ASIAN AMERICAN WOMEN

Thuc Doan Nguyen

The author investigates how Asian American women have been represented by Asian American women in AudreyMagazine.com.

Who pops into your mind when you think of the name "Audrey"? If you're like many, it's Audrey Hepburn—well kept in appearance, tame, Hollywood princess of an earlier generation. Now, Asian American women can think of the name (*Audrey*) as a magazine directed at them, but you might not know that right away because the name certainly doesn't tell you it's Asian American. The print version of *Audrey* started in 2003, calling itself a "lifestyle" magazine. *AudreyMagazine.com* was launched in 2009.

In this reading, I'll share some observations I've made as an Asian American woman about *AudreyMagazine.com* and how it represents Asian American women to the public. My analysis is based on current and archived versions of *AudreyMagazine.com* and covers three main themes: the name of the magazine itself, the magazine's selection of cover models, and the types of stories it chooses to cover.

WHAT'S IN A NAME?

Let's face it. "Audrey" is a quintessential European/American name. Why, then, was this name chosen for a magazine targeting Asian American women? It's true that many Asians don't keep their given names, instead changing them to Anglicized names. And many Asians born in the United States are given American names at birth. I find this to be amusing commentary on the power of white-controlled popular culture as an influencer on Asian American names because I have encountered a few Asian American women who are my age (mid-30s) named Sandy, after the character portrayed by Olivia Newton-John in the movie *Grease*.

Recently, politician Betty Brown sparked a controversy when she told Asian American citizens they should change their names to something "easier to deal with" (Ratcliffe, 2009). This sparked a discussion of Asian pride in names and heritage.

Cuong Le (2006) wrote about switching between a Vietnamese name and an American one: "I hope that, in the process of becoming American, they don't forget that they are still Asian as well." Asian names have their own distinct meanings, value, and history. Unlike typical European names such as Tom, Dick, Harry, and Sally, parents carefully choose names to reflect qualities they want to see in their children. For example, my friend's name *Mizuki* means "beautiful as the moon"; my friend *Song*'s name translates to "river" in Vietnamese, generating philosophical connotations of energy and flow.

The name "Audrey" was popularized in an era when women were still expected to be prim and proper and adhere to society's ideas of suitable decorum for females. The majority of Asian and Asian American households encourage daughters to project an image of propriety, not one of individualism. Males are considered more valuable in traditional Asian cultures because they carry the family name, though females also represent their families and have an obligation to not make their parents "lose face." Boaz Keysar and Shali Wu (2005, p. 601) point out, "Members of collectivist cultures tend to be interdependent and to have self-concepts defined in terms of relationships and social obligations." Asian cultures are collectivist, whereas the U.S. is an individualist culture. Keysar and Wu continue: "In contrast, members of individualist cultures tend to strive for independence and have self-concepts defined in terms of their own aspirations and achievements." Asian American women are caught between their traditional collectivist culture, presenting an image of their familial backgrounds, and forging ahead with what they want for themselves in a Western, individualist society.

Some people think that conforming to society's norms is the key to getting ahead in the society—that assimilation is important when trying to fit in as an immigrant. One should adopt the norms of the host society and revoke the norms of one's native culture. Immigrants are often ridiculed for being different. Asian American women continue to face these pressures today. They are targets of derogatory terms from members of both societies—the native ethnic one and the dominant culture of the United States. For example, Asian Americans are sometimes called bananas—yellow on the outside, white on the inside—when they lack pride in their heritage and just want to be white. And of course, there are numerous racist labels applied to Asians in a white-dominated society. Kristin Pensakovic (1992), a Korean adoptee, laments about her personal history of self-contempt for her Asian face, growing up in a white neighborhood in America. Certainly, mainstream media have historically shown that Anglocentric definitions of beauty are preferable to the features more common to minority groups. Importantly, and unfortunately, the cover models on *Audrey* do, too.

Thus, it appears that the name "*Audrey*" reinforces the assimilationist ideal, showing a new generation of Asian American women that they should be just like women of their mother's generation, and of their grandmother's generation before that. *Audrey* seems to want to demonstrate unity with the dominant American culture.

COVER MODELS

Besides its name, "*Audrey*," the magazine seems to want to demonstrate assimilation by its selection of cover models. *Audrey* showcases Asian Americans who are "safe" for consumption in American popular culture. The people it features are not distinctly Asian except by their genealogy. I looked at issues available online at *AudreyMagazine.com* to evaluate the choice of cover models. Of the four covers available (recall the site was launched in 2009), three presented Asians who have more Caucasian-like features than characteristically Asian ones.

The current cover at the time of my analysis, Spring 2011, features Olivia Munn. Munn is a green-eyed hapa, or half Asian and half Caucasian, who stirred up some racial controversy of her own by being the "Senior Asian Correspondent" on *The Jon Stewart Show*. This pokes fun at the idea that many Asian American women choose broadcast journalism for a career, and I'm reminded of the character "Asian Reporter Tricia Takanawa" on *Family Guy* who is never referred to as just "Tricia Takanawa" or even "Reporter Tricia Takanawa."

The Winter 2010 cover features a young woman with long reddish brown hair and long, skinny legs in a provocative pose who does not distinctly appear to be Asian. She simply does not have the usual facial features or body type of women of Asian descent. There is only one headline and it reads "Just Chill" and "Bask in the Halcyon Days of Winter." This woman could be on any magazine. The headline could be on any magazine. Under the magazine's title "*Audrey*," very small text says: "An Asian American Women's Lifestyle Magazine." If I didn't squint, I wouldn't know it was a magazine targeting Asian American women.

The cover of the prior issue, Fall 2010, features a gorgeous woman who does look Asian American—but she's wearing an animal face mask on top of her head. The young woman is shown with white skin, very light brown eyes, dark brown hair, and very red lips. This image seems no different than those on any other fashion magazine. The headline on this cover is "Oh So Fierce" and "Unleash Autumn's Wild Child." Again, the words "An Asian American Women's Lifestyle Magazine" are just tiny.

Fall 2009's cover is the only one that shows a darker, tanned-skinned, obviously Asian model. This is the only issue featuring the words "An Asian American Women's Lifestyle Magazine" in a larger font over the magazine's title. After this issue, this tagline was shrunken to a barely visible font and moved to a less important position on the cover. What was going on here? Why this change? Did *AudreyMagazine.com*, just like thousands of Asian American women, experience an identity crisis? Was *Audrey* suddenly ashamed of, or uncomfortable with, her ethnic identity? The cover itself cannot yield any answers to these questions, but it certainly does spark these and other concerns.

From its covers, it appears that *Audrey* focuses on Asians who are quite assimilable into America's white-dominated society. The most recent covers of *AudreyMagazine.com* seem to almost want to conceal the identity of *Audrey*'s supposed target market—Asian American women—due to the marginalized tagline and the fact that the cover models do not accurately reflect the vast majority of the ethnic groups that form the heterogeneous group "Asian American women."

INSIDE THE COVERS

AudreyMagazine.com includes links to sections called Features, Fashion, Beauty, Multimedia, Archives, and Shop. At the time I conducted this analysis, the Features link was broken, though there were other ways to access the features stories. *Fashion* highlights Asian American designers and provides the sort of commentary on fashion that can be found in any women's magazine. Unfortunately, the clothing presented by the Asian American designers featured in the magazine is made to appeal to the American mainstream. It doesn't show signs of influence from Asian cultures. The opportunity to really highlight Asian American culture, as opposed to American culture, is lost. *Beauty* has posts about products and does feature Asian models. However, just as with the magazine's cover, the models in the beauty section are Caucasian-like. Another opportunity lost. *Multimedia* takes you to a Youtube.com page, mostly of fashion shows and photo shoots with models.

Mainstream lifestyle magazines aimed at women have tried to expand their horizons to cover stories of importance to everyone, not just thin fashionable women. For example, *Marie Claire*'s column by Ashley Falcon, "Big Girl in a Skinny World," discusses the plight of plus-sized young women. *AudreyMagazine.com* attempts to infuse breadth into its coverage with a series called "My Story" in which ordinary Asian Americans share what has happened in their lives. Recently, *Audrey* posted stories about an Asian American lawyer who made it through a difficult time after having a miscarriage, and an Asian American hapa whose mother was a mail-order bride. This provides some balance to the fluffier pieces that are more prominently featured on the Web site. However, these stories were not readily accessible from the main pages of the site. We have to work harder to find them. As a result, *AudreyMagazine.com*'s readers are probably not going to benefit from these stories as much as they could if the stories were more of a focal point than the other features.

Nonetheless, unlike other women's magazines, *Audrey* does address current events besides those that are fashion, beauty, and film related; these pertain specifically to the Asian American community, although these are links from other sites and not stories written by *Audrey* staff. This shows that *Audrey* pays attention to what other Asian American Web sites are saying. For example, *AudreyMagazine.com* re-posted an iamkoream.com (yes, Kore-am, not Korean) story in March 2011. *Audrey* quoted angryasianman.com in a post about UCLA student Alexandra Wallace (who posted a video discussing "the hordes of Asian people" admitted to UCLA and how rude Asian people are in the library checking on tsunami victims in Japan with their "ching-chong ting tong"). It's positive that *Audrey* keeps with up and shows solidarity regarding problems affecting the whole Asian American community, though I hope that the magazine eventually devotes more resources to these issues by presenting articles written by its own staff.

Audrey doesn't seem to provide any representation of role models for Asian American female readers other than actresses, singers, and clothing designers. I grew up in the United States, but I still cannot give you examples of household names of Asian American women who are prominent in fields, such as math and science, philanthropy, non profits, publishing, politics, screenwriting, or directing. These women are not represented in the mainstream media—but they're not in *AudreyMagazine.com* either.

It's not only that this breadth of potential role model isn't portrayed in the magazine; *Audrey* doesn't portray controversial Asian Americans, either. *Audrey* doesn't cover people such as Jenny Shimizu, who was popular in the 1990s—an Asian American lesbian with a shaved head and tattoos. The women presented in *Audrey* provide "safe" images of Asian American women. *Audrey* shows only the "perfect" side of Asian American women, thereby fueling the internal struggles of Asian women who have long been forced to bottle up their feelings in order to "save face" or keep "respect." It would be more interesting if Audrey showed Asian American female role models who are not afraid to challenge the status quo or society's prevailing conception of the minority group—that of well-put-together pleasers. I know Asian American women who are lesbians, who defy gender roles, and who challenge unfair labor practices imposed by people who think an Asian American woman will shut up and put up when told to do work that is beyond the scope of her position—but *Audrey* doesn't write about them. *Audrey* doesn't choose to delve into the daily struggles of Asian American women, but instead chooses to highlight the glitzy lifestyles that only the members of the wealthy minority get to experience. The magazine presents an upper class lifestyle as if it is the norm. Coupled with this, the overall tone of *Audrey* is passive—it shows Asian American women in fashionable and acceptable situations, as if encased in a nice glass display, but doesn't show any strife behind the facades.

STRONGER ADVOCACY FOR ISSUES AFFECTING REGULAR ASIAN AMERICAN WOMEN

The representation of Asian American women in *Audrey* is the same as on white-oriented Web sites: that of a minority that is happy and perky, putting its best foot forward, not a "problematic" minority group that stands up for itself and its equal rights.

AudreyMagazine.com seems to strive to maintain this unrealistic image of Asian American women, an image with which the dominant culture is so enamored. Sonia Shah (1997) argues that "White feminists and other liberals advanced [a] feel-good fantasy with celebrations of Asian American culture and people. The result was a triple pressure on Asian women to conform to the docile, warm, upwardly mobile stereotype that liberals, conservatives, and their own community members all wanted to promote."

Asian women in media and those who are on the privileged side of the digital divide should do their part to help prevent these sorts of overt and covert racism. If we do nothing, we are condoning victimization and misrepresentation.

Because *Audrey* explicitly bills itself as a lifestyle magazine for Asian American women, the standards by which it must be judged are in some ways different than those applied to women's magazines in general. Of course, many of the criticisms of those magazines are also applicable to *Audrey*. But, in addition, other issues need to be examined.

Ultimately, I can only conclude that *Audrey* is not meeting its stated goal of serving as a lifestyle magazine for Asian American women. The magazine reflects an upper class, individualistic, hedonistic, and self-centered take on the American lifestyle, not an Asian American lifestyle. It has failed to live up to its responsibility of choosing content that reflects its espoused mission; it is not serving Asian American women very well at all. Besides reinforcing much of the harmful material found in mainstream women's magazines (particularly the visual representations of women and the focus on beauty and consumption as ends in and of themselves), *Audrey* seems to be telling Asian American women that in order to advance in the United States, they should look more Caucasian and assimilate to the dominant culture. *Audrey* doesn't show examples of Asian American women speaking out and standing out about issues beyond the superficial in the United States.

IT'S YOUR TURN: WHAT DO YOU THINK? WHAT WILL YOU FIND?

1. What if you grew up with an Anglo name, moved to Asia, and were told you should change your name to an Asian one to make it easier for everyone there? Would that make you feel like you lost any of your personal or cultural identity? How would you think of people with European features getting things like eye and nose surgery to look more like Asian people?

2. What can Web sites such as *AudreyMagazine.com* do to discourage whites from perceiving Asian American women as "ching chong ting tong" people, and as those who are just "cute" and "submissive," or the subjects of exotic sexual fantasies, or other stereotypes?

3. Compare *AudreyMagazine.com* to a site called *Disgrasian.com*. Discuss the differences in content and tone.

4. Go to *AudreyMagazine.com* and see for yourself—do you agree with the author? Compare *Audrey*'s content to that of other fashion magazines. How are they similar or different? Finally, consider whether it's fair to ask *Audrey* to do more than other fashion/lifestyle magazines.

REFERENCES

Keysar, B., & Wu, S. (2005). The effect of culture on perspective taking. *Psychological Science*, *18*(7), 600–607. Retrieved April 26, 2011, from http://psychology.uchicago.edu/people/faculty/keysar/27_wukeysarps.pdf

Le, C. (2006). *Changing names among Asian Americans*. Retrieved April 26, 2011, from http://www.asian-nation.org/headlines/2006/01/changing-names-among-asian-americans/

Pensakovic, K. (1992). *Confessions of a banana*. Retrieved April 26, 2011, from http://www.hcs.harvard.edu/~yisei/issues/spring_92/ys92_35.html

Ratcliffe, R.G. (2009). Lawmaker defends comment on Asians. *Houston Chronicle*. Retrieved April 26, 2011, from http://www.chron.com/disp/story.mpl/metropolitan/6365320.html

Shah, S. (1997). Women and gender issues. *Asian-Nation: The Landscape of Asian America*. Retrieved April 26, 2011, from http://www.asian-nation.org/gender.shtml

7.6 GENDER AND RACE AS MEANING SYSTEMS: UNDERSTANDING THEORETICAL, HISTORICAL, AND INSTITUTIONAL IMPLICATIONS OF SEXUALIZED IMAGERY IN RAP MUSIC

Kiana Cox

> *The author analyzes the songs on* Billboard's *"Hot Rap Singles" charts, and explores implications of the sexualization of African American women in rap music.*

In what ways do images matter? More specifically, in what ways to do images of particular gender and racial groups matter? In this reading, I explore some theoretical, historical, and policy implications of the sexualization of African American women in rap. We'll consider the historic roots of the imagery seen in contemporary rap music videos; the ways in which gendered, racialized, and even sexist meanings have been attached to African American women's bodies; how these meanings show up in institutions that actually affect many aspects of African American women's daily lives; and ultimately, how media play a role in reflecting, constructing, and maintaining these systems of meaning.

HEGEMONIC FEMININITY AND SEXUAL REPRESENTATIONS OF AFRICAN AMERICAN WOMEN

Aside from being axes of stratification that differentially affect people's life chances, race and gender are also systems of meaning that are applied to bodies and actions (Collins, 2004). These systems of meaning are not random sets of race and gender signifiers. Rather, they are organized components of hegemonic ideologies. Collins advances a theory of hegemonic femininity which will serve as the theoretical foundation for this article. Hegemonic femininity is a set of characteristics, behaviors, and interactions that represent the totality of "normal" womanhood. These characteristics, behaviors, and interactions are standards against which the femininity of all women is measured. They are hegemonic in that only particular women can achieve them, though all women tend to deem them normal and accurate. In the United States, "normal" femininity is fully embodied in the form of white, middle-class, heterosexual womanhood. In the history of African American women's representations, there are two aspects of hegemonic femininity that are at the forefront: physical characteristics and sexual uses of the body.

Within the context of hegemonic femininity, physical characteristics serve as a primary marker of proper womanhood. True women should not be mistaken for men, and therefore should have visible breasts, hips, and round butts. Beauty is also a very important physical aspect of hegemonic femininity. The epitome of a beautiful woman in this hegemonic system of femininity is a young and slim white woman. Therefore, a woman's level of beauty is highly contingent upon her body type and race. Hegemonic femininity also sets the boundaries for acceptable actions of the body, specifically how the body is used sexually and how the woman acts in relation to men. Overall, a woman's actions in relation to men are more feminine if she is submissive and deferential to male authority. This also includes sex, in which a truly feminine woman only allows heterosexual men access to her body and that access must occur within the confines of marriage (Collins, 2004).

Historically, stereotypical images have depicted women of African descent as violating these tenets of normal femininity. The European *Hottentot Venus* and the American *Jezebel* are specific sexualized representations of women of African descent that were used to juxtapose normal and deviant notions of femininity and sexuality. The Hottentot Venus is the coalescing of myths and facts about African women. In ancient times, European philosophers attempted to explain Africa's warm climate by arguing that the continent was ruled by the love goddess Venus (Hobson, 2005). Therefore, anyone who was native to that continent was assumed to be overtly sexual. Additionally, the term "Hottentot" was used to describe groups of Africans who were claimed to have a "savage and wild" sexual appetite. European explorers cited physical characteristics, such as the large buttocks of certain African women, as proof of their wild and deviant sexuality (Hobson, 2005). In fact, in 1810 South African woman Saartjie (Sara) Baartman was brought to France in order to fully personify myths about African sexual difference. Because of Baartman's large breasts and buttocks, she was put on display in European social clubs and freak shows. Even upon her death in 1816, famed anatomist George Cuvier dissected, preserved, and displayed her genitals in an attempt to find scientific evidence of African racial and sexual difference. In fact, a life-sized cast of Baartman's body, her skeleton, and preserved genitals remained property of the Musée de l'Homme in Paris until 2002, when they were returned to Cape Town, South Africa, for burial (Hobson, 2005).

In Europe, Saartjie Baartman was the real-life embodiment of racist and sexist notions of physical difference. Her body represents a violation of hegemonic femininity in that it is too feminine—her breasts, hips, and buttocks are too large. However, the American controlling image of Jezebel is also a deviation from "normal" femininity. In addition to prescribing how the body should look, hegemonic femininity also sets the boundaries for acceptable actions of the body, specifically how the body is used sexually and how the woman acts in relation to men. It is in this dimension that Jezebel fails to live up to hegemonic femininity. Jezebel is the historical image of the youthful African American woman. She is usually portrayed as a light skinned African American woman with European features, such as long, straight hair, thin lips, thin nose, and a relatively slim body (Jewell, 1993). She is the African American embodiment of the standard of beauty set by white womanhood. Despite her lighter skin, Jezebel's multiple sexual relationships cause her to miss the mark of true femininity. She is the antithesis to traditional Victorian womanhood, which was characterized by gentility and chastity (Morton, 1991). The Jezebel image emerged in the nineteenth century, and it was used to justify the sexual relationships that masters had with their female slaves. Because of Jezebel's incessant need for sex, she was portrayed as a seductress and her master as the unwilling victim of sexual contact (Jewell, 1993).

REPRESENTATIONS OF AFRICAN AMERICAN WOMEN IN RAP MUSIC

Both the Hottentot Venus and Jezebel provide historical context to the sexualized images of African American women that we see in contemporary rap music. Rap music is now one of the most dominant and widely disseminated aspects of American popular culture. In fact, it has overtaken rock as the most lucrative and influential form of pop music (Tate, 2003). Billboard's 2010 Year End charts (Billboard Magazine Online, 2011) bear this out: 20 of the Top 50 Pop Artists were rap and rap-influenced R&B acts, 39 of the Top 200 Albums were rap and rap-influenced R&B albums, and 56 of the Hot 100 Songs were rap and rap-influenced R&B songs. The 2010 charts' numbers are much higher than those found in the 1992 charts, where only 8 of the Top 100 Albums and 11 of the top 50 artists were rap and rap-influenced R&B.

This overwhelming success and global appeal of rap make it a useful site to examine hegemonic ideologies. What types of images of African American women predominate in contemporary rap music, and how do they compare to the historic images of the Hottentot Venus and Jezebel? In order to answer this question, I used *Billboard* Magazine's Year End "Hot Rap Singles" charts for the years 2005-2010. Although the magazine presents many aspects of the music industry, it is best known for its charts, which are used to track the sales and Internet digital downloads of popular music. Although *Billboard* is not the only compiler of music charts and rankings, it is judged by experts to be the fairest and least subjective (Lena, 2006). The "Hot Rap Singles" charts list, in order of sales and popularity, the top 25 rap songs for each year. Eliminating songs that charted more than once, I had a sample of 144 songs. I used the Black Youth Project's (2010) online lyric database and A–Z Lyrics Universe, an online comprehensive music lyric database in order to locate and download lyrics.

JEZEBEL AND THE HOTTENTOT VENUS RE-INVENTED?

I conducted a close reading of the lyrics for the songs in my sample in two phases. First, I examined each song's lyrics looking for any references to women. Once these songs were identified, the second phase of analysis included a close examination of these songs' lyrics based on the tenets of hegemonic femininity indicated above: physical characteristics and appropriate uses of the female body. I operationalized these tenets further by creating three categories: *body size, and shape*, where I paid specific attention to how the rappers described women's bodies; *interactions,* paying particular attention how and where rappers interact with women and how their bodies are observed; and *sex acts*, with special attention to how sexual encounters are described. On the basis of these categories, my close reading of the lyrics revealed nuanced themes in the representations of African American women in contemporary rap music that are similar to the Hottentot Venus and Jezebel images. These themes include special attention to the African American woman's hips, thighs, and buttocks; treating the African American woman and her body's movements as sexual spectacles; and explicit descriptions of sexual encounters. Overall, 87 of the 144 (60.4%) songs include references to at least one of these categories.

The Lower Body

While Saartjie Baartman's larger lower body was considered unattractive and even grotesque by European standards, this same body type is the most desirable in contemporary rap music. Forty-six songs analyzed (32%) contain specific references to the size and shape of African American women's hips, thighs, and butts. In "U and Dat", which ranked #11 on the 2006 chart (henceforth presented as #11/2006), rappers E-40 and T-Pain talk about the desirability of an African American woman's posterior. The song is set in a nightclub, and they are trying their best to maneuver through the crowd to reach a particular woman whose butt is so large that E-40 claims that he can balance a drinking glass on it. Similarly, in "I Know You Want Me" (#18/2009), reggaeton rapper Pitbull compares a woman to several wild animals and specifically states that her rear end is comparable to that of donkey. Also, in "Pimpin' All Over the World" (#19/2005), Ludacris raps about how a woman's hips and butt are so big that they can stop rush-hour traffic. In each of these examples, contemporary rap music has reframed a particular body type that is rejected as hegemonically feminine, making it preferable and highly sought after.

The Body as Sexual Spectacle

Along with paying special attention to the size and shape of the African American woman's lower body, contemporary rap music also treats African American women and their bodily movements as sexual spectacles. Forty-three of the 144 songs (29.8%) contained these types of depictions of African American women. Many of these types of representations refer to strippers. For example, in "Badd" (#24/2005), the Ying Yang Twins, Mike Jones, and Mr. Collipark challenge a stripper to dance and shake as hard as she can in order to justify them leaving her a tip. Similarly, in "Pop, Lock, and Drop It" (#12/2007), rapper Huey encourages women to go beyond their usual dance limits and to perform handstands for his pleasure.

In both of these examples, the women are aware that they are spectacles and they are expected to dance longer and harder in order to get more money. However, most African American women are not strippers; therefore, she is more likely to be unknowingly treated as a spectacle as she goes about everyday activities. In "Some Cut" (#11/2005), rap group Trillville not only describes seeing an attractive woman in a shopping mall, but also how they have been watching and following her all day. Only after his watching and following does Trillville group member Mr. Funkadelic rap about approaching her and make his interest known. There is no response from the woman in the song, but given Mr. Funkadelic's description, it seems that she was unknowingly being watched. The purpose of Mr. Funkadelic's gazing is revealed at the end of the song, where he states that he wants to take the woman home to have sex. Therefore, the woman's lack of awareness of herself as a spectacle does not change the end result. Her body is being viewed and imagined for the purposes of male sexual pleasure.

Sexual Encounters

The final major theme in the representations of African American women in contemporary rap music is also sexual. Seventy-five of the 144 songs (52%) include references to actual or imagined sex acts. The references depict sexual encounters as pornographic and aggressive, with a particular focus on various types of sex and sexual positions. Rap super group Young Money's "Every Girl" (#5/2009) is a bold statement of sexual adventure. The rappers spend over five verses declaring how much they want to "f*ck" every woman in the world, no matter her race. This same group also put an aggressively sexual spin on a classic cartoon in "Bedrock" (#2/2010). One of the sub-themes of this category is a particular focus on oral sex, namely fellatio. Lil Wayne's also takes a childhood icon and recasts it as sexual in his song "Lollipop" (#1/2008), which is entirely about receiving oral sex. Similarly, in "I Know You See It" (#16/2006), Yung Joc uses little girl's jump rope chants to rap about receiving oral sex from a stripper.

In summary, the representations of African American women in contemporary rap music follow similar patterns of sexualization as define the Hottentot Venus and Jezebel. Key findings indicate that special attention is paid to the African American woman's lower body; her body is treated as a sexual spectacle, much like Saartjie Baartman; and she is overwhelmingly depicted as a subordinate sexual partner to African American men, who take great sexual liberties with her body. What is interesting is that rappers have taken what have historically been constructed as violations of femininity and re-centered them as desirable. The Hottentot Venus' large hips, thighs, and butt and Jezebel's aggressive sexual appetite were based on racist and sexist ideologies whose purpose was to cast African and African American women as sexually deviant. However, this particular body type and form of sex is preferred in rap music. Rarely is an African American woman in rap music not depicted as a source of sexual spectacle and fulfillment. It is this focus on African American women's sexuality that leads us to the institutional implications of such images.

INSTITUTIONAL AND SOCIETAL IMPLICATIONS OF SEXUALIZED IMAGES OF AFRICAN AMERICAN WOMEN

In institutions, contemporary sexualized images and their intersections with social class have been used to frame African American women in two ways: as welfare and crack mothers who are less deserving of societal resources and as poor women who occupy a certain "place" in the social hierarchy. The welfare mother is an updated version of the breeder image of African American women, a stereotype which developed during slavery. The breeder image depicted African American women as a sort of animal who could easily bear children. The welfare mother is the stereotypical image of the lazy African American woman who is unwilling to work. She has multiple children, receives welfare benefits, and continues to birth (i.e., breed) children in order to continue receiving these benefits. The welfare mother is viewed as a threat to the nation's political and economic stability because of her dependence on welfare (Collins, 2000). Similar to the welfare mother/queen, the crack mother is the image of the selfish African American mother whose irresponsible and criminal behavior causes her to give birth to drug dependent children who must be supported by the state. Both the welfare mother and crack mother images were created to justify the rejection of working class African American women from institutions and resources that could benefit them (Collins, 2004).

Just as the welfare mother/queen and the crack mother have been used in politics to frame African American women as less deserving of societal resources, stereotypes have also been used to frame African American women as occupying a lower status in U.S. society. Newsome (2003) examines the intersection of race, class, and gender in informal U.S. Customs detainment policies. She argues that U.S. Customs agents use stereotypes as a basis for detaining African American women. Specifically, African American women who travel internationally have been harassed and searched for drugs without probable cause. Newsome (2003) argues that African American women are subjected to this because stereotypes of them dictate that they are poor and therefore, financially unable to travel internationally, unless it involves drug trafficking. She argues that agents use profiling as a form of social control; to remind African American women of their place.

Why do images matter? In what ways do images of specific racial and gender groups matter? Now we should be able to see that gender and race are specific sets of ideologies that allow us to attach meanings to bodies and actions. Ideologies exist in order to reinforce a society's social order and to protect and conceal the power of the privileged (Jewell, 1993). In contemporary times, popular culture is a site where oppressive racial and gender ideologies are reproduced and contested. This is particularly true for African American women, who have endured and contested the reproduction of sexualized images. These images have been used as a justification for continuing to deny African American women access to institutional resources that could benefit them.

In the United States, there exists an inequitable distribution of society's resources (e.g. access to and attainment of wealth, power, adequate employment, quality education, politics, and other societal institutions), such that privileged groups have a systematic and institutionally supported dominance over wealth and power. These groups seek to sustain their privilege, however, they must justify the inequity in the distribution of resources and access to them. In the course of this justification, the privileged seek to frame themselves and those with similar social locations as rightfully deserving of their privileges due to hard work and intellectual ability. Simultaneously, those that are socially, economically, educationally, politically, and otherwise disadvantaged are framed as the creators of their own misfortune and rightfully deserving of their often depressed social locations (Jewell, 1993). Therefore, sexualized images and the mass media that disseminate them are powerful tools in the hands of those who seek to maintain their privilege. It is the through the repeated creation and dissemination of certain types of images, the messages that these images send about the groups they are claimed to represent, and the "commonsense" nature of these images that inequality is justified and maintained.

IT'S YOUR TURN: WHAT DO YOU THINK? WHAT WILL YOU FIND?

In addition to gender and race, almost any other "social location" (including but not limited to sexuality and sexual orientation, social class, disability status, and age) can operate as a meaning system. To analyze their meaning and the inequality that might result from them, select a social location and explore the meanings that location holds.

1. First, *identify the hegemonic ideology* (or the set of characteristics, behaviors, etc. that define what is "normal" for that social location) by answering questions such as: What physical characteristics, behaviors, and interactions govern "normal" membership in this social category? What "should" __ people look like? How "should" they act in relation to in-group members and out-group members? What happens when members of these categories do not stay within these boundaries? Is it possible for every member of this category to meet these expectations? Who is most likely to meet these expectations? Who is most likely to violate these expectations?

2. Using the same social location, provide historical and institutional context for what you've found, by answering questions such as: Have these characteristics remained the same over time? How have people who violate these characteristics been treated historically? What types of pictures and language were used in order to depict violators? What types of laws and policies were enacted to "control" violators?

3. Try to answer these same questions as they pertain to the dominant social group. In the U.S., this includes straight, white, middle class males. Is it easier or harder to answer the same questions? Why? What does that tell you about the different social locations, and hegemonic ideology, in our society?

REFERENCES

Billboard Magazine Online. (2011). *Year End Charts*. Retrieved from http://www.billboard.biz/bbbiz/charts/yearendcharts

Collins, P. (2004). *Black sexual politics: African Americans, gender, and the new racism*. New York: Routledge.

Collins, P. (2000). *Black feminist thought: Knowledge, consciousness, and the politics of empowerment* (2nd ed.). New York: Routledge.

Jewell, K. (1993). *From Mammy to Miss America and beyond: Cultural images and the shaping of U.S. social policy*. New York: Routledge.

Hobson, J. (2005). *Venus in the dark: Blackness and beauty in popular culture*. New York: Routledge.

Lena, J. (2006). Social context and musical content of rap music, 1979–1995. *Social Forces, 85*, 479–495.

Morton, P. (1991). *Disfigured images: The historical assault on Afro-American women*. New York: Greenwood Press.

Newsome, Y. (2003). Border patrol: The U.S customs service and the racial profiling of African American women. *Journal of African American Studies, 7*, 31–57.

Tate, G. (2003). *Everything but the burden: What white people are taking from Black culture*. New York: Broadway Books.

7.7   CONFLICT DIAMONDS, GLOBALIZATION, AND CONSUMPTION: AN EXAMINATION OF KANYE WEST'S *DIAMONDS FROM SIERRA LEONE*

Michael Adorjan and Athena Elafros[1]

> The authors offer a close reading of Kanye West's track Diamonds from Sierra Leone, *from his second studio album* Late Registration.

The entrepreneur, the showman, the artist, the superstar: Kanye West is one of the most popular and best selling current hip hop artists. From his distinct style of dress, egotistical self-confidence, to his political views (noting on a televised Hurricane Katrina Fundraiser that "George Bush doesn't care about black people"), Kanye West has made his definitive mark on the music industry.

West recorded two versions of *Diamonds from Sierra Leone*—one released as a single, and the more political version we analyze here. This track illuminates how West frames the relationship between the local consumption of diamonds by African Americans within the United States and the global diamond trade. We also examine how West critically interrogates three interrelated issues surrounding the purchase of diamonds: how he examines the vexing relationship between diamonds, Black masculinity, and social status; how he frames conflict diamonds as a social problem; and how he connects the purchase of diamonds (locally) and the continuation of racism and social inequality (globally).

Kanye West's rise to success in the music industry is somewhat different from the career trajectories of other well-known hip hop artists. From his style of dress (Polo shirts and Gucci loafers) to his middle-class upbringing, Kanye West is not your stereotypical hip hop artist. His parents, who separated when he was 11 months old, have strongly influenced his sense of identity, rap content, and style. His mother was an English professor at Chicago State University, while his father was a former Black Panther and award-winning photographer.

West has built a reputation for blending pop with politics as he touches nerves and generates controversy. His choice to rap about conflict diamonds would not surprise his fans. The social problem of conflict diamonds, in contrast to other issues in African countries such as debt relief, has recently attracted widespread concern. The conflict refers to the illegal trade of diamonds within areas of Africa (e.g., Angola, Sierra Leone, Liberia, and the Democratic Republic of Congo) mired in internal conflict and civil war (Taylor & Mokhawa, 2003). Although diamonds are harvested around the world, scholars (Lujala, Gleditsch, & Gilmore, 2005) have found strong relationships between the harvest of illegally traded diamonds and the onset of ethnic civil war, especially in countries already divided among ethnic lines. Before we consider West's discussion of conflict diamonds specifically, we explore how his arguments connect to broader issues related to Black masculinity and social status.

DIAMONDS, BLACK MASCULINITY, AND SOCIAL STATUS

As Roopali Mukherjee (2006) notes, diamond jewelry, minks, luxury cars, designer labels, fur coats, and gold (often referred to as *bling*) are cultural signifiers of what is termed the "ghetto fabulous" aesthetic. These are symbols which convey a positive and emphatic affirmation of working class, urban, Black life. Since bling as a concept emerged in the late 1990s, white pop culture icons such as Madonna, Paris Hilton, and soccer superstar David Beckham have all "mined its au courant elements for their performative repertoire," but, Mukherjee argues, "the appeal of 'bling' remains its showy 'ghetto fabulous' stance, its elevation of the black urban experience as ultimate crucible of cool" (2006, p. 600). Thus, the ultimate role of bling and the ghetto fabulous aesthetic is to perform "specifically racial work, positing blackness as social asset and the ghetto as reservoir of rebellious creativity and stylish daring" (Mukherjee, 2006, p. 600).

It is in this context of the cultural appropriation and co-optation of African American working class cultural forms within the popular North American mainstream that the problem of conflict diamonds needs to be situated. In addition, we also need to position Kanye West, who was raised in the suburbs of Chicago and had a middle-class upbringing, as one of the central figures of the Black bourgeoisie who has taken many of the signifiers of working class, urban, Black life and appropriated them into his own unique style and persona (pink Polo shirts, loafers, etc.). This persona, writer Todd Dills (2007, p. 556) notes, is the direct opposite of the "rough-hewn gangsta character" of many of the rappers on Roc-A-Fella Records, which resulted in the initial reluctance of Jay-Z and others at the label to take him seriously as a rapper.

FORMING CONFLICT DIAMONDS AS A SOCIAL PROBLEM

Having outlined the role that conflict diamonds have played in Sierra Leone, having situated diamonds as a specific marker of social status within hip hop culture, and having placed Kanye West as a key producer and rapper who uses bling as an integral element of his rapping persona, we are now better able to understand how Kanye West interrogates three interrelated issues surrounding the purchase of diamonds in his track *Diamonds from Sierra Leone*. The song heavily samples Shirley Bassey's theme song for the 1971 James Bond movie *Diamonds Are Forever*, and highlights the central role that diamonds, as a quintessential type of bling, play as markers of social status and wealth within North America. In the song, diamonds are represented in several overlapping yet complementary ways—as symbols of social status, as a symbol for Roc-A-Fella Records, and as a symbolic representation of romantic commitment.

Similar to West's references in the song to Yves Saint Laurent glasses, Porsches, and Hennessey, diamonds are markers of social distinction which are part of Kanye West's image as a successful hip hop producer and rapper. From his Jesus Piece—which made RealTalkNY's (2011) list of the 10 most gaudy chains in hip hop—to his diamond earring, to the recent replacement of his bottom row of teeth with diamonds, diamonds play a central role in West's self-presentation. Diamonds as emblems of wealth and status may also be one of the reasons that they are the symbol of Roc-A-Fella Records.

Diamonds are also a socially constructed symbol of romantic commitment. The Shirley Bassey sample in the song *Diamonds Are Forever* references the original De Beers advertising line "a diamond is forever" which was one of the most successful marketing campaigns of diamonds as symbols of love and commitment. However, both Bassey and West's lyrics "flip the script" on this symbolic representation of diamonds. Although they may agree that diamonds are forever, they are not so certain about love and commitment. The *Diamonds Are Forever* theme song begins with Bassey singing about the longevity and dependability of diamonds, reflecting on the idea that although diamonds may very well be forever, people on the other hand are much less trustworthy and reliable. West echoes this statement in the chorus where, signifying off of OutKast's "Ms. Jackson," he rhetorically asks the listener what "forever" actually means when he repeatedly, and challengingly, juxtaposes the words "forever" and "ever," thereby prodding us to question whether forever is actually forever. So, although diamonds are gifts most often purchased and given by men to women, their eternal quality is also symbolic: the relationship which turns into coal is substituted by the diamond—the unwavering "rock" of support that will never waver. Husbands, wives, lovers may come and go, but diamonds are forever.

BRIDGING THE LOCAL WITH THE GLOBAL

Keeping in mind the aforementioned discussion about diamonds as symbols of social status, hip hop machismo, and conflicted emblems of commitment and love, we turn to engage in a broader discussion about the relationship between diamonds, black masculinity, and social status. In the track, featuring Jay-Z, West clearly outlines the moral dilemma he encounters as an African American who enjoys diamonds. In the opening verse, he sets the tone for the song by painting a vivid picture outlining the connections between warfare, mutilation, Sierra Leone, and the diamonds purchased by North Americans. West compares the horrendous loss of limb suffered by the people of Sierra Leone to the lengthy conflict in Vietnam, and admits that there is a linkage to these people's pain and our own—and his own—bling.

Here conflict diamonds are not framed as an issue of individual choice. They are framed as a social problem connecting the consumption practices of North Americans with the labor practices of the people of Sierra Leone. The song acts as a type of consciousness raising and education tool as he directs his message to other African Americans, and, most important, includes himself as part of the problem.

Although West is brave enough to be real about the conflict in his heart regarding conflict diamonds, he is also aware that this conflict mirrors the concerns of many in North America who have become aware of this social problem. West implicates himself with this problem as much as everyone else. In an almost philosophic way, he ponders the source of the problem and ways to overcome it—the source being linked to preconceptions about needs and wants as they are associated with African American masculine identity. Part of him still wants the diamonds, because it is easy not to think about the social injustice, exploitation, and suffering of the diamond trade which is so far away. However, West acknowledges the very real connection between the local consumption of diamonds within North America and the global perpetuation of injustice abroad. He turns a critical eye inward and rhetorically asks himself, how can he remain awash in bling if he knows about blood diamonds? These thoughts are echoed once again when he makes connections between the harmless consumption of luxury goods, such as the aforementioned Jesus Piece, and the mutilation of a child overseas. West raps that seeing a photograph of an armless child in Sierra Leone forced him to make this linkage.

However, West goes even further than merely noting how the purchase of diamonds in North America is connected to the murder and mutilation of Africans in Sierra Leone. This is accomplished when he makes an even more explicit and political connection between African Americans in the United States and Africans in Sierra Leone. Specifically, he raps about the drug trade and how both the use and sale of drugs bring about pain and death.

In his lyrics, West is drawing a clear relationship between the injustices faced by African Americans within the United States and the injustices faced by Africans overseas. He is illustrating the dire consequences of the uninterrupted flow of goods and global capital across borders by making the link between the local desire for luxury goods and jewelry and how this results in the disenfranchisement of whole populations of Africans. By drawing together these two divergent experiences (the local and the global), West also draws connections between the racism and classism experienced by Africans in a transnational context as a result of the processes of globalization. Over here, African Americans die from drugs; over there, Africans die from what African Americans (indeed, all Americans) buy from drugs. In both instances, Africans are dying due to racial and class inequalities.

Perhaps most significantly, West outlines the "real" conflict near the end of the first verse, when he questions whether African Americans *inherently* desire gold, diamonds—bling. He also notes that after working so hard for so long, it's only natural to enjoy the well-deserved fruits of one's labors. The gratification derived from bling, however, does not remain innocent; on the contrary, it's highly problematic. West directly forces us to assess why, if we know it's wrong, we find it so pleasurable.

The question is thrown down like an existential gauntlet: what is the nature of the relationship between African American identity and material possessions, such as diamonds? West tightrope walks the knife edge between posing a question and making a statement about African American identity. If individuals are to challenge the injustices of conflict diamonds, they must challenge material needs and wants as they relate to African Americans and North Americans more broadly.

However, it also seems as though West has his tongue firmly in his cheek here, especially given his repetition of the word "right"—right? The second "right" is directed to the African American listener, someone who may acknowledge the existence of conflict diamonds but can't shake off the desire to obtain more—a desire likely reinforced by social pressures from others in the community: family, friends, lovers, spouses, etc. Furthermore, the African American listener in this instance is not just any listener. The listener is gendered as male through West's reference to wearing a Polo rugby shirt which is a style that West himself has pioneered as part of his image as a "different sort of rapper" (Dills, 2007, p. 556). This is not to say that women cannot wear Polo shirts, but given West's own affinities with this style of dress, and the central role that West's fashion plays in his performance of a different type of African American masculinity, it makes sense that he is addressing an African American *male* audience. But, unlike the version of the song released as a single, in this politicized version West makes much more explicit connections between the individual choices of African Americans and the impact these choices have on Africans overseas.

NOT POLITICAL ENOUGH?

So, what does West suggest is to be done? Here he plays more of a messenger role rather than resolver. He makes it clear that despite his awareness of the problem, he is going to keep his Jesus Piece. Evidently, West has no compelling desire to rid himself of all of his bling simply as a statement of protest. True to form, he is not concerned about his audiences' judgments of him in this regard. Instead, he presents the question, but leaves the answer to his listeners. It is in this regard, however, that West's discussion of conflict diamonds is limited. Although he draws attention to the social problem of conflict diamonds and the direct links of inequality between Africans and African Americans, he does not challenge conspicuous consumption practices, and offers no broader suggestions for social change. In addition, one could also ask why the less political version of the song—which did not make such explicit references to conflict diamonds—was the one released as the single.

These questions should be directed toward contemporary hip hop as a whole, which acts as a cultural juggernaut for this and future generations. The commodification of hip hop has arguably overshadowed more politically oriented artists (e.g., dead prez, Talib Kweli, Mos Def, K-OS). Individual artists may express intermittent transmissions to "shut 'em down,' yet they are ensconced within a system of big business and expectations of commercial performance. The direction hip hop heads toward will be influenced by how these linkages between politics and commerce are mitigated. One possibility is that commercial interests will not be usurped by politics, but rather efficacious political activism will be linked to viable commercial intellectual property. This may be the avenue followed by Kanye West and others given that West's commercial success is linked to his forthright openness regarding religion, materialism, racism, and the needs and wants of African Americans and, indeed, North Americans more broadly.

NOTE

1. Both authors contributed equally to this paper.

IT'S YOUR TURN: WHAT DO YOU THINK? WHAT WILL YOU FIND?

1. Compare and contrast the lyrics between the "political" and "single" versions of *Diamonds from Sierra Leone*. Is West selling out by releasing the less political/activist track as the major commercial single? Explain your answer with reference to hip hop in general. Is hip hop maintaining its political activism or gravitating toward commercialism? Is it possible for hip hop to be political and commercial at the same time?

2. How are material luxuries (such as Gucci loafers, Polo shirts, and Hennessey) raced, classed, and gendered? How does Kanye West's persona reinforce and/or challenge these associations?

3. What is the difference between your needs and wants? Make a list of 10 things you need and 10 things you want. Then get together with a small group of classmates or peers, and have everyone review their list. Are there items that are listed as needs that may more accurately be described as wants, and vice versa? Are there items of overlap on peoples' lists? For example, are men more likely to list certain types of items, while women list others? In other words, how are our needs and wants gendered in ways which reinforce and/or challenge patriarchy? How do various media (music, movies, television, etc.) shape our needs and wants?

4. How do the items on the lists you made reflect your own social classes? What might be on the list of people of social classes different from our own (consider people of both higher- and lower socioeconomic status)? What does that tell you about the existence of social classes in America?

REFERENCES

Dills, T. (2007). Kanye West. In M. Hess (Ed.), *Icons of hip hop: An encyclopedia of the movement, music, and culture* (pp. 555–577). Westport, CT: Greenwood Press.

Lujala, P., Gleditsch N.P., & Gilmore E. (2005). A diamond curse? Civil war and a lootable resource. *The Journal of Conflict Resolution, 49*(4), 538–562.

Mukherjee, R. (2006). The ghetto fabulous aesthetic in contemporary black culture. *Cultural Studies, 20*(6), 599–629.

RealTalkNY (2011). Top 10 most gaudy chains in hip hop. Retrieved October 9, 2011, from http://realtalkny.uproxx.com/?s=10+most+gaudy+chains+in+hip+hop

Taylor, I., & Mokhawa G. (2003). Not forever: Botswana, conflict diamonds and the Bushmen. *African Affairs, 102*(407), 261–283.

7.8   RESIDENT RACIST: EMBODIMENT AND GAME CONTROLLER MECHANICS

Eric Freedman

This reading focuses on the conflicted nature of popular game discourse and the question of racial centeredness. The author believes that the most forceful examinations of race, gender, ethnicity, and class call attention to the matter of industry, connect imaging practices to questions of political economy, and examine the commercial and industrial imperatives affecting the creation and use of images.

In interviews Jun Takeuchi, the creative lead of the *Resident Evil 5* development team, has repeatedly defended the game against charges of racism, speaking directly about the game's setting (Africa) and its infected antagonists (predominantly Black Africans). Referencing generational violence, discrimination and occupation, and speaking to his own country's ancestral relations with the United States, Takeuchi has remarked that the Japanese company's games are designed to entertain and are not laden with political intent, and has suggested that despite any longstanding history of racial or ethnic discrimination in the world at large, self-censorship in game production can be limiting (Narcisse, 2009). Takeuchi claims that too much sensitivity can cripple game design. Pushing further, and defending the *Resident Evil* franchise, he argues that in contrast to the Africans in the world of *Resident Evil 5* (who have lost their humanity to a parasitic infection), the Japanese soldiers common to World War II-themed games are both berserk and human, and this insistence on their humanity is far more damaging than Capcom's fantastical projection of a biologically contaminated Third World zombie populace.

Hutchinson (2009) took an opposing stance, condemning the game for its racism, and for propagating ancient stereotypes against Africans. Despite the assurance of Capcom CEO Kenzo Tsujimoto that there was no intention to racially demean anyone and that the controversy could simply be ascribed to cultural differences and perceptions, Hutchinson countered Tsujimoto's position and aligned it with the rhetorical posturing of most Japanese product manufacturers, many of whom had been similarly called out for producing offensive, racially charged items, such as character dolls and cartoons.

The controversy surrounding *Resident Evil 5* originated with the premiere of the game's trailer in July 2007. The earliest backlash was built around the game's cinematics (narrative cutscenes that advance or frame the story) and in-house demo footage, rather than actual gameplay, and read the imagery for what seemed obvious clues to its disposition. In the trailer, the game's white American male paramilitary protagonist runs around gunning down hordes of Black African villagers. The images evoke primal fears of contagion (both viral and racial) associated with the "dark continent," and seem to align the game's action and mythology with broad sweeping cultural paranoia—the historical legacy that has grievously aligned Blackness with monstrosity and otherness. The evil in the trailer is decidedly human—ominous tones (and ancestral rhythms) ring out as the aerial camera descends into the streets of a local African village. In a pivotal scene, villagers force-feed a parasite to one of their own. Blood begins to pour from his eyes, marking the onset of his grotesque transformation into a monstrous other; yet his transformation is precipitated by what appears to be communal strife. At this point, the trailer's up-tempo adrenaline-charged combat scenes begin. The empty streets yield to an angry civilian mob, brandishing machetes, hatchets, pitchforks, and sickles; their instruments of labor have become weapons. Absent a clearly defined narrative, their violence seems primitively innate.

Even at such an early stage of reception, the discourse surrounding the game was conflicted. Not surprisingly, with the game's release 2 years later, and with gamers now actively embroiled in the *RE5* narrative, the dialogue became even more fractious. The flurry of replies to Hutchinson's commentary, mostly from gamers familiar with the history of the *Resident Evil* series, spins the game quite differently. Many draw attention to the game's larger plotline—the focus of which is a secret organization experimenting with biological weapons on an unsuspecting nation (the attention here is drawn to capitalistic and militaristic exploitation, and the reading emphasizes a victimized African nation)—and the franchise's larger serial structure (the origin story is set in a fictional Midwest American town, later migrating to Spain in *Resident Evil 4*). Several gamers also hold up the game's secondary protagonist, Sheva Alomar, as a positive (and playable) representation of Africanness; she is an African native, but as a controllable character built in the model of Lara Croft, she is unlike the crazed villagers who litter the streets of the game's earliest shanty towns (enemy hordes that are irrevocably mapped by the software's AI). The players' responses and redirections are equally dismissive of the charges of racism, and equally invested in restoring the game's virtue.

Studies of interactive media emphasize that consumers do not simply read images, they occupy and play through (or with) them; and the narrative space is often conflicted, the contextual elements and plot details never fully sewn up. Game narratives are often purposefully messy, and the discussions about images and stories are an important aspect of framing any consideration of the representational practices of particular media economies. What these discussions often reveal is the degree to which people feel personally empowered in their everyday lives.

The traditional cinematic accounts of pleasure and identification may fail to translate to an interactive medium. The avatar's body is not simply watched, but played. But there are other bodies too—those secondary and tertiary characters that frame, interact with, and quite often pose a literal threat to the primary (played) body. Most of the analyses of race relations in the recent installment of the *Resident Evil* series follow a long tradition of studying representations and spectators. Yet the more complex dynamics of narrativity, seriality, genre, and industrial relations must also be considered in any discussion of images.

My interest in this analysis is the unique subject/object relations of video games. My focus is not simply the implications of interactivity but the hardware and software of control mechanisms—the myriad incarnations of the video game controller and its coded response mechanics. I consider the ideological inflections of gaming hardware, connecting technological progress to cultural progress and reform. As a starting point, this case study seeks to understand the player/played body, which occupies a space somewhere between the screen and the controller. Our bodies are not simply at play; we are also projected (read by the industry and asked to engage in specific ways with its commodities) and projecting (caught in the act of revealing our fears and desires). I confront the ongoing controversy surrounding the assumed race relations in the *Resident Evil* game franchise and focus on the all-important material relations enabled by gameplay mechanics (conditions that are largely determined by designers, programmers, and developers) that situate the player's body in relation to what is often misunderstood as televisual and/or cinematic screen space. To what end are the questions of identity politics raised by traditional screen studies satisfactorily mapped onto the material relations embodied by video gameplay, and readily synthesized with the various industrial discourses that drive game production?

This essay tackles the coded rules of engagement (the script that drives the interface and the computational rules that shape the consumer's physical and mental attachments) that are a fundamental part of the industrial processes of development and fabrication. Just as character skins are laid onto armatures (wire frames), and setting and location are the products of environmental mesh, the game world itself is (from a meta-practical perspective) the formal outline of an engine—in this case Capcom's proprietary MT Framework. The MT Framework is a multiplatform engine and allows Capcom to distribute its content across the major next generation consoles, and influence production and reception across the board.

To find meaning, to deconstruct the question of race, is to engage with the more general study of games as a form. Video game studies is a rather young field, and has presented a number of dichotomies (Juul, 2005). Do we focus on the games or the players? On the underlying rules and mechanics or the fiction? On the game as a unique object or as yet another storytelling medium? The aesthetic conventions or the machinery? The game as a self-contained text or an object embedded in the broader culture? Video games are one fragment of a grander enterprise of transmedia (moving between media) storytelling in a transmedia economy. The game industry is not simply a sum total of its software enterprises and its serialized intellectual properties; it is also an arena of hardware development and licensing. The brand name is not simply attached to game franchises, but also to engines that govern the physics-based properties of characters and, by extension, those players who read and engage them. The player and the developer form a circuit of relations as the technical apparatus supports and structures gameplay.

Ignoring the industrial mechanisms of game production, which form a pipeline (laid by the governing policies of a corporation) that gets more narrow as it proceeds from broad concept art, the racial read of video games is commonly done on cinematics and story rather than gameplay. We must move beyond the surface, taking a multilevel approach without losing the image. Theorists such as Janet Murray (1997) argue that a game is not simply a text to be read, but an experience to be had; such analyses offer context, point to narrative, history, and interaction, foreground the performative nature of gameplay, and emphasize the value of individual agency. We must push further to consider how performance is contoured.

Our relationship to the image in a game's cinematic differs from that developed in gameplay, though both constitute the narrative. This divide is becoming less overt in games with quick time events (interactive cinematics), yet gameplay proper invokes more developed forms of agency. The melee attack or the attack with weapons is the most frequent gesture facilitated by standard control schemes in action-oriented games such as the *Resident Evil* series. But, as Gregersen and Grodal (2009) note, this is a limited form of embodiment that lacks the experience of reception, or being acted upon, and at best it is linked to only minimal somatosensory stimulation such as the "rumble" motors inside controllers. Action and reaction may also register formally, as an algorithm, in the heads-up display (HUD), as we receive or impart damage; our well-being is often translated into color-coded status bars. Even the most fully developed biomechanical interfaces produce a fairly limited range of isomorphisms (one-to-one correspondences) related to human agency; developers of controller-free games are currently exploring this gap.

System input (acting on) remains privileged over output (being acted upon, which is usually a consequence of not acting, or acting incorrectly), an imbalance reinforced by the common dependence on practiced bodily mechanics. As we peruse walkthroughs or blindly repeat failed actions, we become conscious of our interaction with both body and control mechanism.

Narrative action, cause, and effect are reduced to a set of required and practiced gestures. Taking ownership of an avatar is commonly more pronounced in third person games, such as *Resident Evil*, than in first-person shooters because one can evidence the body's destruction. But such ownership is still removed from being an object of embodied actions. We do not confuse ourselves with our avatars, however pronounced the dread of being told that "You are dead." The inequities highlighted in the discussion of race cannot be readily synthesized with any studied attention to motor realism, where all bodies can be acted upon equally.

Although themselves of conflicted zombie status (not properly undead), the parasitically infected Majini (Swahili for "evil spirit") of *Resident Evil 5* and Ganados (Spanish for "cattle") of *Resident Evil 4* draw their power from the allegorical models developed in other media, including cinema, that suggest the perversion of the normative order, contagion, and science run amok. Yet situated in survival horror, and located as the target of the first- or third-person shooter, they are aligned with a more generalized character position that drains them of their abject status; we know them and understand their function. They assume a category of being in game-level design—the boss of the boss fight, or the horde of regenerating enemies. But at the same time, they lose their status as pure other in the newer installments of *Resident Evil* as they are situated as a culturally determined other—the African or the Spaniard (in contrast to the generic everyman of the fictional America of Raccoon City). Inside a space over-determined by genre conventions, the Majini are interchangeable (although they vary in type, from civilians to tribespeople, in a manner dictated by environmental level design), but their physiognomy returns with a vengeance in popular discourse, making them contested subjects. This shift in emphasis is made all the more explicit in *RE5*'s "mercenaries" mini-game, a series of timed-challenges; within this mode, players are rewarded for their kill counts. Because the story has already been played through the main game, understanding the narrative gives way to understanding the environment; to succeed, the player must move expeditiously and develop a mental map of the playable space. As story yields to play, the characters are simply understood as targets with point values.

Yet playing through the game and its unlockable mercenaries mode, we may become acutely aware of this shift in attention. The overall play arc situates the indigenous population as central and marginal, villain and victim; gameplay is a dynamic event, and this shift in emphasis accompanies our movement through each environment and our overall progress. As narrative cues accumulate, our understanding of characters and events may evolve—an evolution that cannot occur if we remain outside the game or the genre. Survival horror games foreground the status of our bodies, not those of others; the HUD makes us keenly aware of our health and our odds of survival, and while it suggests our avatar has a decided physicality, it also reminds us of the game's user interface. As an instantaneous biofeedback mechanism, the HUD works toward immersion, but it also reminds us of the surface of things and the specificities of game design. The tension between image and interaction (as the privileged position to read the text) parallels the tension between the pleasure of play and story—between fighting to stay alive, making it through a level, and situating the level as a placeholder in a larger narrative framework.

The bodies in *Resident Evil 5* and *Resident Evil 4* speak to the abject—that which is outside of the symbolic order, or which transgresses boundaries and is marginalized. The abject is a concept often used to describe the status of oppressed groups, and the parallel need to seal over cracks in the existing social order. The parasite takes over and explodes its host body; humans birth monsters. These bodies without boundaries defy categorization and must be eradicated, or they will consume us as well. Yet at the level of story, these bodies also speak to the parasitic nature of colonization (narratively coded as bioterrorism and pharmacological experimentation), which similarly destroys the body of its host (nation).

Games are not simply representational products, they are also player-centric; and while we may not let go of the stereotypical nature of their representations, we must pay attention to the structure of the player's (designed) experience. The game engine allows the insertion of an infinite variety of assets that may perform the same way; but at the same time, the engine provides the syntax and produces the relative openness of the game universe. To connect the game engine to a reading of race, we might suggest that it is ultimately the engine that allows or disallows shifts in the vocabulary of race relations. The engine controls the soft and hard physics, determines the relative utility of exploration, and emits the signals of agency—the engine determines the relative impact (and realness) of our (avatar's) presence on the world we inhabit. By posing certain functional limits while celebrating certain capabilities, the engine contours the discourse. It not only shapes the characters, the field of play, and the environmental mechanics, but it also shapes the player's interaction by contouring the visual and physical experience. To truly understand game space, and to develop a fully articulated critique, we must approach games as rule-based, mediated, fictive, playful, and social enterprises. The game theorist must move beyond the study of representations to consider actions and the worlds in which they transpire. The game theorist must also consider the manner in which the engine, code, and 3D design, bound together in the game production pipeline, introduce operational limits.

Resident Evil 5 resonates with the commonplace patterns of human-computer interaction that govern our everyday lives. An ideological critique of the game must attend to its underlying informatics (data-driven technical protocols). The more one examines the actual construction of racial identity in the game, looking at character construction, for example, the more one sees that software programming (the matter of game design) drives identity itself. Identity is a data type, an easily adjusted mathematical variable. Likewise, the playable body is bound to the player's body through coding; scripting structures our interaction. The informatic mode has recolonized identity and agency (Galloway, 2006). To be more forceful in our critique, we must situate each representation in space and time, and we must understand that each representation is driven by an engine.

Rather than looking at and evaluating the representation on screen, we need to explore the cultural dimensions of technology. Gameplay is a social practice, not a closed text. We need to read across image, interface, and interaction, and examine the industrial frameworks that contour our technologies of play. Is *Resident Evil 5* a racist game? To answer this question, we need to understand the game as an industrial product, rather than read it as a series of images. And to pose a productive solution, to interrogate and erase the residual traces of racism, and to propose alternative models of image production, we need to explore the operational limits imposed in conception and development. Technologies are cultural practices, and as such they are never ideologically neutral. To simply read the image as a playable surface is to overlook the importance of what lies underneath. We need to develop an informed critique of the established design tropes (the artisanal conventions that shape such aspects as character and environment) and the commercial imperatives that fuel the engine-based mechanics of engagement. These are the matters of the intellectual property, and the market force that rules our play, shapes our response, and, in the case of survival horror, dictates what we fear.

IT'S YOUR TURN: WHAT DO YOU THINK? WHAT WILL YOU FIND?

1. Gamers often claim that video games are simply entertainment, implying that race, gender, and politics don't matter. Do you agree? Why or why not? What might be the dangers of not considering why certain representations seem to prevail in video games?

2. Have you played any games that seem to challenge the general claims of racism and sexism? If so, how did these games avoid racial and gendered stereotyping? Are there any representations that seem noticeably absent from video games? Why might these images be hard to find?

3. Consider the central characters in two video games that you have played recently. Did the physical manner that you controlled and interacted with the character shape your relationship to the character? Some games offer significant freedom in choosing or refining in-game characters. Examine the choices you made to personalize your avatar.

4. This case study focused on racial and ethnic stereotypes in one game/genre. Does this analysis work equally well for other stereotypes or video games/genres? How might the claims need to be adjusted for other game forms? Point to specific examples. Look at online reviews, discussion boards, or game journals for the games you have chosen as examples. Do the comments seem to mirror the discussions surrounding *Resident Evil 5*? What are the common arguments? What are the unique arguments?

REFERENCES

Galloway, A. R. (2006). *Gaming: Essays on algorithmic culture.* Minneapolis: University of Minnesota Press.

Gregersen, A., & Grodal, T. (2009). Embodiment and interface. In B. Perron & M. J. P. Wolf (Eds.), *The video game theory reader 2* (pp. 65–83). New York: Routledge.

Hutchinson, E. O. (2009, March 14). Resident Evil Racism. *The Huffington Post.* Retrieved October 8, 2011, from http://www.huffingtonpost.com/earl-ofari-hutchinson/resident-evil-racism_b_175010.html?view=screen

Juul, J. (2005). *Half-real: Video games between real rules and fiction worlds.* Cambridge, MA: MIT Press.

Murray, J. H. (1997). *Hamlet on the holodeck: The future of narrative in cyberspace.* Cambridge, MA: MIT Press.

Narcisse, E. (2009, March 2). Uncomfortable echoes: A conversation with *Resident Evil 5* Director Jun Takeuchi. *Crispy Gamer.* Retrieved October 8, 2011, from http://www.crispygamer.com/interviews/2009-03-02/uncomfortable-echoes-a-conversation-with-resident-evil-5-director-jun-takeuchi

PRODUCTION

Films, TV shows, newspapers, and Web sites don't appear out of thin air; they exist because people create them. While that statement may appear so obvious that it borders on the absurd, the fact remains that we often do forget about the constructed nature of all media messages. Someone decides on the topic and the goal of the message; someone writes it; someone prepares its audiovisual elements; someone distributes it. Who produces the content consumed by media audiences? What pressures do they face?

In this age of mergers and acquisitions, the majority of mainstream media content is produced by individuals or teams working for large corporations that are increasingly interested in the bottom line. But that doesn't mean everything is mainstream. New media and the Internet have made it possible for regular people such as you and me to produce and distribute our own mediated messages (e.g., *produsage*; see Chapter 4). Independent filmmakers still strive to realize their dreams and visions. And it doesn't mean that everything mainstream is profit driven, nor that profit is attainable only at the sacrifice of social responsibility.

If you've ever been involved in media production, you probably learned how to operate equipment (camera, audio recorder, computer, etc.); how to tell a story; and how various elements of sight, sound, and motion can help you convey your message. You've probably also considered your target audience, so that the media text you create will serve the audience's needs, desires, and interests. Even if you haven't been involved in media production, you may understand that the process of producing media texts is often complex and always involves a wide range of activities: conceptualizing, writing, revising, planning desired audio or visual elements, recording/creating raw materials, editing, adding audio or visual effects, and the like.

This section isn't going to address things such as whether female producers have a different working style than men do, or whether people of color or of lower socio-economic status employ various production aesthetics in an identifiable or unique style. We won't do much with the technical side of things, or in terms of making direct comparisons across types of people. Instead, these readings present glimpses into a variety of situations in which real people, creating real media content, have found themselves. They shed light on certain aspects of the production process—perhaps aspects you haven't yet considered.

Specifically, in this section, authors discuss race, gender, and class in media production by addressing the reality of what it's like to create various types of content and by examining media professionals or media organizations to illuminate the environment in which these people work. As with the other sections, the alternate table of contents will indicate which readings address social class.

The seven readings in this section fall into two chapters. The first, *Producing Media Content*, contains four readings looking at how media content is created in a variety of real-life contexts. In Reading 8.1, TV reporter Mark Saxenmeyer shares his vision for and experiences with creating meaningful and substantive reality-television-inspired news and documentary content, focusing on his award-winning *Experiment: Gay and Straight*. Dwight Brooks and George Daniels (Reading 8.2) consider how radio host Tom Joyner uses the *Tom Joyner Morning Show* to accomplish an urban activist mission, and investigate the show's success in light of several radio trends. In reading 8.3, radio reporter Natalie Moore reflects on the unique opportunity of being assigned to a "community bureau," and discusses how her assignment allows her to cover "invisible news" and to "give voice to the voiceless." In Reading 8.4, Cynthia Conti illustrates the technique of participatory cinema—which allows a film's subjects to have input into their representation. She also discusses some ethical and other challenges she faced when producing her documentary film *Out of Bounds*.

Chapter 9, *Media/Communication Organizations*, includes three readings. It begins with Cindy Vincent's ethnographic analysis (Reading 9.1) of *POOR Magazine*, which is led by poor and indigenous people, and which provides media access, education, and advocacy to people in poverty. Robert Papper, in Reading 9.2, reviews his many years researching race and gender in newsroom employment in the United States and provides an overview of some of the key findings on women journalists. In Reading 9.3, Donnalyn Pompper reports on what she learned about the importance of role models for women in communication, from interviewing women of varied ethnic and cultural identities who have succeeded in journalism, public relations, and telecommunications.

If you're interested in becoming involved in any aspect of producing media messages— whether under the auspices of an established media organization or on your own using new media or the Internet—you should find these readings enlightening and informative. Even if you don't plan to be involved in message production, they should help you become informed of the social reality within which media content is created and as a result be a more critical audience member.

Producing Media Content

8.1   EXPLORING GAY/STRAIGHT RELATIONSHIPS ON LOCAL TELEVISION NEWS

Mark Saxenmeyer

> *The author has been a television broadcaster for 23 years, 17 of them at FOX News Chicago (WFLD-TV), where he served as executive producer of* Experiment: Gay and Straight. *He explains how the project came to be, the commitment required to complete it, and the hurdles jumped along the way.*

Is it truly possible to mention the words "reality TV" and "meaningful dialogue" in the same sentence? If you've ever watched these shows—the dating shows (*The Bachelor, Rock of Love*), the competition shows (*Survivor, Project Runway*), the lifestyle shows (*The Real Housewives of Orange County/New York/Atlanta* etc.)—you might easily answer with a resounding "no." Reality TV seems to have become filled with over-the-top characters (or caricatures) dropped into increasingly contrived, staged, manipulated, and even scripted scenarios to create outlandish drama for the viewer/voyeur.

Yet as an admitted connoisseur of the genre at its purest levels, I've always appreciated producers' ability to turn on the cameras, to capture "average Joes" speaking their minds, and to weave the results into compelling stories. Reality TV, in many respects, is an amplified version of traditional documentaries. They're fanciful embellishments of the kind of work TV journalists produce every day.

And, as a news guy, there came a time when I felt as if I'd covered almost every imaginable story in every imaginable way, and I yearned to do something different, creative, original. So in 2002, I pitched *Experiment: Gay and Straight* to my bosses at FOX Chicago News.

As someone who came of age when the granddaddy of all reality shows, *The Real World*, premiered in the early 1990s, I wanted to harken back to that series' early seasons, when the young strangers who were brought together engaged in substantive conversations that shed light on their differences, revealed their similarities, and generally helped them grow into more fully evolved human beings.

I also wanted to emulate components of *Big Brother*, a show that locks up a disparate group of people inside a home for a pre-determined period of time (but for purposes other than plotting to win a cash prize by deceiving, backstabbing, and ultimately eliminating fellow contestants). My goal was a bit loftier. I wanted to create and encourage an environment for ordinary Chicagoans to openly and honestly discuss the serious and sometimes explosive issues involving sexuality, human rights, and discrimination. To make sure that they stuck to the plan, I liked the idea of sequestering them from the outside world for one entire week.

My ultimate hope was that those watching this *Experiment* might then be prompted to engage in similar dialogue in their own lives—to begin similar conversations with their own friends and family members, neighbors, and coworkers.

I called it "reality TV with a purpose."

BUT FIRST, A RACE RELATIONS *EXPERIMENT*

I had previously produced *The Experiment in Black and White,* using the same format and dealing with race relations. Five Black and five white Chicago-area residents lived together in a home for one week and, with the guidance of myself (white) and another reporter from FOX Chicago (Black), engaged in lively, eye-opening debates about everything from affirmative action, slavery reparations and racial profiling, to discrimination, crime, and stereotypes.

Many journalism critics and awards panels lauded this project. It won a national Emmy, the national Edward R. Murrow Award, and the national Scripps Howard Foundation Award, among others. A judge in the Scripps Howard Foundation contest declared, "It brings to light racial hot points so near the surface that the revelations are both alarming and enlightening."

Still, *The Experiment in Black and White* was no bonanza for FOX Chicago in the all-important Nielsen ratings. Turns out that no matter how interestingly or differently or thought-provokingly the subject of race relations is presented, it's still an automatic turn-off for some.

And, of course, the same could be said for homosexuality.

I ASKED AND, EVENTUALLY, WAS ALLOWED TO TELL

The general manager at FOX Chicago at that time was reluctant to proceed for two reasons—surprisingly, the prior *Experiment's* lackluster ratings wasn't really one of them. She and the other managers at the station were progressive thinkers who, like me, were always quick to back creative ideas. They didn't deem the Nielsens the sole arbiter of quality TV or broadcasting success.

No, her first concern was monetary. To rent a home, furnish it, and provide food for 10 people for a week wasn't cheap to begin with; throw in the salaries of the staff who'd be devoted exclusively to this project for anywhere from 5 days to a month (for pre- and post-production), and the price tag for the first *Experiment* approached $20,000—no drop in the bucket, even for a station in the third largest market during flourishing economic times. Her second concern, however, surprised me. I'm paraphrasing here but I distinctly recall her saying something to me along the lines of: "Do straight people really even have issues with gay people any more?"

As a gay man myself, I responded (probably rather incredulously), "Ah, yeah, they do."

In my general manager's worldview, race relations (especially in an extraordinarily segregated city such as Chicago) were much more tense and divided than gay/straight relations. She was someone who had many gay friends and had hired many gay employees who all seemed to work in perfect harmony with the straight people, so she wasn't feeling the same need for this project as the first *Experiment.*

To welcome her to the not-quite-as-enlightened world that I lived in, I rattled off some of the issues that I saw us discussing in this *Experiment:* gay marriage and parenting, harassment and violence, homosexuality and religion, genetic and environmental influences, whether being gay is a choice, whether gays can be "changed", homophobia, gay sex leading to HIV and AIDS, gays on the "down-low" or in the closet, gays' impact on American culture, gays being rejected and disowned by their families, gay kids committing suicide. I'm not sure if I just wore down her defenses, or that she ultimately just trusted me, but *Experiment: Gay and Straight* got the green light.

THE PEOPLE MAKE THE PROJECT

The most important part in putting together this kind of project is the selection of the participants. I needed people who were smart, articulate, engaging, uninhibited, and unafraid to voice their opinions—informed opinions. They also needed to know how to listen, and be willing to learn. This was a chance to let their guards down, to throw "political correctness" to the wind, to delve into subjects often considered taboo for polite discussion, and to cast away their fears about being labeled ignorant, a "hater", or perverted. Perhaps most important, though, I had to make sure that we weeded out closed-minded zealots and activists with specific agendas, or this *Experiment* simply wouldn't work.

It was also extremely important to me not to cast gay stereotypes, such as the overly effeminate man with a lisp, or the androgynous lesbian with a man-hating attitude. Too many reality-based programs seemed to be filled only with flamboyant, over-the-top characters that—while they exist—simply aren't representative of the gay community as a whole.

So, I put together a report announcing and explaining the project, and it aired on our newscasts. Within days, more than 800 people had filled out a lengthy application I created. I selected about 100 people for long in-person, on-camera interviews (by both me and another FOX Chicago reporter who is straight). Next, we introduced 28 of the strongest candidates (seven each of gay and straight men, lesbians, and straight women) to our audience through on-air reports and Internet biographies. More than 1,800 viewers submitted comments about the prospective housemates. And then, after extensive criminal background checks, we selected our 10 finalists.

The participants (all strangers to one another) included three gay men, two straight men, three straight women, and two lesbians. They came from all corners of the Chicago area, were of varied educational, socio economic, ethnic, racial and religious backgrounds, and ranged in age from 23 to 47.

They included Darlene, a straight woman whose grown son had recently been gay bashed; Larry, whose family was unwilling to acknowledge his relationship with his male partner; Frank, a dad who said he'd find it virtually impossible to accept his newborn son if he grew up to be gay; Chris, an out-and-proud college senior who refused to live in the closet despite finding many of his gay peers felt otherwise; Jennifer, who despite her friendships with gay men found lesbian relationships offensive and unrealistic; Deo, a lesbian mom in search of a suitable sperm donor to father another baby for her and her partner; Brandon, a divorced father of two teenagers struggling with the fact his wife left him for a woman; Kyla, a devoted Christian with an unwavering belief that homosexuality is a sin; Andrea, an unapologetic young lesbian searching for both love and her father's approval; and Greg, an HIV patient who had tried and failed to exorcise his homosexuality through a religion-based "ex-gay" program.

LIGHTS, CAMERAS, HOUSE, ACTION

The participants moved into a three-bedroom, three-bathroom house for 7 straight days. They ate, slept, cooked, cleaned, and socialized together; they entered the arrangement fully aware that they'd be entirely cut off from the outside world—no phones, computers, newspapers, radio, television, etc. They were given daily assignments, tasks, and challenges, and were guided through in-depth conversations about sexuality—every hot button topic imaginable.

The ensuing results were recorded 24 hours a day by several videographers, audio technicians, and mounted cameras. Were the housemates influenced or affected by the constant presence of these people and this equipment? At first, most definitely. But after a while, they truly became accustomed, if not oblivious, to it. (The crew was not allowed to interact with the participants.)

For me, the most moving and memorable moments of the week were Frank's emotional upheaval when confronted with a question about whether he would have aborted his son if it were possible to know a child's eventual sexual orientation while still in the womb, the deep bond that grew between Darlene and Greg when she revealed to him that her son was also HIV positive, the literal breakdown of a usually stoic Larry when he verbalized his depression over the fact that no one in his family was willing to attend his commitment ceremony, and the virtual standoff between Kyla and the rest of the housemates over whether God condemned homosexuals.

SEX SELLS, BUT DOES SEXUALITY?

We left the house with 164 hours of digital Beta tapes and camcorder cassettes and began logging, examining, and molding them into the multi-part series that aired on our main newscast, and later, as a 90-minute documentary. It was an enormous and daunting challenge.

Because of the lackluster ratings for the first *Experiment*, I felt pressure from the news director to make this project "sing," right out of the gate. My preference would have been to start the series by introducing the participants to viewers, one by one, taking time to develop a sense of who they were and what they stood for before they even entered the house. But the boss wanted to delve immediately into some of most heated discussions and most controversial issues. (I might add that one of the promotions for the project went like this: "One House, One Week, Ten Strangers, Five Gay, Five Straight, Living Together. Think you could handle it?" This sensationalistic approach, in my opinion, was to try to appeal to every possible homophobe on the most primal of levels.)

When I watch the completed project today, 8 years later, I'm frustrated by some of the editing and pacing choices that were made as a result of this pressure. There is a cloying urgency to the first parts, especially. It's as if I'm trying to convince people who might have absolutely no interest in watching to stay tuned—almost tugging at their shirt sleeves saying, *"Hey, this is gonna be worth your while, really! If you don't like THIS part, you're sure to get a kick out of what's coming up in just a second! So don't turn that channel, buddy!"*

Such are the limits and drawbacks of local television news. On one hand, there's a built-in loyal audience of thousands, accustomed to tuning in at the same time, and the same station, night after night. But in its fickle, trigger-happy hand is a remote control ready to explore umpteen other channels should boredom, unease, or annoyance set in.

Even though FOX Chicago News at 9 p.m. is an hour in length (a fact that has always enabled my reports to run much longer than those on competing channels), it was still difficult to bring the appropriate and necessary context and pathos to each of the individual segments (which aired over five nights, at a total running time of nearly one hour). *Experiment: Gay and Straight* resonates much more strongly as a self-contained documentary, shown uninterrupted and with additional material.

Yet sadly, that was never to be—at least not on FOX Chicago. Despite all the time, the effort, the money, and the hard work put into the project, the top brass at the station seemed to want to backpedal as far away from it as possible after the news series aired. The general manager chose not to have me produce a documentary version, at first asserting there were no time slots available (as if we couldn't pre-empt reruns of *Home Improvement*), and then later claimed it was simply too tough a sell for advertisers.

I was furious. The facts, I felt, suggested otherwise.

THE VIEWERS AND THE CRITICS REACT

The Nielsen ratings for *Experiment: Gay and Straight* were decent, especially in the coveted younger demographics (highest in women aged 18 to 34, and all ages between 12 and 24). As for total household numbers, the final segment garnered a 4% share of the audience, and a 5 rating (translating into about 17,500 homes). And most important, there was no perceivable drop-off of viewers during the newscast when the segments aired over the course of 5 straight nights in November 2002.

Overall, viewer response was phenomenally supportive. The housemates each received hundreds of personal e-mails (we set up addresses for them on our Web site), and the station received well over a thousand. These numbers are virtually unheard of. Here's a sampling from positive viewer e-mails: "Responsible, interesting, serving a higher purpose. Thank you for daring to be different, and for providing one of the greatest cities on earth a push ahead on a very important issue." "If there was ever a way to help the pain from being gay, this news series was it." "Thank you also for helping gay people understand how straight people feels." Thank you for being my inspiration and my reason for coming out of the closet. Just by watching, you all have shown me that there truly is a happy life awaiting me."

Following the broadcasts, the housemates and I spoke about the project on radio stations, at high schools, universities, and at a wide variety of gay and lesbian organizations.

Coverage of the series by other media was extensive, with generally favorable articles written about it in gay publications such as *The Windy City Times*, *The Chicago Free Press*, *She*, *Instinct*, and *The Advocate*, as well as mainstream print and Web-based press such as the *Chicago Sun-Times*, *Red Streak*, *Electronic Media*, *People*, and *USA Today*.

The Gay and Lesbian Alliance Against Defamation (GLAAD) spoke out about the program's importance, and the news series won regional awards from the National Academy of

Television Arts and Sciences (the Emmy Award), the Associated Press, and the Society of Professional Journalists. The National Lesbian and Gay Journalists Association also honored it with a Seigenthaler/NLGJA Excellence in Television Award.

American Journalism Review (AJR) wrote, "Reporter Mark Saxenmeyer . . . knows full well the traditional news brigade will scoff themselves silly over this -- and he doesn't seem to care. What matters, Saxenmeyer says, is that people actually watch the thing, and maybe even lose a prejudice or two" (Rosen, 2002).

And sure enough, those traditionalists did indeed weigh in. *The Chicago Tribune*'s media columnist, Steve Johnson, told *AJR*, "It's as if I enlisted somebody to run through downtown Chicago in a chicken suit, then presented it as a news story." . . . " There are probably more responsible ways to address gay versus straight issues rather than jamming people together and waiting for the fireworks" (Rosen, 2002).

Of course, some viewers weren't fans either: "Why is it I have to be subjected to this during the news? It is not news." "It absolutely disgusts me that a NEWS broadcast is having its very own *Real World* series! This is pathetic! Not to mention, completely biased. It is only for the cause of gay rights!" "It serves no purpose other than to boost ratings of a network historically known for airing shows geared towards the less educated/intelligent people who don't even know who they are." "Being gay is a social disorder. It's not natural. What is Fox going to have next—*Experiment in Child Molester and Non-Child Molester?*"

My final response to the critics: Yep, I took an unorthodox approach. It's because I believed (then, and most definitely now) that most television news coverage of serious subject matter is stale, dull, and redundant. *Experiment: Gay and Straight* was a fresh voice, an intriguing alternative, delivered with integrity, and poised to redefine the parameters of substantive journalism. The *Experiment* might be a gimmick, but if so it's a gimmick that helped our participants and our viewers scrutinize their beliefs in a way never before attempted by a local TV news station.

SO, I'M DOING IT ANYWAY

Just because FOX Chicago didn't want a documentary didn't mean I wasn't going to make one. On my own time, I poured through the logs of all our tapes and wrote the 90-minute version of *Experiment: Gay and Straight*. Out of my own pocket, I spent thousands of dollars to pay videotape editors to help construct it, and to advertise and promote it. It eventually aired several times (with FOX Chicago's permission), on CAN-TV, a cable access channel in Chicago.

I entered the documentary into gay and lesbian-themed film festivals around the world. It was accepted and shown in Auckland, Austin, Breckenridge, Brussels, Cape Town, Dallas, Denver, Montreal, San Francisco, Seattle, and Washington D.C—to name just a few. *Experiment: Gay and Straight* was named by audiences as one of the "Best Documentary" winners in Indianapolis, and both "Best Documentary" and "Best 'Feel-Good Film'" winner in Sydney. It won the juried prize for best documentary in New Orleans.

As a result of the exposure from the festival circuit, I was approached by three different home video companies, and by Canadian Television executives interested in buying and rebroadcasting the program but, unfortunately, because I used contemporary music in the production, I couldn't afford the rights to those songs for widespread distribution.

The documentary won national awards such as the "American Scene" prize from the American Federation of Television and Radio Artists (AFTRA); the National Accolade Competition gave it top honors in the "contemporary issues/awareness raising" category. It also won the Gracie Allen Award from the American Women in Radio and Television (best reality television program), a Hugo Award from the Chicago International Television Competition (educational/adult audience category), and the national "Unity Award in Media" from Lincoln University of Missouri (outstanding public affairs/ social issues reporting).

When all was said and done, I felt more than vindicated. To bring this vision to such incredible fruition was not only empowering, it was—without a doubt—the high point of my broadcasting career thus far.

A LASTING IMPACT

More than 8 years after this project premiered, it continues to have an impact, resonating with people all over the globe. Hundreds of educators from churches, workplaces, schools, and universities around the globe (it's been translated into other languages and subtitled) use the program in sexuality, psychology, sociology, journalism, conflict resolution, and diversity/ sensitivity training classes. PFLAG (Parents and Friends of Lesbians and Gays) chapters around the country keep *Experiment: Gay and Straight* in their libraries, showing and discussing it at meetings.

There's no doubt that many issues were left unresolved when the participants ended their week together. But there's also no doubt that rational compromises were made. And there's *absolutely* no doubt that both the gay and straight participants in this project, and the gay and straight audience members who watched it (and continue to watch it), gained a better understanding of one another. In the end, *Experiment: Gay and Straight* was simply about bridging a divide. Reality television, sprinkled with a healthy dose of journalism, can indeed have a purpose.

IT'S YOUR TURN: WHAT DO YOU THINK? WHAT WILL YOU FIND?

1. Does this kind of "reality TV"-based project truly have a place on a nightly local television newscast? Why or why not?

2. What other divisive social issues and subjects, if any, could you see the *Experiment* format tackling in a meaningful way?

3. What do you consider to be the benefits, as well as the drawbacks, of sequestering the participants for this project?

4. How do you think the constant presence of cameras, microphones, and producers (and the knowledge their views and actions would be televised) might have affected the participants' discussions and reactions?

5. What is your perception of the way gay and lesbian participants on reality television shows are typically depicted?

REFERENCE

Rosen, J. (2002, October). Dose of reality. *American Journalism Review*. Retrieved April 27, 2011, from http://www.ajr.org/article.asp?id=2647

8.2   THE TOM JOYNER MORNING SHOW: ACTIVIST URBAN RADIO IN THE AGE OF CONSOLIDATION

Dwight E. Brooks and George L. Daniels

> *This reading introduces you to the* Tom Joyner Morning Show (TJMS) *and its activist community-oriented programming in an era of consolidation whereby media properties tend to focus on the bottom line. By examining the* TJMS *in this context, you'll understand how this syndicated morning show has combined entertainment and community service into a commercially successful formula. Following a discussion of the* TJMS *and its unique brand of community service and activism, the authors look at the show in terms of radio consolidation issues and trends.*

Tom Joyner, the self-proclaimed "hardest working man in radio," has become a household name within African American communities. Joyner is the first African American elected to the National Association of Broadcasters Hall of Fame. Although Joyner's radio audience is twice Don Imus', comparable to Howard Stern's, and more than half of Rush Limbaugh's, Joyner does not receive comparable attention from "mainstream" media (di Leonardo, 2008). Joyner's Dallas-based program was owned by and syndicated (1994-2003) through ABC Radio Networks. In 2003, Joyner bought it through his Reach Media Company and in 2004, signed a collaboration agreement with Black-owned media conglomerate Radio One. *The Tom Joyner Morning Show* (TJMS) has cultivated audience growth from 5 million in 1998, 7 million by 2001, and currently reaches more than 8 million listeners—nearly one in four African Americans (di Leonardo, 2008; Reach Media, 2011).

THE *TOM JOYNER MORNING SHOW*

The *TJMS* attracts a relatively older, affluent, and responsive listening audience for its roster of blue-chip advertisers such as Southwest Airlines and McDonalds. From Monday through Friday from 6:00 to 10:00 a.m. EST, the *TJMS* presents "old-school" music, news and information, guests from politics and entertainment, and an assortment of segments including open telephone lines, humorous advice, and social commentaries.

Sybil Wilkes and J. Anthony Brown serve as co-hosts for the *TJMS*. The list of regular contributors is topped by Roland Martin, who appears daily with interviews and commentary, and includes Reverend Al Sharpton and D.L. Hughley. Weekly *TJMS* features include "Real Fathers, Real Men" and "The Thursday Morning Mom"—each recognizing fathers and mothers who affect their families and communities in positive ways. The *TJMS* has a weekly segment called "Christmas Wish" to grant wishes to individuals and groups who serve their communities. And the popular daily feature "Little Known Black History Fact" celebrates Black culture through storytelling. Joyner sums up the strategic goal for his show in simple terms: "First we get people to listen, second we get 'em laughing, and then we get them involved. If I can reach people, then they begin to think, and that's when they start making a difference in their communities."[1]

Two of the *TJMS'* most ambitious projects are non broadcast events: the annual Fantastic Voyage cruise and the Tom Joyner Family Reunion. The 7-day cruise prior to Memorial Day offers non stop entertainment, educational and cultural activities, seminars, and even town halls such as CNN's "Black in America 2" with Soledad O'Brien. Well-known entertainers perform for the 4,000 guests who in turn raise millions for the Tom Joyner Foundation. Since 2003, the annual Tom Joyner Family Reunion during Labor Day weekend in Orlando, Florida, has featured family activities, seminars, and concerts by top entertainers. More than 12,000 guests attend the family reunion held at Disney World. Both events receive extensive coverage on the *TJMS* through Joyner's constant updates on cabin sales, and the lineup of entertainers. In fact, big-name performers lobby on the show for a chance to attend—and perform. Joyner characterizes these events as "parties with a purpose." The *TJMS* branding statement "Party with a Purpose" originated with *TJMS* "Sky Shows."

TJMS: ACTIVISM ON THE AIR

Sky Shows originated in 1996 when Joyner and Tavis Smiley wanted to use the morning show to increase voting in African American communities. The *TJMS* encouraged listeners to come to the broadcast venue, register to vote in the upcoming election, and have a good time. In 1999, Southwest Airlines became the title sponsor of Sky Shows—live broadcasts of the *TJMS* several times a year in front of large audiences and featuring a national recording artist or group. Crowds of 3,000 people arrive in the early morning hours, wait in line before entering the arena to be entertained and enlightened by the *TJMS* cast and guests. During one Sky Show, a performance by an old-school funk band was followed by an exchange between Joyner and Tavis Smiley, who at the time provided commentary twice a week on the *TJMS*. Joyner and Smiley discussed the key purpose of holding the Sky Shows—registering people to vote—and stressed how important it was for the Black audience to participate in elections, to effect change. In fact, the TJMS partners with the NAACP to conduct voter registration at the Sky Shows, and even has a 24-hour hotline for people to register by phone.

Another regular component of Sky Shows is recognition of corporate donations for college scholarships awarded by the Tom Joyner Foundation. Each month the *TJMS* features a different historically Black college or university (HBCU) and awards scholarships to students attending that institution.

TJMS voter registration and voting rights initiatives accompany national elections. Prior to the 2004 Presidential election, Tom and his crew marched with filmmaker Michael Moore from the Gleason Theater to voting booths in Miami. During both U.S. Presidential election days in 2004 and 2008, the show aired continuous reports of voter "irregularities" throughout the country.

Besides voter registration efforts and college scholarships, the *TJMS*'s unique approach to community service programming is evident in its activist campaigns—mostly against some aspect of racism in American society. Among the earliest examples was the 1997 movement sparked by the Manhattan auctioneer Christie's decision to sell nineteenth-century slavery documents and memorabilia. After the *TJMS* gave the telephone number of the auction house over the air, thousands phoned in their objections and Christie's president appeared on the *TJMS* to announce changes in the company's policy.

Another example was a 1999 campaign targeting CompUSA for not advertising to Black consumers. *TJMS* listeners mailed in sales receipts to CompUSA to demonstrate that African Americans shopped at the computer store and affected the company's bottom line. ABC (then owner of *TJMS*) allegedly ordered Joyner and Smiley to back down on the CompUSA campaign and even threatened to cancel the program. Upon hearing of the threat, callers flooded the switchboards at both ABC and Comp USA, resulting in an appearance on the *TJMS* by the CompUSA president with an apology for the "misunderstanding," and a promise to hire a Black-owned advertising agency.

Among the more noteworthy instances of the *TJMS*'s on-air activism and service began on the last week in August 2005. The show joined U.S. media in issuing weather warnings as a Category 3 storm named Katrina approached the Gulf Coast. However, the *TJMS* may have been alone in connecting the hurricane's potential damage to the country's wars in Iraq and Afghanistan:

> **Joyner:**   30 billion estimated in claims for Hurricane Katrina. I just want to know Sybil, how much is the war in Iraq costing?
>
> **Sybil:**   Oh my goodness, I don't know.
>
> **Joyner:**   I'm just asking', why can't all that money go towards people lives in the path of the hurricane? (di Leonardo, 2008, p. 19)

As Hurricane Katrina ripped through New Orleans and brought the entire Gulf Coast region to a tragic halt, the *TJMS* devoted most of its programming efforts on the failure to protect residents of New Orleans and evacuate the overwhelmingly Black and poor citizens. The *TJMS* organized it own relief efforts and critiqued media coverage of the disaster. This brief exchange between Tom and Sybil was one day after President Bush's second visit to the region and almost simultaneously with his announcement that he would lead an investigation into what went wrong in the hurricane relief efforts (Tuesday, September 6):

> **Joyner:**   Turn the TV off, will you?
>
> **Sybil:**   Stop watching it! It's like crack!
>
> **Joyner:**   I know, and I'm getting depressed watching it. And they don't have but five pictures . . . . Here's what we've come with. The families who've taken in families can't get any form of relief. So we're gonna help the people who're trying to help the people who have no hope. (di Leonardo, 2008, p. 19)

Joyner explained the show's decision to give out prepaid credit cards to individuals who registered through any church (because of tax law restrictions). Following an initial $80,000 pledge by the show's crew, the 3-day total was $580,000. Two weeks later, they had amassed $1.5 million and sent out more than 500 credit cards with another 300 prepared for the mail (di Leonardo, 2008). In its support of Black colleges (left out of the initial federal relief), the crew pledged $1 million of their own money to award $1,000 scholarships to 1,000 displaced college students. By mid-October, they gave out $2.4 million.

Two years later, the *TJMS* played a major role in rallying more than 100,000 people to ascend on a little-known community of Jena, Louisiana, to call for justice for six Black teenagers convicted as adults for aggravated assault of a White student. Civil rights activist Rev. Al Sharpton was a frequent guest on the *TJMS* as it provided daily updates on the case.

The *TJMS*'s extensive coverage of the 2008 Presidential campaign and election comes as no surprise. Besides appearances on the show by Hillary and Bill Clinton and Michelle and Barack Obama, there were daily commentaries on behalf or against most of the major candidates. What may surprise some is that the Presidential campaign contributed to the resignation of one of the central cast members of the *TJMS*. For nearly 12 years, Tavis Smiley partnered with Tom Joyner in disseminating information to audiences and championing issues and causes on behalf of African Americans. Since the beginning of the Barack Obama Presidential campaign, Smiley was vocal about Black people's support for Obama without focusing on whether he addresses issues of import to Black communities. Despite Joyner's strong support for Obama, Smiley had harsh words for the Presidential candidate on the *TJMS* when Obama did not appear at Smiley's "State of the Black Union" conference in February.

In April (2008), Smiley announced that he was leaving the *TJMS* due to fatigue and other things going on in his life. On the other hand, there is evidence that Smiley's resignation was due to the criticism he received from *TJMS* listeners. According to a Joyner blog posted on blAcka-mericanweb.com: "The real reason is that he can't take the hate he's been getting regarding the Barack issue . . . He loves black American and black American has been very critical of him"

Talk radio is known for the political views of its hosts and listeners, but few entertainment-oriented programs are as politically active as the *TJMS*. The show is described by one political scientist as the "single most recognizable form of black talk in black America today" (Harris-Lacewell, 2004, p. 237). The *TJMS* is consistent with the "public sphere" that focuses on media's public interest role. The public sphere model argues that society's needs cannot be met entirely through a market system emphasizing business success via profit. Thus, the media (also should) become central elements in a vibrant public sphere (Croteau & Hoynes, 2001). Because both the market model and the public sphere are important in understanding the media, we'll examine the *TJMS* in the context of the market model and, more specifically, some of the trends and issues that have emerged from this model—the dominant business model within media industries.

THE MARKET MODEL: DEREGULATION AND CONSOLIDATION

The market model suggests that society's needs are best met through a relatively unregulated process of exchange based on the dynamics of supply and demand. In broadcasting, policymakers believed this could best be achieved through deregulation. Deregulation relies on the marketplace, rather than government intervention, to establish priorities and standards of business conduct. Deregulation intensified in the 1980s when policymakers argued that most media regulation was not in the public interest (Croteau & Hoynes, 2001). By the 1990s, the rise of new digital technologies led to increasing expansion of media industries. As more media conglomerates emerged from a decade of market-oriented media policy, many argued for a wholesale rewriting of the laws and regulations that drive U.S. media policy.

The result was the Telecommunications Act of 1996, which led to major changes in the media industries such as more intense consolidation—the rise of media conglomerates of un-precedented size. In terms of radio, the Act removed limits on the number of stations a company could own and sparked a wave of mergers among radio companies. Staff and other resources were consolidated. Stations are increasingly part of regional or national ownership "groups"; by 1999, some groups had more than 1,000 AM and FM stations under their control. Even within a single market, one owner could hold up to eight radio outlets. Many policymakers and media companies claimed that greater concentration of broadcast outlets meant good business: media conglomerates create economies of scale that allow them to better compete with expanding information and entertainment distribution platforms, such as satellite TV and the Internet.

By 2001, the nation's largest radio group (Clear Channel Communications) owned 19 of the 110 stations that carried the *TJMS*. Some feared such consolidation would hurt racial minorities, many of whom owned stations likely to carry an urban/Black radio program such as the

TJMS. A decade later in 2011, minority-owned Radio One owns the largest number of stations carrying *TJMS*, exceeding Clear Channel, which is still the largest radio station owner in the United States. While the majority of the more than 100+ stations that carry the *TJMS* are located in the South, Radio One owns most of the stations that carry the show outside of the region in cities such as St. Louis, Indianapolis, Detroit, Cincinnati, Cleveland, Boston, and Philadelphia. As a large, vertically integrated station group, Radio One not only has part ownership of the *TJMS,* but control over many of the local stations in which the show is broadcast. Not only is there insufficient evidence to conclude that consolidation has hurt Black radio station ownership, it does not appear to have had an adverse impact on diversity.

DIVERSITY

The FCC's efforts to increase minority ownership were directed at increasing workforce diversity and, ultimately, greater content diversity. However, even if the owners of most *TJMS* affiliates are not African American, mostly racial minorities staff the 100+ stations that air the show. In addition, the *TJMS* represents workforce diversity because the majority of the show's staff is African American. Besides this type of workforce diversity, the show contributes to diversity in radio in other ways. Few shows regularly take on causes such as supporting African American fathers, raising funds for HBCUs, or recognizing trailblazers in Black history such as Rosa Parks. Beyond the show's overt diverse content, it also has contributed to radio content diversity in terms of competing shows.

The *TJMS* is just one of the many choices listeners have during morning drive, traditionally the time period when listenership is highest and thus most lucrative for radio owners. One of few morning drive national competitors for this market of adult (working class) African Americans with an extraordinarily high commitment to radio listening, steady income and significant purchasing power is Steve Harvey. *The Steve Harvey Morning Show* (*SHMS*) is less political than *TJMS*, with its focus on personal (relationship) issues. From 2000-05 the show was syndicated by Radio One, when Harvey signed a joint syndication deal in 2005 with Premiere Radio Networks and Inner City Broadcasting Corporation for a new incarnation of *SHMS*. In 2009, it was announced that the *SHMS* would replace the *TJMS* in Chicago on WVAZ, which had been one of Joyner's flagship stations.

Another show competing—albeit during afternoon drive—for the same audience is *The Michael Baisden Show* (*MBS*), launched by ABC Radio Networks (now Citadel Media) in 2005. Baisden, an air personality at New York's WRKS, is also an author, TV talk show personality, and emerging community leader. The MBS airs weekdays from 3 to 7 p.m. and offers what Baisden calls "grown folks radio"—music, comedy, personal fulfillment, and social outreach to inspire change in local Black communities.

LOCALISM

For its first 50 years of existence, station radio programming thrived on localism, or programming to meet the needs of the public in the area in which the station has been licensed to broadcast. Many critics predicted that consolidation would lessen radio stations' commitment to localism. For urban radio stations carrying the *TJMS*, localism isn't a problem because it's part of the show's formula for success. Despite being distributed to more than 100 stations across the nation, Tom Joyner makes a concerted effort to allow affiliates to maintain a local flavor throughout the show. In fact, some listeners have said the show sounds like it is broadcast from a station in their local area. This is one of the major appeals of the show.

From his Dallas studio, Joyner records customized announcements and introductions of local air personalities daily for each of his affiliates. These elements go beyond traditional customized promotional "drop-ins" (5- to 10-second messages played between songs and announcements) provided by satellite radio announcers. In the case of the *TJMS*, local drop-ins are recorded and updated daily to give the show a live and local flavor. Besides these drop-ins, the show also allows ample time for local news, traffic, weather, and other information throughout the 4 hours. At one time Joyner put his show together as a "national show that sounded like it was local" (Farber, 2000, p. 136), although he now admits there is less of an effort to sound local. In cities where the *TJMS* is not available from a broadcast station, people can listen on the Internet. This leads to another trend in radio's consolidation era—webcasting.

WEBCASTING

When a radio station "streams" its broadcast signals over the Internet for individual reception on computers, we call that "webcasting." Don't confuse this with "Internet radio," in which programming is available *only* online. While many stations have extended their Web sites beyond static marketing pages to active places where consumers may hear the radio signal even as it is broadcast, the *TJMS* utilizes this technology to reach African Americans—especially in areas where the show is unavailable.

The *TJMS* Web site can be found on blAckamericaweb.com, which was launched in 2001 by Tom Joyner as a broad-based effort to become an interactive, timely, and credible source for news and information for African Americans. In addition to live streaming audio of the *TJMS*, the Web site also allows visitors to download segments of previous shows. The *TJMS* Web site's main top menu bar includes tabs for "news," "money," "life and style," "college fair," "sports," "dating," "TJ Foundation," "photos," "blogs," and the home page for blAckamericaweb.com. The *TJMS* Web site also features information about the cast and crew, links to Facebook, *TJMS* segments such as "The Tide (sponsor) Thursday Morning Mom", and blAckamericaweb.com message boards. The site also has advertisements for feature films, credit cards, and products such as LifeLock (identity theft prevention).

THE BOTTOM LINE

We concluded our look at a few radio trends and issues with webcasting because it is a technology that is evolving—as is the era of consolidation. In fact, the impact of consolidation on such trends as minority ownership, the media workforce, and content diversity, and microformatting remains to be seen. What is more certain, the *TJMS*—even when affiliated stations are not minority owned—with its community service and activism, will continue to be an attractive media product because of its commercial appeal and active audience.

In many ways, Tom Joyner demonstrates the financial rewards from integrating public service programming with entertainment. However, Joyner's commitment to serving Black communities has been a foundation of both Black-owned stations and Black/urban radio formats since their inception.[2]

In conclusion, while the two models used here to examine a media product—the market and public sphere—are both necessary in understanding media, we contend the *TJMS* illustrates the limitations of a strict market model approach. Media businesses should not be judged solely by market profitability because markets tend to produce inequities and they rarely meet democratic needs. According to the public sphere model, the media are more than just profit-making components of large conglomerates. For a participatory democracy to function, citizens must have access to the resources necessary for meaningful participation. As media play crucial roles in preparing citizens for active participation in our democracy, the *TJMS*, as a vibrant participant in the public sphere, strengthens our democratic society.

NOTES

1. Unless indicated otherwise, all quotations from Tom Joyner were obtained from an interview conducted by the authors on July 21, 2001.

2. For more on the tradition of Black/urban radio, see Barlow (1999) and Williams (1998).

IT'S YOUR TURN: WHAT DO YOU THINK? WHAT WILL YOU FIND?

1. The *TJMS* has been mistakenly labeled a "talk show" even though it has considerable music and entertainment. Can you name other entertainment-oriented radio programs that also have an activist theme? What are those themes? Would you listen to those programs? Why or why not?

2. Identify the closest station to you that carries the *TJMS*. List the station's call letters, location, and format. Listen to the show for an hour and compile a "log" of its program elements (song, commercial, news break, etc.) Use this log to analyze the show's content in terms of its combination of entertainment and community service programming. If no station in your area carries the show, you can listen to the show on the *TJMS* Web site (http://www.blAckamericaweb.com).

3. Again, listen to the *TJMS* for an hour. How many references to "race," "African Americans," or "whites" did you hear? Describe the way(s) race was referenced (jokes, serious commentary, news content, etc.). Did anything make you feel uncomfortable? If so, do you think the source of discomfort was because of your own racial background or identity? If not, do you think this suggests your comfort level is high in dealing with issues of race? Why or why not?

REFERENCES

Barlow, W. (1999). *Voice over: The making of Black radio.* Philadelphia: Temple University Press.

Croteau, D., & Hoynes, W. (2001). *The business of media: Corporate media and the public interest.* Thousand Oaks, CA: Pine Forge Press.

di Leonardo, M. (2008). Neoliberalism, nostalgia, race politics, and the American public sphere: The case of the Tim Joyner Morning Show. *Cultural Studies, 22:* 1–34.

Farber, E. (2000, April 7). Publisher's profile: Tom Joyner. *Radio & Records*, p. 136.

Harris-Lacewell, M.V. (2004). *Barbershops, bibles and BET: Everyday talk and black political thought.* Princeton: Princeton University Press.

Reach Media. (2011). Retrieved May 3, 2011, from *www. reachmediainc.com*.

Williams, G. (1998). *Legendary pioneers of Black radio.* Westport, CT: Praeger.

8.3   REFLECTIONS ON BEING A COMMUNITY JOURNALIST

Natalie Y. Moore

> *The author, a radio reporter, discusses what being a community journalist means to her, and to the community at large, in terms of covering news that remains invisible to mainstream media.*

I was destined to become a reporter. As a child, I loved reading and writing. At age 13, I would circle errors in the *Chicago Defender*, the city's storied Black newspaper that helped usher in the Great Migration. My father told me that if I was so interested in pointing out problems, I should work on becoming a solution! This was the signpost of when journalism first appealed to me.

I joined WBEZ-Chicago Public Radio—a National Public Radio member station—in May 2007. It was my first radio job. I had worked for corporate chain newspapers, dabbled in free-lance magazine writing, and co-authored a book about Black masculinity in the hip-hop genera-tion. I envisioned my career early on as a newspaper executive. Changes in the profession and economy led me toward another path as a radio reporter and producer.

WBEZ realized that it needed to do a better job of covering Chicago communities—not just institutions like schools, cops, and courts. So the station opened up *community bureaus* in the re-gion. Mine opened third on the South Side of Chicago. The office is a former storefront church in Englewood, a high-poverty, high-crime neighborhood. The office is not just a space where I write scripts and edit audio. We see ourselves as a community space, too. We've hosted events—some of them live and straight to air—and use the studio to conduct interviews. We want people on the greater South Side to see the WBEZ investment and look at us as a resource.

Being assigned to a community bureau allows me to tell stories such as the one about Gloria Allen, a slender, attractive woman who loves stylish jewelry. She has caramel-colored skin and strawberry blond hair. She's 64 years old and has been living as a woman since ever she was 24 years old. She lives in senior public housing in Chicago and was facing discrimina-tion from a fellow tenant. The man allegedly attacked her with a crutch, calling Allen a "nig-ger bitch." Chicago public housing officials at the time said they were in the process of taking "corrective actions" and that Allen didn't deserve to live under threatening circumstances. I did the story because the federal government was embarking on a national study about transgender housing discrimination—the first of its kind. In my research, I learned that around the country transgender people have significant housing instability, including eviction and homelessness.

Interviewing Allen was a treat, and it personalized a potentially wonky story. She was thoughtful, descriptive, and open in relaying her story to me. As a medium, radio provides inti-macy and Allen deftly told her story with conviction. It was one of those moments where I, as the reporter, needed to get out the way and let listeners connect with her steady voice. No need for fancy writing or clever turns of phrases.

One of the best professional compliments I have ever received came from a listener who heard Allen's story. The listener said he admired my work because I always report on "invisible news." I've been lucky to win several national awards for my work at WBEZ. But comments such as these are what keep me motivated in journalism and the work I do in my hometown.

My colleagues in our other WBEZ community bureaus have the same commitment to "invis-ible news." And we're lucky to work for an institution that values this kind of work. It's not easy to find a news organization whose values jibe with your own. I don't know of any other news organization—regardless of the medium—in the country that has embarked on a community bureau journalism endeavor like ours.

There's an adage in my profession that says, "Afflict the comfortable and comfort the afflicted." My addendum to that is to *be a voice to the voiceless*.

Community bureaus are possible because WBEZ operates on a nonprofit model. We don't have to appeal to the highest income earning listeners—the kind that advertisers want. Instead, the staff goes on air during pledge drives to ask listeners for donations. It cuts into programming, but it's necessary. The public radio audience believes in our mission that says we serve "the public interest by producing and delivering diverse, compelling content of multiple viewpoints and expression. We act as the circuit that connects residents of our region to one another, to the nation, and to the world in a relevant and evocative way. We are a regional resource fostering full and active citizenship by creating connections and remaining present and involved broadly in community life" (WBEZ.org). People are willing to pay for the service. They appreciate that there are no commercials and we aren't beholden to advertisers. We simply do stories that matter.

People often ask how I find story ideas. It's a combination of curiosity, observation, press releases, and people pitching ideas. Although some journalists claim to be "objective," I believe there's no such thing as objectivity. We all have subjective experiences. However, I do strive to be fair and balanced. I see my job as neither positive nor negative; life is way too complicated for such neat boxes. I do human-interest narratives on people such as Gloria Allen. Journalists are watchdogs, so I follow policy stories and the ensuing implications. I cover public housing, gentrification, and the intersection of race and class. There's a mix of investigative journalism and sweet audio postcards.

One of the many complaints people have about the news media in general is that we cover too much "negative" news. It's true that "good news" doesn't often make the news. Conflict, proximity, timeliness, and prominence are factors that guide news judgment. But I understand some of the sweeping generalizations made about certain neighborhoods in large cities without regard to the complexity and diversity of the communities. The South Side of Chicago, for example, is not one big ghetto. Not all Black people are poor. Not everything that happens on the South Side is on a police scanner. After all, our forty president of the United States, Barack Obama, calls the South Side home. Yet such narratives play out in many minority–majority cities in the United States.

At times, "diversity" becomes a buzzword when discussing the performance of newspapers and electronic media. But the truth is, there's no grand conspiracy to omit people of color or portray groups in a certain light. Editors don't stand around rubbing their hands together as they plot how to bring down a race. Newsrooms are too disorganized to be that duplicitous. That doesn't mean bias and stereotypes don't seep into news coverage. In a perfect world, a newsroom should be a marketplace of ideas with all kinds of people. When you don't have that mix, stereotypes can thrive.

However, newsrooms don't always get it right even when the intentions are good. I worked in a city where there was a large Somali population in the region. The newspaper rightfully wanted to cover stories about the community and I believe we struggled early on. We ran a story with a side bar explaining what Somalis ate and their customs, and such. It read like text in a museum exhibit. I realize that a general audience might need some schooling on culture, but I doubt that Somali readers gained anything from that type of news coverage. What the newspaper did was write *about* a community rather than *for* a community. The distinction is stark.

In writing for a community, I've constantly had to get out of my comfort zone as a reporter and take notes along the way. When I did the story on Gloria Allen and the transgender discrimination she faced, I referenced that she used to be George Allen. I received a call from someone who enjoyed the story but said one should never refer to a person's former gender. I had never thought about that, and I appreciated our exchange. When I started covering public housing, I thought people would be happy to leave the rickety high rises that had become a national symbol of urban housing policy failures. Nope. Because this was home to people.

In both of these cases, I had to recognize my own bias and value system. And I like to think that I quickly changed course by telling a story that was not from my own perspective. Ultimately, I'm a storyteller. Or a midwife here to deliver news that's "invisible."

IT'S YOUR TURN: WHAT DO YOU THINK? WHAT WILL YOU FIND?

1. Go to WBEZ-FM online (www.wbez.org) and listen for yourself. What do you think of the local news? How does it compare to the news in your community?

2. Find something about your community that's interesting or important, yet remains "invisible." How could you tell that story? If possible, actually write and produce the story, preferably with audio and/or video.

3. Do you, or any of your friends, want to be journalists? How might you consider some using some of the points presented here in your own career?

4. Discuss how learning about "invisible news" in a community can have a positive effect on the community, especially in terms of race, gender, and class relations?

REFERENCE

WBEZ.org (n.d.) Mission. Retrieved March 30, 2011, from http://chicagopublicmedia.org/about/mission

8.4 LOCATING BUTCH IN *OUT OF BOUNDS*: FEMALE FOOTBALL PLAYERS, EXPRESSIONS OF MASCULINITY, AND PARTICIPATORY CINEMA

Cynthia Conti

> *Here is a first-person account of a documentarian's use of participatory cinema to provide a voice for her subjects. Note also the consideration of gender identity as much broader, and reflecting more of a continuum, than the bipolar "masculine" and "feminine."*

In October 2000, I began work on a documentary about a women's flag football team in the Jamaica Plain Women's Flag Football League (JPWFFL) of Boston, Massachusetts. The league has 150 members in 10 teams. One of these, Team Nemesis, consists of about 15 players diversified in age, race, profession, sexual orientation, class, and gender identity. Every Sunday in the fall, the women of Nemesis gather as fierce athletes to engage in some of the most aggressive aspects of professional football, such as full-contact blocking, diving for passes, and rushing at the one-yard line, notably without helmets and pads. Inspired to start attending games when my girlfriend joined Nemesis, at first sight I was struck by the intense physicality with which the teams play. I was even more surprised to find myself enjoying the game, considering I am not much of a sports fan. There was something about watching women playing a sport that has been culturally designated for men that intrigued me. I wanted to know more about the team members and why they played the game.

During this time, I entered my second year of graduate school in media studies. Feeling distanced from the theories of media, cultural, and queer studies that I was constantly immersed in, I was frustrated with the direction of my academic career. I rarely found any opportunities to apply this type of intellectual thought to my own life and my own surroundings. To deal with my feelings of unfulfillment, I decided to dedicate the next semester to a project that would allow me to bring theory into practice, one in which theories of gender and media would unfold as I went deeper into research. I believed I would find such a project in Nemesis—by making a documentary about the team, I would explore issues of gender identity among the members. Sensing it as a way to take an intellectual leap in my relationship to theory, I decided to use the medium of digital video to examine how gender manifests for these women on and off the football field.

This essay is a reflection on my experiences during the first 4 months of production for *Out of Bounds*. I detail the ways digital video was used to explore team members' notions of gender identity, and how I applied Judith Halberstam's theory of female masculinity to help me better understand women's interest in football. Additionally, I discuss the ethical dilemma of representation that documentary filmmakers frequently confront, something that arose for me through exploring Halberstam's theory. Along the same lines, I discuss the techniques of participatory cinema that I implemented in an effort to treat my subjects fairly, and filmmaker Jean Rouch's influence in this endeavor. Finally, I demonstrate how participatory cinema contributed to my original exploration by revealing important information about team members' attitudes about gender identity.

EXPLORING FEMALE MASCULINITY THROUGH DIGITAL VIDEO

I immediately saw the football field as a rich space for exploring gender identity. Whether they are conscious of it or not, every time the members of Nemesis play football, they subvert traditional beliefs that males are naturally masculine, not feminine, and females are naturally feminine, not masculine. In other words, they challenge the binary alignment of sex and gender by engaging in a masculine activity such as football. Halberstam's concept of "female masculinity" concerns this specific form of gender subversion, referring to the masculinity that many women feel and embody. Halberstam calls for a separation of gender (masculinity) from sex (male) by presenting historical and cultural examples of females who refuse to conform to social expectations of femininity. These "alternative masculinities" range from tomboys to drag kings. By doing this, Halberstam makes an academic effort to remove the stigma from women who are not feminine, asserting that the masculine gender does not solely belong to men, but is legitimately experienced by all sexes. She pointed out that this is something even the most liberal individuals fail to recognize, as demonstrated by the rejection of women who assumed the gender identity of "butch" by many members of the lesbian feminist movement during the 1970s (Halberstam, 1998, p. 121).

Although "butch" is a popular term to describe women "who are more comfortable with masculine gender codes, styles, or identities, than with feminine ones" (Rubin, 1992, p. 467), many have misunderstood it to mean a female who desires to be male, rather than a woman who possesses an organic sense of masculinity—which is independent from maleness. Additionally, butch-femme lesbian couples (in which one woman is masculine and the other feminine) have historically been frowned upon within the lesbian feminist movement, read as "a gross mimicry of heterosexuality" (Halberstam, 1998, p.121). Halberstam challenges such outdated stigmas by applying a fresh perspective to interpreting expressions of masculinity in the lesbian community, one represented in the use of the term "female masculinity."

Through making *Out Of Bounds*, I examine how Halberstam's notion of female masculinity manifests among one particular group of female athletes. To reveal team members' feelings toward masculinity, I use footage of games and interviews which I shot and edited using digital video production and post-production equipment, including a Sony TRV900 camcorder, a G4 Macintosh, and Final Cut Pro software. Much of the footage consists of Nemesis playing football against other JPWFFL teams. During each game, I captured a number of action shots, including attempts to run the ball down the field, quarterbacks passing to receivers, defensive blocks, and players grabbing others' flags, as well as sideline shots of players cheering, slapping hands, and strategizing with others. Each of these shots depicts the competitive edge surfacing in every player on the field, often manifesting as aggressive physical behavior. This is most evident during line blocks when two players come head to head, with one attempting to push the other out of the way to get to the quarterback and the other acting as guard for her team. I interpreted these actions as masculine, and after shooting a few games I was convinced that during interviews players would discuss the masculinity that is expressed on the field.

However, despite what I perceived as clear evidence of masculinity in the field footage, interviews revealed that most of the 10 players I spoke to didn't think about football in relation to gender. Mel, a player on the defensive team, said she doesn't see "any of that [gender] stuff going on [while we're playing] because we're all women. . . . I think people might see it differently if it was co-ed flag football and we were playing with the guys, and we had to think about the gender." Speaking for other team members as well, Mel pointed out how sex and gender are seen as closely linked, and by not having to confront this binary difference—male and female—among players on the field, issues of gender are avoided. Instead of perceiving the game as an expression of gender identity, half the team members I spoke to said football is just something they want to play. As Laura explained: "It is sort of progressive in some ways, you know, women playing football, but . . . it's kind of like the way I was brought up playing sports. It's just . . . an extension of myself. For me, it's not a big deal."

Notably, with one exception, players such as Laura who see football as unrelated to their gender identity do not identify themselves as butch. Of these players, a couple took offense at the suggestion of a connection between football and masculinity. As Jenn explained, discussing the game as a masculine sport unjustly perpetuates a stereotype that all female football players identify as butch: "I don't really feel like I'm this . . . butch lesbian, at all. But I guess stereotypically people are like bad-ass bull-dykes on the field, but I mean, not everyone's a lesbian that plays football, so it's not fair." Kim echoed this sentiment when she said she likes the league because women do not have to be butch to play: "That's what I love about our team and most of the teams. People think that girls who are going to be playing football are just like really butch. You know but, we're not, and I'm not."

Although Jenn, Kim, and the majority of women I interviewed said they don't think about playing football in relation to their gender identity, the two members of Nemesis who identify themselves as butch lesbians understand football and gender as intricately connected. In fact, Kath directly locates the game in her butch coming-out process:

> Once I found that label [butch] and thought that it fit me and wanted to take that on, that was when I began to really feel like I could fill myself out. Like I felt like I had been holding parts of myself back, and that's when I began to research things that I really wanted to do, that I had *always* wanted to do, that didn't feel like that I really could because they were too . . . over on the male side of the spectrum. So I started doing things like . . . accepting the stuff that my father had taught me about plumbing, and carpentry, and all those sorts of things that he had taught me as a kid, but I was sort of pushing aside because I had thought that it was too outside of the ordinary, and football fit right into that.

Like Kath, Chris became interested in the game while developing her masculine gender identity. After a girlfriend gave her a football to show support for "what she considered my butchness," Chris casually played around with it, only to discover an affinity for the game. Eventually, she came to realize that football is indeed a part of her identity, something her girlfriend had a sense of when giving her the gift: "I think [she] was like, 'this is you.' [Later on] I was like, 'Yeah, this is me.'"

Unlike Chris and Kath, half the players I interviewed don't perceive football as a masculine act. Furthermore, the vast majority doesn't see masculinity as part of their own gender—a point that I interpret as connected to Halberstam's notion of a masculinity continuum. In discussing a social tendency to narrowly define gender identities, she conceives of a continuum that showcases categories of queer females and their traditional meanings in relation to masculinity, with "androgyny" on the "not masculine" end, "Female-to-Male" (transgendered) on the other, and "butch" in the middle. Besides limiting how a person can define herself, such strictly outlined categories perpetuate the stigmatization of women who do identify as masculine, presenting it as something that is experienced by only a small amount of women. For this reason, it makes sense to me that most of the players don't see themselves as experiencing masculinity when they play football. If they did, they'd be vulnerable to criticism from both the straight and queer communities.

In my mind, the footage from the field strengthened this interpretation. With all players participating in masculine acts of aggression and competition, I found it hard to understand why most of the players I interviewed didn't see masculinity as an important component of their identity. While an interesting point of research, the content disparity between the masculine messages of the field footage and most players' opinions that football is not gendered presented a challenge. It created an ethical dilemma for me as a filmmaker. During post-production I realized that by juxtaposing scenes from the field and interviews, I potentially threatened the assertions of the subjects. To some viewers (including myself), images of aggressive behavior such as blocking, diving, and screaming may undermine the players' verbal denials of masculinity. This might portray them as out of touch with aspects of the game, or even their own self-identity. I wondered if these or other edits would leave players feeling misrepresented. Because the members of Nemesis trusted me to represent them fairly, I wanted to take steps to ensure that this unspoken agreement be respected.

TECHNIQUES OF PARTICIPATORY CINEMA

After some research into different methods of documentary filmmaking, I found that many filmmakers have attempted to achieve fair representation by giving their subjects some degree of editorial control, otherwise known as techniques of "participatory cinema." A special approach named by ethnographic filmmaker David MacDougall (1995), participatory cinema occurs when a film's subject actively contributes to the production process by taking on the role of filmmaker, editor, and/or critic at various times during filmmaking. In this way, the subject transcends her traditional role of passivity—as someone whom the filmmaker uses to convey a message—and ultimately exercises some degree of control over the final cut.

One of the first practitioners of this collaborative approach to filmmaking was the anthropologist-turned-ethnographic filmmaker Jean Rouch. In 1954, Rouch initiated what he called "shared cinema-anthropology" with the Songhay fisherman of Niger. Three years after shooting the fishermen hunting a hippopotamus, Rouch returned to them with a projector and a cut of a film about this event (an early version of *Bataille sur le grande fleuve* from 1951). To his surprise, the subjects had a great deal to say after viewing his film, a response he detailed in *Our Totemic Ancestors and Crazed Masters*: "They saw their own image in the film, they discovered film language, they looked at the film over and over again, and suddenly they started to offer criticisms, telling me what was wrong with it" (1995, p. 224). Based on their feedback, Rouch came to better understand the Songhay people, and eventually changed the soundtrack to more accurately depict their culture.

In *Chronicle of a Summer*, made in 1961with sociologist Edgar Morin, Rouch documented this technique of participatory cinema. The second to last scene depicts a group of his subjects watching images of themselves during a short cut compiled from the film's rushes. After the screening, the filmmakers listen to subjects' thoughts regarding how they and their peers were represented.

I was inspired by the honest discussion between filmmaker and subject that such a situation could evoke, so I organized a feedback session with the members of Nemesis. A few weeks after the season ended, 14 team members, several guests, and I gathered at one of the player's homes to watch and discuss a 30-minute rough cut of *Out of Bounds*. For research purposes, I recorded the discussion with two digital video cameras. One was designated to capture both video and audio from the perspective of one of the subjects, Kim, who some days earlier had expressed an interest in filmmaking. I used the other to record the audio of the discussion that followed the screening. Whereas players had become comfortable with the camera on the football field by the end of the season, they clearly felt uneasy around it in other settings, becoming silent in its presence at social events. Because it might have inhibited the discussion, I decided not to hold a camera in their faces when asking them to speak about such sensitive topics as their representation in the film and gender identity. Instead, I recorded players' voices by holding a shotgun microphone connected to a camera which sat behind a wall. This setup was a compromise between my desires to document the discussion and increase the subjects' comfort.

The technical setup proved successful and resulted in a full hour of discussion about the rough cut—a dialogue that helped me better understand my subjects, especially in relation to gender identity. Far from my expectations, none of the players directly voiced concerns about their representation in *Out of Bounds*. However, what many questioned was my decision to present equal amounts of interview segments containing discussions of gender identity and action shots from the field. These players thought it would be better to prioritize one type of footage over the other. Fran, who has played on Nemesis for four years, suggested choosing between the topics, a point echoed by a guest at the screening who considered football to be the more interesting subject of the two: "Women have struggled with labels [like butch] for decades now. . . . And I think what's new is football. So the newer explanation I think you can have in the video is about football." Team member Carolyn seconded this when she said: "The whole essence of the film is that these are women that are very physical, so you want to show that physicality more, and blend that in with what they're talking about." Through these comments, players encouraged me to reevaluate the emphasis of the film, suggesting that I make the action of football the focus. It is in these moments that the team members assumed the position of the filmmaker and participatory cinema was achieved.

Continuing to think as the filmmakers of *Out of Bounds*, the players moved to a discussion of gender identity. When addressing team members' differing opinions about football's relation to gender identity, the players asked whether it's better to show each individual's perspective or leave some out for the sake of continuity. For example, they wondered if I should exclude a player's interview from the video because she suggests there is no such thing as butch identity, while the others that were interviewed all recognize its existence. One player suggested prioritizing continuity, only to have several teammates quickly disagree with her, saying this edit could conceivably make them all look the same. Ironically, a player received the concerns of misrepresentation that I had expected would be directed at me. Discussions such as this taught me a lot about Nemesis, specifically that the majority of players believe misrepresentation derives from absence of voices rather than inclusion. In other words, contradictory opinions are seen not as vulnerabilities, but strengths. This knowledge alleviated many of my worries about juxtaposing field footage with testimonies of non-masculinity because I recognized that players didn't find such discrepancies threatening; rather, they saw them as adding dimension to the team.

CONTINUING WITH PARTICIPATORY CINEMA

Because *Out of Bounds* is a documentary-in-progress, I feel content in saying that I still don't entirely understand the place of female masculinity in relation to the members of Nemesis. However, although I don't yet have an answer to the initial question that sparked this project, the first 4 months of production uncovered information I never anticipated, as well as challenges I never expected to confront. By applying Halberstam's theory of masculinity to the footage I was collecting, I interpreted the disparity between the masculinity of the field footage and comments of non-masculinity as deriving from players' fear of stigmatization. This inspired me to consider how to fairly represent the perspective of each team member. In searching for ways to address this concern, I was inspired to incorporate techniques of participatory cinema into the production process. To my surprise, the feedback session yielded important information regarding gender identities, particularly that the members of Nemesis recognize they are varied and prefer showing everyone's identity, rather than leaving people out.

As I continue to work on *Out of Bounds*, I will use this information to guide the direction of the project. This experience has taught me to continue to embrace disparities in footage because they may contain compelling details. Additionally, I learned that participatory cinema is not only a way to respect my subjects, but also a means of getting to know them. I believe that if I continue on this path of subject participation, I will move closer to understanding female masculinity in team Nemesis among the players of the team.

IT'S YOUR TURN: WHAT DO YOU THINK? WHAT WILL YOU FIND?

1. Describe the main point the author makes about academic theory. Do you think she succeeds in using theory to inform practice? Why or why not? To what extent might using theory to inform practice result in a better film?

2. Imagine you're a filmmaker making a documentary about a social group you belong to, and you want to incorporate techniques of participatory cinema into the production process. Knowing what you do about this community, how would you go about

achieving participatory cinema with them? List the ways you'd involve your subjects in the production process, and why you chose these methods.

3. What might be some of the negative aspects of participatory cinema? In other words, what are some complications that might result from involving subjects in the production process? How may filmmakers resolve these issues?

4. Consider the gender identities of women and men represented in the media today. To what extent do these representations reflect traditional bipolar "masculine" and "feminine" identities? To what extent do they reflect gender identity as falling along more of a continuum? What do you think are the ramifications of these representations?

REFERENCES

Halberstam, J. (1998). *Female masculinity*. Durham: Duke University Press.

MacDougall, D. (1995). Beyond observational cinema. In P. Hockings (Ed.), *Principles of visual anthropology* (2nd ed., pp. 109–124). New York: Mouton de Gruyter.

Rouch, J. (1995). Our totemic ancestors and crazed masters. In P. Hockings (Ed.), *Principles of visual anthropology* (2nd ed., pp. 217–232). New York: Mouton de Gruyter.

Rubin, G. (1992). Of Catamites and kings: Reflections on butch, gender, and boundaries. In J. Nestle (Ed.), *The persistent desire: A femme-butch reader* (pp. 466–482). Boston: Alyson Publications.

Media/Communication Organizations

9.1 *POOR MAGAZINE* AND CIVIC ENGAGEMENT THROUGH COMMUNITY MEDIA

Cindy S. Vincent

The author reports on her ethnographic study of POOR Magazine, *a non profit arts, education, and media organization led by poor and indigenous people.* POOR Magazine *is dedicated to providing media access, education, and advocacy to people in poverty.*

The United States is one of the largest economies in the world based on gross domestic product, second only to the coalition of countries comprising the European Union's single economy (Central Intelligence Agency, 2010). This apparently robust economic status, however, obscures another startling statistic: from 2008 to 2009, the number of people in the United States struggling with poverty increased from 39.8 million to 43.6 million people (U.S. Census Bureau, 2010). We live in one of the richest countries in the world, but a significant number of our fellow Americans still struggle to make the bare minimum to support themselves and their families. However, in mainstream media coverage this population generally does not appear, or is not taken seriously, so which media serve the needs and express the perspectives and experiences of these 43.6 million people? The sphere of media, or the mediascape, is diverse and consists of several categories: *commercial* (for-profit), including most mainstream media; *public* (partially government-supported) such as the Public Broadcasting Service; and *community* media, in which people create and control media that reflects their own community's needs and experiences. Of these types, it is usually only in community media that we are able to hear the perspectives of people living in poverty.

The class system in contemporary American society can be seen through the lenses of two powerful dynamics: the overwhelming presence of mainstream media in society and the immense power these media have to maintain and strengthen dominant ideologies and social structures. For years, scholars have demonstrated how mainstream commercial media reinforce unequal class structures and dominant ideologies, and marginalize ethnic, gender, class, and sexual communities (Marx, 1978; Said, 1997; Downing, 2001). There is, however, a bright light in this dark tunnel of social inequality. A survey of current media scholarship reveals a number of organizations, educators, and active citizens are using community media to bypass mainstream media's monopoly of control and to engage in social justice activism. These engaged citizens are creating alternative forms of communication to reach out and encourage unengaged individuals to become active participants in social and political processes. Such media-driven outreach and civic engagement strengthens social movements, cultivates grassroots organizations, and alters class structures and communication flows. But how do community media engage individuals who are normally ignored or vilified by the mainstream media? What role do community media educators play in encouraging civic engagement? Using Clemencia Rodríguez's (2001) concept of citizens' media, I sought to answer these questions by conducting ethnographic fieldwork with the community media organization *POOR Magazine*.

POOR Magazine is a poor people/indigenous people-led grassroots, non profit arts organization dedicated to providing revolutionary media access, education, arts, and advocacy to youth, adults, and elders in poverty. The concept of revolution is at the root of *POOR*'s mission because the organization believes it is engaging oppressed people in new and dramatic ways. *POOR* is located in San Francisco, and works to promote positive social change for citizens whose lives are marked by struggles with homelessness, poverty, racism, classism, disability, immigration, incarceration, and discrimination in general. The organization was created by Tiny, aka Lisa Gray-García, and her mother Dee in 1996. They launched a concept known as poverty scholarship, and they were in fact poverty scholars. Through poverty scholarship, *POOR* builds power with the recognition of scholarship and knowledge already held by the students at *POOR* (Tiny, 2011). True to its namesake, *POOR Magazine* could initially only afford to print a few issues before its budget was exhausted. However, thanks to the accessibility of new media technologies, *POOR* has been able to continue its mission with online publishing.

Apart from producing community media, *POOR Magazine* also provides both media education and media access to people struggling with poverty. Thanks to *POOR Magazine*, community members are able to voice their stories, ideas, and opinions in a variety of media, including books, radio programs, blogs, videos, and news articles on the *POOR* Web site and in local publications. *POOR Magazine* also offers courses on media production (radio, television, and publication) and investigative journalism ("digital resistance"), as well as courses on research methods, awareness of systematic oppression, and constructive ways to resist oppression through media and education. Community members are able to take advantage of these opportunities through the personal support *POOR* provides in addition to education and media production. For example, *POOR* provides transportation for students and their children, child care, meals, direct legal advocacy, and monetary stipends for time spent learning with *POOR*. Through these initiatives, *POOR Magazine* works to create change models for long-term economic sustainability and attempts to facilitate agency for people in struggle from many different cultures, races and generations.

CITIZENS' MEDIA THROUGH NEW MEDIA

Alternative and community media play a vital role in helping people in struggle create opportunities to express their voice. According to Rennie (2009), alternative media exist as a direct challenge to mainstream media and dominant information and communication systems. *POOR Magazine* is a good example of a community medium challenging social injustice structures and processes. Not only does *POOR* create revolutionary access for community voices, it also gives citizens an opportunity to examine and challenge the social, political, and economic causes of their conditions of poverty. According to Rodríguez (2001), oppressed peoples can re-appropriate power through strategic use of alternative media. Through this reappropriation, citizens can then engage other passive community members. This engagement happens when citizens create their own media and broadcast their own histories, voices, and cultures. As community broadcasts enter the mediascape, the larger dominant society is forced to take notice of them. The new audibility of these voices can then begin processes of increasing the power of these previously silent populations.

The term *citizens' media* can help us understand how media use can promote citizen engagement in political democracy. Rodríguez (2001) defines a *citizen* as someone who enacts her/his citizenry through everyday life practices of dialogue and action that, ultimately, shape the local social fabric, and argues that passive individuals become active citizens when they become immersed in regular participation in local decision-making processes. Passive people do not civically engage with their communities or political systems. Importantly, by encouraging passive people to express their voices and articulate their perspectives and points of view, community media can become citizen's media; they are uniquely positioned to trigger the transformation of passive individuals into engaged active citizens who can build and shape their own communities.

POOR MAGAZINE: COMMUNITY MEDIA PRODUCER AND EDUCATOR

In its efforts to engage and build power with its demographic audience, composed of under-represented, misrepresented, and silenced communities of color in the San Francisco Bay Area, *POOR* provides PeopleSkool/Escuela de la Gente, an educational initiative designed to teach community media production. I enrolled in Escuela de la Gente to observe this educational process firsthand. I watched and participated alongside local community members as they learned to use new media technologies, including blog writing and video production, and also to respond to the mainstream media's misrepresentations and stereotyping of their communities. In my ethnographic fieldwork, I embraced a Freirean approach to shared knowledge and dialogue of equals (Freire, 1998). In my interactions with *POOR Magazine* staff and community members, rather than assuming any superior knowledge, I attempted to create a dialogue of knowledges. I sought engaged conversation between my academic perspective and the experiential knowledge and understanding of *POOR* participants. Listening to *POOR* participants as legitimate producers of their own knowledge and perspectives allowed me to form a greater understanding of the organizational process and the participants' experiences as will be detailed later in this chapter.

In my participation and observation with *POOR Magazine*, I attended classes, observed protests, wrote articles, recorded press conferences, assisted with F.A.M.I.L.Y. Project (an arts/education initiative for the children of Escuela de la Gente students), and taught video production, among other activities. Escuela de la Gente provides education for people with limited access to formal education channels. The program runs for 9 weeks and provides training in art and media production and courses in language domination, bilingual education, and class struggles from the poor perspective. Once students complete the initial program, they have the option to continue in an advanced program that includes book publishing and advanced media production. After completion of the advanced program, they are also eligible to work as reporters for *POOR*

Magazine. During my enrollment, the *POOR Magazine* office was filled with both first-time and advanced students.

While enrolled in Escuela de la Gente, I observed students transitioning from passivity into active citizenship. Step by step, I saw *POOR* participants progressing from novices to advanced students and finally becoming reporters of *POOR Magazine*. I saw this process following four distinct steps: (1) students articulating their voice and crafting/creating their message, (2) students learning journalism and media skills, (3) students passively using journalism/media skills for class assignments, and finally (4) students actively using their journalism/media skills to express their own perspective and personal struggles. The entire process occurred cyclically as students returned to various phases throughout their participation in the program.

Phase 1: Voice Articulation

In the first phase, students learn to reflect on their personal experiences with poverty and homelessness, and to shape the story of their struggle. These burgeoning voices of resistance are informed and articulated through directed guidance in media education/training courses and class teachings on *POOR* ideologies. For example, a theater class revolves around helping students shape their voices, enabling them to express their own experiences, feelings, and emotions about controversial issues such as homelessness, poverty, and welfare. In the first theater class, students are asked to think of examples of negative media depictions of people like themselves. The students respond with media stereotypes such as: "Welfare mothers are lazy," "Immigrants steal our jobs," "Illegals are just that–illegal," "All crimes are committed by brown and black people," or "People on welfare should just get a job." Afterwards, students are given time to formulate a response based on their own experiences and perspectives and then share their responses with the class. Responses are personal and use personal experience to demonstrate that the negative media depictions are untrue. One student, responding to media images of "welfare mothers," observed that mothers on welfare could not possibly be lazy because being a poor mother is a full-time job. Another student responded to messages about illegal immigrants by observing that immigrants do not steal work from anyone; they actually take the jobs that nobody else in society wants such as harvesting fruit or providing childcare. In this process, as each student confronts a negative stereotype, she is forced to address it with a personal response that stems from her own struggle.

Phase 2: Journalism and Media Skill Cultivation

As students learn how to find and shape their own voices, they are simultaneously learning the skills of "revolutionary journalism" and media that enable them to broadcast their personal stories. Again, revolutionary stems from the concept of creating dramatic change using unique journalism techniques such as guerrilla press conferences and blogging. Journalism and media skills are taught through classes such as Revolutionary Media for Skolaz #101, Radio/Video production, Language Domination, and Po'Poets/Theater. In these classes, students learn basic computer skills, how to write revolutionary blogs, how to conduct revolutionary journalism reporting and interviewing, basic radio production (audio and interview recording), basic video production (camera operation and audio recording), and theatrical skills for corporate media infiltration (similar to the concept of culture jamming).

For example, I assisted the main instructor in the video production class in introducing the students to video camera basics. When he entered the room, rather than dictating a lecture, he sat down in a chair with the students, asking questions and soliciting responses from students who already know about the camera. He created a Freirian class atmosphere where teacher and students are equal by having the students speak as often as the instructor, encouraging shared knowledge. Together, students and instructors go over the basic features of the camera. Each student handles the camera and plays with the buttons to learn by doing. We cover operation of the camera, angles, props, perspective, and lighting, and then have the students practice shooting profiles of each other while figuring out the most comfortable way to hold the camera while still getting the best image.

Phase 3: Passive Application of Journalism and Media Skills

Once students learn the necessary journalism skills and media techniques, they are given class assignments to exercise and strengthen these new skills. Exercises include introspective writing assignments on personal struggles, creating video profiles, and recording audio sound bites. One example of passive journalism/media use is the introspective writing assignment. For this assignment, students write an example of their personal struggle in blog format. One of the immigrant students describes her struggle of her arrival in the United States. Upon her arrival, she lived with her sister and brother-in-law who kept her in captivity by threatening her deportation if she left. While living there, she was forced to clean the house and provide child care for only $100 a month. Out of fear, she did not leave the house and in turn became a prisoner of her family. She eventually could no longer deal with her entrapment and voluntarily placed herself in the foster care system to leave her abusive family. While the student shares her story, the instructor listens and provides insight into how the student can format the struggle into a compelling blog. She gives guidance for the class to begin with attention-getting lines and create empathy by "dropping" the reader into their experience. These exercises build on the skills the students previously learn and begin to incorporate the students' voices and personal struggles.

Phase 4: Active Application of Journalism and Media Skills

As students begin to use journalism and media skills shaped by their individual voices, experiences, and struggles to address important social issues, they enter the fourth stage of transformation from passive to engaged citizenship. Class exercises become complex responses to larger social issues, such as blog campaigns to collectively address issues affecting the students' daily lives, for example, slumlords evicting the elderly. Other exercises include holding press conferences to confront local politicians and the mainstream media about issues concerning the poor, and staging theatrical performances as part of corporate media infiltration. For *POOR*, corporate media infiltration is a type of guerrilla journalism in which citizen journalists use mainstream media against mainstream media and dominant social ideologies. For example, *POOR* sets up instant "guerilla" press conferences in public areas to attract the attention of the public and the mainstream media, in order to get the stories covered in the evening news.

To actively engage the students in a larger social issue, *POOR* created a blog campaign to address a local initiative to improve the CalWorks Community Jobs Program (a program that allows people to earn a living wage without requiring a college degree). For this campaign, students write blogs, send letters, and make phone calls to local government offices to voice their support for the measure. One student writes a blog detailing her struggle with homelessness, hunger, and illness. The bright light in her struggle is the CalWorks Community Jobs Program because it provides her work experience that raises her self-esteem and allows her to earn $400 a month to support her family. In addition to the blogs posted on *POOR*'s Web site, students write letters to the local offices of congressional representatives. The letters provide an overview of the students' struggles and invite elected officials to visit *POOR*'s Web site and read all of the students' blogs of support for the initiative. As part of the campaign, the students and staff members also make phone calls to the politicians' offices. The calls are not easily made because of language barriers but the students are able to overcome adversity and leave their messages of support. Did this make a difference? Perhaps. The month after the blog campaign was launched, Congresswoman Pelosi's office phoned *POOR Magazine* to thank them for writing their blogs and voicing their perspectives.

ACTIVE ENGAGEMENT: AN AFTERTHOUGHT

During these phases, students begin to use new media technologies, interwoven with their life experiences and struggles, and shaped by their own voices to become active engaged citizens. The last phase of active citizenship is built on the first three. Students first articulate their voices, learn journalism and media skills, and then apply these skills. Finally, students take what they have learned and transition from passive to active citizens through the passion they bring to their assignments and merge with their own painful struggles. In this last phase, *POOR* cultivates engaged citizens by providing opportunities for students to express their voices and their stories. *POOR* affords oppressed people the opportunity to join in the mainstream media's exclusive conversation through the power of their own unique voices and stories.

Through this process, we see the power of community media. Through articulating the voices of subjects that have been historically ignored and misrepresented, community media engender communication processes based on empathy, allowing viewers, readers, and listeners to understand the experiences and struggles of these people. In recent years, movements that include African American, Asian American, and Native American perspectives into history books have succeeded in unearthing lost voices. However, many overlooked groups, including the homeless, disabled, and elderly, among others, still struggle to be heard on a daily basis. Through citizens' media and community media education, *POOR Magazine* provides a forum for people to articulate their own voices and allow their stories to break through barriers of oppression.

IT'S YOUR TURN: WHAT DO YOU THINK? WHAT WILL YOU FIND?

1. Compare the coverage of issues in *POOR Magazine* (www.poormagazine.org) with recent issues of mainstream news magazines and television news broadcasts. How are the *POOR Magazine* articles expressing the journalists' own voices? How do these compare with the perspectives and voices prominent in mainstream media? What does this comparison teach you about the class system currently operating in the United States?

2. The digital divide is defined as the gap between people who have access to advancing technology and those who do not. *POOR Magazine* is one example of a way to create media literacy, or the ability to know and use new media technologies, that bridges the digital divide. What are some other ways media scholars can advance media literacy? How does the existence of the digital divide prevent this?

3. Are there any community media organizations where you live? If so, identify them and evaluate how their content and style of production differ from that of mainstream media organizations. How, if at all, do you think these differences affect the potential impact of the community media?

4. Generate a proposal for creating a community media organization to serve a currently underserved group in your area. What medium will you use? What population will you serve? How will you meet their needs? What obstacles will you face, and how will you overcome them?

REFERENCES

Central Intelligence Agency. (2010). *The world factbook.* Retrieved April 4, 2011, from https://www.cia.gov/library/publications/the-world-factbook/rankorder/2001rank.html

Downing, J.D.H. (2001). *Radical media: Rebellious communication and social movements.* Thousand Oaks, CA: Sage.

Freire, P. (1998). *Pedagogy of freedom: Ethics, democracy, and civic courage.* Lanham, MD: Rowman & Littlefield.

Marx, K. (1978). *The German ideology: Part I.* In R.C. Tucker (Ed.), *The Marx-Engels reader* (pp. 146–200). New York: W.W. Norton & Co.

Rennie, E. (2009). Examining internal structures, dynamics and forms: Introduction. In C. Rodriguez, D. Kidd, & L. Stein (Eds.), *Making our media: Global initiatives toward a democratic public sphere: Vol. 1. Creating new communication spaces* (p. 156–161). Cresskill, NJ: Hampton.

Rodriguez, C. (2001). *Fissures in the mediascape: An international study of citizens' media.* Cresskill, NJ: Hampton.

Said, E.W. (1997). *Covering Islam.* New York: Vintage Books.

Tiny. (2011). *Poverty Scholarship #101: A 21st century Friere re-mix: The population brings the popular education.* Unpublished manuscript.

U.S. Census Bureau. (2010). *Income, poverty and health insurance in the United States: 2009 – Highlights.* Retrieved October 8, 2011, from http://www.census.gov/ hhes/www/poverty/data/incpovhlth/2009/highlights.html

9.2   WOMEN IN TV AND RADIO NEWS

Robert A. Papper

> *The author has been investigating race and gender in newsroom employment for 17 years, and has conducted more than two dozen studies of working journalists. This reading presents an overview of some of the most telling results of his and previous research into women's employment patterns, salaries, and obstacles to success.*

Change came quickly for women in radio and television news back in the 1970s; it has been slower and more complex in the years since. In fact, the percentage of women in television news has been largely unchanged in more than a decade, but that's just the big picture. The details reveal a slow evolution in terms of women's roles in TV news. Radio is more complex still. Deregulation efforts—beginning with the Carter administration in the 1970s and continuing with the reforms of the Telecommunications Act in 1996—revolutionized radio and radio news, and everyone—including women—has been affected.

SOME HISTORY

Broadcasting was among the first fields to mandate equal employment opportunity. In 1969, the Federal Communications Commission installed Equal Employment Opportunity (EEO) rules that required radio and television stations to conduct, track, and report special efforts to recruit minorities. In 1971, the FCC extended that rule to include women.

The regulation was revolutionary. Stations which had no minorities and few—if any—women outside of secretaries suddenly found themselves on recruiting binges in search of women and minorities. The station where I worked (WCCO-TV, Minneapolis), one of the largest CBS stations in the country, had just one woman reporter on the air and no minorities at all. Under the new mandate, the percentage of women (and minorities) in radio and television news soared. Within a decade, you could find women in significant numbers in every position except top newsroom and station management. Growth has been slower ever since.

In 1972, Vernon Stone conducted the first of his studies of local radio and television news for the Radio Television News Directors Association (Stone, 1973). He found that about 10% of the news staffs in both radio and TV were women. By the end of the decade in 1979, both radio and TV news had grown to 26% women (Stone, 1987). The 1980s saw continuing—but much slower—growth, and by 1988, Stone found that women made up 33% of the TV news workforce and 31% of the radio news workforce (Stone, 1988).

Although the landmark 1971 EEO rules encouraged the hiring of women, three major legal and legislative changes since then have affected the gender landscape in broadcasting.

In 1979, toward the end of the Carter Administration, the FCC began its deregulation move into what became known as "marketplace" regulation. The idea was that rather than have the government impose rules about station operation, the marketplace itself—consumer demand—would take care of that. It was a concept that the succeeding Reagan Administration embraced and pursued across much of government. Part of that deregulation included eliminating the requirement that radio stations run local news. Some might quibble with that wording because, technically, the FCC never required stations to run news. But the industry understood the FCC's unpublished quota for the percentage of total air time that was to be devoted to news on AM and FM stations. With that requirement gone, many radio stations cut back or even dropped local news completely. Before deregulation, every radio station in America had a news department, and even small stations employed several newspeople. Radio news staffing—and the consequent opportunities for both genders—has generally gone downhill ever since.

The Telecommunications Act of 1996 further deregulated radio (among many other things). Perhaps most critically—at least as far as radio was concerned—it allowed for significant consolidation. Based on the Communications Act of 1934, a single company could own no more than seven AM stations and seven FM stations all told and no more than one AM and one FM in the same market. The FCC liberalized those restrictions somewhat in the 1980s and 1990s; but under the deregulated landscape of the 1996 Act, there was virtually no limit on the total number of radio stations a single company could acquire, and companies started collecting hundreds—and in the case of Clear Channel, more than 1,000 stations all across the country. In the deregulated landscape after 1996, a single company could own as many as eight stations in a single market (depending on certain market conditions).

The result was a predictable consolidation of news departments. Why support eight separate news departments when a company could have one unit with two or three people handling news for about half of the stations? The others could drop news completely. This consolidation further eroded the opportunities for everyone in radio news—including women.

The last significant change came in 1998 as a result of a ruling by the U.S. Court of Appeals for the D.C. Circuit. Long a critic of the FCC and what the Court felt was frequent lack of justification for the FCC's rules and regulations, the Court used what was, at its core, a religious case to strike down those EEO rules from the 1960s and early 1970s. In *Lutheran Church-Missouri Synod v. FCC*, a radio station filed suit against the FCC saying that the rules against discriminatory hiring prevented it from hiring people whose religious convictions matched the radio station's religious orientation. The Court said that preventing discrimination was acceptable but that the FCC's rules went beyond that to promote the hiring of certain groups.

The ruling could have been appealed to the U.S. Supreme Court, but wasn't because the Clinton Administration believed that the conservative Supreme Court would probably side with the Court of Appeals. This leaves open the possibility that a later, more liberal Supreme Court, might take a different view.

The effect of that ruling was felt more by minorities in radio than any other segment of the population, but women were certainly also affected by the end of EEO regulations.

In the 1990s, women continued to grow as a percentage of the TV news workforce, but slowly. By the end of the decade, women were 39% of the TV news workforce—up 18% in the previous 10 years. However, in radio news, women dropped to 29% of the workforce—a 6% drop during the decade (Papper & Gerhard, 1999).

By the late 1990s, market forces may have changed the broadcasting landscape more than the EEO rules had. When those EEO rules first came out, women suddenly had an advocate in the FCC—an advocate that was virtually non existent in any other field. Over time, as other fields opened up, women had more employment options than ever before. Now the marketplace largely determines employment.

While there are jobs in radio, it's been many years since radio could be considered a "growth" industry. Most radio hiring today involves replacement for people who have moved up or moved out.

Television has been a different story. The lure of TV remains high, despite punishingly low starting salaries. Overall, television employment moved up fairly steadily until the housing bust and recession that started in late 2007. That resulted in staffing cutbacks across the board in almost every profession, including broadcasting. Technically, the recession ended in mid-2009, but unemployment has remained high. Although 2010 has seen increased employment in television, staffing levels have not returned to the 2007 levels.

Most of the rest of this reading is based on surveys conducted on behalf of the Radio Television Digital News Association (RTDNA). I took over the responsibility of the annual survey in 1994, and in 1996 I began collecting data for women (and minorities) by specific position—every few years. For detailed results and statistics, visit http://www.rtdna.org/pages/research.php. Unless other sources are cited, the data that follow come from 2010 RTDNA surveys (Papper, 2010 April; Papper, 2010 August).

TELEVISION NEWS TODAY

As far as women in local broadcast news, the new century looks a lot like the end of the last one. In television news, the workforce has stabilized at just about 40% women. That's the figure for 2010, which is essentially where it ended the 1990s. According to the U.S. Bureau of Labor

Statistics (2011), as of March 2011, women make up 41.1% of the full time U.S. workforce, so, overall, TV news isn't far behind.

There is a perception that the number of women in TV news is steadily increasing. That's not correct, but the roles women occupy within the newsroom have certainly changed.

Women are nearly two-thirds (64.2%) of all TV news producers—but that's actually been true for a dozen years. The biggest change involves women reporters and anchors. Women ended the 1990s as a majority of both groups, but that majority position has edged up steadily. The latest figures (2010) put women news anchors at 56.8% and women news reporters at 56.7%. And while pairing women anchors on any show was virtually unthinkable as recently as the 1990s, it's more and more common among secondary news broadcasts: morning, noon, and 5 p.m. It's still rare to see two women co-anchors for main newscasts, and there's an increasing trend toward solo anchors on the weekend as a cost-cutting measure. Women have made some progress in the traditional male strongholds of sports and weather, but the numbers are still small. Women are 21.6% of weathercasters, 18.7% of sports reporters, and 7.8% of sports anchors. Women do better among writers, associate producers/news assistants, executive producers, and the assignment desk. Women have also made grudging progress as news directors.

If women have generally increased among so many of the positions in the newsroom, why are the overall numbers not higher? That's because of the decline in women photographers. The percentage of women photographers has dropped steadily over the last 15 years, to 6.8%, and because the typical TV news department has more photographers than any other single position, a drop there has offset the gains elsewhere. The drop in women photographers is particularly interesting because it coincides with a drop in the size and weight of the equipment that a photographer has to carry around. Still, the photographer position is frequently considered the blue-collar bastion of the newsroom, along with tape editor, while virtually all other newsroom positions mandate a college degree.

Although the percentages vary from survey to survey, the general trends are fairly clear. Women are more likely to be managers at every level than in the mid-1990s, but progress varies by position. A majority of executive producers are women, as are almost half the assistant news directors. But just over 30% of managing editors are women.

RADIO NEWS TODAY

In radio, since 2000, the percentage of women in news has tended to bounce up and down, but the general trend is down. In 2010, the most recent year for which numbers are available, the radio workforce was just above 29% (29.2%) women.

From 2000 through 2002, women were in the low- to mid-30% range in the radio workforce. After that, however, the number slid into the mid-20s before moving up into the high 20s today. Although there is some evidence that women have been more affected than men by the consolidation of radio news, it is far from conclusive.

Even less clear is how many women in radio news are more "sidekick" than news people—part of a morning "zoo" where the woman provides less news than feature material and a different voice to contrast with a male announcer team. Some women at contemporary radio stations have argued that they get the title of "news director" instead of the same money received by the men on the air. There's no empirical evidence on that, one way or the other.

TV NEWS DIRECTORS

Even as women have made gains in a variety of TV news positions, those gains have been more grudging at the top than most other areas. Stone's first survey in 1972 found only two women television news directors—under 1% of the total. By 1976, that number had risen to 4%, but most of those were at small, independent stations.

By 1986, the percentage of women news directors had grown to 14%. It went up again to 16% in 1990 and 21% in 1994 (Papper & Sharma, 1995). Admittedly in fits and starts, but the number has generally edged up to 28.4% in 2010. That's just behind the all-time peak of 29.1% in 2009.

At least as importantly, female news directors are no longer mostly found in smaller markets and at smaller stations. Today, women are more than a quarter of the news directors in the 25 largest markets, and over 20% of the news directors at the largest news departments in the country. At this writing, women make up half the television news directors at the big four network affiliates (ABC, CBS, Fox, and NBC) in all three of the nation's largest markets: New York, Los Angeles, and Chicago. And at this writing, women make up exactly 40% of the TV news directors at the four network affiliates in the country's 10 largest markets.

RADIO NEWS DIRECTORS

In Stone's first RTNDA survey in 1972, he found just 4% of radio news directors were women. Those numbers jumped to 16% in 1981 and 27% in 1986. The percentage stayed in the mid- to upper 20s through 1994 but generally hasn't been that high since. Over the last decade, women news directors in radio have ranged from the high teens to the mid-20th percentile range. The most recent survey in 2010 put women radio news directors at 18.1%—the lowest level in quite a few years.

GENERAL MANAGERS

I started asking about the gender (and ethnicity) of radio and television general managers in 2000, so there's no data before that available for comparison. In 2000, we found 14% of TV general managers were women. The number has held steady between 12% and 16% every year—sometimes up a little, sometimes down. In 2010, the percentage of women general managers was 16.5%.

In 2000, 12% of radio general managers were women. Through 2004, the radio figure generally held in the 11% to 13% range. But in 2005—and for the next 2 years—the number jumped to about 20%, and the 2010 number is nearly that, at 18.8%.

It's important to remember two things about those numbers. First, it's the news director who's filling out that data, not the general manager himself or herself. Second, the data only apply to radio and television stations that run news because the survey is just among radio and television news directors. That doesn't mean that the numbers don't apply to the larger station universe (including the ones that do not run news)—just that I don't know for sure.

SALARIES

There's little data available on this. I gather data for men and women in various positions, and I gather data on salaries, but I don't combine them because of how difficult and time-consuming that would be. The only place to directly compare women versus men is in the position of news director, because that's the only position in a newsroom where there's always only one.

When Stone looked at gender and salaries in the early 1990s, he found that age and experience accounted for any salary differences between men and women (Stone, 1993). When we analyzed salaries for men and women news directors in this century, we found that the only variables to determine the salary of a TV news director were market size (how big is the city where the station is located?) and staff size (how big is the station within that city?). No other factors came into play.

Does that mean there's no discrimination against women in TV news? No, it doesn't. First, women make up 40% of the TV workforce but only 28% of TV news directors. Second, women are still, overall, at least slightly more likely to be news directors at smaller stations. So, yes, there's still discrimination—it's just not directly based on salary.

THE FUTURE

The first decade of the new century has not given us meaningful changes in the percentages of women in radio or television news.

In radio, women have moved up among general managers, but the general shrinkage of radio news and consolidation of companies controlling radio stations have left radio news a static business at best. Few stations make new hires in radio; almost all hiring involves replacement positions for people who have moved up or out. We're now seeing some early signs of backing away from consolidation. Clear Channel, the country's largest radio owner, now operates 850 stations—well down from its peak in the mid-2000s. But overall, the RTDNA Annual Surveys show relatively little change in radio news from one year to the next.

More changes are taking place in television, and its future and opportunities are far less clear. On the one hand, local television news cut 5.8% of its workforce in 2008 and 2009. That wasn't much worse than the economy overall, and it's well below the 24.5% cut in newspaper staff between 2007 and 2009. But even as TV news cut staff, it also increased the amount of news—up an average of about an hour per weekday in the last 3 years. TV news has become the poster child for doing more with less. As TV news again expands in employment, slowly, in 2010, its place within the TV/Internet/mobile marketplace is far from clear.

The increasing number of stations running news, the increasing amount of news, and the increasing number of video outlets presenting news and information have led to an increasing fragmentation of the audience. Thus, as the total audience for video news and information has grown, the audience size for any given news program has generally been shrinking. And as media choices expand, media advertising choices do as well. More and more advertising dollars have been going into the Internet, mobile video and information, and other new technology areas, and it's clearly affecting advertising income for both radio and television. Those changes are not gender-based; whatever the impact, it's likely to affect men and women in much the same way.

As we look to the future, it's likely that women will increase in both sports and weather, which has the potential to raise the overall percentage of women in TV news. There is some evidence that we may see an increase in multimedia or backpack journalists—those who operate on their own, both shooting and reporting stories. The use of those "one-person bands" in TV has gone up about 9% in the last 3 years, but it's skyrocketing on the Web.

Overall, I think that we're at a temporary plateau for women in TV news at 40%, but that the percentage will start to go up again, slowly, and edge up to as much as 45% by 2020. No one area will account for the increase, I predict; rather almost all areas will contribute to the growth.

IT'S YOUR TURN: WHAT DO YOU THINK? WHAT WILL YOU FIND?

1. Watch different TV newscasts in your area. Compare the gender pairings from one station to the next and one newscast to the next. Do you see differences? Why?

2. In your local area, compare the number of women as opposed to men in TV news who anchor the weather and sports. Why the differences?

3. Talk to one or more of the women in your local TV news who are doing jobs that are mostly held by men. Ask what their experiences have been in getting where they are.

4. Are there women in radio news in your area? If so, ask them about their experiences in the male-dominated world of radio.

5. How have the obstacles and progress of women in broadcast journalism reflected the status of women in our society as a whole?

6. Are there ways in which you see or suspect discrimination against women in radio or TV news? Could you design a research project to determine the answers?

REFERENCES

Papper, B. (2010, April). *Staffing and profitability*. RTDNA. Retrieved April 30, 2011, from http://www.rtdna.org/pages/media_items/2010-tv-and-radio-news-staffing-and-profitability-survey1943.php?id=1943

Papper, B. (2010, August). *Women and minorities data*. RTDNA. Retrieved April 30, 2011, from http://www.rtdna.org/pages/research/women-and-minorities.php

Papper, B., & Sharma, A. (1995, October). Newsroom diversity remains elusive goal. *RTNDA Communicator*, 18–25.

Papper, B., & Gerhard, M. (1999, July). Making a difference. *RTNDA Communicator*, 26–37.

Stone, V. A. (1973, June). Radio-television news directors and operations. *RTNDA Communicator*, 5–12.

Stone, V. A. (1987). Changing profiles of news directors of radio and TV stations, 1972–1986. *Journalism Quarterly, 64*(4), 745–749.

Stone, V. A. (1988). Trends in the status of minorities and women in broadcast news. *Journalism Quarterly, 65*(2), 288–293.

Stone, V. A. (1993). *Let's talk pay in television and radio news*. Chicago: Bonus Books.

U.S. Bureau of Labor Statistics (2011, March). *Persons at work by occupation, sex, and usual full- or part-time status*. Retrieved April 30, 2011, from www.bls.gov/web/empsit/cpseea28.pdf

---

9.3 PLANNING TO SUCCEED: ROLE MODELS OF WOMEN WORKING IN MEDIATED MESSAGE INDUSTRIES

Donnalyn Pompper

This reading examines how 37 professional women of multiple ethnic and cultural identities across the United States described role models who have inspired them to achieve success throughout long careers in journalism, public relations, and telecommunications—and to balance public and private spheres.

The act of serving as a role model for others often is associated with the patriarchal idea that women are naturally giving, nurturing, and mothering (Ruddick, 1989). Yet researchers in recent decades have found that workplace structures and routines complicate the issue for women who want to give *and* to receive support and encouragement.

Since the 1980s, having a role model has been key to women's and ethnic minorities' success in media and related fields like public relations. Navigating career plans by modeling a successful person has helped working women to overcome barriers to advancement—namely in organizations run by powerful men—in order to achieve their full potential. This has been especially true for women of color encountering racism at work.

BREAKING THE GLASS CEILING

By demonstrating competence in occupations traditionally dominated by men, highly successful women may undermine ongoing gender stereotypes and break through the glass ceiling by following role models' examples.

Among survey findings of Fortune 1000 company executives, 46% cited lack of role models as an explanation for career advancement inequity between men and women (Wellington, Kiopf, & Gerkovich, 2003). The opportunity gap wherein women fail to advance in their careers at the same rate as men has been a problem in journalism and related occupations since the Kerner Commission advocated 50 years ago for greater hiring of minorities and women in newsrooms and other mediated message industries that (re)present group identities and set news agendas. When women and ethnic minorities cannot find people like themselves in organizations, a dampening effect may make it hard to envision themselves as leaders (Kern-Foxworth, 2004).

Today's journalism students see possible role models amidst both traditional and digital/social media producers—but Bulkeley (2004) is cautiously optimistic and Beasley (2007) encouraged journalism educators to help their female students identify suitable role models. Among journalists, women working in newspapers experience too few role models and other glass ceiling barriers to advancement, as well as work-family balance issues. Women who work in online news environments, however, suggest that less-hierarchical structures afford them greater opportunities to serve as role models (Stern, 2007).

In public relations, men dominated the field until the 1970s when it became more "feminized"; now at 70% women (PRSA/IABC Salary Survey, 2000). Still, men fill highest management levels—especially in public relations agencies, where only four women lead agencies with more than $100 million in global revenue (Lee, 2011). Public relations protégés seek mentors who are good role models—insightful (appreciate individuality, recognize potential, believe in me, take a personal interest in me) and patient (supportive, helpful, inspire confidence, good listening skills, understand mistakes) (Pompper & Adams, 2006).

BENEFITS AND CHALLENGES OF ROLE MODELING

Role models serve as "proxies," guides, or benchmarks by which one can compare/contrast ability to perform tasks for career growth. Strategically, protégés may discover a role model in the person who occupies the position in an organization to which they most immediately aspire. Indeed, role modeling can provide for career and psychosocial functions. Career functions involve preparing protégés for advancement (e.g., sponsorship, exposure, visibility, coaching, protection, challenging assignments), and psychosocial functions enhance protégés' sense of competence and self image (e.g., friendship, counseling, acceptance, confirmation) (Kammeyer-Mueller & Judge, 2008).

Given the advantages to having a role model when choosing a career and in charting for success, it seems a straightforward process—but women and ethnic minorities face unique challenges. Should women select another woman as a role model, or a man? Some suggest that women are more inspired by outstanding women role models (Lockwood, 2006), report better role modeling by other women (Ragins & McFarlin, 1990), and that role-modeled women generally are at mid- to late-career stages (Vincent & Seymour, 1995) with many experiences to share. Other studies find that gender matching is unimportant when selecting a role model (Allen & Eby, 2004). Meanwhile it seems that *in*formal role model relationships that occur spontaneously are better than those created by formal programs in organizations (Scandura & Williams, 2001).

Regarding ethnic compositions in role model dyads, some people of color prefer role models of similar backgrounds because they are inspired by an in-group member or assume that they need to know someone like themselves to succeed (Lockwood, 2006). On the other hand, a study found no race differences in role-modeling functions (Lankau, Riordan, & Thomas, 2005) even though Bonilla-Silva (2009) emphasized that we live in a highly racialized society where social networks are more likely to form within racial groups. For example, role modeling behaviors among Black youth suggest that they better relate to same-race adults "because they believe that White adults cannot relate to the pressures they face as Blacks" (Ainsworth, 2010, pp. 404).

Early research on career advancement according to gender found that women had a limited pool of female role models—and those who *do* make it to the top may not always have the time to mentor younger protégés. In law firms, senior-level women struggle to stay above the glass ceiling and often are unavailable to support junior-level women (Ely, 1994). According to Morrison, White, and Van Velsor (1987): "The unfortunate fact is that pioneer women are often unable to coach and advocate others because of the intense and constant pressures on them to be good team players and consistently outstanding performers" (p. 161). Moreover, women who "forged their own professional identities" are challenged, at midlife, to find role models or social support networks for themselves (Trethewey, 2001, p. 206).

So, should a role model be someone we know in *real life* or a *vicarious* public figure or celebrity? Renowned psychologist Albert Bandura (1986) suggested that anyone could be a socialization agent when he or she motivates us to adopt certain self-images and lifestyle patterns. Hence, parents, teachers, peers, or other relatives can significantly affect young adults' career aspirations. Notably, women high school teachers provide role models for young women (Nixon & Robinson, 2009) and female college professors can influence student interest in a subject like journalism (Bettinger & Long, 2005). Regarding parents as role models, Sonnert (2009) found that women scientists more often identified fathers than mothers.

Often, individuals of outstanding achievement such as entertainers and sports celebrities are considered role models who can affect young people's career choices (Coram, 2007). Some cultural critics suggest that females are presented with a limited range of female role models from an early age—evidenced by nearly no female action figure toys, and dolls that represent "perfect-looking models that [seem] to encourage only consumerism, mindlessness, or obsession with men" (Averett, 2009, p. 365). Female role models can help counter female socialization effects—such as when girls are positively influenced by increasingly greater numbers of women politicians (Campbell & Wolbrecht, 2006) and a politically active mother (Gidengil, O'Neill, & Young, 2010).

ABOUT RESEARCH PARTICIPANTS

To discover more about role models who have inspired powerful professional women to achieve success in mediated message industry careers, in-depth telephone interviews were conducted with 37 women who self-described their ethnic identity as African American (11), Asian American (7), Caucasian/white (7), Hispanic (9), and mixed ethnicity (3: African American Caucasian, Japanese African American, Caucasian Mexican). Their mean age was 49.8, and most were married with children. All women were college graduates and categorized their socio-economic status (SES) as middle- (n = 27) or upper-class (n = 10). All women interviewed held vice president-level corporate, agency, or mid-to-senior-level news production positions in journalism (n = 12), public relations (n = 16), and telecommunications (n = 9) with a mean of 22.4 years working in a mediated message industry.

To protect research participants' confidentiality, no names are used and workplaces are generically described as journalism (newspapers, radio, and television stations), public relations (agencies, corporations, and not-for-profits), and telecommunications (cable companies, Web site providers) in major U.S. cities (Atlanta, Chicago, Washington, D.C., Houston, Los Angeles, Miami, New York, Orlando, Philadelphia, Seattle). A snowball sampling technique was used wherein participants also recommended other women for interviews. Web sites of trade organizations were mined for seed telephone numbers, such as Asian-American Journalists Association, National Association of Hispanic Journalists, National Association of Minority Media Executives, and Public Relations Society of America.

THEMES AMONG VOICES

Findings are steeped in women's voices as they discussed, in their own words, specific women *and* men who have served as role models at various stages of their career: (a) family members; (b) colleagues, bosses, teachers; (c) politicians, business leaders, social activists; (d) nationally known journalists; and (e) celebrities.

Real-Life Role Models

The most frequently identified role models among women interviewed were people in their private spheres: mothers, fathers, sisters, grandmothers, and cousins. An African American Los Angeles television news broadcaster said of her mother: "She had three girls; single mom in a very tough environment. So, she had a very tough go of it . . . What I am today . . . is her, within me." A Taiwanese American telecommunications vice president in Boston identified both of her parents as role models due to their "integrity, hard work and perseverance." A Caucasian/white public relations agency founder in New Jersey spoke of her father: "[He] taught me to stand up for what was right, to speak out as long as it was the truth, and to persevere no matter what obstacles are in your way. He urged me to be my own person."

Several women also told of former and current colleagues and supervisors as role models. An Argentinean American senior editor in Atlanta reflected on a former boss: "She is not only a very knowledgeable professional, but she's a caring warm person who truly cares about people on a personal level. She's great in managing . . . but still keeps a space to care for people and for what's happening in their lives." An African American Philadelphia-based communications consultant said: "It was very rare to have a Black woman the head of a major agency . . . Your role models have to be people who have had to fight the same kinds of battles and go through the same kinds of insults and exclusions." A Washington, D.C.-based Caucasian Mexican American radio journalist described her role models: " . . . good friends, people I've worked with. Both men and women who have integrity, work ethic, humor, honesty – those are the main things for me."

Teachers and civic leaders also topped women's role model lists. An African American telecommunications executive in Los Angles recalled a high school English teacher: "She helped me understand who I was . . . helped me find the words to express what I was feeling." A Korean American vice president based at a New York cable television network described civic leaders who have influenced her: "Community could be anything from their environment at work or the place they live . . . people that are giving, more conscious of their surroundings . . . taught me that there's things bigger than myself and we're not in this world for ourselves only."

Vicarious Role Models

Also listed among role models were women business leaders, politicians, social activists, and journalists (including many women of color who were "firsts"): Madeline Albright, Adelfa Callejo, Hillary Clinton, Lydia Cunard, Carly Fiorino, Barbara Jordan, Andrea Jung, Anita Martinez, Mother Teresa, Nancy Pilosi, Ann Richards, and Eleanor Roosevelt. One male cited in this category was John F. Kennedy. Women journalist role models included Katie Couric, Anne Curry, Charlayne Hunter-Gault, Nichelle Norris, Diane Sawyer, Ida Tarbell, Barbara Walters, and Beverly White. Three male journalists were named: Carl Bernstein, Ernest Hemmingway, and Bob Woodward.

Women celebrity role models were: Jane Fonda, Carole King, Madonna, and Melba Moore. A Caucasian/white corporate public relations executive in New Jersey explained her admiration for popular celebrity singer-activists: "They all have had courage to speak up for their causes and were not afraid to be their authentic selves despite what others may have said or done."

FEMALE ROLE MODELS AND THE BALANCING ACT

Women professionals in journalism, public relations, and telecommunications careers recommended that young women consider role models who are "intelligent" and "successful"—in the workplace *and* in balancing work with family life. A Caucasian/white public relations consultant in New Jersey lamented about early phases of her career: "In the agency world, there were very few women who effectively managed senior responsibilities with kids, home, and a *life*." An African American Los Angeles-based print journalist defined what she considered to be an ideal role model: "Someone who has managed to keep it all together. She has a family, a husband, a successful career – but is *true*, somebody you can look up to."

Other admirable qualities of role models shared were: talented, intellectual, dignified, risk taker, authentic, resilient, intuitive, consistent, respectful, honest, courageous, determined, ethical, integrity, compassionate, activist, civic minded, outspoken, decisive, loyal, generous, patient, charismatic, and fabulous dresser.

WHAT DOES IT ALL MEAN?

Sentiments of the 37 career women working in journalism, public relations, and telecommunications who were interviewed for the current study suggest that they draw from both real-life role models at home, work, in their industry, and among community leaders—as well as vicarious role models. Usually women were identified as the most influential role models, but sometimes men were named, too. Even a number of celebrated figures have served as role models—a predictable outcome given that all women interviewed are at midlife and experienced firsthand 1960s social movements to advance the status of women and ethnic minorities.

Women across ethnic and cultural identities spoke of gratification in "giving back"—now serving as role models who mentor young women. In conclusion, it seems as though women select different role models at various ages and career stages so that seeking *and* being a role model is a circuitous, lifelong process.

IT'S YOUR TURN: WHAT DO YOU THINK? WHAT WILL YOU FIND?

1. Interview someone—preferably someone you'd consider an individual of outstanding achievement, or at least someone with a fair amount of experience—who works in the field you wish to enter upon graduation. Find out how that person got his/her start, and how he/she was able to advance. How important were mentors to that person? If she/he had a mentor, how did mentors help? How might things have been different for her/him if she/he hadn't had a mentor? If he/she he didn't have a mentor, how did that affect his/her career? What advice does he/she have for you as you prepare to enter the field of his/her expertise?

2. What did you learn from your interviewee that you'll be able to incorporate into your own career planning? What qualities does your interviewee possess that you want to develop in yourself?

3. Once you enter the field, what will be your strategy for identifying "individuals of outstanding achievement" for role models?

4. In what ways might *social class* factor into a need/desire for a role model or those whom you choose?

REFERENCES

Ainsworth, J. W. (2010). Does the race of neighborhood role models matter? Collective socialization effects on educational achievement. *Urban Education*, *45*(4), 401–423.

Allen, T. D., & Eby, L. T. (2004). Factors related to mentor reports of mentoring functions provided: Gender and relational characteristics. *Sex Roles: A Journal of Research*, *50*(1/2), 129–139.

Averett, P. (2009). The search for Wonder Woman: An autoethnography of feminist identity. *Affilia*, *24*(4), 360–368.

Bandura, A. (1986). *Social foundations of thought and action: A social cognitive theory*. Englewood Cliffs, NJ: Prentice Hall.

Beasley, M. H. (2007). How to stir up a hornets' nest: Studying the implications of women journalism majors. In P. J. Creedon & J. Cramer (Eds.), *Women in mass communication* (3rd ed., pp. 23–32). Thousand Oaks, CA: Sage.

Bettinger, E. P., & Long, B. T. (2005). Do faculty serve as role models? The impact of instructor gender on female students. *American Economic Review*, *95*(2), 152–157.

Bonilla-Silva, E. (2009). *Racism without racists: Color-blind racism and the persistence of racial inequality in the United States* (3rd ed.). Lanham, MD: Rowman & Littlefield.

Bulkeley, C. C. (2004). Whose news? Progress and status of women in newspapers (mostly) and television news. In R. R. Rush, C. E. Oukrop, & P. J. Creedon (Eds.), *Seeking equity for women in journalism and mass communication education: A 30-year update* (pp. 183–204). Mahwah, NJ: Lawrence Erlbaum Associates.

Campbell, D. E., & Wolbrecht, C. (2006). See Jane run: Women politicians as role models for adolescents. *The Journal of Politics, 68*(2), 233–247.

Coram, S. (2007). Performative pedagogy and the creation of desire: The indigenous athlete/role model and implications for learning. *The Australian Journal of Indigenous Education, 36*, 56–64.

Ely, R. J. (1994). The effects of organizational demographics and social identity on relationships among professional women. *Administrative Science Quarterly, 39*(2), 203–238.

Gidengil, E., O'Neill, B., & Young, L. (2010). Her mother's daughter? The influence on childhood socialization on women's political engagement. *Journal of Women, Politics & Policy, 31*, 334–355.

Kammeyer-Mueller, J. D., & Judge, T. A. (2008). A quantitative review of mentoring research: Test of a model. *Journal of Vocational Behavior, 72*, 269–283.

Kern-Foxworth, M. (2004). Women of color on the frontline in the mass communication professions. In R. R. Rush, C. E. Oukrop, & P. J. Creedon (Eds.), *Seeking equity for women in journalism and mass communication education: A 30-year update* (pp. 205–222). Mahwah, NJ: Lawrence Erlbaum Associates.

Lankau, M. J., Riordan, C. M., & Thomas, C. H. (2005). The effects of similarity and liking in formal mentoring relationships between mentors and protégés. *Journal of Vocational Behavior, 67*, 252–265.

Lee, J. (2011, March 4). Diversity of agency leadership remains up for debate. Retrieved March 6, 2011, from *PR Week*, http://www.prweekus.com/pages/login. aspx?returl=/diversity-of-agency-leadership-remains-up-for-debate/article/197584/&pagetypeid=28&articl eid=197584&accesslevel=2&expireddays=0&access AndPrice=0.

Lockwood, P. (2006). 'Someone like me can be successful': Do college students need same-gender role models? *Psychology of Women Quarterly, 30*, 36–46.

Morrison, A. M., White, R. P., & Van Velsor, E. (1987). *Breaking the glass ceiling: Can women reach the top of America's largest corporations?* Reading, MA: Addison-Wesley.

Nixon, L. A., & Robinson, M. D. (2009). The educational attainment of young women: Role model effects of female high school faculty. *Demography, 36*(2), 185–194.

Pompper, D., & Adams, J. (2006). Under the microscope: Gender & mentor-protégé relationships in public relations. *Public Relations Review, 32*(3), 309–315.

PRSA/IABC Salary Survey 2000. (2000). Public Relations Society of America. Retrieved February 23, 2001, from http://www.prsa.org./salser/secure/tempfile/index.html

Ragins, B. R., & McFarlin, D. B. (1990). Perceptions of mentor roles in cross-gender mentoring relationships. *Journal of Vocational Behavior, 37*, 321–339.

Ruddick, S. (1989). *Maternal thinking: Toward a politics of peace.* Boston: Beacon Press.

Scandura, T. A., & Williams, E. A. (2001). An investigation of the moderating effects of genderon the relationships between mentorship initiation and protégé perceptions of mentoring functions. *Journal of Vocational Behavior, 59*, 342–363.

Sonnert, G. (2009). Parents who influence their children to become scientists: Effects of gender and parental education. *Social Studies of Science, 39*, 927–941.

Stern, S. T. (2007). Increased legitimacy, fewer women? Analyzing editorial leadership and gender in online journalism. In P. J. Creedon & J. Cramer (Eds.), *Women in mass communication* (3rd ed., pp. 133–145). Thousand Oaks, CA: Sage.

Trethewey, A. (2001). Reproducing and resisting the master narrative of decline: Midlife professional women's experiences of aging. *Management Communication Quarterly, 15*(2), 183–226.

Vincent, A., & Seymour, J. (1995). Profile of women mentors: A national survey. *SAM Advanced Management Journal, 60*, 4–10.

Wellington, S., Kiopf, M. B., & Gerkovich, P. R. (2003). What's holding women back? *Harvard Business Review, 81*, 38–39.

Epilogue and Resources

Now that you've read these chapters, think again about some questions raised in the introduction to this book: Does the social scientific or the critical/cultural studies approach seem to make more sense to you? Why? What do you think are the strengths and weaknesses of each approach? If you were going to investigate media effects, how would you approach the subject? Which types of questions (narrow or broad) do you think are more important? Which do you think are easier to answer? Which methods provide more valid and valuable results? Is it possible to maintain one's objectivity while studying human beings? What is lost, and what is gained, by holding one perspective (social scientific) over the other (critical/cultural)? Can researchers borrow from both traditions? Should they? If so, how? What would be gained? At what cost? The answers to these and other questions will influence how you interpret the scholarship you engage as you continue through school, and beyond. As you ask these questions, you are being a critical participant in our academic system/tradition of scholarship and research.

Being a critical participant in our media system means constantly asking questions. The readings in this book have presented you with a kaleidoscope of questions to consider—questions about media production, media content, and media audiences. Which ones did you enjoy the most? Why? What additional questions did you think of? How have you seen your own media literacy increase as you thought about the issues presented here, and as you have brought the question-asking process to your own media use? How have you become a more active and empowered member of the media audience? How can you bring what you've learned to any future media production you might undertake?

Ultimately, the media in our lives constitute a powerful social institution—not the only one, but the one most of us spend most of our time with. What the media tell us about our social world has a profound effect on our understanding of that social world. Even though your time in this class has come to an end, never stop questioning the media and the image of our world they offer us; the way the messages are constructed and by whom; and the way we receive, interpret, use, and are affected by the media. The media do matter. And so does your ability to ask questions, to be a literate and critical participant in the media system.

FOR MORE INFORMATION

What follows are some resources you might find helpful as you continue your studies of media production, content, and audiences. As are all such lists, it's incomplete—in this case, limited by available space—but it's a starting point.

Books

Adamo, G. (2010). *African Americans in television*. New York: Peter Lang.

Albarran, A. (Ed.). (2009). *The handbook of Spanish language media*. New York: Routledge.

Alia, V. (2009). *The new media nation: Indigenous peoples and global communication*. New York: Berghahn Books.

Alia, V., & Bull, S. (2005). *Media and ethnic minorities*. Harrogate, North Yorkshire: Edinburgh University Press.

Allport, G. (1954). *The nature of prejudice*. Cambridge, MA: Addison-Wesley.

Ang, I. (1991). *Desperately seeking the audience*. London: Routledge.

Ang, I. (1997). *Living room wars: Rethinking media audiences for a postmodern world*. London: Routledge.

Alonso, A., & Oiarzabal, P. J. (Eds.). (2010). *Diasporas in the new media age: Identity, politics, and community*. Reno, NV: University of Nevada Press.

Alwood, E. (1996). *Straight news: Gays, lesbians, and the news media*. New York: Columbia University Press.

Barnhurst, K. G. (2007). *Media Q, media/queered: Visibility and its discontents*. New York: Peter Lang.

Beasley, M. H., & Gibbons, S. J. (2002). *Taking their place: A history of women and journalism* (2nd ed.). State College, PA: Strata Publishing.

Beltran, M. C. (2009). *Latina/o stars in U.S. Eyes: The making and meanings of film and TV stardom*. Chicago: University of Illinois Press.

Benshoff, H. M., & Griffin, S. (2005). *Queer images: A history of gay and lesbian film in America*. Lanham, MD: Rowman & Littlefield.

Benwell, B. (Ed.). (2003). *Masculinity and men's lifestyle magazines*. Hoboken, NJ: Wiley-Blackwell.

Berger, M. (2000). *White lies: Race and the myths of whiteness*. New York: Farrar, Straus and Giroux.

Berry, C., Martin, F., & Yue, A. (2003). *Mobile cultures: New media in queer Asia*. Durham, NC: Duke University Press.

Bobo, J. (1995). Black women as cultural readers . New York: Columbia University Press.

Bobo, J. (1998). Black women film and video artists . New York: Routledge.

Bogle, D. (2001). Primetime blues: African Americans on network television. New York: Farrar, Straus & Giroux.

Bogle, D. (2003). Toms, coons, mulattoes, mammies, and bucks: An interpretive history of Blacks in American films (4th ed.). New York: Continuum International Publishing.

Bogle, D. (2005). Bright boulevards, bold dreams: The story of black Hollywood . New York: One World Books.

Bonilla-Silva, E. (2009). Racism without racists: Color-blind racism and the persistence of racial inequality in the United States (3rd ed.). Lanham, MD: Rowman & Littlefield.

Braziel, J. E., & Mannur, A. (Eds.). (2003). Theorizing diaspora: A reader . Hoboken, NJ: Wiley-Blackwell.

Brinkerhoff, J. M. (2009). *Digital diasporas: Identity and transnational engagement*. Cambridge: Cambridge University Press.

Browne, D. R. (1996). *Electronic media and indigenous peoples: A voice of our own?* Ames, IA: Iowa State University Press.

Browne, D. R. (2005). *Ethnic minorities, electronic media and the public sphere.* Cresskill, NJ: Hampton Press.

Bruns, A. (2008). *Blogs, Wikipedia, Second life, and beyond: From production to produsage.* New York: Peter Lang.

Bruns, A. (2005). *Gatewatching: Collaborative online news production.* New York: Peter Lang.

Byerly, C. M., & Ross, K. (2006). *Women & media: A critical introduction.* Malden, MA: Blackwell.

Campbell, C. P., LeDuff, K., Jenkins, C. D., & Brown, R. A. (2011). *Race and news: Critical perspectives.* New York: Routledge.

Carrington, B. (2010). *Race, sport and politics: The sporting black diaspora.* London: Sage.

Castañeda, L., & Campbell, S. B. (Eds.). (2005). *News and sexuality: Media portraits of diversity.* Thousand Oaks, CA: Sage.

Carstarphen, M. G., & Zavoina, S. C. (2000). *Sexual rhetoric: Media perspectives on sexuality, gender and identity.* Westport, CT: Greenwood Press.

Cobas, J. A., Duany, J., & Feagin, J. R. (Eds.). (2009). *How the United States racializes Latinos: White hegemony and its consequences.* Boulder, CO: Paradigm Publishers.

Collins, P.H. (2008). *Black feminist thought: Knowledge, consciousness, and the politics of empowerment.* New York: Routledge.

Collins, P. H. (2010). *Another kind of public education: Race, schools, the media, and democratic possibilities.* Boston, MA: Beacon Press.

Cortese, A. J. (2007) Provacateur: *Images of women and minorities in advertising.* Lanham, MD: Rowman & Littlefield.

Craig, S. (1992). *Men, masculinity, and the media.* Newbury Park, CA: Sage.

Creedon, P. J., & Cramer, J. (Eds.). (2006). *Women in mass communication* (3rd ed.). Newbury Park, CA: Sage.

Curren, R., & Bobo, J. (Eds.). (2001). *Black feminist cultural criticism.* Hoboken, NJ: Wiley-Blackwell.

Dávila, A. (2008). *Latino spin: Public image and the whitewashing of race.* New York: New York University Press.

Dennis, J. (2006). *Queering teen culture: All-American boys and same-sex desire in film and television.* New York: Routledge.

Derné, S. D. (2008). *Globalization on the ground: New media and the transformation of culture, class, and gender in India.* New Delhi: Sage.

Dines, G. (2010). *Pornland: How porn has hijacked our sexuality.* Boston: Beacon Press.

Dotson, E. W. (1999). *Behold the man: The hype and selling of male beauty in media and culture.* New York: Haworth Press.

Durham, M. G. (2008). *The Lolita Effect: The media sexualization of young girls and five keys to fixing it.* Woodstock, NY: Overlook Press.

Enteen, J. B. (Ed.). (2010). *Virtual English: Queer internets and digital creolization.* New York: Routledge.

Entman, R. M., & Rojecki, A. (2001). *The Black image in the White mind: Media and race in America.* Chicago: University of Chicago Press.

Everett, A. (2009). *Digital diaspora: A race for cyberspace.* Albany, NY: SUNY Press.

Everett, A. (Ed.). (2007). *Learning race and ethnicity: Youth and digital media.* Cambridge, MA: MIT Press.

Fiske, J. (1996). *Media matters.* Minneapolis: University of Minnesota Press.

Georgiou, M. (2006). *Diaspora, identity and the media.* Cresskill, NJ: Hampton Press.

Gilens, M. (2002). *Why Americans hate welfare: Race, media, and the politics of antipoverty policy.* Chicago: University of Chicago Press.

Gill, R. (2007). *Gender and the media.* Cambridge, UK: Polity.

Gopinath, G. (2005). *Impossible desires: Queer diasporas and South Asian public cultures.* Durham, NC: Duke University Press.

Gray, H. (2004). *Watching race: Television and the struggle for "Blackness."* Minneapolis: University of Minnesota Press.

Gross, L. (2002). *Up from invisibility: Lesbians, gay men, and the media in America*. New York: Columbia University Press.

Gutierrez, E., Moreno, R., & Armillas, C. (2001). *Suave: The Latin male*. New York: Universe Publishing.

Herman, E. S., & Chomsky, N. (2002). *Manufactuing consent: The political economy of mass media*. New York: Pantheon.

Hogg, J., & Garside, P. (2007). *Women, feminism and the media*. Harrogate, North Yorkshire: Edinburgh University Press.

hooks, b. (1996). *Reel to real: Race, sex and class at the movies*. New York: Routledge.

Jackson, R. L. II. (2006). *Scripting the black masculine body: Identity, discourse, and racial politics in popular media*. Albany, NY: SUNY Press.

Jenkins, H. (2006). *Fans, bloggers, and gamers: Exploring participatory culture*. New York: New York University Press.

Jensen, R. (2005). *The heart of Whiteness: Confronting race, racism and White privilege*. San Francisco: City Lights.

Jensen, R. (2007). *Getting off: Pornography and the end of masculinity*. Cambridge, MA: South End Press.

Johnson, M. L. (2007). *Third wave feminism: Jane puts it in a box*. London: I. B. Tauris.

Johnson, P., & Keith, M. C. (2001). *Queer airwaves: The story of gay and lesbian broadcasting*. Armonk, NY: M. E. Sharpe.

Jones, S. (1998). *CyberSociety 2.0: Revisiting computer-mediated communication and community*. Thousand Oaks, CA: Sage.

Keever, B. A. D., Martindale, C., & Weston, M. A. (1997). *U. S. News coverage of racial minorities: A sourcebook, 1934–1996*. Westport, CT: Greenwood Press.

Kendall, D. (2011). *Framing class: Media representations of wealth and poverty in America* (2nd ed.). Lanham, MD: Rowman & Littlefield.

King, C. R. (2010). *The Native American mascot controversy: A handbook*. Lanham, MD: The Scarecrow Press.

King, C. R., & Springwood, C. F. (2001). *Team spirits: The Native American mascots controversy*. Lincoln: University of Nebraska Press.

Klein, A. G. (2010). *A space for hate: The white power movement's adaptation into cyberspace*. Duluth, MN: Litwin Books.

Kohnen, M. (2011). *Queer representation, visibility, and race in American film and television*: Screening the closet. New York: Routledge.

Larson, S. G. (2005). *Media & minorities: The politics of race in news and entertainment*. Lanham, MD: Rowman & Littlefield.

Lee, R. C. (2003). *Asian American.net: Ethnicity, nationalism, and cyberspace*. New York: Routledge.

Lemish, D. (2010). *Screening gender on children's television: The views of producers around the world*. New York: Routledge.

Levin, D. E., & Kilbourne, J. (2008). *So sexy so soon: The new sexualized childhood and what parents can do to protect their kids*. New York: Ballantine Books.

Lipsitz, G. (2006). *The possessive investment in whiteness: How White people profit from identity politics* (Revised expanded ed.). Philadelphia: Temple University Press.

Lont, C. M. (Ed.). (1995). *Women and media: Content/careers/criticism*. Belmont, CA: Wadsworth.

Lotz, A. D. (2006). *Redesigning women: Television after the network era*. Champaign, IL: University of Illinois Press.

MacDonald, J. F. (1983). *Blacks and White TV: Afro-Americans in television since 1948*. Chicago: Nelson-Hall.

Marciniak, K., Imre, A., & O'Healy, A. (Eds.). (2007). *Transnational feminism in film and media: Visibility, representation, and sexual differences*. New York: Palgrave Macmillan.

Markula, P. (2009). *Olympic women and the media: International perspectives*. New York: Palgrave Macmillan.

Marlane, J. (1999). *Women in television news revisited: Into the twenty-first century.* Austin, TX: University of Texas Press.

Marzolf, M. (1977). *Up from the footnote: A history of women journalists.* New York: Hastings House.

Mask, M. (2009). *Divas on screen: Black women in American film.* Chicago: University of Illinois Press.

Matsaganis, M. D., Katz, V. S., & Ball-Rokeach, S. J. (2010). *Understanding ethnic media: Producers, consumers, and societies.* Thousand Oaks, CA: Sage.

Mayer, V. (2011). *Below the line: Producers and production studies in the new television economy.* Durham, NC: Duke University Press.

McChesney, R. W. (2008). *The political economy of media: Enduring issues, emerging dilemmas.* New York: Monthly Review Press.

Means-Coleman, R. (2002). *Say it loud! African American audiences, identity and media.* New York: Routledge.

Meiss, G. T., & Tait, A. A. (2008). *Ethnic media in America: Building a system of their own.* Dubugue, IA: Kendall Hunt Publishing.

Mendible, M. (2007). *From bananas to buttocks: The Latina body in popular film and culture.* Austin, TX: University of Texas Press.

Meyer, C. J., & Royer, D. (2001). *Selling the Indian: Commercializing & appropriating American Indian cultures.* Tucson: University of Arizona Press.

Miller, M. (2008). *Branding miss g__: Third wave feminists and the media.* Toronto: Sumach Press.

Montagu, A. (1997). *Man's most dangerous myth: The fallacy of race* (6th ed.). Walnut Creek, CA: AltaMira press.

Moran, K. C. (2011). *Listening to Latina/o youth: Television consumption within families.* New York: Peter Lang Publishing.

Morey, P., & Yagin, A. (2011). *Framing Muslims: Stereotyping and representation after 9/11.* Cambridge, MA: Harvard.

Morgan, A. N., Piper, A. I., & Woods, K. (Eds.). (2006). *The authentic voice. The best reporting on race and ethnicity.* New York: Columbia University Press.

Morrison, T. G. (2004). *Eclectic views of gay male pornography: Pornucopia.* New York: Routledge.

Nakamura, L. (2007). *Digitizing race: Visual cultures of the Internet.* Minneapolis: University of Minnesota Press.

Nakamura, L., & Chow-White, P. (2011). *Race after the Internet.* New York: Routledge.

Nicholson, J. O., Creedon, P. J., Lloyd, W. S., & Johnson, P. J. (Eds.). (2009). *The edge of change: Women in the twenty-first-century-press.* Champaign, IL: University of Illinois Press.

Omi, M., & Winant, H. (1986). *Racial formation in the United States: From the 1960s to the 1980s.* New York: Routledge & Kegan Paul.

Ono, K. A., & Pham, V. (2009). *Asian Americans and the media.* Malden, MA: Polity

O'Riordan, K., & Phillips, D. J. (2007). *Queer online: Media technology and sexuality.* New York: Peter Lang.

Papacharissi, Z. A. (2011). *A networked self: Identity, community and culture on social network sites.* New York: Routledge.

Papacharissi, Z. A. (2010). *A private sphere; Democracy in a digital age.* Cambridge: Polity.

Peach, L. J. (Ed.). 1998. *Women in culture: A women's studies anthology.* Malden, MA: Blackwell.

Peele, T. (Ed.). (2011). *Queer popular culture: Literature, media, film, and television.* New York: Palgrave Macmillan.

Pullen, C. (2007). *Documenting gay men: Identity and performance in reality television and documentary film.* Jefferson, NC: McFarland.

Pullen, C., & Cooper, M. (Eds.). (2010). *LGBT identity and online new media.* New York: Routledge.

Riley, C. A., II. (2005). *Disability and the media: Prescriptions for change.* Lebanon, NH: UPNE.

Roberts, G., & Klibanoff, H. (2007). *The race beat: The press, the civil rights struggle, and the awakening of a nation.* New York: Vintage.

Roediger, D. R., & Cleaver, K. (2007). *The wages of Whiteness: Race and the making of the American working class* (2nd ed.). New York: Verso.

Rose, T. (2008). *The hip hop wars: What we talk about when we talk about hip hop – and why it matters.* New York: Basic Civitas Books.

Rush, R. R., Oukrop, C. E., & Creedon, P. J. (2004). *Seeking equity for women in journalism and mass communication education: A 30-year update.* Philadelphia: Lawrence Erlbaum Associates.

Said, E. W. (1997). *Covering Islam: How the media and the experts determine how we see the rest of the world* (Revised ed.). New York: Vintage Books.

Sender, K. (2005). *Business, not politics: The making of the gay market.* New York: Columbia University Press.

Signorile, M. (2003). *Queer in America: Sex, the media, and the closets of power* (3rd ed.). Madison: University of Wisconsin Press.

Spence, L. K. (2011). *Stare in the darkness: The limits of hip-hop and black politics.* Minneapolis, MN: University of Minnesota Press.

Squires, C. (2009). *African Americans and the media.* Malden, MA: Polity.

Sun, W. (2009). *Maid in China: Media, morality, and the cultural politics of boundaries.* New York: Routledge.

Sun, W. (2006). *Media and the Chinese diaspora: Community, communications, and commerce.* New York: Routledge.

Sylvester, J. (2008). *The media and hurricanes Katrina and Rita: Lost and found.* New York: Palgrave Macmillan.

Thorne, B., & Henley, N. (Eds.). (1973). *Language and sex: Difference and dominance.* Rowley, MA: Newbury House.

Trotta, L. (1991). *Fighting for air: In the trenches with television news.* New York: Simon & Schuster.

Turner, G. (1996). *British cultural studies: An introduction* (2nd ed.). New York: Routledge, Chapman & Hall.

U. S. Commission on Civil Rights. (1977). *Window dressing on the set: Women and minorities in television.* Washington, DC: U. S. Government Printing Office.

U. S. Commission on Civil Rights. (1979). *Window dressing on the set: An update.* Washington, DC: U. S. Government Printing Office.

Valdivia, A. N. (Ed.). (1995). *Feminism, multiculturalism, and the media: Global diversities.* Thousand Oaks, CA: Sage.

Valdivia, A. N. (Ed.). (2008). *Latina/o communication studies today.* New York: Peter Lang.

Valdivia, A. N. (2009). *Latina/os and the media.* Malden, MA: Polity.

van Dijk, T. A. (1987). *Communicating racism: Ethnic prejudice in thought and talk.* Newbury Park, CA: Sage.

Waggoner, E. B. (2010). *Sexual rhetoric in the works of Joss Whedon.* Jefferson, NC: McFarland.

Walker, J. (2004). *Rebels on the air: An alternative history of radio in America.* New York: New York University Press.

Walters, S. D. (2003). *All the rage: The story of gay visibility in America.* Chicago: University of Chicago Press.

Weston, M. A. (1996). *Native Americans in the news: Images of Indians in the twentieth century press.* Westport, CT: Greenwood Press.

Whitt, J. (2008). *Women in American journalism: A new history.* Chicago: University of Illinois Press.

Wilson, P., & Stewart, M. (Eds.). (2008). *Global indigenous media: Cultures, poetics, and politics.* Durham, NC: Duke University Press.

Wilson II, C. C., Gutierrez, F., & Chao, L. M. (2003). *Racism, sexism, and the media: The rise of class communication in multicultural America* (3rd ed.). Thousand Oaks, CA: Sage.

Wolf, M. A., & Kielwasser, A. P. (1991). *Gay people, sex, and the media.* New York: Haworth Press.

Wong, D. (2004). *Speak it louder: Asian Americans making music.* New York: Routledge.

Wood, H. (2009). *Talking with television: Women, talk shows, and modern self-reflexivity.* Urbana, IL: University of Illinois Press.

Wu, H. D., & Lee, T. T. (2009). *Media, politics, and Asian Americans.* New York: Hampton Press.

Wykes, M., & Gunter, B. (2005). *The media and body image: If looks could kill.* Thousand Oaks, CA: Sage.

Zook, K. B. (2008). *I see Black people: The rise and fall of African American owned television and radio minority owned television and radio.* New York: Nation Books.

Zook, K. B. (1999). *Color by Fox: The Fox network and the revolution in Black television.* New York: Oxford University Press.

Journal Articles & Chapters in Edited Volumes

Alexander, C. J., Adamson, A., Daborn, G., Houston, J., & Tootoo, V. (2009). Inuit cyberspace: The struggle for access for Inuit Qaujlmajatuqangit. *Journal of Canadian Studies, 43*(2), 220–250.

Arndt, G. (2010). The making and muting of an indigenous media activist: Imagining and ideology in Charles Round Low Cloud's "Indian News". *American Ethnologist, 37*(3), 499–511.

Avraham, E., First, A. (2010). Can a regular representation of minority groups and fair reflection of cultural diversity in national media programs? Lessons from Israel. *Journal of Broadcasting & Electronic Media, 54*(1), 136–149.

Bai, S. Y. (2010). Constructing racial groups' identities in the diasporic press: Internalization, resonance, transparency, and offset. *Mass Communication and Society, 13*(4), 385–411.

Beaudoin, C. E., & Thorson, E. (2006). The social capital of Blacks and Whites: Differing effects of the mass media in the United States. *Human Communication Research, 32*(2), 157–177.

Behm-Morawitz, E., & Mastro, D. E. (2008). Mean girls? The influence of gender portrayals in teen movies on emerging adults' gender-based attitudes and beliefs. *Journal of Broadcasting Mass Communication Quarterly, 85*(1), 131–146.

Ben-Porath, E. N., & Shaker, L. K. (2010). News images, race, and attribution in the wake of Hurricane Katrina. *Journal of Communication, 60*(3), 466–491.

Bjornstrom, E. E. S., Kaufman, R. L., Peterson, R. D., & Slater, M. D. (2010). Race and ethnic representations of lawbreakers and victims in crime news: A national study of television coverage. *Social Problems, 57*(2), 269–294.

Bonnett, A. (1998). Who was White? The disappearance of non-European White identities and the formation of European racial Whiteness. *Ethnic and Racial Studies, 21*(6), 1029–1055.

Breaux, R. M. (2010). After 75 years of magic: Disney answers its critics, rewrites African American history, and cashes in on its racist past. *Journal of African American Studies, 14*(4), 398–416.

Brown, J. D., & Schulze, L. (1990). The effects of race, gender, and fandom on audience interpretation of Madonna's music videos. *Journal of Communication, 40*(2), 88–103.

Buffington, D., & Fraley, T. (2008). Skill in black and white: Negotiating media images of race in a sporting context. *Journal of Communication Inquiry, 32*(3), 292–310.

Busselle, R., & Crandall, H. (2002). Television viewing and perceptions about race differences in socio-economic success. *Journal of Broadcasting & Electronic Media, 46*(2), 265–282.

Caliendo, S. M., & McIlwain, C. D. (2006). Minority framing, and racial cues in the 2004 election. *Harvard International Journal of Press/Politics, 11*(4), 45–69.

Calzo, J. P., & Ward, L. M. (2009). Media exposure and viewers' attitudes toward homosexuality: Evidence for mainstreaming or resonance? *Journal of Broadcasting & Electronic Media, 53*(2), 280–300.

Caspi, D., & Elias, N. (2011). Don't patronize me: Media-by and media-for minorities. *Ethnic and Racial Studies, 34*(1), 62–83.

Chiricos, T., Eschholz, S., & Gertz, M. (1997). Crime, news and fear of crime: Toward an identification of audience effects. *Social Problems, 44*(3), 342–357.

Conrad, K., Dixon, T. L., & Zhang, Y. (2009). Controversial rap themes, gender portrayals and skin tone distortion: A content analysis of rap music videos. *Journal of Broadcasting & Electronic Media, 53*(1), 134–156.

Correa, T. (2010). Framing Latinas: Hispanic women through the lenses of Spanish-language and English-language news media. *Journalism, 11*(4), 425–443.

Covert, J. J., & Dixon, T. L. (2008). A changing view: Representation and effects of the portrayal of women in mainstream women's magazines. *Communication Research, 35*(2), 232–256.

DeBraganza, N., & Hausenblas, H. A. (2010). Media exposure of the ideal physique on women's body dissatisfaction and mood: The moderating effects of ethnicity. *Journal of Black Studies, 40*(4), 700–716.

Devine, P. G. (1989). Stereotypes and prejudice: Their automatic and controlled components. *Journal of Personality and Social Psychology, 56*, 5–18.

Devine, P. G., & Elliot, A. J. (1995). Are racial stereotypes *really* fading? The Princeton trilogy revisited. *Personality and Social Psychology Bulletin, 21*(11), 1139–1150.

Dixon, T. L. (2006). Schemas as average conceptions: Skin tone, television news exposure, and culpability judgments. *Journalism & Mass Communication Quarterly, 83*, 131–149.

Dixon, T. L. (2008). Crime news and racialized beliefs: Understanding the relationship between local news viewing and perceptions of African Americans and crime. *Journal of Communication, 58*(1), 106–125.

Dixon, T. L., & Linz, D. (2002). Television news, prejudicial pretrial publicity, and the depiction of race. *Journal of Broadcasting & Electronic Media, 46*(1), 112–136.

Dixon, T. L., Zhang, Y., & Conrad, K. (2009). Self-esteem, misogyny and afrocentricity: An examination of the relationship between rap music consumption and African American perceptions. *Group Processes Intergroup Relations, 12*(3), 345–360.

Domke, D. (1997). Journalists, framing, and discourse about race relations. *Journalism and Mass Communication Monographs, 164*, 1–55.

Domke, D. (2001). The press, race relations, and social change. *Journal of Communication, 51*(2), 317–344.

Domke, D., McCoy, K., & Torres, M. (1999). News media, racial perceptions and political cognition. *Communication Research, 26*(5), 570–607.

Draper, J. (2010). "Gay or not?!": Gay men, straight masculinities, and the construction of the *Details* audience. *Critical Studies in Media Communication, 27*(4), 357–375.

Drew, E. M. (2011). Pretending to be "postracial": The spectacularization of race in reality TV's *Survivor*. *Television New Media, 12*(3).

Dunaway, J., Branton, R. P., & Abrajano, M. A. (2010). Agenda setting, public opinion, and the issue of immigration reform. *Social Science Quarterly, 91*(2), 359–378.

Dunbar-Hester, C. (2010). Beyond "dudecore"? Challenging gendered and "raced" technologies through media activism. *Journal of Broadcasting & Electronic Media. 54*(1). 121–135.

England, D. E., Descartes, L., & Collier-Meek, M. A. (2011). Gender role portrayal and the Disney princesses. *Sex Roles, 64*(7–8), 555–567.

Entman, R. M. (1990). Modern racism and the images of blacks in local television news. *Critical Studies in Mass Communication, 7*, 332–345.

Entman, R. M. (1992). Blacks in the news: Television, modern racism, and cultural change. *Journalism Quarterly, 69*(2), 341–361.

Esposito, J. (2009). What does race have to do with *Ugly Betty*? An analysis of privilege and postracial(?) representations on a television sitcom. *Television New Media, 10*(6), 521–535.

Evuleocha, S. U., & Ugbah, S. D. (1989). Stereotypes, counter-stereotypes, and Black television images in the 1990s. *Western Journal of Black Studies, 13*(4), 197–205

Faber, R. J., O'Guinn, T. C., & Meyer, T. P. (1987). Televised portrayals of Hispanics: A comparison of ethnic perceptions. *International Journal of Intercultural Relations, 11*, 155–169.

Fuchs, C. (2010). Class, knowledge and new media. *Media, Culture & Society, 32*(1), 141–50.

Fujikoka, Y., Ryan, E., Agle, M., Legaspi, M., & Toohey, R. (2009). The role of racial identity in responses to thin media ideals: Differences between white and black college women. *Communication Research, 36*(4), 451–24.

Fung, A., & Zhang, X. (2011). The Chinese *Ugly Betty*: TV cloning and local modernity. *International Journal of Cultural Studies, 14*(3), 265–276.

Gaertner, S. L., & Dovidio, J. F. (2005). Understanding and addressing contemporary racism: From aversive racism to the common ingroup identity model. *Journal of Social Issues, 61*, 615–639.

Gentles, K. A., & Harrison, K. (2006). Television and perceived peer expectations of body size among African American adolescent girls. *Howard Journal of Communication, 17*(1), 39–55.

Gilliam, F. D., Jr., Valentino, N. A., & Beckmann, M. N. (2002). Where you live and what you watch: The impact of racial proximity and local television news on attitudes about race and crime. *Political Research Quarterly, 55*, 755–780.

Gilliam, F. D., Jr., Iyengar, S., Simon, A., & Wright, O. (1996). Crime in black and white: The violent, scary world of local news. *Press/Politics, 1*(3), 6–23.

Giroux, H. A. (1997). Rewriting the discourse of racial identity: Towards a pedagogy and politics of Whiteness. *Harvard Educational Review, 67*(2), 285–320.

Gorham, B. W. (2006). News media's relationship with stereotyping: The linguistic intergroup bias in response to crime news. *Journal of Communication, 56*(2), 289–308.

Gorham, B. W. (1999). Stereotypes in the media: So what? *The Howard Journal of Communication, 10*(2), 229–247.

Gray, H. (1989). Television, Black Americans and the American dream. *Critical Studies in Mass Communication, 6*, 376–386.

Greer, J. D., Hardin, M., & Homan, C. (2009). "Naturally" less exciting? Visual production of men's and women's track and field coverage during the 2004 Olympics. *Journal of Broadcasting & Electronic Media, 53*(2), 173–190.

Gregory, S. M. (2010). Disney's second line: New Orleans, racial masquerade, reproduction of whiteness in *The Princess and the Frog. Journal of African American Studies, 14*(4), 432–449.

Gruenewald, J., Pizarro, J., & Chermak, S. M. (2009). Race, gender, and the newsworthiness of homicide incidents. *Journal of Criminal Justice, 37*(3), 262–272.

Guidotti-Hernández, N. M. (2007). *Dora The Explorer*, constructing "Latinidades" and the politics of global citizenship. *Latino Studies, 5*, 209–232.

Hardin, M., & Greer, J. D. (2009). The influence of gender-role socialization, media use and sports participation on perceptions of gender-appropriate sports. *Journal of Sports Behavior, 32*(2), 207–227.

Harrison, K. (2000). The body electric: Thin-ideal media and eating disorders in adolescents. *Journal of Communization, 50*(3), 119–143.

Harrison, K., & Cantor, J. (1997). The relationship between media consumption and eating disorders. *Journal of Communication, 47*(1), 40–67.

Harrison, K., Taylor, L. D., & Marske, A. L. (2006). Women's and men's eating behavior following exposure to ideal-body images and text. *Communication Research, 33*(6), 507–529.

Hasinoff, A. A. (2008). Fashioning race for the free market on *America's Next Top Model. Critical Studies in Media Communication, 25*(3), 324–343.

Heavner, B. M. (2007). Liminality and normative Whiteness: A critical reading of poor White trash. *Ohio Communication Journal, 45*, 65–80.

Henderson, C. E. (2010). "King Kong ain't got sh** on me": Allegories, anxieties, and the performance of race in mass media. *Journal of Popular Culture, 43*(6), 1207–1222.

Henderson, J. J., & Baldasty, G. J. (2003). Race, advertising, and prime-time television. *Howard Journal of Communications, 14*(2), 97–112.

Hendriks, A. (2002). Examining the effects of female bodies on television: A call for theory and programmatic research. *Critical Studies in Mass Communication, 19*(1), 106–123.

hooks, b. (1992). Representing Whiteness in the Black imagination. In L. Grossberg, C. Nelson, & P. Treichler (Eds.), *Cultural studies*. London: Routledge.

Howard, J. W. III & Prividera, L. C. (2008). The fallen women archetype: Media representations of Lynndie England, gender, and (ab)uses of U.S. female soldiers. *Women's Studies in Communication, 31*(3), 287–312.

Iyengar, S. (1990). Framing responsibility for political issues: The case of poverty. *Political Behavior, 12,* 19–40.

Jane, D. M., Hunter, G. C., & Lozzi, B. M. (1999). Do Cuban American women suffer from eating disorders? Effects of media exposure and acculturation. *Hispanic Journal of Behavioral Sciences, 21*(2) 212–219.

Johnson, J. D., Adams, M. S., Hall, W., & Ashburn, L. (1997). Race, media, and violence: Differential racial effects of exposure to violent news stories. *Basic and Applied Social Psychology, 19*(1), 81–90.

Johnson, K. A. (1991). Objective news and other myths: The poisoning of young Black minds. *Journal of Negro Education, 60*(3), 328–341.

Kian, E. M., Mondello, M., & Vincent, J. (2009). ESPN—the women's sports network? A content analysis of Internet coverage of March madness. *Journal of Broadcasting & Electronic Media,* 53 (3), 477–496.

Kiecolt, K. J., & Sayles, M. (1988). Television and the cultivation of attitudes toward subordinate groups. *Sociological Spectrum, 8,* 19–33.

Kim, S. H., Carvalho, J. P., & Davis, A. G. (2010). Talking about poverty: News framing of who is responsible for causing and fixing the problem. *Journalism & Mass Communication Quarterly, 87*(3–4), 563–582.

Kinders, D. R., & Sears, D. O. (1981). Prejudice and politics: Symbolic racism versus racial threats to the good life. *Journal of Personality and Social Psychology, 40,* 414–431.

Knobloch-Westerwick, S., Appiah, O., & Alter, S. (2008). News selection patterns as a function of race: The discerning minority and the indiscriminating majority. *Media Psychology, 11*(3), 400–417.

Kretsedemas, P. (2010). "But she's not black!" Viewer interpretations of "angry black women" on prime time TV. *Journal of African American Studies, 14*(2), 149–171.

Lee, L. (2008). Understanding gender through Disney's marriages: A study of young Korean immigrant girls. *Early Childhood Education Journal, 36*(1), 11–18.

Lind, R. A. (2002). Speaking of culture: The relevance of cultural identity as Afro-, Latin-, and Euro-American laypeople plan a television newscast. *Journalism and Communication Monographs,* 3 , 111–145.

Lind, R. A., & Danowski, J. A. (1998). The representation of Arabs in U.S. electronic media. In Y. R. Kamalipour & T. Carelli (Eds.), *Cultural diversity and the U.S. media* (pp. 157 – 167). Albany, NY: SUNY Press.

Lind, R. A., & Salo, C. (2002). The framing of feminists and feminism in news and public affairs programs in U.S. electronic media. *Journal of Communication, 52,* 211–228.

Littlefield, M. B. (2008). The media as a system of racialization: Exploring images of African American women and the new racism. *American Behavioral Scientist, 51*(5), 675–686.

Mahtani, M. (2009). The racialized geographies of news consumption and production: Contaminated memories and racialized silences. *GeoJournal, 74*(3), 257–265.

Martins, N., & Harrison, K. (2011). Racial and gender differences in the relationship between children's television use and self-esteem: A longitudinal panel study. *Communication Research, 38 (2).*

Martins, N., Willaims, D. C., Ratan, R. A., & Harrison, K. (2010). Virtual muscularity: A content analysis of male video game characters. *Body Image , 8* (1), 43–51.

Marwick, A. (2010). There's a beautiful girl under all of this: Performing hegemonic femininity in reality television. *Critical Studies in Media Communication, 27*(3), 251–266.

Mastro, D. E., & Morawitz, E. A. (2005). Latino representation on primetime television. *Journalism and Mass Communication Quarter , 82* (4), 110–130.

Mastro, D. E., & Ortiz, M. (2008). A content analysis of social groups in prime-time Spanish-language television. *Journal of Broadcasting & Electronic Media , 52* (1), 101–118.

Master, D. E., & Stern, S. R. (2003). Representations of race in television commercials: A content analysis of prime-time advertising. *Journal of Broadcasting & Electronic Media, 47*(4), 638–647.

Mastro, D. E., Behm-Morawitz, E., & Kopacz, M. A. (2008). Exposure to television portrayals of Latinos: The implications of aversive racism and social identity theory. *Human Communication Research, 34*(1), 1–27.

Mastro, D., Lapinski, M. K., Kopacz, M. A., & Behm-Morawitz, E. (2009). The influence of exposure to depictions of race and crime in TV news on viewer's social judgments. *Journal of Broadcasting & Electronic Media, 53*(4), 615–635.

Mazie, M., Palmer, P., Pimentel, M., Rogers, S., Ruderfer, S., & Sokolowski, M. (1993). To deconstruct race, deconstruct Whiteness. *American Quarterly, 45*(2), 281–294.

McIlwain, C. D. (2011). Racialized media coverage of minority candidates in the 2008 democratic presidential primary. American Behavioral Scientist , 55 (4), 371–389.

McIlwain, C. D., & Caliendo, S. M. (2009). Black messages, white messages: The differential use of racial appeals by black and white candidates. Journal of Black Studies , 39 (5), 732–743.

McIntosh, P. (2002). White privilege, color, and crime: A personal account. In C. Mann & M. Zatz (Eds.), *Images of color, images of crime* (2nd ed). Los Angeles: Roxbury.

McRobbie, A. (2008). Young women and consumer culture: An intervention. *Cultural Studies, 22*(5), 531–550.

Means Coleman, R. R. (2006). The gentrification of "Black" in Black popular communication in the new millennium. *Popular Communication, 4*(2), 79–94.

Miller, D. (2009). Media power and class power: Overplaying ideology. *Socialist Register, 38*. Retrieved from http://socialistregister.com/index.php/srv/article/view/5786

Mitra, R. (2010). Resisting the spectacle of pride: Queer Indian bloggers as interpretive communities. *Journal of Broadcasting & Electronic Media, 54*(1), 163–178.

Monteath, S. A., & McCabe, M. P. (1997). The influence of societal factors on female body image. *The Journal of Social Psychology, 137*(6), 708–727.

Morgan, M. (2005). Hip-hop women shredding the veil: Race and class in popular feminist identity. *South Atlantic Quarterly, 104*(3), 425–444.

Moscowitz, L. M. (2010). Gay marriage in television news: Voice and visual representation in the same-sex marriage debate. *Journal of Broadcasting & Electronic Media, 54*(1), 24–40.

Muller, F. (2009). Entertaining anti-racism: Multicultural television drama, identification and perceptions of ethnic threat. *Communications, 34*(3), 239–257.

Myers, P. N., Jr., & Biocca, F. A. (1992). The elastic body image: The effect of television advertising and programming on body image distortions in young women. *Journal of Communication, 42*(3), 108–133.

Neuendorf, K. A., Gore, T. D., Dalessandro, A., Janstova, P, & Snyder-Suhy, S. (2009). Shaken and stirred: A content analysis of women's portrayals in James Bond films. *Sex Roles, 62*(11–12), 747–761.

Nishikawa, K. A., Towner, T. L., Clawson, R. A., & Waltenburg, E. N. (2009). Interviewing the interviewers: Journalistic norms and racial diversity in the newsroom. *Howard Journal of Communications, 20*(3), 242–259.

Ogunyemi, O. (2007). The Black popular press. *Journalism Studies, 8*(1), 13–27.

Oh, D. C. (2011). Complementary objectivity and ideology: Reifying white capitalist hierarchies in Time's Magazine's construction of Michelle Rhee. *Journal of Communication Inquiry, 34*(2), 151–167.

Oliver, M. B. (1994). Portrayals of crime, race, and aggression in "reality-based" police shows: A content analysis. *Journal of Broadcasting & Electronic Media, 38*(2), 179–192.

Oliver, M. B. (1999). Caucasian viewers' memory of Black and White criminal suspects. *Journal of Communication, 49*(3), 46–60.

Osucha, E. (2009). The whiteness of privacy: Race, media, law. *Camera Obscura, 70*, 66–106.

Parker, S., Nichter, M., Nichter, M., Vuckovic, N., Sims, C., & Ritenbaugh, C. (1995). Body image and weight concerns among African American and White adolescent females: Differences that make a difference. *Human Organization, 54*(2), 103–114.

Peffley, M., Shields, T., & Williams, B. (1996). The intersection of race and crime in television news stories: An experimental study. *Political Communication, 13*, 309–327.

Piñon, J. (2011). The unexplored challenges of television distribution: The case of Azteca America. *Television New Media, 12*(1), 66–90.

Poindexter, P. M., Smith, L., & Heider, D. (2003). Race and ethnicity in local television news: Framing, story assignments, and source selections, *Journal of Broadcasting & Electronic Media, 47*(4), 524–536.

Pritchard, D., & Stonbely, S. (2007). Racial profiling in the newsroom. *Journalism & Mass Communication Quarterly, 84*(2), 231–248.

Railton, D., & Watson, P. (2005). Naughty girls and red blooded women: Representations of female heterosexuality in music video. *Feminist Media Studies, 5*(1), 51–63.

Ramasubramanian, S. (2010). Television viewing, racial attitudes, and policy preferences: Exploring the role of social identity and intergroup emotions in influencing support for affirmative action. *Communication Monographs, 77*(1), 102–121.

Richardson, E. (2007). "She was workin like foreal": Critical literacy and discourse practices of African American females in the age of hip hop. *Discourse & Society, 18*(6), 789–809.

Reep, D. C., & Dambrot, F. H. (1989). Effects of frequent television viewing on stereotypes: "Drip, drip" or "drench"? *Journalism Quarterly, 66*, 542–550, 556.

Reep, D. C., & Dambrot, F. H. (1994). TV parents: Fathers (and now mothers) know best. *Journal of Popular Culture, 28*(2), 13–23.

Roth, W. D. (2009). "Latino before the world": The transnational extension of panethnicity. *Ethnic and Racial Studies, 32*(6), 927–948.

Seiter, E. (1986). Stereotypes and the media: A re-evaluation. *Journal of Communication, 36*(2), 16–26.

Sender, K. (2003). Sex sells: Sex, class, and taste in commercial gay and lesbian media. *GLQ: A Journal of Lesbian and Gay Studies, 9*(3), 331–365.

Shah, H., & Thornton, M. C. (1994). Racial ideology in U.S. mainstream news magazine coverage of Black–Latino interaction, 1980–1992. *Critical Studies in Mass Communication, 11*, 141–161.

Simpson, J. L. (2008). The color-blind double bind: Whiteness and the (im)possibility of dialogue. *Communication Theory, 18*(1), 139–159.

Tyler, I., & Bennett, B. (2010). 'Celebrity chav': Fame, femininity and social class. *European Journal of Cultural Studies, 13*(3), 375–393.

Velez, V., Huber, L. P., Lopez, C. B., de la Luz, A., & Solorzano, D. G. (2008). Battling for human rights and social justice: A Latina/o critical race media analysis of Latina/o student youth activism in the wake of 2006 anti-immigrant sentiment. *Social Justice, 35*(1), 7–28.

Van Sterkenburg, J., Knoppers, A., & De Leeuw, S. (2010). Race, ethnicity, and contents analysis of the sports media: A critical reflection. *Media, Culture & Society, 32*(5), 819–839.

Ward, M. L., Hansbrough, E., & Walker, E. (2005). Contributions of music video exposure to Black adolescents' gender and sexual schemas. *Journal of Adolescent Research, 20*(2), 143–166.

Winslow, L. (2010). Comforting the comfortable: *Extreme Makeover Home Edition's* ideological conquest. *Critical Studies in Media Communication. 27*(3), 267–290.

Wohlwend, K. E. (2009). Damsels in discourse: Girls consuming and producing identity texts through Disney Princess play. *Reading Research Quarterly, 44*(1), 57–84.

Wong, W. (1994). Covering the invisible "model minority." *Media Studies Journal, 8*, 49–59.

Yao, M. Z., Mahood, C., & Linz, D. (2010). Sexual priming, gender stereotyping, and likelihood to sexually harass: Examining the cognitive effects of playing a sexually-explicit video game. *Sex Roles, 62*(1–2), 77–88.

Yu, S. (2009). Re-evaluating the 'alternative' role of ethnic media in the US: The case of Chinese-language press and working-class women readers. *Media, Culture & Society, 31*(4), 597–616.

Yuanyuan, Z, Dixon, T. L., & Conrad, K. (2009). Rap music videos and African American women's body image: The moderating role of ethnic identity. *Journal of Communication, 59*(2), 262–279.

Zhang, Y., Dixon, T. L., & Conrad, K. (2010). Female body image as a function of themes in rap music videos: A content analysis. *Sex Roles, 62*(11–12), 787–797.

Zimmerman, A., & Dahlberg, J. (2008). The sexual objectification of women in advertising: A contemporary cultural perspective. *Journal of Advertising Research, 48*(1), 71–79.

Zurbriggen, E. L., & Sherman, A. M. (2010). Race and gender in the 2008 U.S. presidential election: A content analysis of editorial cartoons. *Analyses of Social Issues and Public Policy. 10*(1), 223–248.

Web Sites

Adbusters. *www.adbusters.org/home/*
Advocate. *www.advocate.com/*
Against the Current. *www.solidarity.us.org/atc*
AlterNet. *www.alternet.org/*
Asian American Journalists Association. *www.aaja.org*
Black Public Media.Org. *www.blackpublicmedia.org/*
Body Image Site. *www.bodyimagesite.com*
Center for Media Literacy. *www.medialit.org*
China Media News. *www.chinamedianews.net/*
Citizens for Media Literacy. *www.main.nc.us/cml/*
Common Dreams.Org. *www.commondreams.org*
Directory of Media Literacy Sites Worldwide. *www.chebucto.ns.ca/CommunitySupport/AMLNS/internet.html*
Fairness and Accuracy in Reporting. *www.fair.org*
Feminist Media Project. *www.feministmediaproject.com/*
Frameline. *www.frameline.org/*
The Freedom Forum. *www.freedomforum.org*
Gay & Lesbian Alliance Against Defamation. *www.glaad.org/*
GLAAD's Advertising Media Program. *http://www.commercialcloset.org/*
Hispanic Digital Media. *http://hispanicdigital.blogspot.com/*
Hispanic Trending: A Latino Marketing & Advertising Blog. *http://juantornoe.blogs.com/*
I Want Media: *www.iwantmedia.com/resources/index.html*
Index of Native American Media Resources on the Internet. *www.hanksville.org/NAresources/indices/NAmedia.html*
International Women's Media Foundation. *www.iwmf.org/*
Jean Kilbourne (women & media). *www.jeankilbourne.com*
Labor Beat! *www.laborbeat.org*
Media Awareness Network. *www.media-awareness.ca/english*
Media Matters for America. *http://mediamatters.org/*
Media Report to Women. *www.mediareporttowomen.com/*
The Media Resources Center of the Library at the University of California at Berkeley (films by and about people of color). *www.lib.berkeley.edu/MRC/EthnicImagesVid.html*
The Media Resources Center of the Library at the University of California at Berkeley (films dealing with gender issues). *www.lib.berkeley.edu/MRC/WomenVid.html*
Media Watch. *www.mediawatch.com/*
Media Education Foundation. *www.mediaed.org*
Model Minority. *www.modelminority.com/*
The National Association for the Advancement of Colored People. *www.naacp.org*
The National Association of Black Journalists. *www.nabj.org*
The National Association of Hispanic Journalists. *www.nahj.org*
National Hispanic Media Coalition. *www.nhmc.org/*
The National Lesbian & Gay Journalists Association. *www.nlgja.org*
National Organization for Women. *www.now.org*
National Radio Project. *www.radioproject.org*
Native American Journalists Association. *www.naja.com*
The New Press. *www.thenewpress.com/*
NOMAS: National Organization for Men Against Sexism. *http://www.nomas.org/*
Out Front Blog. *www.fhoutfront.com/2008/03/gay-media-matte.html*

Poynter Institute. *www.poynter.org*
RaceProject.org: *www.raceproject.org/*
The Radio-Television Digital News Association. *www.rtdna.org*
Selected women and gender resources on the Web: *http://womenst.library.wisc.edu/*
Seven Stories Press. *www.sevenstories.com*
South End Press. *www.southendpress.org*
Southern Poverty Law Center. *www.splcenter.org.*
    Also see *www.tolerance.org*
The University of Iowa, Communication Studies Department (much information about gender, race, and
    the media). *www.uiowa.edu/~commstud/resources/GenderMedia/*
The Women's Media Center. *www.womensmediacenter.com/*
Women, Action, & the Media. *http://www.womenactionmedia.org/*
Women in Media & News. *www.wimnonline.org/WIMNsVoicesBlog/*

Films/Videos (Distributors; date; run time in minutes)

Arresting Ana: Anorexia Online. (Women Make Movies; 2009; 25.)
The Beauty Backlash. (Films for the Humanities & Sciences; 2006; 29)
Beauty Mark: Body Image & the Race for Perfection. (Media Education Foundation; 2008; 50.)
bell hooks on Video: Cultural Criticism and Transformation. (Media Education Foundation; 1997; 66)
Black Is . . . Black Ain't: A Personal Journey Through Black Identity. (California Newsreel; 1995; 87)
The Black Press: Soldiers Without Swords. (California Newsreel; 1998; 86)
Blacking Up: Hip-Hop's Remix of Race and Identity. (California Newsreel; 2010; 57.)
Blacks and Jews. (California Newsreel; 1997; 85.)
Boys Will be Men. (Bullfrog Films, 2001, 57.)
Blue Eyed. (California Newsreel; 1996; 93)
Bollywood Bound: Finding Fame and Identity in India's Filmmaking Capital. (Films for the Humanities &
    Sciences; 2002; 57)
Calling the Shots. (Direct Cinema Ltd.; 2007; 118.)
Casting Calls: Hollywood and the Ethnic Villain. (Films for the Humanities & Sciences; 2004; 47)
The Celluloid Closet. (Columbia Tristar Home Entertainment; 1995; 101)
Class Dismissed: How TV Frames the Working Class. (Media Education Foundation; 2005; 62.)
The Codes of Gender: Identity and Performance in Pop Culture. (Media Education Foundation; 2009; 73
    [46 abridged].)
The Color of Fear. (StirFry Seminars & Consulting; 1994; 90)
Color Adjustment. (California Newsreel; 1991; 88)
Covering Girl Culture: Awakening the Media Generation. (Women Make Movies; 2009; 80.)
Dishing Democracy: Arab Social Reform via Satellite TV. (Films for the Humanities & Sciences 2007; 58)
Dreamworlds 3: Sex, Desire, & Power in Music Video. (Media Education Foundation; 2007; 55 [35 abridged])
Enough Man. (Frameline Home Video; 2005; 61)
Ethnic Notions: Black People in White Minds. (California Newsreel; 1987; 56)
The Eye of the Storm. (Center for the Humanities; 1991; 26)
Facing Racism. (Films for the Humanities and Sciences; 1996; 57)
For the Bible Tells Me So. (First Run Features, 2007, 98)
Further off the Straight & Narrow: New Gay Visibility on Television 1998–2006. (Media Education Foun-
    dation; 2006; 61)
Game Over: Gender, Race & Violence in Video Games. (Media Education Foundation; 2000; 41)
Generation M. (Media Education Foundation; 2008; 60.)
Girls: Moving Beyond Myth. (Media Education Foundation; 2004; 28)

Hate and the Internet: Web Sites and the Issue of Free Speech. (Films for the Humanities & Sciences; 1998; 21)

The Heretics. (Women Make Movies; 2009; 95.)

Hip-Hip: Beyond Beats & Rhymes. (Media Education Foundation; 2006; 60)

I Was a Teenage Feminist. (Women Make Movies, 2006, 62).

Killing Us Softly 4: Advertising's Image of Women. (Media Education Foundation; 2010; 45.)

The Looking Glass: Inside TV News. (Films for the Humanities & Sciences; 1996; 60)

Ma Vie En Rose (Sony Pictures Classics, 1997, 88)

Made in L.A. (California Newsreel; 2007; 70.)

The Media and Democracy in the Arab World. (Films for the Humanities & Sciences; 1999; 45)

Media Literacy in the 21st-Century Classroom. (Films for the Humanities & Sciences; 2009; 40.)

Nollywood Lady. (Women Make Movies; 2008; 52.)

Playing Unfair: The Media Image of the Female Athlete. (Media Education Foundation; 2002; 30)

Price of Pleasure: Pornography, Sexuality & Relationships. (Media Education Foundation; 2008; 55.)

Race: The Power of an Illusion. (California Newsreel; 2003; 3 episodes 56.)

Race and Local TV News. (Films for the Humanities & Sciences; 1998; 21)

Racial Stereotypes in the Media. (Films for the Humanities & Sciences; 2008; 42)

Reel Bad Arabs: How Hollywood Vilifies a People. (Media Education Foundation; 2006; 50.)

Say My Name. (Women Make Movies; 2009; 73.)

The Sexting Crisis Video Clip Collection. (Films for the Humanities & Sciences; 2010; 23.)

Sexual Stereotypes in the Media. (Films for the Humanities & Sciences; 2008; 38)

Sexy Inc.: A Critical Look at the Hypersexualization of Childhood. (Films for the Humanities & Sciences; 2007; 27.)

Slaying the Dragon. (Women Make Movies; 2007/1988; 60)

Slim Hopes: Advertising & the Obsession With Thinness. (Media Education Foundation; 1995; 30)

Small Steps, Big Strides: The Black Experience in Hollywood. (20th Century Fox Home Entertainment; 1998; 58)

The Strength to Resist: The Media's Impact on Women and Girls. (Cambridge Documentary Films; 2000; 35)

Telenovelas: Love, TV, and Power. (Films for the Humanities & Sciences; 1995; 59)

Tim Wise on White Privilege: Racism, White Denial & the Costs of Inequality. (Media Education Foundation; 2008; 57.)

This is Nollywood. (California Newsreel; 2007; 56)

Tomboys! Feisty Girls and Spirited Women. (Women Make Movies; 2004; 28.)

Tongues Untied. (Frameline; 2008; 55.)

Tough Guise: Media Images and the Crisis in Masculinity. (Media Education Foundation; 1999; 87 [56 abridged])

Transparent. (Frameline; 2010; 62.)

Understanding Media Literacy. (Films for the Humanities & Sciences; 2007; 35)

Unnatural Causes. (California Newsreel; 2008; 1 episode 56, 6 episodes 26.)

What a Girl Wants. (Media Education Foundation; 2001; 33.)

Who Is Albert Woo?: Defying the Stereotypes of Asian Men. (Films for the Humanities & Sciences; 2000; 51)

CONTRIBUTORS

Michael Adorjan is an assistant professor in the department of sociology and Centre for Criminology, the University of Hong Kong. His research interests include comparative youth justice systems and youth crime debates, media representations of crime and moral panics, and debates about public sociology and public criminology.

Neil M. Alperstein is a professor of communication at Loyola University Maryland. His research interests include masculine gender identity, dreams and fantasies, and imaginary social relationships we have with celebrities as they relate to advertising and popular culture.

Colleen Salo Aravena was an undergraduate in communication at the University of Illinois at Chicago while working on this research. She is a senior e-commerce marketing specialist at Space Coast Credit Union in Melbourne, FL.

Cory L. Armstrong is an associate professor in the University of Florida College of Journalism and Communications. She has more than 8 years of professional journalism experience. Her research interests are influences on news content, media credibility, gender and media, and effects of news coverage.

Lori Bindig is an assistant professor of communication and media studies at Sacred Heart University, Fairfield, CT. She is the author of *Dawson's Creek: A Critical Understanding*. Her research interests include critical cultural studies and media literacy particularly dealing with the construction and commodification of young femininity.

Sitthivorada Boupha, MA, is a human resources executive at Millicom Lao Co., Ltd. in Vientiane Capital, Lao PDR. His research interests include cross-cultural communication and relational and organizational communication.

Dwight E. Brooks is a professor and director of the School of Journalism at Middle Tennessee State University. His teaching and research examine representations of race and gender in media, media literacy, and electronic media program management.

Patti Brown is an adjunct instructor in the departments of sociology and political science at Des Moines Area Community College, and a PhD student in rhetoric and professional communication at Iowa State University.

Xiaomei Cai is an associate professor of communication at George Mason University. Her research interests are children and media, media uses and gratifications and privacy issues.

andré m. carrington, PhD, has taught American studies, art history, literature, African cultures, gender and sexuality studies, and media studies at New York University and Skidmore College. His current research engages with the representation of Blackness, gender, space, and history in visual art and popular texts across the African diaspora. His most recent book project analyzes the politics of race and cultural production in twentieth-century science fiction and fantasy and their fan cultures.

Lauren Chartier was an undergraduate student at Emmanuel College (Boston) when she worked on this research. She served as an English tutor and earned her BA in English communications and sociology. She is interested in issues of inequality within the media and more generally throughout society.

Allen Conkle is a graduate student at San Francisco State University. His interests include media and cultural studies, queer theory, and performance studies.

Chiung Hwang Chen is an associate professor of international cultural studies at Brigham Young University, Hawaii. Her research areas and publications include cultural studies, gender/race issues in the media, religion and media, journalism narratives, and media/journalism systems in Chinese-speaking countries. She is developing a new expertise on the Pacific region.

Cynthia Conti is a doctoral candidate in media, culture, and communication at New York University. Her interests are community media, radio history, and broadcast regulations. Her dissertation presents a cultural analysis of low power FM service by investigating the conceptions and lived practices of localism at licensed LPFM stations.

Cynthia A. Cooper is an associate professor and chairperson in the department of mass communication and communication studies at Towson University. Her research interests are media regulation, First Amendment law, hate speech, and media effects.

Diego Costa is a filmmaker and PhD candidate in the interdivisional program in media arts and practice (iMAP) at the University of Southern California. His research interests include queer theory, psychoanalysis, fashion theory, barebacking, and dolls. www.diego-costa.com

Kiana Cox is a PhD candidate in sociology with a concentration in race/ethnicity and gender at the University of Illinois at Chicago. Her research and teaching interests are organized around how race and gender intersect for African American women, theories of race/ethnicity, feminist theory, and media/popular culture; and epistemologies and statistics.

David Cuillier is an associate professor of journalism at the University of Arizona. His research interests include the state of freedom of information and public attitudes toward open government and psychological influences in producing and perceiving news.

George L. Daniels is an associate professor of journalism at the University of Alabama in Tuscaloosa. His research interests include media management and the role of diversity in the media workplace.

Travis L. Dixon is an associate professor of communication studies at UCLA. He is primarily interested in the portrayal of people of color in the mass media and the effects of these images on audiences.

Athena Elafros recently defended her doctoral dissertation, *Global Music, Local Culture: Popular Music Making in Canada and Greece*, in the department of sociology at McMaster University, Canada. Her research interests include cultural sociology, the sociology of music, diaspora, and cultural production.

Eric Freedman is an associate professor of communication and multimedia studies at Florida Atlantic University. He is the author of *Transient Images: Personal Media in Public Frameworks*.

Becca Gercken is an associate professor of English and American Indian studies at the University of Minnesota Morris. Her research interests are American Indian literature, representations of American Indian in popular culture, and Plains Indian ledger art.

Bradley W. Gorham is an associate professor and chair of the communications department at the S.I. Newhouse School of Public Communications, Syracuse University. His research centers around the reception and effects of media messages about social groups.

Rachel Alicia Griffin is an assistant professor of speech communication at Southern Illinois University at Carbondale. Her research interests include critical race theory, Black feminist thought, popular culture, gender violence, and pedagogy.

Leslie A. Grinner is a doctoral candidate in cultural foundations of education at Syracuse University. Her research interests include feminist pedagogy, media and cultural studies, power and privilege, ideology, and ending oppression.

Ashley D. Grisso, PhD, is an independent scholar. Her research interests include the interrelationship of culture, communication, and media, with an emphasis on gender and youth culture. ashvoice@earthlink.net

Travis L. Gosa is an assistant professor of social science at Cornell University. His research examines the social worlds of African American youth, new racial politics, music, and digital inequality.

Aymen Abdel Halim is a graduate student in broadcast and electronic communication arts at San Francisco State University. His research interests include Arab and Muslim representation in U.S. electronic media (and its effects), and socio-political aspects of U.S. electronic media. He is a producer for *Arab Talk* on KPOO in San Francisco, and is producing a documentary film about Palestinian issues in the West Bank and Gaza.

Helen K. Ho received her PhD in communication studies at the University of Michigan. Her research is devoted to issues of race, ethnicity, and gender; how media narratives are implicated in identity formation; and how representations of race and gender are understood, sanctioned, or censored.

Dina Ibrahim is an associate professor of broadcast and electronic communication arts at San Francisco State University. Her research interests are in the psychological impact of television depictions on audiences in the United States, the Middle East, and Southeast Asia, as well as analyzing the visual framing of U.S. television news representations of Islam and Arab countries.

Stacey Irwin is an assistant professor of communication and theatre at Millersville University, PA. Her research interests are philosophy of technology, media philosophy, gender studies, hermeneutic phenomenology, and curriculum studies.

Jean Kilbourne is internationally recognized for her pioneering work on alcohol and tobacco advertising and the image of women in advertising. She is the creator of the award-winning film series *Killing Us Softly: Advertising's Image of Women* and the author of *Can't Buy My Love: How Advertising Changes the Way We Think and Feel* and *So Sexy So Soon: The New Sexualized Childhood and What Parents Can Do to Protect Their Kids*.

C. Richard King is a professor and chair of comparative ethnic studies at Washington State University. He has written extensively on the colonial legacies and postcolonial predicaments of American culture, with special interest in the racial politics of expressive culture.

Jennifer S. Kramer is an assistant professor of communication at The College of St. Benedict & St. John's University. Her research interests include women's gendered communication and patient/physician communication about chronic pain.

Katherine J. Lehman is an assistant professor of communications at Albright College, Reading, PA. She is the author of *That Girl: Single Women in Sixties and Seventies Popular Culture*.

Rebecca Ann Lind is an assistant professor of communication and associate dean of the College of Liberal Arts and Sciences at the University of Illinois at Chicago. Her research interests are race and gender in media, audience studies, journalism, ethics, and new media.

Christine McKenna Lok is an assistant professor of sociology at Emmanuel College, Boston. With a professional background as a social worker, her research focuses on the social policymaking process, particularly regarding gender and poverty.

Cindy M. Lont is a professor of communication and director of film and video studies at George Mason University. Her research interests are women and media, women's music, and visual communication.

Inas Y. Mahfouz is an assistant professor of computational linguistics in the English department, Ain Shams University, Egypt. She has published the *Process Type Database* to facilitate automatic transitivity analysis. Her fields of interest include the computational analysis of language, lexicography, and systemic functional grammar.

Sheena Malhotra is a professor and chair of gender and women's studies at CSU, Northridge. She has worked in the commercial film and television industry in India and on documentary films in the United States. Her research interests are race, gender, and nation in mediated contexts, with a particular focus on India and the Indian diaspora.

Mindy McAdams is a professor of journalism and Knight Chair at the University of Florida. She teaches courses about online journalism. With more than 20 years' experience in journalism, she is the author of *Flash Journalism: How to Create Multimedia News Packages*.

Robert Mejia is a doctoral candidate in the Institute of Communications Research at the University of Illinois at Urbana-Champaign. His research interests include cultural studies; media history; memory studies; technology studies; and histories of class, gender, and race.

Natalie Y. Moore is a journalist at WBEZ-FM in Chicago, and co-author of *Deconstructing Tyrone: A New Look at Black Masculinity in the Hip-Hop Generation* and *The Almighty Black P Stone Nation: The Rise, Fall and Resurgence of an American Gang*.

John Morris, MA, is a freelance copy writer. His research interests include media portrayals of sex, gender, and sexuality, as well as corporate diversity communication.

Jody D. Morrison is an associate professor and the internship and practicum director in the department of communication at Salisbury University in Maryland. Her research interests include interpersonal/relational communication, communication education, and conversation analysis.

Thuc Doan Ngyuen holds a master's in public administration and is working on a master of fine arts.

Robert A. (Bob) Papper is the Lawrence Stessin Distinguished Professor of Journalism and chair of the department of journalism, media studies, and public relations at Hofstra University. He's founder and co-editor of the journal *Electronic News* and studies audience in addition to his cataloguing the state of local radio and TV news for the Radio Television Digital News Association.

Joshua Daniel Phillips is a doctoral student of speech communication at Southern Illinois University, Carbondale. As a student, author, and national speaker, his research interests include rhetoric, gender communication, and gender violence. He is especially interested in men's activist groups aimed at ending men's violence against women.

Lea M. Popielinski is a PhD candidate in the department of women's studies at the Ohio State University. She is writing her dissertation on gender and embodiment in online graphical virtual worlds, with her research focusing on Second Life.

Donnalyn Pompper is an associate professior and directs the master of science in communication management program in the department of strategic communication at Temple University. Her research interests are age, ethnicity, and gender in media representation and organizations.

Naomi Rockler-Gladen is an instructional designer at Capella University and a freelance writer.

John R. Rodriguez is an assistant professor of digital media, in the mass communications program at the University of Louisiana Monroe. His interests are visual arts in new media, environmental impact studies, Hispanic cultures, and communication design.

Ryan Rogers is a doctoral student and Roy H. Park fellow in the School of Journalism and Mass Communication at the University of North Carolina at Chapel Hill. His research interests include media effects, specifically video game effects.

Susan Dente Ross is a professor of English at Washington State University, a Fulbright Scholar, and the director of Paxim, a peace research group. A writer of creative nonfiction, her research encompasses media criticism, peace communication, and the freedoms of speech and press. Her recent books include *Images that Injure (3ed)* co-edited with Paul Martin Lester.

Jonathan Paul Rossing is an assistant professor of communication studies at Indiana University (Purdue University, Indianapolis. His research interests include race and critical race theory, humor, rhetoric, and critical pedagogy.

Terri L. Russ is an assistant professor of communication studies at Saint Mary's College in Notre Dame, Indiana. Her research interests focus on the ways various cultural and other discourses are realized in individual identity, as well as how these discourses serve to subjugate marginalized groups.

John Philip Sanchez is an associate professor of communications at the Pennsylvania State University. His research is focused at the intersection of American Indian cultures and the American media.

Mark Saxenmeyer is the executive director of *The Reporters Inc.*, a non-profit production company devoted to producing projects either ignored or overlooked by the mainstream media. As a television news reporter for more than two decades in Wisconsin, California, and Chicago, he's been recognized with both a national Emmy and Edward R. Murrow Award.

Melinda Schulte Krakow is a doctoral student of communication at the University of Utah, where she studies issues in mass communication, gender, technology, and health.

Rebecca Taff earned her MA from San Francisco State University. Her research interests vary from women in media to marriage and humor.

Pamela J. Tracy is an associate professor of communication studies at Longwood University. Her research interests include studying identity and difference within the context of children and media interpretation, ethnographic audience studies, and media pedagogy.

Cindy S. Vincent is a doctoral student of communication at the University of Oklahoma. Her research interests include class representation in the media, new media technologies, citizens' media, participatory culture, and civic engagement.

Lynne M. Webb is a professor of communication, University of Arkansas. She conducts research on young adults' interpersonal communication in romantic and family contexts, including computer-mediated communication in personal relationships.

Michelle A. Wolf is a professor of broadcast and electronic communication arts at San Francisco State University. Her research interests include representation of race, gender, class, disability, sexuality, and sexual orientation in media; audience studies; media power and control; media pedagogy; and qualitative research.

Gust A. Yep is a professor of communication studies, core graduate faculty of sexuality studies, and faculty of the EdD program in educational leadership at San Francisco State University. Widely published in inter/disciplinary journals and anthologies, his research focuses on communication at the intersections of race, class, gender, sexuality, and nation.

Monica Zakeri, MA, works in the programming division at iN DEMAND Networks, specializing in communication and marketing.

APPENDIX

ALTERNATE TABLES OF CONTENTS

ALTERNATE TABLE OF CONTENTS 1: BY SITE OF STRUGGLE (RACE, GENDER, CLASS, OR A COMBINATION)

· The Relative Presence of the Various Sites of Struggle, When a Combination Is Present, Varies.

SITE OF STRUGGLE*	READING #	AUTHORS	TITLE
G	2.4	Cory L. Armstrong and Mindy McAdams	Believing Blogs: Does a Blogger's Gender Influence Credibility?
G	3.1	Michelle A. Wolf, Melinda S. Krakow, and Rebecca Taff	Women with Physical Disabilities, Body Image, Media, and Self-Conception
G	5.3	Rebecca Ann Lind and Colleen Salo Aravena	Framing Feminism
G	5.9	Jean Kilbourne	"The More You Subtract the More You Add": Cutting Girls Down to Size in Advertising
G	7.1	Cynthia A. Cooper	Anti-Gay Speech on the Internet and the Movement to Counteract Cyber-Hate
G	7.2	Inas Y. Mahfouz	Mining the Opinion of the Globe
G	7.4	Rachel Alicia Griffin and Joshua Daniel Phillips	Eminem's *Love the Way You Lie* and the Normalization of Men's Violence against Women
G	8.1	Mark Saxenmeyer	Exploring Gay/Straight Relationships on Local Television News
G	8.4	Cynthia Conti	Locating Butch in *Out of Bounds*: Female Football Players, Expressions of Masculinity, and Participatory Cinema
G	9.2	Robert A. Papper	Women in TV and Radio News
GC	2.3	Lori Bindig	Media Literacy in Eating Disorder Treatment
GC	3.3	Neil Alperstein	Man Up: Viewer Responses to Images of Less than Ideal Males in Advertising
GC	5.4	Chiung Hwang Chen	"Outwhiting the Whites": An Examination of the Persistence of Asian American Model Minority Discourse

(continued)

SITE OF STRUGGLE*	READING #	AUTHORS	TITLE
GC	6.5	Jennifer S. Kramer	It's Okay That We Backstab Each Other: Cultural Myths That Fuel the Battling Female in *The Bachelor*
GC	6.7	Gust A. Yep and Allen Conkle	The New Gay Domesticity: Homonormativity in ABC's *Brothers and Sisters*
GC	6.9	Stacey Irwin	Mothers in Media
GR	2.1	Bradley W. Gorham	The Social Psychology of Stereotypes: Implications for Media Audiences
GR	2.5	Ryan Rogers	Video Game Design and Acceptance of Hate Speech in Online Gaming
GR	3.6	Pamela J. Tracy	"Why Don't You Act Your Color?": Pre-Teen Girls, Identity, and Popular Music
GR	5.5	Xiaomei Cai and Cynthia M. Lont	The Unchanging Face of the News: A Content Analysis of Online News Sites
GR	7.3	Jody D. Morrison	Community Blogging as Relational and Identity Resolution: Gender, Race and the *PostSecret* Phenomenon
GRC	3.2	Helen K. Ho	Negotiating the Mediascape: Asian American Men and American Mass Media
GRC	3.5	Sheena Malhotra	Finding Home in a Song and a Dance: Nation, Culture, Bollywood
GRC	4.1	andré m. carrington	Dreaming in Colour: Fan Fiction as Critical Reception
GRC	4.4	Robert Mejia	"Walking in the City" in an Age of Mobile Technologies
GRC	4.5	Diego Costa	Becoming Modular: The (Re-)Assembled Queer "Male" Body and Its Digitally Enabled Sexual Economy
GRC	5.1	Christine McKenna Lok and Lauren Chartier	Why Are Some Bullying Victims More Newsworthy Than Others?
GRC	6.1	Jonathan P. Rossing	"People Tell Me I'm White": Stephen Colbert and Comic Deconstruction of Colorblindness
GRC	6.3	Leslie A. Grinner	Bella's Choice: Deconstructing Ideology and Power in *The Twilight Saga*
GRC	6.6	Terri L. Russ	Is Daddy's Little Girl a Bitch or a Princess?: Narratives of Female Identity on *My Super Sweet 16*
GRC	6.8	Katherine J. Lehman	Fragmented Femininity: Postfeminism, Motherhood and Multiple Personalities on Prime-Time Television
GRC	6.10	Lea M. Popielinski	Wicked Stepmothers Wear Dior: Hollywood's Modern Fairy Tales

*G = Gender; R = Race; C = Class

ALTERNATE TABLE OF CONTENTS 2: BY MEDIUM

The Relative Presence of the Various Media, When a Combination Is Present, Varies.

MEDIUM*	READING #	AUTHORS	TITLE
N	2.4	Cory L. Armstrong and Mindy McAdams	Believing Blogs: Does a Blogger's Gender Influence Credibility?
N	2.5	Ryan Rogers	Video Game Design and Acceptance of Hate Speech in Online Gaming
N	3.7	C. Richard King	Arguing over Images: Native American Mascots and Race
N	4.1	andré m. carrington	Dreaming in Colour: Fan Fiction as Critical Reception
N	4.2	Travis L. Gosa	Crank Dat Barack Obama! Social Media and the 2008 Presidential Election
N	4.3	Sitthivorada Boupha, Ashley D. Grisso, John Morris, Lynne M. Webb, and Monica Zakeri	How College Students Display Ethnic Identity on Facebook
N	4.4	Robert Mejia	"Walking in the City" in an Age of Mobile Technologies
N	4.5	Diego Costa	Becoming Modular: The (Re-)Assembled Queer "Male" Body and Its Digitally Enabled Sexual Economy
N	5.5	Xiaomei Cai and Cynthia M. Lont	The Unchanging Face of the News: A Content Analysis of Online News Sites
N	5.6	Susan Dente Ross and David Cuillier	Gambling with Identity: American Indian Self-Representations on Tribal Web Sites
N	7.1	Cynthia A. Cooper	Anti-Gay Speech on the Internet and the Movement to Counteract Cyber-Hate
N	7.2	Inas Y. Mahfouz	Mining the Opinion of the Globe
N	7.3	Jody D. Morrison	Community Blogging as Relational and Identity Resolution: Gender, Race and the *PostSecret* Phenomenon
N	7.5	Thuc Doan Nguyen	*AudreyMagazine.com*: Portrayals of Asian American Women Online by Asian American Women
N	7.8	Eric Freedman	Resident Racist: Embodiment and Game Controller Mechanics
N	9.1	Cindy S. Vincent	*POOR Magazine* and Civic Engagement through Community Media
P	5.1	Christine McKenna Lok and Lauren Chartier	Why Are Some Bullying Victims More Newsworthy Than Others?
P	5.2	Patti Brown	What's in a Name?: Framing the Immigration Story
P	5.4	Chiung Hwang Chen	"Outwhiting the Whites": An Examination of the Persistence of Asian American Model Minority Discourse

(*continued*)

MEDIUM*	READING #	AUTHORS	TITLE
PT	2.2	Travis L. Dixon	"He Was a Black Guy:" How the News Continues to Create Fear of Blacks
PT	3.1	Michelle A. Wolf, Melinda S. Krakow, and Rebecca Taff	Women with Physical Disabilities, Body Image, Media, and Self-Conception
PT	3.3	Neil Alperstein	Man Up: Viewer Responses to Images of Less than Ideal Males in Advertising
PT	5.8	John R. Rodriguez	Advertising and Hispanic Culture
PT	5.9	Jean Kilbourne	"The More You Subtract the More You Add": Cutting Girls Down to Size in Advertising
PT	6.4	John Phillip Sanchez	Mass Media, Mass Media Indians and American Indians
PT	6.9	Stacey Irwin	Mothers in Media
T	3.4	Dina Ibrahim and Aymen Adbel Halim	How TV Makes Arabs and Muslims Feel about Themselves
T	6.1	Jonathan P. Rossing	"People Tell Me I'm White": Stephen Colbert and Comic Deconstruction of Colorblindness
T	6.5	Jennifer S. Kramer	It's Okay That We Backstab Each Other: Cultural Myths That Fuel the Battling Female in *The Bachelor*
T	6.6	Terri L. Russ	Is Daddy's Little Girl a Bitch or a Princess?: Narratives of Female Identity on *My Super Sweet 16*
T	6.7	Gust A.Yep and Allen Conkle	The New Gay Domesticity: Homonormativity in ABC's *Brothers and Sisters*
T	6.8	Katherine J. Lehman	Fragmented Femininity: Postfeminism, Motherhood and Multiple Personalities on Prime-Time Television
T	8.1	Mark Saxenmeyer	Exploring Gay/Straight Relationships on Local Television News

*A = Audio; F = Film; G = General Media; N = New Media; P = Print Media; T = Television

ALTERNATE TABLE OF CONTENTS 3: BY ARENA (ENTERTAINMENT, JOURNALISM/PR/ADVERTISING)

The Relative Presence of the Various Arenas, When a Combination Is Present, Varies.

ARENA*	READING #	AUTHORS	TITLE
E	2.5	Ryan Rogers	Video Game Design and Acceptance of Hate Speech in Online Gaming
E	3.2	Helen K. Ho	Negotiating the Mediascape: Asian American Men and American Mass Media
E	3.3	Neil Alperstein	Man Up: Viewer Responses to Images of Less than Ideal Males in Advertising
E	3.5	Sheena Malhotra	Finding Home in a Song and a Dance: Nation, Culture, Bollywood
E	3.6	Pamela J. Tracy	"Why Don't You Act Your Color?": Pre-Teen Girls, Identity, and Popular Music
E	4.1	andré m. carrington	Dreaming in Colour: Fan Fiction as Critical Reception
E	4.3	Sitthivorada Boupha, Ashley D. Grisso, John Morris, Lynne M. Webb, and Monica Zakeri	How College Students Display Ethnic Identity on Facebook
E	4.4	Robert Mejia	"Walking in the City" in an Age of Mobile Technologies
E	4.5	Diego Costa	Becoming Modular: The (Re-)Assembled Queer "Male" Body and Its Digitally Enabled Sexual Economy
E	6.1	Jonathan P. Rossing	"People Tell Me I'm White": Stephen Colbert and Comic Deconstruction of Colorblindness
E	6.2	Naomi Rockler-Gladen	Race, Hierarchy, and Hyenaphobia in *The Lion King*
E	6.3	Leslie A. Grinner	Bella's Choice: Deconstructing Ideology and Power in *The Twilight Saga*
E	6.5	Jennifer S. Kramer	It's Okay That We Backstab Each Other: Cultural Myths That Fuel the Battling Female in *The Bachelor*
E	6.6	Terri L. Russ	Is Daddy's Little Girl a Bitch or a Princess?: Narratives of Female Identity on *My Super Sweet 16*
E	6.7	Gust A. Yep and Allen Conkle	The New Gay Domesticity: Homonormativity in ABC's *Brothers and Sisters*
E	6.8	Katherine J. Lehman	Fragmented Femininity: Postfeminism, Motherhood and Multiple Personalities on Prime-Time Television

(continued)

ARENA*	READING #	AUTHORS	TITLE
J	5.1	Christine McKenna Lok and Lauren Chartier	Why Are Some Bullying Victims More Newsworthy Than Others?
J	5.2	Patti Brown	What's in a Name?: Framing the Immigration Story
J	5.3	Rebecca Ann Lind and Colleen Salo Aravena	Framing Feminism
J	5.4	Chiung Hwang Chen	"Outwhiting the Whites": An Examination of the Persistence of Asian American Model Minority Discourse
J	5.5	Xiaomei Cai and Cynthia M. Lont	The Unchanging Face of the News: A Content Analysis of Online News Sites
J	5.6	Susan Dente Ross and David Cuillier	Gambling with Identity: American Indian Self-Representations on Tribal Web Sites
J	5.8	John R. Rodriguez	Advertising and Hispanic Culture
J	5.9	Jean Kilbourne	"The More You Subtract the More You Add": Cutting Girls Down to Size in Advertising
J	7.5	Thuc Doan Nguyen	*AudreyMagazine.com*: Portrayals of Asian American Women Online by Asian American Women
J	8.1	Mark Saxenmeyer	Exploring Gay/Straight Relationships on Local Television News
J	8.3	Natalie Y. Moore	Reflections on Being a Community Journalist
J	8.4	Cynthia Conti	Locating Butch in *Out of Bounds*: Female Football Players, Expressions of Masculinity, and Participatory Cinema
J	9.1	Cindy S. Vincent	*POOR Magazine* and Civic Engagement through Community Media
J	9.2	Robert A. Papper	Women in TV and Radio News
J	9.3	Donnalyn Pompper	Planning to Succeed: Role Models of Women Working in Mediated Message Industries

*E = Entertainment; J = Journalism/Advertising/Public Relations